Praise for Ellie Quigley's Books

"I picked up a copy of *JavaScript by Example* over the weekend and wanted to thank you for putting out a book that makes JavaScript easy to understand. I've been a developer for several years now and JS has always been the 'monster under the bed,' so to speak. Your book has answered a lot of questions I've had about the inner workings of JS but was afraid to ask. Now all I need is a book that covers Ajax and Coldfusion. Thanks again for putting together an outstanding book."

—*Chris Gomez, Web services manager,*
Zunch Worldwide, Inc.

"I have been reading your *UNIX® Shells by Example* book, and I must say, it is brilliant. Most other books do not cover all the shells, and when you have to constantly work in an organization that uses tcsh, bash, and korn, it can become very difficult. However, your book has been indispensable to me in learning the various shells and the differences between them…so I thought I'd email you, just to let you know what a great job you have done!"

—*Farogh-Ahmed Usmani, B.Sc. (Honors), M.Sc., DIC,*
project consultant (Billing Solutions), Comverse

"I have been learning Perl for about two months now; I have a little shell scripting experience but that is it. I first started with *Learning Perl* by O'Reilly. Good book but lacking on the examples. I then went to *Programming Perl* by Larry Wall, a great book for intermediate to advanced, didn't help me much beginning Perl. I then picked up *Perl by Example, Third Edition*—this book is a superb, well-written programming book. I have read many computer books and this definitely ranks in the top two, in my opinion. The examples are excellent. The author shows you the code, the output of each line, and then explains each line in every example."

—*Dan Patterson, software engineer,*
GuideWorks, LLC

"Ellie Quigley has written an outstanding introduction to Perl, which I used to learn the language from scratch. All one has to do is work through her examples, putz around with them, and before long, you're relatively proficient at using the language. Even though I've graduated to using *Programming Perl* by Wall et al., I still find Quigley's book a most useful reference."

—*Casey Machula, support systems analyst,*
Northern Arizona University, College of Health and Human Services

"When I look at my bookshelf, I see eleven books on Perl programming. *Perl by Example, Third Edition*, isn't on the shelf; it sits on my desk, where I use it almost daily. When I bought my copy I had not programmed in several years and my programming was mostly in COBOL so I was a rank beginner at Perl. I had at that time purchased several popular books on Perl but nothing that really put it together for me. I am still no pro, but my book has many dog-eared pages and each one is a lesson I have learned and will certainly remember.

"I still think it is the best Perl book on the market for anyone from a beginner to a seasoned programmer using Perl almost daily."

—Bill Maples, network design tools and automations analyst,
Fidelity National Information Services

"We are rewriting our intro to OS scripting course and selected your text for the course. [*UNIX® Shells by Example* is] an exceptional book. The last time we considered it was a few years ago (second edition). The debugging and system administrator chapters at the end nailed it for us."

—Jim Leone, Ph.D., professor and chair, Information Technology,
Rochester Institute of Technology

"Quigley's [*PHP and MySQL by Example*] acknowledges a major usage of PHP. To write some kind of front end user interface program that hooks to a back end MySQL database. Both are free and open source, and the combination has proved popular. Especially where the front end involves making an HTML web page with embedded PHP commands.

"Not every example involves both PHP and MySQL. Though all examples have PHP. Many demonstrate how to use PHP inside an HTML file. Like writing user-defined functions, or nesting functions. Or making or using function libraries. The functions are a key idea in PHP, that take you beyond the elementary syntax. Functions also let you gainfully use code by other PHP programmers. Important if you are part of a coding group that has to divide up the programming effort in some manner."

—Dr. Wes Boudville, CTO,
Metaswarm Inc.

Perl by Example

Fifth Edition

Perl by Example
Fifth Edition

Ellie Quigley

PRENTICE
HALL

Upper Saddle River, NJ • Boston • Indianapolis • San Francisco
New York • Toronto • Montreal • London • Munich • Paris • Madrid
Capetown • Sydney • Tokyo • Singapore • Mexico City

Many of the designations used by manufacturers and sellers to distinguish their products are claimed as trademarks. Where those designations appear in this book, and the publisher was aware of a trademark claim, the designations have been printed with initial capital letters or in all capitals.

The author and publisher have taken care in the preparation of this book, but make no expressed or implied warranty of any kind and assume no responsibility for errors or omissions. No liability is assumed for incidental or consequential damages in connection with or arising out of the use of the information or programs contained herein.

For information about buying this title in bulk quantities, or for special sales opportunities (which may include electronic versions; custom cover designs; and content particular to your business, training goals, marketing focus, or branding interests), please contact our corporate sales department at corpsales@pearsoned.com or (800) 382-3419.

For government sales inquiries, please contact governmentsales@pearsoned.com.

For questions about sales outside the U.S., please contact international@pearsoned.com.

Visit us on the Web: informit.com/ph

Library of Congress Cataloging-in-Publication Data

Quigley, Ellie.
    Perl by example / Ellie Quigley.—Fifth edition.
        pages   cm
    Includes index.
    ISBN 978-0-13-376081-1 (pbk. : alk. paper)
    1. Perl (Computer program language) I. Title.
    QA76.73.P22Q53 2015
    005.13'3—dc23
                                2014036613

ISBN-13: 978-0-13-376081-1
ISBN-10:   0-13-376081-2

Text printed in the United States on recycled paper at Edwards Brothers Malloy in Ann Arbor, Michigan.
First printing, December 2014

Editor-in-Chief
Mark L. Taub

Development Editors
Michael Thurston
Chris Zahn

Managing Editor
John Fuller

**Full-Service
Production Manager**
Julie B. Nahil

Project Manager
Moore Media, Inc.

Copy Editor
Moore Media, Inc.

Indexer
Larry Sweazy

Proofreader
Pam Palmer

Cover Designer
Chuti Prasertsith

Composition
Moore Media, Inc.

Contents

Preface

"You may wonder, why a new edition of *Perl by Example*?" That's how the preface for the fourth edition (2007) opened. So here we are again with a fifth edition and the twentieth anniversary since the first edition of *Perl by Example*, published in 1994. Same question: Why another edition? Perl 5 is still Perl 5.

First of all, a lot has been happening since the release of Perl 5.10. Many of the ideas from Perl 6 have been backported to Perl 5 as we await the official release of Perl 6. And as new features are added, there have been a number of incremental version changes, the latest version number being Perl 5.21. In fact, version 5.10 was what has been called the beginning of "modern Perl." CPAN has added a number of new modules that have spiked interest in Perl, among them Moose, Mojolicious, Dancer, DBIx::Class, and more; and Core Perl has gained many new modules as well, such as List::Util, Time::Piece, autodie, and so on. Those incremental changes to Perl 5 continue to enhance Core Perl and all the many new modules that deal with modern projects and technology. Perl 6 is still a work in progress. To see the roadmap for Perl 6 development, you can go to github.com or you can participate in the development process by going to perl6.org. But the fact is, we're still entrenched in Perl 5 while we wait. This book addresses new features that have been added since the last edition, revitalizes and updates some of the older examples, and trims some of those topics that are not applicable in modern Perl.

As you read this, I am still teaching Perl University of California, Santa Clara (UCSC) extension in Sunnyvale, California, to groups of professionals coming from all around Silicon Valley. I always ask at the beginning of a class, "So why do you want to learn Perl?" The predominate response today: for automation and testing, not CGI or biotech, not even for completing a resume now that the Valley is on an upswing, but primarily for automation and testing. The legacy code remains for those companies that started with Perl, and it continues to grow. No matter what anyone tells you, Perl is still in demand. I know. I teach it, not only at UCSC, but to those major companies that use Perl and require their employees to learn it as part of their training path.

Perl by Example is not just a beginner's guide but a complete guide to Perl. It covers many aspects of what Perl can do, from basic syntax to regular expression handling, files, references, objects, working with databases, and much more. Perl also has a rich variety of functions for handling strings, arrays, hashes, and the like. This book will teach you Perl by using complete, working, numbered examples and output with explanations for each line, and avoids veering off into other areas or using complicated explanations that send you off to your favorite search engine in order to figure out what's going on. It helps if you have some programming background, but it is not assumed that you are an experienced programmer or a guru. Anyone reading, writing, or just maintaining Perl programs can greatly profit from this text.

The appendices contain a complete list of functions and definitions, command-line switches, special variables, popular modules, and the Perl debugger; a tutorial to introduce Moose for object-oriented programming; a tutorial covering the Web application framework, Dancer, to replace the need for the Common Gateway Interface; and a guide for using PerlBrew and CPAN ("the gateway to all things Perl") and how to effectively download modules.

I was fortunate to have been introduced to Alastair McGowan-Douglas as the technical expert for reviewing and critiquing this edition. He went well beyond the line of duty and has contributed greatly to not only transforming this book, but to adding his own writing for the tutorials in the appendices, correcting errors, and introducing modern Perl practices. His extensive knowledge and dedication have been invaluable. When we started the project, Alastair wrote to me:

> ". . . I should note that 'modern Perl' refers to the era since 5.10, where practices and conventions got a massive overhaul within the community, as Perl itself had a resurgence in development on it (the language and binary themselves). The previous edition, of course, predates this sea-change, which it seems like the rug has somewhat been swept out from under us.
>
> No matter! We shall prevail, as they say."

And that is precisely what this edition has attempted to do!

—Ellie Quigley
September 2014

Acknowledgments

I'd like to acknowledge the following people for their contributions to the fifth edition.

Thank you, Mark Taub, an editor-in-chief to be praised for being very cool in every step of the process from the signing of the contract to the final book that you have now in your hand. Mark has a way of making such an arduous task seem possible; he soft-talks impossible deadlines, keeps up a steady pressure, and doesn't get crazy over missed deadlines, quietly achieving his goal and always with a subtle sense of humor. Thank you, Mark, for being the driving force behind this new edition!

Of course, none of this would have been possible without the contributions of the Perl pioneers—Larry Wall, Randal Schwartz, and Tom Christiansen. Their books are must reading and include *Learning Perl* by Randal Schwartz and *Programming Perl* by Larry Wall, Tom Christiansen, and Jon Orwant.

Thank you, Vanessa Moore, the project manager and compositor who has been working with me for the past 20 years on making the *by Example* books look beautiful. She excels in her ability to do editing, layout, and artwork, and also in her ability to find errors that most programmers wouldn't see, not to mention an abundance of patience and sense of humor. Without her, this book would be like a painting without color. She's the best!

Also a big thanks to Daniel Holmes from NetApp (RTP) who contributed to the sections on Moose and wrote the final example; and Alastair McGowan-Douglas whose technical expertise was invaluable.

And last, but certainly not least, a huge thanks to all the students, worldwide, who have done all the real troubleshooting and kept the subject alive.

chapter

1

The Practical Extraction and Report Language

1.1 What Is Perl?

"Laziness, impatience, and hubris. Great Perl programmers embrace those virtues."

—Larry Wall

Perl is an all-purpose, open-source (free software) interpreted language maintained and enhanced by a core development team called the Perl Porters. It is used primarily as a scripting language and runs on a number of platforms. Although initially designed for the UNIX operating system, Perl is renowned for its portability and now comes bundled with most operating systems, including RedHat Linux, Solaris, FreeBSD, Macintosh, and more. Due to its versatility, Perl is often referred to as the Swiss Army Knife of programming languages.

Larry Wall wrote the Perl language to manage log files and reports scattered over the network. According to *Wikipedia. org*, Perl was originally named "Pearl," but when Larry Wall realized that PEARL was another programing language that had been around since 1977, he simply dropped the "a" and the name became "Perl." Perl was later dubbed the Practical Extraction and Report Language, and by some, it is referred to as the Pathologically Eclectic Rubbish Lister. Perl is really much more than a practical reporting language or eclectic rubbish lister, as you'll soon see. Perl makes programming easy, flexible, and fast. Those who use it, love it. And those who use it range from experienced programmers to novices with little computer background at all. The number of users continues to grow at a phenomenal rate.[1]

---

1. Perl is spelled "Perl" when referring to the language, and "perl" when referring to the interpreter.

Perl's heritage is UNIX. Perl scripts are functionally similar to UNIX *awk*, *sed*, shell scripts, and *C* programs. Shell scripts consist primarily of UNIX commands; Perl scripts do not. Whereas *sed* and *awk* are used to edit and report on files, Perl does not require a file in order to function. Whereas *C* has none of the pattern matching and wildcard metacharacters of the shells, *sed*, and *awk*, Perl has an extended set of characters. Perl was originally written to manipulate text in files, extract data from files, and write reports, but through continued development, it can manipulate processes, perform networking tasks, process Web pages, talk to databases, and analyze scientific data. Perl is truly the Swiss Army Knife of programming languages; there is a tool for everyone.

The examples in this book were created on systems running Solaris, Linux, Macintosh, UNIX, and Win32.

Perl is often associated with a camel symbol, a trademark of O'Reilly Media, which published the first book on Perl called *Programming Perl* by Larry Wall and Randal Schwartz (also referred to as "the Camel Book").

1.2 What Is an Interpreted Language?

To write Perl programs, you need two things: a text editor and a perl interpreter, which you can download very quickly from any number of Web sites, including *perl.org*, *cpan.org*, and *activestate.com*. Unlike with compiled languages, such as *C++* and *Java*, you do not need to first compile your program into machine-readable code before executing it. The perl interpreter does it all; it handles the compilation, interpretation, and execution of your program. Advantages of using an interpreted language such as Perl is that it runs on almost every platform, is relatively easy to learn, and is very fast and flexible.

Languages such as Python, JavaScript, and Perl are interpreted languages that use an intermediate representation, which combines both compilation and interpretation. It compiles the user's code into an internal condensed format called bytecode, or threaded code, which is then executed by the interpreter. When you run Perl programs, you need to be aware of two phases: the compilation phase, and then the run phase where you will see the program results. If you have syntax errors, such as a misspelled keyword or a missing quote, the compiler will send an error. If you pass the compiler phase, you could have other problems when the program starts running. If you pass both of these phases, you will probably start working on formatting to make the output look nicer, improving the program to make it more efficient, and so forth.

The interpreter also provides a number of command-line switches (options) to control its behavior. There are switches to check syntax, send warnings, loop through files, execute statements, turn on the debugger, and so forth. You will learn about these options throughout the following chapters.

1.3 Who Uses Perl?

Because Perl has built-in functions to easily manipulate processes and files, and because Perl is portable (that is, it can run on a number of different platforms), it is especially popular with system administrators, who often oversee one or more systems of different types. The phenomenal growth of the World Wide Web greatly increased interest in Perl, which was the most popular language for writing CGI scripts to generate dynamic Web pages. Even today, with the advent of other languages focused on processing Web pages, such as Ruby, Node, and ASP.net, Perl continues its popularity with system and database administrators, scientists, geneticists, and anyone who has a need to collect data from files and manipulate it.

Anyone can use Perl, but it is easier to learn if you are already experienced in writing UNIX shell scripts or languages derived from *C*, such as *C++* and *Java*. For these people, the migration to Perl will be relatively easy. For those who have little programming experience, the learning curve might be a little steeper, but after learning Perl, there may be no reason to ever use anything else.

If you are familiar with UNIX utilities such as *awk*, *grep*, *sed*, and *tr*, you know that they don't share the same syntax; the options and arguments are handled differently, and the rules change from one utility to the other. If you are a shell programmer, you usually go through the grueling task of learning a variety of utilities, shell metacharacters, regular expression metacharacters, quotes, more quotes, and so forth. Also, shell programs are limited and slow. To perform more complex mathematical tasks and to handle interprocess communication and binary data, for example, you may have to turn to a higher-level language, such as *C*, *C++*, or *Java*. If you know *C*, you also know that searching for patterns in files and interfacing with the operating system to process files and execute commands are not always easy tasks.

Perl integrates the best features of shell programming, *C*, and the UNIX utilities *awk*, *grep*, *sed*, and *tr*. Because it is fast and not limited to chunks of data of a particular size, many system administrators and database administrators have switched from the traditional shell scripting to Perl. *C++* and *Java* programmers can enjoy the object-oriented features added in Perl 5, including the ability to create reusable, extensible modules. Now, with Perl you can generate Perl in other languages, and you can embed other languages in Perl. There is something for everyone who uses Perl, and for every task. As Larry Wall says, "There's more than one way to do it."[2]

You don't have to know everything about Perl to start writing scripts. You don't even have to be a programmer. This book will help you get a good jump-start, and you will quickly see some of its many capabilities and advantages. Then you can decide how far you want to go with Perl. If nothing else, Perl is fun!

---

2. Larry Wall, "Diligence, Patience, and Humility," *http://www.oreilly.com/catalog/opensources/book/larry.html*.

1.3.1 Which Perl?

Perl has been through a number of revisions. The last version of Perl 4 was Perl 4, patchlevel 36 (Perl 4.036), released in 1992, making it ancient. Perl 5.000 (also ancient), introduced in fall 1994, was a complete rewrite of the Perl source code that optimized the language and introduced objects and many other features. Despite these changes, Perl 5 remains highly compatible with the previous releases. As of this writing, the current stable version of Perl is 5.20, actively maintained by a large group of voluntary contributors listed at *www.ohloh.net/p/perl/contributors*. Perl 6 is the next generation of another Perl redesign and does not have an official release date. It has new features, but the basic components of the Perl language you learn here will be essentially the same.

From Wikipedia:

> Some observers credit the release of Perl 5.10 with the start of the Modern Perl movement. In particular, this phrase describes a style of development which embraces the use of the CPAN, takes advantage of recent developments in the language (see Table 1.1), and is rigorous about creating high-quality code.[3]

Table 1.1   Release Dates and Recent Developments

Major Version	Latest Update	Status
5.5	02/23/2004	Old version
5.6	11/15/2003	Old version
5.8	12/14/2008	Old version
5.10	08/23/2009	Old version
5.12	11/10/2012	Old version
5.14	03/10/2013	Old version
5.16	03/11/2013	Old version
5.18	01/07/2014	Older version, but still supported
5.20	05/27/2014	Current version

1.3.2 What Are Perl 6, Rakudo Perl, and Parrot?

"Perl 5 was my rewrite of Perl. I want Perl 6 to be the community's rewrite of Perl and of the community."

—Larry Wall, State of the Onion speech, TPC4

Perl 6 is essentially Perl 5 with many new features. Although they continue to develop in parallel, Perl 6 will not supersede Perl 5. The basic language syntax, features, and purpose

---

3. Wikipedia.org, "Perl," *http://en.wikipedia.org/wiki/Perl.*

will be the same. If you know Perl, you will still know Perl. If you learn Perl from this book, you will be prepared to jump into Perl 6 when it is released. Perl 6 has been described by Perl.org as learning Australian English if you speak American English, rather than trying to switch from English to Chinese.

Rakudo Star, a useful and usable distribution of Perl 6 that runs on the Parrot virtual machine, was recently released in October 2013. To find out more go to *http://rakudo.org*.

Parrot is a virtual machine designed to efficiently compile and execute bytecode for dynamic languages. Parrot currently hosts a variety of language implementations in various stages of completion, including Tcl, JavaScript, Ruby, Lua, Scheme, PHP, Python, Perl 6, APL, and a .NET bytecode translator.[4]

To learn more about the latest Perl core development with Perl 6, Rakudo, and Parrot, go to *http://dev.perl.org* (see Figure 1.1).

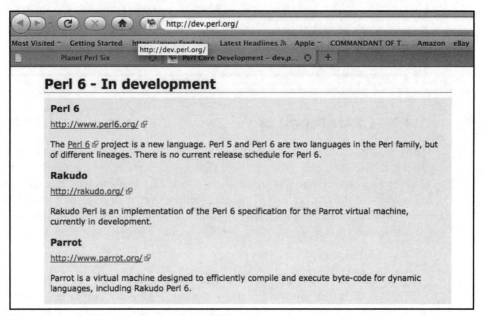

Figure 1.1   The Perl 6 development Web site.

And for a biographical sketch of Larry Wall and the history of Perl, go to *http://www.softpanorama.org/People/Wall/index.shtml#Perl_history*.

---

4. Parrot Speaks Your Language, *http://parrot.org*.

1.4   Where to Get Perl

Perl downloading and instructions are available from a number of sources. You can check the following popular sites for a Perl distribution for your computer: *cpan.org*, *perl.org*, and *activestate.com*, and *strawberryperl.com*.

> **What Is Strawberry Perl?**
> Strawberry Perl is Perl for the Microsoft Windows platform. While most other distributions rely on the user having software development tools already set up to install certain Perl components, Strawberry Perl ships with the most commonly used tools preconfigured and packaged, including Perl binaries, the gcc compiler, all external libraries, all bundled database clients, and more. The latest version, as of this writing, is Strawberry Perl 5.20.1.1, for both 32- and 64-bit versions of Windows. (You can download it at *http://strawberryperl.com*). Larry Wall says, "When I'm on Windows, I use Strawberry Perl."

1.4.1   CPAN (cpan.org)

The primary source for Perl distribution is CPAN, which is available at *www.cpan.org* (see Figure 1.2). CPAN, the "gateway to all things Perl," stands for the Comprehensive Perl Archive Network, a Web site that houses all the free Perl material you will ever need, including documentation, FAQs, modules and scripts, binary distributions and source code, and announcements. CPAN is mirrored all over the world, and you can find the nearest mirror at

- *www.perl.com/CPAN*
- *www.cpan.org*

CPAN is the place you will go to if you want to find modules to help you with your work. The CPAN search engine will let you find modules under a large number of categories. Modules are discussed in Chapter 13, "Modularize It, Package It, and Send It to the Library!"

Go to *www.cpan.org/ports* to find out more about what's available for your platform, of which Perl supports more than 100.

Figure 1.2   The CPAN Web site. Click on the Ports tab to find your platform.

1.4.2   Downloads and Other Resources for Perl (perl.org)

The official Perl home page, run by O'Reilly Media, Inc. is *www.perl.com*, but it seems that everything you will need is found at *www.perl.org* (see Figure 1.3).

Figure 1.3 The Perl.org Web site.

1.4.3   ActivePerl (activestate.com)

If you want to install Perl quickly and easily, ActivePerl is a complete, self-installing distribution of Perl based on the standard Perl sources for Windows, Mac OS X, Linux, Solaris, AIX, and HP-UX. It is distributed online at the ActiveState site (*www.activestate. com*). The complete ActivePerl package contains the binary of the core Perl distribution, complete online documentation, and all the essential tools for Perl development, including PPM, a handy perl package manager. This is available at *www.activestate.com/activeperl* (see Figure 1.4).

Figure 1.4 The ActiveState Web site, where you can download ActivePerl.

1.4.4   What Version Do I Have?

To obtain your Perl version, date the binary version was built, patches, and some copyright information, type the line shown in Example 1.1 (the dollar sign is the shell prompt).

EXAMPLE 1.1

```
1 $ perl -v

This is perl 5, version 18, subversion 2 (v5.18.2) built for darwin-
thread-multi-2level (with 2 registered patches, see perl -V for more
detail)

Copyright 1987-2013, Larry Wall

Perl may be copied only under the terms of either the Artistic License or
the GNU General Public License, which may be found in the Perl 5 source
kit.

Complete documentation for Perl, including FAQ lists, should be found on
this system using "man perl" or "perldoc perl".  If you have access to the
Internet, point your browser at http://www.perl.org/, the Perl Home Page.
```

EXPLANATION

1   This version of Perl is 5.16. for the Mac.
2   Larry Wall, the author of Perl, owns the copyright.
3   Perl may be copied under the terms specified by the Artistic License or GNU. Perl is distributed under GNU, the Free Software Foundation, meaning that Perl is free.

1.5   Perl Documentation

Today, you can find answers to any Perl questions simply by using your favorite search engine or going to the Perl.org Web site. Most Perl distributions also come with full documentation in both HTML and PDF formats.

1.5.1   Where to Find the Most Complete Documentation from Perl

For the most complete documentation, type the Perl function you are looking for in your search engine or just go directly to *perldoc.perl.org* (see Figure 1.5) for all the complete documentation for any version of Perl.

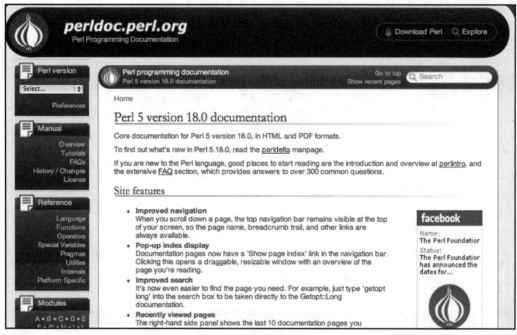

Figure 1.5   Documentation at perldoc.perl.org.

1.5.2   Perl *man* Pages

The standard Perl distribution comes with complete online documentation, called *man* pages, which provide help for all the standard utilities. (The name derives from the UNIX *man* [manual] pages.) Perl has divided its *man* pages into categories. If you type the following at your command-line prompt:

```
man perl
```

you will get a list of all the sections by category. So, if you want help on how to use Perl's regular expressions, you would type:

```
man perlre
```

and if you want help on subroutines, you would type:

```
man perlsub
```

The Perl categories are listed in Table 1.2, with the following sections available only in the online reference manual.

Table 1.2 Perl Categories

Category	What It's Used For
perlbot	Object-oriented tricks and examples
perldebug	Debugging
perldiag	Diagnostic messages
perldsc	Data structures: intro
perlform	Formats
perlfunc	Built-in functions
perlipc	Interprocess communication
perllol	Data structures: lists of lists
perlmod	Modules
perlobj	Objects
perlop	Operators and precedence
perlpod	Plain old documentation
perlre	Regular expressions
perlref	References
perlsock	Extension for socket support
perlstyle	Style guide
perlsub	Subroutines
perltie	Objects hidden behind simple variables
perltrap	Traps for the unwary
perlvar	Predefined variables

If you are trying to find out how a particular library module works, you can use the *perldoc* command to get the documentation. (This command will give you documentation for the version of Perl you are currently using, whereas the *man* pages refer to the system Perl.) For example, if you want to know about the *Moose* module, type at the command line:

```
perldoc Moose
```

and the documentation for the *Moose.pm* module will be displayed. If you type:

```
perldoc Carp
```

the documentation for the *Carp.pm* module will be displayed.

To get documentation on a specific Perl function, type *perldoc -f* and the name of the function. For example, to find out about the *localtime* function, you would execute the following command at your command-line prompt (you may have to set your UNIX/DOS path to execute this program directly):

```
perldoc -f localtime
localtime EXPR
localtime
        Converts a time as returned by the time function to a 9-element
        list with the time analyzed for the local time zone. Typically
        used as follows:
            #   0    1     2      3      4      5      6      7      8
            ($sec,$min,$hour,$mday,$mon,$year,$wday,$yday,$isdst) =
                                                    localtime(time);

<continues>
```

1.5.3   Online Documentation

ActivePerl provides excellent documentation (from *ActiveState.com*) when you download Perl from its site. As shown in Figure 1.6, there are links to everything you need to know about Perl.

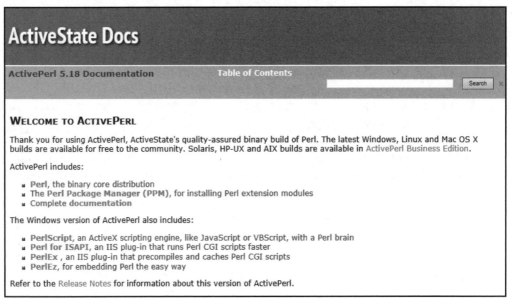

Figure 1.6   Perl documentation from ActiveState.

1.6 **What You Should Know**

1. Who wrote Perl?

2. What does Perl stand for?

3. What is the meaning of "open source"?

4. What is the current release?

5. What is Perl used for?

6. What is an interpreted language?

7. Where can you get Perl?

8. What is Strawberry Perl?

9. What is ActivePerl?

10. What is CPAN?

11. Where do you get documentation?

12. How would you find documentation for a specific Perl function?

1.7 **What's Next?**

In the next chapter, you will learn how to create basic Perl scripts and execute them. You will learn what goes in a Perl script, and about Perl syntax, statements, and comments. You will learn how to check for syntax errors and how to execute Perl at the command line with a number of Perl options.

chapter
2

Perl Quick Start

2.1 Quick Start, Quick Reference

The following reference gives you a general overview of Perl constructs and syntax. It can be used later as a cheat sheet to help you quickly refresh your memory without searching through chapters for a simple concept.

2.1.1 A Note to Programmers

If you have had previous programming experience in another language (such as Visual Basic, *C/C++, C#, Java*, Python, or PHP), and you are familiar with basic concepts (such as variables, loops, conditional statements, and functions), Table 2.1 will give you a quick overview of the constructs and syntax of the Perl language.

At the end of each section, you will be given the chapter number that describes the particular construct and a short, fully functional Perl example designed to illustrate how that construct is used.

2.1.2 A Note to Non-Programmers

If you are not familiar with programming, skip this chapter and go to Chapter 5, "What's in a Name?" You may want to refer to this chapter later for a quick reference.

2.1.3 Perl Syntax and Constructs

Table 2.1 summarizes the Perl concepts discussed throughout this book. If applicable, cross-references are given, as to where you can read further on these topics.

15

Table 2.1 Perl Syntax and Constructs

The Script File	A Perl script is created in a text editor. Normally, there is no special extension required in the filename, unless specified by the application running the script (for example, if running under Apache as a *cgi* program, the filename may require a *.pl* or *.cgi* extension).
	See Chapter 3, "Perl Scripts."
Comments	Perl comments are preceded by a # sign. They are ignored by the interpreter. They can be anywhere on the line and span only one line.
	See Section 3.3.2, "Comments."

EXAMPLE

```
print "Hello, world";  # This is a comment
#  And this is a comment
```

Free Form	Perl is a free-form language. Statements must be terminated with a semicolon but can be anywhere on the line and span multiple lines.
	See Section 3.3.3, "Perl Statements."
Printing Output	The *print*, *say*, and *printf* functions are built-in functions used to display output. The *print* function arguments consist of a comma-separated list of strings and/or numbers.
	The *say* function (Perl 5.10.1) is the same as the *print* function except it automatically appends a newline at the end of the string.
	The *printf* function is similar to the C *printf()* function and is used for formatting output.
	Parentheses are not required around the argument list.
	See Chapter 4, "Getting a Handle on Printing."

FORMAT

```
print value, value, value;
printf ( string format [, mixed args [, mixed ...]] );
```

EXAMPLE

```
use v5.10;  # To enable say function
print "Hello, world\n";
print "Hello,", " world\n";
say "Hello,", " world";  # adds a newline; new feature
                         # in version 5.10.1
print ("It's such a perfect day!\n");  # Parens optional
print "The the date and time are: ", scalar localtime, "\n";
printf "Meet %s:Age 5d%:Salary \$%10.2f\n", "John", 40,
    55000;  # formatting strings and numbers
```

(continued)

Table 2.1   Perl Syntax and Constructs (continued)

Variables	Perl supports three basic variable types: scalars, arrays, and hashes (associative arrays). Perl does not have a native Boolean data type such as true or false, but does comparison with strings and integers to get the same behavior.
	Perl variables don't have to be declared before being used.
	Variable names start with a "funny character" (also called a sigil) followed by a letter and any number of alphanumeric characters (the identifier), including the underscore. The funny character represents the data type and context. The characters following the funny symbol are case-sensitive.
	If a variable name starts with a letter, it may consist of any number of letters (an underscore counts as a letter) and/or digits. If the variable does not start with a letter, it must consist of only one character.
	See Chapter 5, "What's in a Name?"
Scalar	A scalar variable holds a single value, a single string, a number, and so forth.
	The name of the scalar variable is preceded by a $ sign. Scalar context means that *one* value is being used.
	See Chapter 5, "What's in a Name?"
	EXAMPLE

```
$first_name = "Melanie";
$last_name = "Quigley";
$salary = 125000.00;
print $first_name, $last_name, $salary;
```

Array	An array holds an *ordered list* of scalars; that is, strings and/or numbers. The elements of the array are indexed by integers starting at 0. The name of the array is preceded by an @ sign.
	Some commonly used built-in array functions:

- *delete*   removes a value from an element of the array
- *pop*   removes last element
- *push*   adds new elements to the end of the array
- *shift*   removes first element
- *sort*   sorts the elements of an array
- *splice*   removes or adds elements from some position in the array
- *unshift*   adds new elements to the beginning of the array

See Section 5.3, "Array Functions."

EXAMPLE

```
@names = ( "Jessica", "Michelle", "Linda" );
print "@names";  # Prints array with elements separated by a space
print "$names[0] and $names[2]"; # Prints "Jessica" and "Linda"
print "$names[-1]\n";  # Prints "Linda"
$names[3]="Nicole";    # Assign a new value as the 4th element
```

(continued)

Table 2.1   Perl Syntax and Constructs (continued)

Hash	An associative array, called a hash, is an unordered list of key/value pairs, indexed by strings. The name of the hash is preceded by a % symbol. (The % is not evaluated when enclosed in either single or double quotes.) The keys <u>do not have to be quoted</u> as long as they don't begin with a number or contain spaces, internal hyphens, or special characters.

Some commonly used built-in hash functions:

- *keys*   retrieves all the keys in a hash
- *values*   retrieves all the values in a hash
- *each*   retrieves a key/value pair from a hash
- *delete*   removes a key/value pair
- *exists*   tests existence of key

See Section 5.4, "Hash (Associative Array) Functions."

EXAMPLE

```
%employee =  (
    "Name"      => "Jessica Savage",
    "Phone"     => "(925) 555-1274",
    "Position"  => "CEO"
);
print "$employee{'Name'}";  # Print a value
$employee{"SSN"}="999-333-2345";  # Assign a key/value
```

Predefined   Perl provides a large number of predefined variables. The following is a list of some
Variables   common predefined variables:

- *$_*   The default input and pattern-searching space.
- *$.*   Current line number for the last filehandle accessed.
- *$@*   The Perl syntax error message from the last *eval()* operator.
- *$!*   Yields the current value of the error message, used with *die*.
- *$0*   Contains the name of the program being executed.
- *$$*   The process number of the Perl running this script.
- *@ARGV*   Contains the command-line arguments.
- *ARGV*   A special filehandle that iterates over command-line filenames in *@ARGV*.
- *@INC*   The search path for library files.
- *@_*   Within a subroutine, the array @_ contains the parameters passed to that subroutine.
- *%ENV*   The hash *%ENV* contains your current environment.
- *%SIG*   The hash *%SIG, when set,* contains signal handlers for signals.

See Section A.2, "Special Variables," in Appendix A.

Constants   A constant value, once set, cannot be modified. An example of a constant is Pi or the num-
(Literals)   ber of feet in a mile. It doesn't change. Constants are defined with the *constant* pragma,
              shown as follows in the example.

(continued)

Table 2.1   Perl Syntax and Constructs (continued)

	EXAMPLE
	
	``perl
	use constant BUFFER_SIZE => 4096;
	use constant Pi => 4 * atan2 1, 1;
	use constant DEBUGGING => 0;
	use constant ISBN => "0-13-028251-0";
	Pi=6; # Cannot modify Pi; produces an error.
	``

Numbers	Perl supports integers (decimal, octal, hexadecimal), floating-point numbers, scientific notation.
	
	See Section 4.3.2, "Literals (Numeric, String, and Special)."
	
	EXAMPLE
	
	``perl
	$year = 2016; # integer
	$mode = 0775; # octal number in base 8
	$product_price = 29.95; # floating-point number in base 10
	$favorite_color = 0x33CC99; # integer in base 16 (hexadecimal)
	$distance_to_moon=3.844e+5; # floating-point in scientific notation
	$bits = 0b10110110; # binary number
	``

Strings and Quotes	A string is a sequence of characters enclosed in quotes. The quotes must be matched; for example, *"string"* or *'string'*. Scalar and array variables (*$x*, *@name*) and backslash sequences (\n, \t, \", etc.) are interpreted within double quotes; a backslash will escape a quotation mark; a single quote can be embedded in a set of double quotes; and a double quote can be embedded in a set of single quotes. A *here document* is a block of text embedded between user-defined tags, the first tag preceded by <<. The following shows three ways to quote a string:
	
	• Single quotes: `'It rains in Spain';`
	• Double quotes: `"It rains in Spain";`
	• *here document*: `print <<EOF;`
	              `It rains in Spain`
	         `EOF`
	
	See Section 4.3.1, "Quotes Matter!" and Section 4.3.3, "Printing Without Quotes—The *here document*."
	
	EXAMPLE
	
	``perl
	$question = 'He asked her if she wouldn\'t mind going to Spain';
	                                        # Single quotes
	$answer = 'She said: "No, but it rains in Spain."'; # Single quotes
	$line = "\tHe said he wouldn't take her to Spain\n";
	$temperature = 78;
	print "It is currently $temperature degrees.";
	     # Prints: "It is currently 78 degrees." because variables are
	     # interpreted when enclosed in double quotes, but not single
	print <<END;
	     It
	     rains in
	     Spain
	END
	# Prints: "It rains in Spain"
	``

(continued)

Table 2.1   Perl Syntax and Constructs (continued)

Alternative Quotes	Perl provides an alternative form of quoting. The string to be quoted is delimited by a non-alphanumeric character or characters that can be paired, such as *( )*, *{ }*, *[ ]*.

The constructs are *qq*, *q*, *qw*, and *qx*.

See the section, "Perl's Alternative Quotes" in Chapter 4.

EXAMPLE

```
print qq/Hello\n/;   # same as: print "Hello\n";
print q/He owes $5.00/, "\n"; # same as: print 'He owes $5.00', "\n";
@states=qw( ME MT CA FL );   # same as ('ME', 'MT', 'CA', 'FL')
$today = qx(date);  # same as $today = `date`; UNIX only
```

Operators	Perl offers many types of operators, but for the most part they are the same as *C/C++/Java* or PHP operators. Types of operators are:

- Assignment   =, +=, -=, *= , %=, ^=, &=, |=, .=, /=, &&=, ||=, >>=, <<=
- Numeric equality   ==, !=, <=>
- String equality   *eq, ne, cmp*
- Relational numeric   >, >= , <, <=
- Relational string   *gt, ge, lt, le*
- Range   *5 .. 10*   (e.g., range between 5 and 10, increment by 1)
- Logical   *&&, and, ||, or, XOR, xor, !*
- Pre/post increment,   ++, --
  decrement
- File   *-r, -w, -x,-o, -e, -z, -s, -f, -d, -l,* etc.
- Bitwise   *~, &, |, ^, <<, >>*
- String concatenation   *.*
- String repetition   *x*
- Arithmetic   *, /, -, +, %*
- Pattern matching   *=~, !~, ~~*

See Chapter 6, "Where's the Operator?"

EXAMPLE

```
print "\nArithmetic Operators\n";
print ((3+2) * (5-3)/2);

print "\nString Operators\n";  # Concatenation
print "\tTommy" . ' ' . "Savage";

print "\nComparison Operators\n";
print 5>=3 , "\n";
print 47==23 , "\n";

print "\nLogical Operators\n";
$x > $y && $y < 100;
$answer eq "yes" || $money == 200;
```

(continued)

Table 2.1   Perl Syntax and Constructs (continued)

```
print "\nCombined Assignment Operators\n";
$a = 47;
$a += 3;    # short for $a = $a + 3
$a++;       # autoincrement
print $a;   # Prints 51
print "\nPattern Matching Operators\n"
$color = "green";
print $color if $color =~ /^gr/;    # $color matches a pattern
                                    # starting with 'gr'
$answer = "Yes";
print "Yes!\n" if $answer !~ /[Yy]/;  # $answer matches a pattern
                                      # containing 'Y' or 'y'
```

Conditionals	*if* Statement—The basic *if* construct evaluates an expression enclosed in parentheses, and if the expression evaluates to true, the block following the construct is executed. Perl also provides *if* and *unless* modifiers.

See Section 7.1.1, "Decision Making—Conditional Constructs."

FORMAT

```
if ( expression ) {
   statements
}
```

EXAMPLE

```
       if ( $x == $y ){ print "$x is equal to $y"; }
```

if/else Statement—The *if/else* block is a two-way decision. If the expression inside the *if* construct is true, that block of statements is executed; if false, the *else* block of statements is executed.

See Section 7.1.1, "Decision Making—Conditional Constructs."

FORMAT

```
if ( expression ){
   statements;
}
else{
   statements;
}
```

EXAMPLE

```
$coin_toss = int (rand(2 )) + 1; # Get random number between 1 and 2
if( $coin_toss == 1 ) {
   print "You tossed HEAD\n";
}
else {
   print "You tossed TAIL\n";
}
```

(continued)

Table 2.1   Perl Syntax and Constructs (continued)

if/elsif/else Statement—The *if/elsif/else* offers multiway branch; if the expression following the *if* is not true, each of the *elsif* expressions is evaluated until one is true; otherwise, the optional *else* statements are executed.

See Section 7.1.1, "Decision Making—Conditional Constructs."

FORMAT

```
if ( expression ){
   statements;
}
elsif ( expression ){
   statements;
}
elsif (expression){
   statements;
}
else{
   statements;
}
```

EXAMPLE

```
$day_of_week = int(rand(7)) + 1;   # 1 is Monday, 7 Sunday
print "Today is: $day_of_week\n";
if ( $day_of_week >=1 && $day_of_week <=4 ) {
   print "Business hours are from 9 am to 9 pm\n";
}
elsif ( $day_of_week == 5) {
   print "Business hours are from 9 am to 6 pm\n";
}
else {
   print "We are closed on weekends\n";
}
```

Conditional Operator	Like *C/C++*, Perl also offers a shortform of the *if/else* syntax, which uses three operands and two operators (also called the ternary operator). The question mark is followed by a statement that is executed if the condition being tested is true, and the colon is followed by a statement that is executed if the condition is false.

(condition) ? statement_if_true : statement_if_false;

See Section 6.3.4, "Conditional Ooperators."

EXAMPLE

```
$coin_toss = int rand(2) + 1;  # Generate a random number
                               # between 1 and 2
print ( $coin_toss == 1 ? "You tossed HEAD\n" : "You tossed TAIL\n" );
```

(continued)

Table 2.1 Perl Syntax and Constructs (continued)

Loops	A loop is a way to specify a piece of code that repeats many times. Perl supports several types of loops: the *while* loop, *do-while* loop, *for* loop, and *foreach* loop. See Chapter 7, "If Only, Unconditionally, Forever."

while Loop—The *while* is followed by an expression enclosed in parentheses, and a block of statements. As long as the expression tests true, the loop continues to iterate.

See Section 7.3.1, "The *while* Loop."

FORMAT

```
while ( conditional expression ) {
        code block A
}
```

EXAMPLE

```
$count=0;  # Initial value
while ($count < 10){  # Test
   print $n;
   $count++;  # Increment value
}
```

until Loop—The *until* is followed by an expression enclosed in parentheses, and a block of statements. As long as the expression tests false, the loop continues to iterate.

See Section 7.3.2, "The *until* Loop."

FORMAT

```
until ( conditional expression ) {
        code block A
}
```

EXAMPLE

```
$count=0;  # Initial value
until ($count == 10){  # Test
   print $n;
   $count++;  # Increment value
}
```

do-while Loop—The *do-while* loop is similar to the *while* loop except it checks its looping expression at the end of the loop block rather than at the beginning, guaranteeing that the loop block is executed at least once.

See Section 7.3.3, "The *do/while* and *do/until* Loops."

FORMAT

```
do {
   code block A
} while (expression);
```

(continued)

Table 2.1   Perl Syntax and Constructs (continued)

EXAMPLE

```
$count=0;  # Initial value
do {
   print "$n ";
   $count++;  # Increment value
} while ($count < 10 );  # Test
```

for Loop—The *for* loop has three expressions to evaluate, each separated by a semicolon. The first initializes a variable and is evaluated only once. The second tests whether the value is true, and if it is true, the block is entered; if not, the loop exits. After the block of statements is executed, control returns to the third expression, which changes the value of the variable being tested. The second expression is tested again, and so forth.

See Section 7.3.4, "The *for* Loop (The Three-Part Loop)."

FORMAT

```
for( initialization; conditional expression; increment/decrement ) {
   block of code
}
```

EXAMPLE

```
for($count = 0; $count < 10; $count++){
   print "$count\n";
}
```

foreach Loop—The *foreach* is used only to iterate through a list, one item at a time setting either $_ or a named variable to each element of the list in turn. It is just the *for* loop using a list context. In fact, you can write the following examples using either *for* or *foreach*.

See Section 7.3.5, "The *foreach (for)* Loop."

FORMAT

```
foreach (1 .. 5){
      print "$_\n";    # prints 1 2 3 4 5
}
foreach $item ( @list ) {
      print $item, "\n";
}
```

EXAMPLE

```
@dessert = ("ice cream", "cake", "pudding", "fruit");
foreach $choice (@dessert){  # Iterates through each element in array
   print "Dessert choice is: $choice\n";
}
```

(continued)

Table 2.1 Perl Syntax and Constructs (continued)

Loop Control—The *last* statement is used to break out of a loop from within the loop block. It is often used to exit an infinite loop. The *next* statement is used to skip over the remaining statements within the loop block and start back at the top of the loop.

See Section 7.4.3, "Loop Control."

EXAMPLE

```
$n=0;
while( $n < 10){
    print $n;
    if ($n == 3){
        last;      # Break out of loop
    }
    $n++;
}
print "Out of the loop.<br>";
```

EXAMPLE

```
for($n=0; $n < 10; $n++){
    if ($n == 3){
        next;       # Start at top of loop;
                    # skip remaining statements in block
    }
    echo "\$n = $n<br>";
}
print "Out of the loop.<br>";
```

Subroutines/ Functions

A function is a block of code that performs a task and can be invoked from another part of the program. Data can be passed to the function via arguments. A function may or may not return a value. Any valid Perl code can make up the definition block of a function. Variables outside the function are available inside the function. The *my* operator will make the specified variables lexical, visible within the block where they are created.

See Chapter 11, "How Do Subroutines Function?"

FORMAT

```
sub function_name{
    block of code
}
```

EXAMPLE

```
sub greetings() {
    print "Welcome to Perl!<\n>";   # Function definition
}
&greetings;    # Function call
greetings();   # Function call most commonly used
```

(continued)

Table 2.1   Perl Syntax and Constructs (continued)

EXAMPLE

```
my_$year = 2000;

if (is_leap_year( $my_year)) {  # Call function with an argument
   print "$my_year is a leap year\n";
}
else {
   print "$my_year is not a leap year";
}

sub is_leap_year {  # Function definition

   my $year = shift(@_);  # Shift off the year from
                          # the parameter list, @_
   return ((($year % 4 == 0) && ($year % 100 != 0)) ||
      ($year % 400 == 0)) ? 1 : 0;  # What is returned
                                    # from the function
}
```

Files   Perl provides the *open* function to open files and pipes for reading, writing, and appending. The *open* function takes a user-defined filehandle as its first argument and a string containing the symbol for read/write/append followed by the real path to the system file

See Chapter 10, "Getting a Handle on Files."

EXAMPLE

To open a file for reading:
```
open(my $fh, "<", "filename");  # Opens "filename" for reading.
open (my $fh, "/home/ellie/myfile") or die "Can't open file: $!\n";
```

To open a file for writing:
```
open(my $fh, ">", "filename");  # Opens "filename" for writing.
                                # Creates or truncates file.
```

To open a file for appending:
```
open(my $fh, ">>", "filename");  # Opens "filename" for appending.
                                 # Creates or appends to file.
```

To open a file for reading and writing:
```
open(my $fh, "+<", "filename");  # Opens "filename" for read,
                                 # then write.
open($fh, "+>", "filename");  # Opens "filename" for write,
                              # then read.
```

(continued)

Table 2.1 Perl Syntax and Constructs (continued)

To close a file:

```
close($fh);
```

To read from a file:

```
while(<$fh>){ print; }  # Read one line at a time from file.

@lines = <$fh>;         # Slurp all lines into an array.
print "@lines\n";
```

To write to a file:

```
open($fh, ">","file") or die "Can't open file: $!\n";
print $fh "This line is written to the file just opened.\n";
print $fh "And this line is also written to the file just opened.\n";
```

EXAMPLE

To test file attributes:

```
print "File is readable, writeable, and executable\n" if -r $file and
-w _ and -x _;
       # Is it readable, writeable, and executable?
print "File was last modified ",-M $file, " days ago.\n";
       # When was it last modified?
print "File is a directory.\n " if -d $file;
       # Is it a directory?
```

Pipes Pipes can be used to send the output from system commands as input to Perl and to send Perl's output as input to a system command. To create a pipe, also called a filter, the *open* system call is used. It takes two arguments: a user-defined handle and the operating system command, either preceded or appended with the | symbol. If the command is preceded with a |, the operating system command reads Perl output. If the command is appended with the | symbol, Perl reads from the pipe; if the command is prepended with |, Perl writes to the pipe.

See Chapter 10, "Getting a Handle on Files."

EXAMPLE

Input filter:

```
open(FOO, "|-", "ls") or die "$!";  # Open a pipe to read from
while(<FOO>){ print ; }   # Prints list of UNIX files
                          # Use dir /b for Windows
```

Output filter:

```
open(SORT, "-|", "sort" ) or die "$!" ;  # Open pipe to write to
print SORT "dogs\ncats\nbirds\n"   # Sorts birds, cats, dogs
                                   # on separate lines.
```

(continued)

Regular Expressions.   A regular expression is set of characters normally enclosed in forward slashes. They are to match patterns in text and to refine searches and substitutions. Perl is best known for its pattern matching (see Chapter 8, "Regular Expressions—Pattern Matching"). Table 2.2 shows a list of metacharacters and what they mean when used in a regular expression.

Table 2.2 • Some Regular Expression Metacharacters

Metacharacter	What It Represents
^	Matches at the beginning of a line
$	Matches at the end of a line
a.c	Matches an *a*, any single character, and a *c*
[abc]	Matches an *a* or *b* or *c*
[^abc]	Matches a character that is not an *a* or *b* or *c*
[0-9]	Matches one digit between *0* and *9*
ab*c	Matches an *a*, followed by zero or more *b*s and a *c*
ab+c	Matches an *a*, followed by one or more *b*s and a *c*
ab?c	Matches an *a*, followed by zero or one *b* and a *c*
(ab)+c	Matches one or more occurrences of group *ab* followed by a *c*
(ab) (c)	Captures *ab* and assigns it to $1, captures *c* and assigns it to $2

```
EXAMPLES
$_ = "looking for a needle in a haystack";
print if /needle/;  # If $_contains needle, the string is printed.

$_ = "looking for a needle in a haystack";  # Using regular expression
                                            # metacharacters
print if  /^[Nn]..dle/;                     # characters

$str = "I am feeling blue, blue, blue..."
$str =~ s/blue/upbeat/;  # Substitute first occurrence of "blue" with "upbeat"
print $str;
I am feeling upbeat, blue, blue...

$str="I am feeling BLue, BLUE...";
$str = ~ s/blue/upbeat/ig;  # Ignore case, global substitution
print $str;
I am feeling upbeat, upbeat...

$str = "Peace and War";
$str =~ s/(Peace) and (War)/$2 and $1/i;  # $1 gets 'Peace', $2 gets 'War'
print $str;
War and Peace.

$str = "He gave me 5 dollars."
$str =~ s/5/6*7/e;  # Rather than string substitution, evaluate replacement side
print $str;
He gave me 42 dollars.
```

Passing Arguments at the Command Line.   The *@ARGV* array is used to hold command-line arguments. If the ARGV filehandle is used, the arguments are treated as files; otherwise, arguments are strings coming in from the command line to be used in a script. (See Chapter 10, "Getting a Handle on Files.")

EXAMPLE 2.1

```
$ perlscript filea fileb filec

(In Script)
print "@ARGV\n";  # lists arguments: filea fileb filec
print scalar @ARGV, "\n";  # Prints the number of arguments
while(<ARGV>){  # filehandle ARGV -- arguments treated as files
   print;  # Print each line of every file listed in @ARGV
}
-------------------------
while(<>){ print; }  # Empty angle brackets implicity use ARGV and STDIN
                     # if no arguments are provided at the command line
```

References and Pointers.   Perl references are also called **pointers** (although they are not to be confused with *C* language pointers). A reference is a scalar variable that contains the address of another variable. To create a reference, the backslash operator is used. References are used to pass arguments as addresses (pass by reference) to functions, create nested data structures, and create objects. (See Chapter 12, "Does This Job Require a Reference?" and Chapter 13, "Modularize It, Package It, and Send It to the Library!")

EXAMPLE 2.2

```
# Create variables
$age = 25;
@siblings = ("Nick", "Chet", "Susan","Dolly");
%home = ("owner" => "Bank of America",
         "price" => "negotiable",
         "style" => "Saltbox",
);

# Create reference
$ref1 = \$age;   # Create reference to scalar
$ref2 = \@siblings;  # Create reference to array
$ref3 = \%home; # Create reference to hash
$arrayref = [ qw(red yellow blue green) ];  # Create a reference to
                                            # an unnamed array.
$hashref = { "Me" => "Maine", "Mt" => "Montana", "Fl" => "Florida" };
            # $hashref is a reference to an unnamed hash.
```

EXAMPLE 2.2 (CONTINUED)

```
# Dereference pointer
print ${$ref1};   # Dereference pointer to scalar; prints: 25
print @{$ref2};   # Dereference pointer to array;
                  # prints: Nick Chet Susan Dolly
print %{$ref3};   # Dereference pointer to hash;
        # prints: styleSaltboxpricenegotiableownerBank of America
print ${ref2}->[1];    # prints "Chet"
print ${ref3}->{"style"}; # prints "Saltbox"
print @{$arrayref};     # prints elements of unnamed array
print %{$hashref};      # prints elements of unnamed hash
```

Objects.   Perl supports objects, a special type of reference. A Perl class is a package containing a collection of variables and functions, called properties and methods. There is no *class* keyword. The properties (also called attributes) describe the object. Methods are special functions that allow you to create and manipulate the object. Objects are created with the *bless* function (see Chapter 14, "Bless Those Things! (Object-Oriented Perl").

Creating a Class

EXAMPLE 2.3

```
package Pet;

sub new{ # Constructor
   my $class = shift;
   my $pet = {
               "Name"  => undef,
               "Owner" => undef,
               "Type"  => undef,
   };
   return bless($pet, $class);  # Returns a reference to the object
}

sub set_pet{  # Accessor methods
    my $self = shift;
    my ($name, $owner, $type)= @_;
    $self->{'Name'} = $name;
    $self->{'Owner'}= $owner;
    $self->{'Type'}= $type;
}

sub display_pet{
   my $self = shift;
   while(($key,$value)=each%($self)){
      print "$key: $value\n";
   }
}
1;
```

Instantiating a Class

```
$cat = Pet->new();  # Create an object with a constructor method
$cat->set_pet("Sneaky", "Mr. Jones", "Siamese");
# Access the object with an instance
$cat->display_pet;
```

Perl also supports method inheritance by placing base classes in the *@ISA* array.

Libraries and Modules.   Library files have modules and "module" is used to refer to a single *.pm* file inside the library. The standard Perl library, prior to version 5.18, included files with the *.pl* extension. Today, *.pm* files are more commonly used than *.pl* files (see Chapter 13, "Modularize It, Package It, and Send It to the Library!").

Path to Libraries

@INC array contains list of paths to standard Perl libraries and can be updated.

To Include a File

To load an external file, the *use* function imports a module and an optional list of subroutine or variable names into the current package.

```
use Moose;  # Loads Moose.pm module at compile time
```

Diagnostics.   To exit a Perl script with the cause of the error, you can use the built-in *die* function or the *exit* function.

```
open($fh, "filename") or die "Couldn't open filename: $!\n";
if ($input !~ /^\d+$/){
   print STDERR "Bad input. Integer required.\n";
   exit(1);
}
```

You can also use the Perl pragmas:

```
use warnings;  # Provides warning messages; does not abort program
use diagnostics; # Provides detailed warnings; does not abort program
use strict; # Checks for global variables, unquoted words, etc.;
            # aborts program
```

2.2 Chapter Summary

This chapter was provided for programmers who need a quick peek at what Perl looks like, its general syntax, and programming constructs. It is an overview. There is a lot more to Perl, as you'll see as you read through the following chapters.

Later, after you have programmed for a while, this chapter can also serve as a little tutorial to refresh your memory without having to search through the index to find what you are looking for.

2.3 What's Next?

In Chapter 3, "Perl Scripts," we will discuss Perl script setup. We will cover how to name a script, execute it, and add comments, statements, and built-in functions. We will also see how to use Perl command-line switches and how to identify certain types of errors.

chapter

3

Perl Scripts

Now it is time to write a Perl script and execute it. By the time you have finished this chapter, you should understand each of the following lines (each line is an entity unto itself):

```perl
#!/usr/bin/perl

# This statement should print the sum of three numbers

$n = localtime;  print "$n\n";

perl -c myscript

(Might be a runaway multi-line "" string…
Argument "6dogs" isn't numeric in addition (+) …
```

Before we get started, please take note that each line of code, in most of the examples throughout this book, is numbered. The output and explanations are also numbered to match the numbers in the code. These numbers are provided to help you understand important lines of each program. When copying examples into your text editor, don't include these numbers, or you will generate many unwanted errors!

3.1   Getting Started

There are several components to creating and running a Perl script that bear explanation before you can do any real scripting. This section will introduce some of the important steps and concepts you will need to get started. The following example illustrates four steps in creating and running a Perl script. At the end of this section, each line of the program called *tryme.plx* will be explained, including:

1. The optional startup line (UNIX)
2. Comments
3. The executable statements in the body of the script
4. The execution of the script in both UNIX and Windows

EXAMPLE 3.1

```
(The Script)
#!/usr/bin/perl  # Startup line
use warnings;
# This script is called tryme.plx  # Comment
print "What is your name? ";          # Executable statements
chomp(my $name = <STDIN>);            # Program waits for user input
print "Welcome, $name, are you ready to learn Perl now? ";
chomp($response = lc($response);   # Response is converted to lowercase
if($response eq "yes" or $response eq "y"){
    print "Great! Let's get started learning Perl by example.\n";
}
else{
    print "O.K. Try again later.\n";
}
$now = localtime;  # Use a Perl function to get the date and time
print "$name, you ran this script on $now.\n";
# Script ends here


-------------------------------------------------


Script Execution At the Command-line

(Output—first run)
$ perl tryme.plx
What is your name? Ellie
Welcome, Ellie, are you ready to learn Perl now? yes
Great! Let's get started learning Perl by example.
Ellie, you ran this script on Fri Oct 17 10:19:43 2014.

(Output—second run)
$ perl tryme.plx
What is your name? Ellie
Welcome, Ellie, are you ready to learn Perl now? no
O.K. Try again later.
Ellie, you ran this script on Fri Oct 17 10:25:48 2014.
```

3.1.1   Finding a Text Editor

Since you will be using a text editor to write Perl scripts, you can use any of the editors
provided by your operating system or download more sophisticated editors specifically
designed for Perl, including third-party editors and Integrated Development Environments
(IDEs). Table 3.1 lists some of the editors available.

Table 3.1 Types of Editors

Editors	Platform
BBEdit, JEdit, TextMate	Macintosh
Notepad++, UltraEdit, vim, PerlEdit, JEdit, TextPad	Windows
pico, vim, emacs, PerlEdit, JEdit	Linux/UNIX
Padre	Linux, MacOS, Windows
Komodo	Linux, MacOS, Windows
OptiPerl, PerlExpress	Windows
Affus	Mac OS X

3.1.2 Naming Perl Scripts

The only naming convention for a Perl script is that it follow the naming conventions for files on your operating system (upper-/lowercase letters, numbers, and so forth). If, for example, you are using Linux, filenames are case-sensitive, and since there are a great number of system commands, you may want to add an extension to your Perl script names to make sure the names are unique. You are not required to add an extension to the filename unless you are creating modules, writing CGI scripts if the server requires a specific extension, or have set up Windows to expect an extension on certain types of files. By adding a unique extension to the name, you can prevent clashes with other programs that might have the same name. For example, UNIX provides a command called *test*. If you name a script "test," which version will be executed? If you're not sure, you can add a *.plx* or *.pl* extension to the end of the Perl script name to give it its own identity.

And of course, give your scripts sensible names that indicate the purpose of the script rather than names like "foo," "foobar," or "testing."

3.1.3 Statements, Whitespace, and Linebreaks

Perl is called a free-form language, meaning you can place statements anywhere on the line and even cross over lines. **Whitespace** refers to spaces, tabs, and newlines. The **newline** is represented in your program as *"\n"* and must be enclosed in double quotes. Whitespace is used to delimit words. Any number of blank spaces are allowed between symbols and words. Whitespace within strings is preserved when enclosed in single or double quote; otherwise, it is ignored.

For example, the following expressions are the same:

```
5+4*2
```

is the same as

```
5          +          4          *          2;
```

And both of the following Perl statements are correct, even though the output will show that the whitespace is preserved when quoted.

```
print "This is a Perl statement.";

    print "This
              is
                also
                  a Perl
                    statement.";
```

Even though you have a lot of freedom when writing Perl scripts, it is better to put statements on their own line and to provide indentation when using blocks of statements (we'll discuss this in Chapter 5, "What's in a Name?"). Of course, annotating your program with comments, so that you and others will understand what is going on, is vitally important. See the next section for more on comments.

3.1.4   Strings and Numbers

Perl strings are characters enclosed in quotes, either single or double quotes (back quotes are used in command substitution). A string can consist of a single character, multiple characters, numbers, or any combination of these. You can think of words as a set of characters delimited by space or punctuation and a group of words as a sentence, but as long as you enclose characters, words, or sentences in a set of matching quotes, it is just a simple string. Some characters in a string may have special meaning; such as a $ or @ or \n. The way the string is quoted (that is, double or single quotes) determines how Perl will interpret the string (see Section 4.3.1, "Quotes Matter!").

For example,

```
"This is a string of 50 characters"
```

and so is this:

```
'This is also a string with more characters'
```

Without quotes, a word is called a **bareword**. In fact, if you don't quote a string, you can expect to get a warning message such as "Bareword found where operator expected."

Perl numbers can be represented as integers (for example, 4, 56, 123) or floating-point numbers (for example, 3.45, 12.1, .66). They can also be represented using different bases such as octal, hexadecimal, binary, and so forth. We will discuss this in Chapter 4, "Getting a Handle on Printing."

3.2 Filehandles

A **filehandle** is a bare word or variable representing the place where Perl gets input, sends output, or sends errors. When you start up a Perl script, you normally inherit three file streams from the parent process, normally the shell. They are *STDIN*, *STDOUT*, and *STDERR*. *STDIN* is tied to your keyboard where you type input that will be received by your script. The output, *STDOUT*, will initially be sent to your terminal screen in these first examples, and later to files or pipes with user-defined filehandles. The Perl built-in functions *print* and *printf* send output to the *STDOUT*, your screen, as a default.

3.3 Variables (Where to Put Data)

Variables are fundamental to all programming languages. They are data containers whose values may change throughout the run of the program, whereas literals or constants remain fixed. An example of a constant would be the value of PI, the number of seconds in a minute, and so forth. Perl stores strings and numbers in variables, which are storage areas in the program's memory.

Perl differentiates between storing a single item or a list of items; that is, a variable called a **scalar** can hold only one value, such as a single number or single string of text, whereas a variable called an **array** or another type called a **hash** (associative arrays), can store lists, such as a list of names, files, colors, addresses, and so forth.

This is a scalar:

```
$name = "John";
$n = 200;
```

This is an array:

```
@colors = ("red", "green", "yellow");
```

This is a hash:

```
%student = ("Name" => "Joe Blow",
            "Subject" => "Perl",
            "Grade" => "A"
           );
```

For now, we will start with scalar variables. When you see a dollar sign preceding a variable name, think ONE, think scalar. Only one string or one number will be stored there. For example:

```
$ch = "M";   # One string
$answer = "Yes";   # One string
$string = "This is a string of beads";   # One string
$number = 3.45;   # One number
$age = 23;   # One number
```

If you want to think in terms of monetary values, then the dollar sign must be protected from interpretation by either using a backslash or single quotes; for example,

```
$money='$5.00';
$cash = "\$100";
```

3.3.1   What Is Context?

"You misinterpreted what I said. You took the whole thing completely out of context."

Perl has functions and operators that behave in a certain way, depending on how you use them, called context. The major two types of context are **scalar** or **list**. A function may return a scalar or a list depending on how you use it. A variable may accept one value or a list of values. You may have either string or numeric context depending on what operators you are using. For example, if you use a +, Perl assumes that you want to add numbers, as in 5 + 12; but if you say, for example:

```
"5cats" + "dogs"
```

the plus sign operator will automatically try to convert its operands to numbers. *"5cats"* will be converted to the number 5, and since there are no initial numbers in the string *"dogs"*, it will be converted to the number 0. The string portion is discarded, and now the + operator can add the numbers as 5 + 0. If, on the other hand, you were trying to concatenate two strings, such as *"hot"* and *"dog"* to *"hotdog"*, you would use Perl's concatenation operator, the dot: *"hot"* . *"dog"*. This operator wants strings. If you say, *55 . 44*, Perl will convert the 55 to *"55"* and the 44 to *"44"* resulting in *"5544"*. (Perl will warn you about mishaps like this if you indicate to *use warnings* at the top of your script.)

There are other types of context, such as Boolean, void, or interpolative context. We will talk about "context" in much more depth throughout this book, but it is important to get an early introduction because it effects much of what you do in Perl and can cause unexpected results when you use operators or functions in the wrong context.

3.3.2   Comments

You may write a very clever Perl script today and in two weeks have no idea what your script was supposed to do. If you pass the script on to someone else, the confusion magnifies. Comments are plain text that allow you to insert documentation in your Perl script with no effect on the execution of the program. They are used to help you and other programmers maintain and debug scripts. Perl comments are preceded by a # mark. They extend across the line, but do not continue onto the next line.

Perl does **not** understand the *C* language comments /* and */ or *C++* comments //.

EXAMPLE 3.2

```
1  # This is a comment

2  print "hello";  # And this is a comment
```

EXPLANATION

1 Comments, as in UNIX shell, *sed*, and *awk* scripts, are lines preceded with the pound sign (#) and can continue to the end of the line.
2 Comments can be anywhere on the line. Here, the comment follows a valid Perl *print* statement.

3.3.3 Perl Statements

Perl executable statements, similar to English sentences, make up most of the Perl script. A statement is an expression, or a series of expressions. Perl statements can be simple or compound, and a variety of operators, modifiers, expressions, and functions make up a statement, as shown in the following example. Simple statements must end in semicolons.

```
print "Hello, to you!\n";
$now = localtime();
print "Today is $now.\n";
$result = 5.5 * 4 / 2;
print "Good-bye.\n";
```

3.3.4 Using Perl Built-in Functions

A big part of any programming language is the set of functions built into the language or packaged in special libraries (see Appendix A, "Perl Built-ins, Pragmas, Modules, and the Debugger"). Perl comes with many useful functions—independent program code that performs some task. When you call a Perl built-in function, you just type its name, or optionally you can type its name followed by a set of parentheses. All function names must be typed in lowercase. Many functions require arguments—messages that you send to the function. For example, the *print* function won't display anything if you don't pass it an argument, such as the string of text you want to print on the screen. If the function requires arguments, then place the arguments, separated by commas, right after the function name. The function usually returns something after it has performed its particular task. For example, the built-in *sqrt* function returns the square root of a give number.

```
$n = sqrt 25;  # The value '5' is returned and assigned to the scalar $n
```

In Example 3.3, we call two built-in Perl functions, *print* and *localtime*. The *print* function takes a string as its argument and displays the string of text on the screen. The *localtime* function, on the other hand, doesn't require an argument and returns the current date and time. Both of the following statements are valid ways to call a function with an argument. The argument is *"Hello, there.\n"*.

EXAMPLE 3.3

```
print("Hello, there.\n");  # Parens are optional
print "Hello, there.\n";   # No parens, same as previous
print "Hello", "there", "\n"; # A comma-separated list of strings
print "The sum is", 5 + 4, "\n"; # A comma-separated list including
                                 # an arithmetic expression
```

The *localtime()* function returns the date and time. What the date and time look like depends on context (that is, what type of return value is expected from localtime, such as whether it is a list or scalar).

```
$now = localtime;   # $now is a scalar; the returned value from
                    # localtime is scalar in context.
print $now;
```

```
(Output)
```

```
Wed Jan 15 10:29:36 2014
```

```
@now = localtime;  # @now is an array; return type from
                   # localtime is list in context.
print @now;
```

```
(Output)
```

```
3930101501143140
```

3.3.5   Script Execution

At the beginning of this section (Example 3.1) we introduced a sample script to give you an idea of what a script looks like and how it is executed. The script was created in a text editor such as one of those listed in Section 3.1.1. (Don't use a word processor such as Microsoft Word or Notepad, as you may get unusual characters in your output). Once the lines of the script were entered, the file was saved with the name *tryme.plx*. Now saved, you would normally go to the command line (either UNIX/Windows), and type at your prompt (in this example, the dollar sign is the prompt):

```
$   perl tryme.plx
```

where *perl* is the name of the perl interpreter and *tryme.plx* is the name of the script, passed to the interpreter as an argument. When you execute a Perl script, it takes just one step on your part, but internally the Perl interpreter takes two steps. First, it compiles the entire program into byte code, an internal representation of the program. After that, Perl's byte code engine runs the byte code line by line. If you have compiler errors, such as a missing semicolon at the end of the line, misspelled keyword, or mismatched quotes, you will get a syntax error.

You can execute Perl script directly at the UNIX **command line** if the *#!* startup line, commonly called the **shebang line**, is included as the first line in your script file and the script has execute permission.

```
$ ./tryme.plx
```

A note about the *shebang* line: The first line of the script contains the *#!* symbols (called the *shebang* line), followed by the full pathname of the file where the Perl executable resides. This tells the UNIX kernel what program is interpreting the script. An example of the startup line might be

```
#!/usr/bin/perl
```

or

```
#!/usr/bin/env perl
```

the latter which allows the user's environment to select which Perl to run, 5.18+.

It is important that the path to the interpreter is entered correctly after the *shebang* (*#!*). Perl may be installed in different directories on different systems. Most Web servers will look for this line when invoking CGI scripts written in Perl. Any inconsistency will cause a fatal error. To find the path to the Perl interpreter on your system, type at your UNIX prompt:[1]

```
$ which perl
```

Mac OS is really just a version of UNIX and comes bundled with Perl 5.16 (as of this writing). You open a terminal and use Perl exactly the same way you would use it for Solaris, Linux, *BSD, HP-UX, AIX OSX, and so forth.

Win32 platforms don't provide the *shebang* syntax or anything like it.[2] For Windows,[3] you can associate a Perl script with extensions such as *.pl* or *.plx* and then run your script directly from the command line. At the command-line prompt or from the system Control Panel, you can set the *PATHEXT* environment variable to the name of the extension that will be associated with Perl scripts:

```
SET PATHEXT=.pl;%PATHEXT%
```

---

1. Another way to find the interpreter would be: *find / -name '*perl*' -print;*
2. Although Win32 platforms don't ordinarily require the *shebang* line, the Apache Web server does, so you will need the *shebang* line if you are writing CGI scripts that will be executed by Apache.
3. File association does not work on Windows 95 unless the program is started from the Explorer window.

Again, the simplest way to execute your script is to pass the script as an argument to the perl interpreter:

```
$ perl scriptname
```

3.4 Summing It Up

Now, let's get a line-by-line explanation of the script that was introduced at the beginning of this section. You should have a better picture of how the script is set up and executed.

EXAMPLE 3.4

```
(The Script)
1   #!/usr/bin/perl
2   # This script is called "tryme.plx"
3   print "What is your name? ";    # Executable statements
4   chomp($name = <STDIN>);  # Program waits for user input from keyboard
    print "Welcome, $name, are you ready to learn Perl now? ";
    chomp($response = <STDIN>);
5   $response=lc($response);  # Response is converted to lowercase
6   if($response eq "yes" or $response eq "y"){
        print "Great! Let's get started learning Perl by example.\n";
    }
    else{
        print "O.K. Try again later.\n";
    }
7   $now = localtime;  # Use a Perl function to get the date and time
    print "$name, you ran this script on $now.\n";
    # Sctipt ends here

(At the command line)
8   $ perl -c tryme.plx
    tryme.plx syntax O.K.

9   $ chmod +x tryme.plx     (UNIX/Linux only)
10  $ ./tryme.plx

(At the Command line for both MS-DOS and Windows)
11  $ perl tryme.plx

Script Execution

(Output—first run)
What is your name? Ellie
Welcome, Ellie, are you ready to learn Perl now? yes
Great! Let's get started learning Perl by example.
Ellie, you ran this script on Fri Oct 17 10:19:43 2014.
```

EXAMPLE 3.4 (CONTINUED)

```
(Output—second run)
$ perl tryme.plx
What is your name? Ellie
Welcome, Ellie, are you ready to learn Perl now? no
O.K. Try again later.
Ellie, you ran this script on Fri Oct 17 10:25:48 2014.
```

EXPLANATION

1   This script is created in your favorite editor. The startup line tells the shell where Perl is located on UNIX-type systems. It is not required unless you are going to run the script directly from the command line as you would any other OS command.

2   A comment starting with a # sign describes information the programmer wants to convey about the script.

3   The *print* function sends its string argument to *STDOUT*.

4   User is prompted to type his name. His input comes from the keyboard through the *STDIN* filehandle. The program will accept input until he presses the Enter/Return key and is accepted as one line (including the newline), stored in the scalar variable, *$name*. The *chomp* function will remove the newline.

5   The input will be converted to lowercase by the *lc* function.

6   This is a test. If the value of *$response* was either "yes" or "y," the block of statements within the curly braces will be entered. Otherwise, the program will jump to the *else* block.

7   The built-in *localtime* function returns the current date and time.

8   The *-c* switch is used to check for syntax errors. Hopefully, everything is "OK." (See Section 3.5, "Perl Switches.")

9   The *chmod* command is for UNIX-type systems and is used to turn on the execute permission on this file in order to run the program directly at the command line.

10 The Perl script is executed by its name. The dot/slash preceding its name tells the UNIX shell that the script is located in the current working directory.

11 This is the way you will normally execute your script if using either MS-DOS or UNIX at the command line. (The path to the Perl interpreter must be set in the environment PATH variable. You normally don't have to worry about this, as it is done by the installation program.)

3.4.1   What Kinds of Errors to Expect

Expect to make errors and maybe lots of them. You may try many times before you actually get a program to run perfectly. Knowing your error messages is like knowing the quirks of your boss, mate, or even yourself. Some programmers make the same error over and over again. Don't worry. In time, you will learn what most of these messages mean and how to prevent them.

EXAMPLE 3.5

```
(The Script)
   print "Hello, world";
1  print "How are you doing?
2  print "Have you found any problems in this script?";


(Output)
Bareword found where operator expected at errors.plx line 3, near "print
"Have"
   (Might be a runaway multi-line "" string starting on line 2)
      (Do you need to predeclare print?)
syntax error at errors.plx line 3, near "print "Have you "
Search pattern not terminated at errors.plx line 3.
```

EXPLANATION

1   This line should have a closing double quote and a terminating semicolon. Since it doesn't end in a double quote, Perl continues onto the next line looking for it.

2   This Perl statement is correct, but Perl is still looking for the closing quote on the previous line and finds it just before the word *Have*. Now the rest of this statement is left hanging without an initial opening quote. Whenever you see the word *runaway* in the error message, it usually means a quote that has "run away" (that is, missing). If you see *Bareword*, it means that a word has no quotes surrounding it.

After the program passes the compile phase (that is, you don't get any syntax errors or complaints from the compiler), then you may get what are called runtime, or logical, errors. These errors are harder to find and are probably caused by not anticipating problems that might occur when the program starts running. Or it's possible that the program has faulty logic in the way it was designed. Runtime errors may be caused if a file or database you're trying to open doesn't exist, a user enters bad input, you get into an infinite loop, or you try to illegally divide by zero. Whatever the case, these problems, called "bugs," are harder to find. Perl comes with a debugger that is helpful in determining what caused these logical errors by letting you step through your program line by line. (See Appendix A, "Perl Built-ins, Pragmas, Modules, and the Debugger," specifically Section A.6, "Debugger.")

3.5 Perl Switches

Although most of your work with Perl will be done in scripts, you can also execute Perl at the command line for simple tasks, such as testing a function, a *print* statement, or simply testing Perl syntax. Perl has a number of command-line switches, also called command-line options, to control or modify its behavior. The switches discussed next are not a complete list (again, see Appendix A), but will demonstrate a little about Perl syntax at the command line.

When working at the command line, you will see a shell prompt. The shell is called a **command interpreter**. UNIX shells such as *Korn* and *bash* display a default $ prompt, and *C* and *tcsh* shell display a % prompt. The UNIX, Linux (*bash* and *tcsh*), and Mac OS shells are quite similar in how they parse the command line. By default, if you are using Windows, the MS-DOS command-line prompt displays a $.[4] The Win32 shell has its own way of parsing the command line. Since most of your Perl programming will be done in script files, you will seldom need to worry about the shell's interaction, but when a script interfaces with the operating system, problems will occur unless you are aware of what commands you have and how the shell executes them on your behalf.

3.5.1 The -e Switch (Quick Test at the Command Line)

The *-e* switch allows Perl to **execute** Perl statements at the command line instead of from a script. This is a good way to test simple Perl statements before putting them into a script file, but the shells for UNIX and MS-DOS don't always parse the command line in the same way, as shown in Example 3.6.

EXAMPLE 3.6

```
1  $ perl -e 'print "hello dolly\n";'       # UNIX/Linux
   hello dolly
2  $ perl -e "print qq/hello dolly\n/;"      # Windows and UNIX/Linux
   hello dolly
```

EXPLANATION

1   Perl prints the string *hello dolly* to the screen followed by a newline \n. The dollar sign ($) is the UNIX shell prompt. The single quotes surrounding the Perl statement protect it from the UNIX shell when it scans and interprets the command line. This will fail to execute on a Windows system.

2   At the MS-DOS prompt, Perl statements must be enclosed in double quotes. The *qq* construct surrounding *hello dolly* is another way Perl represents double quotes. For example, *qq/hello/* is the same as *"hello"*. An error is displayed if you type the following at the MS-DOS prompt:

```
$ perl -e 'print "hello dolly\n";'
```

Can't find string terminator "" anywhere before EOF at -e line 1.

Note: UNIX systems can use this format as well.

---

4. It is possible that your command-line prompt has been customized to contain the current directory, history number, drive number, and so forth.

3.5.2   The -c Switch (Check Syntax)

As we demonstrated earlier in this chapter, the -c switch is used to **check** the Perl syntax without actually executing the Perl commands. If the syntax is correct, Perl will tell you so. It is a good idea to always check scripts with the -c switch. This is especially important with CGI scripts written in Perl, because error messages that are normally sent to the terminal screen are sent to a log file instead. (See also the -w switch in Chapter 4, "Getting a Handle on Printing.")

EXAMPLE 3.7

```
1   print "hello';
    Can't find string terminator '"' anywhere before EOF at test.plx


2   print "hello";
    test.plx syntax OK
```

EXPLANATION

1   The string *"hello'* starts with a double quote but ends with a single quote. The quotes should be matched—that is, the first double quote should be matched at the end of the string with another double quote but instead ends with a single quote. With the -c switch, Perl will complain if it finds syntax errors while compiling.
2   After correcting the previous problem, Perl lets you know that the syntax is correct.

3.5.3   The -w Switch (Warnings)

Even though your script may pass the compile test, when you run it, something seems strange; for example, perhaps a variable doesn't have a value or an operation isn't producing what you expected. The -w switch sends warning messages if you have, for example, misused operators, or if you have variables used only once, or scalar variables used before they are set, or references to undefined filehandles, and so forth.

A warning is just that: a warning. It doesn't mean that your program has syntax errors; it means you are doing something questionable and your output might reflect that. It is a good practice to use warnings in your scripts rather than at the command line. We'll have more about warnings and the use of the warnings pragma in Chapter 4. (See perldiag documentation for more detail.)

```
1   $sum = "dogs" + "5cats\n";   # trying to add two strings;
                                 # should be numbers
2   print "The sum is $sum.\n";

3   $name="Jack";
4   print "I know $nime well.\n";   # Misspelled variable;
                                    # should be $name, not $nime
```

```
(At the Command line)
perl -w  context.plx
Name "main::nime" used only once: possible typo at context line 4.
Argument "5cats\n" isn't numeric in addition (+) at context line 1.
Argument "dogs" isn't numeric in addition (+) at context line 1.
The sum is 5.
Use of uninitialized value $nime in concatenation (.) or string at context
line 4.
I know  well.
```

3.6 What You Should Know

1. How do you set up a script?

2. How do you name a script?

3. How are statements terminated?

4. What is whitespace?

5. What is meant by free form?

6. What is a variable?

7. What is a built-in function?

8. What is the #! line?

9. What is meant by scalar or list context?

10. How do you make a script executable?

11. Why use comments?

12. How do you execute a Perl script if not using the *shebang* line.

13. What command-line option lets you check Perl syntax?

14. What is the -w switch for?

3.7 What's Next?

If you can't print what your program is supposed to do, it's like trying to read the mind of a person who can't speak. In the next chapter, we discuss Perl functions to print output to the screen (*stdout*) and how to format the output. You will learn how Perl views words, whitespace, literals, backslash sequences, numbers, and strings. You will learn how to use single, double, and backquotes and their alternative form. We will discuss *here documents* and how to use them in CGI scripts. You will also learn how to use warnings and diagnostics to help debug your scripts.

EXERCISE 3
Getting with It Syntactically

1. At the command-line prompt, write a Perl statement that will print

```
Hello world!!
Welcome to Perl programming.
```

2. Execute a Perl command that will display the version of the Perl distribution you are currently using.

3. Copy the program sample from Example 3.1 into your editor, save it, check the syntax, and execute it.

4. Fix errors in the following script. Use the -c and the -w switches, and execute it.

```
# This is a comment
to explain what I'm tying to do.
$name=John Doe
print Welcome to Perl!, $nime."
$today=localtime;
print 'The time is $today\n';
```

chapter

4

Getting a Handle on Printing

When you complete this chapter, you should be able to explain each of the following statements (each statement is an entity unto itself):

```
printf "%-10s\t\$%d%10.2f\t%b\t%x\t%o\n", "Jack", 15,15,15,15,15;

print 'She cried, "I can\'t help you!"'," \n";

$str = sprintf "\$%.2f", $sal;
print  qq!\u$name, the local time is !, scalar localtime, "\n";

use feature qw(say);

say "The sum is ", 5 + 4;
say "No more! "
```

Before we get started, please take note that each line of code, in most of the examples throughout this book, is numbered. The output and explanations are also numbered to match the numbers in the code. These numbers are provided to help you understand important lines of each program. When copying examples into your text editor, don't include these numbers, or you will generate many unwanted errors!

4.1 The Special Filehandles *STDOUT, STDIN, STDERR*

In Chapter 3, "Perl Scripts," we briefly introduced standard I/O. By convention, whenever your program starts execution, the parent process (normally a shell program) opens three predefined streams called *stdin, stdout,* and *stderr.* All three of these streams are connected to your terminal by default.

stdin is the place where input comes from, the terminal keyboard; *stdout* is where output normally goes, the screen; and *stderr* is where errors from your program are printed, also the screen.

Perl inherits *stdin*, *stdout*, and *stderr* from the shell. Perl does not access these streams directly but gives them names called **filehandles**. Perl accesses the streams via the filehandle. The filehandle for *stdin* is called *STDIN*; the filehandle for *stdout* is called *STDOUT*; and the filehandle for *stderr* is called *STDERR*. *STDERR* is a separate stream that sends its output to the screen and allows you to redirect those errors to, for example, an error log in order to find out what went wrong. Later, we'll use Perl techniques to deal with errors and error messages. (See Figure 4.1.)

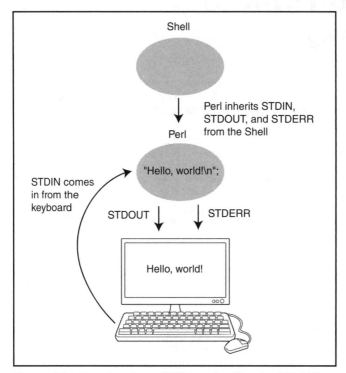

Figure 4.1   Reading from *STDIN* and writing to *STDOUT*.

In Chapter 10, "Getting a Handle on Files," we'll see how you can create your own filehandles, but for now we'll stick with those that are predefined.

The *print* and *printf* functions, by default, send their output to the *STDOUT* filehandle, your screen. For example:

```
print "Give me your name";
chomp($name = <STDIN>);
# User is prompted to enter something at the keyboard,
# until he presses the return key. The chomp function removes the newline.
    if ( $name eq "") { print STDERR "You didn't enter anything.
        \$name is empty.\n";
        exit 1; }
```

```
print STDOUT "Hello, $name\n";   # A string of output is sent to screen.
print "Hello back to you.\n";    # STDOUT is the default for the print
                                 # function.
```

4.2 Words

When printing, it is helpful to understand how Perl views words. A word is a sequence of characters with a unit of meaning, much like words in English. Perl words are not restricted to just alpha characters, but they cannot contain whitespace unless quoted. A string is a word or words enclosed in matching quotes (for example, *"This is the life!"*). You can use an unquoted word to identify filehandles, functions, labels, and other reserved words; for example, with *print STDERR "Error\n"*, *print* is a function, *STDERR* is a filehandle, and *"Error\n"* is a string. If the word has no special meaning to Perl, it will be treated as if surrounded by single quotes and is called a **bareword**.

4.3 The *print* Function

You will probably use the built-in *print* function more than any of the printing options provided by Perl because it is efficient and easy to use. The *print* function prints a string or a list of comma-separated words to the Perl filehandle *STDOUT*. If successful, the *print* function returns 1.

The string literal \n adds a newline to the string. You can embed it in the string or treat it as a separate string. (Perl requires that escape sequences like \n be enclosed in double quotes.) The *say* function (version 5.10) is just like *print* but appends a newline for you. (See Section 4.4.2, "The No Newline *say* Function," later in this chapter.)

EXAMPLE 4.1

```
(The Script)
1   print "Hello", "world", "\n";
2   print "Hello world\n";

(Output)
1   Helloworld
2   Hello world
```

EXPLANATION

1   Each string passed to the *print* function is enclosed in double quotes and separated by a comma. To print whitespace, the whitespace must be enclosed within the quotes. The \n escape sequence must be enclosed in double quotes for it to be interpreted as a newline character.
2   The entire string is enclosed in double quotes and printed to standard output.

EXAMPLE 4.2

```
(The Script)
1  print Hello, world, "\n";

(Output)
1  No comma allowed after filehandle at ./perl.st line 1
```

EXPLANATION

1   If the strings are not quoted, the filehandle *STDOUT* must be specified, or the *print* function will treat the first word it encounters as a filehandle (that is, the word *Hello* would be treated as a filehandle). The comma is not allowed after a filehandle; it is used only to separate strings that are to be printed.

4.3.1 Quotes Matter!

Since quoting affects the way in which variables are interpreted, this is a good time to review Perl's quoting rules. It is often difficult to determine which quotes to use, where to use them, and how to find the culprit if they are misused; in other words, it can be a real debugging nightmare.[1] To lighten things up a little, Perl offers an alternative method of quoting, but you still have to fully understand quoting rules before the alternative is useful.[2] You can use the backslash (\) to quote a special character such as $ or @ and it behaves as a set of single quotes, as '$' or '@'.

Perl has three types of quotes and all three types have a different function. They are **single quotes**, **double quotes**, and **backquotes**. Quotes come in pairs and must be matched. For example:

```
print "This is a quoted string. Some characters are special;
e.g., $var, @list and \t are interpreted within double quotes.\n";

print 'This is also a quoted string. All characters are literal within
single quotes; i.e., $, @, and backslash characters are not special';

print "This is an operating system shell command enclosed in back quotes."
, `pwd`;

print "The backslash quotes a single character as in \$5.00. It protects
the $ from interpretation";
```

---

1. Barry Rosenberg, in his book *KornShell Programming Tutorial,* has a chapter titled "The Quotes From Hell."
2. Larry Wall, creator of Perl, calls his alternative quoting method "syntactic sugar."

A pair of single or double quotes may delimit a string of characters. Quotes will either allow the interpretation of special characters or protect special characters from interpretation, depending on the kind of quotes you use.

Single quotes are the "democratic" quotes. All characters enclosed within them are treated equally; in other words, there are no special characters. But the double quotes discriminate. They treat some of the characters in the string as special characters. The special characters include the $ sign, the @ symbol, and escape sequences such as \t and \n.

When backquotes surround an operating system command, the command will be executed by the shell, often called **command substitution**. The output of the command will be returned as a string that can be used in a *print* statement, assigned to a variable, and so forth. If you are using Windows, Linux, or UNIX, the commands enclosed within backquotes must be supported by the particular operating system and will vary from system to system. (If your program is going to be used on several operating systems, using backquotes will affect its portability.)

No matter what kind of quotes you are using, they **must be matched**. Because the quotes mark the beginning and end of a string, Perl will complain about a *"Might be a multiline runaway string"* or *"Execution of quotes aborted..."* or *"Can't find string terminator anywhere before EOF.."* and fail to compile if you forget one of the quotes.

Double Quotes. Double quotes must be matched, unless embedded within single quotes. When a string is enclosed in double quotes, scalar variables (preceded with a $) and arrays (preceded by the @ symbol) are interpolated (that is, the value of the variable replaces the variable name in the string). Hashes (preceded by the % sign) are **not** interpolated within the string enclosed in double quotes.

Strings that contain string literals (such as \t, \n) must be enclosed in double quotes for backslash interpretation.

A single quote may be enclosed in double quotes, as in *"I don't care!"*

EXAMPLE 4.3

```
(The Script)
   use warnings;
   # Double quotes
1  $num=5;
2  @colors=("red","green","blue");
3  print "The number is $num.\n";
4  print "The colors are @colors.\n";
5  print "I need \$5.00.\n";
6  print "\t\tI can't help you.\n";

(Output)
3  The number is 5.
4  The colors are red green blue\n";
5  I need $5.00.
6  I can't help you.
```

1   The scalar variable $num is assigned the value 5.
2   The array is assigned three colors. The @ is a special character used to create a list of values. The @ is interpreted within double quotes.
3   The string is enclosed in double quotes. The value of the scalar variable is printed. The string literal, \n, is interpreted.
4   The @ is evaluated and the array of values is printed.
5   The dollar sign ($) is printed as a literal dollar sign when preceded by a backslash; in other words, variable substitution is ignored.
6   The special literals \t and \n are interpreted when enclosed within double quotes.

Single Quotes.   If a string is enclosed in single quotes, it is printed literally (what you see is what you get).

If a single quote is needed within a string, then it can be embedded within double quotes or backslashed. If double quotes are to be treated literally, they can be embedded within single quotes.

EXAMPLE 4.4

```
(The Script)
    use warnings;
    # Single quotes
1   print 'I need $100.00.', "\n";
2   print 'The string literal, \t, is used to represent a tab.', "\n";
3   print 'She cried, "Help me!"', "\n";

(Output)
1   I need $100.00.
2   The string literal, \t, is used to represent a tab.
3   She cried, "Help me!"
```

1   The dollar sign is interpreted literally. In double quotes, it would be interpreted as a scalar. The \n is in double quotes in order for backslash interpretation to occur.
2   The string literal, \t, is not interpreted to be a tab but is printed literally.
3   The double quotes are protected when enclosed in single quotes (that is, they are printed literally).

Backquotes.   UNIX/Windows[3] commands placed within backquotes are executed by the shell, and the output is returned to the Perl program as a string, usually assigned to a variable or made part of a *print* string. When the output of a command is assigned to a

---

3. If using other operating systems, such as Microsoft or Mac OS 9.1 and below, the OS commands available for your system will differ.

variable, the context is scalar (that is, a single value is assigned).[4] For command substitution to take place, the backquotes cannot be enclosed in either double or single quotes. (Make note, UNIX shell programmers: backquotes cannot be enclosed in double quotes as in shell programs.)

EXAMPLE 4.5

```
(The Script for Unix/Linux)
   use warnings;
   # Backquotes and command substitution
1  print "The date is ", `date`;        # Windows users: `date /T`
2  print "The date is `date`", ".\n";   # Backquotes treated literally
3  $directory=`pwd`;                     # Windows users: `cd`
4  print "\nThe current directory is $directory.";


(Output)
1  The date is Mon Jun 25 17:27:49 PDT 2014.
2  The date is `date`.
4  The current directory is /home/jody/ellie/perl.
```

EXPLANATION

1   The UNIX *date* command will be executed by the shell, and the output will be returned to Perl's *print* string. The output of the *date* command includes the newline character. For Windows users, the command is `date /T`.

2   Command substitution will not take place when the backquotes are enclosed in single or double quotes.

3   The scalar variable *$dir*, including the newline, is assigned the output of the UNIX *pwd* command (that is, the present working directory). For Windows users, the command is `cd`.

4   The value of the scalar, *$dir*, is printed to the screen.

Perl's Alternative Quotes.   Perl provides an alternative form of quoting—the *q*, *qq*, *qx*, and *qw* constructs.

- The *q* represents single quotes.
- The *qq* represents double quotes.
- The *qx* represents backquotes.
- The *qw* represents a quoted list of words. (See Table 4.1.)

---

4. If output of a command is assigned to an array, the first line of output becomes the first element of the array, the second line of output becomes the next element of the array, and so on.

Table 4.1 Alternative Quoting Constructs

Quoting Construct	What It Represents
q/Hello/	'Hello'
qq/Hello/	"Hello"
qx/date/	`date`
@list=**qw**/red yellow blue/;	@list=('red', 'yellow', 'blue');

The string to be quoted is enclosed **in forward slashes**, but you can use alternative delimiters for all four of the *q* constructs. You can use a nonalphanumeric character for the delimiter, such as a # sign, ! point, or paired characters, such as parentheses, square brackets, and so forth. You can also use a single character or paired characters. For example:

> *q/Hello/*
> *q#Hello#*
> *q{Hello}*
> *q[Hello]*
> *q(Hello)*

EXAMPLE 4.6

```
(The Script)
   use warnings;
   # Using alternative quotes
1  print 'She cried, "I can\'t help you!"',"\n";   # Clumsy
2  print qq/She cried, "I can't help you!" \n/;     # qq for double quotes
3  print qq(I need $5.00\n);  # Really need single quotes
                             # for a literal dollar sign to print
4  print q/I need $5.00\n/;   # What about backslash interpretation?
   print qq(I need \$5.00\n); # Can escape the dollar sign
5  print qq/\n/, q/I need $5.00/,"\n";
6  print q!I need $5.00!,"\n";
7  print "The present working directory is ", `pwd`;
8  print qq/Today is /, qx/date/;  # use qx#date /T# (Windows)
9  print "The hour is ", qx{date +%H}; # Unix only

(Output)
1  She cried, "I can't help you!"
2  She cried, "I can't help you!"
3  I need .00
4  I need $5.00\nI need $5.00

5  I need $5.00
6  I need $5.00
7  The present working directory is /home/jody/ellie/perl
8  Today is Mon Jun 25 17:29:34 PDT 2014
9  The hour is 17
```

EXPLANATION

1 The string is enclosed in single quotes. This allows the conversational quotes to be printed as literals. The single quote in *can\'t* is quoted with a backslash so that it will also be printed literally. If it were not quoted, it would be matched with the first single quote. The ending single quote would then have no mate, and, alas, the program would either tell you that you have a runaway quote or search for its mate until it reached the end of file unexpectedly.

2 The *qq* construct replaces double quotes. Now parentheses delimit the string.

3 Because the *qq* is used, the dollar sign ($) in *$5.00* is interpreted as a scalar variable with a null value. The *.00* is printed. (This is not the way to handle your money!)

4 The single *q* replaces single quotes. The *$5* is treated as a literal. Unfortunately, so is the \n because backslash interpretation does not take place within single quotes. Without a newline, the next line is run together with line 4. In the next line, if the dollar sign is preceded by a backslash, the backslash "escapes" the special meaning of the $. Now the string will print correctly.

5 The \n is double quoted with the *qq* construct, the string *I need $5.00* is single quoted with the *q* construct, and old-fashioned double quotes are used for the second \n.

6 An alternative delimiter, the exclamation point (!), is used with the *q* construct (instead of the forward slash) to delimit the string.

7 The string *The present working directory is* is enclosed in double quotes; the UNIX command *pwd* is enclosed in backquotes for command substitution.

8 The *qq* construct quotes *Today is*; the *qx* construct replaces the backquotes used for command substitution. Note: To get the same results for MS-DOS, the date command takes the /T option. A different delimiter is used because of the slash in /T. Typing *qx/ date /T/* would produce an error, so change the delimiter to something else, in this case a #.

9 Alternative delimiters, the curly braces, are used with the *qx* construct (instead of the forward slash). The output of the UNIX *date* command is printed.

Quoting rules affect almost everything you do in Perl, especially when printing a string of words. Strings are normally delimited by a matched pair of either double or single quotes. When a string is enclosed in single quotes, all characters are treated as literals. When a string is enclosed in double quotes, however, <u>almost</u> all characters are treated as literals, with the exception of those characters that are used for variable substitution and special escape sequences. We will look at the special escape sequences in this chapter and discuss quoting and variables in Chapter 5, "What's in a Name?"

Perl uses some characters for special purposes, such as the dollar sign ($) and the at (@) sign. If these special characters are to be treated as literal characters, they may be preceded by a backslash (\) or enclosed within single quotes (' '). Use the backslash to quote a single character rather than a string of characters.

EXAMPLE 4.7

```
(The Script)
   use warnings;
1  $name="Ellie";
2  print "Hello, $name.\n";  # $name and \n evaluated
3  print 'Hello, $name.\n';  # String is literal; newline not interpreted

4  print "I don't care!\n";
5  print 'I don\'t care!', "\n";  # Backslash protects single quote in 't

(Output)
2    Hello, Ellie.
3,4  Hello, $name.\nI don't care!
5    I don't care!
```

EXPLANATION

1   The string *"Ellie"* is assigned to the scalar variable *$name*.
2   A string is enclosed in double quotes. The variable *$name* is interpolated and printed.
3   A string is enclosed in single quotes. All characters are printed as is.
4   Single quotes can be embedded within double quotes.
5   Quotes are matched from left to right. The backslash preceding the second single quote prevents it from being interpreted so that the closing single quote will be matched.

It is so common to make mistakes with quoting that we will introduce here the most common error messages you will receive resulting from mismatched quotes and bare words.

Think of quotes as being the "clothes" for Perl strings. If you take them off, you may get a "Bareword" message such as:

Bareword "there" not allowed while "strict subs" in use at try.pl line 3. Execution of program.pl aborted due to compilation errors.

Also think of quotes as being mates. A double quote is mated with a matching double quote, and a single quote with a matching single quote. If you don't match the quotes, if one is missing, the missing quote has "run away." Where did the mate go? You may receive an error like this:

*(Might be a **runaway** multi-line "" string starting on line 3)*

EXAMPLE 4.8

```
(The Script)
   use warnings;
   # Program to illustrate printing literals
1  print "Hello, "I can't go there";  # Unmatched quotes
2  print "Good-bye";
```

EXAMPLE 4.8 (CONTINUED)

```
(Output)
Bareword found where operator expected at qtest.plx line 2, near ""Hello,
"I"
        (Missing operator before I?)
Bareword found where operator expected at qtest.plx line 3, near "print
"Good"
   (Might be a runaway multi-line "" string starting on line 2)
        (Do you need to predeclare print?)
String found where operator expected at qtest.plx line 3, at end of line
        (Missing semicolon on previous line?)
syntax error at qtest.plx line 2, near ""Hello, "I can't "
Can't find string terminator '"' anywhere before EOF at qtest.plx line 3
```

EXPLANATION

1 The string *"Hello* starts with an opening double quote but is missing the ending quote. This cascades into a barrage of troubles. Perl assumes the double quote preceding the word *I* is the mate for the first quote in *"Hello.* That leaves the rest of the string *"I can't go there"* exposed as a bare string. The double quote at the end of the line will be mated with the double quote on the next line. Not good.

2 The word *Good-bye* is considered a bareword because Perl can't find an opening quote. The double quote at the end of *there"* on line 1 has been matched with the double quote at the beginning of *"Good-bye,* leaving *Good-bye* exposed and bare, with an unmatched quote at the end of the string. Ugh!

4.3.2 Literals (Numeric, String, and Special)

When assigning literal values[5] to variables or printing literals, you can represent the literals numerically as integers in decimal, octal, or hexadecimal or as floats in floating-point or scientific notation.

Strings enclosed in double quotes may contain string literals, such as \n for the newline character, \t for a tab character, or \e for an escape character. String literals are alphanumeric (**and only alphanumeric**) characters preceded by a backslash. They may be represented in decimal, octal, or hexadecimal, or as control characters.

Perl also supports special literals for representing the current script name, the line number of the current script, and the logical end of the current script.

Since you will be using literals with the *print* and *printf* functions, let's see what these literals look like.

---

5. Literals may also be called "constants," but the Perl experts prefer the term "literal," so in deference to them, we'll use the term "literal."

Numeric Literals.   You can represent literal numbers as positive or negative integers in decimal, octal, or hexadecimal (see Table 4.2). You can represent floats in floating-point notation or scientific notation. Octal numbers contain a leading *0* (zero), hex numbers a leading *0x* (zero and x), and numbers represented in scientific notation contain a trailing *E*, followed by a negative or positive number representing the exponent.

Table 4.2   Numeric Literals

Example	Description
12345	Integer
0b1101	Binary
0x456fff	Hex
0777	Octal
23.45	Float
.234E-2	Scientific notation

Printing Numeric Literals

EXAMPLE 4.9

```
(The Script)
1  use warnings;
   # Program to illustrate printing literals
2  print "The price is $100.\n";
3  print "The price is \$100.\n";
4  print "The price is \$",100, ".\n";
5  print "The binary number is converted to: ",0b10001,".\n";
6  print "The octal number is converted to: ",0777,".\n";
7  print "The hexadecimal number is converted to: ",0xAbcF,".\n";
8  print "The unformatted number is ", 14.56, ".\n";
9  $now = localtime(); # A Perl built-in function
10 $name = "Ellie"; # A string is assigned to a Perl variable
11 print "Today is $now, $name.";
12 print 'Today is $now, $name.';

(Output)
   Use of uninitialized value $100 in concatenation (.) or string at
   warn.plx line 4.
2  The price is .
3  The price is $100.
4  The price is $100.
5  The binary number is converted to: 17.
6  The octal number is converted to: 511.
7  The hexadecimal number is converted to: 43983.
8  The unformatted number is 14.56.
11 Today is Sat Mar 24 15:46:08 2014, Ellie.
12 Today is $now, $name.
```

EXPLANATION

1. Turning on *warnings* will make Perl complain at a *huge* variety of things that are almost always sources of bugs in your programs; in this example, the fact that an uninitialized variable is used in the next line.

2. The string *The price is $100* is enclosed in double quotes. The dollar sign is a special Perl character. It is used to reference scalar variables, not money. Therefore, since there is no variable called *$100*, nothing prints. Since single quotes protect all characters from interpretation, they would have sufficed here, or the dollar sign could have been preceded with a backslash. But when surrounded by single quotes, the \n will be treated literally rather than as a newline character.

3. The backslash quotes the dollar sign, so it is treated as a literal.

4. To be treated as a numeric literal, rather than a string, the number *100* is a single word. The dollar sign must be escaped even if it is not followed by a variable name. The \n must be enclosed within double quotes if it is to be interpreted as a special string literal.

5. The number is represented as a binary number because of the leading *0b* (zero and b). The decimal value is printed.

6. The number is represented as an octal value because of the leading *0* (zero). The decimal value is printed.

7. The number is represented as a hexadecimal number because of the leading *0x* (zero and x). The decimal value is printed.

8. The number, represented as *14.56*, is printed as is. The *print* function does not format output.

9. Perl has a large set of functions. You have already learned about the *print* function. The *localtime()* function is another. (The parentheses are optional for all functions.) This functions returns the current date and time. We are assigning the result to a Perl scalar variable called *$now*. You will learn more about variables in the next chapter.

10. The variable *$name* is assigned the string *"Ellie"*.

11. When the string is enclosed in double quotes, the *print* function will display the value of the variables *$now* and *$name*.

12. When the string is enclosed in single quotes, the *print* function prints all characters literally.

String Literals. Like shell strings, Perl strings are normally one or more characters delimited by either single or double quotes; for example, *"This is a literal string"* and *'so is this a literal string'*. Escape sequences, (single characters that when preceded by a backslash don't represent themselves) are interpreted only if enclosed in double quotes (see Table 4.3). *"This is a literal string with an escape sequence \n\n"*.

Table 4.3 Escape Sequences

Escape Sequence	Descriptions (ASCII Name)
\t	Tab
\n	Newline
\r	Carriage return
\f	Form feed
\b	Backspace
\a	Alarm/bell
\e	Escape
\033	Octal character
\xff	Hexadecimal character
\c[	Control character
\l	Next character is converted to lowercase
\u	Next character is converted to uppercase
\L	Next characters are converted to lowercase until \E is found
\U	Next characters are converted to uppercase until \E is found
\Q	Backslash all following nonalphanumeric characters until \E is found
\E	Ends upper- or lowercase conversion started with \L or \U
\	Backslash

EXAMPLE 4.10

```
print "This string contains \t\ttwo tabs and a newline.\n" # Double quotes

(Output)
This string contains        two tabs and a newline.

print 'This string contains\t\ttwo tabs and a newline.\n'; # Single quotes

(Output)
This string contains\t\ttwo tabs and a newline.\n
```

Printing String Literals

EXAMPLE 4.11

```
(The Script)
    use warnings;
1   print "***\tIn double quotes\t***\n";   # Escape sequence backslash
                                             # interpretation
2   print '%%%\t\tIn single quotes\t\t%%%\n'; # All characters are
                                             # printed as literals

3   print "\n";

(Output)
1   ***     In double quotes         ***
2   %%%\t\tIn single quotes\t\t%%%\n
3
```

EXPLANATION

1 When a string is enclosed in double quotes, backslash interpretation is performed. The \t is a string literal and produces a tab; the \n produces a newline.
2 When enclosed within single quotes, the special string literals \t and \n are not interpreted. They will be printed as is.
3 The newline \n must be enclosed in double quotes to be interpreted. A \n produces a newline.

Special Literals. Perl's special literals _ _LINE_ _ and _ _FILE_ _ are used as separate words and will **not** be interpreted if enclosed in quotes, single or double. They represent the current line number of your script and the name of the script, respectively. These special literals are equivalent to the predefined special macros used in the C language.

The _ _END_ _ special literal is used in scripts to represent the logical end of the file. Any trailing text following the _ _END_ _ literal will be ignored, just as if it had been commented. The control sequences for end of input in UNIX are <CTRL>+D (\004), and <CTRL>+Z (\032) in MS-DOS; both are synonyms for _ _END_ _.

The _ _DATA_ _ special literal is used as a filehandle to allow you to process textual data from within the script instead of from an external file. This can be useful in testing samples of data from files rather than working on the entire file. See Chapter 5, "What's in a Name?" for some examples.

There are two underscores on either side of the special literals. See Table 4.4 for a description of them all.

EXAMPLE 4.12

```
print "The script is called", __FILE__, "and we are on line number ",
__LINE__,"\n";

(Output)
The script is called ./testing.plx and we are on line number 2
```

Table 4.4 Special Literals

Literal	Description
_ _LINE_ _	Represents the current line number
_ _FILE_ _	Represents the current filename
_ _END_ _	Represents the logical end of the script; trailing garbage is ignored
_ _DATA_ _	Represents a special filehandle
_ _PACKAGE_ _	Represents the current package; default package is *main*

EXAMPLE 4.13

```
(The Script)
  use warnings;
1 print "\a\t\tThe \Unumber\E \LIS\E ",0777,".\n";

(Output)
1 (BEEP)        The NUMBER is 511.
```

EXPLANATION

1 The \a produces an alarm or beep sound, followed by \t\t (two tabs). \U causes the string to be printed in uppercase until \E is reached or the line terminates. The string *number* is printed in uppercase until the \E is reached. The string *is* is to be printed in lowercase, until the \E is reached, and the decimal value for octal *0777* is printed, followed by a period and a newline character.

Printing Special Literals

EXAMPLE 4.14

```
(The Script)
   use warnings;
   # Program, named literals.perl, written to test special literals

1  print "The name of this file is ",__FILE__,".\n";
2  print "The default package is ", __PACKAGE__,".\n";
3  print "We are on line number ", __LINE__, ".\n";
4  __END__
   You must have this literal on its own line. This text is whatever you
   want it to be and is ignored by Perl. It is quite helpful for debugging
   as you can move this literal above a line where you are having syntax
   trouble. Keep moving __END__ until your program runs. It will help
   you discover the line that is broken.

   The __END__ literal is like Ctrl-d or \004.*
```

```
(Output)
1  The name of this file is literals.perl.
2  The default package is main.
3  We are on line number 3.
4  Nothing is printed below the __END__ special literal.
```

_____

* See the -x switch in Appendix A for discarding leading garbage.

EXPLANATION

1   The special literal _ _LINE_ _ cannot be enclosed in quotes if it is to be interpreted. It holds the current line number of the Perl script.
2   The name of this script is _literals.perl_. The special literal _ _FILE_ _ holds the name of the current Perl script.
3   The special literal _ _END_ _ represents the logical end of the script and must be on its own line. It tells Perl to ignore any characters that follow it.

EXAMPLE 4.15

```
(The Script)
   # written to test special literal __DATA__
1  while(<DATA>){  # loop until there is no more data
2     print;       # Reading from DATA and printing each line
   }
3  __DATA__
   This line will be printed.
   And so will this one.
```

```
(Output)
This line will be printed.
And so will this one.
```

EXPLANATION

1   The special literal *<DATA>* is enclosed in angle brackets, meaning "read from DATA"; that is, get input from below the word _ _DATA_ _ until the end of the file. (Without the while loop, only one line of data would be read.) The *print* function will display whatever text is found under the special literal _ _DATA_ _.

2   This is the data that is used by the *<DATA>* filehandle. (You could use _ _END_ _ instead of _ _DATA_ _ to get the same results.)

4.3.3 Printing Without Quotes—The *here document*

The Perl *here document* is derived from the UNIX shell *here document*. It allows you to quote a whole block of text enclosed between words called user-defined terminators. From the first terminator to the last terminator, the text is quoted, or you could say "from *here* to *here*" the text is quoted. The *here document* is a line-oriented form of quoting, requiring the << operator followed by an initial terminating word and a semicolon. There can be no spaces after the << unless the terminator itself is quoted.

If the starting terminating word is not quoted or double quoted, variable expansion is performed. If the starting word is singly quoted, variable expansion is not performed. Each line of text is inserted between the first and last terminating word. The final terminating word must be on a line by itself, with no surrounding whitespace.

Perl does not perform command substitution (backquotes) in the text of a *here document*. Perl, on the other hand, does allow you to execute commands in the *here document* if the terminator is enclosed in backquotes. (Not a good idea.)

Here documents are used extensively in CGI scripts for enclosing large chunks of HTML documents for printing.

EXAMPLE 4.16

```
(The Script)
   use warnings;
1  $price=1000;   # A variable is assigned a value.
2  print <<EOF;
3  The consumer commented, "As I look over my budget, I'd say
4  the price of $price is right. I'll give you \$500 to start."\n
5  EOF

6  print <<'FINIS';
   The consumer commented, "As I look over my budget, I'd say
7  the price of $price is too much.\n I'll settle for $500."
8  FINIS
```

EXPLANATION

1   A scalar variable, *$price*, is assigned the value *1000*.
2   Start of *here document*. *EOF* is the terminator. The block is treated as if in double quotes. If there is any space preceding the terminator, then enclose the terminator in double quotes, such as *"EOF"*.
3   All text in the body of the *here document* is quoted as though the whole block of text were surrounded by double quotes.
4   The dollar sign has a special meaning when enclosed in double quotes. Since the text in this *here document* is treated as if in double quotes, the variable has special meaning here as well. The $ is used to indicate that a scalar variable is being used. The value of the variable will be interpreted. If a backslash precedes the dollar sign, it will be treated as a literal. If special backslash sequences are used, such as \n, they will be interpreted.
5   End of *here document* marked by matching terminator, *EOF*. There can be no space surrounding the terminator.
6   By surrounding the terminator, *FINIS*, with single quotes, the text that follows will be treated literally, turning off the meaning of any special characters, such as the dollar sign or backslash sequences.
7   Text is treated as if in single quotes.
8   Closing terminator marks the end of the *here document*.

here documents and **CGI.** The following program is called a CGI (Common Gateway Interface) program, a simple Perl program executed by a Web server rather than by the shell. It is just like any other Perl script with two exceptions:

- There is a line called the MIME line (for example, *Content-type: text/html*) that describes what kind of content will be sent back to the browser.
- The document consists of text embedded with HTML tags, the language used by browsers to render text in different colors, font faces, types, and so forth. The *here document* avoids using the *print* function for every line of the program.

CGI programs are stored in a special directory called *cgi-bin,* which is normally found under the Web server's root directory.

The following is a simple example of how Perl interacts with a Web server, but "Perl's CGI.pm performs very well in a vanilla CGI.pm environment and also comes with built-in support for mod_perl and mod_perl2 as well" (see FastCGI. *http://perldoc.perl.org/CGI.html#SYNOPSIS* in the Perl 5.18 documentation).

To execute the following script, you will start up your Web browser and type in the Location box: *http://servername/cgi-bin/scriptname.*[6]

---

6. You must supply the correct server name for your system and the correct filename. Some CGI files must have a *.cgi* or *.pl* extension.

EXAMPLE 4.17

```
1   #!c:/Perl/bin/perl.exe
    # The HTML tags are embedded in the here document to avoid using
    # multiple print statements
    $now=localtime;
2   print "Content-type: text/html\n\n";
3   print <<EOF; # here document in a CGI script
    <html><head><title>Town Crier</title></head>
    <body bgColor="lightgreen">
    <div align="center"> <h1>Hear ye, hear ye, Sir Richard cometh!!</h1>
    <img src="http://localhost/sir-richard-grenville.jpg">
    <h2>Today is $now. </h2> </div>
    </body>
    </html>
4   EOF
```

Output from this example is shown in Figure 4.2.

EXPLANATION

1   The shebang line is required by the Web server, Apache, so that it can locate the Perl interpreter in order to execute the script.
2   This line tells the browser that the type of content being sent is text mixed with HTML tags. This line **must** be followed by a blank line.
3   The *here document* starts here. The terminating word is *EOF*. The *print* function will receive everything from *EOF* to *EOF*.
    The body of the document consists of text and HTML tags.
4   The word *EOF* marks the end of the *here document*. It must be on its own line and at the left margin with no leading spaces.

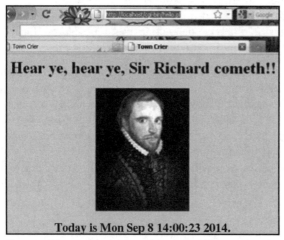

Figure 4.2 Output from Example 4.17.

4.4 Fancy Formatting with the *printf* Function

Perl provides the built-in *printf* function if you want to format strings or numbers with specific field sizes, left or right field designators, the different number bases, decimal point precision, and so forth. The *printf* function prints a formatted string to the selected filehandle, the default being *STDOUT*. It is like the *printf* function used in the *C* language and many other languages derived from *C*. The return value is *1* if *printf* is successful and *0* if it fails.

The *printf* function consists of a quoted control string that may include format specifications. The quoted string is followed by a comma and a list of comma-separated arguments, which are simply expressions.

The format specifiers are preceded by a % sign. For each % sign and format specifier, there must be a corresponding argument. (See Tables 4.5 and 4.6.)

Placing the quoted string and expressions within parentheses is optional.

EXAMPLE 4.18

```
printf("The name is %s and the number is %d\n", "John", 50);
          This is the control  string with
          format specifiers, %s and %d.
```

EXPLANATION

1   The string to be printed is enclosed in double quotes. The first format specifier is %s. It has a corresponding argument, *John*, positioned directly to the right of the comma after the closing quote in the control string. The *s* following the percent sign is called a **conversion character**. The *s* means *string* conversion will take place at this spot. In this case, *John* will replace the %s when the string is printed.

2   The %d format specifies that the decimal (integer) value *50* will be printed in its place within the string.

Table 4.5 Format Specifiers

Conversion	Definition
%b	Unsigned binary integer
%c	Character
%d, %i	Decimal number
%e	Floating-point number in scientific notation
%E	Floating-point number in scientific notation using capital *E*
%f, %F	Floating-point number
%g	Floating-point number using either e or f conversion, whichever takes the least space

(continued)

Table 4.5 Format Specifiers (continued)

Conversion	Definition
%G	Floating-point number using either e or f conversion, whichever takes the least space
%ld, %D	Long decimal number
%lu, %U	Long unsigned decimal number
%lo, %O	Long octal number
%p	Pointer (hexadecimal)
%s	String
%u	Unsigned decimal number
%x	Hexadecimal number
%X	Hexadecimal number using capital X
%lx	Long hexidecimal number
%%	Print a literal percent sign

Flag modifiers are used after the % to further define the printing; for example, *%-20s* represents a 20-character left-justified field.

Table 4.6 Flag Modifiers

Conversion	Definition
%-	Left-justification modifier; for example, *%-30s* is a left-justified, 30-space string.
%#	Integers in octal format are displayed with a leading *0*; integers in hexadecimal form are displayed with a leading *0x*.
%+	For conversions using *d, e, f,* and *g*, integers are displayed with a numeric sign, + or -.
%0	The displayed value is padded with zeros instead of whitespace.
%number	Maximum field width; for example, if number is *6*, as in *%6d*, maximum field width is six digits.
%.number	Precision of a floating-point number; for example, *%.2f* specifies a precision of two digits to the right of the decimal point, and *%8.2* represents a maximum field width of eight, where one of the characters is a decimal point followed by two digits after the decimal point.

When an argument is printed, the field holds the value that will be printed, and the width of the field is the number of characters the field should contain. The width of a field is specified by a percent sign and a number representing the maximum field width, followed by the conversion character. Example 4.19 shows how this works.

EXAMPLE 4.19

```
$name="Thomas Savage";
$phone="206-456-1234";
$salary=95200.00

printf "%25s%25s\n", $name, $phone;  # 25-space, right-justified strings
(Ouput)
                          Thomas Savage             206-456-1234

printf "%-25s%-25s\n", $name, $phone;  # 25-space, left-justified strings

(Output)
Thomas Savage            206-456-1234

printf "His salary is \$%10.2f\n", $salary; # right-justified field width
                               # of 10 including decimal point and precision
                               # two numbers to right of decimal point

(Output)
His salary is $  95200.00
```

Note that if the argument exceeds the maximum field width, *printf* will **not** truncate the number, but your formatting may not look nice. If the number to the right of the decimal point is truncated, it will be rounded up; for example, if the formatting instruction is %.2f, the corresponding argument, 56.555555, would be printed as 56.6.

EXAMPLE 4.20

```
(The Script)
  use warnings;
1 printf "Hello to you and yours %s!\n","Sam McGoo!";
2 printf("%-15s%-20s\n", "Jack", "Sprat");
3 printf "The number in decimal is %d\n", 45;
4 printf "The formatted number is |%10d|\n", 100;
5 printf "The number printed with leading zeros is |%010d|\n", 5;
6 printf "Left-justified the number is |%-10d|\n", 100;
7 printf "The number in octal is %o\n",15;
8 printf "The number in hexadecimal is %x\n", 15;
9 printf "The formatted floating point number is |%8.2f|\n", 14.3456;
```

EXAMPLE 4.20 (CONTINUED)

```
10 printf "The floating point number is |%8f|\n", 15;
11 printf "The character is %c\n", 65;
```

(Output)
```
1  Hello to you and yours Sam McGoo!
2  Jack            Sprat
3  The number in decimal is 45
4  The formatted number is |       100|
5  The number printed with leading zeros is |0000000005|.
6  Left-justified the number is |100       |
7  The number in octal is 17
8  The number in hexadecimal is f
9  The formatted floating point number is |   14.35|
10 The floating point number is |15.000000|
11 The character is A
```

EXPLANATION

1   The quoted string contains the *%s* format conversion specifier. The string *Sam Magoo* is converted to a string and replaces the *%s* in the printed output.

2   The string *Jack* has a field width of 15 characters and is left-justified. The string *Sprat* has a field width of 20 characters and is also left-justified. Parentheses are optional.

3   The number *45* is printed in decimal format.

4   The number *100* has a field width of 10 and is right-justified.

5   The number *5* has a field width of 10, is right-justified, and is preceded by leading zeroes rather than whitespace. If the modifier *0* is placed before the number representing the field width, the number printed will be padded with leading zeroes if it takes up less space than it needs.

6   The number *100* has a field width of 10 and is left-justified.

7   The number *15* is printed in octal.

8   The number *15* is printed in hexadecimal.

9   The number *14.3456* is given a field width of eight characters. One of them is the decimal point; the fractional part is given a precision of two decimal places. The number is then rounded up.

10   The number *15* is given a field width of eight characters, right-justified. The default precision is six decimal places to the right of the decimal point.

11   The number *65* is converted to the ASCII character *A* and printed.

4.4.1 Saving Formatting with the *sprintf* Function

The *sprintf* function is just like the *printf* function, except it allows you to save the formatting to a variable to be printed at some later time. Both functions, *sprintf* and *printf*, use the same conversion tables. Variables are discussed in Chapter 5, "What's in a Name?"

EXAMPLE 4.21

```
(The Script)
1   $string = sprintf("The name is: %10s\nThe number is: %8.2f\n",
                       "Ellie", 33);
2   print "$string";

(Output)
2   The name is:      Ellie
    The number is:    33.00
```

EXPLANATION

1   The *sprintf* function follows the same rules as *printf* for conversion of characters, strings, and numbers. The only real difference is that *sprintf* allows you to store the formatted output in a variable. In this example, the formatted output is stored in the scalar variable *$string*. The \n inserted in the string causes the remaining portion of the string to be printed on the next line. (Scalar variables are discussed in Chapter 5.) Parentheses are optional.

2   The value of the variable is printed showing the formatted output produced by *sprintf*.

4.4.2 The No Newline *say* Function

The *say* function is just like the *print* function. It also prints a comma-separated list of arguments, except it automatically appends a newline to the end of its list, so you don't have to remember to do it. It may save you a little time when debugging. This feature is not available in versions of Perl before release 5.10, so you must enable it. There are several ways to do this:

```
use feature 'say';    # See pragmas in the next section
```

or

```
use feature ':5.10';
```

or

```
use v5.10;
```

EXAMPLE 4.22

```
(The Script)
1   use feature 'say';
2   say "What were you thinking?";
    say "Not much.";
    say "The sum is ", 5 + 4;


(Output)
What were you thinking?
Not much.
The sum is 9
```

EXPLANATION

1   By using *feature 'say'*, Perl will enable this feature if you have installed Perl 5.10 or above.

2   The *say* function is just like the *print* function, but will add a newline at the end of the string so that you don't have to remember to do it.

4.5   What Are Pragmas?

A pragma is a special Perl module that comes with each distribution of Perl and hints to the compiler something about how your program code should be compiled. You can use this type of module to help control the way your program behaves such as discovering context errors, global variables, misused references, operators, and to implement new features.

4.5.1   The *feature* Pragma

The *feature* pragma is used to load features particular to a newer release of Perl, features that may break older versions.

```
use feature ':5.10';  # loads all features available in perl 5.10

use v5.10;            # implicitly loads :5.10 feature bundle

use feature qw(say switch state);  # Adds functions by name new since 5.10.
```

Here is a description of the *feature* pragma from the Perl documentation:

It is usually impossible to add new syntax to Perl without breaking some existing programs. This pragma provides a way to minimize that risk. New syntactic constructs, or new semantic meanings to older constructs, can be enabled by *"use feature 'foo'"*, and will be parsed only when the appropriate feature pragma is in scope. (Nevertheless, the *"CORE::"* prefix provides access to all Perl keywords, regardless of this pragma.)

4.5.2 The *warnings* Pragma

In Chapter 3, "Perl Scripts," we talked about the *-w* switch used to warn you about the possibility of using future reserved words, misspelled variables, misused operators, and a number of other problems that may cause problems in the program. (Often, these warnings are rather cryptic and hard to understand if you are new to programming.)

Larry Wall says in the Perl 5 *man* pages, "Whenever you get mysterious behavior, try the *-w* switch! Whenever you don't get mysterious behavior, try the *-w* switch anyway."

You can use the *-w* switch either as a command-line option to Perl, as:

```
perl -w <scriptname>
```

or after the *shebang* line in the Perl script, such as:

```
#!/usr/bin/perl -w
```

or since version 5.10:

```
#!/usr/bin/env perl -w
```

Starting with Perl 5.6.0, *warnings.pm* was added to the standard Perl library; similar to the *-w* switch, it is a pragma that allows you to control the types of warnings printed.

To see more about how the warnings pragma works, use the *perldoc* command at the command line:

```
perldoc warnings;
```

In your programs, add the following line under the *#!* line or, if not using the *#!* line, at the top of the script:

```
use warnings;
```

This enables all possible warnings. To turn off warnings, simply add as a line in your script:

```
no warnings;
```

This disables all possible warnings for the rest of the script.

EXAMPLE 4.23

```
(The Script)
1  use warnings;
2  print "What is your name? ";
3  chomp($name = <STDIN>);
4  print "$nime, welcome!\n";  # Misspelled $name


   # Scriptname: warnme


(Output)
Name "main::name" used only once: possible typo at warnme.plx line 3.
Name "main::nime" used only once: possible typo at warnme.plx line 4.
What is your name? Joe Shmoe
Use of uninitialized value $nime in concatenation (.) or string at warnme.
plx line 4, <STDIN> line 1.
, welcome!
```

EXPLANATION

1   In Perl versions 5.6 and later, you can use the *warnings* pragma instead of the *-w* switch. The *-w* switch produced warnings for the entire script, whereas the *warnings* pragma can be limited to the enclosing block. When you say *use warnings*, that tells Perl that you want to use a module called *warnings.pm* from the Standard Perl Library. If you want to turn warnings off, just type *no warnings* on a line by itself.

4   The variable *$nime* is a misspelling. It should have been spelled *$name*. Perl lets you know by saying you only used the variable once in the string. The program still runs, but the string is missing the value of *$name*.

4.5.3   The *diagnostics* Pragma

This special pragma enhances the warning messages to a more verbose explanation of what went wrong in your program. Like the *warnings* pragma, it affects the compilation phase of your program, but unlike the *warnings* pragma, it attempts to give you an explanation that doesn't assume you are an experienced programmer.

EXAMPLE 4.24

```
(The Script)
1  use diagnostics;
2  print "Hello there';  # Unmatched quote
3  print "We are on line number ", __LINE__,"\n";
```

EXAMPLE 4.24 (CONTINUED)

```
(The output)
Bareword found where operator expected at test.plx line 3, near "$now =
"Ellie"
  (Might be a runaway multi-line "" string starting on line 2) (#1)
    (S syntax) The Perl lexer knows whether to expect a term or an
operator.
      If it sees what it knows to be a term when it was expecting to see
      an operator, it gives you this warning.  Usually it indicates that
      an operator or delimiter was omitted, such as a semicolon.

Missing operator before Ellie?)
String found where operator expected at test.plx line 3, at end of line
(#1)
        (Missing semicolon on previous line?)

syntax error at test.plx line 3, near "$now = "Ellie"
Can't find string terminator '"' anywhere before EOF at test.plx line 3
(#2)
    (F) Probably means you had a syntax error.  Common reasons include:

        A keyword is misspelled.
        A semicolon is missing.
        A comma is missing.
        An opening or closing parenthesis is missing.
print "hello there';
print "We are on line number ", __LINE__,"\n";
```

EXPLANATION

In Perl versions 5.6 and later, the *diagnostics* pragma is used instead of the -w switch or the *warnings* pragma. This special Perl module sends detailed messages about the problems that occurred in the script. Since the string *"Hello there'* does not contain matched quotes, the *diagnostics* pragma issues a list of all the potential causes for the failed program. The compiler expects the string to be terminated with another double quote.

4.5.4 The *strict* Pragma and Words

Another important pragma is the *strict* pragma. If your program disobeys the restrictions placed on it, it won't compile. There are three possible ways that being strict will cause your program to abort given the arguments: *"subs"*, *"vars"*, and *"refs"*. Using *strict* without arguments get you all three. If, for example, there is a chance that you might have used barewords (that is, unquoted words, as in *Hello*), the *strict* pragma with *sub* as the argument will catch it, and your program will abort until you quote the word, *"Hello"*. When creating modules, *strict* is also used to enforce privately scoped variables and catch symbolic references, a topic we cover in Chapter 5, "What's in a Name?"

EXAMPLE 4.25

```
(The Script)
   # Program: stricts.test
   # Script to demonstrate the strict pragma
1  use strict "subs";
2  $name = Ellie;              # Unquoted word Ellie
3  print "Hi $name.\n";

(Output)
$ stricts.test
  Bareword "Ellie" not allowed while "strict subs" in use at ./stricts.
test line 5.
  Execution of stricts.test aborted due to compilation errors.
```

EXPLANATION

1   The *use* function allows you to use modules located in the standard Perl library. When the *strict* pragma takes *subs* as an argument, it will catch any barewords found in the program while it is being internally compiled. If a bareword is found, the program will be aborted with an error message.

4.6 What You Should Know

1. How do you define *stdin*, *stdout*, and *stderr*?

2. What is meant by the term **filehandle**?

3. How do you represent a number in octal, hexadecimal, or binary?

4. What is the main difference between the *print, say,* and *printf* functions?

5. How do double and single quotes differ in the way they treat a string?

6. What are *q* and *qq* used for?

7. What are **literals**?

8. What is the use of _ _END_ _?

9. What are backslash sequences?

10. What is the purpose of the *sprintf* function?

11. What does *strict* do?

12. What is a pragma? What does the *feature* pragma do?

13. How can you check to make sure your syntax is ok? How can you check for a spelling error?

14. What is a *here document*? How is it useful in CGI programs?

4.7 What's Next?

In the next chapter, you will learn about Perl variables and the meaning of the "funny characters." You will be able to create and access scalars, arrays, and hashes and understand context and namespaces. You will also learn how to get input from a user and why we need to *chomp*. A number of array and hash functions will be introduced.

EXERCISE 4
A String of Perls

1. Use the *print, printf,* or *say* function to output the following string:

   "Ouch," cried Mrs. O'Neil, "You mustn't do that Mr. O'Neil!"

2. Use the *sprintf* function to format $34.666666 as $34.67 and store it in a variable. Print the value of the variable with the *say* function.

3. Write a Perl script called *literals.plx* that will print the following:

   ```
   $ perl literals
   Today is Mon Mar 12 12:58:04 PDT 2014   (Use localtime())
   The name of this PERL SCRIPT is literals.
   Hello. The number we will examine is 125.5.
   The NUMBER in decimal is 125.
   The following number is taking up 20 spaces and is right justified.
   |                    125|
              The number in hex is 7d
              The number in octal is 175
   The number in scientific notation is 1.255000e+02
   The unformatted number is 125.500000
   The formatted number is 125.50
   My boss just said, "Can't you loan me $12.50 for my lunch?"
   I flatly said, "No way!"
   Good-bye (Makes a beep sound)
   ```

   Note: The words *PERL SCRIPT* and *NUMBER* are capitalized by using string literal escape sequences.

   What command-line option would you use to check the syntax of your script?

4. Add to your literals script a *here document* to print:

   Life is good with Perl.
   I have just completed my second exercise!

5. What is the *feature* pragma used for?

6. How would you turn on warnings in the script? How would you turn them off? How would you turn on diagnostics?

chapter
5

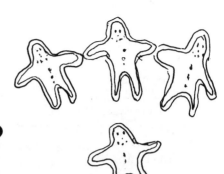

What's in a Name?

5.1 More About Data Types

By the end of this chapter, you will be able to read the following Perl code:

```
use strict;
use warnings;
my @l = qw/a b c d d a e b a b d e f/;
my %hash=();

foreach my $key (@l){
    $hash{$key} = $key;
}
print join(" ",sort keys %hash),"\n";
```

Again, please take note that each line of code, in most of the examples throughout this book, is numbered. The output and explanations are also numbered to match the numbers in the code. When copying examples into your text editor, don't include these numbers, or you will generate errors.

5.1.1 Basic Data Types (Scalar, Array, Hash)

In Chapter 3, "Perl Scripts," we briefly discussed scalars. In this chapter, we will cover scalars in more depth, as well as arrays and hashes. It should be noted that Perl does not provide the traditional data types, such as *int*, *float*, *double*, *char*, and so on. It bundles all these types into one type, the scalar. A scalar can represent an integer, float, string, and so on, and can also be used to create aggregate or composite types, such as arrays and hashes.

Unlike *C* or *Java*, Perl variables don't have to be declared before being used, and you do not have to specify what kind data will be stored there. Variables spring to life just by the mere mention of them. You can assign strings, numbers, or a combination of these to Perl variables and Perl will figure out what the type is. You may store a number or a list of numbers in a variable and then later change your mind and store a string there. Perl doesn't care.

A scalar variable contains a single value (for example, one string or one number), an array variable contains an ordered list of values indexed by a positive number, and a hash contains an unordered set of key/value pairs indexed by a string (the key) that is associated with a corresponding value (see Figure 5.1). (See Section 5.2, "Scalars, Arrays, and Hashes.")

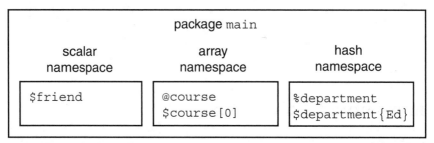

Figure 5.1 Namespaces for scalars, arrays, and hashes in package *main*.

5.1.2 Package, Scope, Privacy, and Strictness

Package and Scope. The Perl sample programs you have seen in the previous chapters are compiled internally into what is called a **package**, which provides a **namespace** for variables.

An analogy often used to describe a package is the naming of a person. In the Johnson family, there is a boy named James. James is known to his family and does not have to qualify his name with a last name every time he is being called to dinner. "James, sit down at the table" is enough. However, in the school he attends there are several boys named James. The correct James is identified by his last name, for example, "James Johnson, go to the principal's office."

In a Perl program, "James" represents a variable and his family name, "Johnson," a package. The default package is called *main*. If you create a variable, *$name*, for example, *$name* belongs to the *main* package and could be identified as *$main::name*, but qualifying the variable at this point is unnecessary as long as we are working in a single file and using the default package, *main*. Later when working with modules, we will step outside of the package *main*. This would be like James going to school. Then we could have a conflict if two variables from different packages had the same name and would have to qualify which package they belong to. For now, we will stay in the *main* package. When you see the word *main* in a warning or error message, just be aware that it is a reference to something going on in your *main* package.

The scope of a variable determines where it is visible in the program. In the Perl scripts you have seen so far, the variables live in the package *main* and are visible to the entire script file (that is, global in scope). Global variables, also called package variables, can be changed anywhere within the current package (and other packages), and the change will permanently affect the variable. To keep variables totally hidden within their file, block, or subroutine programs, we can define lexical variables. One way Perl does this is with the *my* operator. An entire file can be thought of as a block, but we normally think of a block as a set of statements enclosed within curly braces. If a variable is declared as a *my* variable within a block, it is visible (that is, accessible within that block and any nested blocks). It is not visible outside the block. If a variable is declared with *my* at the file level, then the variable is visible throughout the file. See Example 5.1.

EXAMPLE 5.1

```
  # We are in package main
1 no warnings;   # warnings turned off so that output is
                 # not clouded with warning messages

2 my $family="Johnson";  # file scope
3 {  my $mother="Mama";   # block scope
      my $father="Papa";
      my ($cousin, $sister, $brother);
4     my $family="McDonald";   # new variable
5     print "The $family family is visible here.\n";
   }
6 print "$mother and $father are not visible here.\n";
7 print "The $family family is back.\n";

(Output)
5 The McDonald family is visible here.
6    and are not visible here.
7 The Johnson family is back.
```

EXPLANATION

1   *warnings* are turned off so that you can see what's going on without being interrupted with warning messages. If *warnings* had been turned on, you would have seen the following:

```
Name "main::father" used only once: possible typo at my.plx line 10.
Name "main::mother" used only once: possible typo at my.plx line 10.
The McDonald family is visible here.
Use of uninitialized value $mother in concatenation (.) or string at
        my.plx line 10.
Use of uninitialized value $father in concatenation (.) or string at
        my.plx line 10.
And are not visible here.
The Johnson family is back.
```

The messages are telling you that for package *main*, the *$mother* and *$father* variables were used only once. That is because they are not visible outside of the block where they were defined, and by being mentioned outside the block, they are new uninitialized variables.

EXPLANATION (CONTINUED)

2   The *$family* variable is declared as a lexical *my* variable at the beginning of the program. The file is considered a block for this variable giving it file scope; that is, visible for the entire file, even within blocks. If changed within a block, it will be changed for the rest of the file.

3   We enter a block. The *my* variables within this block are private to this block, visible here and in any nested blocks, and will go out of scope (become invisible) when the block exits.

4   This is a brand new lexical *$family* variable (*McDonald*). It has nothing to do with the one created on line 2. The first one (*Johnson*) will be visible again after we exit this block.

6   The *my* variables defined within the block are not visible here; that is, they have gone out of scope. These are brand new variables, created on the fly, and have no value.

7   The Johnson family is back. It is visible in the outer scope.

The purpose in mentioning packages and scope now is to let you know that the default scope of variables in the default *main* package, your script, is global; that is, accessible throughout the script. To help avoid the future problems caused by global variables, it is a good habit (and often a required practice) to keep variables private by using the *my* operator. This is where the *strict* pragma comes in.

The *strict* pragma (a pragma is a compiler directive) is a special Perl module that directs the compiler to abort the program if certain conditions are not met. It targets barewords, symbolic references, and global variables. For small practice scripts within a single file, using *strict* isn't necessary, but it is a good, and often required, practice to use it (a topic you can expect to come up in a Perl job interview!).

In the following examples, we will use *strict* primarily to target global variables, causing your program to abort if you don't use the *my* operator when declaring them.

EXAMPLE 5.2

```
1   use strict;
2   use warnings;
3   $family="Johnson";  # Whoops! global scope
4   $mother="Mama";
5   $father="Papa";
6   print "$mother and $father are here.\n"; # global
7   print "The $family family is here.\n";

(Output)
Global symbol "$family" requires explicit package name at strictex.plx
line 3.
Global symbol "$mother" requires explicit package name at strictex.plx
line 4.
Global symbol "$father" requires explicit package name at strictex.plx
line 5.
```

EXAMPLE 5.2 (CONTINUED)

```
Global symbol "$mother" requires explicit package name at strictex.plx
line 6.
Global symbol "$father" requires explicit package name at strictex.plx
line 6.
Global symbol "$family" requires explicit package name at strictex.plx
line 7.
Execution of strictex.plx aborted due to compilation errors.
```

EXPLANATION

1 The *strict* pragma is being used to restrict all "unsafe constructs." To see all the restrictions, type the following at your command-line:

```
perldoc strict
```

If you just want to target global variables, you would use *strict* with an argument in your program, such as:

```
use strict 'vars'
```

2 The *warnings* pragma is turned on, but will not issue warnings because *strict* will supersede it, causing the program to abort first.

3 This is a global variable in the program, but it sets off a plethora of complaints from *strict* everywhere it is used. By preceding *$family* and the variables *$mother* and *$father* with the *my* operator, all will go well. (You can also explicitly name the package and the variable, as *$main::family* to satisfy *strict*. But then, the *warnings* pragma will start complaining about other things, as discussed in the previous example.)

6, 7 Global variables again! *strict* complains, and the program is aborted.

The *warnings* and *strict* pragmas together are used to help you find typos, spelling errors, and global variables. Although using warnings will not cause your program to die, with *strict* turned on, it will, if you disobey its restrictions. With the small examples in this book, the *warnings* are always turned on, but we will not turn on *strict* until later.

5.1.3 Naming Conventions

Variables are identified by the "funny characters" that precede them. Scalar variables are preceded by a $ sign, array variables are preceded by an @ sign, and hash variables are preceded by a % sign. Since the "funny characters" (properly called **sigils**) indicate what type of variable you are using, you can use the same name for a scalar, array, or hash (or a function, filehandle, and so on) and not worry about a naming conflict. For example, *$name*, *@name*, and *%name* are all different variables; the first is a scalar, the second is an array, and the last is a hash.[1]

---

1. Using the same name is perfectly legal, but not recommended; it makes reading the program too confusing.

Since reserved words and filehandles are not preceded by a special character, variable names will not conflict with them. Names are **case sensitive**. The variables named *$Num*, *$num*, and *$NUM* are all different. If a variable starts with a letter, it may consist of any number of letters (an underscore counts as a letter) and/or digits. If the variable does not start with a letter, it must consist of only one character. Perl has a set of special variables (for example, *$_*, *$^*, *$.*, *$1*, *$2*) that fall into this category. (See Section A.2, "Special Variables," in Appendix A.) In special cases, variables may also be preceded with a single quote, but only when packages are used. An uninitialized variable will get a value of zero or *undef*, depending on whether its context is numeric or string.

5.1.4 Assignment Statements

The assignment operator, the equal sign (=), is used to assign the value on its right-hand side to a variable on its left-hand side. Any value that can be "assigned to" represents a named region of storage and is called an *lvalue*.[2] Perl reports an error if the operand on the left-hand side of the assignment operator does not represent an *lvalue*.

When assigning a value or values to a variable, if the variable on the left-hand side of the equal sign is a scalar, Perl evaluates the expression on the right-hand side in a scalar context. If the variable on the left of the equal sign is an array, then Perl evaluates the expression on the right in an array or list context (see Section 5.2, "Scalars, Arrays, and Hashes").

EXAMPLE 5.3

```
(The Script)
   use warnings;
   # Scalar, array, and hash assignment
1  my $salary=50000;                   # Scalar assignment
2  my @months=('Mar', 'Apr', 'May');   # Array assignment
3  my %states= (                       # Hash assignment
      CA => 'California',
      ME => 'Maine',
      MT => 'Montana',
      NM => 'New Mexico',
   );
4  print "$salary\n";
5  print "@months\n";
6  print "$months[0], $months[1], $months[2]\n";
7  print "$states{'CA'}, $states{'NM'}\n";
8  print $x + 3, "\n";                 # $x just came to life!
9  print "***$name***\n";              # $name is born!
```

---

2. The value on the left-hand side of the equal sign is called an *lvalue*, and the value on the right-hand side is called an *rvalue*.

EXAMPLE 5.3 (CONTINUED)

```
(Output)
4   50000
5   Mar Apr May
6   Mar, Apr, May
7   California, New Mexico
8   3
9   ******
```

EXPLANATION

1   The scalar variable *$salary* is assigned the numeric literal *50000.**

2   The array *@months* is assigned the comma-separated list, *'Mar ', ' Apr ', May '*. The list is enclosed in parentheses and each list item is quoted.

3   The hash, *%states*, is assigned a list consisting of a set of strings separated by either a digraph symbol (=>) or a comma. The string on the left is called the key and it is not required that you quote the key, unless it starts with a number. The string to the right is called the value. The key is associated with its value.

5   The *@months* array is printed. The double quotes preserve spaces between each element.

6   The individual elements of the array, *@months*, are scalars and are thus preceded by a dollar sign ($). The array index starts at zero.

7   The *key* elements of the hash, *%states*, are enclosed in curly braces ({}). The associated *value* is printed. Each *value* is a single value, a scalar. The *value* is preceded by a dollar sign ($).

8   The scalar variable, *$x*, is referenced for the first time with an initial value of *undef*. Because the number 3 is added to *$x*, the context is numeric. *$x* then gets an initial value of 0 in order to perform arithmetic. Initially *$x* is null.

9   The scalar variable, *$name*, is referenced for the first time with an undefined value. The context is string.

---

* The comma can be used in both Perl 4 and Perl 5. The => symbol was introduced in Perl 5.

5.2 Scalars, Arrays, and Hashes

Now that we have discussed the basics of Perl variables (types, visibility, funny characters, and so forth), we can look at them in more depth. Perhaps a review of the quoting rules detailed in Chapter 4, "Getting a Handle on Printing," would be helpful at this time.

5.2.1 Scalar Variables

Scalar variables hold a single number or string[3] and are preceded by a dollar sign ($). Perl scalars need a preceding dollar sign whenever the variable is referenced, even when the scalar is being assigned a value.

Assignment.   When making an assignment, the value on the right-hand side of the equal sign is evaluated as a single value (that is, its context is scalar). A quoted string, then, is considered a single value even if it contains many words.

EXAMPLE 5.4

```
1   $number = 150;   # Number
2   $name = "Jody Savage"; # String
3   $today = localtime();  # Function
```

EXPLANATION

1   The numeric literal, *150*, is assigned to the scalar variable *$number*.
2   The string literal *Jody Savage* is assigned to the scalar *$name* as a single string.
3   The output of Perl's *localtime* function will be assigned as a string to *$today*. (The return value of *localtime* is string context here and if assigned to an array its return value is an array of numbers. See perldoc *-f localtime*.)

EXAMPLE 5.5

```
(The Script)
    use warnings;
    # Initializing scalars and printing their values
1   my $num = 5;
2   my $friend = "John Smith";
3   my $money = 125.75;
4   my $now = localtime;          # localtime is a Perl function
5   my $month="Jan";
6   print "$num\n";
7   print "$friend\n";
8   print "I need \$$money.\n";      # Protecting our money
9   print qq/$friend gave me \$$money.\n/;
10  print qq/The time is $now\n/;
11  print "The month is ${month}uary.\n";   # Curly braces shield
                                            # the variable
12  print "The month is $month" . "uary.\n"; # Concatenate
```

---

3. References are also stored as string variables.

EXAMPLE 5.5 (CONTINUED)

```
(Output)
6   5
7   John Smith
8   I need $125.75.
9   John Smith gave me $125.75.
10  The time is Sat Jan 24 16:12:49 2014.
11  The month is January.
12  The month is January.
```

EXPLANATION

1   The scalar *$num* is assigned the numeric literal, *5*.
2   The scalar *$friend* is assigned the string literal, *John Smith*.
3   The scalar *$money* is assigned the numeric floating point literal, *125.75*.
4   The scalar *$now* is assigned the output of Perl's built-in *localtime* function.
5   The scalar *$month* is assigned *Jan*.
8   The quoted string is printed. The backslash allows the first dollar sign ($) to be printed literally; the value of *$money* is interpolated within double quotes, and its value printed.
9   The Perl *qq* construct replaces double quotes. The string to be quoted is enclosed in forward slashes. The value of the scalar *$friend* is interpolated; a literal dollar sign precedes the value of the scalar interpolated variable, *$money*.
10 The quoted string is printed as if in double quotes. The *$now* variable is interpolated.
11 Curly braces can be used to shield the variable from characters that are appended to it. *January* will be printed.
12 Normally, two strings or expressions are joined together with the dot operator (see Chapter 6, "Where's the Operator?"), called the concatenation operator.

The *defined* Function.   If a scalar has neither a valid string nor a valid numeric value, it is undefined. The *defined* function allows you to check for the validity of a variable's value. It returns 1 if the variable has a value (other than *undef*) and nothing if it does not.

EXAMPLE 5.6

```
.
$name="Tommy";
print "OK \n" if defined $name;
```

The *undef* Function.   When you define a variable without giving it a value, such as

```
my $name;
```

the initial value is *undef*.

You can use the *undef* function to undefine an already defined variable. It releases whatever memory that was allocated for the variable. The function returns the undefined value. This function also releases storage associated with arrays and subroutines.

EXAMPLE 5.7

```
undef $name;
```

The $_ Scalar Variable.   The $_ (called a **topic** variable[4]) is a ubiquitous little character. Although it is very useful in Perl scripts, it is often not seen, somewhat like your shadow—sometimes you see it; sometimes you don't. It is used as the default pattern space for searches, for functions that require a scalar argument, and to hold the current line when looping through a file. Once a value is assigned to $_, functions such as *chomp*, *split*, and *print* will use $_ as an argument. You will learn more about functions and their arguments later, but for now, consider the following example.

EXAMPLE 5.8

```
1   $_ = "Donald Duck\n";
2   chomp;    # The newline is removed from $_
3   print;    # The value of $_ is printed

(Output)
Donald Duck
```

EXPLANATION

1   The $_ scalar variable is assigned the string *"Donald Duck\n"*. Now you see it!
2   The *chomp* function removes the newline from $_, the default scalar. Now you don't!
3   The *print* function has been given nothing to print, so it will print $_, the default scalar, without a trailing newline.

The $_ Scalar and Reading Input from Files

When looping through a file, the $_ is often used as a holding place for each line as it is read. In the following example, a text file called *datebook.txt* is opened for reading. The filehandle is *$fh*, a user-defined variable to represent the real file, *datebook.txt*. Each time the loop is entered, a line is read from the file. But where does the line go? It is implicitly assigned to the $_ variable. The next time the loop is entered, a new line is read from the file and assigned to $_, overwriting the previous line stored there. The loop ends when the end of file is reached. The *print* function, although it appears to be printing nothing, will print the value of $_ each time the loop block is entered.

_____

4. A topic variable is a special variable with a very short name, which in many cases can be omitted.

EXAMPLE 5.9

```
(The Script)
   use warnings;
   # Reading input from a file
1  open(my $fh, "<", "datebook.txt") or die $!;
2  while(<$fh>){   # loops through the file a line at a time storing
                   # each line in $_
3      print;      # prints the value stored in $_
4  }
5  close $fh;

(Output)
Jon DeLoach:408-253-3122:123 Park St., San Jose, CA 04086:7/25/53:85100
Karen Evich:284-758-2857:23 Edgecliff Place, Lincoln, NB
92086:7/25/53:85100
Karen Evich:284-758-2867:23 Edgecliff Place, Lincoln, NB
92743:11/3/35:58200
Karen Evich:284-758-2867:23 Edgecliff Place, Lincoln, NB
92743:11/3/35:58200
Fred Fardbarkle:674-843-1385:20 Parak Lane, DeLuth, MN
23850:4/12/23:780900
```

EXPLANATION

1   A user-defined filehandle is a Perl way of associating a real file with an internal Perl structure by a name. In this example, *$fh* is a lexically scoped filehandle used to represent the real file, *datebook.txt*, which is opened for reading. If the file doesn't exist or is unreadable, the program will "die" (exit) with the reason it died (*$!*).

2   The *while* loop is entered. Perl will read the first line from the file and implicitly assign its value to $_, and if successful enter the body of the loop. The angle brackets (<>) are used for reading, as we saw when reading from *STDIN*.

3   Every time the loop is entered, a new line from the file is stored in $_, overwriting the previous line that was stored there, and each time the current value of $_ is printed.

4   This is the closing brace for the block of the loop. When the file has no more lines, the read will fail, and the loop will end.

5   Once finished with the file, it is closed via the filehandle. (See Chapter 10, "Getting a Handle on Files," for a complete discussion on filehandles.)

5.2.2 Arrays

Let's say when you moved into town, you made one friend. That friend can be stored in a scalar as *$friend="John"*. Now let's say a few months have gone by since you moved, and now you have a whole bunch of new friends. In that case, you could create a list of friends, give the list one name, and store your friends in a Perl array; for example, *@pals=("John", "Mary", "Sanjay", "Archie")*.

When you have a collection of similar data elements, it is easier to use an array than to create a separate variable for each of the elements. The array name allows you to associate a single variable name with a list of data elements. Each of the elements in the list is referenced by its name and a subscript (also called an **index**).

Perl, unlike *C*-like languages, doesn't care whether the elements of an array are of the same data type. They can be a mix of numbers and strings. To Perl, **an array is a list containing an ordered set of scalars.** The name of the array starts with an @ sign and the list is enclosed in parentheses, each element assigned an index value starting at zero (see Figure 5.2).

Assignment.   If the array is initialized, the elements are enclosed in parentheses, and each element is separated by a comma. The list is parenthesized due to the lower precedence of the comma operator over the assignment operator. Elements in an array are simply scalars.

The *qw* construct can also be used to quote words in a list (similar to *qq*, *q*, and *qx*). The items in the list are treated as singly quoted words and the comma is also provided.

```
$pal = "John";  # Scalar holds one value
@pals = ("John", "Sam", "Nicky", "Jake" );  # Array holds a list of values
@pals = qw(John Sam Nicky Jake);  # qw means quote word and include comma
```

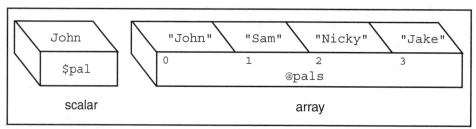

Figure 5.2 A scalar variable and an array variable.

EXAMPLE 5.10

```
1   @name=("Guy", "Tom", "Dan", "Roy");
2   @list=(2..10);
3   @grades=(100, 90, 65, 96, 40, 75);
4   @items=($a, $b, $c);
5   @empty=();
6   $size=@items;
7   @mammals = qw/dogs cats cows/;
8   @fruit = qw(apples pears peaches);
```

EXPLANATION

1   The array *@name* is initialized with a list of four string literals.
2   The array *@list* is assigned numbers ranging from *2* through *10*.
3   The array *@grades* is initialized with a list of six numeric literals.

4   The array @*items* is initialized with the values of three scalar variables.

5   The array @*empty* is assigned an empty list.

6   The array @*items* is assigned to the scalar variable $*size*. The value of the scalar is the number of elements in the array (in this example, 3).

7   The *qw* (quote word) construct is followed by a delimiter of your choice and a string. *qw()* extracts words out of your string using embedded whitespace as the delimiter and returns the words as a list. Variables are not interpolated. Each word in the list is treated as a singly quoted word. The list is terminated with a closing delimiter. This example could be written like so:

```
@mammals = ('cats', 'dogs', 'cows' );
```

8   The *qw* construct accepts paired characters ( ), { },< >, and [ ], as optional delimiters.

Output and Input Special Variables ($, and $").   The $, is a special default global variable, called the **output field separator**. When used by the *print* function to print a list or an array (not enclosed in quotes), this variable separates the elements and is initially set to *undef*. For example, *print 1,2,3* would ouput *123*. Although you can assign a different value to the $, it's not a good idea, as once changed, it will affect your whole program. (The *join* function would provide a better solution.)

EXAMPLE 5.11

```
1   use warnings;
2   my @pets=("Smokey", "Fido", "Gills", "Skiddy");
3   print @pets, "\n";  # Output separator is undef
4   $,="****";   # Changes the output field separator
5   print @pets,"\n";  # no quotes; **** replaces undef
6   print 1,2,3, "\n";

(Output)
SmokeyFidoGillsSKiddy
Smokey****Fido****Gills****Skiddy****
  1****2****3****
```

3   The array of pets is printed. The value of of $, is used to separate elements of an unquoted list for the *print* function and is initially set to undef .

4   The $, variable is reset to *"****"*.

5   Now, when the *print* function displays an unquoted list, the list items are separated by that string.

6   The comma evaluates to *"****"* in the *print* function.

The $" is a special scalar variable, called the **list separator**, used to separate the elements of a list in an array, and is by default a single space. For example, when you print an array enclosed in double quotes, the value of $" will be preserved, and you will have a space between the elements.

EXAMPLE 5.12

```
1  @grocery_list=qw(meat potatoes rice beans spinach milk);
2  print "@grocery_list\n";  # The list separator is a space
3  $" = "---";  # Change the list separator
4  print "@grocery_list\n"; # The list separator has been changed
5  $, = "||";  # change print's separator
6  print @grocery, "\n";  # no quotes
```

(Ouput)
```
2  meat potatoes rice beans spinach milk
4  meat---potatoes---rice---beans---spinach---milk
5  meat||potatotes||rice||beans||spinach||milk
```

EXPLANATION

2 The $" variable is called the list separator and is initially set to a space. Unless the array is enclosed in double quotes, the space is lost.

3 You can change the $" variable by assigning it a string.

4 Now you can see when we print the quoted array, the array separator between the elements has been changed.

5 Now the print separator is changed to "||". If the quotes are removed, the *print* function will display the list with the new separator.

Array Size. $#arrayname returns the largest index value in the array; that is, the index value of its last element. Since the array indices start at zero, this value is one less than the array size. The $#arrayname variable can also be used to shorten or truncate the size of the array.

To get the size of an array, you can assign it to a scalar or use the built-in *scalar* function which used with an array, forces scalar context. It returns the size of the array, one value. (This is defined as a unary operator. See perlop for more details.)

EXAMPLE 5.13

```
   use warnings;
1  my @grades = (90,89,78,100,87);
2  print "The original array is: @grades\n";
3  print "The number of the last index is $#grades\n";
4  print "The value of the last element in the array is
       $grades[$#grades]\n";

5  print "The size of the array is ", scalar @grades, "\n";
   # my $size = @grades;  # Get the size of the array
6  @grades=();
   print "The array is completely truncated: @grades\n";
```

(Output)
```
2  The original array is: 90 89 78 100 87
3  The number of the last index is 4
4  The value of the last element of the array is 87
5  The size of the array is 5
6  The array is completely truncated:
```

EXPLANATION

1   The array *@grades* is assigned a list of five numbers.
2   The $# construct gets the index value of the last element in the array.
3   By using $#*grades* as an index value, the expression would evaluate to $*grades[4]*.
4   The built-in *scalar* function forces the array to be in scalar context and returns the number of elements in the array. You could also assign the array to a scalar variable, as in $*size* = *@grades*, to produce the same result as shown in line 6.
6   Using an empty list causes the array to be completely truncated to an empty list.

The Range Operator and Array Assignment.   The .. operator, called the **range** operator, when used in a list context, returns a list of values starting from the left value to the right value, counting by ones.

EXAMPLE 5.14

```
    use warnings;
1   my @digits=(0 .. 10);
2   my @letters=( 'A' .. 'Z' );
3   my @alpha=( 'A' .. 'Z', 'a' .. 'z' );
4   my @n=( -5 .. 20 );
```

EXPLANATION

1   The array *@digits* is assigned a list of numbers, *0* incremented by 1 until 10 is reached.
2   The array *@letters* is assigned a list of capital letters, *A* through *Z* (ASCII values of A through Z).
3   The array *@alpha* is assigned a list of uppercase and lowercase letters.
4   The array *@n* is assigned a list of numbers, *-5* through *20*.

Accessing Elements.   An array is an ordered list of scalars. To reference the individual elements in an array, each element (a scalar) is preceded by a dollar sign. The index starts at 0, followed by positive whole numbers. For example, in the array *@colors*, the first element in the array is $*colors[0]*, the next element is $*colors[1]*, and so forth. You can also access elements starting at the end of an array with the index value of –1 and continue downward; for example, –2, –3, and so forth.

1. To assign a list of values to an array:

   ```
   @colors = qw( green red blue yellow);
   ```

2. To print the whole array, use the @:

   ```
   print "@colors\n";
   ```

3. To print single elements of the array:

   ```
   print "$colors[0]   $colors[1]\n";
   ```

4. To print more than one element (meaning, a list):

```
print "@colors[1,3]\n";   # Now the index values are in a list,
                          # requiring the @ rather than the $ sign.
```

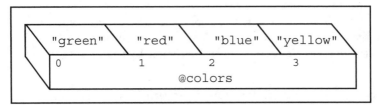

Figure 5.3 Array elements.

```
(The Script)
   use warnings;

   # Populating an array and printing its values
1  my @names=('John', 'Joe', 'Jake');      # @names=qw/John Joe Jake/;
2  print @names, "\n";  # prints without the separator
3  print "Hi $names[0], $names[1], and $names[2]!\n";
4  my $number=@names;          # The scalar is assigned the number
                               # of elements in the array
5  print "There are $number elements in the \@names array.\n";
6  print "The last element of the array is $names[$number -1].\n";
7  print "The last element of the array is $names[$#names].\n";
                            # Remember, the array index starts at zero!
8  my @fruit = qw(apples pears peaches plums);
9  print "The first element of the \@fruit array  is $fruit[0];
      the second element is $fruit[1].\n";
10  print "Starting at the end of the array; @fruit[-1, -3]\n";

(Output)
2  JohnJoeJake
3  Hi John, Joe, and Jake!
5  There are 3 elements in the @names array.
6  The last element of the array is Jake.
7  The last element of the array is Jake.
9  The first element of the @fruit array is apples; the second element is
   pears.
10 Starting at the end of the array: plums pears
```

EXPLANATION

1 The @names array is initialized with three strings: *John, Joe,* and *Jake*.

2 The entire array is displayed without a space between the individual elements. The input field separator, a space, is preserved when the array is enclosed in double quotes: *"@names"*.

3 Each element of the array is printed, starting with subscript number zero.

4 The scalar variable *$number* is assigned the array *@names*. The value assigned is the number of elements in the array *@names*. You can also use the built-in scalar function to get the size of an array; for example: *$size = scalar @names;*

5 The last element of the array is printed. Since index values start at zero, the number of elements in the array decremented by one evaluates to the number of the last subscript.

6 The last element of the array is printed. The *$#names* value evaluates to the number of the last subscript in the array. This value used as a subscript will retrieve the last element in the *@names* array.

8 The *qw* construct creates an array of **singly** quoted words from the string provided to it, using space as the word separator. (You don't enclose the words in quotes or separate the words with commas.) The *qw* delimiter is any pair of nonalphanumeric characters.

9 The first two elements of the *@fruit* array are printed.

10 With a negative offset as an index value, the elements of the array are selected from the end of the array. The last element (*$fruit[-1]*) is *plums*, and the third element from the end (*$fruit[-3]*) is *pears*. Note that when both index values are within the same set of brackets, as in *@fruit[-1,-3]*, the reference is to a list, not a scalar; that is why the @ symbol precedes the name of the array, rather than the $.

Looping Through an Array with the *foreach* Loop. One of the best ways to traverse the elements of an array is with Perl's *foreach* loop. (See Chapter 7, "If Only, Unconditionally, Forever," for a thorough discussion.)

This control structure steps through each element of a list (enclosed in parentheses) using a scalar variable as a loop variable. The loop variable references, one at a time, each element in the list, and for each element, the block of statements following the list is executed. When all of the list items have been processed, the loop ends. If the loop variable is missing, $_, the default scalar, is used. You can use a named array or create a list within parentheses.

You may also see code where the word *for* is used instead of *foreach*. This is because *for* and *foreach* are synonyms. In these examples, *foreach* is used simply to make it clear that we are going through a list, one element at a time; that is, "for each" element in the list.

EXAMPLE 5.16

```
(The Script)
   use warnings;
   # Array slices
1  my @names=('Tom', 'Dick', 'Harry', 'Pete' );
2  foreach $pal (@names){
3     print "$pal\n";
   }

4  foreach ("red", "green", "yellow", "blue"){
5     print "$_ \n";
   }
```

```
(Output)
3  Tom
   Dick
   Harry
   Pete

5  red
   green
   Yellow
   blue
```

EXPLANATION

1   The array @*names* is assigned a list: *'Tom', 'Dick', 'Harry', 'Pete'*.
2   The *foreach* loop is used to walk through the list, one word at a time.
3   The $*pal* scalar is used as a loop variable, called an iterator; that is, it points to each successive element of the list for each iteration of the loop. If you don't provide the iterator variable, Perl uses the topic variable $_ instead. For each iteration of the loop, the block of statements enclosed in curly braces is executed.
4   In this example, the *foreach* loop is not given an iterator variable, so Perl uses the $_ variable instead, even though you can't see it.
5   The value of $_ is printed each time through the loop. (This time we have to explicitly use $_ because we have added the \n to the string.)

Array Copy and Slices.   When you assign one array to another array, a copy is made. It's that simple. Unlike many languages, you are not responsible for the type of data the new array will hold or how many elements it will need. Perl handles the memory allocation and the type of data that will be stored in each element of the new array.

A **slice** accesses several elements of a list, an array, or a hash simultaneously using a list of index values. You can use a slice to copy some elements of an array into another and also assign values to a slice. If the array on the right-hand side of the assignment operator is larger than the array on the left-hand side, the unused values are discarded. If it is smaller, the values assigned are undefined. As indicated in the following example, the array indices in the slice do not have to be consecutively numbered; each element is assigned the corresponding value from the array on the right-hand side of the assignment operator.

EXAMPLE 5.17

```
(The Script)
   use warnings;
   # Array copy and slice
1  my @names=('Tom', 'Dick', 'Harry', 'Pete' );
2  @newnames = @names;  # Array copy
3  print "@newnames\n";
4  @pal=@names[1,2,3];  # Array slice -- @names[1..3] also okay
5  print "@pal\n\n";

6  ($friend[0,1,2])=@names;  # Assign to an array slice
7  print "@friend\n";

(Output)
3  Tom Dick Harry Pete
5  Dick Harry Pete
7  Tom Dick Harry
```

EXPLANATION

1   The array *@names* is assigned the elements *'Tom'*, *'Dick'*, *'Harry'*, and *'Pete'*.

4   The array *@pal* is assigned the elements *1*, *2*, and *3* of the *@names* array. The elements of the *@names* array are selected and copied in the *@pal* array.

6   The *@friend* array is created by copying all the values from the *@names* array and assigning them to *@friend* elements *0*, *1*, and *2*.

Multidimensional Arrays—Lists of Lists. Multidimensional arrays are sometimes called **tables** or **matrices**. They consist of rows and columns and can be represented with multiple subscripts. In a two-dimensional array, the first subscript represents the row, and the second subscript represents the column.

Perl allows this type of array, but it requires an understanding of references. We will cover this in detail in Chapter 12, "Does This Job Require a Reference?"

5.2.3 Hashes—Unordered Lists

A **hash** (in some languages called an associative array, map, table, or dictionary) is a variable consisting of one or more pairs of scalars—either strings or numbers. Hashes are often used to create tables, complex data structures, find duplicate entries in a file or array, or to create Perl objects. We will cover objects in detail in Chapter 14, "Bless Those Things! (Object-Oriented Perl)."

Hashes are defined as an unordered list of key/value pairs, similar to a table where the keys are on the left-hand side and the values associated with those keys are on the right-hand side. The name of the hash is preceded by the % and the keys and values are separated by a => , called the **fat comma** or **digraph** operator.

Whereas arrays are ordered lists with numeric indices starting at 0, hashes are unordered lists with string indices, called keys, stored randomly. (When you print out the hash, don't expect to see the output ordered just as you typed it!)

To summarize, the keys in a hash must be unique. The keys need not be quoted unless they begin with a number or contain hyphens, spaces, or special characters. Since the keys are really just strings, to be safe, quoting the keys (either single or double quotes) can prevent unwanted side effects. It's up to you. The values associated with the key can be much more complex that what we are showing here, and require an understanding of Perl references. These complex types are discussed in Chapter 12, "Does This Job Require a Reference?"

```
my %pet = ("Name"  => "Sneaky",
           "Type"  => "cat",
           "Owner" => "Carol",
           "Color" => "yellow",
          );
```

So for this example, the keys and values for the hash called *%pet*, are as follows:

Keys	Values
"Name"	"Sneaky"
"Type"	"cat"
"Owner"	"Carol"
"Color"	"yellow"

Assignment.   As in scalars and arrays, a hash variable must be defined before its elements can be referenced. Since a hash consists of pairs of values, indexed by the first element of each pair, if one of the elements in a pair is missing, the association of the keys and their respective values will be affected. When assigning keys and values, make sure you have a key associated with its corresponding value. When indexing a hash, curly braces are used instead of square brackets.

EXAMPLE 5.18

```
1   my %seasons=("Sp" => "Spring",
                 "Su" => "Summer",
                 "F"  => "Fall",
                 "W"  => "Winter",
                );
```

EXAMPLE 5.18 (CONTINUED)

```
2   my %days=("Mon" => "Monday",
              "Tue" => "Tuesday",
              "Wed" => undef,
              );
3   $days{"Wed"}="Wednesday";
```

EXPLANATION

1   The hash *%seasons* is assigned keys and values. Each key and value is separated by the fat comma, =>. The string *"Sp"* is the key with a corresponding value of *"Spring"*, the string *"Su"* is the key for its corresponding value *"Summer"*, and so on. It is not necessary to quote the key if it is a single word and does not begin with a number or contain spaces.

2   The hash *%days* is assigned keys and values. The third key, *"Wed"*, is assigned *undef*. The *undef* function evaluates to an undefined value; in this example, it serves as a placeholder with an empty value to be filled in later.

3   Individual elements of a hash are scalars. The key *"Wed"* is assigned the string value *"Wednesday"*. The index is enclosed in curly braces. Note: the keys do not have any consecutive numbering order and the pairs can consist of numbers and/or strings.

Accessing Hash Values.   When accessing the values of a hash, the subscript or index consists of the key enclosed in curly braces. Perl provides a set of functions to list the keys, values, and each of the elements of the hash.

Due to the internal hashing techniques used to store the keys, Perl does not guarantee the order in which an entire hash is printed.

EXAMPLE 5.19

```
    (The Script)
    use warnings;
    # Assigning keys and values to a hash
    my(%department,$department,$school);  # Declare variables
1   %department = (
2       "Eng" => "Engineering",    # keys do not require quotes
        "M"   => "Math",
        "S"   => "Science",
        "CS"  => "Computer Science",
        "Ed"  => "Education",
3   );
4   $department = $department{'M'};  # Either single, double quotes
5   $school = $department{'Ed'};
6   print "I work in the $department section\n" ;
7   print "Funds in the $school department are being cut.\n";
8   print qq/I'm currently enrolled in a $department{'CS'} course.\n/;
9   print qq/The department hash looks like this:\n/;
```

EXAMPLE 5.19 (CONTINUED)

```
10 print %department, "\n";    # The printout is not in the expected
                               # order due to internal hashing

(Output)
6  I work in the Math section

7  Funds in the Education department are being cut.
8  I'm currently enrolled in a Computer Science course.
9  The department hash looks like this:
10 SScienceCSComputer ScienceEdEducationMMathEngEngineering
```

EXPLANATION

1   The hash is called *%department*. It is assigned keys and values.
2   The first **key** is the string *Eng*, and the **value** associated with it is *Engineering*.
3   The closing parenthesis and semicolon end the assignment.
4   The scalar *$department* is assigned *Math*, the value associated with the *M* key. It's sometimes confusing to name different types of variables by the same name. In this example, it might be better to change *$department* to *$subject* or *$course*, for example.
5   The scalar *$school* is assigned *Education*, the value associated with the *Ed* key.
6   The quoted string is printed; the scalar *$department* is interpolated.
7   The quoted string is printed; the scalar *$school* is interpolated.
8   The quoted string and the value associated with the *CS* key are printed.
9, 10   The entire hash is printed, with keys and values packed together and not in any specific order. A key and its value, however, will always remain paired.

Hash Slices.   A hash slice is a list of hash keys. The hash name is preceded by the @ symbol and assigned a list of hash keys enclosed in curly braces. The hash slice lets you access one or more hash elements in one statement, rather than by going through a loop.

EXAMPLE 5.20

```
(The Script)
   use warnings;
   # Hash slices
1  my %officer= ("name" => "Tom Savage",
                 "rank" => "Colonel",
                 "dob"  => "05/19/66"
   );
2  my @info=@officer{"name","rank","dob"};  # Hash slice
3  print "@info\n";
4  @officer{'phone','base'}=('730-123-4455','Camp Lejeune');
5  print %officer, "\n";

(Output)
2  Tom Savage Colonel 05/19/66
6  baseCamp Lejeunedob05/19/66nameTom Savagephone730-123-4455rankColonel
```

EXPLANATION

1 The hash *%officer* is assigned keys and values.

2 This is an example of a hash slice. The list of hash keys, *"name"*, *"rank"*, and *"dob"* are assigned to the *@info* array. The name of the hash is prepended with an @ because this is a list of keys. The *values* corresponding to the list of keys are assigned to *@info*.

3 The keys and their corresponding values are printed. Using the slice is sometimes easier than using a loop to do the same thing.

4 Now using a slice in the assignment, we can create two new entries in the hash.

Removing Duplicates from a List Using a Hash. Because all keys in a hash must be unique, one way to remove duplicates from a list, whether an array or file, is to list items as keys in a hash. The values can be used to keep track of the number of duplicates or simply left undefined. The keys of the new hash will contain no duplicates. See the section, "The *map* Function," later in this chapter, for more examples.

EXAMPLE 5.21

```
(The Script)
    use warnings;
1   my %dup=();  # Create an empty hash.
2   my @colors=qw(red blue red green yellow green red orange);

3   foreach my $color (@colors){
       $dup{$color} = $dup{$color}++;    # Adds one to the value side of
                                          # the hash. May be written
                                          # $dup{$color}=$dup{$color}+1
    }
    printf"Color   Number of Occurrences\n";
4   while((my $key, my $value)=each %dup){
        printf"%-12s%-s\n",$key, $value;
    }
5   @colors = sort keys %dup;
    print "Duplicates removed: @colors\n";

(Output)
perl dup.plx
    Color   Number of Occurrences
3   green       2
    blue        1
    orange      1
    red         3
    yellow      1
5   Duplicates removed: blue green orange red yellow
```

EXPLANATION

1   This is the declaration for an empty hash called *%dup()*.
2   The array of colors contains a number of duplicate entries, as shown in Figure 5.4.
3   For each item in the array of colors, a key and value are assigned to the *%dup* hash. The first time the color is seen, it is created as a key in the hash; its value is incremented by 1, starting at 0 (that is, the key is the color and the value is the number of times the color occurs). Because the key must be unique, if a second color occurs and is a duplicate, the first occurrence will be overwritten by the duplicate and the value associated with it will increase by one.
4   The built-in *each* function is used as an expression in the *while* loop. It will retrieve and assign each key and each value from the hash to *$key* and *$value* respectively, and a pair is printed each time through the loop.
5   The keys of *%dup* hash are a unique list of colors. They are sorted and assigned to the *@colors* array.

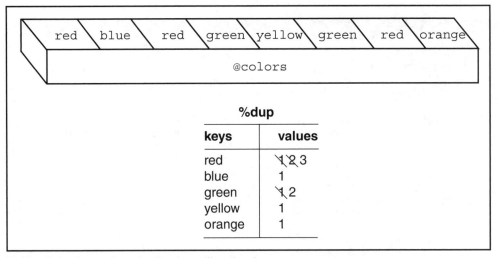

Figure 5.4   Removing duplicates with a hash.

5.2.4   Complex Data Structures

By combining arrays and hashes, you can make more complex data structures, such as arrays of hashes, hashes with nested hashes, arrays of arrays, and so on. Here is an example of an array of arrays requiring references.

```
my $matrix = [
              [ 0, 2, 4 ],
              [ 4, 1, 32 ],
              [ 12, 15, 17 ]
            ] ;
```

To create these structures, you should have an understanding of how Perl references and complex data structures are used. (See Chapter 12, "Does This Job Require a Reference?")

5.3 Array Functions

Arrays can grow and shrink. The Perl array functions allow you to insert or delete elements of the array from the front, middle, or end of the list, to sort arrays, perform calculations on elements, to search for patterns, and more.

5.3.1 Adding Elements to an Array

The *push* Function.   The *push* function pushes values onto the end of an array, thereby increasing the length of the array (see Figure 5.5).

FORMAT

```
push(ARRAY, LIST)
```

EXAMPLE 5.22

```
(In Script)
   use warnings;
   # Adding elements to the end of a list
1  my @names=("Bob", "Dan", "Tom", "Guy");
2  push(@names, "Jim", "Joseph", "Archie");
3  print "@names \n";

(Output)
2  Bob Dan Tom Guy Jim Joseph Archie
```

EXPLANATION

1   The array *@names* is assigned list values.
2   The *push* function pushes three more elements onto the end of the array.
3   The new array has three more elements appended to it.

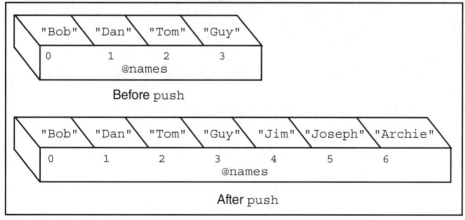

Figure 5.5 Adding elements to an array.

The _unshift_ Function.   The _unshift_ function prepends _LIST_ to the front of the array (see Figure 5.6).

FORMAT

```
unshift(ARRAY, LIST)
```

EXAMPLE 5.23

```
(In Script)
   use warnings;
   # Putting new elements at the front of a list
1  my @names=("Jody", "Bert", "Tom") ;
2  unshift(@names, "Liz", "Daniel");
3  print "@names\n";

(Output)
3  Liz Daniel Jody Bert Tom
```

EXPLANATION

1   The array _@names_ is assigned three values, _"Jody"_, _"Bert"_, and _"Tom"_.
2   The _unshift_ function will prepend _"Liz"_ and _"Daniel"_ to the array.

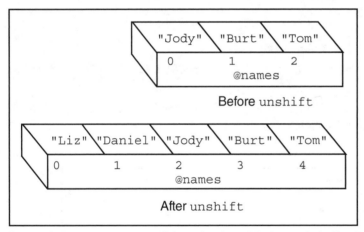

Figure 5.6   Using the _unshift_ function to add elements to the beginning of an array.

5.3.2   Removing and Replacing Elements

The _delete_ Function.   If you have a row of shoeboxes and take a pair of shoes from one of the boxes, the number of shoeboxes remains the same, but one of them is now empty. That is how _delete_ works with arrays. The _delete_ function allows you to remove a value from an element of an array, but not the element itself. The value deleted is simply undefined. (See Figure 5.7.) But if you find it in older programs, perldoc.perl.org warns not to use it for arrays, but rather for deleting elements from a hash. In fact, perldoc.perl.org warns that calling _delete_ on array values is deprecated and likely to be removed in a future version of Perl.

Instead, use the *splice* function to delete and replace elements from an array, while at the same time renumbering the index values.

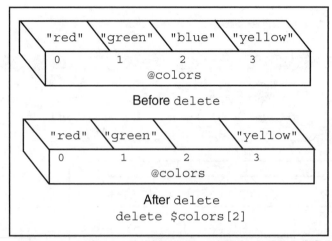

Figure 5.7 Using the *delete* function to remove elements from an array.

The *splice* Function. For the *delete* function, we described a row of shoeboxes in which a pair of shoes was removed from one of the boxes, but the box itself remained in the row. With *splice*, the box and its shoes can be removed and the remaining boxes pushed into place. (See Figure 5.8.) We could even take out a pair of shoes and replace them with a different pair (see Figure 5.9), or add a new box of shoes anywhere in the row. Put simply, the *splice* function removes and replaces elements in an array. The *OFFSET* is the starting position where elements are to be removed. The *LENGTH* is the number of items from the *OFFSET* position to be removed. The *LIST* consists of an optional new elements that are to replace the old ones. All index values are renumbered for the new array.

FORMAT

```
splice(ARRAY, OFFSET, LENGTH, LIST)
splice(ARRAY, OFFSET, LENGTH)
splice(ARRAY, OFFSET)
```

EXAMPLE 5.24

```
(The Script)
   use warnings;
   # Splicing out elements of a list
1  my @colors=("red", "green", "purple", "blue", "brown");
2  print "The original array is @colors\n";
3  my @discarded = splice(@colors, 2, 2);
4  print "The elements removed after the splice are: @discarded.\n";
5  print "The spliced array is now @colors.\n";
```

EXAMPLE 5.24 (CONTINUED)

(Output)
2 *The original array is red green purple blue brown.*
4 *The elements removed after the splice are: purple blue.*
5 *The spliced array is now red green brown.*

EXPLANATION

1 An array of five colors is created.
3 The *splice* function removes elements *purple* and *blue* from the array and returns
   them to *@discarded*, starting at index position two, *$colors[2]*, with a length of two
   elements.

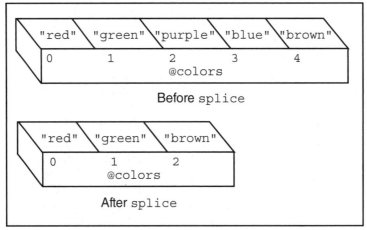

Figure 5.8   Using the *splice* function to remove or replace elements in an array.

EXAMPLE 5.25

```
(The Script)
    use warnings;
    # Splicing and replacing elements of a list
1   my @colors=("red", "green", "purple", "blue", "brown");
2   print "The original array is @colors\n";
3   my @lostcolors=splice(@colors, 2, 3, "yellow", "orange");
4   print "The removed items are @lostcolors\n";
5   print "The spliced array is now @colors\n";

(Output)
2   The original array is red green purple blue brown
4   The removed items are purple blue brown
5   The spliced array is now red green yellow orange
```

1   An array of five colors is created.
2   The original array is printed.
3   The *splice* function will delete elements starting at *$colors[2]* and remove the next three elements. The removed elements (*purple*, *blue*, and *brown*) are stored in *@lostcolors*. The colors *yellow* and *orange* will replace the ones that were removed.
4   The values that were removed are stored in *@lostcolors* and printed.
5   The new array, after the splice, is printed.

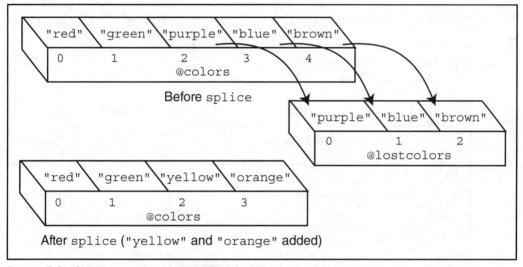

Figure 5.9   Splicing and replacing elements in an array.

The *pop* Function.   The *pop* function pops off the last element of an array and returns it. The array size is subsequently decreased by one. (See Figure 5.10.)

```
pop(ARRAY)
pop ARRAY
```

```
(In Script)
    use warnings;
    # Removing an element from the end of a list
1   my @names=("Bob", "Dan", "Tom", "Guy");
2   print "@names\n";
3   my $got = pop @names;    # Pops off last element of the array
4   print "$got\n";
5   print "@names\n";
```

EXAMPLE 5.26 (CONTINUED)

```
(Output)
2   Bob Dan Tom Guy
4   Guy
5   Bob Dan Tom
```

EXPLANATION

1   The *@name* array is assigned a list of elements.
2   The array is printed.
3   The *pop* function removes the last element of the array and returns the popped item.
4   The *$got* scalar contains the popped item, *Guy*.
5   The new array is printed.

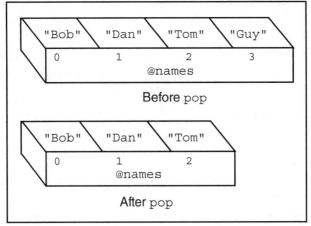

Figure 5.10   Using the *pop* function to pop the last element off the array.

The *shift* Function.   The *shift* function shifts off and returns the first element of an array, decreasing the size of the array by one element. (See Figure 5.11.) If *ARRAY* is omitted, then the *@ARGV* array is shifted. If in a subroutine, the argument list, stored in the *@_* array is shifted.

FORMAT

```
shift(ARRAY)
shift ARRAY
shift
```

EXAMPLE 5.27

```
(In Script)
   use warnings;
   # Removing elements from front of a list
1  my @names=("Bob", "Dan", "Tom", "Guy");
2  my $ret = shift @names;
3  print "@names\n";
4  print "The item shifted is $ret.\n";

(Output)
3  Dan Tom Guy
4  The item shifted is Bob.
```

EXPLANATION

1. The array *@names* is assigned list values.
2. The *shift* function removes the first element of the array and returns that element to the scalar *$ret*, which is *Bob*.
3. The new array has been shortened by one element.

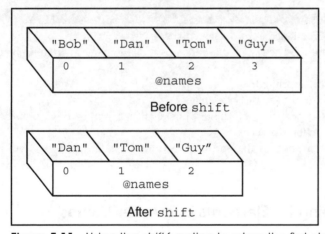

Figure 5.11 Using the *shift* function to return the first element of an array.

5.3.3 Deleting Newlines

The *chop* and *chomp* Functions (with Lists).   The *chop* function chops off the last character of a string and returns the chopped character, usually for removing the newline after input is assigned to a scalar variable. If a list is chopped, *chop* will remove the last letter of each string in the list.

The *chomp* function removes a newline character at the end of a string or for each element in a list.

FORMAT

```
chop(LIST)
chomp(LIST)
```

EXAMPLE 5.28

```
(In the Script)
   use warnings;
   # Chopping and chomping a list
1  my @line=("red", "green", "orange");
2  chop(@line);    # Chops the last character off each
                   # string in the list
3  print "@line";
4  @line=( "red\n", "green\n", "orange\n");
5  chomp(@line);   # Chomps the newline off each string in the list
6  print "@line";

(Output)
3  re gree orang
6  red green orange
```

EXPLANATION

1 The array *@line* is assigned a list of elements.
2 The array is chopped. The *chop* function chops the last character from each element of the array.
3 The chopped array is printed.
4 The array *@line* is assigned a list of elements.
5 The *chomp* function will chop off the newline character from each word in the array. This is a safer function than *chop*.
6 If there are no newlines on the end of the words in the array, *chomp* will not do anything.

5.3.4   Searching for Elements and Index Values

The *grep* Function.   The *grep* function is similar to the UNIX *grep* command in that it searches for patterns of characters, called **regular expressions**. However, unlike the UNIX *grep*, it is not limited to using regular expressions. Perl's *grep* evaluates the expression (*EXPR*) for each element of the array (*LIST*), locally setting $_ to each element. The return value is another array consisting of those elements for which the expression evaluated as true. As a scalar value, the return value is the number of times the expression was true (that is, the number of times the pattern was found).

FORMAT

```
grep BLOCK LIST
grep(EXPR,LIST)
```

EXAMPLE 5.29

```
(The Script)
    use warnings;
    # Searching for patterns in a list
1   my @list = ("tomatoes", "tomorrow", "potatoes", "phantom", "Tommy");

2   my $count = grep($_ =~ /tom/i, @list);
    # $count = grep(/tom/i, @list);
3   @items= grep(/tom/i, @list); # Could say: grep {/tom/i} @list;

4   print "Found items: @items\nNumber found: $count\n";

(Output)
4   Found items: tomatoes tomorrow phantom Tommy
    Number found: 4
```

EXPLANATION

1   The array *@list* is assigned a list of elements.
2   The *grep* function searches for the pattern (regular expression) *tom*. The *$_* scalar is used as a placeholder for each item in the iterator *@list*. (*$_* is also an alias to each of the list values, so it can modify the list values.) Although omitted in the next example, it is still being used. The *i* turns off case sensitivity. When the return value is assigned to a scalar, the result is the number of times the regular expression was matched.
3   *grep* again searches for *tom*. The *i* turns off case sensitivity. When the return value is assigned to an array, the result is a list of the matched items.

The next example shows you how to find the index value(s) for specific elements in an array using the built-in *grep* function. (If you have version 5.10+, you may want to use the more efficient *List::MoreUtils* module from the standard Perl libaray, or from CPAN.)

EXAMPLE 5.30

```
(The Script)
    use warnings;
    my(@colors, $index);
    # Searching for the index value where a pattern is found.
1   @colors = qw(red green blue orange blueblack);
2   @index_vals = grep( $colors[$_] =~ /blue/, (0..$#colors));
3   print "Found index values: @index_vals where blue was found.\n";

(Output)
3   Found index values: 2 4 where blue was found.
```

EXPLANATION

1   The array *@colors* is assigned a list of elements.
2   The *grep* function searches for the pattern *blue* in each element of *@colors*. (See Chapter 8, "Regular Expressions—Pattern Matching," for a detailed discussion on pattern matching.) The list (0 .. *$#colors*) represents the index values of *@colors*. *$_* holds one value at a time from the list starting with 0. If, for example, in the first iteration, *grep* searches for the pattern *blue* in *$colors[0]*, and finds *red*, nothing is returned because it doesn't match. (=~ is the bind operator.) Then, the next item is checked. Does the value *$colors[1]*, *green*, match *blue*? No. Then, the next item is checked. Does *$colors[2]* match *blue*? Yes it does. 2 is returned and stored in *@index_vals*. Another match for *blue* is true when *$colors[4]*, *blueblack*, is matched against *blue*. 4 is added to *@index_vals*.
3   When the *grep* function finishes iterating over the list of index values, the results stored in *@index_vals* are printed.

5.3.5 Creating a List from a Scalar

The *split* Function.   The *split* function splits up a string (*EXPR*) by some delimiter (whitespace, by default) and returns a list. (See Figure 5.12.) The first argument is the delimiter, and the second is the string to be split. The Perl *split* function can be used to create fields when processing files, just as you would with the UNIX *awk* command. If a string is not supplied as the expression, the *$_* string is split.

The *DELIMITER* statement matches the delimiters that are used to separate the fields. If *DELIMITER* is omitted, the delimiter defaults to whitespace (spaces, tabs, or newlines). If the *DELIMITER* doesn't match a delimiter, *split* returns the original string. You can specify more than one delimiter, using the regular expression metacharacter *[ ]*. For example, *[+\t:]* represents zero or more spaces or a tab or a colon.

To split on a dot (.), use ∧./ to escape the dot from its regular expression metacharacter.

LIMIT specifies the number of fields that can be split. If there are more than *LIMIT* fields, the remaining fields will all be part of the last one. If the *LIMIT* is omitted, the *split* function has its own *LIMIT*, which is one more than the number of fields in *EXPR*. (See the *-a* switch for autosplit mode, in Appendix A, "Perl Built-ins, Pragmas, Modules, and the Debugger.")

FORMAT

```
split("DELIMITER",EXPR,LIMIT)
split(/DELIMITER/,EXPR,LIMIT)
split(/DELIMITER/,EXPR)
split("DELIMITER",EXPR)
split(/DELIMITER/)
split
```

EXAMPLE 5.31

```
(The Script)
   use warnings;
   # Splitting a scalar on whitespace and creating a list
1  my $line="a b c d e";
2  my @letter=split(' ',$line);
3  print "The first letter is $letter[0]\n";
4  print "The second letter is $letter[1]\n";

(Output)
3  The first letter is a
4  The second letter is b
```

EXPLANATION

1   The scalar variable *$line* is assigned the string *a b c d e*.
2   The value in *$line* (scalar) is a single string of letters. The *split* function will split the string, using whitespace as a delimiter. The *@letter* array will be assigned the individual elements *a*, *b*, *c*, *d*, and *e*. Using single quotes as the delimiter is **not** the same as using the regular expression / /. The ' ' resembles *awk* in splitting lines on whitespace. Leading whitespace is ignored. The regular expression / / includes leading whitespace, creating as many null initial fields as there are whitespaces.
3   The first element of the *@letter* array is printed.
4   The second element of the *@letter* array is printed.

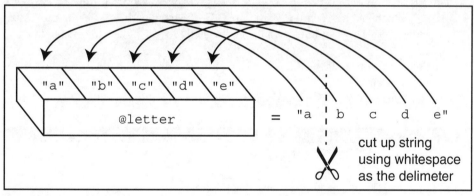

Figure 5.12   Using the *split* function to create an array from a scalar.

EXAMPLE 5.32

```
(The Script)
   use warnings;
   # Splitting up $_
   my @line;
1  while(<DATA>){
2      @line=split(":");         # or split (/:/, $_);
3      print "$line[0]\n";
   }

__DATA__
Betty Boop:245-836-8357:635 Cutesy Lane, Hollywood, CA 91464:6/23/23:14500
Igor Chevsky:385-375-8395:3567 Populus Place, Caldwell, NJ
23875:6/18/68:23400
Norma Corder:397-857-2735:74 Pine Street, Dearborn, MI
23874:3/28/45:245700
Jennifer Cowan:548-834-2348:583 Laurel Ave., Kingsville, TX
83745:10/1/35:58900
Fred Fardbarkle:674-843-1385:20 Park Lane, Duluth, MN 23850:4/12/23:78900

(Output)
Betty Boop
Igor Chevsky
Norma Corder
Jennifer Cowan
Fred Fardbarkle
```

EXPLANATION

1   The $_ variable holds each line of the file *DATA* filehandle; the data being processed is below the _ _DATA_ _ line. Each line is assigned to $_. $_ is also the default line for *split*.

2   The *split* function splits the line, ($_), using the : as a delimiter and returns the line to the array, *@line*.

3   The first element of the *@line* array, *line[0]*, is printed.

EXAMPLE 5.33

```
(The Script)
   use warnings;
   my($name, $phone, $address, $bd, $sal);
   # Splitting up $_ and creating an unnamed list
   while(<DATA>){
1      ($name,$phone,$address,$bd,$sal)=split(":");
2      print "$name\t $phone\n" ;
   }
```

EXAMPLE 5.33 (CONTINUED)

```
__DATA__
Betty Boop:245-836-8357:635 Cutesy Lane, Hollywood, CA 91464:6/23/23:14500
Igor Chevsky:385-375-8395:3567 Populus Place, Caldwell, NJ
23875:6/18/68:23400
Norma Corder:397-857-2735:74 Pine Street, Dearborn, MI
23874:3/28/45:245700
Jennifer Cowan:548-834-2348:583 Laurel Ave., Kingsville, TX
83745:10/1/35:58900
Fred Fardbarkle:674-843-1385:20 Park Lane, Duluth, MN 23850:4/12/23:78900

(Output)
2 Betty Boop  245-836-8357
  Igor Chevsky        385-375-8395
  Norma Corder        397-857-2735
  Jennifer Cowan      548-834-2348
  Fred Fardbarkle     674-843-1385
```

EXPLANATION

1 Perl loops through the *DATA* filehandle one line at a time from _ _DATA_ _, storing each successive item in the $_ variable, overwriting what was previously stored there. The *split* function splits each line in $_, using the colon as a delimiter.

2 The returned list consists of five scalars, *$name*, *$phone*, *$address*, *$bd*, and *$sal*. The values of *$name* and *$phone* are printed.

EXAMPLE 5.34

```
(The Script)
   use warnings;
   # Many ways to split a scalar to create a list
1  my $string= "Joe Blow:11/12/86:10 Main St.:Boston, MA:02530";
2  my @line=split(":", $string);   # The string delimiter is a colon
3  print @line,"\n";
4  print "The guy's name is $line[0].\n";
5  print "The birthday is $line[1].\n\n";

6  @line=split(":", $string, 2);
7  print $line[0],"\n";  # The first element of the array
8  print $line[1],"\n";  # The rest of the array because limit is 2
9  print $line[2],"\n";  # Nothing is printed

10 ($name, $birth, $address)=split(":", $string);

11 print $name,"\n";
12 print $birth,"\n";
13 print $address,"\n";
```

EXAMPLE 5.34 (CONTINUED)

```
(Output)
3   Joe Blow11/12/8610 Main St.Boston, MA02530
4   The guy's name is Joe Blow.
5   The birthday is 11/12/86.

7   Joe Blow
8   11/12/86:10 Main St.:Boston, MA:02530
9
11  Joe Blow
12  11/12/86
13  10 Main St.
```

EXPLANATION

1   The scalar *$string* is split at each colon.
2   The delimiter is a colon. The limit is 2.
6   The string is split by colons and given a limit of two, meaning that the text up to the first colon will become the first element of the array; in this case, *$line[0]* and the rest of the string will be assigned to *$line[1]*. *LIMIT*, if not stated, will be one more than the total number of fields.
10 The string is split by colons and returns a list of scalars. This may make the code easier to read.

5.3.6 Creating a Scalar from a List

The *join* Function.   The *join* function joins the elements of an array into a single string and separates each element of the array with a given delimiter, sometimes called the "glue" character(s) since it glues together the items in a list (opposite of *split*). (See Figure 5.13.) The expression *DELIMITER* is the value of the string that will join the array elements in *LIST*.

FORMAT

```
join(DELIMITER, LIST)
```

EXAMPLE 5.35

```
(The Script)
   use warnings;
   my(@colors, $color_string);
   # Joining each elements of a list with commas
1  @colors = qw( red green blue);

2  $color_string = join(", ",@colors); # Create a string from an array
3  print "The new string is: $color_string\n";

(Output)
3  The new string is: red, green, blue
```

1 An array is assigned three colors.
2 The *join* function joins the three elements of the *@colors* array, using a comma and space as the delimiter returning a string, which is then assigned to *$color_string*.
3 The new string with commas is printed.

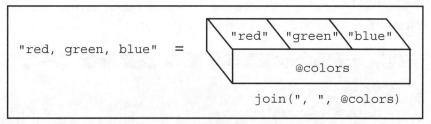

Figure 5.13 Using the *join* function to join elements of an array with a comma.

EXAMPLE 5.36

```
(The Script)
    use warnings;
    # Joining each element of a list with a newline
1   my @names= qw(Dan Dee Scotty Liz Tom);
2   @names=join("\n", sort(@names));
3   print @names,"\n";

(Output)
3   Dan
    Dee
    Liz
    Scotty
    Tom
```

1 The array *@names* is assigned a list of strings.
2 The *join* function will *join* each word in the list with a newline (*\n*) after the list has been sorted alphabetically.
3 The sorted list is printed with each element of the array on a line of its own.

5.3.7 Transforming an Array

The *map* Function.   If you have an array and want to perform the same action on each element of the array without using a *for* loop, the *map* function may be an option. The *map* function maps each of the values in an array to an expression or block, returning another list with the results of the mapping. It lets you change the values of the original list.

FORMAT

```
map EXPR, LIST;
map {BLOCK} LIST;
```

Using *map* to Change All Elements of an Array

In the following example, the *chr* function is applied or mapped to each element of an array and returns a new array showing the results. (See Figure 5.14.)

EXAMPLE 5.37

```
(The Script)
   use warnings;
   my(@list, @words, @n);
   # Mapping a list to an expression
1  my @list=(0x53,0x77,0x65,0x64,0x65,0x6e,012);
2  my @letters = map chr $_, @list;
3  print @letters;
4  my @n = (2, 4, 6, 8);
5  @n = map $_ * 2 + 6, @n;
6  print "@n\n";

(Output)
3  Sweden
6  10 14 18 22
```

EXPLANATION

1 The array *@list* consists of six hexadecimal numbers and one octal number.

2 The *map* function maps each item in *@list* to its corresponding *chr* (character) value and returns a new list, assigned to *@letters*. (According to *perldoc.perl.org*, the *chr* function "returns the character represented by that NUMBER in the character set. For example, chr(65) is "A" in either ASCII or Unicode, and chr(0x263a) is a Unicode smiley face.")

3 The new list is printed. Each numeric value was converted with the *chr* function to a character corresponding to its ASCII value; for example, *chr(65)* returns ASCII value *"A"*.

4 The array *@n* consists of a list of integers.

5 The *map* function evaluates the expression for each element in the *@n* array and returns the result to the new array *@n*.

6 The results of the mapping are printed, showing that the original list has been changed.

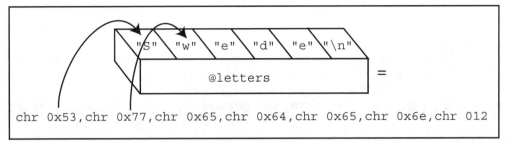

Figure 5.14 Using the *map* function to change elements in an array.

Using *map* to Remove Duplicates from an Array

The *map* function can be used to create a hash from an array. If you are using the array elements as keys for the new hash, any duplicates will be eliminated.

EXAMPLE 5.38

```
(The Script)
   use warnings;
   my(@courses, %c);
1  @courses=qw( C++ C Perl Python French C C Perl);
2  %c = map { $_ => undef } @courses;   # Create a unique list of keys
3  @courses = keys %c;
4  print "@courses\n";

(Output)
Python, French, Perl, C, C++
```

EXPLANATION

1 The array of courses contains duplicates.
2 The *map* function is used to create a hash called *%c*. Each element in the array *@courses* is assigned in turn to *$_*. *$_* serves as the key to the new *%c* hash. The value is left undefined since the keys are all we need to get a list of unique courses.
3 The keys in the *%c* hash are assigned to *@courses*, overwriting what was there. The new list will have no duplicate entries, although it will be unordered, as are all hashes.

5.3.8 Sorting an Array

The *sort* Function. The *sort* function sorts and returns a sorted list. Its default is to sort alphabetically, but you can define how you want to sort by using different comparison operators. If *SUBROUTINE* is specified, the first argument to *sort* is the name of the subroutine, followed by a list of values to be sorted. If the string *cmp* operator is used, the values in the list will be sorted alphabetically (ASCII sort), and if the <=> operator (called the **space ship** operator) is used, the values will be sorted numerically. The values are passed to the subroutine by reference and are received by the special Perl variables *$a* and $b, not the normal @_ array. (See Chapter 11, "How Do Subroutines Function?" for further discussion.) Do not try to modify $a or $b, as they represent the values that are being sorted.

If you want Perl to sort your data according to a particular locale, your program should include the *use locale* pragma. For a complete discussion, see *perldoc.perl.org/perllocale*.

FORMAT

```
sort (SUBROUTINE LIST)
sort (LIST)
sort SUBROUTINE LIST
sort LIST
```

EXAMPLE 5.39

```
(The Script)
   use warnings;
   # Simple alphabetic sort
1  my @list=("dog","cat","bird","snake" );
   print "Original list: @list\n";
2  my @sorted = sort @list;
3  print "ASCII sort: @sorted\n";

   # Reversed alphabetic sort
4  @sorted = reverse sort @list;
   print "Reversed ASCII sort: @sorted\n";

(Output)
Original list: dog cat bird snake
ASCII sort: bird cat dog snake
Reversed ASCII sort: snake dog cat bird
```

EXPLANATION

1   The *@list* array will contain a list of items to be sorted.
2   The *sort* function performs a string (lexographical for current locale) sort on the items. The sorted values must be assigned to another list or the same list. The *sort* function doesn't change the original list.
3   The sorted string is printed.
4   This list is sorted alphabetically and then reversed.

ASCII and Numeric Sort Using Subroutine

You can either define a subroutine or use an inline function to perform customized sorting, as shown in the following examples. A note about $a and $b: they are special global Perl variables used by the *sort* function for comparing values. If you need more information on the operators used, see Chapter 6, "Where's the Operator?"

EXAMPLE 5.40

```
(The Script)
   use warnings;
1  my @list=("dog","cat", "bird","snake" );
   print "Original list: @list\n";
   # ASCII sort using a subroutine
2  sub asc_sort{
3     $a cmp $b;  # Sort ascending order
   }
4  @sorted_list=sort asc_sort(@list);
   print "ASCII sort: @sorted_list\n";

   # Numeric sort using subroutine
5  sub numeric_sort {
      $a <=> $b ;
   } # $a and $b are compared numerically

6  @number_sort=sort numeric_sort 10, 0, 5, 9.5, 10, 1000;
   print "Numeric sort: @number_sort.\n";

(Output)
Original list: dog cat bird snake
ASCII sort: bird cat dog snake
Numeric sort: 0 5 9.5 10 10 1000.
```

EXPLANATION

1   The @list array will contain a list of items to be sorted.

2   The subroutine asc_sort() is sent a list of strings to be sorted.

3   The special global variables $a and $b are used when comparing the items to be sorted in ascending order. If $a and $b are reversed (for example, $b cmp $a), then the sort is done in descending order. The cmp operator is used when comparing strings.

4   The sort function sends a list to the asc_sort(), user-defined subroutine, where the sorting is done. The sorted list will be returned and stored in @sorted_list.

5   This is a user-defined subroutine, called numeric_sort(). The special variables $a and $b compare the items to be sorted numerically, in ascending order. If $a and $b are reversed (for example, $b <=> $a), then the sort is done in numeric descending order. The <=> operator is used when comparing numbers.

6   The sort function sends a list of numbers to the numeric_sort() function and gets back a list of sorted numbers, stored in the @number_sort array.

EXAMPLE 5.41

```
(The Script)
    use warnings;
    # Sorting numbers with block
1   my @sorted_numbers = sort {$a <=> $b} (3,4,1,2);
2   print "The sorted numbers are: @sorted_numbers", ".\n";

(Output)
2   The sorted numbers are: 1 2 3 4.
```

EXPLANATION

1   The *sort* function is given a block, also called an **inline subroutine**, to sort a list of numbers passed as arguments. The <=> operator is used with variables $a and $b to compare the numbers. The sorted numeric list is returned and stored in the array *@sorted_numbers*. (See *http://perldoc.perl.org/functions/sort.html* for more on the *sort* function.)

2   The sorted list is printed.

5.3.9 Checking the Existence of an Array Index Value

The *exists* Function.   The *exists* function returns **true** if an array index (or hash key) has been defined, and **false** if it has not. It is most commonly used when testing a hash key's existence.

FORMAT

```
    exists $ARRAY[index];
```

EXAMPLE 5.42

```
    use warnings;
1   my @names = qw(Tom Raul Steve Jon);
2   print "Hello $names[1]\n", if exists $names[1];
3   print "Out of range!\n", if not exists $names[5];

(Output)
2   Hello Raul
3   Out of range!
```

EXPLANATION

1   An array of names is assigned to *@names*.
2   If the index *1* is defined, the *exists* function returns true and the string is printed.
3   If the index *5* does not exist (and in this example it doesn't), then the string *Out of range!* is printed.

5.3.10 Reversing an Array

The *reverse* Function. The *reverse* function reverses the elements in a list, so that if the values appeared in descending order, now they are in ascending order, or vice versa. In scalar context, it concatenates the list elements and returns a string with all the characters reversed; for example, in scalar context *Hello, there!* reverses to *!ereht ,olleH*.

FORMAT

```
reverse(LIST)
reverse LIST
```

EXAMPLE 5.43

```
(In Script)
    use warnings;
    my(@names, @reversed);
    # Reversing the elements of an array
1   @names=("Bob", "Dan", "Tom", "Guy");
2   print "@names \n";
3   my @reversed=reverse @names,"\n";
4   print "@reversed\n";

(Output)
2   Bob Dan Tom Guy
4   Guy Tom Dan Bob
```

EXPLANATION

1   The array *@names* is assigned list values.
2   The original array is printed.
3   The *reverse* function reverses the elements in the list and returns the reversed list. It does not change the original array; that is, the array *@names* is not changed. The reversed items are stored in *@reversed*.
4   The reversed array is printed.

5.4 Hash (Associative Array) Functions

5.4.1 The *keys* Function

The *keys* function returns, in random order, an array whose elements are the keys of a hash (see also Section 5.4.2, "The *values* Function," and Section 5.4.3, "The *each* Function"). Starting with Perl 5.12, *keys* also returns the index values of an array. In scalar context, it returns the number of keys (or indices).

FORMAT

```
keys(ASSOC_ARRAY)
keys ASSOC_ARRAY
```

EXAMPLE 5.44

```
(In Script)
    use warnings;
    my(%weekday, @daynumber, $key);
    # The keys function returns the keys of a hash
1   my %weekday= (
        '1'=>'Monday',
        '2'=>'Tuesday',
        '3'=>'Wednesday',
        '4'=>'Thursday',
        '5'=>'Friday',
        '6'=>'Saturday',
        '7'=>'Sunday',
    );
2   my @daynumber = keys(%weekday);
3   print "@daynumber\n";

4   foreach $key ( keys(%weekday) ){print "$key ";}
    print "\n";

5   foreach $key ( sort keys(%weekday) ){print "$key ";}
    print "\n";

(Output)
6 4 1 3 7 2 5
6 4 1 3 7 2 5
1 2 3 4 5 6 7
```

EXPLANATION

1   The hash *%weekday* is assigned keys and values.
2   The *keys* function returns a list of all the keys in a hash. In this example, *@daynumber* is an unordered list of all the keys in the *%weekday* hash.
4   The *keys* function returns a list of keys. The *foreach* loop will traverse the list of keys, one at a time, printing the keys.
5   The *keys* function returns a list of keys in *%weekday* hash. The list will then be sorted, and finally the *foreach* loop will traverse the sorted list of keys, one at a time, printing each key.

5.4.2 The *values* Function

The *values* function returns, in random order, a list consisting of all the values of a named hash. (After Perl 5.12, it will also return the values of an array.) In scalar context, it returns the number of values.

FORMAT

```
values(ASSOC_ARRAY)
values ASSOC_ARRAY
```

EXAMPLE 5.45

```
(In Script)
    use warnings;

    # The values function returns the values in a hash
1   my %weekday= (
        '1'=>'Monday',
        '2'=>'Tuesday',
        '3'=>'Wednesday',
        '4'=>'Thursday',
        '5'=>'Friday',
        '6'=>'Saturday',
        '7'=>'Sunday',
    );
2   foreach my $val ( values(%weekday)){print "$val";}
    print "\n";

(Output)
2   Saturday Thursday Monday Wednesday Sunday Tuesday Friday
```

EXPLANATION

1   The hash *%weekday* is assigned keys and values.
2   The *values* function returns a list of values from the hash *%weekday*. The *foreach* is used to loop through the list of values, one at a time, using *$val* as its loop variable.

Since hashes are stored in a random order, to get the hash values in the order in which they were assigned, you can use a hash slice as shown in the following example.

EXAMPLE 5.46

```
(In Script)
    use warnings;

    # Use a hash slice to get the values returned in order.
1   my %weekday= (
        '1'=>'Monday',
        '2'=>'Tuesday',
        '3'=>'Wednesday',
        '4'=>'Thursday',
        '5'=>'Friday',
        '6'=>'Saturday',
        '7'=>'Sunday',
    );
```

EXAMPLE 5.46 (CONTINUED)

```
2   my @days = @weekday{1..7};
    print "@days\n";
```

```
(Output)
2   Monday Tuesday Wednesday Thursday Friday Saturday Sunday
```

EXPLANATION

1 The hash *%weekday* is assigned keys and values.
2 CA hash slice is a way of referring to one or more elements of the hash in one statement, to get a list of values, or to assign a list of values, and because it is using a list
   of keys, the list is preceded by the @ sign and the list is enclosed in curly braces to
   indicate that your are indexing a hash.*

---

* To preserve the insert order of hash keys, see *Tie::InsertOrderHash* at the Comprehensive Perl Archive
   Network—CPAN (*http://search.cpan.org*).

5.4.3 The *each* Function

The *each* function returns, in random order, a two-element list whose elements are the *key*
and the corresponding *value* of a hash. It must be called multiple times to get each key/
value pair, as it only returns one set each time it is called, somewhat like reading lines from
a file, one at a time.

FORMAT

```
each(ASSOC_ARRAY)
each ASSOC_ARRAY
```

EXAMPLE 5.47

```
(In Script)
   use warnings;
   my(%weekday $key, $value);
   # The each function retrieves both keys and values from a hash
1  %weekday=(
      'Mon' => 'Monday',
      'Tue' => 'Tuesday',
      'Wed' => 'Wednesday',
      'Thu' => 'Thursday',
      'Fri' => 'Friday',
      'Sat' => 'Saturday',
      'Sun' => 'Sunday',
   );
2  while(($key,$value)=each(%weekday)){
3     print "$key = $value\n";
   }
```

EXAMPLE 5.47 (CONTINUED)

```
(Output)
3  Sat = Saturday
   Fri = Friday
   Sun = Sunday
   Thu = Thursday
   Wed = Wednesday
   Tue = Tuesday
   Mon = Monday
```

EXPLANATION

1   The hash *%weekday* is assigned keys and values.
2   The *each* function returns a list consisting of each key and its associated *value* from the
    %weekday hash. They are assigned to the scalars *$key* and *$value*, respectively.
3   The keys and values are printed, but in an unordered way. You can order them as
    shown in Example 5.46 or use a *foreach* loop with an ordered list of keys:

```
foreach $key( 1..7){
    print $weekday{$key},"\n";
}
```

5.4.4 Removing Duplicates from a List with a Hash

Earlier, we used a hash to remove duplicate entries in an array. In the following example,
the built-in *map* function is used to map each element of an array into a hash to create
unique hash keys.

EXAMPLE 5.48

```
(The Script)
  use warnings;  .
  my(@list, @uniq);
  # Using the map function with a hash
  @list = qw/a b c d d a e b a b d e f/;
1 @uniq = keys %{{ map {$_ => 1 } @list }};
2 print "@list\n@uniq\n";

(Output)
a b c d d a e b a b d e f
e c a b d f
```

EXPLANATION

1   The *map* function iterates through the values in the *@list* array to create a hash where
    each element in *@list* becomes a key, *$_*, to an unnamed hash with each key getting a
    corresponding value of *1*. After the hash is created, the built-in *keys* function returns
    a list of the unique keys which are assigned to the array *@uniq*.
2   Both the original list, *@list*, and the new list, *@uniq*, are printed, showing that the
    duplicate values in the original list have been removed.

5.4.5   Sorting a Hash by Keys and Values

When sorting a hash, you can sort the keys alphabetically very easily by using the built-in *sort* command, as we did with arrays in the preceding section. But you may want to sort the keys numerically or sort the hash by its values. To do this requires a little more work.

You can define a subroutine to compare the keys or values. (See Chapter 11, "How Do Subroutines Function?") The subroutine will be called by the built-in *sort* function. It will be sent a list of keys or values to be compared. The comparison is either an ASCII (alphabetic) or a numeric comparison, depending upon the operator used. The *cmp* operator is used for comparing strings, and the <=> operator is used for comparing numbers. The reserved global scalars $a, and $b are used in the subroutine to hold the values as they are being compared. The names of these scalars cannot be changed.

Sort Hash by Keys in Ascending Order.   To perform an ASCII, or alphabetic, sort on the keys in a hash is relatively easy. Perl's *sort* function is given a list of keys and returns them sorted in ascending order. A *foreach* loop is used to loop through the hash keys, one key at a time.

EXAMPLE 5.49

```
(In Script)
    use warnings;
1   my %wins = (
        "Portland Panthers"   => 10,
        "Sunnyvale Sluggers"  => 12,
        "Chico Wildcats"      => 5,
        "Stevensville Tigers" => 6,
        "Lewiston Blazers"    => 11,
        "Danville Terriors"   => 8,
    );
    print "\n\tSort Teams in Ascending Order:\n\n";
2   foreach my $key(sort keys %wins) {
3       printf "\t% -20s%5d\n", $key, $wins{$key};
    }

(Output)

Sort Teams in Ascending  Order:

        Chico Wildcats        5
        Danville Terriors     8
        Lewiston Blazers      11
        Portland Panthers     10
        Stevensville Tigers   6
        Sunnyvale Sluggers    12
```

1   A hash called *%wins* is assigned key/value pairs.
2   The *foreach* loop will be used to iterate through each of an alphabetically sorted list of keys from a hash called *%wins*.
3   The *printf()* function formats and prints the sorted keys and its values.

Sort Hash by Keys in Reverse Order.   To sort a hash by keys alphabetically and in descending order, just add the built-in *reverse* function to the previous example. The *foreach* loop is used to get each key from the hash, one at a time, after the reversed sort.

```
(In Script)
   use warnings;
1  my %wins = (
       "Portland Panthers"    => 10,
       "Sunnyvale Sluggers"   => 12,
       "Chico Wildcats"       => 5,
       "Stevensville Tigers"  => 6,
       "Lewiston Blazers"     => 11,
       "Danville Terriors"    => 8,
   );
   print "\n\tSort Teams in Descending/Reverse Order:\n\n";
2  foreach my $key (reverse sort keys %wins) {
3      printf "\t% -20s%5d\n", $key, $wins{$key};
   }

(Output)

Sort Teams in Descending/Reverse Order:

       Sunnyvale Sluggers    12
       Stevensville Tigers    6
       Portland Panthers     10
       Lewiston Blazers      11
       Danville Terriors      8
       Chico Wildcats         5
```

1   A hash called *%wins* is assigned key/value pairs.
2   The *foreach* loop will be used to iterate through each of the elements in the hash. The *reverse* function takes the alphabetically sorted list returned from the *sort* function and reverses it.
3   The *printf()* function formats and prints the keys and sorted values.

Sort Hash by Keys Numerically.   A user-defined subroutine is used to sort a hash by keys numerically. In the subroutine, Perl's special $a and $b variables are used to hold the value being compared with the appropriate operator. For numeric comparison, the <=> operator is used, and for string comparison, the *cmp* operator is used. The *sort* function will send a list of keys to the user-defined subroutine. The sorted list is returned.

EXAMPLE 5.51

```
(In Script)
    use warnings;
1   sub desc_sort_subject {
2       $b <=> $a;                # Numeric sort descending
    }
3   sub asc_sort_subject{
4       $a <=> $b;                # Numeric sort ascending
    }

5   my %courses = (
        "101" => "Intro to Computer Science",
        "221" => "Linguistics",
        "300" => "Astronomy",
        "102" => "Perl",
        "103" => "PHP",
        "200" => "Language arts",
    );
    print "\n\tCourses in Ascending Numeric Order:\n";
6   foreach my $key (sort asc_sort_subject(keys %courses)) {
7       printf "\t%-5d%s\n", $key, $courses{"$key"};
    }
8   print "\n\tCourses in Descending Numeric Order:\n";
    foreach my $key (sort desc_sort_subject(keys %courses)) {
        printf "\t%-5d%s\n", $key, $courses{"$key"};
    }

(Output)
Courses in Ascending Numeric Order:
        101   Intro to Computer Science
        102   Perl
        103   PHP
        200   Language arts
        221   Linguistics
        300   Astronomy

Courses in Descending Numeric Order:
        300   Astronomy
        221   Linguistics
        200   Language arts
        103   PHP
        102   Perl
        101   Intro to Computer Science
```

EXPLANATION

1   This is a user-defined subroutine called *desc_sort_subject*. When its name is given to the *sort* function, this function will be used to compare the keys passed to it. It will sort the keys numerically.

2   The special Perl variables *$a* and *$b* are used to compare the values of the keys from the hash called *%courses*. The <=> operator is a numeric comparison operator that will compare each of the keys to be sorted as numbers. In the previous examples, we sorted the keys alphabetically. Since *$b* precedes *$a*, the sort is descending.

3   This is also a user-defined subroutine called *asc_sort_subject*. This function is identical to the previous function on line 1, except it will sort the keys of the hash in ascending numeric order rather than descending.

4   . In this function, the special variables *$a* and *$b* have been reversed, causing the sort after the comparison to be in ascending order.

5   The hash called *%courses* is defined with key/value pairs.

6   The *foreach* loop will be used to iterate through each of the keys in the hash. It receives its list from the output of the *sort* command.

7, 8   The *printf* function formats and prints the keys and sorted values.

Numerically Sort a Hash by Values in Ascending Order.   To sort a hash by its values, a user-defined function is also defined. The values of the hash are compared by the special variables *$a* and *$b*. If *$a* is on the left-hand side of the comparison operator, the sort is in ascending order, and if *$b* is on the left-hand side, then the sort is in descending order. The <=> operator compares its operands numerically.

EXAMPLE 5.52

```
(In Script)
   use warnings;
1  sub asc_sort_wins {
2     $wins{$a} <=> $wins{$b};
   }
3  my %wins = (
      "Portland Panthers"    => 10,
      "Sunnyvale Sluggers"   => 12,
      "Chico Wildcats"       => 5,
      "Stevensville Tigers"  => 6,
      "Lewiston Blazers"     => 11,
      "Danville Terriors"    => 8,
   );
   print "\n\tWins in Ascending Numeric Order:\n\n";
4  foreach my $key (sort asc_sort_wins(keys %wins)) {
5     printf "\t% -20s%5d\n", $key, $wins{$key};
   }
```

EXAMPLE 5.52 (CONTINUED)

```
(Output)

Wins in Ascending Numeric Order:

        Chico Wildcats        5
        Stevensville Tigers   6
        Danville Terriors     8
        Portland Panthers     10
        Lewiston Blazers      11
        Sunnyvale Sluggers    12
```

EXPLANATION

1 This is a user-defined subroutine called *asc_sort_wins*. When its name is given to the *sort* function, this function will be used to compare the hash values passed to it. It will sort the values by value, numerically.

2 The special Perl variables $a and $b are used to compare the values of the hash called $wins. The <=> operator is a numeric comparison operator that will compare each of the values to be sorted. To compare strings, the *cmp* operator is used.

3 The hash called %wins is assigned key/value pairs.

4 The *foreach* loop iterates through each of the elements in the hash. It receives its list from what is returned from the *sort* function.

5 The *printf* function formats and prints the keys and sorted values.

Numerically Sort a Hash by Values in Descending Order.   To sort a hash numerically and in descending order by its values, a user-defined function is created as in the previous example. However, this time the $b variable is on the left-hand side of the <=> numeric operator, and the $a variable is on the right-hand side. This causes the *sort* function to sort in descending order.

EXAMPLE 5.53

```
(In Script)
  use warnings;
  # Sorting a hash by value in descending order

1  sub desc_sort_wins {
2     $wins{$b} <=> $wins{$a};  # Reverse $a and $b
   }

3  my %wins = (
       "Portland Panthers"    => 10,
       "Sunnyvale Sluggers"   => 12,
       "Chico Wildcats"       => 5,
       "Stevensville Tigers"  => 6,
       "Lewiston Blazers"     => 11,
       "Danville Terriors"    => 8,
   );
```

EXAMPLE 5.53 (CONTINUED)

```
        print "\n\tWins in Descending Numeric Order:\n\n";
4   foreach my $key (sort desc_sort_wins(keys %wins)){
5       printf "\t% -20s%5d\n", $key, $wins{$key};
    }
```

(Output)

```
Wins in Descending Numeric Order:

        Sunnyvale Sluggers     12
        Lewiston Blazers       11
        Portland Panthers      10
        Danville Terriors       8
        Stevensville Tigers     6
        Chico Wildcats          5
```

EXPLANATION

1   This is a user-defined subroutine called *desc_sort_wins*. When its name is given to the *sort* function, this function will be used to compare the hash values passed to it. It will sort the values by value, numerically but in descending order.

2   The special Perl variables *$a* and *$b* are used to compare the values of the hash called *$wins*. The position of *$a* and *$b* determines whether the sort is in ascending or descending order. If *$a* is on the left-hand side of the <=> operator, the sort is a numeric ascending sort; if *$b* is on the left-hand side of the <=> operator, the sort is descending. To compare strings, the *cmp* operator is used.

3   The hash called *%wins* is assigned key/value pairs.

4   The *foreach* loop will be used to iterate through each of the keys in the hash. It receives its list from what is returned from the *sort* function.

5   The *printf* function formats and prints the keys and sorted values.

5.4.6   The *delete* Function

The *delete* function deletes a specified element from a hash. The deleted value is returned if successful.[5]

EXAMPLE 5.54

```
(In Script)
    use warnings;
1   my %employees=(
        "Nightwatchman" => "Joe Blow",
        "Janitor" => "Teddy Plunger",
        "Clerk" => "Sally Olivetti",
    );
```

---

5.   If a value in an *%ENV* hash is deleted, the environment is changed. (See "The *%ENV* Hash" on page 137.)

EXAMPLE 5.54 (CONTINUED)

```
2   my $layoff=delete $employees{"Janitor"};
    print "We had to let $layoff go.\n";
    print "Our remaining staff includes: ";
    print "\n";
    while((my $key, my $value)=each %employees){
       print "$key: $value\n";
    }
```

(Output)
We had to let Teddy Plunger go.
Our remaining staff includes:
Nightwatchman: Joe Blow
Clerk: Sally Olivetti

EXPLANATION

1   A hash is defined with three key/value pairs.
2   The *delete* function deletes an element from the specified hash by specifying the key. *Janitor* is the key. Both key and value are removed. The hash value associated with the key *Janitor* is removed and returned. The value *Teddy Plunger* is returned and assigned to the scalar *$layoff*.

5.4.7   The *exists* Function

The *exists* function returns true if a hash key (or array index) exists, and false if not.

FORMAT

```
exists $ASSOC_ARRAY{KEY}
```

EXAMPLE 5.55

```
    use warnings;

1   my %employees=(
        "Nightwatchman" => "Joe Blow",
        "Janitor" => "Teddy Plunger",
        "Clerk" => "Sally Olivetti",
    );

2   print "The Nightwatchman exists.\n" if exists
        $employees{"Nightwatchman"};
3   print "The Clerk exists.\n" if exists $employees{"Clerk"};
4   print "The Boss does not exist.\n" if not exists $employees{"Boss"};
```

(Output)
2   *The Nightwatchman exists.*
3   *The Clerk exists.*
4   *The Boss does not exist.*

1   A hash is defined with three key/value pairs.
2   If a key *"Nightwatchman"* exists, the *exists* function returns true.
3   If a key *"Clerk"* exists, the exists function returns true.
4   If the key *"Clerk"* does **not** exist, the inverted value of the *exists* function is false.

5.4.8 Special Hashes

The *%ENV* Hash.   The *%ENV* hash contains the environment variables handed to Perl from the parent process; for example, a shell or a Web server. The key is the name of the environment variable, and the value is what was assigned to it. If you change the value of *%ENV*, you will alter the environment for your Perl script and any processes spawned from it, but not the parent process. Environment variables play a significant roll in CGI Perl scripts.

EXAMPLE 5.56

```
(In Script)
   use warnings;
1  foreach my $key (keys %ENV){
2      print "$key\n";
   }
3  print "\nYour login name $ENV{'LOGNAME'}\n";
4  my $pwd = $ENV{'PWD'};
5  print "\n", $pwd, "\n";

(Output)
2  OPENWINHOME
   MANPATH
   FONTPATH
   LOGNAME
   USER
   TERMCAP
   TERM
   SHELL
   PWD
   HOME
   PATH
   WINDOW_PARENT
   WMGR_ENV_PLACEHOLDER

3  Your login name is ellie

5  /home/jody/home
```

EXPLANATION

1   The *foreach* loop iterates through the keys of the *%ENV* hash.
3   Print the value of the key *LOGNAME*.
4   Assign the value of the key *PWD* to *$pwd*.
5   Print the value of *$pwd*, the present working directory.

The *%SIG* Hash.   The *%SIG* hash allows you to set signal handlers for signals. If, for example, you press <CTRL>+C when your program is running, that is a signal, identified by the name *SIGINT*. (See UNIX manual pages for a complete list of signals.) The default action of *SIGINT* is to interrupt your process. The signal handler is a subroutine that is automatically called when a signal is sent to the process. Normally, the handler is used to perform a clean-up operation or to check some flag value before the script aborts. (All signal handlers are assumed to be set in the *main* package.)

The *%SIG* hash contains values only for signals set within the Perl script.

EXAMPLE 5.57

```
(In Script)
   use warnings;
1  sub handler{
2     local($sig) = @_;  # First argument is signal name
3     print "Caught SIG$sig -- shutting down\n";
      exit(0);
   }
4  SIG{'INT'} = 'handler';  # Catch <CTRL>+C
   print "Here I am!\n";
5  sleep(10);
6  $SIG{'INT'}='DEFAULT';
7  $SIG{'INT'}='IGNORE';
   < Program continues here >
```

EXPLANATION

1   *handler* is the name of the subroutine. The subroutine is defined.
2   *$sig* is a local variable and will be assigned the signal name.
3   When the *SIGINT* signal arrives, this message will appear, and the script will exit.
4   The value assigned to the key *INT* is the name of the subroutine, *handler*. When the signal arrives, the handler is called.
5   The *sleep* function gives you 10 seconds to press <CTRL>+C to see what happens.
6   The default action is restored. The default action is to abort the process if the user presses <CTRL>+C.
7   If you assign the value *IGNORE* to the *$SIG* hash, then <CTRL>+C will be completely ignored and the program will continue.

The %INC Hash. The *%INC* hash contains the entries for each filename that has been included via the *use* or *require* functions. The **key** is the filename; the **value** is the location of the actual file found.

5.4.9 Context Revisited

In summary, the way Perl evaluates variables depends on how the variables are being used; they are evaluated by context, either scalar, list, or void.

If the value on the left-hand side of an assignment statement is a scalar, the expression on the right-hand side is evaluated in a **scalar** context; whereas if the value on the left-hand side is an array, the right-hand side is evaluated in a **list** context.

Void context is a special form of scalar context. It is defined by the Perl monks as a "context that doesn't have an operator working on it. The value of a thing in void context is discarded, not used for anything…" An example of void context is when you assign a list to a scalar separating the elements with a comma. The comma operator evaluates its left argument in void context, throws it away, then evaluates the right argument, and so on, until it reaches the end of the list, discarding all but the last one.

```
$fruit = ("apple","pear","peach");  # $fruit is assigned "peach";
                                     # "apple" and "pear" are discarded
                                     # as useless use in void context
```

You'll see examples throughout the rest of this book where context plays a major role.

EXAMPLE 5.58

```
(The perldoc function describes how reverse works)
1  $ perldoc -f reverse
   reverse LIST
          In list context, returns a list value consisting of the
   elements of LIST in the opposite order. In scalar context, concatenates
   the elements of LIST and returns a string value with all characters in the
   opposite order.
      ......
```

EXAMPLE 5.59

```
(The Perl Script)
   use warnings;
1  my @list = (90,89,78,100,87);
2  my $str="Hello, world";
3  print "Original array: @list\n";
4  print "Original string: $str\n";
5  my @revlist = reverse @list;
```

EXAMPLE 5.59 (CONTINUED)

```
6  my $revstr = reverse $str;
7  print "Reversed array is: @revlist\n";
8  print "Reversed string is: $revstr\n";
9  my $newstring = reverse @list;
10 print "List reversed, context string: $newstring\n";
11 "Later, going into the Void!!!!\n";  # Void context
```

```
(Output)
11 Useless use of a constant ("Later, going into the void\n")
   in void context at Example line 13.
3  Original array: 90 89 78 100 87
4  Original string: Hello, world
7  Reversed array is: 87 100 78 89 90
8  Reversed string is: dlrow ,olleH
10 List reversed, context string: 78001879809
```

EXPLANATION

11 This is a case where you will see a warning message about using *void* context when you have a string constant that is not being used in assignment, print out, or doesn't return anything, and appears to be doing nothing. It doesn't have any side effects and doesn't break the program, but demonstrates a case where Perl views *void* context.

5 Context is demonstrated in the documentation for Perl's built-in *reverse* function.

6 The *reverse* function reverses the elements of an array and returns the reversed elements to another array. Context is list.

8 This time, the *reverse* function reverses the characters in a string. It returns the reverse string as a scalar. Context is scalar.

9 Here the *reverse* function reverses the array again, but the returned value will be assigned to a string. The context being scalar, the function will reverse the array elements and convert the list into a string of characters.

5.5 What You Should Know

1. If you don't give a variable a value, what will Perl assign to it?

2. What are "funny characters"? What is a sigil?

3. What data types are interpreted within double quotes?

4. How many numbers or strings can you store in a scalar variable?

5. In a hash, can you have more than one key with the same name? What about more than one value with the same name?

6. What function would you use to find the index value of an array if you know the value of the data stored there?

7. How does the *scalar* function evaluate an expression if it's an array?

8. How do you find the size of an array?

9. What does the $" special variable do?

10. When are elements of an array or hash preceded by a $ (dollar sign)?

11. What is the difference between *chop* and *chomp?*

12. What is the difference between *splice* and *slice?*

13. What does the *map* function do?

14. How do you sort a numeric array? How do you sort a hash by value?

15. What function extracts both keys and values from a hash?

16. How can you remove duplicates in an array?

17. What is meant by the term **scope**?

18. What is "scalar" context, "list" context, "void" context? Would you be able to write an example to demonstrate how they differ?

5.6 What's Next?

In the next chapter, we discuss the Perl operators. We will cover the different types of assignment operators, comparison and logical operators, arithmetic and bitwise operators, how Perl sees strings and numbers, how to create a range of numbers, how to generate random numbers, and some special string functions.

EXERCISE 5
The Funny Characters

1. Write a script that will ask the user for his five favorite foods (read from *STDIN*). The foods will be stored as a string in a scalar, each food separated by a comma.

   a. Split the scalar by the comma and create an array.

   b. Print the array.

   c. Print the first and last elements of the array.

   d. Print the number of elements in the array.

   e. Use an array slice of three elements in the *food* array and assign those values to another array. Print the new array with spaces between each of the elements.

2. Given the array @names=qw(Nick Susan Chet Dolly Bill), write a statement that would do the following:

   a. Replace *Susan* and *Chet* with *Ellie*, *Beatrice*, and *Charles*.

   b. Remove *Bill* from the array.

   c. Add *Lewis* and *Izzy* to the end of the array.

   d. Remove *Nick* from the beginning of the array.

   e. Reverse the array.

   f. Add *Archie* to the beginning of the array.

   g. Sort the array.

   h. Remove *Chet* and *Dolly* and replace them with *Christian* and *Daniel*.

3. Write a script called *elective* that will contain a hash. The keys will be code numbers—*2CPR2B, 1UNX1B, 3SH414, 4PL400*. The values will be course names—*C Language, Intro to UNIX, Shell Programming, Perl Programming*.

   a. Sort the hash by values and print it.

   b. Ask the user to type the code number for the course he plans to take this semester and print a line resembling the following:

   You will be taking Shell Programming this semester.

4. Modify your *elective* script to produce output resembling the output below. The user will be asked to enter registration information and to select an EDP number from a menu. The course name will be printed. It doesn't matter if the user types in the EDP number with upper- or lowercase letters. A message will confirm the user's address and thank him for enrolling.

   Output should resemble the following:

   REGISTRATION INFORMATION FOR SPRING QUARTER
   Today's date is Wed Apr 19 17:40:19 PDT 2014
   Please enter the following information:
   Your full name: Fred Z. Stachelin
   What is your Social Security Number (xxx-xx-xxxx): 004-34-1234
   Your address:
       StreetHobartSt
       CityStateZipChicoCA

"EDP" NUMBERS AND ELECTIVES:

2CPR2B | C Programming

1UNX1B | Intro to UNIX

4PL400 | Perl Programming

3SH414 | Shell Programming

What is the EDP number of the course you wish to take? 4pl400
The course you will be taking is "Perl Programming."

Registration confirmation will be sent to your address at
  1424 HOBART ST.
  CHICO, CA 95926

Thank you, Fred, for enrolling.

5. Write a script called *findem* that will do the following:

   a. Assign the contents of the *datebook* file to an array. (The *datebook* file is on the CD that accompanies this book.)

   b. Ask the user for the name of a person to find. Use the built-in *grep* function to find the elements of the array that contain the person and number of times that person is found in the array. The search will ignore case.

   c. Use the *split* function to get the current phone number.

   d. Use the *splice* function to replace the current phone number with the new phone number, or use any of the other built-in array functions to produce output that resembles the following:

   Who are you searching for? Karen

   What is the new phone number for Karen? 530-222-1255

   Karen's phone number is currently 284-758-2857.
   Here is the line showing the new phone number:

   Karen Evich:530-222-1255:23 Edgecliff Place, Lincoln, NB 92086:7/25/53:85100
   Karen was found in the array three times.

6. Write a script called *tellme* that will print out the names, phones, and salaries of all the people in the *datebook* file. To execute, type the following at the command line:

tellme datebook

Output should resemble the following:

Salary: 14500
Name: Betty Boop
Phone: 245-836-8357

7. The following array contains a list of values with duplicates.

@animals=qw(cat dog bird cat bird monkey elephant cat elephant pig horse cat);

a. Remove the duplicates with the built-in *map* function.

b. Sort the list.

c. Use the built-in *grep* function to get the index value for the *monkey*.

chapter

6

Where's the Operator?

In the real world, there are operators who operate switchboards, computers, bulldozers, tanks, and so forth. In Perl, operators operate on numbers and strings, or a combination of them. Operators are symbols, such as +, -, =, >, <, that produce a result based on some rules. This chapter is all about Perl operators, their use, and their rules.

By the end of this chapter, you should be able to explain how Perl evaluates the following example:

```
$year=(localtime)[5] + 1900;
$year % 100 == 0 && $year % 400 == 0 || $year % 100 != 0 &&
$year % 4 == 0? printf "Year %d is leap year.\n",$year :
                printf "\nYear %d is not a leap year.\n", $year;
```

6.1   About Perl Operators—More Context

Before getting into the nitty gritty of Perl operators, consider the following Example 6.1. The user is asked a question and his answer is tested. The results would normally be unexpected unless you have a good grasp on how Perl operators handle context, a subject we have been discussing from the beginning. The problem with this example is the use of the == operator, the equality operator used to test whether two numbers are equal. But in the example, the operators are used incorrectly to evaluate the equality of two strings.

EXAMPLE 6.1

```
(The Script)
   print "Did Larry Wall write Perl? ";
   chomp($answer = <STDIN>);

1  if ( $answer == "yes" or $answer == "y" ){
2     print "$answer is correct! Hooray for you!\n";
   }
   else {
3     print "Wrong! Try again.\n";
   }
```

```
(Output)
   Did Larry Wall write Perl? no
1  no is correct! Hooray for you!

   Did Larry Wall write Perl? maybe
1  maybe is correct! Hooray for you!

   Did Larry Wall write Perl? yes
1  yes is correct! Hooray for you!

   Did Larry Wall write Perl? 3
3  Wrong! Try again.
```

EXPLANATION

1   User typed *no* and the expression evaluated as *true* because the == operator is used
    to test for the equality of numbers; that is, the context is numeric. Since *no* is a string
    and has no leading numbers, Perl converts it to a number, 0. (If the string had started
    with a number, such as *3no*, then *3no* would have been converted to 3.) *$answer* has
    the value *no*, which will be converted to 0, *yes* will be converted to 0, resulting in 0 ==
    0; the expression evaluates to true, and line 2 is executed. This same situation occurs
    for a response of *yes*, *maybe*, or any string not starting with a number.

3   The only way the condition in line 1 will be evaluated as false is if the input string
    starts with a number. Perl will keep the number and discard the rest of the string; for
    example, if *$answer* is *3no*, Perl will keep the 3 and throw away the rest of the string,
    resulting in *if (3 == 0)*, which is false, so the *else* block is entered.

Now we will add one line to the program in Example 6.1. The *warnings* pragma will warn
you that the == operator expects numeric data, and *$answer* is not numeric.

EXAMPLE 6.2

```
(The Script)
    use warnings;

    print "Did Larry Wall write Perl? ";
    chomp($answer = <STDIN>);

1   if ( $answer == "yes" or $answer == "y" ){
2       print "$answer is correct! Hooray for you!\n";
    }
    else {
3       print "Wrong! Try again.\n";
    }

(Output)
Did Larry Wall write Perl? no
Argument "yes" isn't numeric in numeric eq (==) at yesno line 5, <STDIN>
line 1.
Argument "no" isn't numeric in numeric eq (==) at yesno line 5, <STDIN>
line 1.
no is correct! Hooray for you!
```

6.1.1 Evaluating an Expression

A Perl **operator** manipulates data items called **operands**; for example, 5 and 4 are operands in the expression 5 + 4. Operators and operands are found in expressions. An **expression** combines a group of values and returns something. A **statement** tells the computer to do something; for example:

```
$n = 5 + 4;
```

gets the return value from the expression 5 + 4 and assigns it to n. Perl statements end with a semicolon.

In the numeric expression, 5 + 4 - 2, three numbers are combined. The operators are the + and - signs. The operands for the + sign are 5 and 4. After that part of the expression is evaluated to 9, the expression becomes 9 - 2. After evaluating the complete expression, the result is 7.

Because the plus and minus operators each manipulate two operands, they are called **binary operators**. If there is only one operand, the operator is called a **unary operator**; and if there are three operands, it is called a **ternary operator**. We'll see examples of these operators later in the chapter.

Most of the Perl operators are borrowed from the C language, although Perl has some additional operators of its own.

6.2   Mixing Types

As Example 6.3 demonstrates, if you have operands of mixed types (that is, numbers and strings), Perl will make the appropriate conversion by testing whether the operator expects a number or a string for an operand. This is called **coercion**.

If the operator is a numeric operator, such as an arithmetic operator, and the operand(s) is a string, Perl will treat the string as a decimal floating-point value. Undefined values will become zero. If there is leading whitespace or trailing non-numeric characters, they will be ignored, and if a string cannot be converted to a number, it will be converted to zero. (See Table 6.1.)

```
$string1 = "5 dogs ";
$string2 = 4;
$number = $string1 + $string2;   # Numeric context
print "Number is $number.\n";    # Result is 9
```

Likewise, if Perl encounters a string operator and the operand(s) is numeric, Perl will treat the number as a string. The concatenation operator, for example, expects to join two strings together.

```
$number1 = 55;
$number2 = "22";
$string = $number1 . $number2;   # Context is string
print "String is string.\n"      # Result is "5522"
```

Table 6.1 How Strings Are Converted to Numbers

String	Converts to	Number
"123 go! "	⟶	*123*
"hi therev"	⟶	*0*
"4e3"	⟶	*4000*
"-6**3xyz"	⟶	*-6*
" .456!! "	⟶	*0.456*
"x.1234"	⟶	*0*
"0xf "	⟶	*0*

EXAMPLE 6.3

```
(The Script)
   use warnings;
 1 $x = "     12hello!!" + "4abc\n";   # Perl will remove leading
                                       # whitespace and trailing
                                       # non-numeric characters
```

EXAMPLE 6.3 (CONTINUED)

```
2   print "$x";
3   print "\n";

4   $y = "ZAP" . 5.5;
5   print "$y\n";

(Output)
2   16
5   ZAP5.5
```

EXPLANATION

1   The plus sign (+) is a numeric operator. The strings " 12hello!!" and "4abc\n" are converted to numbers (leading whitespace and trailing non-numeric characters are removed) and addition is performed. The result is stored in the scalar $x.

2   The scalar $x is printed.

3   Since the \n was stripped from the string 4\n in order to convert it to a number, another \n is needed to get the newline in the printout.

4   The period (.), when surrounded by whitespace, is a string operator. It concatenates two strings. The number 5.5 is converted to a string and concatenated to the string "ZAP". (In expression 5.5, the dot is used as the decimal point for the floating-point number because it is not surrounded by spaces.)

5   The value of the scalar $y is printed.

6.3 Precedence and Associativity

Which piece has the higher precedence (most power) in a game of chess? The queen or the bishop? The bishop or the pawn? These pieces have rules on how they move across the board. In programming languages, a table of precedence (see Table 6.2) shows what operators are evaluated before others and whether the evaluation is from left to right or vice-versa.

When an expression contains a number of operators and operands, and the result of the operation is potentially ambiguous, then the order of precedence and associativity determines how Perl will evaluate such an expression. **Precedence** refers to the way in which the operator binds to its operand. The multiplication operator binds more tightly to its operands than the addition operator, so it is of higher precedence; whereas the assignment operators are low in precedence and thus bind loosely to their operands. Parentheses are of the highest precedence and are used to control the way an expression is evaluated. When parentheses are nested, the expression contained within the innermost set of parentheses is evaluated first.

Associativity refers to the order in which a sequence of operators with the same precedence evaluates its operands: left to right, in no specified order, or right to left.

In the following example, how is the expression evaluated? Is addition, multiplication, or division done first? And in what order—right to left or left to right?

EXAMPLE 6.4

```
(The Script)
    use warnings;
1   $x = 5 + 4 * 12 / 4;
2   print "The result is  $x\n";


(Output)
2   The result is 17
```

EXPLANATION

1   Associativity affects multiplication and division in this example because they are used in sequence. The precedence affects the rest.

To illustrate precedence, we'll use parentheses to group the operands as they are handled by the compiler. In fact, if you want to force precedence, use the parentheses around the expression to group the operands in the way you want them evaluated.

```
$x = (5 + ( ( 4 * 12 ) / 4));
```

2   The expression is evaluated and the result is printed to *STDOUT*.

Table 6.2 summarizes the rules of precedence and associativity for the Perl operators. The operators on the same line are of equal precedence. The rows are in order of highest to lowest precedence.

Table 6.2 Precedence and Associativity (Highest to Lowest)

Operator	Description	Associativity
() [] {}	Function call, array subscripts	Left to right
->	Dereferencing operator	Left to right
++ - -	Autoincrement, autodecrement	None
**	Exponentiation	Right to left
! ~ \ + -	Logical *not*, bitwise *not*, reference backslash, unary plus, unary minus	Right to left
=~ !~	Match and not match	Left to right
* / % x	Multiply, divide, modulo, repetition	Left to right
+ - .	Add, subtract, string concatenation	Left to right
<<	Bitwise left shift, right shift	Left to right
-r -w -x -o (and so forth)	Named unary operators; for example, file test operators	None

(continued)

Table 6.2 Precedence and Associativity (Highest to Lowest) (continued)

Operator	Description	Associativity
< = = lt le gt ge	Numeric and string tests; for example, less than, greater than, and so forth	None
== != <=> eq ne ~~ cmp	Numeric and string tests; for example, equal to, not equal to, smartmatch, and so forth	None
&	Bitwise *and*	Left to right
| ^	Bitwise *or*, exclusive *or* (*xor*)	Left to right
&&	Logical *and*	Left to right
||	Logical *or*	Left to right
.. ...	Range operator, flip-flop operator	None
? :	Ternary conditional	Right to left
= += -= *= /= %=	Assignment, and so forth.	Right to left
, =>	Evaluate left operand, discard it, and evaluate right operand	Left to right
not	Synonym for *!* with lower precedence	Right
and	Synonym for &&	Left to right
or xor	Synonym for ||, ^	Left to right

6.3.1 Assignment Operators

The = sign is an assignment operator. The value on the right-hand side of the equal sign is assigned to the variable on the left-hand side. Table 6.3 illustrates assignment and shortcut assignment statements borrowed from the *C* language.

Table 6.3 Assignment Operators

Operator	Example	Meaning
=	$var = 5;	Assign 5 to $var
+=	$var += 3;	Add 3 to $var and assign result to $var
-=	$var -= 2;	Subtract 2 from $var and assign result to $var
.=	$str .= "ing";	Concatenate *ing* to $str and assign result to $str
*=	$var *= 4;	Multiply $var by 4 and assign result to $var
/=	$var /= 2;	Divide $var by 2 and assign result to $var
**=	$var **= 2;	Square $var and assign result to $var
%=	$var %= 2;	Divide $var by 2 and assign remainder to $var

(continued)

Table 6.3 Assignment Operators (continued)

Operator	Example	Meaning
x=	$str x= 20;	Repeat value of $str 20 times and assign result to $str
<<=	$var <<= 1;	Left-shift bits in $var one position and assign result to $var
>>=	$var>>= 2;	Right-shift bits in $var two positions and assign result to $var
&=	$var &= 1;	One is bitwise-ANDed to $var and the result is assigned to $var
|=	$var |= 2;	Two is bitwise-ORed to $var and the result is assigned to $var
^=	$var ^= 2;	Two is bitwise-exclusive ORed to $var and the result is assigned to $var

---

EXAMPLE 6.5

```
(The Script)
    use warnings;
1   $name="Dan";
    $line="*";
    $var=0;          # Assign 0 to var

2   $var += 3;       # Add 3 to $var; same as $var=$var+3
    print  "\$var += 3 is $var \n";

3   $var -= 1;       # Subtract 1 from $var
    print "\$var -= 1 is $var\n";

4   $var **= 2;          # Square $var
    print "\$var squared is $var\n";

5   $var %= 3;          # Modulus
    print "The remainder of \$var/3 is $var\n";

6   $name .= "ielle";   # Concatenate string "Dan" and "ielle"
    print "$name is the girl's version of Dan.\n";

7   $line x= 10;        # Repetition; print 10 stars
    print "$line\n";

8   printf "\$var is %.2f\n", $var=4.2 + 4.69;

(Output)
2   $var += 3 is 3
3   $var -=1 is 2
4   $var squared is 4
5   The remainder of $var/3 is 1
6   Danielle is the girl's version of Dan.
7   **********
8   $var is 8.89
```

EXPLANATION

1   Values on the right-hand side of the equal sign are assigned to scalar variables on the left-hand side of the equal sign.

2   The shortcut assignment operator, +=, adds 3 to the scalar $var. This is equivalent to $var = $var + 3; .

3   The shortcut assignment operator, -=, subtracts 1 from the scalar $var. This is equivalent to $var = $var - 1; .

4   The shortcut assignment operator, **=, squares the scalar $var. This is equivalent to $var = $var ** 2; .

5   The shortcut assignment modulo operator, %=, yields the integer amount that remains after the scalar $var is divided by 3. The operator is called the modulus operator, or remainder operator. The expression $var% = 3 is equivalent to $var = $var % 3; .

6   The shortcut assignment operator, . , concatenates the string *"ielle"* to the string value of the scalar, $name. This is equivalent to $name = $name . "ielle".

7   The repetition operator takes two operands. The operand on the right is the number of times the string operand on the left is repeated. The value of the scalar $line, an asterisk (*), is repeated 10 times.

8   The *printf* function is used to format and print the result of the addition of two floating-point numbers.

6.3.2 Boolean

Perl does not have a special Boolean type, *true* or *false*, but does use Boolean context when evaluating expressions. To quote the Perl documentation:

> The number 0, the strings '0' and '', the empty list "()", and "undef" are all false in a Boolean context. All other values are true. Negation of a true value by "!" or "not" returns a special false value. When evaluated as a string, it is treated as "", but as a number, it is treated as 0.[1]

So what does that mean? Although Perl does not have specific Boolean types, every value in scalar context, if checked using *if*, will be either true or false.

```
if ($x == 10) {print "true\n";}

if ($x){print "true\n";}
```

The first example will check if the value $x is equal to *10* and if true, will return 1; if false, 0. If true, the block is entered.

The second example checks to see if $x itself is true or false; only false if it evaluates to *0*, *"0"*, the empty string or *undef*.

---

1. From perlsyn under "Truth and Falsehood," *http://perldoc.perl.org/perlsyn.html#Truth-and-Falsehood*.

6.3.3   Relational Operators

Relational operators are used to compare operands. The result of the comparison is either 1 (**true**) or the empty string " " (**false**). Perl has two classes of relational operators: one set that compares numbers and another that compares strings. Normally, these operators are used to test a condition when using *if/else* loops, *while* loops, and so forth; for example:

```
if ( $x > $b ){ print "$x is greater.\n"; }
```

The expression (5 > 4 > 2) would have produced a syntax error because there is no associativity. (See Table 6.2.) We will discuss conditionals in more detail in Chapter 7, "If Only, Unconditionally, Forever."

Numeric.   Table 6.4 contains a list of numeric relational operators.

Table 6.4   Relational Operators and Numeric Values

Operator	Example	Meaning
>	$x > $y	$x is greater than $y
>=	$x >= $y	$x is greater than or equal to $y
<	$x < $y	$x is less than $y
<=	$x <= $y	$x is less than or equal to $y

EXAMPLE   6.6

```
(The Script)
    use warnings;
    $x = 5;
    $y = 4;
1   $result = $x > $y ;
2   print "$result\n";
3   $result = $x < $y;
4   print $result;

(Output)
2   1
4
```

EXPLANATION

1   If $x is greater than $y, the value *1* (true) is returned and stored in $result; otherwise, *0* (false) is returned.
2   Since the expression was true, the value of $result, *1*, is printed to *STDOUT*.
3   If $x is less than $y, the value *1* (true) is returned and stored in $result; otherwise, *0* (false) is returned.
4   Since the expression was false, the value of $result, Perl prints the empty string (that is, no output).

String. The string relational operators evaluate their operands (strings) by comparing the alphabetic value of each character in the first string with the corresponding character in the second string. The comparison (called **lexagraphical ordering**) includes trailing whitespace.

If the first string contains a character that is of a higher or lower alphabetic value than the corresponding character in the second string, the value 1 is returned; otherwise, the empty string or 0 is returned.

Table 6.5 contains a list of relational string operators.

Table 6.5 Relational Operators and String Values

Operator	Example	Meaning
gt	$str1 gt $str2	$str1 is greater than $str2
ge	$str1 ge $str2	$str1 is greater than or equal to $str2
lt	$str1 lt $str2	$str1 is less than $str2
le	$str1 le $str2	$str1 is less than or equal to $str2

EXAMPLE 6.7

```
(The Script)
    use warnings;
1   $fruit1 = "pear";
2   $fruit2 = "peaR";
3   $result = $fruit1 gt $fruit2;
4   print "$result\n";

5   $result = $fruit1 lt $fruit2;
6   print "$result\n";

(Output)
4   1
6
```

EXPLANATION

1   The scalar $fruit1 is assigned the string value *pear*.
2   The scalar $fruit2 is assigned the string value *peaR*.
3   When lexicographically comparing each of the characters in $fruit1 and $fruit2, all of the characters are equal until the *r* and *R* are compared. The ASCII value of the lower-case *r* is 114, and the ASCII value of the uppercase *R* is 82. Since 114 is greater than 82, the result of evaluating the strings is *1* (true); that is, *pear* is greater than *peaR*.
4   Since the expression was true, the value of $result, *1*, is printed to *STDOUT*.
5   This is the reverse of line 3. The alphabetic value of uppercase *R* (82) is less than the value of the lowercase *r* (114). The result of evaluating the two strings is *0* (false); that is, *pear* is less than *peaR*.
6   Since the expression was false, the value of $result, the empty string, is printed to *STDOUT*.

6.3.4 Conditional Operators

The conditional operator is another taken from the *C* language. It requires three operands and, thus, it is often called the **ternary** conditional operator. It is used to evaluate expressions, a shortcut for the *if/else* construct.

FORMAT

```
conditional expression ? expression : expression
```

EXAMPLE 6.8

```
$result = $x > $y ? $y : $z;
is equivalent to:
if( $x > $y ){ $result = $y; } else { $result = $z; }
```

EXPLANATION

If $x > $y evaluates to true, $y becomes the value of the entire expression and its value is assigned to *$result*; otherwise, *$z* becomes the value of the expression. If $x > $y evaluates to false, $z becomes the value of the expression and assigned to *$result*.

EXAMPLE 6.9

```
(The Script)
    use warnings;
1   print "What is your age? ";
2   chomp($age=<STDIN>);
3   $price=($age > 60 ) ? 0 : 5.55;
4   printf "You will pay \$%.2f.\n", $price;

(Output)
1   What is your age? 44
4   You will pay $5.55.

(Output)
1   What is your age? 77
4   You will pay $0.00.
```

EXPLANATION

1   The string *What is your age?* is printed to *STDOUT*.
2   The input is read from the terminal and stored in the scalar *$age*. The newline is *chomp*ed.
3   The scalar *$price* is assigned the result of the conditional operator. If the age is greater than *60*, the price is assigned the value to the right of the question mark (*?*). Otherwise, the value after the colon (*:*) is assigned to the scalar *$price*.
4   The *printf* function prints the formatted string to *STDOUT*.

EXAMPLE 6.10

```
(The Script)
   use warnings;
1  print "What was your grade? ";
2  $grade = <STDIN>;
3  print $grade > 60 ? "Passed.\n" : "Failed.\n";

(Output)
1    What was your grade? 76
3    Passed.

(Output)
1    What was your grade? 34
3    Failed.
```

EXPLANATION

1   The user is asked for input.
2   The input is assigned to the scalar *$grade*.
3   The *print* function takes as its argument the result of the conditional expression. If the grade is greater than *60*, *Passed.* is printed; otherwise, *Failed.* is printed.

6.3.5   Equality Operators

The equality operators test numeric operands and string operands (see Tables 6.6 and 6.7). Be sure when you are testing equality that you use the string operators for strings and the numeric operators for numbers! If, for example, you have the expression

```
"5 cats" == "5 dogs"
```

the expression will evaluate to true. Why? Because Perl sees a numeric operator, ==. The == operator expects its operands to be numbers, not strings. Perl will then convert the *"5 cats"* to the number 5 (throwing away all non-numeric characters) and the string *"5 dogs"* to the number 5, resulting in 5 == 5, which evaluates to true. In the conversion, Perl starts on the left-hand side of the string and looks for a number; if there is a number, Perl keeps it. As soon as a non-number is found, the conversion stops. If the string starts with a non-number, the result is 0.

Numeric.   The numeric equality operators evaluate their operands (numbers) by comparing their numeric values. If the operands are equal, *1* (true) is returned; if the operands are not equal, *0* (false) is returned.

The numeric comparison operator evaluates its operands, returning a *-1* if the first operand is less than the second operand, *0* if the numbers are equal, or *1* if the first operand is greater than the second.

Table 6.6 Equality Operators and Numeric Values

Operator	Example	Meaning
==	$num1 == $num2	$num1 is equal to $num2
!=	$num1 != $num2	$num1 is not equal to $num2
<=>	$num1 <=> $num2	$num1 is compared to $num2 with a signed return; 1 if $num1 is greater than $num2, 0 if $num1 is equal to $num2, and -1 if $num1 is less than $num2

EXAMPLE 6.11

```
(The Script)
   use warnings;
   $x = 5;
   $y = 4;
1  $result = $x == $y;
2  print "$result\n";

3  $result = $x != $y;
4  print "$result\n";

5  $result = $x <=> $y;
6  print "$result\n";

7  $result = $y <=> $x;
8  print "$result\n";

(Output)
2  0
4  1
6  1
8  -1
```

EXPLANATION

1   If $x is equal to $y, the value 1 (true) is returned and stored in $result; otherwise, 0 (false) is returned.

2   Since the expression was not true, the value of $result, 0, is printed to STDOUT.

3   If $x is not equal to $y, the value 1 (true) is returned and stored in $result; otherwise, 0 (false) is returned.

4   Since the expression was true, the value of $result, 1, is printed to STDOUT.

5   The scalars, $x and $y, are compared. If $x is greater than $y, 1 is returned; if $x is equal to $y, 0 is returned; if $x is less than $y, a signed -1 is returned.

6   Since $x is greater than $y, the value of $result, 1, is printed to STDOUT.

7   The scalars $x and $y are compared (<=> is called the spaceship operator). If $y is greater than $x, 1 is returned; if $x is equal to $y, 0 is returned; if $y is less than $x, a signed -1 is returned.

8   Since $x is less than $y, the value of $result, -1, is printed to STDOUT.

String. The string equality operators evaluate their operands (strings) by comparing the ASCII value of each character in the first string with the corresponding character in the second string. The comparison includes trailing whitespace.

If the first string contains a character that is of a higher ASCII value than the corresponding character in the second string, the value *1* is returned; if the strings are equal, *0* is returned; if the first string character has a lesser ASCII value than the corresponding character in the second string, *-1* is returned (see Table 6.7).

Table 6.7 Equality Operators and String Values

Operator	Example	Meaning
eq	$str1 eq $str2	$str1 is equal to $str2
ne	$str1 ne $str2	$str1 is not equal to $str2
cmp	$str1 cmp $str2	$str1 is compared to $str2, with a signed return

---

EXAMPLE 6.12

```
(The Script)
    use warnings;
1   $str1 = "A";
    $str2 = "C";
    $result = $str1 eq $str2;
    print "$result\n";

2   $result = $str1 ne $str2;
    print "$result\n";

3   $result = $str1 cmp $str2;
    print "$result\n";

4   $result = $str2 cmp $str1;
    print "$result\n";

5   $str1 = "C";          # Now both strings are equal
6   $result = $str1 cmp $str2;
    print "$result\n";

(Output)
1
2   1
3   -1
4   1
6   0
```

EXPLANATION

1   The scalar $str1 is assigned the value *A*, and scalar $str2 is assigned the value *C*. If $str1 is **equal** to $str2, the value *1* (true) is returned, assigned to $result, and printed.

2   If $str1 is **not equal** to $str2, the value *1* (true) is returned, assigned to $result, and printed.

3   If $str1 is compared with $str2 (that is, an ASCII comparison is made on each character), and all characters are the same, the value *0* is returned and assigned to $result. If $str1 is greater than $str2, the value *1* is returned, and if $str1 is less than $str2, *-1* is returned. In this example, $str1 is less than $str2. The value of $result is printed.

4   In this example, we reverse the order of comparison. Since $str2 is greater than $str1, the result is *1*. The value of $result is printed.

5   $str1 is assigned *C*. It has the same value as $str2.

6   Now $str1 and $str2 are equal. Since all of the characters are the same, the value *0* is returned and assigned to $result. The value of $result is printed.

EXAMPLE 6.13

```
(The Script)
    # Don't use == when you should use eq!
1   $answer = "no";
2   print $answer == "yes"?"$answer is YES":"$answer is NO", "\n";

(Output)
2   no is YES
```

EXPLANATION

1   The scalar *$answer* is assigned the string *"no"*.

2   The numeric equality operator, ==, is being used incorrectly to test the equality of two strings in a conditional statement. The strings are converted to numbers. Since the characters are non-numeric, the result is to convert each string to *0* (zero). *0* is equal to *0*, resulting in *1* (true). The string equality operator *eq* should have been used in this test: *print $answer eq "yes"?"$answer is YES":"$answer is NO", "\n";*

6.3.6 The Smartmatch Operator

As of Perl 5.10.1, the quirky smartmatch operator (still experimental) provides you a way to compare two operands without imposing context on them, as we saw in the previous section with == and *eq*.

The smartmatch operator infers the type that should be used. According to the Perl documentation for Perl 5 version 18.2 at perldoc.perl.org, "The behavior of a smartmatch depends on what type of 'things' (scalars, arrays, hashes) its arguments are."

For example, in the expression *"yes" == "no"*, the == operator forces numeric context, converting both *"yes"* and *"no"* to 0, because the == takes only numeric values as its operands. The *eq* operator should have been used when testing the equality of two strings.

But the smartmatch operator infers what the operands should be by how they are used. The smartmatch operator returns 1 if true, and " " if false.

EXAMPLE 6.14

```
1  use warnings;
2  use v5.14;
   $str = "Boston";
3  if($str == "San Francisco"){
4     print qq(The == operator says: "$str" is equal to "San
           Francisco".\n);
   }
   else{ print qq("$str" is not equal to "San Francisco".\n);}

5  if($str ~~ "San Francisco"){
      print qq(The smartmatch operator says: "$str" is equal to "San
   Francisco".\n);
    }
6  else{ print qq(The smartmatch operator says: "$str" is not equal to
           "San Francisco".\n);}
```

(Output)
```
1  Argument "San Francisco" isn't numeric in numeric eq (==) at smartmatch
   line 4.
   Argument "Boston" isn't numeric in numeric eq (==) at smartmatch line 4.
4  The == operator says: Boston" is equal to "San Francisco".
6  The smartmatch operator says: "Boston" is not equal to "San Francisco".
```

EXPLANATION

1   With *warnings* turned on, Perl will complain when you use strings with a numeric operator and warn you that *"San Francisco"* and *"Boston"* should use the *eq* rather than == operator.

2   By specifying the version number, we enable the use of the smartmatch operator as it became available in Perl 5.10.1.

3   Here, we see the use of the numeric == operator, which forces its operands to be numeric even if they're not meant to be, and in this example will convert both strings to 0 (since neither start with a number). Doing this triggers a warning message, but the program will still run. The statement reads *if (0 == 0)*, execute the following block.

4   This statement is executed and printed due to the test on the previous line. 0 is equal to 0.

5   The smartmatch operator, unlike the equality operators, doesn't force the operand to become a number or string because it expects a certain context, but infers by the type of the operands how to best compare them. Should I be comparing these values as numbers or as strings? Which one seems appropriate here? Since *"Boston"* and *"San Francisco"* are both strings, the smartmatch operator compares them with the *eq* operator and line 6 is printed.

The smartmatch operator also compares different types of operands, such as arrays, hashes, regular expressions, and so forth. To understand how this works, ask yourself, "Does the value on the left-hand side match the value on the right-hand side, and if the right-hand side is an array, does the value match any of the elements in the array? Or if the value on the right-hand side is a hash, does the value on the left match any of the keys in the hash?" The smaller thing is usually on the left-hand side of the ~~ and the larger thing on the right.

EXAMPLE 6.15

```
    use warnings;
1   @n = ("5", 100 , 20, "alice");
2   if ( 5 ~~ @n ){ print qq/5 matched\n/; }
3   if ( "20" ~~ @n ){ print qq/20 matched\n/; }
4   if ( 10 ~~ @n ){ print qq/10 matched\n/; } else{ print "10 is
       not a match\n"      ;}
5   if ( "alice" ~~ @n){ print "matched alice\n";}
       else{print "didn't match alice\n";}
6   %h = (Name=>"Tom",
          Id=>"123B",
          Age=>undef,
       );

7   if (Name ~~ %h){print qq(The hash key 'Name' matched.\n);}
       # Matched the key
8   if ($h{Age} ~~ undef) { print qq(The hash key 'Age' matched.\n);}
```

(Output)
5 matched
20 matched
10 is not a match
Argument "alice" isn't numeric in smart match at smartmatch line 21.
matched alice
The hash key 'Name' matched.
The hash key 'Age' matched.

6.3.7 Logical Operators (Short-Circuit Operators)

The short-circuit operators evaluate their operands, from left to right, testing the truth or falsity of each operand, in turn. There is no further evaluation once a true or false condition is satisfied. Unlike *C*, the short-circuit operators do not return *0* (false) or *1* (true) but rather the **value** of the last operand evaluated. These operators are most often used in conditional statements. (See Chapter 7, "If Only, Unconditionally, Forever.")

If the expression on the left-hand side of the *&&* evaluates to false, the expression is false and that value is returned. If the expression on the left-hand side of the operator evaluates to true (nonzero), the right-hand side is evaluated and its value is returned.

The logical operators can also be represented as *and*, *or*, or *not*, but the precedence for them is **lower**. If the expression on the left-hand side of the || operator is evaluated as true (nonzero), the value of the expression is returned. If the value on the left-hand side of the || is false, the value of the expression on the right-hand side of the operator is evaluated, and its value is returned.

A list of logical operators is shown in Table 6.8.

Table 6.8 Logical Operators (Short-Circuit Operators)

Operator	Alternative Form	Example	Meaning
&&	and	$x && $y	If $x is true, evaluate $y and return $y
			$x and $y	If $x is false, evaluate $x and return $x
||	or	$x || $y	If $x is true, evaluate $x and return $x
			$x or $y	If $x is false, evaluate $y and return $y
	xor	$x xor $y	True if $x or $y is true, but not both
!	not	! $x	Not $x; true if $x is not true, false if $x is true; returns 1 or 0
		not $x	Same as ! $x

EXAMPLE 6.16

```
(The Script)
    use warnings;
    # Short-circuit operators
1   $num1=50;
2   $num2=100;
3   $num3=0;

4   print $num1 && $num3, "\n";      # result is 0
5   print $num3 && $num1, "\n";      # result is 0
6   print $num1 && $num2, "\n";      # result is 100
7   print $num2 && $num1, "\n\n";    # result is 50

8   print $num1 || $num3, "\n";      # result is 50
9   print $num3 || $num1, "\n";      # result is 50
10  print $num1 || $num2, "\n";      # result is 50
11  print $num2 || $num1, "\n";      # result is 100

(Output)
4   0
5   0
6   100
7   50
8   50
9   50
10  50
11  100
```

EXPLANATION

1   Because the expression to the left of the *&&* operator, *$num1*, is nonzero (true), the expression to the right of the *&&*, *$num3*, is returned.

2   Because the expression to the left of the *&&* operator, *$num3*, is zero (false), the expression *$num3* is returned.

3   Because the expression to the left of the *&&* operator, *$num1*, is true (true), the expression on the right-hand side of the *&&* operator, *$num2*, is returned.

4   Because the expression to the left of the *&&* operator, *$num2*, is true (true), the expression on the right-hand side of the *&&* operator, *$num1*, is returned.

5   Because the expression to the left of the *||* operator, *$num1*, is nonzero (true), the expression *$num1* is returned.

6   Because the expression to the left of the *||* operator, *$num3*, is zero (false), the expression to the right of the *||* operator, *$num1*, is returned.

7   Because the expression to the left of the *||* operator, *$num1*, is nonzero (true), the expression *$num1* is returned.

8   Because the expression to the left of the *||* operator, *$num2*, is nonzero (true), the expression *$num2* is returned.

6.3.8 Logical Word Operators

These logical operators are of lower precedence than the short-circuit operators, but basically work the same way and make the program easier to read, and they also short-circuit. In addition to the short-circuit operators, the *xor* (exclusive *or*) operator has been added to the logical word operators.

EXAMPLE 6.17

```
    # Examples using the word operators
    use warnings;
1   $num1=50;
    $num2=100;
    $num3=0;
    print "\nOutput using the word operators.\n\n";
2   print "\n$num1 and $num2: ",($num1 and $num2);, "\n";
3   print "\n$num1 or $num3: ", ($num1 or $num3), "\n";
4   print "\n$num1 xor $num3: ",($num1 xor $num3), "\n";
5   print "\nnot $num3: ", not $num3;
    print "\n";
```

EXAMPLE 6.17 (CONTINUED)

```
(Output)
    Output using the word operators.

2   50 and 100: 100

3   50 or 0: 50

4   50 xor  0: 1

5   not 0: 1
```

EXPLANATION

1   Initial values are assigned to $num1, $num2, and $num3.

2   The *and* operator evaluates its operands. $num1 and $num2 are both true, resulting in the value of the last expression evaluated, *100*. Since *100* is a nonzero value, the expression is true.

3   The *or* operator evaluates its operands. $num1 is true. The word operators also short-circuit, so that if the first expression is true, there is no need to continue evaluating. The result returned is *50*, which is true.

4   The exclusive *xor* operator evaluates both its operands. It does not short-circuit. If one of the operands is *true*, then the expression is true and *1* is returned; if both sides are either true or false, the result is false.

5   The logical *not* operator evaluates the operand to the right; if it is true, false is returned; if false, true is returned.

EXAMPLE 6.18

```
(The Script)
    use warnings;  # line 2 will produce a warning when warnings are on
    # Precedence with word operators and short-circuit operators
    $x=5;
    $y=6;
    $z=0;
1   $result=$x && $y && $z;        # Precedence of = lower than &&
    print "Result: $result\n";

2   $result2 = $x and $y and $z;   # Precedence of = higher than and
    print "Result: $result2\n";

3   $result3 = ( $x and $y and $z );
    print "Result: $result3\n";

(Output)
1   Result: 0
2   Result: 5
3   Result: 0
```

1   The logical short-circuit operators evaluate each of the expressions and return the value of the last expression evaluated. The value *0* is assigned to *$result*. Since *&&* is higher in precedence than the equal sign, the logical operators evaluated their expressions first.

2   Check Perl's precedence table for this one. The word operators are used here, but they are lower in precedence than the equal sign. The first expression to the right of the equal sign is assigned to *$result2*.

3   By adding parentheses to the expression on the right-hand side of the equal sign, that expression is evaluated first and the result assigned to *$result3*.

6.3.9   Arithmetic Operators and Functions

Perl comes with the standard set of arithmetic operators found in most languages, plus some of its own. It also provides for a number of built-in functions for handling mathematical operations such as finding the square root of a number, producing random numbers, getting an absolute value, and so forth.

Arithmetic Operators.   Perl's arithmetic operators are listed in Table 6.9.

Table 6.9   Arithmetic Operators

Operator	Example	Meaning
+	$x + $y	Addition
–	$x - $y	Subtraction
*	$x * $y	Multiplication
/	$x / $y	Division
%	$x % $y	Modulo
**	$x ** $y	Exponentiation

```
(The Script)
   use warnings;
1  printf "%d\n", 4 * 5 / 2;
2  printf "%d\n", 5 ** 3;
3  printf "%d\n", 5 + 4 - 2 * 10;
4  printf "%d\n", (5 + 4 - 2 ) * 10;
5  printf "%d\n", 11 % 2;  # Get the remainder after division
```

EXAMPLE 6.19 (CONTINUED)

```
(Output)
1   10
2   125
3   -11
4   70
5   1
```

EXPLANATION

1   The *printf* function formats the result of the arithmetic expression in decimal. Multiplication and division are performed. Operators are of the same precedence, left-to-right associativity. This is the same as *(4 * 5) / 2.*

2   The *printf* function formats the result of the arithmetic expression in decimal. The exponentiation operator cubes its operand, 5, same as 5^3.

3   The *printf* function formats the result of the arithmetic expression in decimal. Since the multiplication operator is of higher precedence than the addition and subtraction operators, multiplication is performed first, left-to-right associativity. This is the same as *5 + 4 - (2 * 10).*

4   The *printf* function formats the result of the arithmetic expression in decimal. Since the parentheses are of highest precedence, the expression enclosed in parentheses is calculated first.

5   The *printf* function formats the result of the arithmetic expression in decimal. The modulo operator produces the remainder after performing division on its operands.

Arithmetic Functions.   In addition to arithmetic operators, Perl provides a number of built-in functions to evaluate arithmetic expressions (see Table 6.10).

There are also a number of general utility functions provided by CPAN in a module called *List::Util*, including *first, max, maxstr, min, minstr, reduce, shuffle,* and *sum.*[2] Now this module is part of the standard Perl library. Type *perldoc List::Util* at your prompt and you will see the following output:

NAME
    List::Util - A selection of general-utility list subroutines

SYNOPSIS
    use **List::Util** qw(first max maxstr min minstr reduce shuffle sum);

DESCRIPTION
    "List::Util" contains a selection of subroutines that people have
    expressed would be nice to have in the perl core, but the usage would
    not really be high enough to warrant the use of a keyword, and the size
    so small such that being individual extensions would be wasteful.
        < Continues here>

---

2. See *http://perldoc.perl.org/List/Util.html#DESCRIPTION.*

Table 6.10   Built-in Perl Arithmetic Functions

Function	Meaning
abs VALUE	Returns the absolute value of its argument. Returns the absolute value of $_.
atan2(Y,X)	Returns the arctangent of *Y/X* in the range -Pi to Pi.
cos EXPR	Returns the cosine of *EXPR* (expressed in radians). If *EXPR* is omitted, takes cosine of $_.
exp EXPR	Returns e to the power of *EXPR*. If *EXPR* is omitted, gives *exp($_)*.
hex EXPR	Interprets *EXPR* as a hex string and returns the corresponding value. (To convert strings that might start with either *0, 0x* , or *0b*, see *http://perldoc.perl.org/functions/oct.html*.) If EXPR is omitted, uses $_.
int EXPR	Returns the integer portion of *EXPR*. If *EXPR* is omitted, uses $_.
log EXPR	Returns logarithm (base e) of *EXPR*. If *EXPR* is omitted, returns log of $_.
oct EXPR	Interprets *EXPR* as an octal string and returns the corresponding value. (If *EXPR* happens to start off with *0x*, interprets it as a hex string. If *EXPR* starts off with *0b*, it is interpreted as a binary string. Leading whitespace is ignored in all three cases.)
rand EXPR	Returns a random fractional number between 0 and the value of *EXPR*. (*EXPR* should be positive.) If *EXPR* is omitted, returns a value between 0 and 1. See also *srand()*.
sin EXPR	Returns the sine of *EXPR* (expressed in radians). If *EXPR* is omitted, returns sine of $_.
sqrt EXPR	Return the square root of *EXPR*. If *EXPR* is omitted, returns square root of $_.
ssrand EXPR	Sets the random number seed for the *rand* operator. If *EXPR* is omitted, does *srand(time)*.

Generating Random Numbers

When looking for a good description of random number generation on the Web, one of the related topics is *Games>Gambling>Lotteries>Ticket Generators*. Games and lotteries depend on the use of random number generation and so do more sophisticated programs, such as cryptographic protocols that use unpredictable encrypted keys to ensure security when passing information back and forth on the Web.

Random numbers produced by programs are called **pseudo-random** numbers. As described in an article by Ian Goldberg and David Wagner concerning Web security, truly random numbers can be found only in nature, such as the rate of decay of a radioactive element. Apart from using external sources, computers must generate these numbers themselves, but since computers are deterministic, these numbers will not be truly random. Perl programs that need to generate pseudo-random numbers can use the built-in *rand* function described next.

The *rand/srand* Functions

The *rand* function returns a pseudo-random fractional number between 0 and 1. If *EXPR* has a positive value, *rand* returns a fractional number between 0 and *EXPR*. The *srand* function sets the random number seed for the *rand* function but is no longer required if you are using a version of Perl greater than 5.004, which you should be. A seed is a random number itself that is fed to the random number generator as the starting number from which new random numbers are produced. The *rand* function is given a seed and, using a complex algorithm, produces random numbers within some range. If the same seed is fed to the *rand* function each time it is called, the same series of numbers will be produced. A different seed will produce a different series of random numbers. The default seed value used to be the time of day, but now a more unpredictable number is selected for you by Perl.

You may want to set the seed with *srand()*. For example, when performing simulations, you might use a different seed for each simulation and when a problem occurs, save the seed, and then reset that seed to reproduce the error.

FORMAT

```
rand(EXPR)
rand EXPR
rand

srand(EXPR)
srand EXPR
```

EXAMPLE 6.20

```
    $n = 0;
1   while ($n < 10){
2       print rand,"\n";
        $n++;
    }

(Output)
0.137701336600916
0.634569291581528
0.906979192552296
0.924376643119963
0.388869890605822
0.840094240134917
0.22705622776115
0.753856265492765
0.628500061799432
0.101241892495409
```

EXPLANATION

1   The *while* loop will iterate 10 times.
2   Each time through the loop, a new random number is printed. This number is a fractional number between 0 and 1, not including 1.

EXAMPLE 6.21

```
(The Script)
   use warnings;
1  $num=10;
2  srand(time|$$); # Seed rand with the time or'ed to
                    # the pid of this process
3  while($num){     # srand not necessary in versions 5.004 and above
4     $lotto = int (rand 10);
                    # Returns a random number between 0 and 10
5     print "The random number is $lotto\n";
      sleep 3;
      $num--;
   }

(Output)
5  The random number is 7
   The random number is 4
   The random number is 3
   The random number is 5
   The random number is 3
   The random number is 6
   The random number is 8
   The random number is 0
   The random number is 6
   The random number is 8
```

EXPLANATION

1   The value of *$num* will be used in the *while* loop on line 7, which will iterate 10 times.
2   The *srand* function allows you to set the seed for the *rand* function, in this example to a unique starting point, the return value of the built-in *time* function bitwise *ored* to the process identification number of this Perl program (*$$*). Perl will set the seed for you, so this step in unnecessary unless you want to control the randomness for simulations or tests as mentioned previously.
3   The *while* loop will iterate 10 times.
4   The *rand* function will return an integer value between 0 and 9, inclusive. The value will be assigned to *$lotto*. Just add 1 if you want to start with 1 to 10.
5   The value of the random number is printed.

EXAMPLE 6.22

```
(The Script)
   use warnings;
1  $x=5 ;     # Starting point in a range of numbers
2  $y=15;     # Ending point

   # Formula to produce random numbers between 5 and 15 inclusive
   # $random = int(rand($y - $x + 1)) + $x;
   # $random = int(rand(15 - 5 + 1)) + 5

3  while(1){
4     print int(rand($y - $x + 1)) + $x , "\n";
5     sleep 1;
   }

(Output)
15
14
5
10
11
6
12
6
7
10
6
8
6
15
11
```

EXPLANATION

1 The scalar $x is assigned the starting value in the range of numbers produced by the *rand* function.

2 The scalar $y is assigned the ending value of the range of numbers produced by the *rand* function.

3 An infinite *while* loop is started. To exit, the user must type <CTRL>+D (UNIX) or <CTRL>+Z (Windows).

4 *rand* is used *in* a formula that will produce random integers between 1 and 15, but it is *given* (the result of) a formula that will produce a number between 0 and 11.

5 The *sleep* function causes the program to pause for 1 second.

6.3.10 Autoincrement and Autodecrement Operators

The autoincrement and autodecrement operators are taken straight from the C language The autoincrement operator adds 1 to the value of a variable, and the autodecrement operator subtracts 1 from the value of a variable. When used with a single variable, these operators are just shortcuts for the traditional method of adding and subtracting 1. However, if used in an assignment statement or if combined with other operators, the end result depends on the placement of the operator (see Table 6.11). Consider the following example:

```
$i = 4;
printf  "%d\n", $i++;

printf "%d\n", ++$i;
```

The first example is a post increment operation; that is, $i won't be incremented until after its value is printed, resulting in 4 being printed.

Now if we set $i back to 4 and go to the second example, $i is pre-incremented before it is printed, resulting in 5.

Don't use these operators unless you know what to expect. For example, the following statement is frivolous and the results are based on how the *printf* function internally evaluates its arguments:

```
$x = 5;
printf "%d   %d   %d   %d\n", $x++, --$x, $x--, ++$x;
```

Table 6.11 Autoincrement and Autodecrement Operators and Assignment

Example	Description	Equivalence	Result
If $y is 0 and $x is 0: $y = $x++;	Assign the value of $x to $y, then increment $x	$y = $x; $x = $x + 1;	$y is 0 $x is 1
If $y is 0 and $x is 0: $y = ++$x;	Increment $x, then assign $x to $y	$x = $x + 1; $y = $x;	$x is 1 $y is 1
If $y is 0 and $x is 0: $y = $x--;	Assign the value of $x to $y, then decrement $x	$y = $x; $x = $x - 1;	$y is 0 $x is -1
If $y is 0 and $x is 0: $y = --$x;	Decrement $x, then assign $x to $y	$x = $x - 1; $y = $x;	$x is -1 $y is -1

The most common use for these operators is within loops. It's a quick way to add or subtract 1 from a value. See Example 6.23.

EXAMPLE 6.23

```
(The Script)
   use warnings;
   my $n = 0;
1  while ($n < 10 ){
      print "$n ";
      $n++;
   }
   print "\n\n";

2  for(my $i = 20; $i >= 0; $i--){
      print "$i  ";
   }
   print "\n";

(Output)
1 2 3 4 5 6 7 8 9

20 19 18 17 16 15 14 13 12 11 10 9 8 7 6 5 4 3 2 1 0
```

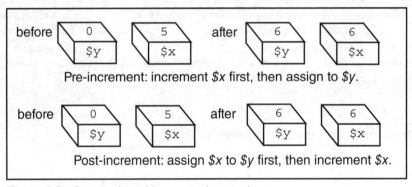

Figure 6.1 Pre- and post-increment operators.

6.3.11 Bitwise Logical Operators

A Little Bit About Bits.   People represent numbers in decimal, or base 10, a numbering system based on 10 values starting from 0 to 9; for example, $100,000 and 1955. The HTML color codes are represented in hexadecimal, base 16, values ranging from 0 to 15; for example, #00FFFF is cyan and #FF00FF is fuchsia.

Computers, on the other hand, store everything in binary, or base 2. A binary numbering system represents numbers in two values, 0 or 1. Each of the individual 1s and 0s are called bits. All the data you use is stored in your computer using bits. A byte is made up of 8 bits, a word is 2 bytes, or 16 bits, and finally, two words together are called a double word, or dword, which is a 32-bit value. The reason a computer uses only 0s and 1s for everything is because a binary digit is represented by the presence of an electric current. If the level of electricity reaches a certain level, the digit is 1. Otherwise, the digit is a 0. Using just two numbers makes building hardware less difficult and cheaper than if electrical levels were represented by a bigger combination of bits, like base 10 (decimal) or base 16 (hexadecimal). Hence, computers store everything in binary.

Bitwise Operators.   Most processors today are built to operate on 32-bit numbers. For example, the term "Win32" is derived from the fact that an integer on a Win32 compiler defaults to 32 bits. Bitwise operators allow you to turn on or off specific bits within an integer. For example, if you are setting a read-only flag on a file, you need only two values, on or off, represented as 1 or 0. And if both the left- and right-hand parameters are strings, the bitwise operator will operate on the characters within the string.

Bitwise operators treat their operands as a set of 64 bits (0s and 1s), rather than as decimal, hexadecimal, or octal numbers. For example, the decimal number 9 has a binary representation of 1001. Although bitwise operators perform their operations on expressions containing bit strings, they return standard Perl numerical values, as shown in Table 6.13. If you are working with graphics, games, encryption, registers, setting switches, or any operation that requires "twiddling bits," then the bitwise operators may become useful. Generally speaking, those types of operations are more fitting for such languages as C or Java.

When you're ready to manipulate integer values at the bit level, the bitwise logical operators are used. The bitwise operators are binary operators and manipulate their operands in terms of the internal binary representation of those operands. A bit-by-bit comparison is made on each of the corresponding operands, producing its result as the binary value (see Tables 6.12 and 6.13).

Table 6.12   Bitwise Logical Operators

Operator	Example	Meaning
&	$x & $y	Bitwise *and*
|	$x | $y	Bitwise *or*
^	$x ^ $y	Bitwise exclusive *or*
~	~$x	Bitwise *not* or complement
<<	$x << 1	Bitwise left shift, integer multiply by two
>>	$x >> 1	Bitwise right shift, integer divide by two

Table 6.13   Resulting Values of Bitwise Operators

$x	$y	$x & $y	$x | $y	$x ^ $y
0	0	0	0	0
0	1	0	1	1
1	0	0	1	1
1	1	1	1	0

```
      $x = 7;
  1   $x <<= 1;
      printf "Left shift 7 * 2: %d  %b\n", $x, $x;
  2   $x = 16;
      $x >>= 1;
      printf "Right shift 16/2: %d  %b\n", $x, $x;

(Output)
Left shift 7 * 2: 14  1110
Right shift 16/2: 8  1000
```

1   The left and right shift bitwise operators move all the bits in a number to the left or right a given amount of times. Bitwise shifted to the left moves each bit over to the left one position. These operators are often used to quickly divide or multiply integers. In this example, $x is assigned the value 7 which is 111 in bits. Moving all the bits to the left by one results in 1110 or 14.

2   When shifting all bits to the right by 1 the result is to divide the integer value by 2 Starting with the number 16 in bits, 10000 and shifting bits by one to the right, the rightmost bit is shifted off and all the rest of the bits are moved to the right resulting in 01000. Shifting right by 2 would result in dividing 16 by 4.

6.3.12 Range Operator

The range operator is used in both scalar and array context. In a scalar context, the value returned is a Boolean, _1_ or _0_. In an array context, it returns a list of items starting on the left side of the operator and counting by ones until the value on the right-hand side is reached.

```
  1   @num = (0 .. 10);
      print "@num\n";
      0 1 2 3 4 5 6 7 8 9 10
  2   @alpha=('A' .. 'Z'); print "@alpha\n";
      A B C D E F G H I J K L M N O P Q R S T U V W X Y Z
  3   @letters=('a'..'z', 'A'..'Z'); print "@letters\n";
      a b c d e f g h i j k l m n o p q r s t u v w x y z A B C D E F G H I
      J K L M N O P Q R S T U V W X Y Z
  4   @n=( -5 .. 20 ); print "@n\n";l
      -5 -4 -3 -2 -1 0 1 2 3 4 5 6 7 8 9 10 11 12 13 14 15 16 17 18 19 20
```

1   Print the numbers _0_ to _10_.

2   Create an array called _@alpha_ and store all uppercase letters in the array in the range from _A_ to _Z_. The context is list. Print the array.

3   Create an array called *@letters*. The range operator creates two lists, one of lowercase letters and one of uppercase letters. The comma concatenates the two lists. The letters are assigned to *@letters* and the array is printed.

4   Create an array called *@n* and store all numbers in the range between *-5* and *20*. Print the array.

6.3.13   Special String Operators and Functions

A number of operations can be performed on strings. For example, the concatenation operator joins two strings together, and the string repetition operator concatenates as many copies of its operand as specified.

Perl also supports some special functions for manipulating strings (see Table 6.14). The *substr* function returns a substring found within an original string, starting at a character offset in the original string and ending with the number of character positions to the right of that offset. The *index* function returns the character offset of the first character of a substring found within the original string. The *length* function returns the number of characters in a given expression.

Table 6.14   String Operations

Example	Meaning
$str1 . $str2	Concatenate strings *$str1* and *$str2*.
$str1 x $num	Repeat *$str1*, *$num* times.
substr($str1, $offset, $len)	Substring of *$str1* at *$offset* for *$len* bytes.
index($str1, $str2)	Character offset of string *$str2* in string *$str1*.
length($str)	Returns the length in characters of expression, *$str*.
rindex($str, $substr, POSITION)	Returns the position of the last occurrence of *$substr* in *$str*. If *POSITION* is specified, start looking there. If *POSITION* is not specified, start at the end of the string.
chr(NUMBER)	Returns the character represented by that *NUMBER* in the Unicode character set. For example, *chr(65)* is the letter *A* and *chr(0x263a)* is a Unicode smiley face.
lc($str)	Returns a lowercase string.
uc($str)	Returns an uppercase string.

EXAMPLE 6.26

```
(The Script)
   use warnings;
1  my $x="pop";
2  my $y="corn";
3  my $z="*";
4  print $z x 10, "\n";          # Print 10 stars; repetition operator
5  print $x . $y, "\n";          # Concatenate "pop" and "corn"
6  print $z x 10, "\n";          # Print 10 stars

7  print uc($x . $y), "!\n";     # Convert string to uppercase

(Output)
4  **********
5  popcorn
6  **********
7  POPCORN!
```

EXPLANATION

1   The scalar $x is assigned *pop*.
2   The scalar $y is assigned *corn*.
3   The scalar $z is assigned *.
4   The string * is repeated 10 times and printed to *STDOUT*.
5   The value of $x, string *pop*, and the value of $y, string *corn*, are concatenated and printed to *STDOUT*.
6   The value of $x, string *, is repeated 10 times and printed to *STDOUT*.
7   The *uc* function converts and returns the string in uppercase. The *lc* function will convert a string to lowercase.

EXAMPLE 6.27

```
(The Script)
   use warnings;
1  my $line="Happy New Year";
2  print substr($line, 6, 3),"\n";        # Offset starts at zero
3  print index($line, "Year"),"\n";
4  print substr($line, index($line, "Year")),"\n";
5  substr($line, 0, 0)="Fred, ";
6  print $line,"\n";
7  substr($line, 0, 1)="Ethel";
8  print $line,"\n";
9  substr($line, -1, 1)="r to you!";
10 print $line,"\n";
11 my $string="I'll eat a tomato tomorrow.\n";
12 print rindex($string, "tom"), "\n";
```

EXAMPLE 6.27 (CONTINUED)

```
(Output)
2   New
3   10
4   Year
6   Fred, Happy New Year
8   Ethelred, Happy New Year
9   Ethelred, Happy New Year to you!
12  18
```

EXPLANATION

1   The scalar *$line* is assigned *Happy New Year*.

2   The substring *New* of the original string *Happy New Year* is printed. The offset starts at position 0. The beginning of the substring is position 6, the *N* in *New*, and the length of the substring is 3, (i.e., three characters to the right of *N*). The substring *New* is returned.

3   The *index* function returns the first position in the string where the substring is found. The substring *Year* starts at position 10. Remember, the offset starts at 0.

4   The *substr* and *index* functions are used together. The *index* function returns the starting position of the substring *Year*. The *substr* function uses the return value from the *index* function as the starting position for the *substring*. The *substring* returned is *Year*.

5   The substring *Fred* is inserted at starting position *0*, and over length *0* of the scalar *$line*; that is, at the beginning of the string.

6   The new value of *$line* is printed to *STDOUT*.

7   The substring *Ethel* is inserted at starting position, byte *0*, and over length *1* of the scalar *$line*.

8   The new value of *$line, Ethelred, Happy New Year*, is printed to *STDOUT*.

9   The substring, *r to you!*, is appended to the scalar *$line* starting at the end (*-1*) of the substring, over one character.

10 The new value of *$line, Ethelred, Happy New Year to you!*, is printed to *STDOUT*.

11 The *$string* scalar is assigned.

12 The *rindex* function finds the index of the **rightmost** substring, *tom*, and returns the index position where it found the substring. That position, *18*, is the number of characters starting at the zero position from the beginning of the string to the substring *tom* in *tomorrow*.

6.4   What You Should Know

1. What is meant by the term *operand*?

2. How does Perl treat the expression *"5cats" + 21*?

3. How does Perl treat the expression *23 . 43*?

4. What is an autoincrement operator?

5. What is a pseudorandom number?

6. What is the difference between *eq* and ==?

7. Are *and* and *&&* the same?

8. What is the *&* operator?

9. What is a ternary operator?

10. How does Perl use relational operators to compare strings?

11. What is the difference between *and* and *or*?

12. Where is the equal sign in the precedence table?

13. Does the equal sign associate right to left or left to right?

14. What Perl string function lets you extract a piece of a string?

15. What function converts a string to uppercase?

16. What operator allows you to repeat a string?

17. What operator allows you to concatenate strings together?

6.5 What's Next?

In the next chapter, we discuss the Perl control structures, how to test whether a condition is true or false with *if* and *unless* constructs, how to block statements, how to use loops to repeat a statement(s), and how to break out of loops, use labels, and nest loops.

EXERCISE 6
Operator, Operator

---

1. Use *printf* to print the average of three floating-point numbers with a precision of two decimal places.

2. What are two other ways you could write $x = $x + 1;?

3. Write the following expression using a shortcut: $y = $y + 5;

4. Calculate the volume of a room that is 12.5 ft. long, 9.8 ft. wide, and 10.5 ft. high. Square the number 15 and print the result.

5. How do the ~~, ==, and *eq* differ? Give an example of each.

6. What would the following program print?

```
$x = 15; $b = 4; $c = 25.0; $d = 3.0;
printf "4 + c / 4 * d = %f\n", 4 + $c / 4 * $d;
printf "x / d * x + c = %.2f\n", $x / $d * $x + $c;
printf "%d\n", $result = $c / 5 - 2;
```

```
printf "%d = %d + %f\n", $result = $b + $c, $b, $c;
printf "%d\n", $result == $d;
```

7. Given the values of *$x=10*, *$b=3*, *$c=7*, and *$d=20*, print the value of *$result*:

```
$result = ( $x >= $b ) && ( $c < $d ); print "$result\n";
$result = ( $x >= $b ) and ( $c < $d ); print "$result\n";
$result = ( $x < $b) || ( $c <= $d ); print "$result\n";
$result = ( $x < $b) or ( $c <= $d ); print "$result\n";
$result = $x % $b;
```

8. Write a program called *convert* that converts a Fahrenheit temperature to Celsius using the following formula: $C = (F - 32) / 1.8$

9. Create an array of five sayings:

   "An apple a day keeps the doctor away"
   "Procrastination is the thief of time"
   "The early bird catches the worm"
   "Handsome is as handsome does"
   "Too many cooks spoil the broth"

   Each time you run your script, a random saying will be printed. Hint: the index of the array will hold a random number.

10. What's wrong with this statement?

```
$x = 5;
$y = 13;
$z = 3;
print  ($x + $y) / $z;
```

   Turn on warnings. What is the meaning of the warning?

11. The following formula is used to calculate the fixed monthly payment required to fully amortize a loan over a term of months at a monthly interest rate. Write a Perl expression to represent the following formula where: *P* = principal amount borrowed, *r* = periodic interest rate (annual interest rate divided by 12), *n* = total number of payments (for a 30-year loan with monthly payments, *n* = 30 years × 12 months = 360), and *A* = periodic payment.

$$P = A \cdot \frac{1 - \dfrac{1}{(1 + r)^n}}{r}$$

12. At the start of this chapter, there was an example that calculates whether or not this is a leap year. In your browser's search box, type the following:

   How do I determine a leap year--Perl monks

   You can download their example and test it. The Perl monks are devoted to answering questions related to Perl and offer many solutions.

chapter

7

If Only, Unconditionally, Forever

By the end of this chapter, you will be able to read and write the following Perl code:

```perl
use warnings;
use feature qw(say);
my %guests=("Joe"=>"pizza",
            "Medhi"=>"veggies",
            "Dat"=>"rice",
            "Vipul"=>"meat",
            "Anna"=>"sandwiches",
            "Peter"=>"dessert",
            );
my $place="Golden Gate Park";
my $when = "Tomorrow, noon";
foreach (keys %guests){
    if ($_ eq "Anna"){ next; }
    my $message=<<EOF;
    Hello, $_. Please join me at the $place at $when for
    a picnic. You will bring $guests{$_} and I'll bring
    the drinks. RSPV if you can't make it.
    Later,
    ellieq\@gamil.edu
EOF
    say $message;
}
```

7.1 Control Structures, Blocks, and Compound Statements

People plan their lives by making decisions, and so do programs. Figure 7.1 is a flow chart. A flow chart is defined as a pictorial representation of how to plan the stages of a program. It helps you to visualize what decisions need to be made to accomplish a task. According to computer science books, a good language allows you to control the flow of your program in three ways:

- Execute a sequence of statements.
- Based on the results of a test, branch to an alternative sequence of statements.
- Repeat a sequence of statements until some condition is met.

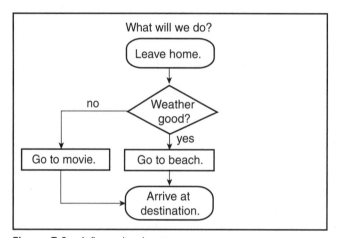

Figure 7.1   A flow chart.

So far, we have seen script examples that are linear in structure; that is, simple statements that are executed in sequence, one after the other. Control structures, such as branching and looping statements, allow the flow of the program's control to change depending on some conditional expression.

The decision-making constructs (*if, if/else, if/elsif/else, unless,* and so forth) contain a control expression that determines whether a block of statements will be executed.

The looping constructs (*while, until, for, foreach*) allow the program to repetitively execute a statement block until some condition is satisfied.

A compound statement, or block, consists of a group of statements surrounded by curly braces and usually follows an *if, else, while,* or *for* construct. But unlike C, where curly braces are not always required, Perl requires them, even with one statement when that statement comes after the *if, else, while,* and so forth. The conditional modifiers, discussed in Chapter 8, "Regular Expressions—Pattern Matching," can be used when a condition is evaluated within a **single** statement.

7.1.1   Decision Making—Conditional Constructs

if and *unless* Statements.   The *if* and *unless* constructs are followed by an expression surrounded by parentheses and followed by a block of one more statements. The block of statements are always enclosed in curly braces.

An *if* statement is a conditional statement. It allows you to test an expression and, based on the results of the test, make a decision. The expression is enclosed in parentheses and Perl evaluates the expression in a string context. If the string is not empty, the expression is true; otherwise, the expression is false. If the expression is evaluated to be true, the next statement block is executed; if the condition is false, Perl will skip the block associated with the expression and go on to the next executable statement within the script.

The *unless* statement is constructed exactly the same as the *if* statement; the results of the test are simply reversed. If the expression is evaluated to be false, the next statement block is executed; if the expression is evaluated to be true, Perl will ignore the block of statements controlled by the expression.

The *if* Construct.   The *if* statement consists of the keyword *if*, followed by a conditional expression, followed by a block of one or more statements enclosed in curly braces. Each statement within the block is terminated with a semicolon (;). The block of statements collectively is often called a **compound statement**. Make sure when you are testing strings that you use the string operators shown in Table 6.7, "Equality Operators and String Values," and that if testing numbers, you use the numeric operators also shown in Table 6.6, "Equality Operators and Numeric Values." Perl converts strings and numbers to conform to what the operator expects, so be careful. A test such as *"yes" == "no"* is incorrect. It should be *"yes" eq "no"*.

FORMAT

```
if (Expression) {Block}
if (Expression) {Block} else {Block}
if (Expression) {Block} elsif (Expression)
   {Block}... else {Block}
```

EXAMPLE 7.1

```
(The Script)
  use warnings;
1  print "How old are you? ";
2  chomp(my $age = <STDIN>);
3  if ($age >= 21 ){   # If true, enter the block
4     print "Let's party!\n";
   }
5  print "You said you were $age.\n";
```

EXAMPLE 7.1 (CONTINUED)

```
(Output)
1   How old are you? 32
4   Let's party!
5   You said you were 32.


------------Run the program again-------------
(Output)
1   How old are you? 10
5   You said you were 10.
```

EXPLANATION

1   The user is asked for his age.
2   The scalar $age is assigned a value.
3   The scalar $age is tested. If its value is greater than or equal to 21 (that is, the expression evaluates to true), then the block is entered and line 4 is executed.
4   If the user is older than 21, this line is printed. The curly braces enclosing the block after the *if* are not optional. They are required!
5   Program control continues here whether or not the *if* block was executed.

The *if/else* Construct.   Another form of the *if* statement is the *if/else* construct. This construct allows for a two-way decision. If the first conditional expression following the *if* keyword is true, the block of statements following the *if* are executed. Otherwise, if the conditional expression following the *if* keyword is false, control branches to the *else*, and the block of statements following the *else* are executed. The *else* statement is never an independent statement. It must follow an *if* statement. When the *if* statements are nested within other *if* statements, the *else* statement is associated with the closest previous *if* statement. (Review the ternary operator in Section 6.3.4, "Conditional Operators," for an alternative to a simple *if/else* block.)

FORMAT

```
if (Expression)
    {Block}
else
    {Block}
```

EXAMPLE 7.2

```
(The Script)
    use warnings;
1   print "What version of the operating system are you using? ";
2   chomp(my $os=<STDIN>);
3   if ($os > 2.2) {print "Most of the bugs have been worked out!\n";}
    }
4   else {
        print "Expect some problems.\n";}
    }
```

EXAMPLE 7.2 (CONTINUED)

```
(Output)
1  What version of the operating system are you using?  2.4
3  Most of the bugs have been worked out!

(Output)
1  What version of the operating system are you using?  2.0
4  Expect some problems.
```

EXPLANATION

1   The user is asked for input.
2   The newline is removed.
3   If the value of $os is greater than 2.2, the block enclosed in curly braces is executed. If not, program control goes to the *else* on line 4.
4   If $os is not greater than 2.2, this block is executed.

The *if/elsif/else* Construct.   Yet another form of the *if* statement is the *if/elsif/else* construct. This construct provides a multiway decision structure. If the first conditional expression following the *if* keyword is true, the block of statements following the *if* is executed. Otherwise, the first *elsif* statement is tested. If the conditional expression following the first *elsif* is false, the next *elsif* is tested, and so forth. If all of the conditional expressions following the *elsifs* are false, the block after the *else* is executed; this is the default action.

FORMAT

```
if (Expression1)
    {Block}
elsif (Expression2)
    {Block}
elsif (Expression3)
    {Block}
else
    {Block}
```

EXAMPLE 7.3

```
(The Script)
    use warnings;
1   my $hour=(localtime)[2];
2   if ($hour >= 0 && $hour < 12){print "Good-morning!\n";}
3   elsif ($hour == 12){print "Lunch time.\n";}
4   elsif ($hour > 12 && $hour < 17) {print "Siesta time.\n";}
5   else {print "Goodnight. Sweet dreams.\n";}

(Output)
4   Siesta time
```

EXPLANATION

1   The scalar $hour is set to the current hour. The *localtime* built-in function returns the hour, the third element of the array of time values.

2   The *if* statement tests whether the value of $hour is greater than or equal to *0* and less than *12*. The result of the evaluation is true, so the block following the control expression is executed (that is, the *print* statement is executed).

3   If the first *if* test is false, this expression is tested. If the value of $hour is equal to *12*, the *print* statement is executed.

4   If the previous *elsif* test failed, and this *elsif* expression evaluates to true, the *print* statement will be executed.

5   If none of the above statements is true, the *else* statement, the default action, is executed.

The *unless* Construct.   The *unless* statement is similar to the *if* statement, except that the control expression after the *unless* is tested for the reverse condition; that is, if the conditional expression following the *unless* is false, the statement block is executed.

The *unless/else* and *unless/elsif* behave in the same way as the *if/else* and *if /elsif* statements with the same reversed test as previously stated.

FORMAT

```
unless (Expression) {Block}
unless (Expression) {Block} else {Block}
unless (Expression) {Block} elsif (Expression)
   {Block}... else {Block}
```

EXAMPLE 7.4

```
(The Script)
   use warnings;
1  print "How old are you? ";
2  chomp($age = <STDIN>);
3  unless ($age <= 21 ){  # If false, enter the block
4     print "Let's party!\n";
   }
5  print "You said you were $age.\n";

(Output)
1  How old are you? 32
4  Let's party!
5  You said you were 32.
------------Run the program again-------------
(Output)
1  How old are you? 10
5  You said you were 10.
```

EXPLANATION

1. This example is exactly like Example 7.1 except the logic in the condition is reversed. We will test for false rather than true. The user is asked for his age.
2. The scalar *$age* is assigned a value.
3. The scalar *$age* is tested. Unless its value is less than or equal to *21* (that is, the expression evaluates to false), then the block is entered and line 4 is executed.
4. If the user is not *21* or older, this line is printed. The curly braces enclosing the block after the *if* are not optional. They are required!
5. Program control continues here whether or not the *if* block was executed.

EXAMPLE 7.5

```
(The Script)
   use warnings;
   open(my $fh, "<", "excluder.plx") or die $!;
1  while(<>){
2      ($name, $phone)=split(/:/);
3      unless($name eq "barbara"){
          $record="$name\t$phone";
4          print "$record";
       }
   }
5  print "\n$name has moved from this district.\n";

(Output)
$ perl excluder.plx names
igor chevsky     408-123-4533
paco gutierrez   510-453-2776
ephram hardy     916-235-4455
james ikeda      415-449-0066
barbara kerz     207-398-6755
jose Santiago    408-876-5899
tommy savage     408-876-1725
lizzy stachelin  415-555-1234

barbara has moved from this district.
```

EXPLANATION

1. The *while* loop is entered. It will read one line at a time from whatever filename is given as a command-line argument to this script. The argument file is called *names*.
2. Each line is split by a colon delimiter. The first field is assigned to *$name* and the second field to *$phone*.
3. The *unless* statement is executed. It reads: unless *$name* evaluates to *barbara*, enter the block; in other words, anyone except *barbara* is okay.
4. All names and phones are printed with the exception of *barbara*.
5. When the loop exits, this line is printed.

7.2   Statement Modifiers and Simple Statements

In English, a modifier is an adjective or adverb; for example:

He ran. (without an adverb)

He ran quickly. (with an adverb)

Perl modifiers are like adverbs in that they modify the way a function behaves, and like most adverbs, they are tacked onto the end of a statement. They allow you to evaluate a statement based on some condition, and are simpler to use than the full-blown conditional construct. The modifier and its expression are always terminated with a semicolon. Perl provides the following modifiers. We'll discuss the conditional modifiers now and the loop modifiers later.

- *if*
- *unless*
- *while*
- *until*
- *foreach*

7.2.1   The *if* Modifier

The *if* modifier is used to control a simple statement consisting of two expressions. If *Expression1* is true, *Expression2* is executed. *Expression2* cannot contain multiple statements. If it does, then you will need to use the traditional conditional with a block of statements, such as, *if* (*Expression1*){ *Statement1*; *Statement2*, and so forth }.

FORMAT

```
Expression2 if Expression1;
```

EXAMPLE 7.6

```
(In Script)
1   $x = 5;
2   print $x if $x == 5;

(Output)
5
```

EXPLANATION

1   $x is assigned 5. The value of $x is printed only if $x is equal to 5.
2   The *if* modifier must be placed at the end of a statement and, in this example, controls the *print* function. If the expression $x == 5 is true, then the value of $x is printed. It could be written *if* ($x == 5) {print $x;}.

EXAMPLE 7.7

```
(The Script)
   use warnings;
1  open(my $fh,"datebook") or die;
2  while(<$fh>){
3     (my $name,my $phone)=split(":", $_);
4     print "$phone\n" if $name eq "Betty Boop";
   }
5  close $fh;

(Output)
245-836-8357
```

EXPLANATION

1 *$fh* is a lexical, user-defined filehandle that Perl will use to associate itself with the external *datebook* file. The file is opened for reading.
2 The *while* loop is entered. A line is read from the *datebook* file and implicitly assigned to $_.
3 The line is split up by colons to create two scalars, *$name* and *$phone*.
4 The modifying *if* controls what the print function will display; in this example, the values of *$name* and *$phone* only if *$name* is exactly equal to the string *"Betty Boop"*.

7.2.2 The *unless* Modifier

The *unless* modifier is used to control a simple statement consisting of two expressions. If *Expression1* is false, *Expression2* is executed. Like the *if* modifier, *unless* is placed at the end of the statement.

FORMAT

```
Expression2 unless Expression1;
```

EXAMPLE 7.8

```
(The Script)
1  $x=5;
2  print $x unless $x == 6;

(Output)
5

(The Script)
1  $x=5;
2  print $x unless $x == 6;

(Output)
5
```

EXAMPLE 7.8 (CONTINUED)

```
(The Script)
   use warnings;
1  open(my $fh,"datebook") or die $!;
2  while(<$fh>){
3     (my $name,my $phone)=split(":", $_);
4     print "$phone\n" unless $name eq "Betty Boop";
   }
5  close FH;

(Output)
238-923-7366
385-375-8395
397-857-2735
548-834-2348
408-253-3122
   < more numbers printed here>
```

EXPLANATION

1   This example is exactly like the previous one, except instead of using the *if* modifier, the *unless* modifier is used. The *print* function displays all lines where the name is not *Betty Boop*.

7.3   Repetition with Loops

Sometimes, you may want to repeat a statement or group of statements until some condition is met; for example, continue to ask the user a question until he gives the correct response, or you may want to create a timer that counts down from 10 to 0, or you may want to modify each item in a list, until you reach the end of the list. This is where loops come in. They are used to execute a segment of code repeatedly. Perl's basic looping constructs are as follows:

- *while*
- *until*
- *for*
- *foreach*

Each loop is followed by a block of statements enclosed in curly braces.

7.3.1   The *while* Loop

The *while* statement executes the block as long as the control expression after the *while* is true. An expression is true if it evaluates to nonzero (true); *while*(1) is always true and loops forever. An expression is false if it evaluates to zero; *while*(0) is false and never loops. See Figure 7.2.

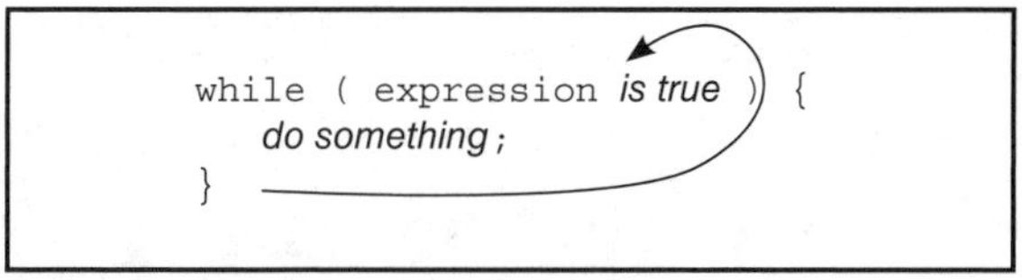

Figure 7.2   How the *while* loop works.

FORMAT

```
while (Expression) {Block}
```

EXAMPLE 7.9

```
(The Script)
   use warnings;
1  my $num=0;             # Initialize $num
2  while ($num < 10){     # Test expression
   # Loop quits when expression is false or 0

3     print "$num ";
4     $num++;   # Update the loop variable $num; increment $num
5  }
6  print "\nOut of the loop.\n";

(Output)
3  0 1 2 3 4 5 6 7 8 9
6  Out of the loop.
```

EXPLANATION

1   The scalar $num is initialized. The initialization takes place before entering the loop.
2   The test expression is evaluated. If the result is true, the block of statements in curly braces is executed.
3   The scalar $num is incremented. If not, the test expression would always yield a true value, and the loop would never end.

EXAMPLE 7.10

```
(The Script)
   use warnings;
   my($count, $beers, $remain, $where);
1  $count=1;        # Initialize variables
   $beers=10;
   $remain=$beers;
   $where="on the shelf";
2  while ($count <= $beers) {
      if ($remain == 1){print "$remain bottle of beer $where ." ;}
      else {print "$remain bottles of beer $where $where .";}
      print " Take one down and pass it all around.\n";
      print "Now ", $beers - $count , " bottles of beer $where!\n";
```

EXAMPLE 7.10 (CONTINUED)

```
3      $count++;
4      $remain--;
5      if ($count > 10){print "Party's over. \n";}
    }
   print "\n";
```

(Output)
10 bottles on the shelf on the shelf. Take one down and pass it all
around.
Now 9 bottles of beer on the shelf!
9 bottles on the shelf on the shelf. Take one down and pass it all around.
Now 8 bottles of beer on the shelf!
8 bottles on the shelf on the shelf. Take one down and pass it all around.
Now 7 bottles of beer on the shelf!
7 bottles on the shelf on the shelf. Take one down and pass it all around.
Now 6 bottles of beer on the shelf!
6 bottles on the shelf on the shelf. Take one down and pass it all around.
Now 5 bottles of beer on the shelf!
5 bottles on the shelf on the shelf. Take one down and pass it all around.
Now 4 bottles of beer on the shelf!
4 bottles on the shelf on the shelf. Take one down and pass it all around.
Now 3 bottles of beer on the shelf!
3 bottles on the shelf on the shelf. Take one down and pass it all around.
Now 2 bottles of beer on the shelf!
2 bottles on the shelf on the shelf. Take one down and pass it all around.
Now 1 bottle of beer on the shelf!
1 bottle of beer on the shelf on the shelf. Take one down and pass it all
around.
Now 0 bottles of beer on the shelf!
Party's over.

EXPLANATION

1   The scalars $count, $beers, $remain, and $where are initialized.
2   The *while* loop is entered; the control expression is tested and evaluated.
3   The scalar $count is incremented.
4   The scalar $remain is decremented.
5   When the value of $count is greater than *10*, this line is printed.

7.3.2   The *until* Loop

The *until* statement executes the block as long as the control expression after the *until* is false. When the expression evaluates to true, the loop exits. See Figure 7.3.

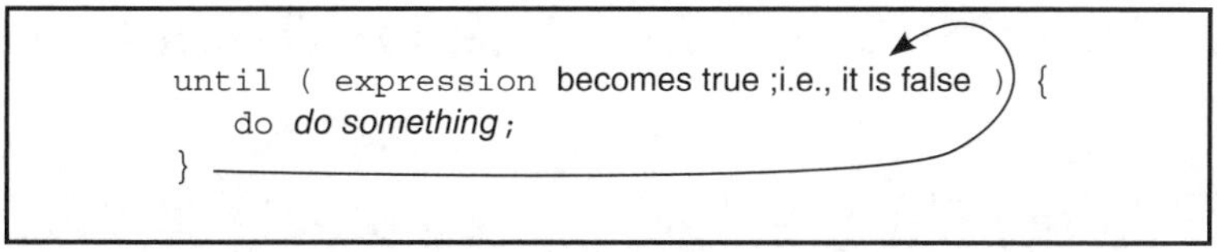

Figure 7.3 How the *until* loop works.

FORMAT

```
until (Expression) {Block}
```

EXAMPLE 7.11

```
(The Script)
    use warnings;
1   $num=0;        # initialize
2   until ($num == 10){
         # Test expression; loop quits when expression is true or 1
3        print "$num ";
4        $num++;    # Update the loop variable $num; increment $num
5   }
6   print "\nOut of the loop.\n";

(Output)
3   0 1 2 3 4 5 6 7 8 9
6   Out of the loop.
```

EXPLANATION

1   The scalar *$num* is initialized. The initialization takes place before entering the loop.
2   The test expression is evaluated. If the result is false, the block of statements in curly braces is executed. When *$num* is equal to *10*, the loop exits.
3   The scalar *$num* is incremented. If not, the test expression would always yield a false value and the loop would never end.

EXAMPLE 7.12

```
(The Script)
    use warnings;
1   print "Are you o.k.? ";
2   chomp($answer=<STDIN>);
3   until ($answer eq "yes"){
4       sleep(1);
5       print "Are you o.k. yet? ";
6       chomp($answer=<STDIN>);
7   }
8   print "Glad to hear it!\n";
```

EXAMPLE 7.12 (CONTINUED)

```
(Output)
1   Are you o.k.? n
1   Are you o.k. yet? nope
1   Are you o.k. yet? yup
1   Are you o.k. yet? yes
8   Glad to hear it!
```

EXPLANATION

1   The user is asked an initial question.
2   The user's response is taken from standard input and stored in the scalar *$answer*. The newline is *chomped*.
3   The *until* loop checks the expression enclosed in parentheses, and if the value of *$answer* is not exactly equal to the string *yes*, the block following the expression will be entered. When *$answer* evaluates to *yes*, the loop exits and control begins at line 8.
4   If the value of *$answer* is not equal to *yes*, this line will be executed; in other words, the program will pause for one minute (*sleep 1*). This gives the user time before being asked the question again.
5   The user is asked again if he is okay.
6   The user's response is read again from *STDIN* and stored in *$answer*. This line is very important. If the value of *$answer* never changes, the loop will go on forever.
7   The closing curly brace marks the end of the block connected to the *until* loop. Control will return to line 3 and the expression will be tested again. If the value of *$answer* is *yes*, control will go to line 8; otherwise, the statements in the block will be reexecuted.
8   When the loop exits, this line is executed; in other words, when the value of *$answer* is equal to *yes*.

7.3.3 The *do/while* and *do/until* Loops

The *do/while* or *do/until* loops evaluate the conditional expression for true and false just as in the *while* and *until* loop statements. However, the expression is not evaluated until after the block is executed at least once.

FORMAT

```
do {Block} while (Expression);
do {Block} until (Expression);
```

EXAMPLE 7.13

```
(The Script)
   use warnings;
1  my $x = 1;
2  do {
3     print "$x ";
4     $x++;
5  } while ($x <= 10); # Test after the do block has executed
   print "\n";

6  $y = 1;
7  do {
8     print "$y " ;
9     $y++;
10 } until ($y > 10);
```

```
(Output)
3    1 2 3 4 5 6 7 8 9 10
8    1 2 3 4 5 6 7 8 9 10
```

EXPLANATION

1 The scalar $x is assigned the value 1.
2 The *do/while* loop statement starts.
3 The block of statements is executed before the expression within the *while* loop is tested.
4 The scalar $x is incremented once.
5 The conditional expression following the *while* is evaluated. If true, the block of statements is executed again, and so on.
6 The scalar $y is assigned the value 1.
7 The *do/until* loop statement starts.
8 The block of statements is executed.
9 The scalar $y is incremented once.
10 The conditional expression following the *until* is evaluated. If false, the block of statements is executed again, and so on.

EXAMPLE 7.14

```
    use warnings;
1   my  $n=0;
2   do {
3     print $n++ == 0?"Anybody out there? ": "Anybody out there yet?";
      chomp($input = <STDIN>);
4     $input = lc $input;
5     sleep 1;
6   } until ( $input eq "yes" );
    print "Welcome home!\n";
```

```
(Output)
Anybody out there? No
Anybody out there yet? not yet
Anybody out there yet? yup
Anybody out there yet? Yes
Welcome home!
```

EXPLANATION

1   Initialize $n to zero.

2–5   The first time in the loop, $n will evaluate to zero and the program prints *Anybody out there?*. Because this is a post increment ++, $n will be incremented **after** it is evaluated, and thereafter $n will be greater than 0, *Anybody out there* **yet?** will be displayed until the value of *$input* equals the string *yes*. The builtin sleep function causes the program to pause for one second.

6   The expression in the until loop is tested and if it tests false, the do block will be executed again.

7.3.4 The *for* Loop (The Three-Part Loop)

The *for* statement is like the *for* loop in C. The *for* keyword is followed by three expressions separated by semicolons and enclosed within parentheses. You can omit any or all of the expressions, but not the two semicolons. The first expression is used to set the initial value of variables, the second expression is used to test whether the loop should continue or stop, and the third expression updates the loop variables. See Figure 7.4.

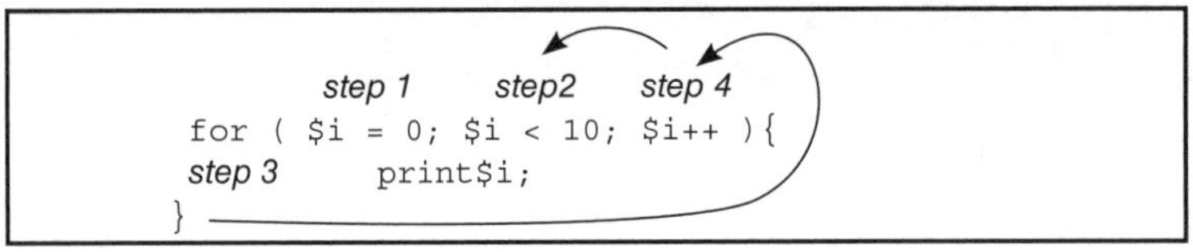

Figure 7.4 How the three-part *for* loop works.

FORMAT

```
for (Expression1;Expression2;Expression3) {Block}
```

The above format is equivalent to the following *while* statement:

```
Expression1;
while (Expression2)
   {Block; Expression3};
```

EXAMPLE 7.15

```
(The Script)
   use warnings;
1  for (my $i=0; $i<10; $i++){    # Initialize, test, and increment $i
2    print "$i ";
   }
3  print "\nOut of the loop.\n";

(Output)
2  0 1 2 3 4 5 6 7 8 9
3  Out of the loop.
```

EXPLANATION

1   The *for* loop contains three expressions. In the first expression, the scalar $i is assigned the value *0*. This statement is executed just once. The second expression tests whether $i is less than *10*, and if so, the block statements are executed (that is, the value of $i is printed). The last expression increments the value of $i by 1. The second expression is again tested, and the block is executed, $i is incremented, and so on, until the test evaluates to false.

2   The value of $i is printed each time through the loop.

EXAMPLE 7.16

```
(The Script)
   use warnings;
   # Initialization, test, and increment, decrement of
   # counters is done in one step.
1  for (my $count=1, my $beers=10,  my $remain=$beers,
       my $where="on the shelf";
       $count <= $beers; $count++, $remain--)
       {
2      if ($remain == 1){
          print "$remain bottle of beer $where $where " ;
       }
       else {
          print "$remain bottles of beer $where $where.";
       }
       print " Take one down and pass it all around.\n";
       print "Now ", $beers - $count , " bottles of beer $where!\n";
3      if ($count == 10 ){print "Party's over.\n";}
   }
```

EXAMPLE 7.16 (CONTINUED)

```
(Output)
10 bottles of beer on the shelf on the shelf. Take one down and pass it
all around.
Now 9 bottles of beer on the shelf!
9 bottles of beer on the shelf on the shelf. Take one down and pass it all
around.
Now 8 bottles of beer on the shelf!
8 bottles of beer on the shelf on the shelf. Take one down and pass it all
around.
Now 7 bottles of beer on the shelf!


  < continues >


2 bottles of beer on the shelf on the shelf. Take one down and pass it all
around.
Now 1 bottle of beer on the shelf!
1 bottle of beer on the shelf on the shelf. Take one down and pass it all
around.
Now 0 bottles of beer on the shelf!
Party's over.
```

EXPLANATION

1   The initialization of all scalars is done in the first expression of the *for* loop. Each initialization is separated by a comma, and the expression is terminated with a semicolon. The first expression is executed only once, when the loop starts. The second expression is the test. If it evaluates to true, the statements in the block are executed. After the last statement in the block is executed, the third expression is evaluated. The control is then passed to the second expression in the *for* loop, and so on.

2   The block is executed if the second expression in the *for* loop is evaluated as true.

3   This statement will be tested and, if the condition is true, the statement will be executed and control will go to the third expression within the *for* loop, incrementing *$count* for the last time.

7.3.5   The *foreach* (*for*) Loop

If you need to iterate through an array or hash such as a list of files, IP or email addresses, keys, values from a hash, and so forth, then the *foreach* loop, as its name implies, is a control structure designed just for you.

The *foreach* loop (a synonym for *for*) iterates over each element in the parenthesized list or an array, aliasing each element of the list to a scalar variable, one after the other, until the end of the list.

The *VARIABLE* is local to the *foreach* block. It will regain its former value when the loop is exited. Any changes made when assigning values to *VARIABLE* will, in turn, affect the individual elements of the array. If *VARIABLE* is not present, the $_ special scalar variable is implicitly used.

FORMAT

```
foreach VARIABLE (LIST) {BLOCK}
for (LIST) {BLOCK}
```

EXAMPLE 7.17

```
(The Script)
    use warnings;
1   foreach my $pal ('Tom', 'Dick', 'Harry', 'Pete') {
2       print "Hi $pal!\n";
    }

(Output)
2   Hi Tom!
    Hi Dick!
    Hi Harry!
    Hi Pete!
```

EXPLANATION

1   The *foreach* is followed by the scalar *$pal* and a list of names. *$pal* points to each name in the list, starting with *Tom*. You can think of *$pal* as an alias, or reference, for each item in the list. Each time the loop is entered, *$pal* goes to the next item in the list and gets that value. So, for example, after *Tom*, *Dick* is fetched, then *Harry*, and so on until all list items have been used, at which time the loop exits.

2   Each time through the loop, the value referenced by *$pal* is printed. (See Figure 7.5.)

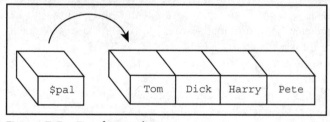

Figure 7.5 The *foreach* loop.

EXAMPLE 7.18

```
(The Script)
    use warnings;
1   foreach my $hour (1 .. 24){  # The range operator is used here
2       if ($hour > 0 && $hour < 12) {print "Good-morning.\n";}
3       elsif ($hour == 12) {print "Happy Lunch.\n";}
4       elsif ($hour > 12 && $hour < 17) {print "Good afternoon.\n";}
5       else {print "Good-night.\n";}
    }
```

EXAMPLE 7.18 (CONTINUED)

```
(Output)
2  Good-morning.
   Good-morning.
   Good-morning.
   Good-morning.
   Good-morning.
   Good-morning.
   Good-morning.
   Good-morning.
   Good-morning.
   Good-morning.
   Good-morning.
3  Happy Lunch.
4  Good afternoon.
   Good afternoon.
   Good afternoon.
   Good afternoon.
5  Good-night.
   Good-night.
   Good-night.
   Good-night.
   Good-night.
   Good-night.
   Good-night.
   Good-night.
```

EXPLANATION

1   The list *(1 .. 24)* is a range of list items starting with *1* and ending with 24. Each of those values is referenced in turn by the scalar *$hour*. The block is executed, and the next item in the list is assigned to *$hour*, and so on.

2   The scalar *$hour* is tested, and if the value is greater than *0* and less than *12*, the *print* statement is executed.

3   If the previous *elsif* statement is false, this statement is tested. If the scalar *$hour* is equal to *12*, the *print* statement is executed.

4   If the previous *elsif* statement is false, this statement is tested. If the scalar *$hour* is greater than *12* and less than *17*, the *print* statement is executed.

5   If all of the previous statements are false, the *else,* or default statement, is executed.

EXAMPLE 7.19

```
(The Script)
   use warnings;
1  my $val="hello";
2  my @numbers = (1, 3, 5, 7, 9);
3  print "The scalar \$val is initially $val.\n";
4  print "The array \@numbers is initially @numbers.\n";

5  foreach $val (@numbers ){
6     $val+=5;
7     print "$val\n";
8  }
9  print "Out of the loop--\$val is $val.\n";
10 print "Out of the loop--The array \@numbers is now @numbers.\n";

(Output)
3  The scalar $val is initially hello.
4  The array @numbers is initially 1 3 5 7 9.
7  6
   8
   10
   12
   14
9  Out of the loop--$val is hello.
10 Out of the loop--The array @numbers is now 6 8 10 12 14.
```

EXPLANATION

1   The scalar $val is assigned the string *hello*.
2   The array *@numbers* is assigned the list of numbers: *1, 3, 5, 7,* and *9*.
3   The *print* function prints the initial value of *$val* to *STDOUT*.
4   The *print* function prints the initial value of *@numbers* to *STDOUT*.
5   The *foreach* statement assigns, in turn, each element in the list to *$val*. The variable *$val* is local to the loop and references each item in the list so that whatever is done to *$val* will affect the array *@numbers*. When the loop exits, *$val* will regain its former value.
6   Each time through the loop, the value referenced by *$val* is incremented by 5.
7   The *print* function prints the new value of *$val* to *STDOUT*.
8   After exiting the loop, the original value of *$val* is printed to *STDOUT*.
9   After exiting the loop, the new and modified values of the *@number* array are printed to *STDOUT*.

EXAMPLE 7.20

```
(The Script)
   use warnings;
1  my @colors=("red", "green", "blue", "brown");
2  for (@colors) {
3     print "$_ ";
4     $_="YUCKY";      # Don't assign
   }
5  print "\n@colors\n";

(Output)
3  red green blue brown
5  YUCKY  YUCKY  YUCKY  YUCKY
```

EXPLANATION

1   The array @colors is initialized.

2   The foreach loop is not followed by an explicit variable, but it does have a list. Since the variable is missing, the $_ special scalar is used implicitly.

3   $_ is really a reference to the item in the list that is currently being evaluated. As each item of the list @colors is referenced by the $_ variable, the value is printed to STDOUT.

4   The $_ variable is assigned the string YUCKY. Each original element in the array @colors will be replaced permanently by the value YUCKY, in turn.

5   The @color array has really been changed. The $_ variable is null, its value before entering the loop. Moral to the story: when looping through a named array, don't assign values to the loop variable, as it will modify the original array.

7.4   Looping Modifiers

In this section we will discuss looping modifiers and various control statements you can use for increased file manipulation.

7.4.1   The *while* Modifier

The *while* modifier repeatedly executes the second expression as long as the first expression is true.

FORMAT

```
Expression2 while Expression1
```

EXAMPLE 7.21

```
(The Script)
1  $x=1;
2  print $x++,"\n" while $x != 5;

(Output)
1
2
3
4
```

EXPLANATION

Perl prints the value of x while x is not 5.

FORMAT

```
Expression2 until Expression1;
```

EXAMPLE 7.22

```
(The Script)
1  $x=1;
2  print $x++,"\n" until $x == 5;

(Output)
1
2
3
4
```

EXPLANATION

1   x is assigned an initial value of *1*.
2   Perl prints the value of x until x is equal to 5. The variable x is set to *1* and then incremented. Be careful that you don't get yourself into an infinite loop.

7.4.2   The *foreach* Modifier

The *foreach* modifier evaluates once for each element in its list, with $_ aliased to each element of the list, in turn.

EXAMPLE 7.23

```
(The Script)
1  my @alpha=("a" .. "z", "\n");
2  print foreach @alpha;

(Output)
abcdefghijklmnopqrstuvwxyz
```

EXPLANATION

1   A list of lowercase letters is assigned to array *@alpha*.
2   Each item in the list is aliased to $_ and printed, one at a time, until there are no more items in the list. Could also say: *print for @alpha;*

7.4.3   Loop Control

To interrupt the normal flow of control within a loop, Perl provides labels and simple control statements. These statements are used for controlling a loop when some condition is reached; that is, the control is transferred directly to either the bottom or the top of the loop, skipping any statements that follow the control statement condition.

Labels.   Labels are optional but you can use them to control the flow of a loop. (Note that you can attach them to any statement, not just loops.) By themselves, labels do nothing. They are used with the loop control modifiers, listed next. A block by itself, whether or not it has a label, is equivalent to a loop that executes only **once**. If labels are capitalized, they will not be confused with reserved words.

EXAMPLE 7.24

```
LABEL: while (Expression){Block}
LABEL: while (Expression) {Block} continue{Block}
LABEL: for (Expression; Expression; Expression)
   {BLOCK}
LABEL: foreach Variable (Array){Block}
LABEL: {Block} continue {Block}
```

To control the flow of loops, the following simple statements may be used within the block:

```
next next LABEL
last
last LABEL
redo
redo LABEL
goto LABEL
```

The *next* statement restarts the next iteration of the loop, skipping over the rest of the statements in the loop and reevaluating the loop expression, like a *C, awk,* or shell *continue* statement. Since a block is a loop that iterates once, you can use *next* (with a *continue* block, if provided) to exit the block early.

The *last* statement leaves or breaks out of a loop and is like the *break* statement in *C, awk,* and shell. Since a block is a loop that iterates once, you can use *last* to break out of a block.

The *redo* statement restarts the block without evaluating the loop expression again.

The *continue* block is executed just before the conditional expression is about to be evaluated again.

The *goto* statement, although frowned upon by most programmers, is allowed in Perl programs. It takes a label as its argument and jumps to the label when the *goto* statement is executed. The label can be anywhere in your script but does not work when it appears inside a *do* statement or within a subroutine.

The *redo* and *goto* Statements.   A block is like a loop that executes once. You can label a block. The *redo* statement causes control to start at the top of the innermost or labeled block without reevaluating the loop expression if there is one (similar to a *goto*). The *goto* finds the label and resumes execution at that point. It can go almost anywhere within the script scope, including getting out of subroutines.

EXAMPLE 7.25

```
(The Script)
    use warnings;
    # Program that uses a label without a loop and the redo statement
1   ATTEMPT: {
2      print "Are you a great person? ";
       chomp(my $answer = <STDIN>);
       $answer = lc $answer;    # Convert to lowercase
3      unless ($answer eq "yes"){redo ATTEMPT ;}
       else{ goto BYE; }  # go to the label
    }
4   print "I'm here \n";

5   BYE: { print "Branched here\n"; }
    }

(Output)
2  Are you a great person? Nope
2  Are you a great person? Sometimes
2  Are you a great person? Yes
5  Branched here
```

EXPLANATION

1   The label is user-defined. It precedes a block. It is as though you had named the block *ATTEMPT*.
2   The user is asked for input.
3   The *redo* statement restarts the block unless the *$answer* evaluates to *yes*.
4   This statement will not be executed because the *goto* will cause the program to branch to the *BYE* label.

EXAMPLE 7.26

```
(The Script)
   use warnings;
1  while(1){   # start an infinite loop

2     print "What was your grade? ";
      my $grade = <STDIN>;

3     if ($grade < 0 || $grade > 100) {
         print "Illegal choice\n";
4        next; }    # start control at the beginning of
                    # the innermost loop; i.e. line 1
5     if($grade  > 89 && $grade < 101) {print "A\n";}
      elsif($grade > 79 && $grade < 90) {print "B\n";}
      elsif($grade > 69 && $grade < 80) {print "C\n";}
      elsif($grade > 59 && $grade < 70) {print "D\n";}
      else{print "You Failed."};
6     print "Do you want to enter another grade? (y/n) ";
      chomp(my $choice = <STDIN>);
7     if($choice ne "y"){last ;}   # break out of the innermost
                                   # loop if the condition is true; i.e.,
                                   # break out of the while loop, line 1

   }


(Output)
2  What was your grade? 94
   A
6  Do you want to enter another grade (y/n)?  y
2  What was your grade? 66
   D
6  Do you want to enter another grade (y/n)?  n
```

EXPLANATION

1   Start an infinite loop.
2   Ask for user input.
3   Logical test. If the value of *$grade* is less than *0* or greater than *100*.
4   If the test yields *false*, control starts again at the beginning of the *while* loop.
5   Test each of the *if* conditional statements.
6   Ask for user input.
7   Break out of the innermost loop if the conditional tests true.

EXAMPLE 7.27

```
(The Script)
    use warnings;
    my( %department, $course, $answer, $number, $key );
    %department=();   # Declare and empty hash
1   ATTEMPT:{
2       print "What is the course number? ";
        chomp($number = <STDIN>);
        print "What is the course name? ";
        chomp($course = <STDIN>);

3       $department{$number} = $course;

        print "\nReady to quit? ";
        chomp($answer = <STDIN>);
        $answer=lc($answer);   # Convert to lowercase
4       if ($answer eq  "yes" or $answer eq "y") {last;}
5       redo ATTEMPT;
    }
        # Out of block, program continues
6   foreach $key (keys %department){
        printf "%-6s%-s\n", $key, $department{$key};
    }
```

```
(Output)
2   What is the course number? 101
    What is the course name?  CIS342
3   Ready to quit? n
2   What is the course number? 201
    What is the course name? BIO211
3   Ready to quit? n
2   What is the course number? 301
    What is the course name? ENG120
3   Ready to quit? yes
6   201    BIO211
    101    CIS342
    301    ENG120
```

EXPLANATION

1   The label *ATTEMPT* prepends the block. A block without a looping construct is like a loop that executes only once.

2   The script gets user input in order to fill an associative array. Both the key and value are provided by the user.

3   The hash *%department* is assigned a value.

4   If the user is ready to quit, the *last* statement sends the control out of the block.

5   The *redo* statement returns control to the top of the labeled block at the opening curly brace. Each of the statements is executed again.

6   After breaking out of the block with the *last* statement (line 4), the program continues. The *foreach* loop iterates through the *%department* hash so that we can print out each key and value that was entered by the user. (Remember, hashes are unordered lists of key/value pairs.)

Nested Loops and Labels.   A loop within a loop is a **nested loop**. The outside loop is initialized and tested, the inside loop then iterates completely through all of its cycles, and the outside loop starts again where it left off. The inside loop moves faster than the outside loop.

EXAMPLE 7.28

```
(The Script)
    use warnings;
1   for (my $rows=5; $rows>=1; $rows--){
2       for (my $columns=1; $columns<=$rows; $columns++){
3           printf "*";
4       }
5       print "\n";
6   }

(Output)
3   *****
    ****
    ***
    **
    *
```

EXPLANATION

1   The first expression in the outside loop initializes the scalar *$rows* to 5. The variable is tested. Since it is greater than or equal to *1*, the inner loop starts.

2   The first expression in the inner loop initializes the scalar *$columns* to 1. The scalar *$columns* is tested. The inner loop will iterate through all of its cycles. When the inner loop has completed, the outer loop will pick up where it left off; that is, *$rows* will be decremented, then tested, and if true, the block will be executed again, and so on.

3   This statement belongs to the inner *for* loop and is executed for each iteration of the loop.

4   This curly brace closes the inner *for* loop.

5   The *print* statement is executed for each iteration of the outer *for* loop.

6   This curly brace closes the outer *for* loop.

EXAMPLE 7.29

```
      # use warnings;  # Suppress warnings for this example
      # Program to get the average of a list of grades
      # Checks that grades are valid in a nested loop
      my($grades, @listofgrades, $grade, $sum, @valid);
      print "Give me a list of grades from 0 to 100: ";
1     chomp($grades=<STDIN>);
2     @listofgrades=split(" ", $grades);  # Get grades from user
      $sum=0;  # Initialize variable
3     foreach $grade (@listofgrades){  # Go through each grade
4       while(($grade ne "0"&& $grade == 0)||($grade < 0||$grade > 100)){
              # test validity
              print STDERR "$grade is an invalid grade\n";
              print "Give me another grade: ";
              chomp($grade=<STDIN>);
        } # End of inner while loop
5       push(@valid, $grade);  # Make a new list with valid grades
6       $sum+=$grade; # Add the value of $grade to $sum each time
      }   # Exit outer foreach loop
      print "@valid\n";
7     printf "The average is %d.\n", $sum/scalar @valid; # get the average

(Output)
Give me a list of grades from 0 to 100: A 75 100 -6 99 102 88
A is an invalid grade
Give me another grade: 99
-6 is an invalid grade
Give me another grade: 77
102 is an invalid grade
Give me another grade: 66
99 75 100 77 99 66 88
The average is 86
```

EXPLANATION

1   The user is asked for a list of grades ranging from *0* to *100*, each one separated by a space. The list will be stored as a string in the scalar, *$grade*.

2   The *split* function will split the scalar, *$grades*, by whitespace and return an array called *@listofgrades*.

3   The *foreach* loop will iterate through each grade in the list, one at a time until it reaches the end of the list.

4   The inner *while* loop will be used to test the validity of each grade coming from the *foreach* loop. If the user enters a letter, such as "A" or string such as "Passing" for a grade, or a grade with a value of less than 0 or greater than 100, the *while* loop block will be entered and an error will be sent to standard error (the screen). Then the user can enter another grade, which will also be tested. The loop will not exit until he enters a grade that passes the validity test.

5   If the grade is valid, it will pushed onto the *@valid* array.

6   The value of the grade is added to *$sum* each time through the loop.

7   The average of all the grades is calculated by dividing the number of grades (scalar *@grades*) by the sum of the all the grades (*$sum*).

You can nest loops as deeply as you wish, but there are times when it is necessary to terminate the loop when some condition is met. Normally, if you use loop-control statements, such as *next* and *last*, the control is directed to the innermost loop. There are times when it might be necessary to switch control to some outer loop. This is accomplished by using labels.

By prefixing a loop with a label, you can control the flow of the program with *last, next,* and *redo* statements. Labeling a loop is like giving the loop its own name.

When a label is omitted, the loop-control statements *next, last,* and *redo,* reference the innermost loop. When branching out of a nested loop to an outer loop, labels may precede the loop statement.

EXAMPLE 7.30

```
(A Demo Script)
1  OUT: while(1){
2      < Program continues here >
3      MID: while(1){
4          if (<expression is true>) {last OUT;}
           < Program continues here >
5          INNER: while(1){
6              if (<expression is true>) {next OUT;}
               <Program continues here>
           }
       }
   }
7  print "Out of all loops.\n";
```

EXPLANATION

1 The *OUT* label is used to control this infinite *while* loop, if necessary. The label is followed by a colon and the loop statement.
2 The program code continues here.
3 The *MID* label is used to control this inner *while* loop, if necessary.
4 If the expression being evaluated is true, the *last* loop-control statement is executed, breaking from this loop, labeled *OUT*, all the way out to line 7.
5 The innermost *while* loop is labeled *INNER*.
6 This time, the *next* statement with the *OUT* label causes loop control to branch back to line 1.
7 This statement is outside all of the loops and is where the *last* statement branches, if given the *OUT* label.

The *continue* Statement.   When followed by a block, the *continue* statement acts as a flow-control statement. When a *continue* block is attached to the end of a *while* or *foreach* block, it is always executed just before the loop conditional is about to be evaluated again, just like the third part of a *for* loop, and even if there is a *next* statement within the loop, control will go to the *continue* block before re-evaluating the loop condition again.

EXAMPLE 7.31

```
(The Script)
    # Example using the continue block
1   for (my $i=1; $i<=10; $i++) {        # $i is incremented only once
2       if ($i==5){
3           print "\$i == $i\n";
4           next;
        }
5       print "$i ";
    }


    print "\n"; print '=' x 35; print "\n";
# ------------------------------------------------------------

6   my $i=1;
7   while ($i <= 10){
8       if ($i==5){
            print "\$i == $i\n";
9           $i++;       # $i must be incremented here or an
                        # infinite loop will start
10          next;
        }
11      print "$i ";
12      $i++;           # $i is incremented again
    }


    print "\n"; print '=' x 35; print "\n";
    # --------------------------------------------------------
    # The continue block allows the while loop to act like a for loop
    my    $i=1;
13  while ($i <= 10) {
14      if ($i == 5) {
15          print "\$i == $i\n";
16          next;       # control goes to line 18
        }
17      print "$i ";
18  }continue {$i++; }      # $i is incremented only once

(Output)
1 2 3 4 $i == 5
6 7 8 9 10
=================================
1 2 3 4 $i == 5
6 7 8 9 10
=================================
1 2 3 4 $i == 5
6 7 8 9 10
```

EXPLANATION

1   The *for* loop is entered and will loop 10 times.
2   If the value of $i is 5, the block is entered and . . .
3   . . . the value of $i is printed.
4   The *next* statement returns control back to the *for* loop. When control is returned to the *for* loop, the third expression is always evaluated before the second expression is tested. **Before** the second expression is tested, $i is incremented.
5   Each time through the loop, the value of $i is printed unless $i equals 5.
6    $i is initialized to 5.
7   The body of the *while* loop is entered if the expression tested is true.
8   If $i is equal to 5, the value of $i is displayed.
9    $i is incremented by 1. If the $i is not incremented here, it will never be incremented and the program will go into an infinite loop.
10   The *next* statement causes control to start again at the top of the *while* loop, where the expression after *while* is evaluated.
11   The current value of $i is displayed.
12   After $i is incremented, control will go back to the top of the *while* loop and the expression will be tested again.
13   While $i is less than or equal to *10*, enter the loop body.
14   If $i is equal to 5, the block is entered.
15   The current value of $i is displayed.
16   The *next* statement normally causes control to go back to the top of the *while* loop, but because there is a *continue* block at the end of the loop, control will go into the *continue* block first and then back to the top of the *while* loop where the expression will be tested.
17   The value of $i is displayed.
18   The *continue* block is executed at the end of the *while* loop block, before the *next* statement returns control to the top of the loop or, if *next* is not executed, after the last statement in the loop block.

7.4.4 The *switch* Statement (*given/when*)

A *switch* statement is another type of control statement similar to *if/elsif/else* but evaluates an expression by matching the expression to a set of case labels. When a match is found, program control is transferred to that block where the expression matched the label value.

A *switch* statement in the *C* language, Java, *PHP*, and so forth, is designed like so:

```
switch (expression) {
    case value1 :
        /* statements */
        break;
    case value2 :
        /* statements */
        break;
    case value3 :
        /* statements */
        break;
    default:
        /* statements */
        break;
}
```

Although the *switch/case* mechanism is a common control structure provided by most modern programming languages, it is **not** available in core Perl. You can achieve the same goal in Perl with the traditional *if/elsif/else* constructs or by creating labeled blocks, as shown next. Since a block (labeled or not) is equivalent to a loop that executes once, and you can use loop control statements, such as *last*, *next*, and *redo*, within this block, you can create a phony *switch* statement by adding a *do* block, which will execute a sequence of commands within the block (see Example 7.32). Since 5.10.1, the experimental feature from Perl 6 is available enabling a whole new way of creating a *switch*-style statement with new Perl constructs: *given* and *when* (see Examples 7.33 and 7.34).

EXAMPLE 7.32

```
(The Script)
1   my  $hour=0;
2   while($hour < 24) {
3       SWITCH: {        # SWITCH is just a user-defined label
4           $hour < 12                  && do { print "Good-morning!\n";
5                                                last SWITCH;};

6           $hour == 12                 && do { print "Lunch!\n";
                                                last SWITCH;};

7           $hour > 12 && $hour <= 17   && do { print "Siesta time!\n";
                                                last SWITCH;};

8           $hour > 17                  && do { print "Good night.\n";
                                                last SWITCH;};
        } # End of block labeled SWITCH

9       $hour++;
    } # End of loop block
```

EXAMPLE 7.32 (CONTINUED)

```
(Output)
Good-morning!
Good-morning!
Good-morning!

<Output continues>

Good-morning!
Good-morning!
Good-morning!
Lunch!
Siesta time!
Siesta time!
Siesta time!
Siesta time!
Siesta time!
Good night.
Good night.
Good night.
Good night.
Good night.
```

EXPLANATION

1　The *$hour* scalar is assigned an initial value of *0* before entering the loop.

2　The *while* loop expression is evaluated.

3　The label *SWITCH* labels the block. It is simply a label, nothing more.

4　After entering the block, the expression is evaluated. The expression reads *if $hour is less than 12...,* the expression on the right of the *&&* is evaluated. This is a *do* block. Each of the statements within this block is executed in sequence. The value of the last statement evaluated is returned.

5　The *last* statement causes control to branch to the end of this block labeled *SWITCH* to line 8.

6　This statement is evaluated if the expression in the previous statement evaluates to false. The expression reads *if $hour is equal to 12...*

7　This statement is evaluated if the expression in the previous statement evaluates to false. The expression reads *if $hour is greater than 12 and also less than or equal to 17...*

8　If this statement is true, the *do* block is executed. The expression reads *if $hour is greater than 17...*

9　The *$hour* scalar is incremented once each time after going through the loop.

The *switch* Feature (*given/when/say*).　Starting with Perl 5.10.1 and beyond, you can use the experimental *switch* feature which enables the Perl 6 *given/when* construct.

```
use feature qw(switch);
```

You also get the *switch* feature whenever you declare that your code prefers to run under a version of Perl that is 5.10.1 or later. For example:

```
use v5.10.1;
```

The Perl 5 version 18.0 documentation says:

Under the "switch" feature, Perl gains the experimental keywords *given*, *when*, *default*, *continue*, and *break*. Starting from Perl 5.18, you can prefix the *switch* keywords with *CORE::* to access a feature without including the *use* feature. In the following example, each feature is prefixed with the *CORE::* label:

```
CORE::given ( some_variable) {
CORE::when( /abc/) { statements }
```

(The *CORE* namespace gives you access to the original built-in functions of Perl. For more on *CORE*, see *http://perldoc.perl.org/CORE.html*.)

The code in Example 7.33 can be rewritten as shown in Example 7.34.

EXAMPLE 7.33

```
1  use v5.10.1;
2  for (1..24){
3     when([1..11]) { say "Morning" }
       when(12) { say "Lunch"}
       when([13..17]) {say "Afternoon"}
4     default {say "Night"}
   }


(Output)
Morning
Morning
Morning
Morning
Morning
Morning
Morning
Morning
Morning
Morning
Morning
Lunch
Afternoon
Afternoon
Afternoon
Afternoon
Afternoon
Night
Night
Night
Night
Night
Night
Night
```

EXPLANATION

1   Use at least v5.10 to implement the *when* feature.
2   The *for* loop will iterate 24 times.

EXAMPLE 7.34

```
1  use feature qw(switch say);

2    my @week=("Sunday",
              "Monday",
              "Tuesday",
              "Wednesday",
              "Thursday",
              "Friday",
              "Saturday");

3    foreach $wday (0..6){
4        $today=$week[$wday];
5        given ($wday) {
6            when([1..5]) { say "$today is Work, work, work" }
             when (6) {say "$today is Play"}
7            default { say "$today is Rest" }
         }
     }
```

(Output)
Sunday is Rest
Monday is Work, work, work
Tuesday is Work, work, work
Wednesday is Work, work, work
Thursday is Work, work, work
Friday is Work, work, work
Saturday is Play

EXPLANATION

1   You must use Perl 5.10.1 or later to run this script. Use the *feature* module to include *switch* and *say*.
2   The array, *@week*, is defined with a list of days of the week.
3   The *foreach* loop iterates through a list of numbers representing days of the week.
4   Each day of the week is assigned in its string format to *$today*; for example, *"Sunday"*.
5   The arguments to *given* and *when* are in scalar context, and *given* assigns the *$_* variable its topic value.
6   The *when* reads: when the given value matches a number in the range of 1 to 5, enter the following block and say what day it is and *Work, work, work*.
7   If none of the *when* expressions match the *given* value, the *default* block is entered, similar to the *else* in an *if/elsif* conditional construct.

7.5   **What You Should Know**

1. What are control structures?

2. What are blocks?

3. Are curly braces optional after the *if* or *else* constructs?

4. What is the purpose of the *else* block?

5. What construct allows for multiple choices?

6. How does a *while* loop differ from a *do/while*? From an *until*?

7. How do you break out of a loop before you reach the end of the enclosing block?

8. What is a *redo* statement? How does it differ from the *next* statement?

9. Why would you use *next* rather than *redo* to control a loop?

10. What is an infinite loop?

11. How does a *foreach* loop work?

12. Does Perl support a *switch* statement? What is the *switch* feature?

13. What is *CORE::*?

14. What is a *continue* block used for?

7.6   **What's Next?**

In the next chapter, you will learn about pattern matching with regular expressions, one of the best and most important features of the language. You will learn about expression modifiers and how to find patterns in text strings. If you are familiar with the UNIX *grep* or the *vi* editor, you will see how Perl enhances and simplifies the power of pattern matching with its matching and substitution operators and large selection of regular expression metacharacters.

EXERCISE 7
What Are Your Conditions?

1. Physicists tell us that the lowest possible temperature is absolute zero. Absolute zero is -459.69 degrees Fahrenheit.

   a. Accept inputs from the user: a beginning temperature, an ending temperature, and an increment value (all Fahrenheit).

   b. Check for bad input: a temperature less than absolute zero and an ending temperature less than a beginning temperature. The program will send a message to *STDERR* if either condition is detected.

   c. Print a header showing: *Fahrenheit   Celcius*. Print all the values from the beginning to the ending temperatures. Use a looping mechanism. The conversion formula is C = (F - 32) / 1.8.

2. Ask the user for a list of grades, separated by whitespace. The grades will be stored in a string called *$input*.

   a. Split the string *$input* and create an array.

   b. Use the *foreach* loop to get the total sum of all the grades.

   c. Print the average.

3. Write a script that will print 10 random number cards from a deck.

   a. The script will build a deck of 52 cards by using nested *foreach* loops.

   b. The outer loop will iterate through a list consisting of cards for each suit: *clubs, diamonds, hearts, spades*. The inner loop will iterate through a list for each type of card within the suit: *ace, 2 through 10, jack, queen,* and *king*. A card of each suit will be assigned to an array.

   c. The *rand()* function will be used to get a random card from the pack. There should be no duplicates in the 10 cards selected from the deck. (Hint: the splice function is often used to remove the duplicate card.)

4. Remove the colors in *@drop* from the array *@colors*; that is, remove pink and brown from the array *@colors*.

   @colors=qw(red green blue yellow pink purple brown);

   @drop=qw(pink brown);

chapter

8

Regular Expressions— Pattern Matching

By the end of this chapter, you should understand the following Perl code:

```
while(<DATA>){
    ($name,$price)=split(":");
    $price =~ s/$price/$& + ($& * .20)/e;
    printf "%s \$%.2f\n",$name, $price if $price > 35;
}
__DATA__
Ramya:30.25
Lu:12.66
Shiva:65.75
Dee:44.32
```

8.1   What Is a Regular Expression?

This is a regular expression: */love/*. This is also a regular expression: */^.+$/*.

A **regular expression** (regex) is really just a sequence, or pattern, of characters that is matched against a string of text when performing searches and replacements. Regexes have been around for a long time and most modern programming languages have libraries that support them, such as the popular library called PCRE, short for Perl Compatible Regular Expressions, an open-source library compatible with a great number of *C* compilers and operating systems. If you are familiar with UNIX utilities, such as *vi*, *sed*, *grep*, and *awk*, you have already met regular expressions face-to-face. Under Perl, regular expressions have evolved into a powerful tool, unsurpassed by any modern programming language and a major reason for Perl's rise to fame.

A simple regular expression consists of a character or set of characters that matches itself. The regular expression is normally delimited by forward slashes.[1] The special scalar $_ is the default search space where Perl does its pattern matching. $_ is like a shadow. Sometimes you see it; sometimes you don't. Don't worry; all this will become clear as you read through this chapter.

8.1.1   Why Do We Need Regular Expressions?

Before going into the details, you may wonder what regular expressions do. A good example would be the validation of input from a user, searching for sequences in a file, or replacing one value with another based on a specified search criteria. When you fill out a form to buy a product online, a program must be able to validate that the information is correct. Let's say you type in your email address into one of the text boxes in the form. The program running behind the scenes (*JavaScript*, *PHP*, Perl, or the like) will check to see if the email address is valid. How would the program perform the test? Enter regular expressions, commonly called regexes or re's. The following is an example of a regular expression used to validate an email address:

```
/^\w+[\w-\.]*\@\w+((-\w+)|(\w*))\.[a-z]{2,3}$/
```

It looks like gibberish at first sight. The only character you might recognize in the example as part of an email address is the @ symbol. The other characters are special regular expression metacharacters and have a special meaning; for example, the \w+ represents any set of alphanumeric characters (a-z, A-Z, 0-9). This regular expression is designed to search for a specific pattern of characters that would be found in an email address. Finding the exact pattern can be very time-consuming and may not be the correct expression for all valid emails, requiring numerous tests before it is established as a comprehensive validation. You can find various regex libraries on the Web to help you unravel regular expression patterns (see also Chapter 9, "Getting Control—Regular Expression Metacharacters"), such as the example shown previously, and not all of them are that complex.

This chapter will show you how to use regular expressions for simple pattern matching and substitution, how to use them with the conditional and looping modifiers, and how to use the various regex options to further define the expression. In Chapter 9, regular expression **metacharacters** will be explained to let you further control and refine the search pattern as shown in the email example, and that is where the real power of pattern matching lies.

---

1. Actually, you can use any character as a delimiter. See Table 8.1 and Example 8.12.

EXAMPLE 8.1

```
1   /abc/
```

EXPLANATION

1   The pattern *abc* is enclosed in forward slashes, the default delimiters. If searching for this pattern (regular expression) in a string, for example, any string that contains the pattern *abc* will be matched.

8.2 Modifiers and Simple Statements with Regular Expressions

A **simple statement** is an expression terminated with a semicolon. To review from Chapter 7, "If Only, Unconditionally, Forever," we saw that Perl supports a set of modifiers that allow you to further evaluate a statement based on some condition. A simple statement may contain an expression **ending** with a single modifier. The modifying expression is always terminated with a semicolon. When evaluating regular expressions, the modifiers may be simpler to use than the full-blown conditional constructs.

EXAMPLE 8.2

```
(In Script)
1   $_ = "My brother didn't bother to call Mother.";
2   print if /other/;   # Could be written: print $_ if $_ =~ /other/;

(Output)
My brother didn't bother to call Mother.
```

EXPLANATION

1   The $_ scalar variable is assigned a string.
2   When the *if* modifier is followed directly by a regular expression, Perl assumes that the line being matched is $_, the default placeholder for pattern matching. The value of $_, *My brother didn't bother to call Mother*, is printed if the regular expression *other* is matched anywhere in the string.* The search starts at the left-hand side of the string, so that matching *other* in *brother* will produce the true condition before *bother* is reached. The expression could have been written as *if $_ =~ /other/*. Notice that the pattern *other* is found in *brother*, *bother*, and *Mother*. In the next chapter, we will get better control of the search pattern by using regular expression metacharacters.

---

* $_ is the default output for the print function.

8.2.1   Pattern Binding Operators

The **pattern binding** operators are used to bind a string being searched for with the pattern that specifies the search. In the previous examples, most of the pattern searches were done implicitly (or explicitly) on the $_ variable, the default pattern space. That is, each line was stored in the $_ variable when looping through a file. We've also seen that if you store a value in some variable other than $_, you will need the pattern matching operators (see Table 8.1).

Table 8.1 Pattern Matching Operators

Example	Meaning
$name =~ /John/	True if $name matches the pattern. Returns 1 for *true*, or the empty string for *false*.
$name !~ /John/	True if $name does not match pattern.

Instead of using $_ as in the following line:

```
$_  = 5000;
```

you could use another named scalar, like so:

```
$salary = 5000;
```

Then, if a match is performed on *$salary* instead of $, you would use this:

$salary =~ /5/;** or **$salary !~ /5/;

So, if you have a string that is not stored in the $_ variable and need to perform matches or substitutions on that string, the pattern binding operators =~ or !~ are used. They are also used with the *tr* function for string translations (for more on *tr*, see Section 9.2.4, "The *tr* or *y* Operators"). This doesn't mean that you can't use the pattern matching operators with the $_ variable; it just means that if you're not using $_, then you will need them.

EXAMPLE 8.3

```
(In Script)
1  my $line = "My brother didn't bother to call Mother.";
2  print $line if $line =~ /other/;
3  print $line if $line !~ /sister/;

(Output)
My brother didn't bother to call Mother.
My brother didn't bother to call Mother.
```

EXPLANATION

2   In this example, *$line*, rather than *$_*, is used after the *if* modifier, then the =~ pattern matching operator is necessary when evaluating the regular expression.

3   The *!~* pattern matching operator means "not match." The value of *$line* will be printed if it doesn't match the pattern */sister/*.

8.2.2 The *DATA* Filehandle

In the following examples, the special filehandle called *DATA* is used as an expression in a *while* loop. This allows us to directly get the data from the same script that is testing it, rather than reading input from a separate text file. (In fact, you may find this technique handy if you are testing some specific sections of an external file. Just copy the lines in question into your script, place them under the _ _DATA_ _ special literal, and run your tests within the script.) The data itself is located after the _ _DATA_ _² special literal at the bottom of each of the example scripts. The _ _DATA_ _ literal marks the logical end of the script and opens the *DATA* filehandle for reading. Each time a line of input is read from <DATA>, it is assigned by default to the special $_ scalar. Although $_ is implied, you could also use it explicitly, or even some other scalar. The format used is shown in the following examples.

FORMAT

```
while(<DATA>){
    Do something with the data here
}
_ _DATA_ _
    The actual data is stored here
```

Or you could use the $_ explicitly, as follows:

```
while($_ = <DATA>){
    Do something with the data here
}
_ _DATA_ _
    The actual data is stored here
```

Or use another variable instead of $_, as follows:

```
while($inputline = <DATA>){
    Do something with the $inputline here
}
_ _DATA_ _
    The actual data is stored here

(Output)
Norma Cord
```

---

2. Instead of _ _DATA_ _, you can use _ _END_ _, but _ _END_ _ opens the *DATA* filehandle in the *main* package and _ _DATA_ _ in any package.

EXAMPLE 8.4

```
(The Script)
  use warnings;
1 while(<DATA>){
2    print if /Norma/;        # Print the line if it matches Norma
  }
3 __DATA__
  Steve Blenheim
  Betty Boop
  Igor Chevsky
  Norma Cord
  Jon DeLoach
  Karen Evich
```

EXPLANATION

1 The special *DATA* filehandle gets its input from the text after the _ _DATA_ _ token.
   When the *while* loop is entered, a line of input is stored in the $_ scalar variable. The
   first line stored in $_ is *Steve Blenheim*. The next time around the loop, *Betty Boop* is
   stored in $_, and this continues until all of the lines following the _ _DATA_ _ token
   are read and processed.

2 Only the lines containing the regular expression *Norma* are printed. $_ is the default
   for pattern matching; it could also have been written as *print $_ if $_ =~ /Norma/;*.

3 The *DATA* filehandle gets its data from the lines that follow the _ _DATA_ _ token.

EXAMPLE 8.5

```
(The Script)
  use warnings;
1 while(<DATA>){
2    if /Norma/ print;       # Wrong!
  }

3 __DATA__
  Steve Blenheim
  Betty Boop
  Igor Chevsky
  Norma Cord
  Jon DeLoach
  Karen Evich

(Output)
Execution of script aborted due to compilation errors.
```

EXPLANATION

2 The modifier must be at the end of the expression, or a syntax error results. This statement should be *print if /Norma/* or *if(/Norma/) {print;}*. (Similar to the *grep* command
   for UNIX.)

EXAMPLE 8.6

```
(The Script)
    use warnings;
1   while(<DATA>){
2      print unless /Norma/;   # Print line if it doesn't match Norma
    }

3   __DATA__
    Steve Blenheim
    Betty Boop
    Igor Chevsky
    Norma Cord
    Jon DeLoach
    Karen Evich

(Output)
Steve Blenheim
Betty Boop
Igor Chevsky
Jon DeLoach
Karen Evich
```

EXPLANATION

2   All lines that don't contain the pattern *Norma* are matched and printed. (Similar to the *grep -v* command for UNIX.)

3   The *DATA* filehandle gets its data from the lines that follow the *__DATA__* token.

8.3 Regular Expression Operators

The regular expression operators are used for matching patterns in searches and for replacements in substitution operations. The *m* operator is used for matching patterns, and the *s* operator is used when substituting one pattern for another.

8.3.1 The *m* Operator and Pattern Matching

The *m* operator is optional if the delimiters enclosing the regular expression are forward slashes (the forward slash is the default), but required if you change the delimiter. You may want to change the delimiter if the regular expression itself contains forward slashes (for example, when searching for birthdays, such as *3/15/93*, or pathnames, such as */usr/var/ adm*). Matching modifiers are shown in Table 8.2.

FORMAT

```
/Regular Expression/      default delimiter
m#Regular Expression#     optional delimiters
m{regular expression}     pair of delimiters
```

Table 8.2 Matching Modifiers

Modifier	Meaning
i	Turn off case sensitivity.
m	Treat a string as multiple lines.
o	Compile pattern only once. Used to optimize the search.
s	Treat string as a single line when a newline is embedded.
x	Permit comments in a regular expression and ignore whitespace.
g	Match globally; that is, find all occurrences. Return a list if used with an array context, or true or false if a scalar context.

EXAMPLE 8.7

```
1   m/Good morning/
2   /Good evening/
3   /\/usr\/var\/adm/
4   m#/usr/var/adm#
5   m(Good evening)
6   m'$name'
```

EXPLANATION

1   The *m* operator is not needed in this example, since forward slashes delimit the regular expression.

2   The forward slash is the delimiter; therefore, the *m* operator is optional.

3   Each of the forward slashes in the search path is quoted with a backslash so it will not be confused with the forward slash used for the pattern delimiter—a messy approach.

4   The *m* operator is required because the pound sign (#) is used as an alternative to the forward slash. The pound sign delimiter clarifies and simplifies the previous example.

5   If the opening delimiter is a parenthesis, square bracket, angle bracket, or brace, then the closing delimiter must be the corresponding closing character. *m(expression)*, *m[expression]*, *m<expression>*, or *m{expression}*.

6   If the delimiter is a single quote, then variable interpolation is turned off; in other words, *$name* is treated as a literal.

EXAMPLE 8.8

```
(The Script)
   use warnings;
1  while(<DATA>){
2      print if /Betty/;        # Print the line if it matches Betty
   }
3  __DATA__
   Steve Blenheim
   Betty Boop
   Igor Chevsky
   Norma Cord
   Jon DeLoach
   Karen Evich

(Output)
Betty Boop
```

EXPLANATION

2   All lines that match the pattern *Betty* are printed.

3   The *DATA* filehandle gets its data from the lines that follow the _ _DATA_ _ token.

EXAMPLE 8.9

```
(The Script)
   use warnings;
1  while(<DATA>){
2      print unless /Evich/;    # Print line unless it matches Evich
   }
3  __DATA__
   Steve Blenheim
   Betty Boop
   Igor Chevsky
   Norma Cord
   Jon DeLoach
   Karen Evich

(Output)
Steve Blenheim
Betty Boop
Igor Chevsky
Norma Cord
Jon DeLoach
```

EXPLANATION

2   All lines that don't match the pattern *Evich* are printed.

3   The *DATA* filehandle gets its data from the lines that follow the _ _DATA_ _ token.

EXAMPLE 8.10

```
(The Script)
   use warnings;
1  while(<DATA>){
2      print if m#Jon#       # Print the line if it matches Jon
   }
3  __DATA__
   Steve Blenheim
   Betty Boop
   Igor Chevsky
   Norma Cord
   Jon DeLoach
   Karen Evich

(Output)
Jon DeLoach
```

EXPLANATION

2　The *m* (match) operator is necessary because the delimiter has been changed from the default forward slash to a pound sign (#). The line is printed if it matches *Jon*.

3　The *DATA* filehandle gets its data from the lines that follow the _ _DATA_ _ token.

EXAMPLE 8.11

```
(The Script)
   use warnings;
1  while(<DATA>){
2      print if m(Karen E);    # Print the line if it matches Karen E
   }
3  $name="Jon";
4  $_=qq/$name is a good sport.\n/;
5  print if m'$name';
6  print if m"$name";

7  __DATA__
   Steve Blenheim
   Betty Boop
   Igor Chevsky
   Norma Cord
   Jon DeLoach
   Karen Evich

(Output)
2  Karen Evich
5  <No output>
6  Jon is a good sport.
```

EXPLANATION

2   The *m* (match) operator is necessary because the delimiter has been changed from the default forward slash to a set of opening and closing parentheses. Other pairs that could be used are square brackets, curly braces, angle brackets, and single quotes. If single quotes are used, and the regular expression contains variables, the variables will not be interpolated. The line is printed if it matches *Karen E.*

3   The scalar *$name* is assigned *Jon*.

4   *$_* is assigned a string including the scalar *$name*.

5   When the matching delimiter is a set of single quotes, variables in the regular expression are not interpolated. The literal value *$name* is not found in *$_*; therefore, nothing is printed.

6   If double quotes enclose the expression, the variable *$name* will be interpolated. The string assigned to *$_* is printed if it contains *Jon*.

7   The *DATA* filehandle gets its data from the lines that follow the _ _DATA_ _ token.

The *g* Modifier—Global Match.   The *g* modifier is used to cause a global match; in other words, all occurrences of a pattern in the line are matched. Without the *g*, only the first occurrence of a pattern is matched. The *m* operator will return a list of the patterns matched.

FORMAT

```
m/search pattern/g
```

EXAMPLE 8.12

```
(The Script)
   use warnings;
1  $_ = "I lost my gloves in the clover, Love.";
2  my @list=/love/g;
3  print "@list.\n";

(Output)
3  love love.
```

EXPLANATION

1   The *$_* scalar variable is assigned a string of text.

2   If the search is done with the g modifier, in an array context, each match is stored in the *@list* array. The regular expression *love* was found in the string twice, once in *gloves* and once in *clover*. *Love* is not matched, since the *L* is uppercase.

3   The list of matched items is printed.

The *i* Modifier—Case Insensitivity. Perl is sensitive to whether characters are upper- or lowercase when performing matches. If you want to turn off case sensitivity, an *i* (insensitive) is appended to the last delimiter of the match operator.

FORMAT

```
m/search pattern/i
```

EXAMPLE 8.13

```
(The Script)
   use warnings;
1  $_ = "I lost my gloves in the clover, Love.";
2  my @list=/love/gi;
3  print "@list.\n";

(Output)
3  love love Love.
```

EXPLANATION

1 The $_ scalar variable is assigned the string.
2 This time, the *i* modifier is used to turn off the case sensitivity. Both *love* and *Love* will be matched and assigned to the array *@list*.
3 The pattern was found three times. The list is printed.

Special Scalars for Saving Patterns. The $& special scalar is assigned the string that was matched in the last successful search. &` saves what was found preceding the pattern that was matched, and &′ saves what was found after the pattern that was matched.

EXAMPLE 8.14

```
(The Script)
   use warings;
1  $_="San Francisco to Hong Kong\n";

2  /Francisco/;      # Save 'Francisco' in $& if it is found
3  print $&,"\n";

4  /to/;
5  print $`,"\n";    # Save what comes before the string 'to'

6  /to\s/;           # \s represents a space
7  print $', "\n";   # Save what comes after the string 'to'

(Output)
3  Francisco
5  San Francisco
7  Hong Kong
```

EXPLANATION

1   The $_ scalar is assigned a string.
2   The search pattern contains the regular expression *Francisco*. Perl searches for this pattern in the $_ variable. If found, the pattern *Francisco* will be saved in another special scalar, $&.
3   The search pattern *Francisco* was successfully matched, saved in $&, and printed.
4   The search pattern contains the regular expression *to*. Perl searches for this pattern in the $_ variable. If the pattern *to* is matched, the string to the **left** of this pattern, *San Francisco*, is saved in the $` scalar (note the backquote).
5   The value of $` is printed.
6   The search pattern contains the regular expression *to\s* (*to* followed by a space; \s represents a space). Perl searches for this pattern in the $_ variable. If the pattern *to\s* is matched, the string to the **right** of this pattern, *Hong Kong*, is saved in the $' scalar (note the straight quote).
7   The value of &' is printed.

The *x* Modifier—The Expressive Modifier.   The *x* modifier allows you to place comments within the regular expression and add whitespace characters (spaces, tabs, newlines) for clarity without having those characters interpreted as part of the regular expression; in other words, you can *express* your intentions within the regular expression.

EXAMPLE 8.15

```
(The Script)
    use warnings;
1   $_="San Francisco to Hong Kong\n";
2   /Francisco  # Searching for Francisco
    /x;
3   print "Comments and spaces were removed and \$& is $&\n";

(Output)
3   Comments and spaces were removed and $& is Francisco
```

EXPLANATION

1   The $_ scalar is assigned a string.
2   The search pattern consists of *Francisco* followed by a space, comment, and another space. The *x* modifier allows the additional whitespace and comments to be inserted in the pattern space without being interpreted as part of the search pattern.
3   The printed text illustrates that the search was unaffected by the extra spaces and comments. $& holds the value of what was matched as a result of the search.

8.3.2 The *s* Operator and Substitution

The *s* operator is used for **substitutions**. The substitution operator replaces the search pattern in the first set of slashes, and if found, replaces it with what is found within the second set of forward slashes. The delimiter can also be changed. The g modifier placed after the last delimiter stands for **global change** on a line, so that if Perl finds multiple occurrences of the pattern on a line, it will replace all of them, not just the first one it finds. The return value from the *s* operator is the number of substitutions that were made.

The special built-in variable $&, used in the replacement side of the substitution, gets the value of whatever was found in the search string. $& is a read-only variable. It cannot be changed.

FORMAT

```
s/old/new/;
s/old/new/i;
s/old/new/g;
s+old+new+g;
s(old)/new/;    s[old]{new};
s/old/expression to be evaluated/e;
s/old/new/ige;
s/old/new/x;
```

EXAMPLE 8.16

```
s/Igor/Boris/;
s/Igor/Boris/g;
s/norma/Jane/i;
s!Jon!Susan!;
s{Jon} <Susan>;
s/$sal/$sal * 1.1/e
s/dec/"Dec" . "ember"        # Replace "dec" or "Dec" with "December"
 /eigx;
```

8.3.3 The Pattern Binding Operators with Substitution

You can also use the **pattern binding** operators, used to bind the string being searched for with the pattern specifying the search, with substitution. In the previous examples, most of the substitutions were done implicitly (or explicitly) on the $_ variable, the default pattern space. That is, each line was stored in the $_ variable when looping through a file. We've also seen that if you store a value in some variable other than $_, you will need the pattern matching operators (see Table 8.3).

Table 8.3   Pattern Matching Operators with Substitution

Example	Meaning
$name =~ s/John/Sam/	Replace first occurrence of *John* with *Sam*.
$name =~ s/John/Sam/g	Replace all occurrences of *John* with *Sam*.

Instead of

```
$_ = "John";
```

we will use a named variable

```
$name = "John";
```

Then if a substitution is performed on *$name* instead of *$_*, as in

```
print if s/John/Sam/;
```

you would write

```
print if $name =~ s/John/Sam/;
```

EXAMPLE 8.17

```
(The Script)
    use warnings;
1   while(my $line = <DATA>){
2       $line =~ s/Norma/Jane/;   # Substitute Norma with Jane in $line
3       print $line;
    }
4   __DATA__
    Steve Blenheim
    Betty Boop
    Igor Chevsky
    Norma Cord
    Jon DeLoach
    Karen Evich

(Output)
Steve Blenheim
Betty Boop
Igor Chevsky
Jane Cord
Jon DeLoach
Karen Evich
```

EXPLANATION

2   In lines where *$line* contains the regular expression *Norma*, the substitution operator,
     s, will replace *Norma* with *Jane* for the first occurrence of *Norma* on each line. Because
     $line is used as an operand, the pattern matching operator =~ must be used.
3   Each line will be printed, whether or not the substitution occurred.
4   The *DATA* filehandle gets its data from the lines that follow the _ _DATA_ _ token

Changing the Substitution Delimiters. Normally, the forward slash delimiter
encloses both the search pattern and the replacement string. You can use any nonalphanumeric character following the *s* operator in place of the slash. For example, if a #
follows the *s* operator, you must use it as the delimiter for the replacement pattern. If you
use pairs of parentheses, curly braces, square brackets, or angle brackets to delimit the
search pattern, you may use any other type of delimiter for the replacement pattern, such
as *s(John) /Joe/;*.

EXAMPLE 8.18

```
(The Script)
   use warnings;
1  while(<DATA>){
2      s#Igor#Boris#;         # Substitute Igor with Boris
3      print;
   }
4  _ _DATA_ _
   Steve Blenheim
   Betty Boop
   Igor Chevsky
   Norma Cord
   Jon DeLoach
   Karen Evich

(Output)
Steve Blenheim
Betty Boop
Boris Chevsky
Norma Cord
Jon DeLoach
Karen Evich
```

EXPLANATION

1   The special *DATA* filehandle gets its input from the text after the _ _DATA_ _ token.
     The *while* loop is entered and the first line after the _ _DATA_ _ token is read in and
     assigned to $_.
2   The delimiter following the *s* operator has been changed to a pound sign (#). This
     is fine as long as all three delimiters are pound signs. The regular expression *Igor* is
     replaced with *Boris*.
3   The *DATA* filehandle gets its data from the lines that follow the _ _DATA_ _ token.

EXAMPLE 8.19

```
(The Script)
  use warnings;
1 while(<DATA>){
2    s(Blenheim){Dobbins};      # Substitute Blenheim with Dobbins
3    print;
  }
4  __DATA__
  Steve Blenheim
  Betty Boop
  Igor Chevsky
  Norma Cord
  Jon DeLoach
  Karen Evich

(Output)
Steve Dobbins
Betty Boop
Igor Chevsky
Norma Cord
Jon DeLoach
Karen Evich
```

EXPLANATION

2   The search pattern *Blenheim* is delimited with parentheses and the replacement pattern, *Dobbins*, is delimited with forward slashes.
3   The substitution is shown in the printed output. *Blenheim* is replaced with *Dobbins*.
4   The *DATA* filehandle gets its data from the lines that follow the _ _*DATA*_ _ token.

Substitution Modifiers.   You can control the way the substitution is performed by a number of special modifiers; for example, you can turn off case sensitivity, evaluate the replacement side, make global subsitutions, and so forth. Table 8.4 lists those modifiers.

Table 8.4   Substitution Modifiers

Modifier	Meaning
e	Evaluate the replacement side as an expression.
i	Turn off case sensitivity.
m	Treat a string as multiple lines.*
o	Compile pattern only once. Used to optimize the search.
s	Treat string as a single line when newline is embedded.
x	Allow whitespace and comments within the regular expression.
g	Replace globally; that is, find all occurrences.

* The *m*, *s*, and *x* options are defined only for Perl 5.

The *g* Modifier—Global Substitution

The *g* modifier is used to cause a global substitution; that is, all occurrences of a pattern are replaced on the line. Without the *g*, only the first occurrence of a pattern on each line is changed.

FORMAT

```
s/search pattern/replacement string/g;
```

EXAMPLE 8.20

```
(The Script)
   # Without the g option
   use warnings;
1  while(<DATA>){
2     print if s/Tom/Christian/;   # First occurrence of Tom on each
                                    # line is replaced with Christian
   }
3  _ _DATA_ _
   Tom Dave Dan Tom
   Betty Tom Henry Tom
   Igor Norma Tom Tom

(Output)
Christian Dave Dan Tom
Betty Christian Henry Tom
Igor Norma Christian Tom
```

EXPLANATION

2   The **first** occurrence of *Tom* will be replaced with *Christian* for each line that is read.
3   The *DATA* filehandle gets its data from the lines that follow the *_ _DATA_ _* token.

EXAMPLE 8.21

```
(The Script)
   # With the g option
   use warnings;
1  while(<DATA>){
2     print if s/Tom/Christian/g;   # All occurrences of Tom on each
                                     # line are replaced with Christian
   }
3  _ _DATA_ _
   Tom Dave Dan Tom
   Betty Tom Henry Tom
   Igor Norma Tom Tom
```

EXAMPLE 8.21 (CONTINUED)

```
(Output)
Christian Dave Dan Christian
Betty Christian Dick Christian
Igor Norma Christian Christian
```

EXPLANATION

2   With the g option, the substitution is global. **Every** occurrence of *Tom* will be replaced with *Christian* for each line that is read.

3   The *DATA* filehandle gets its data from the lines that follow the _ _DATA_ _ token.

The *i* Modifier—Case Insensitivity

Perl is sensitive to upper- or lowercase characters when performing matches. If you want to turn off case sensitivity, an *i* (insensitive) is appended to the last delimiter of the match or substitution operator and the search pattern will be case insensitive, whereas this has no effect on the replacement side.

FORMAT

```
s/search pattern/replacement string/i;
```

EXAMPLE 8.22

```
(The Script)
   # Matching with the i option
   use warnings;
1  while(<DATA>){
2     print if /norma cord/i;     # Turn off case sensitivity
   }
3  _ _DATA_ _
   Steve Blenheim
   Betty Boop
   Igor Chevsky
   Norma Cord
   Jon DeLoach
   Karen Evich

(Output)
Norma Cord
```

EXPLANATION

2   Without the *i* option, the regular expression */norma cord/* would not be matched, because all the letters are not lowercase in the lines that are read as input. The *i* option turns off case sensitivity.

3   The *DATA* filehandle gets its data from the lines that follow the _ _DATA_ _ token.

EXAMPLE 8.23

```
(The Script)
   use warnings;
1  while(<DATA>){
2      print if s/igor/Daniel/i;    # Substitute igor with Daniel
   }


3  __DATA__
   Steve Blenheim
   Betty Boop
   Igor Chevsky
   Norma Cord
   Jon DeLoach
   Karen Evich

(Output)
Daniel Chevsky
```

EXPLANATION

2   The regular expression in the substitution is also case insensitive, owing to the *i* option. If *igor* or *Igor* (or any combination of upper- and lowercase) is matched, it will be replaced with *Daniel*.

3   The *DATA* filehandle gets its data from the lines that follow the *__DATA__* token.

The *e* Modifier—Evaluating an Expression

On the replacement side of a substitution operation, it is possible to evaluate an expression or a function. The search side is replaced with the result of the evaluation.

FORMAT

```
s/search pattern/replacement string/e;
```

EXAMPLE 8.24

```
(The Script)
   use warnings;
   # The e and g modifiers
1  while(<DATA>){
2      s/6/6 * 7.3/eg;           # Substitute 6 with product of 6 * 7.3

3      print;

   }
   __DATA__
   Steve Blenheim    5
   Betty Boop        4
   Igor Chevsky      6
   Norma Cord        1
   Jon DeLoach       3
   Karen Evich       66
```

EXAMPLE 8.24 (CONTINUED)

```
(Output)
Steve Blenheim      5
Betty Boop          4
Igor Chevsky        43.8
Norma Cord          1
Jon DeLoach         3
Karen Evich         43.843.8
```

EXPLANATION

2   If the $_ scalar contains the number 6, the replacement side of the substitution is evaluated. In other words, the 6 is multiplied by 7.3 (e modifier); the product of the multiplication (43.8) replaces the number 6 each time the number 6 is found (g modifier).

3   Each line is printed. The last line contained two occurrences of 6, causing each 6 to be replaced with 43.8.

EXAMPLE 8.25

```
(The Script)
    use warnings;
    # The e modifier
1   my $number = 5;
2   $number =~ s/5/6 * 4 - 22/e;
3   print "The result is: $number\n";

4   $number = 51055;
5   $number =~ s/5/3 * 2/eg;
6   print "The result is: $number\n";

(Output)
3   The result is: 2
6   The result is: 61066
```

EXPLANATION

1   The $number scalar is assigned 5.

2   The s operator searches for the regular expression 5 in $number. The e modifier evaluates the replacement string as a numeric expression and replaces it with the result of the arithmetic operation, 6 * 4 - 22, that is, 2.

2   $number is assigned 1055.

5   The s operator searches for the regular expression 5 in $number. The e modifier evaluates the replacement string as a numeric expression and replaces it with the product of 3 * 2; that is, every time 5 is found, it is replaced with 6. Since the substitution is global, all occurrences of 5 are replaced with 6.

EXAMPLE 8.26

```
(The Script)
    use warnings;
1   my $line = "knock at heaven's door.\n";
2   $line =~ s/knock/"knock, " x 2  . "knocking"/ei;
3   print "He's $line;

(Output)
He's knock, knock, knocking at heaven's door.
```

EXPLANATION

1   The *$line* variable is the string *"knock at heaven's door.\n"*;
2   The *s* operator searches for the regular expression *knock* in *$line*. The *e* modifier evaluates the replacement string as a string expression and replaces it with *knock x 2* (repeated twice) and concatenates (the dot operator) with the string *knocking*, ignoring case.
3   The resulting string is printed.

Using the Special $& Variable in a Substitution.   The special *$&* variable is used to hold the pattern that is found on the search side of a substitution. Its value is used in the replacement side when performing an evaluation, but it is a read-only variable, meaning you cannot change it; for example, you cannot use *$& += 5*.

EXAMPLE 8.27

```
(The Script)
    use warnings;
1   my $salary=50000;
2   $salary =~ s/$salary/$& * 1.1/e;
3   print "\$& is $&\n";
4   print "The salary is now \$$salary.\n";

5   my $line = "knock at heaven's door.\n";
6   $line =~ s/knock/"$&, " x 2  . "knocking"/ei;
7   print "He's $line;

(Output)
3   $& is 50000
4   The salary is now $55000.
6   He's knock, knock, knocking at heaven's door.
```

EXPLANATION

1   The scalar *$salary* is assigned *50000*.
2   The substitution is performed on *$salary*. The replacement side evaluates the expression. The special variable *$&* holds the value found on the search side. To change the value in *$salary* after the substitution, the pattern matching operator =~ is used. This binds the result of the substitution to the scalar *$salary*.

EXPLANATION (CONTINUED)

3   The $& scalar holds the value of what was found on the search side of the substitution.

4   The scalar $salary has been increased by 10%.

5   The $line scalar is assigned the string "knock at heaven's door.\n".

6   If the search string (knock) is found, it is stored in the $& variable. On the replacement side, the expression is evaluated. So, the value of $& (knock) is replicated twice and concatenated with $&ing (knocking). The new value is substituted for the original value. $line is assigned the new value and printed.

Pattern Matching with a Real File. In all the previous examples, we have been using the *DATA* filehandle for performing pattern matches and substitutions with regular expressions. The following examples demonstrate how you can use pattern matching when working with lines from an external file.

EXAMPLE 8.28

```
(The Script)
   # Using split, an anonymous list, and pattern matching
   my($name,$phone,$address);
1  open(my $fh, "<", "datafile") or die "Can't open file $!";
2  while(<$fh>){
3     ($name, $phone, $address) = split(":", $_);
4     print "$name\n" if $phone =~ /408-/   # Using the pattern
                                             # matching operator
   }
5  close $fh

(The file)
Steve Blenheim:415-444-6677:12 Main St.
Betty Boop:303-223-1234:234 Ethan Ln.
Igor Chevsky:408-567-4444:3456 Mary Way
Norma Cord:555-234-5764:18880 Fiftieth St.
Jon DeLoach:201-444-6556:54 Penny Ln.
Karen Evich:306-333-7654:123 4th Ave.

(Output)
Igor Chevsky
```

EXPLANATION

1   The user-defined lexical variable $fh is associated with the external file, *datafile*. It is opened for reading.

3   The *split* function will split each line, $_, as it is read from the file and return a list consisting of three scalars: $name, $phone, and $address.

4   The pattern /408-/ is matched against the $phone variable. If that pattern is matched, the value of $name is printed. *Igor*'s name is printed because his phone matches the *408* area code. In the next chapter, we will use regular expression metacharacters to control how the pattern is matched; for example, $phone =~ /^408/ will match only if the phone begins with 408. The ^ is the beginning-of-line anchor.

5   The file is closed. The contents of the file that is being used for this example are listed.

EXAMPLE 8.29

```
(The Script)
    use warnings;
    my($name,$phone,$address);
1   open(my $fh, "<", "datafile") or die "Can't open datafile";
2   while(my $inputline=<$fh>){
3       ($name, $phone, $address) = split(":", $inputline);
4       print $inputline if $name =~ /^Karen/;
5       print if /^Norma/;  # $_ is empty
    }
(The datafile)
Steve Blenheim:415-444-6677:12 Main St.
Betty Boop:303-223-1234:234 Ethan Ln.
Igor Chevsky:408-567-4444:3456 Mary Way
Norma Cord:555-234-5764:18880 Fiftieth St.
Jon DeLoach:201-444-6556:54 Penny Ln.
Karen Evich:306-333-7654:123 4th Ave.

(Output)
4   Karen Evich:306-333-7654:123 4th Ave.
5   < No output >
```

EXPLANATION

2   Each line is read from *FH* and stored in $inputline, one after the other, until the end of the file is reached.

3   *$inputfile* will be split at the colons and the value returned stored in an anonymous list consisting of three scalars: $name, $phone, and $address.

4   The value of $inputline is displayed if the value of $name begins with *Karen*.

5   Since $_ is not being used in this example to hold the current line, nothing will print here. The line reads: print the value of $_ if $_ contains the pattern *Norma*.

8.4 **What You Should Know**

1. What is meant by a regular expression? Why do we need them?

2. How are the *if* and *unless* modifiers used?

3. How do you change the forward slash delimiter used in the search pattern to something else?

4. What does the *s* operator do?

5. What is meant by a global search?

6. When do you need the pattern binding operators, =~ and !~ ?

7. What is the default pattern space holder?

8. What is the _ _DATA_ _ filehandle used for?

9. What do the *i, e,* and *g* modifiers mean?

8.5 **What's Next?**

In the next chapter, you will harness the power of pattern matching by learning Perl's plethora of regular expression metacharacters. You will learn how to anchor patterns and how to search for alternating patterns, whitespace characters, sets of characters, repeating patterns, and so forth. You will learn about greedy metacharacters and how to control them. You will learn about capturing and grouping patterns, to look ahead and behind. By the time you complete that chapter, you should be able to search for data by regular expressions based on a specific criterion in order to validate the data and to modify the text that was found.

EXERCISE 8
A Match Made in Heaven

(sample.file found on CD)
Tommy Savage:408-724-0140:1222 Oxbow Court, Sunnyvale,CA 94087:5/19/66:34200
Lesle Kerstin:408-456-1234:4 Harvard Square, Boston, MA 02133:4/22/62:52600
JonDeLoach:408-253-3122:123 Park St., San Jose, CA 94086:7/25/53:85100
Ephram Hardy:293-259-5395:235 Carlton Lane, Joliet, IL 73858:8/12/20:56700
Betty Boop:245-836-8357:635 Cutesy Lane, Hollywood, CA 91464:6/23/23:14500
William Kopf:846-836-2837:6937 Ware Road, Milton, PA 93756:9/21/46:43500
Norma Corder:397-857-2735:74 Pine Street, Dearborn, MI 23874:3/28/45:245700
James Ikeda:834-938-8376:23445 Aster Ave., Allentown, NJ 83745:12/1/38:45000
Lori Gortz:327-832-5728:3465 Mirlo Street, Peabody, MA 34756:10/2/65:35200
Barbara Kerz:385-573-8326:832 Ponce Drive, Gary, IN 83756:12/15/46:268500

1. Print all lines containing the pattern *Street*.

2. Print lines where the first name matches a *B* or *b*.

3. Print last names that match *Ker*.

4. Print phone numbers in the *408* area code.

5. Print Lori Gortz's name and address.

6. Print Ephram's name in capital letters.

7. Print lines that do not contain a *4*.

8. Change William's name to Siegfried.

9. Print Tommy Savage's birthday.

10. Print the names of those making over $40,000.

11. Print the names and birthdays of those people born in June.

12. Print the ZIP Codes for Massachusetts.

chapter
9

Getting Control—
Regular Expression
Metacharacters

By the end of this chapter, you will be able to unravel and use the following regular expressions:

```
die unless (/^.+@[^\.].*\.[a-z]{2,}$/);

$money =~ s/(?<=\d)(?=(\d\d\d)+(?!\d))/,/g
```

9.1 The *RegExLib.com* Library

Before getting deep into the weeds, let's take a look at the *regexlib.com* Web site. This Web site allows you to search for a pattern and will show you a list of regular expression solutions and a rating on how well each one performs its pattern-matching task. Although the Web site may not be 100 percent Perlish in the way it handles regexes, it is certainly a good research tool when you're trying to get some clues on how to write your own. The following is the opening statement found at the home page of *RegExLib.com* (also shown in Figure 9.1).

> Welcome to **RegExLib.com**, the Internet's first Regular Expression Library. Currently we have indexed **3800** expressions from **2172** contributors around the world. We hope you'll find this site useful and come back whenever you need help writing an expression, you're looking for an expression for a particular task, or are ready to contribute new expressions you've just figured out. Thanks!

Figure 9.1   The RegExLib.com home page.

If you look closely at Figure 9.1, you will see a magnifying glass with a search box next to it. In this box, the word *email* has been typed. If the search button is clicked, another page will appear with a variety of regular expressions that have been designed by different programmers to match for a valid email address (see Figure 9.2). The purpose of each regex is defined and given a rating (the number of green boxes) on its quality, much like grading a hotel. The more green boxes, the better the regex—five being the best, as in a five-star hotel.

By the time we finish this chapter, you should be able to read any of the regex examples found here. Once you understand all the metacharacters and how they are used, you can write you own regular expressions or use the ones provided here. Knowing what the regular expression is matching on and being able to test it right at the Web site is a great time-saving tool. In Figure 9.2, you can see some examples of how to validate an email address. Note the ratings, the test box, and the description.

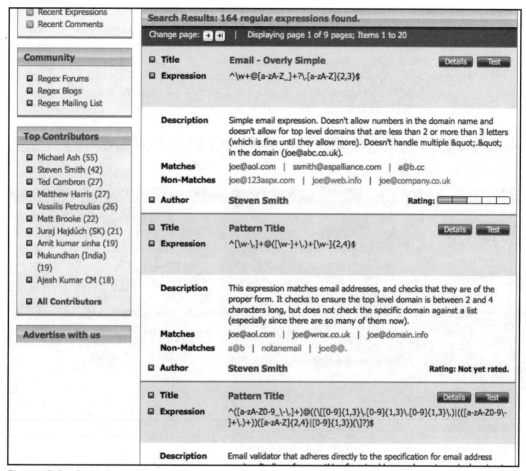

Figure 9.2 Search results.

9.2 Regular Expression Metacharacters

So what are these metacharacters? Regular expression metacharacters are characters that do not represent themselves. They are endowed with special powers to allow you to control the search pattern in some way (for example, find the pattern only at the beginning of the line, or at the end of the line, or only if it starts with an upper- or lowercase letter). Metacharacters lose their special meaning if preceded with a backslash (\). For example, the dot metacharacter represents any single character, but when preceded with a backslash, is just a dot or period.

If you see a backslash preceding a metacharacter, the backslash turns off the meaning of the metacharacter, but if you see a backslash preceding an alphanumeric character in a regular expression, then the backslash means something else; for example, \d means one decimal number. Perl provides a simpler form of some of the metachacters, called **metasymbols**, to represent characters. For example, *[0-9]* represents numbers in the range between 0 and 9, and \d represents the same thing. *[0-9]* uses the bracket metacharacter; \d is a metasymbol. Table 9.1 describes the metacharacters and what they do.

EXAMPLE 9.1

```
/^a...c/
```

EXPLANATION

This regular expression contains metacharacters. (See Table 9.1.) The first one is a caret (^). The caret metacharacter matches for a string only if it is at the beginning of the line. The period (.) is used to match for any single character, including whitespace. This expression contains three periods, representing any three characters. To find a literal period or any other character that does not represent itself, the character must be preceded by a backslash to prevent interpretation.

In Example 9.1, the regular expression reads: search at the beginning of the line for an *a*, followed by any three single characters, followed by a *c*. What comes after the *c* could be any characters. It will match, for example, *abbbc, a123c, a   c,* or *aAx3cde* only if those patterns were found at the beginning of the line.

Table 9.1 Metacharacters

Metacharacter	What It Matches
Character Class: Single Characters and Digits	
.	Matches any character except a newline
[a-z0-9]	Matches any single character in set
[^a-z0-9]	Matches any single character **not** in set
\d	Matches one digit
\D	Matches a nondigit, same as *[^0-9]*
\w	Matches an alphanumeric (word) character
\W	Matches a nonalphanumeric (nonword) character

(continued)

Table 9.1 Metacharacters (continued)

Metacharacter	What It Matches
Character Class: Whitespace Characters	
\s	Matches a whitespace character, such as spaces, tabs, and newlines
\S	Matches nonwhitespace character
\n	Matches a newline
\r	Matches a return
\t	Matches a tab
\f	Matches a form feed
\b	Matches a backspace
\0	Matches a null character
Character Class: Anchored Characters	
\b	Matches a word boundary (when not inside [ ])
\B	Matches a nonword boundary
^	Matches to beginning of line
$	Matches to end of line
\A	Matches the beginning of the string only
\Z	Matches the end of the string or line
\z	Matches the end of string only
\G	Matches where previous $m//g$ left off
Character Class: Repeated Characters	
$x?$	Matches 0 or 1 x
$x*$	Matches 0 or more occurrences of x
$x+$	Matches 1 or more occurrences of x
$(xyz)+$	Matches 1 or more patterns of xyz
$x\{m,n\}$	Matches at least m occurrences of x and no more than n occurrences of x
Character Class: Alternative Characters	
was|were|will	Matches one of *was*, *were*, or *will*

(continued)

Table 9.1   Metacharacters (continued)

Metacharacter	What It Matches
Character Class: Remembered Characters	
(string)	Used for backreferencing
\1 or $1	Matches first set of parentheses*
\2 or $2	Matches second set of parentheses
\3 or $3	Matches third set of parentheses
Character Class: Miscellaneous Characters	
\12	Matches that octal value, up to \377
\x811	Matches that hex value
\cX	Matches that control character; e.g., \cC is <CTRL>+C and \cV is <CTRL>+V
\e	Matches the ASCII ESC character, not backslash
\E	Marks the end of changing case with \U, \L, or \Q
\l	Lowercase the next character only
\L	Lowercase characters until the end of the string or until \E
\N	Matches that named character; e.g., \N{greek:Beta}
\p{PROPERTY}	Matches any character with the named property; e.g., \p{IsAlpha}/
\P{PROPERTY}	Matches any character without the named property
\Q	Quote metacharacters until \E
\u	Titlecase next character only
\U	Uppercase until \E
\x{NUMBER}	Matches Unicode NUMBER given in hexadecimal
\X	Matches Unicode "combining character sequence" string
\[	Matches that metacharacter
\\	Matches a backslash

* \1 and $1 are called backreferences. They differ in that the \1 backreference is valid within a pattern, whereas the $1 notation is valid within the enclosing block or until another successful search.

9.2.1 Metacharacters for Single Characters

If you are searching for a particular character within a regular expression, you can use the **dot** metacharacter to represent a single character or a **character class** that matches one character from a set of characters. In addition to the dot and character class, Perl has added some backslashed symbols (called **metasymbols**) to represent single characters. See Table 9.2.[1]

Table 9.2 Metacharacters for Single Characters

Metacharacter	What It Matches
.	Matches any character except a newline
[a-z0-9_]	Matches any single character in set
[^a-z0-9_]	Matches any single character **not** in set
\d	Matches a single digit
\D	Matches a single nondigit; same as [^0-9]
\w	Matches a single alphanumeric (word) character; same as [a-z0-9_]
\W	Matches a single nonalphanumeric (nonword) character; same as [^a-z0-9_]

The Dot Metacharacter. The dot (.) metacharacter matches any single character with the exception of the newline character. For example, the regular expression /a.b/ is matched if the string contains an *a*, followed by any one single character (except the \n), followed by *b*, whereas the expression /.../ matches any string containing at least three characters.

EXAMPLE 9.2

```
(The Script)
    # The dot metacharacter
    use warnings;
1   while(<DATA>){
2       print "Found Norma!\n" if /N..ma/;
    }
    __DATA__
    Steve Blenheim 101
    Betty Boop 201
    Igor Chevsky 301
    Norma Cord 401
    Jonathan DeLoach 501
    Karen Evich 601
```

---

1. The metasymbols match on more than just the alphanumeric characters; they are "Unicode" aware.

EXAMPLE 9.2 (CONTINUED)

(Output)
Found Norma!

EXPLANATION

1   The special *DATA* filehandle gets its input from the text after the __DATA__ token. The *while* loop is entered and the first line following the __DATA__ token is read in and assigned to $_. Each time the loop is entered, the next line below __DATA__ is assigned to $_ until all the lines have been processed.

2   The string *Found Norma!\n* is printed only if the pattern found in $_ contains an uppercase *N*, followed by any two single characters, followed by an *m* and an *a*. It would find *Norma*, *No man*, *Normandy*, and so forth.

The *s* Modifier—The Dot Metacharacter and the Newline.   Normally, the dot metacharacter does not match the newline character, \n, because it matches only the characters within a string up until the newline is reached. The *s* modifier treats the line with embedded newlines as a single line, rather than a group of multiple lines, and allows the dot metacharacter to treat the newline character the same as any other character it might match. The *s* modifier can be used with both the *m* (match) and the *s* (substitution) operators.

EXAMPLE 9.3

(The Script)
```
   # The s modifier and the newline
1  $_="Sing a song of sixpence\nA pocket full of rye.\n";
2  print $& if /pence./s;
3  print $& if /rye\../s;
4  print if s/sixpence.A/twopence, a/s;
```

(Output)
```
2  pence
3  rye.
4  Sing a song of twopence, a pocket full of rye.
```

EXPLANATION

1   The $_ scalar is assigned; it contains two newlines.

2   The regular expression, */pence./*, contains a dot metacharacter. The dot metacharacter does not match a newline character unless the *s* modifier is used. The *$&* special scalar holds the value the pattern found in the last successful search; that is, *pence\n*.

3   The regular expression */rye\./* contains a literal period (the backslash makes the period literal), followed by the dot metacharacter that will match on the newline, thanks to the *s* modifier. The *$&* special scalar holds the value the pattern found in the last successful search; that is, *rye.\n*.

4   The *s* modifier allows the dot to match on the newline character, \n, found in the search string. The newline will be replaced with a space.

The Character Class.   A character class represents **one** character from a set of characters. For example, *[abc]* matches an *a*, *b*, **or** *c*, and *[a-z]* matches one character from a set of characters in the range from *a* to *z*, and *[0-9]* matches one character in the range of digits between *0* and *9*. If the character class contains a leading caret (^), then the class represents any one character **not** in the set; for example, *[^a-zA-Z]* matches a single character **not** in the range from *a* to *z* or *A* to *Z*, and *[^0-9]* matches a single character not in the range between *0* and *9*.[2] To represent a number between 10 and 13, use *1[0-3]*, not *[10-13]*.

Perl provides additional symbols, **metasymbols**, to represent a character class. The symbols \d and \D represent a single digit and a single nondigit, respectively; they are the same as *[0-9]* and *[^0-9]*. Similarly, \w and \W represent a single word character and a single nonword character, respectively; they are the same as *[A-Za-z_0-9]* and *[^A-Za-z_0-9]*.

EXAMPLE 9.4

```
(From a Script)
    use warnings;
1   while(<DATA>){
2       print if /[A-Z][a-z]eve/;
    }
    __DATA__
    Steve Blenheim 101
    Betty Boop 201
    Igor Chevsky 301
    Norma Cord 401
    Jonathan DeLoach 501
    Karen Evich 601

(Output)
Steve Blenheim 101
```

EXPLANATION

1   The special *DATA* filehandle gets its input from the text after the __DATA__ token. The *while* loop is entered and the first line following the __DATA__ token is read in and assigned to $_. Each time the loop is entered, the next line after __DATA__ is assigned to $_ until all the lines have been processed.

2   The line $_ is printed only if $_contains a pattern matching one uppercase letter *[A-Z]*, followed by one lowercase letter *[a-z]*, and followed by *eve*.

---

2. Don't confuse the caret inside square brackets with the caret used as a beginning of line anchor. See Table 9.7.

EXAMPLE 9.5

```
(The Script)
   use warnings;
   # The bracketed character class
1  while(<DATA>){
2     print if /[A-Za-z0-9_]/;
   }
   __DATA__
   Steve Blenheim 101
   Betty Boop 201
   Igor Chevsky 301
   Norma Cord 401
   Jonathan DeLoach 501
   Karen Evich 601
```

(Output)
Steve Blenheim 101
Betty Boop 201
Igor Chevsky 301
Norma Cord 401
Jonathan DeLoach 501
Karen Evich 601

EXPLANATION

2   The line $_ is printed only if it contains a pattern matching one alphanumeric word character, represented by the character class, *[A-Za-z0-9_]*. All lines are printed.

EXAMPLE 9.6

```
(The Script)
   use warnings;
   # The bracket metacharacters and negation
1  while(<DATA>){
2     print if / [^123]0/
   }
   __DATA__
   Steve Blenheim 101
   Betty Boop 201
   Igor Chevsky 301
   Norma Cord 401
   Jonathan DeLoach 501
   Karen Evich 601
```

(Output)
Norma Cord 401
Jonathan DeLoach 501
Karen Evich 601

EXPLANATION

2   The line $_ is printed only if $_ contains a pattern matching one space, followed by one number **not** in the range between *1* and *3* (not *1*, *2*, or *3*), followed by *0*.

EXAMPLE 9.7

```
(The Script)
    use warnings;
    # The \d metasymbol
1   while(<DATA>){
2       print if /6\d\d/
    }
    _ _DATA_ _
    Steve Blenheim 101
    Betty Boop 201
    Igor Chevsky 301
    Norma Cord 401
    Jonathan DeLoach 501
    Karen Evich 601

(Output)
Karen Evich 601
```

EXPLANATION

2   The line $_ is printed only if it contains a pattern matching the number 6, followed by two single digits. The metasymbol \d represents the character class [0-9].

EXAMPLE 9.8

```
(The Script)
    use warnings;
    # The \D metasymbol
1   while(<DATA>){
2       print if /[ABC]\D/
    }
    _ _DATA_ _
    Steve Blenheim 101
    Betty Boop 201
    Igor Chevsky 301
    Norma Cord 401
    Jonathan DeLoach 501
    Karen Evich 601

(Output)
Steve Blenheim 101
Betty Boop 201
Igor Chevsky 301
Norma Cord 401
```

EXPLANATION

2   The line $_ is printed only if $_ contains a pattern matching an uppercase A, B, or C [ABC], followed by one single **non**digit, \D. The metasymbol \D represents the character class [^0-9]; that is, a number **not** in the range between 0 and 9.

EXAMPLE 9.9

```
(The Script)
   use warnings;
   # The \w metasymbols
1  while(<DATA>){
2     print if / \w\w\w\w \d/
   }
   __DATA__
   Steve Blenheim 101
   Betty Boop 201
   Igor Chevsky 301
   Norma Cord 401
   Jonathan DeLoach 501
   Karen Evich 601

(Output)
Betty Boop 201
Norma Cord 401
```

EXPLANATION

2   The line $_ is printed only if it matches a pattern containing a space, followed by four alphanumeric word characters, \w, followed by a space and a digit, \d. The metasymbol \w represents the character class *[A-Za-z0-9_]*.

EXAMPLE 9.10

```
(The Script)
   # The \W metasymbols
1  while(<DATA>){
2     print if /\W\w\w\w\w\W/
   }
   __DATA__
   Steve Blenheim 101
   Betty Boop 201
   Igor Chevsky 301
   Norma Cord 401
   Jonathan DeLoach 501
   Karen Evich 601

(Output)
Betty Boop 201
Norma Cord 401
```

EXPLANATION

2   The line $_ is printed only if $_ matches a pattern containing a nonalphanumeric word character, followed by four alphanumeric word characters, \w, followed by another nonalphanumeric word character, \W. The metasymbol \W represents the character class *[^A-Za-z0-9_]*. Both *Boop* and *Cord* are four word characters surrounded by whitespace (nonalphanumeric characters).

The POSIX Bracket Expressions. Perl 5.6 introduced the POSIX, a special kind
of character classes, called **bracket expressions**. POSIX (the Portable Operating System
Interface[3]) is an industry standard used to ensure that programs are portable across operating systems. In order to be portable, POSIX recognizes that different countries or locales
may vary in the way characters are encoded, the symbols used to represent currency, and
how times and dates are represented. To handle these different types of characters, POSIX
(the bracketed character class of characters) is used (see Table 9.3). The POSIX module
permits you to access all (or nearly all) the standard POSIX 1003.1 identifiers.

The class *[:alnum:]* is another way of saying *A-Za-z0-9*. To use this class, it must be
enclosed in another set of brackets for it to be recognized as a regular expression. For
example, *A-Za-z0-9,* by itself, is not a regular expression character class, but *[A-Za-z0-9]*
is. Likewise, *[:alnum:]* should be written *[[:alnum:]]*. The difference between using the first
form, *[A-Za-z0-9],* and the bracketed form, *[[:alnum:]],* is that the first form is dependent
on ASCII character encoding, whereas the second form allows characters from other
languages to be represented in the class. (For more on POSIX expressions, see *www.regular-
expressions.info/posixbrackets.html.*)

To negate one of the characters in the POSIX character class, the syntax is as follows:

```
[^[:space:]] - all nonwhitespace characters
```

Table 9.3 The Bracketed Character Class

Bracket Class	Meaning
[:alnum:]	Alphanumeric characters
[:alpha:]	Alphabetic characters
[:ascii]:	Any character with ordinal value between *0* and *127*
[:cntrl:]	Control characters
[:digit:]	Numeric characters, *0* to *9*, or \d
[:graph:]	Nonblank characters (not spaces, control characters, etc.) other than alphanumeric or punctuation characters
[:lower:]	Lowercase letters
[:print:]	Like *[:graph:]* but includes the space character
[:punct:]	Punctuation characters
[:space:]	All whitespace characters (newlines, spaces, tabs); same as \s
[:upper:]	Uppercase letters
[:word:]	Any alphanumeric or underline characters
[:xdigit:]	Allows digits in a hexadecimal number (*0-9a-fA-F*)

---

3. POSIX is a registered trademark of the IEEE. See *http://www.opengroup.org/austin/papers/backgrounder.html.*

EXAMPLE 9.11

```
(In Script)
   use warnings;
   # The POSIX character classes
1  require 5.6.0;
2  while(<DATA>){
3     print if /[[:upper:]][[:alpha:]]+ [[:upper:]][[:lower:]]+/;
   }
   __DATA__
   Steve Blenheim
   Betty Boop
   Igor Chevsky
   Norma Cord
   Jon DeLoach
   joe blow
   Betty Boop
   Karen Evich

(Output)
Steve Blenheim
Betty Boop
Igor Chevsky
Norma Cord
Jon DeLoach
Betty Boop
Karen Evich
```

EXPLANATION

1   Perl 5.6.0 (and above) is needed to use the POSIX character class. (By now, everyone should have a version of Perl higher than 5.6.)

2   The special *DATA* filehandle gets its input from the text after the _ _DATA_ _ token. The *while* loop is entered and the first line after the _ _DATA_ _ token is read in and assigned to $_. Each time the loop is entered, the next line following _ _DATA_ _ is assigned to $_ until all the lines have been processed.

3   The regular expression contains POSIX character classes. The line is printed if $_ contains one uppercase letter, *[[:upper:]]*, followed by one or more (+) alphabetic characters, *[[:alpha:]]*, a space, followed by an uppercase letter, and one or more lowercase alphabetic characters, *[[:lower:]]*. (The + is a regular expression metacharacter representing one or more of the previous characters.) The line *joe blow* does not match this pattern.

9.2.2 Whitespace Metacharacters

A whitespace character represents a space, tab, return, newline, or form feed. The whitespace character can be represented literally, by pressing a Tab key or the spacebar or the Enter key. See Table 9.4.

Table 9.4 Whitespace Metacharacters

Metacharacter	What It Matches
\s	Matches whitespace character, spaces, tabs, and newlines
\S	Matches nonwhitespace character
\n	Matches a newline, the end-of-line character (\015)
\r	Matches a a carriage return or (\ \012)
\t	Matches a tab
\f	Matches a form feed

EXAMPLE 9.12

```
(The Script)
   use warnings;

   # The \s metasymbol and whitespace
1  while(<DATA>){
2      print if s/\s/*/g;       # Substitute all spaces with stars
   }
   _ _DATA_ _
   Steve Blenheim 101
   Betty Boop 201
   Igor Chevsky 301
   Norma Cord 401
   Jonathan DeLoach 501
   Karen Evich 601

(Output)
Steve*Blenheim*101*Betty*Boop*201*Igor*Chevsky*301*Norma*
*Cord*401*Jonathan*DeLoach*501*Karen*Evich*601
```

EXPLANATION

1   The special *DATA* filehandle gets its input from the text after the _ _DATA_ _ token. The *while* loop is entered and the first line after the _ _DATA_ _ token is read in and assigned to $_. Each time the loop is entered, the next line following _ _DATA_ _ is assigned to $_ until all the lines have been processed.

2   The line $_ is printed if it matches a pattern containing a whitespace character (space, tab, newline), \s. All whitespace characters (other than the newline) are replaced with an *.

EXAMPLE 9.13

```
(The Script)
   use warnings;
   # The \S metasymbol and nonwhitespace
1  while(<DATA>){
2      print if s/\S/*/g;
   }
   _ _DATA_ _
   Steve Blenheim 101
   Betty Boop 201
   Igor Chevsky 301
   Norma Cord 401
   Jonathan DeLoach 501
   Karen Evich 601

(Output)
***** ********* ***
***** **** ***
**** ******* ***
***** **** ***
******* ******* ***
***** ****** ***
```

EXPLANATION

The line $_ is printed if $_ matches a pattern containing a nonwhitespace character (**not** a space, tab, or newline), \S. This time, all nonwhitespace characters are replaced with an *. When a metasymbol is capitalized, it negates the meaning of the lowercase version of the metasymbol; \d is a digit; \D is a nondigit.

EXAMPLE 9.14

```
(The Script)
   use warnings;
   # Escape sequences, \n and \t
1  while(<DATA>){
2      print if s/\n/\t/;
   }
   _ _DATA_ _
   Steve Blenheim 101
   Betty Boop 201
   Igor Chevsky 301
   Norma Cord 401
   Jonathan DeLoach 501
   Karen Evich 601

(Output)
Steve Blenheim 101    Betty Boop 201    Igor Chevsky 301
Norma Cord 401    Jon DeLoach 501    Karen Evich 601
```

2   The regular expression contains the \n escape sequence, representing a single newline character. The expression reads: print the line if the substitution is successful; meaning, each newline can be replaced with a tab (\t).

9.2.3 Metacharacters to Repeat Pattern Matches

In the previous examples, the metacharacter matched on a single character. What if you want to match on more than one character? For example, let's say you are looking for all lines containing names, and the first letter must be in uppercase—which can be represented as *[A-Z]*—but the following letters are lowercase, and the number of letters varies in each name. *[a-z]* matches on a single lowercase letter. How can you match on one or more lowercase letters? Or zero or more lowercase letters? To do this, you can use what are called **quantifiers**. To match on one or more lowercase letters, the regular expression can be written */[a-z]+/* where the + sign means "one or more of the previous characters," which in this case is one or more lowercase letters. Perl provides a number of quantifiers, as shown in Table 9.5.

Table 9.5 The Greedy Metacharacters

Metacharacter	*What It Matches*
x?	Matches 0 or 1 occurrences of *x*
(xyz)?	Matches 0 or 1 occurrences of pattern *xyz*
x*	Matches 0 or more occurrences of *x*
(xyz)*	Matches 0 or more occurrences of pattern *xyz*
x+	Matches 1 or more occurrences of *x*
(xyz)+	Matches 1 or more occurrences of pattern *xyz*
x{m,n}	Matches at least *m* occurrences of *x* and no more than *n* occurrences of *x*

The Greed Factor.   Normally, quantifiers are **greedy**; in other words, they match on the largest possible set of characters starting at the left-hand side of the string and searching to the right, look for the last possible character that would satisfy the condition. For example, given the following string:

```
$_="ab123456783445554437AB"
```

and the regular expression

```
s/ab[0-9]*/X/;
```

the search side would match

`ab123456783445554437`

All of this will be replaced with an *X*. After the substitution, *$_* would be

XAB

The asterisk (*) is a greedy metacharacter. It matches for zero or more of the preceding characters. In other words, it attaches itself to the character preceding it and looks only for zero or more occurrences of that character. In the preceding example, the asterisk attaches itself to the character class *[0-9]*. The matching starts on the left, searching for *ab* followed by zero or more numbers in the range between *0* and *9*. The matching continues until the last number is found; in this example, the number *7*. The pattern *ab* and all of the numbers in the range between *0* and *9* are replaced with a single *X*. The trailing characters, *AB*, remain.

Greediness can be turned off so that instead of matching on the greatest number of characters, the match is made on the least number of characters found. This is done by appending a question mark after the greedy metacharacter (see Example 9.23).

EXAMPLE 9.15

```
(The Script)
    use warnings;
    # The zero or one quantifier
1   while(<DATA>){
2       print if / [0-9]\.?/;
    }
    __DATA__
    Steve Blenheim 1.10
    Betty Boop .5
    Igor Chevsky 555.100
    Norma Cord 4.01
    Jonathan DeLoach .501
    Karen Evich 601

(Output)
Steve Blenheim 1.10
Igor Chevsky 555.100
Norma Cord 4.01
Karen Evich 601
```

EXPLANATION

2   The regular expression contains the *?* metacharacter, representing zero or one of the preceding characters. The expression reads: find a space, followed by a number between *0* and *9*, followed by either one literal period or no period at all.

EXAMPLE 9.16

```
(The Script)
   use warnings;
   # The zero or one quantifier
1  while(<DATA>){
2     print if /\sB[a-z]*/;
   }
   __DATA__
   Steve Blenheim 1.10
   Betty Boop .5
   Igor Chevsky 555.100
   Norma Cord 4.01
   Jonathan DeLoach .501
   Karen Evich 601

(Output)
Steve Blenheim 1.10
Betty Boop .5
```

EXPLANATION

2   The regular expression contains the * metacharacter, representing zero or more of the preceding character. The expression reads: Find a space, \s, followed by a B and zero or more lowercase letters [a-z]*.

EXAMPLE 9.17

```
(The Script)
   use warnings;
   # The dot metacharacter and the zero or one quantifier
1  while(<DATA>){
2     print if s/[A-Z].*y/Tom/;
   }
   __DATA__
   Steve Blenheim 101
   Betty Boop 201
   Igor Chevsky 301
   Norma Cord 401
   Jonathan DeLoach 501
   Karen Evich 601

(Output)
Tom Boop 201
Tom 301
```

EXPLANATION

2   The regular expression contains .*, where the * represents zero or more of the previous character. In this example, the previous character is the dot metacharacter, which represents any character at all. This expression reads: find an uppercase letter, *[A-Z]*, followed by zero or more of any character, .*, followed by the letter *y*. If there is more than one *y* on the line, the search will include all characters up until the **last** *y*. Both *Betty* and *Igor Chevsky* are matched. Note that the space in *Igor Chevsky* is included as one of the characters matched by the dot metacharacter.

EXAMPLE 9.18

```
(The Script)
   use warnings;
   # The one or more quantifier
1  while(<DATA>){
2     print if /5+/;
   }
   __DATA__
   Steve Blenheim 1.10
   Betty Boop .5
   Igor Chevsky 555.100
   Norma Cord 4.01
   Jonathan DeLoach .501
   Karen Evich 601

(Output)
Betty Boop .5
Igor Chevsky 555.100
Jonathan DeLoach .501
```

EXPLANATION

2   The regular expression contains the + metacharacter, representing one or more of the preceding characters. The expression reads: Find one or more repeating occurrence of the number 5.

EXAMPLE 9.19

```
(The Script)
   use warnings;
   # The one or more quantifier
1  while(<DATA>){
2     print if s/\w+/X/g;
   }
```

EXAMPLE 9.19 (CONTINUED)

```
    __DATA__
    Steve Blenheim 101
    Betty Boop 201
    Igor Chevsky 301
    Norma Cord 401
    Jonathan DeLoach 501
    Karen Evich 601

(Output)
X X X
X X X
X X X
X X X
X X X
X X X
```

EXPLANATION

The regular expression contains \w followed by a + metacharacter, representing one or more alphanumeric word characters. For example, the first set of alphanumeric word characters is *Steve,* and *Steve* is replaced by an *X*. Since the substitution is global, the next set of alphanumeric characters, *Blenheim*, is replaced by an *X*. Finally, the alphanumeric characters, *101*, are replaced by an *X*.

EXAMPLE 9.20

```
(The Script)
    use warnings;
    # Repeating patterns
1   while(<DATA>){
2       print if /5{1,3}/;
    }
    __DATA__
    Steve Blenheim 1.10
    Betty Boop .5
    Igor Chevsky 555.100
    Norma Cord 4.01
    Jonathan DeLoach .501
    Karen Evich 601

(Output)
Betty Boop .5
Igor Chevsky 555.100
Jonathan DeLoach .501
```

EXPLANATION

2   The regular expression contains the curly brace ({}) metacharacters, representing the number of times the preceding expression will be repeated. The expression reads: find at least one occurrence of the pattern *5* and as many as three in a row.

EXAMPLE 9.21

```
(The Script)
   use warnings;
   # Repeating patterns
1  while(<DATA>){
2     print if /5{3}/;
   }
   __DATA__
   Steve Blenheim 1.10
   Betty Boop .5
   Igor Chevsky 555.100
   Norma Cord 4.01
   Jonathan DeLoach .501
   Karen Evich 601

(Output)
Igor Chevsky 555.100
```

EXPLANATION

The expression reads: find three consecutive occurrences of the pattern 5. This does not mean that the string must contain exactly three, and no more, of the number 5. It just means that there must be **at least** three consecutive occurrences of the number 5. If the string contained 5555555, the match would still be successful. To find exactly three occurrences of the number 5, the pattern would have to be anchored in some way, either by using the ^ and $ anchors or by placing some other character before and after the three occurrences of the number 5; for example, /^5{3}$/ or / 5{3}898/ or /95{3}\.56/.

EXAMPLE 9.22

```
(The Script)
   use warnings;
   # Repeating patterns
1  while(<DATA>){
2     print if /5{1,}/;
   }
   __DATA__
   Steve Blenheim 1.10
   Betty Boop .5
   Igor Chevsky 555.100
   Norma Cord 4.01
   Jonathan DeLoach .501
   Karen Evich 601

(Output)
Betty Boop .5
Igor Chevsky 555.100
Jonathan DeLoach .501
```

EXPLANATION

The expression reads: Find at least one or more repeating occurrences of 5.

Metacharacters That Turn off Greediness. By placing a question mark after a greedy quantifier, the greed is turned off, and the search ends after the first match rather than the last one. Table 9.6 describes the metacharacters that turn off greediness.

EXAMPLE 9.23

```
(The Script)
   use warnings;
   # Greedy and not greedy
1  $_="abcdefghijklmnopqrstuvwxyz";
2  s/[a-z]+/XXX/;
3  print $_, "\n";

4  $_="abcdefghijklmnopqrstuvwxyz";
5  s/[a-z]+?/XXX/;
6  print $_, "\n";

(Output)
3  XXX
6  XXXbcdefghijklmnopqrstuvwxyz
```

EXPLANATION

1   The scalar $_ is assigned a string of lowercase letters.
2   The regular expression reads: search for one or more lowercase letters, and replace them with *XXX*. The + metacharacter is greedy. It takes as many characters as match the expression; meaning, it starts on the left-hand side of the string, grabbing as many lowercase letters as it can find until the end of the string.
3   The value of $_ is printed after the substitution. The whole string has been replaced with *XXX*.
4   The scalar $_ is again assigned a string of lowercase letters.
5   The regular expression reads: search for one or more lowercase letters, and, after finding the first one, <u>stop</u> searching and replace it with *XXX*. The ? affixed to the + turns off the greediness of the metacharacter. The minimal number of characters is searched for. The *a* is replaced with *XXX* and the rest of the string remains untouched.
6   The value of $_ is printed after the substitution.

Table 9.6   Turning off Greediness

Metacharacter	*What It Matches*
x??	Matches 0 or 1 occurrences of *x*
(xyz)??	Matches 0 or 1 occurrences of pattern *xyz*
x?*	Matches 0 or more occurrences of *x*
(xyz)?*	Matches 0 or more occurrences of pattern *xyz*
x+?	Matches 1 or more occurrences of *x*

(continued)

Table 9.6 Turning off Greediness (continued)

Metacharacter	What It Matches
(xyz)+?	Matches 1 or more occurrences of pattern xyz
x{m,n}?	Matches at least m occurrences of x and no more than n occurrences of x
x{m}?	Matches at least m occurrences of x
x{m,}?	Matches at least m times

EXAMPLE 9.24

```
(The Script)
   # A greedy quantifier
1  $string="I got a cupful of sugar and two cups of flour
        from the cupboard.";

2  $string =~ s/cup.*/tablespoon/;
3  print "$string\n";
   # Turning off greed
4  $string="I got a cupful of sugar and two cups of flour
        from the cupboard.";
5  $string =~ s/cup.*?/tablespoon/;
6  print "$string\n";

(Output)
3  I got a tablespoon
6  I got a tablespoonful of sugar and two cups of flour from the cupboard.
```

EXPLANATION

1   The scalar $string$ is assigned a string containing the pattern *cup* three times.

2   The *s* (substitution) operator searches for the pattern *cup* followed by zero or more characters; that is, *cup* and all characters to the end of the line are matched and replaced with the string *tablespoon*. The .* is called a greedy quantifier because it matches for the largest possible pattern.

3   The output shows the result of a greedy substitution.

4   The scalar $string$ is reset.

5   This time the search is not greedy. By appending a question mark to the .*, the smallest pattern that matches *cup*, followed by zero or more characters, is replaced with *tablespoon*. Only the first *cup* will be replaced with *tablespoon* resulting in *tablespoonful*. This example is to demonstrate the way greedy metacharacters work. Another way to write the regex would be: *s/cupful/tablespoonful/*

6   The new string is printed.

Anchoring Metacharacters. Often, it is necessary to anchor a metacharacter so that it matches only if the pattern is found at the beginning or end of a line, word, or string. These metacharacters are based on a position just to the left or to the right of the character that is being matched. Anchors (see Table 9.7) are technically called **zero-width assertions** because they correspond to positions, not actual characters in a string. For example, /^abc/ means: find *abc* at the beginning of the line, where the ^ represents a position, not an actual character.

Table 9.7 Anchors (Assertions)

Metacharacter	What It Matches
^	Matches to beginning of line or beginning of string
$	Matches to end of line or end of a string
\A	Matches the beginning of the string only
\Z	Matches the end of the string or line
\z	Matches the end of string only
\G	Matches where previous *m//g* left off
\b	Matches a word boundary (when not inside *[ ]*)
\B	Matches a nonword boundary

EXAMPLE 9.25

```
(The Script)
    use warnings;
    # Beginning-of-line anchor
1   while(<DATA>){
2       print if /^[JK]/;
    }
    __DATA__
    Steve Blenheim 1.10
    Betty Boop .5
    Igor Chevsky 555.100
    Norma Cord 4.01
    Jonathan DeLoach .501
    Karen Evich 601

(Output)
Jonathan DeLoach .501
Karen Evich 601.100
```

EXPLANATION

The regular expression contains the caret (^) metacharacter, representing the beginning-of-line anchor only when it is the first character in the pattern. The expression reads: find a *J* or *K* at the beginning of the line. \A would produce the same result as the caret in this example. The expression /^[^JK]/ reads: search for a non-*J* or non-*K* character at the beginning of the line. Remember that when the caret is within a character class, it negates the character class. It is a beginning-of-line anchor only when positioned **directly after** the opening delimiter.

EXAMPLE 9.26

```
(The Script)
   use warnings;
   # End-of-line anchor
1  while(<DATA>) {
2     print if /10$/;
   }
   __DATA__
   Steve Blenheim 1.10
   Betty Boop .5
   Igor Chevsky 555.10
   Norma Cord 4.01
   Jonathan DeLoach .501
   Karen Evich 601

(Output)
Steve Blenheim 1.10
Igor Chevsky 555.10
```

EXPLANATION

The regular expression contains the $ metacharacter, representing the end-of-line anchor only when the $ is the last character in the pattern. The expression reads: find a *1* and a *0* followed by a newline.

EXAMPLE 9.27

```
(The Script)
   use warnings;
   # Word anchors or boundaries
1  while(<DATA>) {
2     print if /\bJon/;
   }
```

EXAMPLE 9.27 (CONTINUED)

```
__DATA__
Steve Blenheim 1.10
Betty Boop .5
Igor Chevsky 555.100
Norma Cord 4.01
Jonathan DeLoach .501
Karen Evich 601

(Output)
Jonathan DeLoach .501
```

EXPLANATION

The regular expression contains the \b metacharacter, representing a word boundary. The expression reads: find a word beginning with the pattern *Jon*.

EXAMPLE 9.28

```
(The Script)
    use warnings;
    # Beginning- and end-of-word anchors
1   while(<DATA>){
2       print if /\bJon\b/;
    }
    __DATA__
    Steve Blenheim 1.10
    Betty Boop .5
    Igor Chevsky 555.100
    Norma Cord 4.01
    Jonathan DeLoach .501
    Karen Evich 601

(Output)
<No output>
```

EXPLANATION

The regular expression also contains the \b metacharacter, representing a word boundary. The expression reads: find a word beginning and ending with *Jon*. Nothing is found.

The *m* Modifier.   The *m* modifier is used to control the behavior of the $ and ^ anchor metacharacters. A string containing newlines will be treated as multiple lines. If the regular expression is anchored with the ^ metacharacter, and that pattern is found at the beginning of any one of the multiple lines, the match is successful. Likewise, if the regular expression is anchored by the $ metacharacter (or \Z) at the end of any one of the multiple lines, and the pattern is found, it too will return a successful match. The *m* modifier has no effect with \A and \z.

EXAMPLE 9.29

```
(The Script)
   use warning;
   # Anchors and the m modifier
1  $_="Today is history.\nTomorrow will never be here.\n";
2  print if /^Tomorrow/;     # Embedded newline

3  $_="Today is history.\nTomorrow will never be here.\n";
4  print if /\ATomorrow/;    # Embedded newline

5  $_="Today is history.\nTomorrow will never be here.\n";
6  print if /^Tomorrow/m;

7  $_="Today is history.\nTomorrow will never be here.\n";
8  print if /\ATomorrow/m;

9  $_="Today is history.\nTomorrow will never be here.\n";
10 print if /history\.$/m;

(Output)
6  Today is history.
   Tomorrow will never be here.
10 Today is history.
   Tomorrow will never be here.
```

EXPLANATION

1   The $_ scalar is assigned a string with embedded newlines.

2   The ^ metacharacter anchors the search to the beginning of the line. Since the line does not begin with *Tomorrow,* the search fails and nothing is returned.

3   The $_ scalar is assigned a string with embedded newlines.

4   The \A assertion matches only at the beginning of a string, no matter what. Since the string does not begin with *Tomorrow,* the search fails and nothing is returned.

5   The $_ scalar is assigned a string with embedded newlines.

6   The *m* modifier treats the string as multiple lines, each line ending with a newline. In this example, the ^ anchor matches at the beginning of any of these multiple lines. The pattern /^*Tomorrow*/ is found in the second line.

7   The $_ scalar is assigned a string with embedded newlines.

8   The \A assertion matches only at the beginning of a string, no matter how many newlines are embedded, and the *m* modifier has no effect. Since *Tomorrow* is not found at the beginning of the string, nothing is matched.

9   The $_ scalar is assigned a string with embedded newlines.

10 The $ metacharacter anchors the search to the end of a line. With the *m* modifier, embedded newlines create multiple lines. The pattern /*history*\.$/ is found at the end of the first line. This will also work with the \Z assertion but not with \z.

Alternation.   Alternation allows the regular expression to contain alternative patterns to be matched. For example, the regular expression /John|Karen|Steve/ will match a line containing *John* or *Karen* or *Steve*. If *Karen, John,* or *Steve* are all on different lines, all lines are matched. Each of the alternative expressions is separated by a vertical bar (pipe symbol) and the expressions can consist of any number of characters, unlike the character class that matches for only one character; for example, /a|b|c/ is the same as *[abc]*, whereas /ab|de/ cannot be represented as *[abde]*. The pattern /ab|de/ is either *ab* or *de*, whereas the class *[abcd]* represents only **one** character in the set, *a, b, c,* or *d*.

EXAMPLE 9.30

```
(The Script)
   use warnings;
   # Alternation: this, that, and the other thing
1  while(<DATA>){
2     print if /Steve|Betty|Jon/;
   }
   __DATA__
   Steve Blenheim
   Betty Boop
   Igor Chevsky
   Norma Cord
   Jonathan DeLoach
   Karen Evich

(Output)
2  Steve Blenheim
   Betty Boop
   Jonathan DeLoach
```

EXPLANATION

The pipe symbol, |, is used in the regular expression to match on a set of alternative patterns. If any of the patterns *Steve, Betty,* or *Jon,* are found, the match is successful.

Grouping or Clustering.   If the regular expression pattern is enclosed in parentheses, a subpattern is created. Then, for example, instead of the greedy metacharacters matching on zero, one, or more of the previous single characters, they can match on the previous subpattern. Alternation can also be controlled if the patterns are enclosed in parentheses. This process of grouping characters together is also called **clustering** by the Perl wizards.

EXAMPLE 9.31

```
(The Script)
   use warnings;
   # Clustering or grouping
1  $_=qq/The baby says, "Mama, Mama, I can say Papa!"\n/;
2  print if s/(ma|pa)+/goo/gi;

(Output)
The baby says, "goo, goo, I can say goo!"
```

EXPLANATION

1 The $_ scalar is assigned the doubly quoted string.
2 The regular expression contains a pattern enclosed in parentheses, followed by a +
   metacharacter. The parentheses group the characters that are to be controlled by the +
   metacharacter. The expression reads: find one or more occurrences of the pattern *ma*
   or *pa* and replace that with *goo*.

EXAMPLE 9.32

```
(The Script)
   use warnings;
   # Clustering or grouping
1  while(<DATA>){
2     print if /\s(12){3}$/;
   }
   __DATA__
   Steve Blenheim      121212
   Betty Boop          123
   Igor Chevsky        123444123
   Norma Cord          51235
   Jonathan DeLoach    123456
   Karen Evich         121212456

(Output)
Steve Blenheim  121212
```

EXPLANATION

2 The pattern *12* is grouped in parentheses. It is controlled by the quantifier {3}; meaning, a row of exactly 3 occurrences of the number *12* at the end of the line ($) will be
   matched.

EXAMPLE 9.33

```
(The Script)
   use warnings;
   # Grouping
1  $_="Tom and Dan Savage and Ellie Main are cousins.\n";
2  print if s/Tom|Ellie Main/Archie/g;
```

EXAMPLE 9.33 (CONTINUED)

```
3   $_="Tom and Dan Savage and Ellie Main are cousins.\n";
4   print if s/(Tom|Ellie) Main/Archie/g;
```

(Output)
```
2   Archie and Dan Savage and Archie are cousins.
4   Tom and Dan Savage and Archie are cousins.
```

EXPLANATION

1   The $_ scalar is assigned the string.
2   If either the pattern *Tom* or the pattern *Ellie Main* is matched in $_, both patterns will be replaced with *Archie*.
3   The $_ scalar is assigned the string.
4   By enclosing *Tom* and *Ellie* in parentheses, the alternative now becomes either *Tom Main* or *Ellie Main*. Since the pattern *Ellie Main* is the only one matched in $_, *Ellie Main* is replaced with *Archie*.

EXAMPLE 9.34

```
(The Script)
    use warnings;
    # Grouping and anchors
1   while(<DATA>){
2       # print if /^Steve|Boop/;
3       print if /^(Steve|Boop)/;      # /^Steve|^Boop also works
    }
    __DATA__
    Steve Blenheim
    Betty Boop
    Igor Chevsky
    Norma Cord
    Jonathan DeLoach
    Karen Evich
```

(Output)
Steve Blenheim

EXPLANATION

2   This line has been commented out. It would print any line that begins with *Steve* and any line containing the pattern *Boop*. The beginning-of-line anchor, the caret, applies only to the pattern *Steve*.
3   The line will be printed if it begins with either *Steve* or *Boop*. The parentheses group the two patterns so that the beginning-of-line anchor, the caret, applies to both patterns *Steve* and *Boop*. It could also be written as /(^Steve|^Boop)/.

Remembering or Capturing. If the regular expression pattern is enclosed in parentheses, a subpattern is created. The subpattern is saved in special numbered scalar variables, starting with $1, then $2, and so on. These variables can be used later in the program and will persist until another successful pattern match occurs, at which time they will be cleared. Even if the intention was to use grouping to create as shown in the previous examples, the subpatterns are saved as a side effect.[4]

EXAMPLE 9.35

```
(The Script)
   use warnings;
   # Remembering subpatterns
1  while(<DATA>){
2     s/([Jj]on)/${1}athan/;  # Substitute Jon or jon with
                                # Jonathan or jonathan
3     print;
   }
   __DATA__
   Steve Blenheim
   Betty Boop
   Igor Chevsky
   Norma Cord
   Jon DeLoach
   Karen Evich

(Output)
Steve Blenheim
Betty Boop
Igor Chevsky
Norma Cord
Jonathan DeLoach
Karen Evich
```

EXPLANATION

The regular expression contains the pattern *Jon* enclosed in parentheses. This pattern is captured and stored in a special scalar, $1, so it can be remembered. (The curly braces used here ${1} are not required, but insulate the number 1 from the string that follows it.) If a second pattern is enclosed in parentheses, it will be stored in $2, and so on. The numbers are represented on the replacement side as $1, $2, $3, and so on. The expression reads: find *Jon* or *jon* and replace with either *Jonathan* or *jonathan*, respectively. The special numbered variables are cleared after the next successful search is performed.

---

4. It is possible to prevent a subpattern from being saved.

EXAMPLE 9.36

```
(The Script)
   use warnings;
   # Remembering multiple subpatterns
1  while(<DATA>){
2      print if s/(Steve) (Blenheim)/$2,$1/;
   }
   __DATA__
   Steve Blenheim
   Betty Boop
   Igor Chevsky
   Norma Cord
   Jonathan DeLoach
   Karen Evich

(Output)
Blenheim, Steve
```

EXPLANATION

The regular expression contains two patterns enclosed in parentheses. The first pattern is captured and saved in the special scalar *$1*, and the second pattern is captured and saved in the special scalar *$2*. On the replacement side, since *$2* is referenced first, *Blenheim* is printed first, followed by a comma, and then by *$1*, which is *Steve* (meaning, the effect is to reverse *Steve* and *Blenheim*).

EXAMPLE 9.37

```
(The Script)
   use warnings;
   # Reversing subpatterns
1  while(<DATA>){
2      s/([A-Z][a-z]+)\s([A-Z][a-z]+)/$2, $1/;
                                    # Reverse first and last names
3      print;
   }
   __DATA__
   Steve Blenheim
   Betty Boop
   Igor Chevsky
   Norma Cord
   Jon DeLoach
   Karen Evich

(Output)
Blenheim, Steve
Boop, Betty
Chevsky ,Igor
Cord, Norma
De, JonLoach      # Whoops!
Evich, Karen
```

EXPLANATION

This regular expression also contains two patterns enclosed in parentheses. In this example, metacharacters are used in the pattern-matching process. The first pattern reads: find an uppercase letter followed by one or more lowercase letters. A space follows the remembered pattern. The second pattern reads: find an uppercase letter followed by one or more lowercase letters. The patterns are saved in $1 and $2, respectively, and then reversed on the replacement side. Note the problem that arises with the last name, *DeLoach*. That is because *DeLoach* contains **both** uppercase and lowercase letters after the first uppercase letter in the name. To allow for this case, the pattern should be *s/([A-Z][a-z]+)\s([A-Z][A-Za-z]+)/$2, $1/.*

EXAMPLE 9.38

```
(The Script)
    use warnings;
    # Metasymbols and subpatterns
1   while(<DATA>){
2       s/(\w+)\s(\w+)/$2,$1/;        # Reverse first and last names
3       print;
    }
    __DATA__
    Steve Blenheim
    Betty Boop
    Igor Chevsky
    Norma Cord
    Jon DeLoach
    Betty Boop

(Output)
Blenheim, Steve
Boop, Betty
Chevsky, Igor
Cord, Norma
DeLoach, Jon
Boop, Betty
```

EXPLANATION

2   The regular expression contains two subpatterns enclosed in parentheses. The \w+ represents one or more word characters. The regular expression consists of two parenthesized subpatterns separated by a space (\s). Each subpattern is saved in $1 and $2, respectively. $1 and $2 are used in the replacement side of the substitution to reverse the first and last names.

EXAMPLE 9.39

```
(The Script)
   use warnings;
   # Capturing
   my($first, $last);
1  while(<DATA>){
2     ($first, $last)=/(\w+)\s(\w+)/;     # Could be: (\S+)\s(\S+)/
3     print "$last, $first\n";
   }
   __DATA__
   Steve Blenheim
   Betty Boop
   Igor Chevsky
   Norma Cord
   Jon DeLoach               .
   Betty Boop

(Output)
Blenheim, Steve
Boop, Betty
Chevsky, Igor
Cord, Norma
DeLoach, Jon
Boop, Betty
```

EXPLANATION

2   The regular expression contains two patterns enclosed in parentheses. The \w+ represents one or more word characters. This time, the captured subpatterns are directly assigned to $first$ and $last$, respectively.

3   The values of the variables are printed in reverse for each line of the file.

EXAMPLE 9.40

```
(The Script)
   use warnings;
   # The greedy quantifier
1  my $string="ABCdefghiCxyzwerC YOU!";
2  $string=~s/.*C/HEY/;
3  print "$string", "\n";

(Output)
HEY YOU!
```

EXPLANATION

1   The scalar $string$ is assigned a string containing a number of Cs.

2   The search side of the substitution, /.*C/, reads: find the largest pattern that contains any number of characters ending in C. This search is greedy. It will search from left to right until it reaches the **last** C. The string HEY will replace what was found in $string$.

3   The new string is printed, showing the result of the substitution. Everything up until the last C is replaced with HEY.

Turning off Greed.   Greed can be turned off using the question mark (?) character.

EXAMPLE 9.41

```
(The Script)
   use warnings;
   # Turning off greed
1  my $str="Tom Jones:23 Main St.:Boston, MA";
2  $str=~/(.*):/;      # Capture everything up to the last colon
   print "$1\n";

   $str="Tom Jones:23 Main St.:Boston, MA";
3  $str=~/(.*?):/;     # Capture everything up to the first colon
   print "$1\n";

(Output)
2  Tom Jones:23 Main St.
3  Tom Jones
```

EXPLANATION

1   The scalar $string is assigned the string.
2   The regular expression is enclosed in parentheses. Everything is matched up until the last colon because the .* is greedy. The matched characters are captured and stored in $1.
3   In this example, the greed is turned off with the ? after the .*. Now everything will be matched up until the first colon, then captured, and printed.

EXAMPLE 9.42

```
(The Script)
   use warnings;
   # Capturing and greed
1  my $fruit="apples pears peaches plums";
2  $fruit =~ /(.*)\s(.*)\s(.*)/;
3  print "$1\n";
4  print "$2\n";
5  print "$3\n";
   print "-" x 30, "\n";
6  $fruit="apples pears peaches plums";
7  $fruit =~ /(.*?)\s(.*?)\s(.*?)\s/;   # Turn off greedy quantifier
8  print "$1\n";
9  print "$2\n";
10 print "$3\n";
```

EXAMPLE 9.42 (CONTINUED)

```
(Output)
3    apples pears
4    peaches
5    plums
     - - - - - - - - - - - - - - - - - - - - - - - - - - -
8    apples
9    pears
10   peaches
```

EXPLANATION

1   The scalar *$fruit* is assigned the string.

2   The string is divided into three remembered substrings, each substring enclosed within parentheses. The .* metacharacter sequence reads zero or more of any character. The * always matches for the largest possible pattern. The largest possible pattern would be the whole string. However, there are two whitespaces outside of the parentheses that must also be matched in the string. What is the largest possible pattern that can be saved in *$1* and still leave two spaces in the string? The answer is *apples pears*.

3   The value of *$1* is printed.

4   The first substring was stored in *$1*. *peaches plums* is what remains of the original string. What is the largest possible pattern (.*) that can be matched and still have one whitespace remaining? The answer is *peaches*. *peaches* will be assigned to *$2*. The value of *$2* is printed.

5   The third substring is printed. *plums* is all that is left for *$3*.

6   The scalar *$fruit* is assigned the string again.

7   This time, a question mark follows the greedy quantifier (*). This means that the pattern saved will be the minimal, rather than the maximal, number of characters found. *apples* will be the minimal numbers of characters stored in *$1*, *pears* the minimal number in *$2*, and *peaches* the minimal number of characters in *$3*. The \s is required or the minimal amount of characters would be zero, since the * means zero or more of the preceding character.

8   The value of *$1* is printed.

9   The value of *$2* is printed.

10 The value of *$3* is printed.

Turning off Capturing.   When the only purpose is to use the parentheses for grouping, and you are not interested in saving the subpatterns in *$1*, *$2*, or *$3*, the special *?:* metacharacter can be used to suppress the capturing of the subpattern.

EXAMPLE 9.43

```
(In Script)
    # Turning off capturing
1   $_="Tom Savage and Dan Savage are brothers.\n";
2   print if /(?:D[a-z]*|T[a-z]*) Savage/;    # Perl will not capture
                                              # the pattern

3   print $1,"\n";      # $1 has no value

(Output)
2   Tom Savage and Dan Savage are brothers.
3   <Nothing is printed>
```

EXPLANATION

1   The $_ scalar is assigned a string.
2   The ?: turns off capturing when a pattern is enclosed in parentheses. In this example, alternation is used to search for any of two patterns. If the search is successful, the value of $_ is printed, but whichever pattern is found, it will not be captured and assigned to $1.
3   Without the ?:, the value of $1 would be *Tom*, since it is the first pattern found. ?: says "Don't save the pattern when you find it." Nothing is saved and nothing is printed.

Metacharacters That Look Ahead and Behind.   Suppose you want to find and replace words in a document that are followed by a comma. In your search string, you have the word you are looking for followed by the comma as part of the search criteria, but you want to exclude the comma when replacing the word. Looking ahead for a pattern that will be matched and then excluded, in this case the comma, is called a **positive look ahead**. A **negative look ahead** would look ahead for a character that is not there.

A positive look ahead is an assertion like the ^ and $ anchors in that it represents a position in the search. A regular expression contains the positive look ahead as /regex (?=pattern)/. So for example, if you say s/John (?=Doe)/Jane/, the regex engine will search for *John* and look ahead to see if *Doe* follows, and if it does, then the positive look ahead match is true and *Doe* is completely discarded (and will not be captured in $1). *Doe* will not be included in what is replaced. Only *John* will be replaced with *Jane*.

A negative look ahead looks ahead to see if the pattern (?!pattern) is **not** there, and if it is not, succeeds, discarding the pattern after the ?!.

With a **positive look behind**, Perl looks backward in the string for a pattern (?<=pattern) and if that pattern is found, will then continue pattern matching on the regular expression, discarding the pattern in parentheses. A **negative look behind** looks behind in the string to see if a pattern (?<!pattern) is not there, and if it is not, succeeds in the matching. See Table 9.8.

Table 9.8   Look Around Assertions

Metacharacter	What It Matches
/PATTERN(?=pattern)/	Positive look ahead
/PATTERN(?!pattern)/	Negative look ahead
(?<=pattern)/PATTERN/	Positive look behind
(?<!pattern)/PATTERN/	Negative look behind

EXAMPLE 9.44

```
(The Script)
   use warnings;
   # A positive look ahead
1  my $string="I love chocolate cake and chocolate ice cream.";
2  $string =~ s/chocolate (?=ice)/vanilla/;
3  print "$string\n";
4  $string="Tomorrow night Tom Savage and Tommy Johnson will leave
            for vacation.";
5  $string =~ s/Tom(?=my)/Jere/g;
6  print "$string\n";

(Output)
3   I love chocolate cake and vanilla ice cream.
6   Tomorrow night Tom Savage and Jeremy Johnson will leave for vacation.
```

EXPLANATION

1   The scalar *$string* contains *chocolate* twice; the word *cake* follows the first occurrence of *chocolate*, and the word *ice* follows the second occurrence.

2   This is an example of a **positive look ahead**. The pattern *chocolate* is followed by *(?=ice)*; meaning, if *chocolate* is found, look ahead *(?=)* and see if *ice* is the next pattern. If *ice* is found just ahead of *chocolate*, the match is successful and *chocolate* will be replaced with *vanilla*. The look ahead part, *ice*, is discarded. It is not part of the pattern to be replaced, but only there to help further define which *chocolate* we are looking for.

3   After the substitution on line 2, the new string is printed.

4   The scalar *$string* is assigned a string of text consisting of three words starting with *Tom*.

5   The pattern is matched if it contains *Tom*, only if *Tom* is followed by *my*. If the positive look ahead is successful, then *Tom* will be replaced with *Jere* in the string.

6   After the substitution on line 5, the new string is printed. *Tommy* has been replaced with *Jeremy*.

EXAMPLE 9.45

```
(The Script)
   use warnings;
   # A negative look ahead
1  while(<DATA>){
2     print if /^\w+\s(?![BC])/;
   }
   __DATA__
   Steve Blenheim
   Betty Boop
   Igor Chevsky
   Norma Cord
   Jon DeLoach
   Karen Evich

(Output)
Jon DeLoach
Karen Evich
```

EXPLANATION

2   The regular expression means: search at the beginning of the line for one or more
    word characters (\w+), followed by a space (\s), and look ahead for any character that
    is **not** a *B* or *C*. This is called a **negative look ahead**.

EXAMPLE 9.46

```
(The Script)
   use warnings;
   # A positive look behind
1  my $string="I love chocolate cake, chocolate milk,
           and chocolate ice cream.";
2  $string =~ s/(?<= chocolate) milk/ candy bars/;
3  print "$string\n";

4  $string="I love coffee, I love tea, I love the boys
           and the boys love me.";
5  $string =~ s/(?<=the boys) love/ don't like/;
6  print "$string\n";

(Output)
3  I love chocolate cake, chocolate candy bars, and chocolate ice cream.
6  I love coffee, I love tea, I love the boys and the boys don't like me.
```

EXPLANATION

1 The scalar *$string* is assigned a string with three different occurrences of *chocolate*.
2 The pattern in parentheses is called a **positive look behind,** meaning that Perl looks **backward** in the string to make sure this pattern occurs. If the pattern *milk* is found, Perl will look back in the string to see if it is preceded by *chocolate* and, if so, *milk* will be replaced with *candy bars*. The look behind pattern, *chocolate*, is not affected by the replacement, so now we have *chocolate candy bars*.
3 The string is printed after the substitution.
4 This is another example of a positive look behind. Perl looks backward in the string for the pattern *the boys*, and if the pattern is found, the regular expression *love* will be replaced with *don't like*.

EXAMPLE 9.47

```
(The Script)
    # A negative look behind
1   while(<DATA>){
2      print if /(?<!Betty) B[a-z]*/;
    }
    __DATA__
    Steve Blenheim
    Betty Boop
    Igor Chevsky
    Norma Cord
    Jon DeLoach
    Karen Evich

(Output)
Steve Blenheim
```

EXPLANATION

2 The pattern in parentheses is called a **negative look behind,** meaning that Perl looks **backward** in the string to make sure this pattern does not occur. Any line that contains the letter *B*, followed by zero or more lowercase letters, *[a-z]**, will be printed, as long as the pattern behind it is **not** *Betty*.

9.2.4 The *tr* or *y* Operators

The *tr* operator translates characters on a one-to-one basis. To see what this means, let's compare translation to substitution. You can see in the following example that the syntax for both the *tr* operator and substitution operator look very much the same, but they are really quite different in what they do. Let's take a look at **substitution** first:

```
$str = "Elizabeth likes little baby lizards. ";
$str =~ s/Elizabeth/Christopher/;
print "$str\n";
```

and the result is:

```
Christopher likes little baby lizards.
```

Now let's look at the *tr* function.

```
$str = "Elizabeth likes little baby lizards. ";
$str =~ tr/Elizabeth/Christopher/;
print "$str\n";
```

and the result is:

```
Christoph hrkos hrppho tsty hrisrds.
```

What is different? The *s* operator searches for a pattern and replaces it with a string; meaning, *Elizabeth* is replaced with *Christopher*. The *tr* operator[5] translates characters, on a one-on-one correspondence, from each character in the search string to its corresponding character in the replacement string and returns the number of characters it replaced. In the preceding example, every *E* in *$str*, is translated to a corresponding *C*, every *l* is translated to an *h*, every *i* is transalted to an *r*, and so on.

The *tr* operator does not interpret regular expression metacharacters but allows a dash to represent a range of characters. The letter *y* can be used in place of *tr*. This strangeness comes from UNIX, where the *sed* utility has a *y* command to translate characters, similar to the UNIX *tr*. If you look at the UNIX *tr* man page, you can see that it is very similar to the Perl *tr* function, illustrating the role UNIX has played in the development of Perl.

The *d* option deletes the search string.

The *c* option complements the search string.

The *s* option is called the squeeze option. Multiple occurrences of characters found in the search string are replaced by a single occurrence of that character (for example, you may want to replace multiple tabs with single tabs). See Table 9.9 for a list of modifiers.

Table 9.9   *tr* Modifiers

Modifier	Meaning
d	Delete characters
c	Complement the search list
s	Squeeze out multiple characters to single character

---

5. The Perl *tr* function is derived from the UNIX *tr* command.

FORMAT

```
tr/search/replacement/
tr/search/replacement/d
tr/search/replacement/c
tr/search/replacement/s
y/search/replacement/        (same as tr; uses same modifiers)
```

EXAMPLE 9.48

```
(The Input Data)
    Steve Blenheim 101
    Betty Boop 201
    Igor Chevsky 301
    Norma Cord 401
    Jon DeLoach 501
    Karen Evich 601

(Lines from a Script)
1  tr/a-z/A-Z/;print;

(Output)
STEVE BLENHEIM  101
BETTY BOOP  201
IGOR CHEVSKY  301
NORMA CORD  401
JON DELOACH  501
KAREN EVICH  601


2  tr/0-9/:/; print;

(Output)
Steve Blenheim :::
Betty Boop :::
Igor Chevsky :::
Norma Cord :::
Jon DeLoach :::
Karen Evich :::


3  tr/A-Z/a-c/;print;

(Output)
cteve blenheim 101
betty boop 201
cgor chevsky 301
corma cord 401
con cecoach 501
caren cvich 601
```

EXAMPLE 9.48 (CONTINUED)

```
4  tr/ /#/; print;
```

(Output)
Steve#Blenheim#101
Betty#Boop#201
Igor#Chevsky#301
Norma#Cord#401
Jon#DeLoach#501
Karen#Evich#601

```
5  y/A-Z/a-z/;print;
```

(Output)
steve blenheim 101
betty boop 201
igor chevsky 301
norma cord 401
jon deloach 501
karen evich 601

EXPLANATION

1   The *tr* operator makes a one-on-one correspondence between each character in the search string with each character in the replacement string. Each lowercase letter will be translated to its corresponding uppercase letter.

2   Each number will be translated to a colon.

3   The translation is messy here. Since the search side represents more characters than the replacement side, all letters from *D* to *Z* will be replaced with a *c*.

4   Each space will be replaced with pound signs (*#*).

5   The *y* is a synonym for *tr*. Each uppercase letter is translated to its corresponding lowercase letter.

The *d* Delete Option.   The *d* (delete) option removes all characters in the search string not found in the replacement string.

EXAMPLE 9.49

```
1  tr/ //; print;   # Nothing happens
```

(Output)
1 Steve Blenheim
2 Betty Boop
3 Igor Chevsky
4 Norma Cord
5 Jon DeLoach
6 Karen Evich

EXAMPLE 9.49 (CONTINUED)

```
2  tr/ //d; print;    # Delete spaces

(Output)
1SteveBlenheim
2BettyBoop
3IgorChevsky
4NormaCord
5JonDeLoach
6KarenEvich
```

EXPLANATION

1. In this example, the translation does not take place as it would if you were using *sed* or *vi*.

2. The *d* option is required to delete each space when using the *tr* function.

The *c* Complement Option. The *c* (complement) option complements the search string; that is, it translates each character not listed in this string to its corresponding character in the replacement string.

EXAMPLE 9.50

```
1  tr/0-9/*/; print;

(Output)
* Steve Blenheim
* Betty Boop
* Igor Chevsky
* Norma Cord
* Jon DeLoach
* Karen Evich


2  tr/0-9/*/c; print;

(Output)
1****************2*************3***************4*************5****
*********6*************
```

EXPLANATION

1. Without the *c* option, *tr* translates each number to an asterisk (*).

2. With the *c* option, *tr* translates each character that is **not** a number to an asterisk (*); this includes the newline character.

The s Squeeze Option.   The s (squeeze) option translates all characters that are repeated to a single character and can be used to get rid of excess characters, such as excess
whitespace or delimiters, squeezing these characters down to just one.

EXAMPLE 9.51

```
(The Text File)
1  while (<DATA>){
      tr/:/:/s;
      print;
   {
   __DATA__
   1:::Steve Blenheim
   2::Betty Boop
   3:Igor Chevsky
   4:Norma Cord
   5:::::Jon DeLoach
   6:::Karen Evich

(Output)
1:Steve Blenheim
2:Betty Boop
3:Igor Chevsky
4:Norma Cord
5:Jon DeLoach
6:Karen Evich
```

EXPLANATION

1   The "squeeze" option causes the multiple colons to be translated (squeezed) to single
     colons.

9.3 Unicode

For every character, Unicode specifies a unique identification number called a **code point**
that remains consistent across applications, languages, and platforms.

With the advent of the Internet, it became obvious that the ASCII coding for characters
was insufficient if the whole world were to be included in transferring data from one Web
site to another without corrupting the data. The ASCII sequence of characters consists of
only 256 (one-byte) characters and could hardly accommodate languages like Chinese and
Japanese, where a given symbol is drawn from a set of thousands of characters.

The Unicode standard is an effort to solve the problem by creating new characters sets,
and encoding called UTF8 and UTF16, where characters are not limited to one byte. UTF8,
for example, allows two bytes that can hold up to 65,536 characters, and each character has
a unique number. To remove ambiguity, any given 16-bit value would always represent the

same character, thereby allowing for consistent sorting, searching, displaying, and editing of text. According to the Unicode Consortium,[6] Unicode has the capacity to encode over one million characters, which is sufficient to encompass all the world's written languages. Further, all symbols are treated equally, so that all characters can be accessed without the need for escape sequences or control codes.

9.3.1 Perl and Unicode

"The days of just flinging strings around are over. It's well established that modern programs need to be capable of communicating funny accented letters, and things like euro symbols. This means that programmers need new habits. It's easy to program Unicode capable software, but it does require discipline to do it right."

— Perlunitut

The largest change in Perl 5.6 was to provide UTF8 Unicode support. By default, Perl represents strings internally in Unicode, and all the relevant built-in functions (*length*, *reverse*, *sort*, *tr*) now work on a character-by-character basis instead of on a byte-by-byte basis. Two Perl pragmas are used to turn Unicode settings on and off. The *utf8* pragma turns on the Unicode settings and loads the required character tables, while the *bytes* pragma refers to the old byte meanings, reading one byte at a time. (For a complete discussion of see *perldoc.perl.org/perlunicode.html*.)

To find out what character encoding your version of Perl uses, type at the prompt:

```
$ perl -MEncode -le "print for encodings(':all')"
ascii
ascii-ctrl
iso-8859-1
null
utf-8-strict
utf8
(This output is for Perl5.16 )
```

When *utf8* is turned on, you can specify string literals in Unicode using the \x{Number} notation for characters (called code points) 0xFF and above (see *www.unicode-table.com*) where *Number* is a hexadecimal character code such as \x{395}. See Figure 9.3.

You can also use the \N{U+hexnumber} notation where *hexnumber* in the braces is the hexadecimal number for the Unicode character; for example, a smiley face is \N{U+263A}, or use the official name for the Unicode character, \N{WHITE SMILING FACE}. For a list of Unicode character names, see *www.unicode.org/charts/charindex.html*.

---

6. The Unicode Consortium is a nonprofit organization founded to develop, extend, and promote use of the Unicode standard. For more information on Unicode and the Unicode Consortium, go to *www.unicode.org/ unicode/standard/whatisunicode.html*.

Figure 9.3   The *unicode-table.com* Web site.

```
1  use 5.012;  # use feature 'unicode strings'
2  my $smiley="\N{U+263A}";  # Unicode smiley character
3  utf8::encode($smiley);
4  print "Smiley face is $smiley\n";
5  my $swring="\x{00E5}";  # Unicode for Swedish ring, Decimal 229
6  utf8::encode($swring);
7  print "Swedish ringed a is $swring\n";
   my $symbol = "\N{UMBRELLA}";  # Name the code point
8  utf8::encode $symbol;
9  print "Umbrella is $symbol\n";

(Output)
Smiley face is ☺
Swedish ringed a is å
Umbrella is ☂
```

EXPLANATION

1   From perldoc: In order to preserve backward compatibility, Perl <u>does not</u> turn on full internal Unicode support unless the pragma <u>use</u> feature 'unicode_strings' is specified (automatically selected if you use <u>use</u> 5.012 or higher).
    This example is using 5.016, making this line not necessary.

2   Using the \N notation, the *U+* stands for "add Unicode" and the Unicode character for a smiley character is *263A*. Instead of the number, you could use the name \N{U+WHITE SMILING FACE}.

3   The *utf8* encoding function will encode the smiley face Unicode into a readable character.

4   The Unicode smiley face is printed after encoding.

5   you can use the \x{...} notation for characters 0x100 and above. This time, the notations for a Swedish ring is \x{00E5}.

7   With the \N{...} notation, you can put the official Unicode character name within the braces; in this example, the name for an umbrella symbol.

8   The encode function changes the native bytes of a Perl scalar to UTF-8 bytes. See *http://perldoc.perl.org/5.8.9/utf8.html*.

Unicode also provides support for regular expressions and matching characters based on Unicode properties, some of which are defined by the Unicode standard and some by Perl. The Perl properties are composites of the standard properties; in other words, you can now match any uppercase character in any language with \p{IsUpper}.

Table 9.10 is a list of Perl's composite character classes. If the *p* in \p is capitalized, the meaning is a negation; so, for example, \p{IsASCII} represents an ASCII character, whereas \P{IsASCII} represents a non-ASCII character.

Table 9.10 *utf8* Composite Character Classes

utf8 Property	Meaning
\p{IsASCII}	ASCII character
\p{Cntrl}	Control character
\p{IsDigit}	A digit between 0 and 9
\p{IsGraph}	Alphanumeric or punctuation character
\p{IsLower}	Lowercase letter
\p{IsPrint}	Alphanumeric, punctuation character, or space
\p{IsPunct}	Any punctuation character
\p{IsSpace}	Whitespace character
\p{IsUpper}	Uppercase letter
\p{IsWord}	Alphanumeric word character or underscore
\p{IsXDigit}	Any hexadecimal digit

EXAMPLE 9.53

```
1   use utf8;
2   $chr=11;
3   print "$chr is a digit.\n"if $chr =~ /\p{IsDigit}/;
4   $chr = "junk";
5   print "$chr is not a digit.\n"if $chr =~ /\P{IsDigit}/;
6   print "$chr is not a control character.\n"if $chr =
    ~ /\P{IsCntrl}/;

(Output)
3   11 is a digit.
5   junk is not a digit.
6   junk is not a control character.
```

EXPLANATION

1   The *utf8* pragma is used to turn on the Unicode settings. Even in modern Perl, utf-8 is not a default.

2   Scalar *$chr* is assigned a number.

3   The Perl Unicode property *IsDigit* is used to check for a number between *0* and *9*, the same as using *[0-9]*.

4   Scalar *$chr* is assigned the string *junk*.

5   The \p is now \P, causing the escape sequence to mean **not** a digit, the same as using *[^0-9]*. Since *junk* is not a digit, the condition is true.

6   The opposite of *junk* is not a control character.

9.4 What You Should Know

1. What are metacharacters used for?

2. What is a character class?

3. What is meant by a "greedy" metacharacter?

4. What is an anchoring metacharacter?

5. How do you search for a literal period?

6. What is capturing? Can you turn it off?

7. What is grouping?

8. How does a character class differ from alternation?

9. How do you search for one or more digits?

10. How do you search for zero or one digit?

11. What is a metasymbol?

12. What is the purpose of the "squeeze" option when used with *tr*?

13. What is *utf8*?

9.5 What's Next?

In the next chapter, we discuss how Perl deals with files, how to open them, read from them, write to them, append to them, and close them. You will learn how *die* works. You will learn how to seek to a position within a file, how to rewind back to the top, how to mark a spot for the next read operation. You will learn how to perform file tests to see if a file is readable, writeable, executable, and so forth. We will also discuss pipes, how Perl sends output to a pipe, and how Perl reads from a pipe. You will learn how to pass arguments to a Perl script at the command line and all the variations of *ARGV*.

EXERCISE 9
And the Search Goes On . . .

(Sample file found on CD)
Tommy Savage:408-724-0140:1222 Oxbow Court, Sunnyvale,CA 94087:5/19/66:34200
Lesle Kerstin:408-456-1234:4 Harvard Square, Boston, MA 02133:4/22/62:52600
JonDeLoach:408-253-3122:123 Park St., San Jose, CA 94086:7/25/53:85100
Ephram Hardy:293-259-5395:235 Carlton Lane, Joliet, IL 73858:8/12/20:56700
Betty Boop:245-836-8357:635 Cutesy Lane, Hollywood, CA 91464:6/23/23:14500
Wilhelm Kopf:846-836-2837:6937 Ware Road, Milton, PA 93756:9/21/46:43500
Norma Corder:397-857-2735:74 Pine Street, Dearborn, MI 23874:3/28/45:245700
James Ikeda:834-938-8376:23445 Aster Ave., Allentown, NJ 83745:12/1/38:45000
Lori Gortz:327-832-5728:3465 Mirlo Street, Peabody, MA 34756:10/2/65:35200
Barbara Kerz:385-573-8326:832 Ponce Drive, Gary, IN 83756:12/15/46:268500

1. Print the city and state where Norma lives.

2. Give everyone a $250.00 raise.

3. Calculate Lori's age.

4. Print lines 2 through 6. (The $. variable holds the current line number.)

5. Print names and phone numbers of those in the 408 area code.

6. Print names and salaries in lines 3, 4, and 5.

7. Print a row of stars after line 3.

8. Change *CA* to *California*.

9. Print the file with a row of stars after the last line.

10. Print the names of the people born in March.

11. Print all lines that don't contain *Karen*.

12. Print lines that end in exactly five digits; no more, no less.

13. Print the file with the first and last names reversed with only the first letter of the first name and the full last name; for example, *Savage,*

14. Print all cities in California, and the first names of those people who live there.

15. Without using the split function, print all the lines up to the first colon (just the names).

16. Without using the split function, print the street address; for example, 123 Park St.

17. Create and display a new format for all the phone numbers to look like this:

    (408) 465-1234

18. Print a smiley face, a heart, and a black chess knight after line 6.

chapter
10

Getting a Handle on Files

Now it is time to see how Perl interacts with files, pipes, and command-line arguments. By the time you have finished this chapter, you should be able to explain the following script.

```
use feature 'say';
die "Insufficient arguments" if scalar @ARGV < 1;

while(<>){
    say "$ARGV $. $_ ";
    say "x" x 30 && close ARGV if eof;
}
```

10.1 The User-Defined Filehandle

If you are processing text, you will regularly be opening, closing, reading from, and writing to files. In Perl, we use filehandles to get access to system files.

A **filehandle** is a name for a file, device, pipe, or socket. In Chapter 4, "Getting a Handle on Printing," we discussed the three default filehandles, *STDIN*, *STDOUT*, and *STDERR*. Perl also allows you to create your own filehandles for input and output operations on files, devices, pipes, or sockets. A filehandle allows you to associate the filehandle name with a system file and to use that filehandle to access the file.

10.1.1 Opening Files—The *open* Function

The *open* function lets you name a filehandle and the file you want to attach to that handle. If the filehandle is an undefined scalar variable, a new file filehandle is created (called **autovivification**) as a reference to a new anonymous filehandle. If the filehandle is an expression, it is a symbolic reference to the named file. The file can be opened for reading, writing, or appending (or both reading and writing), and the file can be opened to pipe data to or from a process. The *open* function returns a nonzero result if successful and the undefined value if it fails. Like scalars, arrays, and labels, filehandles have their own namespace. So that they will not be confused with reserved words, it is recommended that you use lexical scalars variables to hold your filehandles (as we will do in most of the examples in this chapter). If you use a bareword name for your filehandle, it is recommended that it be in capital letters (see the *open* function in Appendix A, "Perl Built-ins, Pragmas, Modules, and the Debugger").

When opening text files on Win32 platforms, the \r\n (\r octal \015; and \n octal \012), are characters representing return and newline are translated into \n when text files are read from disk, and the ^Z character is read as an end-of-file (EOF) marker. The following functions for opening files should work fine with text files but will cause a problem with binary files (see Section 10.2.8, "Win32 Binary Files").

10.1.2   Opening for Reading

The following examples illustrate how to open files for reading with both the older style and modern style. Even though the examples represent UNIX files, they will work the same way on Windows, Mac OS, and other systems.

FORMAT

```
1  open(my $fh, "<", "FILENAME");  # Indirect filehandle (Modern style)
2  open(FILEHANDLE, "<FILENAME");  # Simple filehandle (Older style)
```

EXAMPLE 10.1

```
1  open(my $fh, "<", "myfile");    # Indirect filehandle (Modern style)
2  open (FH, "/etc/passwd");       # Simple filehandle (Older style)
```

EXPLANATION

1   This indirect style is recommended. It is a three-part format for opening a file for reading. The *open* function will create a reference to a filehandle, lexical variable *$fh* (any scalar variable name can be used), then the < symbol indicates that the file will be opened for reading, and the third argument is the name of the system file, *myfile*. Since a full pathname is not specified for *myfile*, it must be in the current working directory, and you must have read permission to open it for reading. When leaving the block where *$fh* is defined, the variable will go out of scope and the file will be implicitly closed. This helps reduce the chance of a name clash if you use the same variable later in the file to open another file.

2   This is an alternate way to open a file with two arguments. The *open* function will create the user-defined filehandle *FH* and attach it to the system file */etc/passwd*. The < symbol is not necessary, but may help clarify that this is a *read* operation. The full pathname is specified for *passwd*.

Closing the Filehandle.   The *close* function closes the file, pipe, socket, or device attached to *FILEHANDLE*. Once *FILEHANDLE* is opened, it stays open until it goes out of scope, the script ends, or you call the *open* function again. (The next call to *open* closes *FILEHANDLE* before reopening it.) If you don't explicitly close the file, when you reopen it this way, the line counter variable, $., will not be reset. Closing a pipe causes the process to wait until the pipe is complete and reports the status in the $! variable (see the following section, "The *die* Function" for more about the $! variable). It's a good idea to explicitly close files and handles after you are finished using them, but if using a lexically scoped scalar as the filehandle, it will be closed as soon as it goes out of scope.

FORMAT

```
close $fh;
close FILEHANDLE;
```

EXAMPLE 10.2

```
open(my $fh, "<", "datebook");
close $fh;
```

EXPLANATION

The file associated with *$fh*, which is *datebook*, will be closed.

The *die* Function.   In the following examples, the *die* function is used if a call to the *open* function fails. If Perl cannot open the file, the *die* function is used to exit the Perl script and print a message to *STDERR*, usually the screen.

If you were to go to your shell or MS-DOS prompt and type

```
cat junk    (UNIX)
```

or

```
type junk  (DOS)
```

and if *junk* is a nonexistent file, the following system error would appear on your screen:

```
cat: junk: No such file or directory    (UNIX "cat" command)
The system cannot find the file specified.    (Windows "type" command)
```

When using the *die* function, Perl provides a special variable $! to hold the value of the system error that occurs when you are unable to successfully open a file or execute a system utility. This is very useful for detecting a problem with the filehandle before continuing with the execution of the script.

EXAMPLE 10.3

```
(Line from Script)
1  open(my $fh, "<", "/etc/password") or die "Can't open: $!\n";

(Output)
1  Can't open: No such file or directory

(Line from Script)
2  open(my $fh, "<", "/etc/password") or die "Can't open: $!";

(Output)
2  Can't open: No such file or directory at ./handle line 3.
```

EXPLANATION

1   When trying to open the file */etc/password*, the *open* fails (it should be */etc/passwd*). The *or* operator causes its right operand to execute if the left operand fails. The *die* operator is executed. The string *Can't open:* is printed, followed by the system error *No such file or directory*. The \n suppresses any further output from the *die* function. All of *die*'s output is sent to *STDERR* after the program exits.

2   This is exactly like the first example, except that the \n has been removed from the string *Can't open:*. Omitting the \n causes the *die* function to append a string to the output, indicating the line number in the script where the system error occurred.

10.1.3   Reading from a File and Scalar Assignment

The Filehandle and $_.   In Example 10.4, a file called *datebook* is opened for reading. Each line read is assigned, in turn, to $_, the default scalar that holds what was just read until the end of file is reached.

EXAMPLE 10.4

```
(The Text File: datebook)
    Steve Blenheim
    Betty Boop
    Lori Gortz
    Sir Lancelot
    Norma Cord
    Jon DeLoach
    Karen Evich


    ------------------------------------------------------------


(The Script)
    use warnings;
    # Open a file with a filehandle
```

EXAMPLE 10.4 (CONTINUED)

```
1   open(my $fh, "<", "datebook") || die "Can't open datebook: $!\n";
2   while(<$fh>) { # The $_, hidden variable, gets a line at a time
3       print  if /Sir Lancelot/;
4   }
5   close($fh);
```

(Output)
3   *Sir Lancelot*

EXPLANATION

1   *$fh* is a lexically scoped, user-defined scalar used as a filehandle. The *open* function will attach the system file *datebook* to it and open the file for reading. If *open* fails because the file *datebook* does not exist, the *die* operator will print to the screen, *Can't open datebook: No such file or directory*.

2   The expression in the *while* loop is the filehandle *$fh*, enclosed in angle brackets. The angle bracket operator is used for reading input and not part of the filehandle name. When the loop starts, the first line read will be stored in the $_ scalar variable. (Remember, the $_ variable holds each line of input from the file.) If it has not reached end of file, the loop will continue to take a line of input from the file, execute statements 3 and 4, and continue until end of file is reached.

3   The default input variable $_ is implicitly used to hold the current line of input read from the filehandle. If the line contains the regular expression *Sir Lancelot*, that line (stored in $_) is printed to *STDOUT*. For each loop iteration, the next line read is stored in $_ and tested.

4   At the end of the loop, control will go back to the top of the loop (line 2) and the next line of input will be read from the file; this process will continue until all the lines have been read.

5   After looping through the file, the filehandle is closed.

The Filehandle and a User-Defined Scalar Variable.   In addition to the default $_ variable, Perl allows you to create your own user-defined scalar variables to hold input from a file.

EXAMPLE 10.5

(The Text File: *datebook*)
   Steve Blenheim
   Betty Boop
   Lori Gortz
   Sir Lancelot
   Norma Cord
   Jon DeLoach
   Karen Evich

- -

EXAMPLE 10.5 (CONTINUED)

```
(The Script)
   use warnings;
   # Open a file with a filehandle
1  open(my $fh, "<", "datebook") || die "Can't open datebook: $!\n";
2  while(my $line = <$fh>) { # Each line, in turn, is assigned to $line
3     print "$line" if  $line =~ /^Lori/;
4  }
5  close($fh);
```

```
(Output)
3  Lori Gortz
```

EXPLANATION

1   The *datebook* file is opened for reading.
2   When the *while* loop is entered, a line is read from the file and stored in the scalar *$line*.
3   The value of the scalar *$line* is printed if it contains the pattern *Lori*, and *Lori* is at the beginning of the line.
4   When the closing brace is reached, control goes back to line 2, and another line is read from the file. The loop ends when the file has no more lines.
5   The file is closed by closing the filehandle.

"Slurping" a File into an Array.   When assigning input from a file to an array, Perl takes each line (ending in \n) as an element of the array, "slurping" up each line of the file and adding it to the array until end of file is reached.

EXAMPLE 10.6

```
(The Script)
   use warnings;
   # Open a file with a filehandle
1  open(my $fh, "<", "datebook") || die "Can't open datebook: $!\n";
2  @lines = <$fh>;
3  print @lines;          # Contents of the entire file are printed
4  print "\nThe datebook file contains ", scalar @lines,
          " lines of text.\n";
5  close(FILE);
```

```
(Output)
The datebook file contains 7 lines of text.
```

EXPLANATION

1 The *datebook* file is opened for reading.
2 All of the lines are read from the file, via the filehandle, and assigned to *@lines*, where each line is an element of the array. The newline terminates each element.
3 The array *@lines* is printed.
4 The *scalar* function returns the number of elements (that is, lines) in the array, *@lines*.

Using *map* to Create Fields from a File. You can use the *map* function in conjunction with the *split* function to break up input into several elements of an array.

EXAMPLE 10.7

```
(The Script)
   use warnings;
   my(@lines, @fields, $field, $fh);
   # Map using a block
1  open(my $fh, "<", "datebook.master") or die $!;
2  @lines=<$fh>;
3  @fields = map { split(":") } @lines;
4  foreach $field (@fields){
5     print $field,"\n";
   }
```

```
(Output)
5  Sir Lancelot
   837-835-8257
   474 Camelot Boulevard, Bath, WY 28356
   5/13/69
   24500

   Tommy Savage
   408-724-0140
   1222 Oxbow Court, Sunnyvale, CA 94087
   5/19/66
   34200

   Yukio Takeshida
   387-827-1095
   13 Uno Lane, Asheville, NC 23556
   7/1/29
   57000

   Vinh Tranh
   438-910-7449
   8235 Maple Street, Wilmington, VT 29085
   9/23/63
   68900
```

EXPLANATION

1. The *datebook.master* file is opened for reading from the *$fh* filehandle. Each line consists of colon-separated fields terminated by a newline.
2. The contents of the file are read and assigned to *@lines*. Each line of the file is an element of the array.
3. The *map* function uses the block format. (With the block format, don't put a comma after the close of the block.) The *split* function splits up the input, *@lines*, at colons, resulting in a list where each field becomes an element of the array.
4. The *foreach* loop iterates through the array, assigning each element, in turn, to *$field*.
5. The display demonstrates the results of the mapping. Before mapping, the line was: *Sir Lancelot:837-835-8257:474 Camelot Boulevard, Bath, WY 28356:5/13/69:24500*

Slurping a File into a String with the *read* Function.   The *read* function allows you to read in a specified number of characters, and put them in a variable. It returns the number of characters that were read. If you know the size of a file, you can read the entire file into a string, as shown in the next example.

FORMAT

```
read FILEHANDLE,SCALAR,LENGTH,OFFSET
read FILEHANDLE,SCALAR,LENGTH
```

EXAMPLE 10.8

```
read($fh, $str, 100);
```

EXAMPLE 10.9

```
(The Script)
use warnings;
1  open(my $fh, "<", "datebook") or die;
2  $size = -s $fh;
3  read($fh, $buffer, $size);
4  @fields = split(/\n|:/,$buffer);
5  foreach $f (@fields){
6     print "$f\n";
7     print "-" x 35, "\n" if $f =~ /^\d+$/;
   }
   close $fh;
```

EXAMPLE 10.9 (CONTINUED)

```
(Output)
Steve Blenheim
238-923-7366
95 Latham Lane, Easton, PA 83755
11/12/56
20300
-----------------------------------
Betty Boop
245-836-8357
635 Cutesy Lane, Hollywood, CA 91464
6/23/23
14500
-----------------------------------
Igor Chevsky
385-375-8395
3567 Populus Place, Caldwell, NJ 23875
6/18/68
23400
-----------------------------------
```

EXPLANATION

1   The *datebook* file is opened for reading.
2   The *-s* test option returns the size of the *datebook* file referenced by the filehandle.
3   The *read* function reads *$size* bytes (characters) from the filehandle and stores them in the scalar, *$buffer*. The *read* function treats all characters as characters, including newline, spaces, tabs, and so forth.
4   The first argument to the *split* function is a regular expression matching either a newline or a colon, the delimiter for splitting up the string in *$buffer*, the second argument. (Remember, *split* splits a scalar and returns an array or list.) When either a newline or a colon is matched in *$buffer*, *split* returns an element to be stored in the array *@lines*. The first element of the array will be the name (for example, *Steve Blenheim*), the second element will be Steve's phone number, then the address, the birthday, and salary. When the newline is matched, the next element will be the next name in *$buffer*. When the splitting has completed, a large array will be created.
5   The *foreach* loop is used to iterate through each element of the array.
6   Each element of the array is printed with a newline.
7   When the last field is reached, meaning the field containing the salary, a row of 35 dashes is printed. The salary is represented in the regular expression as "beginning and ending with one or more digits." Since the salary field is the last on the line, it contains a newline. By printing the row of dashes and another newline, the output displays a line separating the records.

10.1.4 Loading a Hash from a File

Loading a hash from a file requires selecting what will be the key and what will be the value
for the hash. Since keys must be unique, this method can be used for removing duplicate
entries based on a key.

EXAMPLE 10.10

```
(The datafile)
Ann Willy:530-444-5678
Joe Shmoe:415-333-4567
Jack Sprat:213-453-1098
Ann Willy:530-444-5678
Jack Sprat:213-453-1098
Jack Sprat:213-453-1098


(The Script)
   open($fh, "<", "datafile") or die "$!";
   while(<$fh>){
1     ($name, $phone)=split(":");
2     $duphash{$name}=$_;
   }
3  foreach $key (sort keys %duphash){
4     print $duphash{$key};
   }
   close $fh;

(Output)
4  Ann Willy:530-444-5678
   Jack Sprat:213-453-1098
   Joe Shmoe:415-333-4567
```

EXPLANATION

1   Each line is split by a colon into two variables, *$name* and *$phone*.
2   A hash, called *%duphash*, is being created on the fly. The unique keys will be the values
    in the name field. The value assigned to the key is the current line.
3   The *sort* function will alphabetically sort all the keys from the newly created hash
    called *%duphash*.
4   The value of the hash is a line from the file. All the lines are printed, the duplicates
    removed.

10.2 Reading from *STDIN*

The three filehandles *STDIN*, *STDOUT*, and *STDERR*, as you may recall, are names given to three predefined streams, *stdin*, *stdout*, and *stderr*. By default, these filehandles are associated with your terminal. When printing output to the terminal screen, *STDOUT* is used. When printing errors, *STDERR* is used. When assigning user input to a variable, *STDIN* is used.

The Perl <> input operator encloses the *STDIN* filehandle so that the next line of standard input can be read from the terminal keyboard and assigned to a variable. Unlike the shell and *C* operations for reading input, Perl retains the newline on the end of the string when reading a line from standard input. If you don't want the newline, then you have to explicitly remove it, or "chomp" it off (see the following Section 10.2.2, "The *chop* and *chomp* Functions").

10.2.1 Assigning Input to a Scalar Variable

When reading input from the filehandle *STDIN*, if the context is scalar, one line of input is read, including the newline, and assigned to a scalar variable as a single string.

EXAMPLE 10.11

```
(The Script)
    # Getting a line of input from the keyboard.
1   print "What is your name?  ";
2   $name = <STDIN>;
3   print "What is your father's name? ";
4   $paname=<>;
5   print "Hello respected one, $paname";

(Output)
1   What is your name? Isabel
3   What is your father's name? Nick
5   Hello respected one, Nick
```

EXPLANATION

1   The string *What is your name?* is sent to *STDOUT*, which is the screen by default.
2   The input operator <> (called the diamond operator) surrounding *STDIN* reads one line of input and assigns that line and its trailing newline to the scalar variable $*name*. When input is assigned to a scalar, characters are read until the user presses the Enter key.
3   The string is printed to *STDOUT*.
4   If the input operator is empty, the next line of input is read from *STDIN*, and the behavior is identical to line 2, except input is assigned to $*paname*.

10.2.2 The *chop* and *chomp* Functions

The *chop* function removes the last character in a scalar variable and the last character of each word in an array. Its return value is the character it chopped. *Chop* is used primarily to remove the newline from the line of input coming into your program, whether it is *STDIN*, a file, or the result of command substitution. When you first start learning Perl, the trailing newline can be a real pain!

The *chomp* function was introduced in Perl 5 to remove the last character in a scalar variable and the last character of each word in an array **only if** that character is the newline (or, to be more precise, the character that represents the input line separator, initially defined as a newline and stored in the $/ variable). It returns the number of characters it chomped. Using *chomp* instead of *chop* protects you from inadvertently removing some character other than the newline.

EXAMPLE 10.12

```
(The Script)
    # Getting rid of the trailing newline. Use chomp instead of chop.
1   print "Hello there, and what is your name? ";
2   $name = <STDIN>;
3   print "$name is a very high class name.\n";
4   chop($name);    # Removes the last character no matter what it is.
5   print "$name is a very high class name.\n\n";
6   chop($name);
7   print "$name has been chopped a little too much.\n";
8   print "What is your age?  ";
9   chomp($age=<STDIN>); # Removes the last character if
                         # it is the newline.
10  chomp($age);         # The last character is not removed
                         # unless a newline.
11  print "For $age, you look so young!\n";

(Output)
1   Hello there, and what is your name? Joe Smith
3   Joe Smith
    is a very high class name.
5   Joe Smith is a very high class name.

7   Joe Smit has been chopped a little too much.

8   What is your age? 25
11  For 25, you look so young!
```

EXPLANATION

1 The quoted string is printed to the screen, *STDOUT*, by default.
2 The scalar variable is assigned a single line of text typed in by the user. The <> operator is used for read operations. In this case, it reads from *STDIN*, which is your keyboard, until the Enter key is pressed. The newline is included in the text that is assigned to the variable *$name*.
3 The value of *$name* is printed. Note that the newline breaks the line after *Joe Smith*, the user's input.
4 The *chop* function removes the last character of the string assigned to *$name*. The character that was chopped is returned.
5 The string is printed again after the *chop* operation. The last character was removed (in this case, the newline).
6 This time *chop* will remove the last character in *Joe Smith's* name, which is the *h* in *Smith*.
7 The quoted string is printed to *STDOUT*, indicating that the last character was removed.
9 The user input is first assigned to the variable *$age*. The trailing newline is chomped. The character whose value is stored in the special variable, *$/*, is removed. This value is, by default, the newline character. The number of characters chomped is returned. Because of the low precedence of the equal (=) operator, parentheses ensure that the assignment occurs before the *chomp* function chomps.
10 The second *chomp* will have no effect. The newline has already been removed, and *chomp* removes only the newline. It's safer than using *chop*.
11 The chomped variable string is printed.

10.2.3 The *read* Function

The *read* function[1] allows you to read a number of characters into a variable from a specified filehandle. (The first character is character 0.) If reading from standard input, the filehandle is *STDIN*. The *read* function returns the number of bytes that were read. You will normally use this function with files or reading input from a server using CGI. To read the entire file you will need to know the size in bytes of that file.

---

1. The *read* function is similar to the *fread* function in the C language.

FORMAT

```
number_of_bytes = read(FILEHANDLE, buffer, how_many_bytes);
```

EXAMPLE 10.13

```
(The Script)
    use warnings;
    # Reading input in a requested number of bytes
1   print "Describe your favorite food in 10 bytes or less.\n";
    print "If you type less than 10 characters, press CTRL+D on a line
        by itself.\n";
2   my $number=read(STDIN, $favorite, 10);
3   print "You just typed: $favorite\n";
4   print "The number of bytes read was $number.\n";


(Output)
1   Describe your favorite food in 10 bytes or less.
    If you type less than 10 characters, press CTRL+D on a line by
    itself.
    apple pie and ice cream         <-user input
3   You just typed: apple pie
4   The number of bytes read was 10.
```

EXPLANATION

1   The user is asked for input. If he types less than 10 characters, he should press <CTRL>+D to exit.

2   The *read* function takes three arguments: the first argument is *STDIN*, the place from where the input is coming; the second argument is the scalar *$favorite*, where the input will be stored; and the third argument is the number of characters (bytes) that will be read.

3   The 10 characters read in are printed. The rest of the characters were left in the buffer and ignored.

4   The number of characters (bytes) actually read was stored in *$number* and is finally printed.

10.2.4   The *getc* Function

The *getc* function gets a single character from the keyboard or from a file. At EOF, *getc* returns a null string.

FORMAT

```
getc(FILEHANDLE)
getc FILEHANDLE
getc
```

EXAMPLE 10.14

```
(The Script)
    use warnings;
    # Getting only one character of input
    print "Answer y or n   ";
1   my $answer=getc;      # Gets one character from stdin
2   $restofit=<>;         # What remains in the input buffer is
                          # assigned to $restofit
3   print "$answer\n";
4   print "The characters left in the input buffer were:
        $restofit\n";

(Output)
1   Answer y or n yessirreebob <ENTER>
3   y
4   The characters left in the input buffer were: essirreebob
```

EXPLANATION

1 Only one character is read from the input buffer by *getc* and stored in the scalar *$answer*.

2 The characters remaining in the input buffer are stored in *$restofit*. This clears the input buffer. Now, if you ask for input later in the program, you will not be picking up those characters that were left hanging around in the buffer.

3 The character that was read in by *getc* is printed.

4 The characters stored in *$restofit* are displayed.

10.2.5 Assigning Input to an Array

When reading input from the filehandle *STDIN*, if the context is an array, then each line is read with its newline and is treated as a single list item, and the read is continued until you press <CTRL>+D (in UNIX) or <CTRL>+Z (in Windows) for end of file (EOF). Normally, you will not assign input to an array, because it could eat up a large amount of memory, or because the user of your program may not realize that he should press <CTRL>+D or <CTRL>+Z to stop reading input.

EXAMPLE 10.15

```
(The Script)
    use warnings;
    # Assigning input to an array
1   print "Tell me everything about yourself.\n ";
2   my @all = <STDIN>;
3   print "@all";
4   print "The number of elements in the array are: ",
          $#all + 1, ".\n";
5   print "The first element of the array is: $all[0]";


(Output)
1   Tell me everything about yourself.
2   OK. Let's see I was born before computers.
    I grew up in the 50s.
    I was in the hippie generation.
    I'm starting to get bored with talking about myself.
    <CTRL>+D

3   OK. Let's see I was born before computers.
    I grew up in the 50s.
    I was in the hippie generation.
    I'm starting to get bored with talking about myself.
4   The number of elements in the array are: 4.
5   The first element of the array is:
    OK. Let's see I was born before computers.
```

EXPLANATION

1   The string *Tell me everything about yourself.* is printed to *STDOUT*.

2   The input operator <> surrounding *STDIN* reads input lines until <CTRL>+D, EOF, is reached. (For Windows, use <CTRL>+Z instead of <CTRL>+D.) Each line and its trailing newline are stored as a list element of the array *@all*.

3   The user input is printed to the screen after the user presses <CTRL>+D or <CTRL>+Z.

4   The $# construct lets you get the last subscript or index value in the array. By adding 1 to $#*all*, the size of the array is obtained; that is, the number of lines that were read.

5   $*all[0]* is the first element of the array that evaluates to the first line of input from the user. Each line read is an element of the array.

10.2.6   Assigning Input to a Hash

Reading input from *STDIN* and assigning it to a hash is like reading from a file. The line read can be assigned as a value corresponding to a hash key or as the key itself.

EXAMPLE 10.16

```
(The Script)
    use warnings;
    # Assign input to a hash
1   my %course=();  # Empty hash
2   my $course_number=101;
3   print "What is the name of course $course_number?";
4   chomp($course{$course_number} = <STDIN>);
5   print %course, "\n";

(Output)
3   What is the name of course 101? Linux Administration
5   101Linux Administration
```

EXPLANATION

1 The hash, *%course*, is declared here. Keys and values will be assigned later.
2 The scalar variable *$course_number* is assigned the value *101*.
3 The string *What is the name of course 101?* is printed to *STDOUT*.
4 The name of the hash is *%course*. We are assigning a value to one of the hash elements. The key is *$course_number* enclosed in curly braces. The *chomp* function will remove the newline from the value assigned by the user.
5 The new hash is printed. It has one key and one value.

10.2.7 Opening for Writing

When opening a file for writing, the file will be created if it does not exist, and if it already exists, it must have write permission. If the file exists, its contents will be overwritten. The filehandle is used to access the system file.

FORMAT

```
1   open(my $filehandle, ">", "FILENAME");   # Three arguments, modern way
2   open(FILEHANDLE, ">FILENAME");           # Bareword, old way
```

EXAMPLE 10.17

```
1   open(my $fh, ">", "temp");
2   open(FH, ">temp");
```

EXPLANATION

1 The user-defined filehandle, *$fh*, will be used to send output to the file called *temp*. As with the shell, the redirection symbol directs the output from the default filehandle, *STDOUT*, to the *temp* file.
2 This is the two-argument older way to create a user-defined handle.

EXAMPLE 10.18

```
(The Script)
   use warnings;
   # Write to a file with a filehandle. Scriptname: file.handle
1  my $file="/home/jody/ellie/perl/newfile";
2  open(my $fh, ">", $file) || die "Can't open newfile: $!\n";

3  print $fh "hello world.\n";
4  print $fh "hello world again.\n";

(At the Command Line)
5  $ perl file.handle
6  $ cat newfile

(Output)
3  hello world.
4  hello world, again.
```

EXPLANATION

1   The scalar variable *$file* is set to the full pathname of a UNIX file called *newfile*. The scalar will be used to represent the name of the UNIX file to which output will be directed via the filehandle. This example will work the same way with Windows, but if you use the backslash as a directory separator, either enclose the path in single quotes, or use two backslashes; for example, *C:\\home\\ellie\\testing*.

2   The user-defined filehandle *$fh* will change the default place to where output normally goes, *STDOUT*, to the file that it represents, *newfile*. The > symbol indicates that *newfile* will be created if it does not exist and opened for writing. If it does exist, it will be opened and any text in it will be **overwritten**, so be careful!

3   The *print* function will send its output to the file, instead of to the screen. The string *hello world.* will be written into *newfile* via the *$fh* filehandle. The file *newfile* will remain open unless it is explicitly closed or the Perl script ends (see "Closing the Filehandle" earlier in this chapter).

4   The *print* function will send its output to the filehandle *$fh* instead of to the screen. The string *hello world, again.* will be written into *newfile* via the *$fh* filehandle. The operating system keeps track of where the last write occurred and will send its next line of output to the location immediately following the last byte written to the file.

5   The script is executed. The output is sent to *newfile*.

6   The contents of the file *newfile* are printed.

10.2.8 Win32 Binary Files

Win32 distinguishes between text and binary files. If ^Z is found, the program may abort prematurely or have problems with the newline translation. When reading and writing Win32 binary files, use the *binmode* function to prevent these problems. The *binmode* function arranges for a specified filehandle to be read or written to in either binary (raw) or text mode. If the discipline argument is not specified, the mode is set to "raw." The discipline is one of *:raw, :crlf, :text, :utf8, :latin1*, and so forth.

FORMAT

```
binmode FILEHANDLE
binmode FILEHANDLE, DISCIPLINE
```

EXAMPLE 10.19

```
  # This script copies one binary file to another.
  # Note its use of binmode to set the mode of the filehandle.
    use warnings;
1   $infile="statsbar.gif";
2   open( my $in, "<" , "$infile" );
3   open( my $out, ">", "outfile.gif" );

4   binmode( $in );      # Crucial for binary files!

5   binmode( $out );
    # binmode should be called after open() but before any I/O
    # is done on the filehandle.

6   while ( read( $in, $buffer, 1024 ) ) {
7      print $out $buffer;
    }

8   close( INFILE );
    close( OUTFILE );
```

EXPLANATION

1   The scalar *$infile* is assigned a *.gif* filename.
2   The file *statsbar.gif* is opened for reading and attached to the *$in* filehandle.
3   The file *outfile.gif* is opened for writing and assigned to the *$out* filehandle.
4   The *binmode* function arranges for the input file to be read as binary text.
5   The *binmode* function arranges for the output file to be written as binary text.
6   The *read* function reads 1,024 bytes at a time, storing the input read in the scalar *$buffer.*
7   After the 1,024 bytes are read in, they are sent out to the output file.
8   Both filehandles are closed. The result was that one binary file was copied to another binary file.

10.2.9   Opening for Appending

When opening a file for appending, the file will be created if it does not exist, and if it already exists, it must have write permission. If the file exists, its contents will be left intact, and the output will be appended to the end of the file. Again, the filehandle is used to access the file rather than accessing it by its real name.

FORMAT

```
1 open(my $filehandle, ">>", FILENAME); # Three arguments, modern way
2 open(FILEHANDLE, ">> FILENAME");       # Bareword, alternate way
```

EXAMPLE 10.20

```
1  open(my $fh, ">>", "temp");
2  open(APPEND, ">> temp");
```

EXPLANATION

1   The lexically scoped scalar, *$fh*, will be used to append output to the file called *temp*. As with the shell, the redirection symbol directs the output from the default, standard out filehandle, *STDOUT*, to the *temp* file.

2   The filehandle *APPEND* is used to append output to the output file called *temp*.

EXAMPLE 10.21

```
(The Text File)
$ cat newfile
hello world.
hello world, again.

(The Script)
   use warnings;
1  open(my $fh, ">>", "newfile") ||
        die print "Can't open newfile: $!\n";
2  print $fh qq(Just appended "hello world" to the end of newfile.\n);

(Output)
$ cat newfile
hello world.
hello world, again.
Just appended "hello world" to the end of newfile.
```

EXPLANATION

1   The user-defined filehandle *$fh* will be used to send and append output to the file called *newfile*. As with the shell, the redirection symbol directs the output from the default filehandle, *STDOUT*, and appends the output to the file *newfile*. If the file cannot be opened because, for example, the write permissions are turned off, the *die* operator will print the error message, *Can't open newfile: Permission denied.*, and the script will exit.

EXPLANATION (CONTINUED)

2   The string, *Just appended "hello world" to the end of newfile*, will be written to end of *newfile* via the *$fh* filehandle.

10.2.10   The *select* Function

The *select* function sets the default output to the specified filehandle and returns the previously selected filehandle. All printing will go to the selected handle. Once you use *select*, you must remember to reset your default ouput to *STDOUT* or all output from your script will continue to be sent to the "selected" filehandle.

EXAMPLE 10.22

```
(The Script)
   use warnings;
1  open (my $fh,">", "newfile") || die "Can't open newfile: $!\n";
2  select $fh;        # Select the new filehandle for output
3  open (my $db, "<", "datebook") || die "Can't open datebook: $!\n";

   while(<$db>) {
4     print ;                  # Output goes to $fh, i.e., newfile
   }
5  select(STDOUT);      # Send output back to the screen
   print "Good-bye.\n";  # Output goes to the screen
```

EXPLANATION

1   *newfile* is opened for writing and assigned to the filehandle *$fh*.
2   The *select* function assigns *$fh* as the current default filehandle for output. The return value from the *select* function is the name of the filehandle that was closed (*STDOUT*) in order to select *$fh*, the one that is now opened for writing.
3   The *$db* filehandle is opened for reading.
4   As each line is read into the *$_* variable from the file referenced by *$db*, it is then printed to the currently selected filehandle, *$fh*. Notice that you don't have to name the filehandle.
5   By selecting *STDOUT*, the rest of the program's output will go to the screen.

10.2.11   File Locking with *flock*

To prevent two programs from writing to a file at the same time, you can lock the file so you have exclusive access to it, and then unlock it when you're finished using it. The *flock* function takes two arguments: a filehandle and a file-locking operation. The operations are listed in Table 10.1.

Table 10.1   File-Locking Operations

Name	Operation	What It Does
lock_sh	1	Creates a shared lock.
lock_ex	2	Creates an exclusive lock.
lock_nb	4	Creates a nonblocking lock.
lock_un	8	Unlocks an existing lock.

Read permission is required on a file to obtain a shared lock, and write permission is required to obtain an exclusive lock. With operations 1 and 2, normally the caller requesting the file will block (wait) until the file is unlocked. If a nonblocking lock is used on a filehandle, an error is produced immediately if a request is made to get the locked file. (See *Fcntl.pm* for a better implementation of locks.)

EXAMPLE 10.23

```
    use warnings;
    # Program that uses file locking -- UNIX
1   $LOCK_EX = 2;
2   $LOCK_UN = 8;

3   print "Adding an entry to the datafile.\n";
    print "Enter the name: ";
    chomp($name=<STDIN>);
    print "Enter the address: ";
    chomp($address=<STDIN>);

4   open(my $fh, ">>", "datafile") || die "Can't open: $!\n";

5   flock($fh, $LOCK_EX) || die ;          # Lock the file

6   print $fh "$name:$address\n";

7   flock($fh, $LOCK_UN) || die;           # Unlock the file

    close $fh;
```

EXPLANATION

1   The scalar is assigned the value of the operation that will be used by the *flock* function to lock the file. This operation is to block (wait) until an exclusive lock can be created. It can be defined by importing the constants from *Fcntl.pm* as use Fcntl qw(:flock);
2   This operation will tell *flock* when to unlock the file so others can write to it.
3   The user is asked for the information to update the file. This information will be appended to the file.

EXPLANATION (CONTINUED)

4   The file is opened for appending.
5   The *flock* function puts an exclusive lock on the file.
6   The data is appended to the file.
7   Once the data has been appended, the file is unlocked so others can access it.

10.2.12 The *seek* and *tell* Functions

The *seek* Function.   *Seek* allows you to randomly access a file. The *seek* function is the same as the *fseek* standard I/O function in C. Rather than closing the file and then reopening it, the *seek* function allows you to move to some byte (not line) position within the file. The *seek* function returns *1* if successful, *0* otherwise.

FORMAT

```
seek(FILEHANDLE, BYTEOFFSET, FILEPOSITION);
```

The *seek* function sets a position in a file, where the first byte is 0. Positions are as follows:

- 0 = Beginning of the file
- 1 = Current position in the file
- 2 = End of the file

The offset is the number of bytes from the file position. A positive offset moves the position forward in the file; a negative offset moves the position backward in the file for position 1 or 2.

The *od* command lets you look at how the characters in a file are stored. This file was created on a Win32 platform; on UNIX systems, the linefeed/newline is one character, \n.

```
$ od -c db
0000000000   S   t   e   v   e       B   l   e   n   h   e   i   m  \r  \n
0000000020   B   e   t   t   y       B   o   o   p  \r  \n   L   o   r   i
0000000040   G   o   r   t   z  \r  \n   S   i   r       L   a   n   c
0000000060   e   l   o   t  \r  \n   N   o   r   m   a       C   o   r   d
0000000100  \r  \n   J   o   n       D   e   L   o   a   c   h  \r  \n   K
0000000120   a   r   e   n       E   v   i   c   h  \r  \n
0000000134
```

EXAMPLE 10.24

```
(The Text File: db)
Steve Blenheim
Betty Boop
Lori Gortz
Sir Lancelot
Norma Cord
Jon DeLoach
Karen Evich


-------------------------------------------------------------------


(The Script)
  use warnings;
    # Example using the seek function
1 open(my $fh, "<", "db") or die "Can't open: $!\n";
2 while($line=<$fh>){          # Loop through the whole file
3    if ($line =~ /^Lori/) { print "--$line--\n";}
  }
4 seek($fh,0,0);               # Start at the beginning of the file
5 while(<$fh>) {
6    print if /Steve/;
  }
  close $fh;

(Output)
3  --Lori Gortz--
6  Steve Blenheim
```

EXPLANATION

1　The *db* file is assigned to the *$fh* filehandle and opened for reading.

2　Each line of the file is assigned, in turn, to the scalar *$line* while looping through the file.

3　If *$line* begins with *Lori*, the *print* statement is executed.

4　The *seek* function causes the file pointer to be positioned at the top of the file (position 0) and starts reading at byte 0, the first character. If you want to get back to the top of the file without using *seek*, the filehandle must first be explicitly closed with the *close* function.

5　Starting at the top of the file, the loop is entered. The first line is read from the filehandle and assigned to $_, the default line holder.

6　If the pattern *Steve* is found in $_, the line will be printed.

EXAMPLE 10.25

```
(The Text File: db)
Steve Blenheim
Betty Boop
Lori Gortz
Sir Lancelot
Norma Cord
Jon DeLoach
Karen Evich

-------------------------------------------------------------

(The Script)
   use warnings;
1  open($fh, "<", "db") or die "Can't open datebook: $!\n";
2  while(<$fh>){
3     last if /Norma/;   # This is the last line that
                         # will be processed
   }
4  seek($fh,0,1) or die;   # Seeking from the current position
5  $line=<$fh>;            # This is where the read starts again
6  print "$line";
7  close $fh;

(Output)
6  Jon DeLoach
```

EXPLANATION

1   The *db* file is opened for reading via the *$fh* filehandle.
2   The *while* loop is entered. A line from the file is read and assigned to $_.
3   When the line containing the pattern *Norma* is reached, the *last* function causes the loop to be exited.
4   The *seek* function will reposition the file pointer at the byte position 0 where the next read operation would have been performed in the file, position 1; in other words, the line right after *Norma*. The byte position could be either a negative or positive value.
5   A line is read from the *db* file and assigned to the scalar *$line*. The line read is the line that would have been read just after the *last* function caused the loop to exit.
6   The value of *$line* is printed.

EXAMPLE 10.26

```
(The Script)
   use warnings;
1  open(my $fh, "<", "db") or die "Can't open datebook: $!\n";
2  seek($fh,-13,2) or die;
3  while(<$fh>){
4      print;
   }
   close $fh;

(Output)
4  Karen Evich
```

EXPLANATION

1 The *db* file is opened for reading via the *$fh* filehandle.

2 The *seek* function starts at the end of the file (position 2) and backs up 13 bytes. The newline (\r\n), although not visible, is represented as the last two bytes in the line (Windows).

3 The *while* loop is entered, and each line, in turn, is read from the filehandle *$fh*.

4 Each line is printed. By backing up 13 characters from the end of the file, *Karen Evich* is printed. Note the output of the *od -c* command and count back 13 characters from the end of the file.

```
0000000000    S   t   e   v   e       B   l   e   n   h   e   i   m  \r  \n
0000000020    B   e   t   t   y       B   o   o   p  \r  \n   L   o   r   i
0000000040        G   o   r   t   z  \r  \n   S   i   r       L   a   n   c
0000000060    e   l   o   t  \r  \n   N   o   r   m   a       C   o   r   d
0000000100   \r  \n   J   o   n       D   e   L   o   a   c   h  \r  \n   K
0000000120    a   r   e   n       E   v   i   c   h  \r  \n
0000000134
```

The *tell* Function.   The *tell* function returns the current byte position in the file and is used with the *seek* function to move to that position in the file. If *FILEHANDLE* is omitted, *tell* returns the position of the file last read.

FORMAT

```
tell(FILEHANDLE);
tell;
```

EXAMPLE 10.27

```
(The Text File: db)
Steve Blenheim
Betty Boop
Lori Gortz
Sir Lancelot
Norma Cord
Jon DeLoach
Karen Evich


-----------------------------------------------------------------


(The Script)
   use warnings;
   # Example using the tell function
1  open(my $fh,"<","db") || die "Can't open: $!\n";
2  while ($line=<$fh>) {        # Loop through the whole file
      chomp($line);
3     if ($line =~ /^Lori/) {
4        $currentpos=tell;
5        print "The current byte position is $currentpos.\n";
6        print "$line\n\n";
      }
   }
7  seek($fh,$currentpos,0);   # Start after the line starting with Lori
8  @lines=(<$fh>);
9  print @lines;
10 close $fh;

(Output)
5  The current byte position is 40.
6  Lori Gortz

9  Sir Lancelot
   Norma Cord
   Jon DeLoach
   Karen Evich
```

EXPLANATION

1   The *db* file is assigned to the *$fh* filehandle and opened for reading.

2   Each line of the file is assigned, in turn, to the scalar *$line* while looping through the file.

3   If the scalar *$line* contains the regular expression *Lori*, the *if* block is entered.

4   The *tell* function is called and returns the current byte position (starting at byte 0) in the file. This represents the position of the first character in the line that was just read in after the line containing *Lori* was processed.

5   The value in bytes is stored in *$currentpos*. It is printed. Byte position 40 represents the position where *Sir Lancelot* starts the line.

EXPLANATION (CONTINUED)

6   The line containing the regular expression *Lori* is printed.

7   The *seek* function will position the file pointer for $fh at the byte offset, $currentpos, 40 bytes from the beginning of the file. Without *seek*, there is no way to go directly to byte 40; the only option would be to start again from the beginning of the file.

8   The lines starting at offset 40 are read in and stored in the array @lines.

9   The array is printed, starting at offset 40.

10.2.13   Opening for Reading and Writing

Two files are used in the next example: a text file, called *visitor.txt*, which has an initital value of 1 as it's only text, and *countem.pl*, the script that will be used to track the number of users who have run the script.

The *visitor_count* file is a Perl script that will add one to the *visitor.txt* file every time the script is executed.

Table 10.2   Reading and Writing Operations

Symbol	Open For
+<	Read first, then write.
+>	Write first, then read (> clobbers your file).
+>>	Append first, then read.

EXAMPLE 10.28

```
(The text file, visitor.txt)
1


(The Script)
   use warnings;
   # Scriptname: countem.pl
   # Open visitor_count for reading first, and then writing
1  open(my $fh, "+<", "visitor.txt") ||
         die "Can't open visitor.txt: $!\n";
2  $count=<$fh>;              # Read a number from from the file
3  print "You are visitor number $count.";
4  $count++;
5  seek($fh, 0,0) || die;  # Seek back to the top of the file
6  print $fh $count;       # Write the new number to the file
7  close $fh;
```

EXAMPLE 10.28 (CONTINUED)

```
(Output)                                    Script
(First run of countem.pl)
You are visitor number 1.           ┌──────────┐        ┌──────────┐
                                    │          │        │    1     │
                                    │  $count  │        │          │
(Second run of countem.pl)          └──────────┘        └──────────┘
You are visitor number 2.            countem.pl         visitor.txt
                                                            file
```

EXPLANATION

1   The file *visitor.txt* is opened for reading first, and then writing. If the file does not exist or is not readable, *die* will cause the program to exit with an error message.
2   A line is read from the *visitor.txt* file. The first time the script is executed, the number *1* is read in from *visitor.txt* file and stored in the scalar *$count*.
3   The value of *$count* is printed.
4   The *$count* scalar is incremented by 1.
5   The *seek* function moves the file pointer to the beginning of the file.
6   The new value of *$count* is written back to the *visitor.txt* file. The number that was there is overwritten by the new value of *$count* each time the script is executed.
7   The file is closed.

EXAMPLE 10.29

```
(The Script)
    # Open for writing first, then reading
    print "\n\n";
1   open(my $fh, "+>","joker") || die;
2   print $fh "This line is written to joker.\n";
3   seek($fh,0,0);              # Go to the beginning of the file
4   while(<$fh>) {
5       print;                 # Reads from joker; the line is in $_
    }
    close fh;

(Output)
5   This line is written to joker.
```

EXPLANATION

1   The filehandle *$fh* is opened for writing first. This means that the file *joker* will be created or, if it already exists, it will be truncated. Be careful not to mix up +< and +>.
2   The output is sent to *joker* via the *$fh* filehandle.
3   The *seek* function moves the filepointer to the beginning of the file.
4   The *while* loop is entered. A line is read from the file *joker* via the *$fh* filehandle and stored in $_.
5   Each line ($_) is printed after it is read until the end of the file is reached.

10.2.14   Opening for Anonymous Pipes

When using a **pipe** (also called a **filter**), a connection is made from one program to another. The program on the left-hand side of a pipe symbol sends its output into a temporary buffer and writes into it. On the other side of the pipe is a program that is a reader. It gets its input from the buffer. Here is an example of a typical UNIX pipe (see Figure 10.1):

```
who | wc -l
```

and an MS-DOS pipe:

```
dir /b | more
```

   The output of the *who* command is sent to the *wc* command. The *who* command sends its output to the pipe; meaning, it writes to the pipe. The *wc* command gets its input from the pipe; it reads from the pipe. (If the *wc* command were not a reader, it would ignore what is in the pipe.) The output of the *wc* command is finally sent to the *STDOUT*, the terminal screen. The number of people logged on is printed.

   When a Perl pipe is opened, the operating system command is either on the left-hand side or right-hand side of the pipe. For example, if you see | *sort*, the OS command is on the right side of the pipe symbol. There is nothing on the left side, which implies that Perl is there and Perl is the writer. Perl sends its output to the pipe and the *sort* command reads from it. On the other hand, if you see *ls* | or *dir* |, the OS command is on the left-hand side of the pipe, implying that Perl is on the right-hand side, making perl the reader.

   (It is important to keep in mind that the process connecting to Perl is an operating system command. If you are running Perl on a UNIX or Linux system, the commands will be different from those on a Windows system, thereby making Perl scripts implementing pipes unportable between systems.)

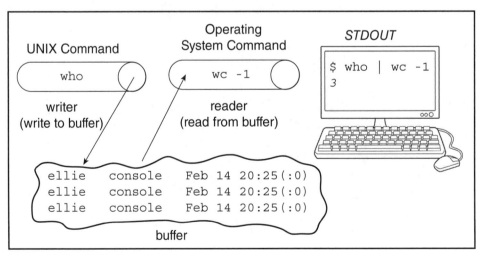

Figure 10.1   UNIX pipe example.

The Output Filter. When creating a handle with the *open* function, you can open a filter so that the output is piped to a system command. The command is preceded by a pipe symbol (|) and replaces the filename argument in the previous examples. The output will be piped to the command and sent to *STDOUT* (see Figure 10.2). You can use the two-argument format or the three-argument format, as shown in the following example. With the three-argument format, your shell (bash, korn, and so on) may be avoided and, thus, shell wildcard expansion, redirection, and multistage pipelines will not be handled.

FORMAT

```
open(PIPE, "|COMMAND");
open ($pipe, "|-", "COMMAND");
```

EXAMPLE 10.30

```
(The Script)
   use warnings;
   # Scriptname: outfilter (UNIX/Windows)
1  open(MYPIPE, "|sort");
2  print MYPIPE "dogs\ncats\nbirds\zebras\";
3  close(MYPIPE);

4  open (my $mypipe, "|-", "sort" );  # Three-argument format
5  print $mypipe "dogs\ncats\nbirds\nzebras";
6  close $mypipe;

(Output)
       birds
       cats
       dogs
       zebras

       birds
       cats
       dogs
       zebra
```

EXPLANATION

1   The user-defined pipe handle *MYPIPE* will be used to pipe output from the Perl script to the OS command *sort*, which sorts lines, hence the newline between each animal.

2   The *print* function sends the output to *MYPIPE* instead of to the screen. The *sort* command on right-hand side of the pipe sorts by lines.

3   After you have finished using the pipe handle, close it. This guarantees that the command will complete before the script exits. If you don't close the handle, the output may not be flushed properly.

4   This is the three-argument style for creating a pipe. The pipe name is a lexical scalar, *$mypipe*, the pipe symbol with a dash on its righthand side, |-, indicates that Perl will be sending output to the pipe where the OS *sort* command is represented by the dash. Perl writes; the *sort* command reads.

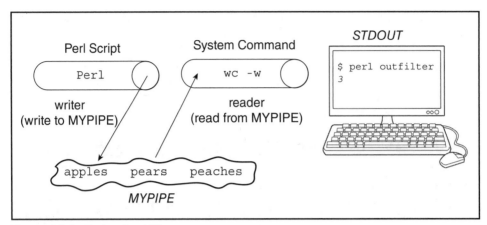

Figure 10.2 Perl output filter.

EXAMPLE 10.31

```
(The Text File)
$ cat emp.names
Steve Blenheim
Betty Boop
Igor Chevsky
Norma Cord
Jon DeLoach
Karen Evich

(The Script)
   use warnings;
   # Reverse first and last names and pipe to the sort command
1  open(FOO,"|sort");    # Open output filter
2  open($db, "<","emp.names") or die;    # Open DB for reading
3  while(<$db>)
4     ($first, $last)= split(" ", $_);
5     print FOO "$last, $first\n";
      }
6  close FOO;
   close $db;

(Output)
       Blenheim, Steve
       Boop, Betty
       Chevsky, Igor
       Cord, Norma
       DeLoach, Jon
       Evich, Karen
```

EXPLANATION

1   The user-defined pipe handle, a bareword *FOO*, will be used to pipe output to the OS *sort* command.
2   The *open* function creates the pipe handle *$db* and attaches it to the UNIX file called *emp.names*.
3   The expression in the *while* loop contains the filehandle *DB*, enclosed in angle brackets, indicating a read operation. The loop will read the first line from the *emp.names* file and store it in the *$_* scalar variable.
4   The *split* function splits each line by whitespace and returns a list consisting of *$first*, the first name, and *$last*, the last name.
5   The first and last names are printed to the *FOO* pipe and then sent to the OS *sort* command, and the output from the sort command will be sent to the screen.
6   The output filter *FOO* is closed.

Sending the Output of a Filter to a File.   In the previous example, what if you had wanted to send the output of the filter to a file intead of to *STDOUT*? You can't send output to a pipe and a filehandle at the same time, but you can redirect *STDOUT* to a filehandle. Since, later in the program, you may want *STDOUT* to be redirected back to the screen, you can first save it or simply reopen *STDOUT* to the terminal device by typing

```
open(STDOUT, ">/dev/tty");
```

The following example can better be accomplished by using *Capture::Tiny* from CPAN. *Capture::Tiny* fixes pitfalls, incuding avoiding accidentally clobbering someone else's global filehandles.

EXAMPLE 10.32

```
    use warnings;
    # Program to redirect STDOUT from filter to a UNIX file
1   $| = 1;                 # Flush buffers
2   my $tmpfile = "temp";
3   open($db, "<","data") || die qq/Can't open "data": $!\n/;
                                        # Open file for reading
4   open(SAVED, ">&STDOUT") || die "$!\n";  # Save stdout
5   open(STDOUT, ">$tmpfile" ) || die "Can't open: $!\n";
6   open(SORT, "| sort ") || die;          # Open output filter
7   while(<$db>){
8       print SORT;    # Output is first sorted and then sent to temp.
9   }
10  close SORT;
    close $db;
11  open(STDOUT, ">&SAVED") || die "Can't open";
12  print "Here we are printing to the screen again.\n";
                       # This output will go to the screen
13  rename("temp","data");
```

1. The $|$ variable guarantees an automatic flush of the output buffer after each *print* statement is executed. (See the *autoflush* module in Appendix A, "Perl Built-ins, Pragmas, Modules, and the Debugger.")

2. The scalar $tmpfile is assigned *temp* to be used later as an output file.

3. The *data* file is opened for reading, and attached to the *DB* filehandle.

4. *STDOUT* is being copied and saved in another filehandle called *SAVED*. Behind the scenes, the file descriptors are being manipulated.

5. The *temp* file is being opened for writing and is assigned to the file descriptor normally reserved for *STDOUT*, the screen. The file descriptor for *STDOUT* has been closed and reopened for *temp*.

6. The output filter will be assigned to *SORT*. Perl's output will be sent to the *sort* utility, which works here for both Windows and UNIX to sort alphabetically from the beginning of the line.

7. The $db filehandle is opened for reading.

8. The output filehandle will be sent to the *temp* file after being sorted.

9. Close the loop.

10. Close the pipe.

11. Open the standard output filehandle so that output is redirected back to the screen.

12. This line prints to the screen because *STDOUT* has been reassigned there.

13. The *temp* file is renamed *data*, overwriting what was in *data* with the contents of *temp*.

Input Filter. When creating a filehandle with the *open* function, you can also open a filter so that input is piped **into** Perl. The OS shell normally handles any special characters that need interpretation during the processing.

If you don't have any need for the shell to process the command in the pipe (meaning you aren't using redirection, wildcard expansion, or multiple pipes), you can use the three-argument format as previously shown in Example 10.30. See Figure 10.3.

FORMAT

```
open(FILEHANDLE, COMMAND|);
open(FILEHANDLE, "-|", COMMAND);
```

EXAMPLE 10.33

```
    use warnings;
    # Scriptname: infilter
1   open(INPIPE, "date +%D|");      # Windows use:  date /T
2   $today = <INPIPE> ;
3   print $today;
4   close(INPIPE);
5   open (my $pipe, "-|", "date +%D");  # three arguments
6   $today = <$pipe>;
    print $today;
    close $pipe;
```

EXAMPLE 10.33 (CONTINUED)

(Output)
Sun Feb 18 14:12:44 PST 2014

EXPLANATION

1   The user-defined pipe handle *INPIPE* will be used to pipe the output from the command as input to Perl. The output of a UNIX *date* command will be used as input by your Perl script via the *INPIPE* pipe handle. Windows users: use *date /T*.

2   The scalar *$today* will receive its input from the *INPIPE* pipe handle; in other words, Perl reads from *INPIPE*.

3   The value of the UNIX *date* command was assigned to *$today* and is displayed.

4   After you have finished using the pipe handle, use the *close* function to close it. This guarantees that the command will complete before the script exits. If you don't close the pipe handle, the output may not be flushed properly.

5   This format became available in version 5.6. It allows you to create lexically scoped pipe handles which will be closed when the handle goes out of scope.

6   Now Perl reads from the pipe, storing the output of the UNIX *date* command in *$today*.

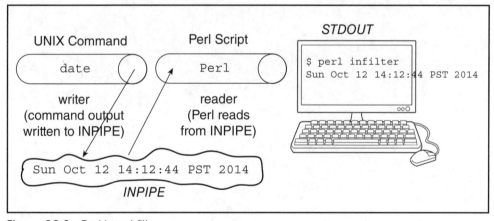

Figure 10.3   Perl input filter.

EXAMPLE 10.34

```
(The Script)
    use warnings;
1   open(LISTDIR, "ls |") or
        die "PIPE failed $!\n";    # See next example for Windows
2   while( $filename = <LISTDIR> ){
3       print $filename;
    }
```

EXAMPLE 10.34 (CONTINUED)

```
(Output)
3    ./perl2
     ./perl3
     ./perl.man
     ./perl.arg
```

EXPLANATION

1   The output of the UNIX *ls* command will be piped as input to *LISTDIR*. When enclosed in angle brackets, the standard input will come from *LISTDIR*. If *open* fails, the *die* operator will print *PIPE failed!* and exit the script.

2   The output from the UNIX *ls* command has been piped into *LISTDIR*. For each iteration of the *while* loop, one line from the *LISTDIR* will be assigned to the scalar variable *$filename* and printed.

EXAMPLE 10.35

```
(The Script)
    use warnings;
    # Opening an input filter on a Win32 platform
1   open(LISTDIR, 'dir "C:\perl" |') || die $!;
2   @filelist = <LISTDIR>;
3   foreach $file ( @filelist ){
        print $file;
    }

(Output)
Volume in drive C is 010599
Volume Serial Number is 2237-130A

Directory of C:\perl

03/31/1999  10:34p     <DIR>          .
03/31/1999  10:34p     <DIR>          ..
03/31/1999  10:37p                30,366 DeIsL1.isu
03/31/1999  10:34p     <DIR>          bin
03/31/1999  10:34p     <DIR>          lib
03/31/1999  10:35p     <DIR>          html
03/31/1999  10:35p     <DIR>          eg
03/31/1999  10:35p     <DIR>          site
              1 File(s)        30,366 bytes
              7 Dir(s)     488,873,984 bytes free
```

EXPLANATION

1   The output of the Windows *dir* command will be piped to *LISTDIR*. When enclosed in angle brackets, the standard input will come from *LISTDIR*. If the open fails, the *die* operator will print an error and exit the script.

EXPLANATION (CONTINUED)

2   The output from the Windows *dir* command has been piped into pipe *LISTDIR*. The input is read from the pipe and assigned to the array *@filelist*. Each element of the array represents one line of input.
3   The *foreach* loop iterates through the array, printing one line at a time until the end of the array.

10.3 Passing Arguments

How does Perl pass command-line arguments to a Perl script? If you are coming from a *C*, *C++*, *awk*, or *C* shell background, at first glance you might think, "Oh, I already know this!" Beware! There are some subtle differences. So, read on.

10.3.1   The *@ARGV* Array

Perl does store arguments in a special array called *@ARGV*. The subscript starts at zero and, unlike *C* and *awk*, *$ARGV[0]* does **not** represent the name of the program; it represents the name of the first word after the script name. Like the shell languages, the *$0* special variable is used to hold the name of the Perl script. Unlike the *C* shell, the *$#ARGV* expression contains the number of the last subscript in the array, **not** the number of elements in the array. The number of arguments is *$#ARGV + 1*. *$#ARGV* initially has a value of *-1*. To get the size of the *@ARGV* array, it is easier to just say *scalar @ARGV*.

When *ARGV*, the filehandle, is enclosed in angle brackets, *<ARGV>*, the command-line argument is treated as a filename. The filename is assigned to *ARGV* and the *@ARGV* array is shifted immediately to the left by one, thereby shortening the *@ARGV* array.

The value that is shifted off the *@ARGV* array is assigned to *$ARGV*. *$ARGV* contains the name of the currently selected filehandle. See Figure 10.4.

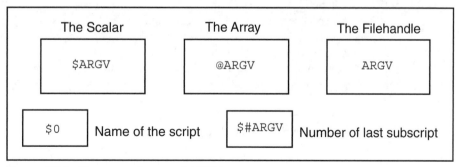

Figure 10.4   The many faces of *ARGV*.

EXAMPLE 10.36

```
(The Script)
   #!/usr/bin/env perl
   use warnings;
1  die "$0 requires an argument.\n" unless @ARGV;
                        # Must have at least one argument
2  print "@ARGV\n";        # Print all arguments
3  print "$ARGV[0]\n";     # Print first argument
4  print "$ARGV[1]\n";     # Print second argument
5  print The number of arguments is ", scalar @ARGV,".\n";
6  print "There are ", $#ARGV + 1," arguments.\n";
                        # $#ARGV is the last index value
7  print "$ARGV[$#ARGV] is the last one.\n";  # Print last arg


(Output)
   $ perl.arg
2  perl.arg requires an argument.

   $ perl.arg f1 f2 f3 f4 f5
2  f1 f2 f3 f4 f5
3  f1
4  f2
5  The number of arguments is 5.
6  There are 5 arguments.
6  f5 is the last one.
```

EXPLANATION

1   If there are no command-line arguments, the *die* function is executed and the script is terminated. The *$0* special variable holds the name of the Perl script, *perl.arg*.

2   The contents of the *@ARGV* array are printed.

3   The first argument, not the script name, is printed.

4   The second argument is printed.

5   The *scalar* function evaluates an expression in scalar context; that is, it returns the size of the array *@ARGV*.

6   The *$#ARGV* variable contains the number value of the last index value. Since the index starts at zero, *$#ARGV + 1* is the total number of arguments, not counting the script name; also the size of the array.

7   Since *$#ARGV* contains the value of the last index value, *$ARGV[$#ARGV]* is the **value** of the last element of the *@ARGV* array.

10.3.2 *ARGV* and the Null Filehandle

When used in loop expressions and enclosed in the input angle brackets (<>), each element of the *@ARGV* array is treated as a **special filehandle**. Perl shifts through the array, storing each element of the array in a variable *$ARGV*. A set of empty angle brackets is using the **null filehandle**, and Perl implicitly uses each element of the *ARGV* array as a filehandle.

When using the input operators <>, either with or without the keyword *ARGV*, Perl shifts through its arguments one at a time, allowing you to process each argument in turn. Once the *ARGV* filehandle has been opened, the arguments are shifted off one at a time, so if they are to be used later, they must be saved in another array.

EXAMPLE 10.37

```
(The Text Files)
$ cat f1
Hello there. Nice day.
$ cat f2
Are you sure about that?
$ cat f3
This is it.
This is the end.

(The  Script)
1  while( <ARGV> ) {print ;}
2  print "The value of \$ARGV[0] is $ARGV[0].\n";

(Output)
#!/usr/bin/env perl
$ argv.test f1 f2 f3
Hello there. Nice day.
Are you sure about that?
This is it.
This is the end.
The value of $ARGV[0] is .
```

EXPLANATION

1   This will print the contents of all the files named at the command line. Once used, the argument is shifted off. The contents of *f1*, *f2*, and *f3* are read and then printed, consecutively.

2   Since the arguments were all shifted off, *$ARGV[0]* has no value and, therefore, nothing is printed.

EXAMPLE 10.38

```
(The Text File: emp.names)
Steve Blenheim
Betty Boop
Igor Chevsky
Norma Cord
Jon DeLoach
Karen Evich
```

EXAMPLE 10.38 (CONTINUED)

```
(The Script)
   #!/usr/bin/env perl
   use warnings;
   # Scriptname: grab.pl
   # Program will behave like grep -- will search for a pattern
   # in any number of files.
1  if ( scalar @ARGV < 2) {die "Usage: $0 pattern filename(s) \n";}
2  my $pattern = shift;  # Implictly shifts @ARGV
3  while(my $line=<ARGV>){
      print "$ARGV: $.:  $line" if $line =~ /$pattern/i;
      close(ARGV) if eof;
   }
```

```
(Output)
   $ grab.pl
1  Usage: grab.pl pattern filenames(s)
   $ grab.pl 'norma' db
2  db:5: Norma Cord
   $ grab.pl 'Sir Lancelot' db
3  db:4: Sir Lancelot
   $ grab.pl '^.... ' db
4  db:3: Lori Gortz
   $ grab.pl Steve d*
5  datebook.master:12: Johann Erickson:Stevensville, Montana
   datafile:8: Steven Daniels:496-456-5676:83755:11/12/56:20300
   db:1: Steve Blenheim
```

EXPLANATION

1   If there are no command-line arguments, the *die* function is executed. *$0* is the current Perl script name.

2   The first argument is shifted from the *@ARGV* array. This should be the pattern that will be searched for.

3   Since the first argument was shifted off the *@ARGV* array and assigned to the scalar *$pattern,* the remaining arguments passed in from the command line are opened in turn to the *ARGV* filehandle. When the *while* loop is entered, a line is read and assigned to *$line*.

4   The *$ARGV* scalar holds the name of the file that is currently being processed. The $. variable holds the current line number. If the value in *$pattern* is matched, the filename where it was found, the number of the line where the pattern was found, and the line itself are printed. The *i* after the last delimiter in the pattern turns off case sensitivity.

5   When the file being processed reaches the end of file (EOF), the *ARGV* filehandle is closed. This causes the $. variable to be reset. If *ARGV* is not closed explicitly here, the $. variable will continue to increment and not be set back to *1* when the next file is read.

EXAMPLE 10.39

```
(The Script)
    #!/usr/bin/env perl
    use warnings;
1   if ( scalar @ARGV < 1 ){ die "Usage: $0 <argument>"; }
2   open(my $pw,"<", "etc/passwd") || die "Can't open /etc/passwd: $!";
3   my $username=shift;    # Same as shift @ARGV
4   while( my $pwline = <$pw>){
5       unless ( $pwline =~ /$username:/){ print "$username is not
                a user here.\n"; next;}


    }
6   close $pw;
7   open(LOGGEDON, "who |" ) || die "Can't execute who $!" ;
8   while($logged = <LOGGEDON> ){
        if ( $logged =~ /$username/){ $logged_on = 1; last;}
    }
9   close LOGGEDON;
    die "$username is not logged on.\n" if ! $logged_on;
    print "$username is logged on and running these processes.\n";
10  open(PROC, "ps -aux|" ) || die "Can't execute ps: $! ";
    while(my $line=<PROC>){
        print "$line" if  $line =~ /$username:/;
    }
11  close PROC;
    print '*' x 80; "\n";
    print "So long.\n";
```

```
(Output)
    $ checkon
1   Usage: checkon <argument>:  at checkon line 6.
    $ checkon joe
5   Joe is not a user here.
    $ checkon ellie
8   ellie is logged on and running these processes:
ellie  3825  6.4  4.5   212   464 p5 R    12:18     0:00 ps -aux
ellie  1383  0.8  8.4   360   876 p4 S    Dec 26 11:34 /usr/local/OW3/bin/xview
ellie   173  0.8 13.4 1932  1392 co S    Dec 20389:19 /usr/local/OW3/bin/xnews
ellie   164  0.0  0.0   100     0 co IW   Dec 20     0:00 -c
< some of the output was cut to save space >
ellie  3822  0.0  0.0     0     0 p5 Z    Dec 20     0:00 <defunct>
ellie  3823  0.0  1.1    28   112 p5 S    12:18     0:00 sh -c ps -aux | grep '^'
ellie  3821  0.0  5.6   144   580 p5 S    12:18     0:00 /bin/perl checkon ellie
ellie  3824  0.0  1.8    32   192 p5 S    12:18     0:00 grep ^ellie
ellie  3815  0.0  1.9    24   196 p4 S    12:18     0:00 script checkon.tsc
****************************************************************************
```

EXPLANATION

1   This script calls for only one argument. If *ARGV* is empty (meaning, no arguments are passed at the command line), the *die* function is executed and the script exits with an error message. (Remember: *$#ARGV* is the number of the last subscript in the *ARGV* array, and *ARGV[0]* is the first argument, not counting the name of the script, which is *$0*.) If more than one argument is passed, the script will also exit with the error message.

2   The */etc/passwd* file is opened for reading via the *$pw* filehandle.

3   The first argument is shifted from *@ARGV* and assigned to *$username*.

4   Each time the *while* loop is entered, a line of the */etc/passwd* file is read via the *$pw* filehandle.

5   The =~ is used to test if the first argument passed matches the *$username*. If a match is not found, the loop is exited.

6   The filehandle is closed.

7   *LOGGEDON* is opened as a pipe to accept input. Output from the UNIX *who* command will be piped to the *LOGGEDON* pipe.

8   Each line of the input from the pipe is tested. If the user is logged on, the scalar *$logged_on* is set to *1*, and the loop is exited.

9   The pipe is closed.

10   *PROC* is opened a pipe to accept input. Output from the UNIX *ps* command will be piped to *PROC*. Each line from the pipe is read in turn and placed in the scalar *$line*. If *$line* contains a match for the user, that line will be printed to *STDOUT*, the screen.

11   The pipe is closed.

10.3.3   The *eof* Function

The *eof* function can be used to test if end of file has been reached. It returns *1* if either the next read operation on a *FILEHANDLE* is at the end of the file, or the file was not opened. Without an argument, the *eof* function returns the *eof* status of the last file read. The *eof* function with parentheses can be used in a loop block to test the end of file when the last filehandle has been read. Without parentheses, each file opened can be tested for end of file.

FORMAT

```
eof(FILEHANDLE)
eof()
eof
```

EXAMPLE 10.40

```
(The Text File: emp.names)
Steve Blenheim
Betty Boop
Igor Chevsky
Norma Cord
Jon DeLoach
Karen Evich

(In Script)
   use warnings;
1  open ( my $fh,"<", "emp.names") || die "Can't open emp.names: $!";
2  while(<$fh>){
3     print if (/Norma/ .. eof);        # .. is the range operator
   }

(Output)
Norma Cord
Jonathan DeLoach
Karen Evitch
```

EXPLANATION

1 The file *emp.names* is opened via the *$fh* filehandle.
2 The *while* loop reads a line at a time from the filehandle *$fh*.
3 When the line containing the regular expression *Norma* is reached, that line and all lines in the range from *Norma* until *eof* (the end of file) are printed.

EXAMPLE 10.41

```
(The Text Files)
$ cat file1
abc
def
ghi

$ cat file2
1234
5678
9101112

(The Script)
   #!/usr/bin/env perl
   use warnings;
   # eof.p script
1  while(<>){
2     print "$.\t$_";
3     if (eof){
         print "-" x 30, "\n";
4        close(ARGV);
      }
   }
```

EXAMPLE 10.41 (CONTINUED)

```
(Output)
$ eof.p file1 file2
1   abc
2   def
3   ghi
    ------------------------------
1   1234
2   5678
3   9101112
    ------------------------------
```

EXPLANATION

1   The first argument stored in the *ARGV* array is *file1*. The null filehandle is used in the *while* expression. The file *file1* is opened for reading.

2   The $. variable is a special variable containing the line number of the currently opened filehandle. It is printed, followed by a tab and then the line itself.

3   If end of file is reached, print a row of 30 dashes.

4   The filehandle is closed in order to reset the $. value back to *1* for the next file that is opened. When *file1* reaches end of file, the next argument, *file2*, is processed, starting at line 1.

10.3.4 The *-i* Switch—Editing Files in Place

The -i option is used to edit files in place. The files are named at the command line and stored in the @ARGV array. Perl will automatically rename the output file to the same name as the input file. The output file will be the selected default file for printing. To ensure that you keep a backup of the original file, you can specify an extension to the -i flag, such as -i.bak. The original file will be renamed *filename.bak*. The file must be assigned to the *ARGV* filehandle when it is being read from. Multiple files can be passed in from the command line and each, in turn, will be edited in place.

EXAMPLE 10.42

```
(The Text File)
1   $ more names.txt
    igor chevsky
    norma corder
    jennifer cowan
    john deloach
    fred fardbarkle
    lori gortz
    paco gutierrez
    ephram hardy
    james ikeda
```

EXAMPLE 10.42 (CONTINUED)

```
(The Script)
   # Scriptname: inplace.plx
2  while(<ARGV>){   # Open ARGV for reading
3    tr/a-z/A-Z/;
4    print;    # Output goes to file currently being read in-place
5    close ARGV if eof;
   }
```

```
(Output)
6  $ perl -i.bak inplace.plx names.txt
   IGOR CHEVSKY
   NORMA CORDER
   JENNIFER COWAN
   JOHN DELOACH
   FRED FARDBARKLE
   LORI GORTZ
   PACO GUTIERREZ
   EPHRAM HARDY
   JAMES IKEDA
7  more names.txt.bak
   igor chevsky
   norma corder
   jennifer cowan
   john deloach
   fred fardbarkle
   lori gortz
   paco gutierrez
   ephram hardy
   james ikeda
```

EXPLANATION

1   The contents of the original text file, called *names.txt*, is printed.

2   The *while* loop is entered. The *ARGV* filehandle will be opened for reading. The *ARGV* filehandle represents the file coming in from the command line, *names.txt*.

3   All lowercase letters are translated to uppercase letters in the file being processed (*tr* function).

4   The *print* function sends its output to the file being processed in place.

5   The *ARGV* filehandle will be closed when the end of file is reached. This makes it possible to reset line numbering for each file when processing multiple files or to mark the end of files when appending.

6   The -i in-place switch is used with an extension, *bak*. The *name.txt* file will be edited in place and the original file will be saved in *names.txt.bak*. The *names.txt* file has been changed, illustrating that the file was modified in place.

7   The *names.txt.bak* file was created as a backup file for the original file. The original file, *names.txt*, was changed in place.

10.4 File Testing

Like the shells, Perl provides a number of file test operators (see Table 10.3) to check for the various attributes of a file, such as existence, access permissions, directories, and so on. Most of the operators return *1* for true and " " (null) for false.

A single underscore can be used to represent the name of the file if the same file is tested more than once. The *stat* structure of the previous file test is used.

Table 10.3   File Test Operators

Operator	Meaning
-r $file	True if $file is a readable file.
-w $file	True if $file is a writeable file.
-x $file	True if $file is an executable file.
-o $file	True if $file is owned by effective uid.
-e $file	True if file exists.
-z $file	True if file is zero in size.
-s $file	Returns the size of the $file in bytes.
-f $file	True if $file is a plain file.
-d $file	True if $file is a directory file.
-l $file	True if $file is a symbolic link.
-p $file	True if $file is a named pipe or *FIFO*.
-S $file	True if $file is a socket.
-b $file	True if $file is a block special file.
-c $file	True if $file is a character special file.
-u $file	True if $file has a *setuid* bit set.
-g $file	True if $file has a *setgid* bit set.
-k $file	True if $file has a sticky bit set.
-t $file	True if $file is opened to a *tty*.
-T $file	True if $file is a text file.
-B $file	True if $file is a binary file.
-M $file	Age of $file in days since modified.
-A $file	Age of $file in days since last accessed.
-C $file	Age of $file in days since the inode changed.

EXAMPLE 10.43

```
(At the Command Line)
1  $ ls -l perl.test
   -rwxr-xr-x  1 ellie         417 Apr 23 13:40 perl.test
2  $ ls -l afile
   -rws--x--x  1 ellie           0 Apr 23 14:07 afile

(In Script)
   use warnings;
   my $file="perl.test";

3  print "File is readable\n" if -r  $file;
   print "File is writeable\n" if -w  $file;
   print "File is executable\n" if -x  $file;
   print "File is a regular file\n" if -f  $file;
   print "File is a directory\n" if -d $file;
   print "File is text file\n" if -T $file;
   printf "File was modified in the last 12 hours\n" if -M $file < .5;
   print "File has been accessed in the last 12 hours.\n" if -M <= 12;

4  print "File has read, write, and execute set.\n"
           if -r $file && -w _ && -x _;
5  stat("afile");  # stat another file
   print "File is a set user id program.\n" if  -u _;
                   # underscore evaluates to last file stat'ed
   print "File is zero size.\n" if -z _;

(Output)
3  File is readable
   File is writeable
   File is executable
   File is a regular file
   *** No print out here because the file is not a directory ***
   File is text file
   File was last modified 0.000035 days ago.
   File has read, write, and execute set.
   File is a set user id program.
   File is zero size.
```

EXPLANATION

1   The permissions, ownership, file size, and so on, on *perl.test* are shown.

2   The permissions, ownership, file size, and so on, on *afile* are shown.

3   The *print* statement is executed if the file is readable, writeable, executable, and so on.

4   Since the same file is checked for more than one attribute, an underscore is appended to the file test operator. The underscore references the *stat* structure, an array that holds information about the file.

5   The *stat* function returns a 13-element array containing the statistics about a file. As long as the underscore is appended to the file test operator, the statistics for *afile* are used in the tests that follow.

10.5 What You Should Know

1. What is a filehandle?

2. What does it mean to open a file for reading?

3. When opened for writing, if the file exists, what happens to it?

4. How does > differ from >> when opening a file?

5. What is the purpose of the *select()* function?

6. What is binmode?

7. What does the *die()* function accomplish when working with files?

8. How do Windows and UNIX differ in how they terminate a line?

9. What is an exclusive lock?

10. What does the *tell()* function return?

11. What is the difference between the +< and +> symbols?

12. What does the *stat()* function do?

13. How do you reposition the file pointer in a file?

14. How does the -*M* switch work when testing a file?

10.6 What's Next?

Until this point, all the functions you have used were provided by Perl. The *print()* and *printf()*, *push()*, *pop()*, and *chomp()* functions are all examples of built-in Perl functions. All you had to know was what they were supposed to do and how to use them. You did not have to know what the Perl authors did to make the function work; you just assumed they knew what they were doing. In the next chapter, you will write your own functions, also called subroutines, and learn how to send messages to them and return some result.

EXERCISE 10
Getting a Handle on Things

Part 1

1. Create a filehandle for reading from the *datebook* file (on the CD); print to another filehandle the names of all those who have a salary greater than $50,000.

2. Ask the user to input data for a new entry in the *datebook* file. (The name, phone, address, and so on, will be stored in separate scalars.) Append the newline to the *datebook* file by using a user-defined filehandle.

Part 2

This problem appeared on a Web site called *daniweb.com*. Can you solve it?

1. We need a Perl program that will check whether or not an IP address entered by a user is valid. The user is to enter the IP address as a command-line parameter. For example, the user could type at the prompt

```
check_ip.pl 192.168.9.23
```

and the script will attempt to validate the IP address 192.168.9.23.

2. The script must first check whether the user has input any data and if not, display an appropriate error message. A valid IP address must have:

   a. Four octets, each separated by a dot.

   b. Only numbers are allowed in each of the four octets (meaning, no alphabetic or punctuation characters are allowed within each octet).

   c. The first octet values are between 1 and 255. The second, third, and fourth octet values are between 0 and 255. Only one IP Address is to be input and validated (meaning, there is no looping through several IP addresses).

Part 3

1. Use a pipe to list all the files in your current directory, and print only those files that are readable text files. Use the *die* function to quit if the open fails. For UNIX users, the command is *ls*. For Windows use *dir /b*. (Hint: Don't forget to *chomp*!)

2. Rewrite the program to test whether any of the files listed have been modified in the last 12 hours. Print the names of those files.

Part 4

1. Sort the *datebook* file by names, using a pipe.

Part 5

1. Create a number of duplicate entries in the *datebook* file. *Fred Fardbarkle*, for example, might appear five times, and *Igor Chevsky* three times. In most editors, this will be a simple copy/paste operation.

   a. Write a program that will assign the name of the *datebook* file to a scalar and check to see if the file exists. If it does exist, the program will check to see if the file is readable and writeable. Use the *die* function to send any errors to the screen. Also tell the user when the *datebook* was last modified.

   b. The program will read each line of the *datebook* file giving each person a 10% raise in salary. If, however, the person appears more than once in the file (assume having the same first and last name means it is a duplicate), he will be given a raise the first time, but if he appears again, he will be skipped. Send each line of output to a file called *raise*. The *raise* file should not contain any person's name more than once. It will also reflect the 10% increase in pay. Display on the screen the average salary for all the people in the *datebook* file. For duplicate entries, print the names of those who appeared in the file more than once, and how many times each appeared.

2. Write a script called *checking* that will take any number of filenames as command-line arguments and will print the names of those files that are readable and writeable text files. The program will print an error message if there are no arguments, and exit.

chapter

11

How Do Subroutines Function?

In computer programming, a **subroutine** is a sequence of program instructions that perform a specific task, packaged as a unit. This unit can then be used in programs wherever that particular task should be performed. Subprograms may be defined within programs, or separately in libraries that can be used by multiple programs. In different programming languages, a subroutine may be called a procedure, a function, a routine, a method, or a subprogram. The generic term callable unit is also sometimes used.[1]

Perl allows you to collect a sequence of statements, give the collection a name, and use the collection just as you use the built-in functions, such as *print* and *localtime*. This collection can be called a subroutine or a function. It doesn't matter.

By the end of this chapter, you should be able to explain each line in the following program.

```
1   use feature 'say';
2
3   print "What is the current Fahrenheit temperature? ";
4   chomp( $fahr = <STDIN> );
5   say "$fahr Fahrenheit converted to Celsius is ", converter($fahr),".";
6   say "program continues here";
7
8   sub converter{
9       my ($ftemp) = @_;
10      if ($ftemp < -459 ){ return "too cold"; }
11      my $celsius = ($ftemp - 32 ) * 5/9;
12      return int $celsius;
13  }
```

---

1. Wikipedia, "Subroutine," *http://en.wikipedia.org/wiki/Subroutine*.

11.1 Subroutines/Functions

We have been using a number of Perl's built-in functions since the beginning of this book. In addition to the large number of Perl functions already available, you can create your own. Some languages distinguish between the terms **function** and **subroutine**. Perl doesn't. Technically, a function is a block of code that returns a value, whereas a subroutine is a block of code that performs some task, but doesn't return anything. Perl subroutines and functions can do both, so we'll use the two terms interchangeably in this text. For now, we'll use the term "subroutine" when referring to user-defined functions.

Let's further define the Wikipedia definition of a subroutine. Subroutines are self-contained units of a program designed to accomplish a specified task, such as calculating a mortgage payment, retrieving data from a database, or checking for valid input. When a subroutine is called in a program, it is like taking a detour from the main part of the program. Perl starts executing the instructions in the subroutine and when finished, returns to the main program and picks up where it left off. You can use subroutines over and over again and thus save you from repetitious programming. They are also used to break up a program into smaller units to keep it better organized and easier to maintain. If the subroutine proves to be useful in other programs, you can store it in a library as a module (discussed in Chapter 13, "Modularize It, Package It, and Send It to the Library!").

The subroutine definition consists of one or more statements enclosed in a block, independent of your program and not executed until it is called. It is often referred to as a **black box**. Information goes into the black box as input (like the calculator or remote control when you push buttons), and the action or value returned from the box is its output (such as a calculation or a different channel, continuing the analogy). What goes on inside the box is transparent to the user. The programmer who writes the subroutine is the only one who cares about those details. When you use Perl's built-in functions, such as *print* or *rand*, you send a string of text or a number to the function, and it sends something back. You don't care how it does its job; you just expect it to work. If you send bad input, you get back bad output or maybe nothing; hence the expression "garbage in, garbage out."

The scope of a subroutine is where it is visible in the program. Up to this point, all scripts have been in the namespace *main*, the *main* package. Subroutines are global in that they are visible or available to the entire script where they are defined. And you can place them anywhere in the script. You can define them in another file, and when coming from another file, they are loaded into the script with the *require* or *use* functions. All variables created within a subroutine or accessed by it are also global, unless specifically made local with either the *local* or *my* operators.

The subroutine is called, or invoked, by appending a set of empty parentheses to the subroutine name. (Rarely you will see a function called by prepending it with an ampersand, but that style is outdated in modern Perl.) If you use a forward reference, neither ampersands nor parentheses are needed to call the subroutine. You can send scalars, arrays, hashes, references, and the like to subroutines in an argument list and receive them by the function. This is all covered in the following pages.

If a nonexistent subroutine is called, the program quits with an error message: *Undefined subroutine in "main::prog"* .... If you want to check whether the subroutine has been defined, you can do so with the built-in *defined* function.

The return value of a subroutine is the value of the last expression evaluated (either a scalar or a list). You can use the *return* function explicitly to return a value or to exit from the subroutine early, based on the result of testing some condition.

If you make the call to the subroutine part of an expression, you can assign the returned value to a variable, thus emulating a function call.

FORMAT

```
Subroutine declaration:
   sub subroutine_name;
Subroutine definition:
   sub subroutine_name { Block }
Subroutine call:
   subroutine_name();
   subroutine_name;
   &subroutine_name;    # Alternate method
Subroutine call with parameters:
   subroutine_name(parameter1, parameter2, ... )
```

11.1.1 Defining and Calling a Subroutine

A **declaration** simply announces to the Perl compiler that a subroutine is going to be defined in the program and may take specified arguments. Declarations are global in scope for a package (we have been working in package *main*). In other words, they are visible no matter where you put them in the program, although it is customary to put declarations at the beginning or end of the program, or in another file. (For now, we will define the subroutines in one file, package *main*.) We will discuss packages in Chapter 13, "Modularize It, Package It, and Send It to the Library!" but it is important to note that when we use the term **global variable**, it is technically called a **package variable**. A subroutine **definition** is a block of statements that follows the subroutine name. A subroutine you do not explicitly **declare** is declared at the same time it is defined.

- **Declaration:** *sub name;*
- **Definition:** *sub name { statement; statement; }*

You can define a subroutine anywhere in your program (or even in another file). The subroutine consists of the keyword *sub* followed by an opening curly brace, a set of statements, and ending in a closing curly brace.

The subroutine and its statements are not executed until called. You can call a subroutine by attaching a set of empty parentheses to its name (called the null parameter list), or by calling it as a built-in function. If you call the subroutine without parentheses, then you must declare it first.[2]

EXAMPLE 11.1

```
(The Script)
1   sub greetme { print "Welcome, Välkommen till, Bienvenue!\n";}
                                       # Define the subroutine

2   &greetme();  # Call the subroutine; could also say &greetme
3   print "Program continues....\n";
4   &greetme if defined &greetme;  # Call to subroutine
5   print "More program here.\n";
6   &bye;  # Older method of calling a subroutine
7   sub bye { print "Bye, adjo, adieu.\n"; }
8   bye();   # Call to subroutine using empty parameter list

(Output)
2   Welcome, Välkommen till, Bienvenue!
3   Program continues....
4   Welcome, Välkommen till, Bienvenue!
5   More program here.
    Bye, adjo, adieu.
    Bye, adjo, adieu.
```

EXPLANATION

1 This is a subroutine definition consisting of the keyword *sub*, followed by the name of the subroutine, *greetme*, and a block of statements that will execute when the subroutine is called. You can place this definition anywhere in your program and it will do nothing until it is called. In this example, there is only one *print* statement that will execute when the function is called.

2 The subroutine *greetme* is called by appending a set of empty parentheses to its name. When called, the program will jump into the subroutine and start executing the statements defined there; in this case, the *Welcome* statement.

4 After the subroutine is called (invoked), program execution starts at the line right after where it was called and continues from there.
   The subroutine *greetme* is called again. The *defined* built-in function is used to check that the subroutine has been defined.
   The program resumes execution after the subroutine exits on line 4.

6 The subroutine *&bye* is called. The definition is found later on line 7. This is an older way of calling a subroutine and rarely used today.

7 Subroutine *bye* is defined. No matter where you place subroutines, the compiler sees them.

8 Subroutine *bye* is called using a null parameter list.

---

2. The sigil for a subroutine is the ampersand (&) and in older programs you may see this used to call a subroutine, as in *&greetme*. Today, the & is used only in special cases with reference.

Forward Declaration. A forward declaration announces to the compiler that the subroutine has been defined somewhere in the program. If no arguments are being passed to the subroutine, the empty parens are not needed to call a subroutine if it has been declared.

EXAMPLE 11.2

```
    (The Script)
1   sub bye;  # Forward declaration

    my $name="Ellie";
2   print "Hello $name.\n";

3   bye;       # Call subroutine without parens; e.g., bye();

4   sub bye{
5      print "Bye\n";
    }

(Output)
2   Hello Ellie.
5   Bye
```

Scope of Variables. Scope describes where a variable is visible in your program. Perl variables are global in scope. They are visible throughout the entire program, even in subroutines. If you declare a variable in a subroutine, it is visible to the entire program. If you change the value of an existing variable from within a subroutine, it will be changed when you exit the subroutine. A local variable is private to the block, subroutine, or file where it is declared. You use the *my* operator to create local, lexically scoped variables, since by default, Perl variables are global in scope.

EXAMPLE 11.3

```
(The Script)
    # Script: perlsub_sub2
    # Variables used in subroutines are global by default
1   sub bye { print "Bye $name\n"; $name="Tom";}  # Subroutine definition
2   $name="Ellie";
3   print "Hello to you and yours!\n";
4   &bye;
5   print "Out of the subroutine. Hello $name.\n";   # $name is now Tom
6   bye;

(Output)
3   Hello to you and yours!
1   Bye Ellie
5   Out of the subroutine. Hello Tom.
1   Bye Tom
```

EXPLANATION

1   The subroutine *bye* is defined. Within the subroutine block, the variable *$name* is assigned the value *Tom*, a global variable visible throughout the program.*

2   Program execution starts here. *$name* is assigned the value *Ellie*.

3   This line is here just to show you the flow of execution.

4   The subroutine *bye* is called. The program jumps into the subroutine on line 1. The value of *$name* is still *Ellie*. After the line *Bye, Ellie* is printed, and the variable *$name* is assigned a new value, *Tom*. The subroutine exits and the program resumes execution at line 5.

5   The value of the global variable *$name* was changed in the subroutine.

6   The subroutine is called again. The value of *$name* is *Tom*.

---

*   We are assuming that the program was compiled into one package, *main*. For more on packages and scope, see Chapter 13, "Modularize It, Package It, and Send It to the Library!"

11.2 Passing Arguments and the @_ Array

If you want to send values to a subroutine, you call it with a comma-separated list of arguments enclosed in parentheses.

The following *feed_me()* function takes three arguments when called:

```
my @fruit=qw(apples pears peaches plums);  # Declare variables
my $veggie="corn";
&feed_me( @fruit, $veggie, "milk" );  # Call subroutine with arguments
```

The arguments can be a combination of numbers, strings, references, lists, hashes, variables, and so forth. They are received by the function in a special Perl array, called the @_ array, as a list of corresponding values called parameters. No matter how many arguments are passed, they will be flattened out into a single list in the @_ array. In this example, *@fruit* will be sent as four values, followed by *$veggie* and the string *"milk"*. That means that six values will be stored in the @_ array. The @_ is populated when the subroutine is entered and cleared when it is exited.

```
sub feed_me{ print join(",", @_),"\n"; }  # Subroutine gets arguments
                                           # in @_ array

Output:  apples, pears, peaches, plums, corn, milk
```

11.2.1 Call-by-Reference and the @_ Array

Arguments, whether scalar values or lists, are passed into the subroutine and stored in the @_ array, whose values consist of implicit references or aliases to the actual parameters. (If you modify the @_ array, you will modify the actual parameters.)

The elements of the @_ array are $_[0], $_[1], $_[2], and so on. If a scalar variable is passed, its value is the first element of the @_ array, $_[0]. If you pass two or more arrays or hashes or any combination of values to the function, they will be flattened out into the @_ as one big array. Perl doesn't care if you don't use all the parameters passed or if you have an insufficient number of parameters. If you *shift* or *pop* the @_ array, you merely lose your reference to the actual arguments.

11.2.2 Assigning Values from @_

When retrieving the values in @_, you may fall into common pitfalls when copying its values into a variable (see Table 11.1).

Table 11.1 Retrieving Values

Example	*What It Does*
my $param = @_;	$param gets the size of the @_ array
my ($param) = @_;	$param gets the first value in the @_ array
my $param = shift;	$param gets the first value in the @_ array
my $param = pop;	$param gets the last value in the @_ array
my @param = @_;	@param gets all values in the @_ array
my ($x, $y, $z) = @_;	$x, $y, $z get the first three elements of @_, respectively
my %param = @_	%param is hash built from the elements of the @_ array

---

EXAMPLE 11.4

```
(The Script)
   use warnings;
   # Passing arguments
1  my $first="Charles";
   my $last="Dobbins";
2  greeting($first, $last);
3  sub greeting{
4     print "@_", "\n";
5     print "Welcome to the club, $_[0] $_[1]!\n";
6  }

(Output)
4  Charles Dobbins
5  Welcome to the club, Charles Dobbins!
```

1   Scalars are assigned values.
2   The *greeting* subroutine is called with two parameters, *$first* and *$last*.
3   The subroutine is declared.
4   The parameters are stored in the @_ array, a local array that is created when the subroutine is entered and is removed when the subroutine exits. It contains references to the *$first* and *$last*.
5   The first two elements of the @_ array are printed. The individual elements are represented as scalars *$_[0]* and *$_[1]*.
6   The closing curly brace marks the end of the subroutine definition. @_ will disappear.

EXAMPLE 11.5

```
(The Script)
# Subroutine to add a list of numbers
  use warnings;
1   my @m = (1..100);  # Create an array of 100 numbers
    my @n = (2..29);

2   addemup(@m, @n);   # Pass two arrays
3   addemup(1,3,5,7);  # Pass a list

4   sub addemup{
5      print "@_\n";    # print values in @_
6      my $sum=0;       # Initialize $sum
7      foreach my $n (@_){
8         $sum += $n;
       }
9      print "The sum is $sum.\n";
       print "-" x 30, "\n";
    }

(Output)
1 2 3 4 5 6 7 8 9 10 11 12 13 14 15 16 17 18 19 20 21 22 23 24 25 26 27 28
29 30 31 32 33 34 35 36 37 38 39 40 41 42 43 44 45 46 47 48 49 50 51 52 53
54 55 56 57 58 59 60 61 62 63 64 65 66 67 68 69 70 71 72 73 74 75 76 77 78
79 80 81 82 83 84 85 86 87 88 89 90 91 92 93 94 95 96 97 98 99 100 2 3 4 5
6 7 8 9 10 11 12 13 14 15 16 17 18 19 20 21 22 23 24 25 26 27 28 29
The sum is 5484.
------------------------------
1 3 5 7
The sum is 16.
------------------------------
```

EXPLANATION

1   Two arrays, @m and @n, are assigned a range of numbers.
2   The *addemup()* subroutine is called with two arrays as arguments (also called actual parameters). The *foreach* loop assigns, in turn, to scalar *$value* each element of the @_ array.

EXPLANATION (CONTINUED)

3   The *addemup()* subroutine is called, this time with a list of numbers.

4   The subroutine is defined here.

5   The values in the @_ array are printed. You can see that when the subroutine is called the first time, all of the array elements are flattened out into the @_ and there is no boundary indicating where one ended and the other began.

6   The lexical scalar, *$sum*, is initialized to 0. Because it is a *my* variable, *$sum* belongs to the subroutine and will go out of scope when the subroutine exits. (If not declared as a lexical variable and not initialized, the variable would not be reset when the subroutine is called again, because it is global in scope.)

7   The *foreach* loop will iterate over all the elements in @_, one at a time.

8   Each time through the loop, the value of *$n* will be added to the sum until all of the values in @_ are totaled.

9   After the sum has been calculated, it is printed. This is a subroutine in that it is not returning a value to the caller.

Passing a Hash to a Subroutine.   When you pass a hash to a subroutine, it is also flattened onto the @_ as a single list. When copied from the @_ into another hash, the hash is recreated with key/value pairs. It is more efficient to send a reference (address). In this way, you would send only the address of the hash, rather than the entire hash. (See Chapter 12, "Does This Job Require a Reference?")

EXAMPLE 11.6

```
(The Script)
    # Create a hash and send it to a function
    use warnings;
1   my %home=("Address" => "1077 Washington St.",
             "Owner" => "B of A",
             "Phone" => "543-213-1234",
            );

2   displayhash(%home);  # Call subroutine, pass a hash

3   sub displayhash{
4     my %h = @_;  # The @_ array contains the key/values as an array
5     foreach my $key (sort keys %h ){
          printf "%-10s%-s\n", $key, $h{$key};
      }
    }

(Output)
Address    1077 Washington St.
Owner      B of A
Phone      543-213-1234
```

EXPLANATION

1   A hash is defined with key/value pairs.
2   The hash is passed to the subroutine, *diplayhash*.
3   The subroutine is defined here.
4   The hash key/value pairs (sent by the caller) are flattened out into the @_ array.
    Perl builds *%h* from keys and values stored in the @_ array.
5   The foreach iterates through the sorted keys in the *%h* hash, and each time through
    the loop the key and value for the hash are printed.

11.2.3   Returning a Value

When a subroutine returns a value to the caller, it behaves as a function. For example, you may call a subroutine from the right-hand side of an assignment statement. The subroutine can then send back a value to the caller which can be assigned to a variable, either scalar or array.

```
    $average   =   ave(3, 5, 6, 20);
returned value      call to subroutine
```

The value returned is really the value of the last expression evaluated within the subroutine.

You can also use the *return* function to return early from the subroutine based on some condition. Your main program will pick up in the line right after where the subroutine was called. If used outside a subroutine, the *return* function causes a fatal error. You could say that the *return* is to a subroutine what an *exit* is to a program. If you use the *exit* function in a subroutine, you will exit the entire program and return to the command line.

EXAMPLE 11.7

```
(The Script)
   use warnings;
   sub MAX {
1      my($max) = shift(@_);
2      foreach my $foo ( @_ ){
3         $max = $foo if $max < $foo;
          print $max,"\n";
       }
       print "-----------------------------\n";
4      $max;
   }
   sub MIN {
       my($min) = pop( @_ );
       foreach my $foo ( @_ ) {
          $min = $foo if $min > $foo;
          print $min,"\n";
       }
```

EXAMPLE 11.7 (CONTINUED)

```
        print "-------------------------------\n";
        return $min;
    }

5   my $biggest = MAX ( 2, 3, 4, 10, 100, 1 );
6   my $smallest= MIN ( 200, 2, 12, 40, 2, 20 );
7   print "The biggest is $biggest and the smallest is $smallest.\n";
```

(Output)
```
    3
    4
    10
    100
    100
    -------------------------------
    200
    2
    2
    2
    2
    -------------------------------
7   The biggest is 100 and the smallest is 2.
```

EXPLANATION

1 The scalar $max is assigned the value of the first element in the array @_. The *my* operator makes $max local to this subroutine. If $max is modified, the original copy is not affected.

2 For each element in the list, the loop will assign, in turn, an element of the list to the scalar $foo.

3 If $max is less than $foo, $max gets $foo.

4 Since the **last statement** executed in subroutine MAX is $max, the value of $max is returned and assigned to $biggest at line 5.

5 The scalar $biggest is assigned the value of the last expression in the MAX subroutine.

6 The scalar $smallest is assigned the return value from function MIN. The return function is explicitly used in subroutine MIN.

11.2.4 Scoping Operators: *local, my, our,* and *state*

Most programming languages provide a way for you to pass arguments by using **call-by-value**, where a copy of the value of the argument is received by the subroutine. If the copy is modified, the original value is untouched. To make copies of values in Perl, the arguments are copied from the @_ array and assigned to local variables. As discussed in Chapter 5, "What's in a Name?" Perl provides two operators (also called keywords or functions) to create local copies, *local* and *my*. The *state* keyword is similar to the *my* operator, but it creates the variable and initializes it only once (similar to a *static* variable in the *C* language) and is only available for versions of Perl starting with 5.10. The *our* function, to put it simply, allows you to create a global variable even when *strict* is turned on.

The *local* Operator. The *local* operator was used to turn on *call-by-value* in Perl programs prior to the Perl 5 release. Although you can still use *local* with special variables and filehandles, the *my* operator is normally used, which further ensures the privacy of variables within a function block. With *strict* turned on, local variables will not be allowed.

   The *local* operator creates local variables from its list. Any variable declared with *local* is said to be dynamically scoped, which means it is visible from within the block where it was created and visible to any functions called from within this block or any blocks (or subroutines) nested within the block where it is defined. If a local variable has the same name as a global variable, the value of the global one is saved and a new local variable is temporarily created. When the local variable goes out of scope, the global variable becomes visible again with its original value(s) restored. After the last statement in a subroutine is executed, its local variables are discarded. For an interesting Web page on when and how to use the *local* operator, see: *http://perl.plover.com/local.html*, particularly "Coping with Scoping."

The *my* Operator. The *my* operator is also used to turn on *call-by-value* and is said to be lexically scoped. Although we have already used *my* variables to declare variables, it bears more discussion here. Lexically scoped means that variables declared as *my* variables are visible from the point of declaration to the end of the innermost enclosing block. That block could be a simple block enclosed in curly braces, a subroutine, *eval*, or a file. A variable declared with the *my* operator is created on a special scratch pad that is private to the block where it was created.[3] Example 11.8 reviews the scope of *my* variables within a block.

EXAMPLE 11.8

```
    (The Script)
    #  The scope of my variables
    use warnings;
1   my $name = "Raimo";  # Visible to the end of the file
2   print "$name\n";
3   {  # Enter block
4        print "My name is $name\n";
5        my $name = "Elizabeth";  # Visible within the block
6        print "Now name is $name\n";
7        my $love = "Christian";
8        print "My love is $love.\n";
9   }  # Exit block
10  print "$name is back.\n";
11  print "I can't see my love,$love, out here.\n";
```

---

3. See Chapter 12, "Does This Job Require a Reference?" for more on *my* variables.

EXAMPLE 11.8 (CONTINUED)

```
(Output)
2  Raimo
5  My name is Raimo
6  Now name is Elizabeth
8  My love is Christian.
10 Raimo is back.
11 I can't see my love,, out here.
```

EXPLANATION

1 The *my* operator is used to create a lexically scoped local variable *$name* assigned the value *Raimo*. The variable is visible from the place where it is created and within any inner blocks. It is placed onto its own private scratch pad.

2 The value of the lexical variable is printed.

3 A new block is entered.

4 The lexical variable, *$name*, is still in scope (it is still visible).

5 A new lexical variable is declared. It gets its own private scratch pad.

6 The new variable, *$name*, is visible and its value is printed.

7 Another lexical variable is declared within the block and given its private scratch pad.

8 The value of *$love, Christian*, is printed. It is visible within this block.

9 The block ends here. The *my* variables will go out of scope.

10 The value of the *$name* variable is now visible. *Raimo* is printed.

11 The *$love* variable has gone out of scope.

Unlike the variables declared with the *local* operator, any variables declared as *my* variables are visible only within the block or subroutine in which they are declared, not in any subroutines called from this subroutine. Now let's take a look at the next example, which shows the scope of *my* variables within a subroutine.

EXAMPLE 11.9

```
(The Script)
1   my $first="Per";
    my $last="Lindberg";
2   &greeting ($first, $last ) ;      # Call the greeting subroutine
3   print "---$fname---\n" if defined $fname;   # $fname is local to
                                                # Subroutine defined

    sub greeting{
4       my($fname, $lname) = @_ ;     # Copy parameters
5       print "Welcome $fname!!\n";   # $fname, $lname only visible
                                      # in this subroutine
    }
```

EXAMPLE 11.9 (CONTINUED)

```
(Output)
5  Welcome Per!!

3  < No output from line 3 >
```

EXPLANATION

1   The lexical scalar variables are assigned values.

2   A call is made to the *greeting* subroutine. Two arguments are passed.

3   This line will execute after returning from the subroutine, but because *$fname* is not defined here, nothing is printed. It was defined as a *my* variable in the subroutine. It is visible only within the *greeting* subroutine. If *warnings* had been turned on, this line would have produced a warning message.

4   The *my* operator takes a list of arguments from the @_ array and creates two private variables, *$fname* and *$lname*, from that list. The values in the *my* variables are **copies** of the values that were passed.

5   The *print* statement is executed. The value of the *my* variable *$fname* is printed, which is a copy of what is in the argument, *$first*.

In the next example, we will examine the difference between *my* and *local* variables in a subroutine.

EXAMPLE 11.10

```
(The Script)
   # Difference between my and local
1  $friend="Louise";        # Global variables
2  $pal="Danny";
3  print "$friend and $pal are global.\n";

4  sub guests {
5     my $friend="Pat";     # Lexically scoped variable
6     local $pal="Chris";   # Dynamically scoped variable
7     print "$friend and $pal are welcome guests.\n";
8     &who_is_it;           # Call subroutine
   }

9  sub who_is_it {
10    print "You still have your global friend, $friend, here.\n";
11    print "But your pal is now $pal.\n";  # Dynamically scoped
   }

12 guests();                # Call subroutine
13 print "Global friends are back: $friend and $pal.\n";
```

EXAMPLE 11.10 (CONTINUED)

```
(Output)
3   Louise and Danny are global.
7   Pat and Chris are welcome guests.
10   You still have your global friend, Louise, here.
11  But your pal is now Chris.
13  Global friends are back: Louise and Danny.
```

EXPLANATION

  1   *$friend* is a global variable.

  2   *$pal* is also global and visible from here to the bottom of the file.

  3   The values are displayed here.

  4   The subroutine, *guests*, is defined.

  5   The lexically scoped *my* variable, *$friend*, is assigned *"Pat"*. It is visible from here until the end of the block; in this case, the end of the subroutine.

  6   The dynamically scoped local variable *$pal* is assigned *"Chris"*. It is also available until the end of the block, but if another subroutine were called from here, the value of *$pal* would be visible there as well. See line 8.

  8   Now we call the subroutine *who_is_it* from within the *guests* subroutine.

9–11   The subroutine *who_is_it* is defined. When called from line 8, the value of *$friend*, reverts back to the global copy containing *Louise* because the lexical variable *$friend* (*Pat*) was declared as a *my* variable in the calling subroutine and is not visible in this subroutine. On the other hand, the dynamic local copy *$pal* retains its value *Chris* from the *guests* subroutine on line 6.

  12   This is where *guests* is first called to produce the output on line 7.

  13   After returning from the subroutine *guests*, the global variables are back in scope.

11.2.5 Using the *strict* Pragma (*my* and *our*)

Although we touched on pragmas, particularly the *warnings* and *strict* pragmas, they are topics that bear repeating when discussing subroutines. You may recall, a pragma is a module that triggers a compiler to behave in a certain way. The *strict* module, *strict.pm*, is part of the standard Perl distribution. If the compiler detects something in your program it considers "unsafe," your program will be aborted. You can use the *strict* pragma with an import list to give specific restrictions, such as:

```
use strict 'vars';   # Must use my, our, state, or use vars.
use strict 'refs';   # Symbolic references not allowed.
use strict 'subs';   # Bareword (identifier without quotes) not allowed
                     # with the exception of subroutines.
```

Without the import list, all restrictions are in effect. Check the full documentation. At your command-line prompt, type *perldoc strict*.

You can use the *strict* pragma to prevent the use of global variables in a program. When you use a global variable, even a variable declared with *local*, the compiler will complain if *strict* has been declared. Only lexically scoped variables are allowed. They are variables that are declared with either the *my* or *our* built-in functions. The *our* built-in (Perl 5.6+) is used when you need a global variable but still want to use the *strict* pragma to protect against accidentally using global variables elsewhere in the program. (For more information about *strict* and packages, see the section, "The *strict* Pragma," in Chapter 12, "Does This Job Require a Reference?")

EXAMPLE 11.11

```
(The Script)
1  use strict "vars";
2  my $name = "Ellie";              # my (lexical) variables are okay
3  @friends = qw(Tom Stefan Bin Marie);
                                    # global variables not allowed
4  local $newspaper = "The Globe"; # local variables are not allowed
5  print "My name is $name and our friends are @friends.\n";


(Output)
3  Global symbol "@friends" requires explicit package name at
      rigid.pl line 3.
4  Global symbol "$newspaper" requires explicit package name at
      rigid.pl line 4.
   In string, @friends now must be written as \@friends at rigid.pl
      line 5, near "$name and our friends our @friends"
   Global symbol "@friends" requires explicit package name at
      rigid.pl line 5.
   Execution of rigid.pl aborted due to compilation errors.
```

EXPLANATION

1   The *strict* pragma is used with *vars* as its argument. This tells the compiler to complain if it spots any global variables; that is, variables must be declared with *my*, *our*, *state*, or listed in the *use vars* directive.

2   The variable *$name* is a lexically scoped *my* variable, which means it is private to the block where it is created. The *strict* pragma likes *my* variables.

3   The array *@friends* is a global variable. The compiler will complain when it sees global variables, as shown in line 3 of the output. By *explicit package name*, the message is saying that you can still use this global variable if you precede its name with the package name and two colons; in other words, *@main::friends* is acceptable.

4   Perl classifies variables declared with the *local* function as dynamically allocated global variables. The compiler again complains because the variable is not declared with *my*. To still use the global and local variables, use the *our* function or be explicit, meaning *@main::friends* and *local $main::newspaper*, where *main* is the name of this package.

5   Due to compiler errors, the program never gets this far.

EXAMPLE 11.12

```
(The First Script)
1  use strict vars;    # Restrict global variables
2  my $name = Ellie;   # Doesn't complain about bareword Ellie
3  our @friends = qw(Tom Stefan Bin Marie);  # Global variable
4  our $newspaper = "The Globe";
5  print "$name and $friends[0] read the $newspaper.\n";

(Output)
5  Ellie and Tom read the The Globe.
---------------------------------------------
(The Second Script)
1  use strict;  # All restrictions apply
2  my $name = Ellie;        # A bareword, Ellie, is used
3  our @friends = qw(Tom Stefan Bin Marie);
4  our $newspaper = "The Globe";
5  print "$name and $friends[0] read the $newspaper.\n";

(Output)
Bareword "Ellie" not allowed while "strict subs" in use at strict.plx
line 2.
Execution of strict.plx aborted due to compilation errors.
```

EXPLANATION

1   In the first script, the *strict* pragma is used with *vars*. The compiler will complain if it spots any variable not declared with *my, our, state,* or the *use vars* directive.

2   In the second example, *use strict* is turned on with all restrictions in effect. Variable *$name* is a lexically scoped *my* variable, but the value, *Ellie*, should be quoted; that is, it is a bare word, producing a compiler error.

The *state* Feature.   The *state* feature, like the *my* operator, creates a lexically scoped variable, but once created, it is not reinitialized when the subroutine is called again; that is, the variable is persistent from one call to the next. This feature was not implemented before Perl 5.10 was released. In order to avoid backward-compatibility problems, you must enable *state* with the *use feature state* pragma.

EXAMPLE 11.13

```
1  use feature ("state","say");
2  use strict;
3  sub countme{
4    state $x = 3;  # Initialized once
5    $x++;
6    return $x;
7  }
8
```

EXAMPLE 11.13 (CONTINUED)

```
9  say countme();
10 say countme();
11 say countme();
12

(Output)
4
5
6
```

EXPLANATION

1   The *use feature* pragma includes both the *state* and *say* keywords.
2   The *strict* pragma allows state variables.
3   The *countme()* subroutine is defined.
4   A *state* variable called $x is assigned the value 3. Once initialized, the value is persistent and will be persistent throughout calls to the subroutine. Each time the subroutine is called, the value of $ is incremented by 1.

11.2.6   Putting It All Together

Example 11.5 was a bare bones sample of how to pass arguments (two arrays) to subroutines. The *strict* pragma was not used. There was no return value. This final version summarizes the steps for defining and invoking a subroutine with a return value.

EXAMPLE 11.14

```
# REDO of Example 11.5
(The Script)
1  use strict;
   use warnings;
2  my @m = (1..100);
3  my @n=  (2..29);
4
5  my $sum = addemup(@m, @n);
6  printf "The sum is %.2f.\n", $sum;
7  print "The sum is ", (5 + 4 * 3), ".\n";
8
9  sub addemup{
10    my @nums = @_;
11    my $sum = 0;
12    foreach my $n (@nums) {
13        $sum += $n;
       }
14    return $sum;
    }
15 }
```

11.2.7 Prototypes

A **prototype** can be described as like a template, and tells the compiler how many and what types of arguments the subroutine should get when it is called. It lets you treat your subroutine just like a Perl built-in function. Note that prototypes are often misused and should only be used to produce special behavior in your subroutine! So be wary.

The prototype is made part of a declaration and is handled at compile time.

Prototype:
```
sub subroutine_name($$);
```
Takes two scalar arguments

```
sub subroutine_name(\@);
```
Argument must be an array, preceded with an \@ symbol

```
sub subroutine_name($$;@)
```
Requires *two scalar arguments and an optional array.*
Anything after the semicolon is optional.

EXAMPLE 11.15

```
     # Filename: prototypes
     # Testing prototyping
     use warnings;
1    my $x=5;
     my $y=6;
     my $z=7;
2    @list=(100,200,300);
3    sub myadd($$) {         # myadd enforces two scalar arguments
         my($xx, $yy)=@_;
         print $xx + $yy,"\n";
     }
4    myadd($x, $y);          # Okay
5    myadd(5, 4);            # Okay
6    myadd($x, $y, $z);      # Too many arguments
```

(Output)
6   *Too many arguments for main::myadd at prototypes line 14,*
     near "$c)" Execution of prototypes aborted due to compilation
     errors.11

EXPLANATION

1   Three scalar variables are declared and assigned values.
2   The array *@list* is assigned values.
3   The subroutine *myadd* is prototyped. Two scalar values are expected as parameters. Any more or less will cause a compiler error.
4   The subroutine is passed two scalar variables. This is okay.
5   The subroutine is passed two numbers. This is okay.
6   The subroutine was prototyped to take two scalars, but three are being passed here. The compiler sends an error message.

EXAMPLE 11.16

```
    # Prototypes
1   sub mynumbs(@$;$);          # Declaration with prototype
2   my @list=(1,2,3);
3   mynumbs(@list, 25);
4   sub mynumbs(@$;$) {         # Match the prototypes
5       my ($scalar)=pop(@_);
6       my(@arr) = @_;
7       print "The array is: @arr","\n";
8       print "The scalar is $scalar\n";
    }

(Output)
7   The array is: 1 2 3
8   The scalar is: 25
```

EXPLANATION

1   This is a declaration with a prototype, asking for an array, a scalar, and an optional scalar. The semicolon is used to indicate that the argument is optional.

2   The array *@list* is assigned values.

3   The *mynumbs* subroutine is called with a list and a scalar value, *25*. Don't use an ampersand when calling prototyped subroutines.

4   The subroutine is defined. Even though the declaration of the subroutine on line 1 established the prototype, it must be repeated again here or the following error will appear: *Prototype mismatch: sub main::mynumbs (@$;$) vs none at prototype line 19.*

5   The last element from the @_array is popped off and assigned to *$scalar*.

6   The rest of the @_array is assigned to *@arr*.

7   The values of the array *@arr* are printed.

8   The value of *$scalar* is printed.

11.2.8   Context and Subroutines

We introduced "context" when discussing variables and operators. Now we will see how context applies to subroutines. There are two main contexts: *scalar* and *list*. When mixing data types, results differ when an expression is evaluated in one or the other context. When a subroutine doesn't return a value, the context is called **void context**.

A good example of context is in array or scalar assignment. Consider the following statements:

```
@list = qw( apples pears peaches plums );  # List context
$number = @list;   # Scalar context
print scalar @list, "\n";  # Use the scalar function
```

In list context, *@list* is assigned an array of the elements, but in scalar context, *$number* produces the number of items in the array *@list*.

We have also seen context when using built-in Perl functions. Consider the *localtime* function. If the return value is assigned to a scalar, the date and time are returned as a string, but if the return value is assigned to an array, each element of the array represents a numeric value for the hour, minute, second, and so forth. The *print* function, on the other hand, expects to receive a list of arguments, in list context. You can use the built-in *scalar* function to explicitly evaluate an expression in a scalar context, as shown in Example 11.17.

EXAMPLE 11.17

```
    # Context
1   my @now = localtime;  # List context
2   print "@now\n";

3   my $now = localtime;  # Scalar context
4   print "$now\n";

5   print localtime, "\n";       # Evaluated in list context
6   print scalar localtime,"\n"; # Forced to scalar context

(Output)
2   22 48 9 8 11 113 0 341 0
4   Sun Dec  8 09:48:22 2013
5   2248981111303410
6   Sun Dec  8 09:48:22 2013
```

EXAMPLE 11.18

```
    # Context
1   print "What is your full name? ";

2   my($first, $middle, $last)=split(" ",<STDIN>); # STDIN scalar context

3   print "Hi $first $last.\n";

(Output)
2   What is your full name? Daniel Leo Stachelin
3   Hi Daniel Stachelin.
```

The *wantarray* Function and User-Defined Subroutines. "He took that totally out of context," is something you might say after hearing an argument based on a news story, the Bible, or a political speech. In Chapter 5, "What's in a Name?" we discussed context, in Perl, which refers to how a variable and values are evaluated. For example, is the context list or scalar? There may be times when you want a subroutine to behave in a certain way based on the context in which it was called. This is where you can use the built-in *wantarray* function. You can use this function to determine whether the subroutine should be returning a list or a scalar. If your subroutine is called in list context (that is, the return value will be assigned to an array), then *wantarray* will return true; otherwise, it will return false. If the context is to return no value (void context), *wantarray* returns the undefined value. (Use this function sparingly; it is not recommended for general use due to unexpected behavior. See *http://en.wikipedia.org/wiki/Principle_of_least_astonishment.*)

EXAMPLE 11.19

```
      use warnings;
      use strict;
      print "What is your full name? ";
      chomp(my $fullname=<STDIN>);

1     my @arrayname = title($fullname); # Context is array
      print "Welcome $arrayname[0] $arrayname[2]!\n";

      print "What is the name of that book you are reading? ";
      chomp(my $($bookname=<STDIN>);
2     my $scalarname = title($bookname);  # Context is string
      print "The book $arrayname[0] is reading is $scalarname.\n";

3     sub title{
         # Function to capitalize the first character of each word
         # in a name and to return a string or an array of words
4        my $text=shift;
         my $newstring;
5        my$text=lc($text);
6        my @newtext=split(" ", $text); # Create a list of words
         foreach my $word ( @newtext ){
            $word = ucfirst($word); # Capitalize the first letter
7           $newstring .= "$word "; # Create a title string
         }
         @newarray = split(" ", $newstring);
8        # Split the string into an array
         chop($newstring); # Remove trailing whitespace

9        return wantarray ? @newarray : $newstring;  # Return either array
         # or scalar based on how the subroutine was called

      }
```

```
(Output)
What is your full name? robert james taylor
Welcome Robert Taylor!
What is the name of that book you are reading? harry potter half blood
prince
The book Robert is reading is Harry Potter Half Blood Prince.
```

11.2.9 Autoloading

The Perl *AUTOLOAD* function is called whenever Perl is told to call a subroutine and the subroutine can't be found. The special variable *$AUTOLOAD* is assigned the name of the undefined subroutine.

You can also use the *AUTOLOAD* function with objects to provide an implementation for calling unnamed methods. (A **method** is a subroutine called on an object.)

EXAMPLE 11.20

```
(The Script)
   use warnings;
1  sub AUTOLOAD {
2      my(@arguments)=@_;
3      my $args=join(', ', @arguments);
4      print "$AUTOLOAD was never defined.\n";
5      print "The arguments passed were $args.\n";
   }

6  my  $driver="Jody";
   my  $miles=50;
   my  $gallons=5;

7  &mileage($driver, $miles, $gallons);  # Call to an undefined
                                         # subroutine
(Output)
4  main::mileage was never defined.
5  The arguments passed were Jody, 50, 5.
```

EXPLANATION

1   The subroutine *AUTOLOAD* is defined.
2   The *AUTOLOAD* subroutine is called with the same arguments as would have been passed to the original subroutine called on line 7.
3   The arguments are joined by commas and stored in the scalar *$args*.
4   The name of the package and the subroutine that was originally called are stored in the *$AUTOLOAD* scalar. (For this example, *main* is the default package.)
5   The arguments are printed.
6   The scalar variables are assigned values.
7   The *mileage* subroutine is called with three arguments. Perl calls the *AUTOLOAD* function if there is a call to an undefined function, passing the same arguments as would have been passed in this example to the *mileage* subroutine.

EXAMPLE 11.21

```
      use warnings;
      # Program to call a subroutine without defining it
1     sub AUTOLOAD {
2        my(@arguments) = @_;
3        my($package, $command)=split("::",$AUTOLOAD,  2);
4        return `$command @arguments`;   # Command substitution
      }
5     my $day=date("+%D");      # date is an undefined subroutine
6     print "Today is $day.\n";
7     print cal(3,2014);        # cal is an undefined subroutine
```

(Output)
Today is 03/26/14.

*   March 2014*
Su Mo Tu We Th Fr Sa
*   1 2 3*
* 4 5 6 7 8 9 10*
11 12 13 14 15 16 17
18 19 20 21 22 23 24
25 26 27 28 29 30 31

EXPLANATION

1　The subroutine *AUTOLOAD* is defined.

2　The *AUTOLOAD* subroutine is called with the same arguments as would have been passed to the original subroutine on lines 5 and 7.

3　The *$AUTOLOAD* variable is *split* into two parts by a double colon delimiter (::). The array returned consists of the package name and the name of the subroutine that was called.

4　The value returned is the name of the function called, which in the first case happens to be a UNIX command and its arguments. The backquotes cause the enclosed string to be executed as a UNIX command. Tricky!

5　The *date* function has never been defined. *AUTOLOAD* will pick its name and assign it to *$AUTOLOAD* in the *AUTOLOAD* function. The *date* function will pass an argument. The argument, *+%D*, is also an argument to the UNIX *date* command. It returns today's date.

6　The returned value is printed.

7　The *cal* function has never been defined. It takes two arguments. *AUTOLOAD* will assign *cal* to *$AUTOLOAD*. The arguments are 3 and 2014 assigned to *@arguments*. They will be passed to the *AUTOLOAD* function and used in line 4. After variable substitution, the backquotes cause the string to be executed. The UNIX command *cal 3 2014* is executed and the result returned to the *print* function.

11.2.10 *BEGIN* and *END* Blocks (Startup and Finish)

The *BEGIN* and *END* special code blocks may remind UNIX programmers of the special *BEGIN* and *END* patterns used in the *awk* programming language.

A *BEGIN* block is executed immediately, before the rest of the file is even parsed. If you have multiple *BEGIN*s, they will be executed in the order they were defined.

The *END* block is executed when all is done; that is, when the program is exiting, even if the *die* function caused the termination. Multiple *END* blocks are executed in reverse order.

EXAMPLE 11.22

```
      use warnings;
      # Program to demonstrate BEGIN and END subroutines
      use warnings;
1     chdir("/stuff") || die "Can't cd: $!\n";
2     BEGIN{ print "Welcome to my Program.\n"};
3     END{ print "Bailing out somewhere near line ",_ _LINE_ _,
                                            " So long.\n"};


(Output)
Welcome to my Program.
Can't cd: No such file or directory
Bailing out somewhere near line 5. So long.
```

EXPLANATION

1. An effort is made to change directories to */stuff*. The *chdir* fails and the *die* is executed. Normally, the program would exit immediately, but this program has defined an *END* block. The *END* block will execute before the program dies.
2. The *BEGIN* block is executed as soon as possible; that is, as soon as it has been defined. This block is executed before anything else in the program happens.
3. The *END* block is always executed when the program is about to exit, even if a *die* is called. The line printed is there just for you *awk* programmers.

11.2.11 The *subs* Function

The *subs* function allows you to predeclare subroutine names. Its arguments are a list of subroutines. This allows you to call a subroutine without the ampersand or parentheses and to override built-in Perl functions.

EXAMPLE 11.23

```
   # The subs module
   use warnings;
1  use subs qw(fun1 fun2 );

2  fun1;
3  fun2;
4  sub fun1{
       print "In fun1\n";
   }
5  sub fun2{
       print "In fun2\n";
   }

(Output)
In fun1
In fun2
```

EXPLANATION

1   The *subs* module is loaded (see the section, "The *use* Function (Modules and Pragmas)," in Chapter 13) into your program and given a list of subroutines.

2   *fun1* is called with neither an ampersand nor parentheses, because it was in the *subs* list. The function is not defined until later.

3   *fun2* is also called before it is defined.

11.3 **What You Should Know**

1. How do you define and call a subroutine?

2. What is the difference between a function and a subroutine?

3. Where do you put a subroutine definition in your Perl script?

4. How do you pass arguments to a subroutine?

5. How does Perl retrieve its parameter list?

6. What is the difference between local and global variables?

7. What is the difference between *my* and *our*?

8. How do you pass a hash to a function?

9. What is a *state* variable?

10. What is the significance of the *return* statement?

11. What is prototyping?

12. What is autoloading?

11.4 **What's Next?**

In the next chapter, you will learn about references and why you need them. A Perl reference is a variable that refers to another one. In short, it contains the address of another variable. Generally, there are three good reasons to use references: to pass arguments by reference to subroutines; to create complex data structures, such as a hash of hashes, an array of arrays, a hash consisting of nested hashes, arrays, subroutines, and so forth; and to create Perl objects.

EXERCISE 11
I Can't Seem to Function Without Subroutines

1. Write a program called *tripper* that will ask the user the number of miles he has driven and the amount of gas he used.

    a. In the *tripper* script, write a subroutine called *mileage* that will calculate and return the user's mileage (miles per gallon). The number of miles driven and the amount of gas used will be passed as arguments. All variables should be *my* variables. The program should test to make sure the user doesn't enter 0 for the amount of gas. (Division by zero is illegal.)

    b. Print the results.

    c. Prototype *tripper*.

2. Hotels are often rated using stars to represent their score. A five-star hotel may have a king-size bed, a kitchen, and two TVs; a one-star hotel may have cockroaches and a leaky roof.

    a. Write a subroutine called *printstar* that will produce a histogram to show the star rating for hotels shown in the following hash. The *printstar* function will be given two parameters: the name of the hotel and the number of its star rating. (Hint: sort the hash keys into an array. Use a loop to iterate through the keys, calling the *printstar* function for each iteration.)

```
%hotels=("Pillowmint Lodge" => "5",
         "Buxton Suites"     => "5",
         "The Middletonian"  => "3",
         "Notchbelow"        => "4",
         "Rancho El Cheapo"  => "1",
         "Pile Inn"          => "2",
        );
```

```
(OUTPUT)
Hotel                    Category
- - - - - - - - - - - - - - - - - - - - - - - - - - - - - - - -
Notchbelow           |****     |
The Middletonian     |***      |
Pillowmint Lodge     |*****    |
Pile Inn             |**       |
Rancho El Cheapo     |*        |
Buxton Suites        |*****    |
- - - - - - - - - - - - - - - - - - - - - - - - - - - - - - - -
```

b. Sort the hotels by stars, five stars first, one star last. Can you sort the hash by values so that the five-star hotels are printed first, then four, and so forth? (See *http://alvinalexander.com/perl/edu/qanda/plqa00016.*)

```
Hotel              Category
------------------------
Buxton Suites     |*****     |
Pillowmint Lodge  |*****     |
Notchbelow        |****      |
The Middletonian  |***       |
Pile Inn          |**        |
Rancho El Cheapo  |*         |
------------------------
```

3. Write a *grades* program to take the course number and the name of a student as command-line arguments. The course numbers are *CS101*, *CS202*, and *CS303*. The program will include three subroutines:

   - Subroutine *ave* to calculate the overall average for a set of grades.
   - Subroutine *highest* to get the highest grade in the set.
   - Subroutine *lowest* to get the lowest grade in the set.

   a. Print the average, the highest score, and the lowest score.

   b. If there were any failures (average below 60), print the name, course number, and a warning to *STDERR* such as: *Be advised: Joe Blow failed CS202.*

   c. Send the name of the failing student and the course number to a file called *failures*. Sort the file by course number.

   d. Use the *AUTOLOAD* function to test that each subroutine has been defined.

4. Write a function to calculate and return the monthly payment on a loan where:

   P = principal, the initial amount of the loan
   I = the annual interest rate (from 1 to 100 percent)
   L = length, the length (in years) of the loan, or at least the length over which the loan is amortized

   The following assumes a typical conventional loan where the interest is compounded monthly. (See *http://www.hughchou.org/calc/formula.html* for tips on how to calculate mortgage loan payments.)

   a. First, define two more variables to make the calculations easier:

      J = monthly interest in decimal form = $I / (12 \times 100)$
      N = number of months over which loan is amortized = $L \times 12$

   b. Create a hash with the values of *P*, *I*, *L*, and pass the hash to the function. Return the monthly payment using the following formula (you must convert the formula to Perl):

      $$M = P * (J / (1 - (1 + J) ** -N))$$

12

Does This Job Require a Reference?

By the time you finish this chapter, you will understand the following Perl statements:

```perl
use Data::Dumper;
use warnings;
use strict;
my $student={  "Name"=>undef,
               "Major"=>undef,
               "Courses"=>[],
               "Stats"=>{},
            };
$student->{"Courses"}=[ qw( French Algebra Chemistry ) ];
$student->{"Stats"}->{"PointAve"}=3.5;
$student->{"Stats"}->{"StartDate"}="09/17/12";
print Dumper $student;
```

12.1 What Is a Reference?

You have a post office box where you receive mail. The address on a letter contains a reference to your mailbox. The postman goes to that address and puts the letter in the box. You go to your mailbox address and pull out the letter. If you didn't have the mailbox, the postman would have to hand you the letter directly. Instead, he did it indirectly by putting it in the box. That's a simplified attempt to explain references.

A Perl reference is a variable that refers to another one. In short, it contains the address of another variable. The terms **reference** and **pointer** are often used interchangeably in Perl, because they both point to something, but they are not really the same, and those in Perl circles avoid using the term **pointer**. The main difference is that pointers in other languages contain the integer value of a memory address (for a specified data type) which you can directly manipulate. For example, with a *C* pointer, you can jump from element to element in an array of integers by performing pointer arithmetic, such as *p++*, where *p* contains the memory address of an array of ints. However, you can't do that with Perl references. As you know, Perl variables can hold any data type at any given time. We don't declare ints, floats, and the like. Perl handles all that. (To see how C, C++, *Java*, and other languages handle pointers and to get a really good introduction to pointers in general, Stanford provides a simple video called "Binky Fun With Pointers" found at *http://cslibrary. stanford.edu/104/.)*

Unlike pointers, Perl references are data structures that are displayed as strings, not integers. They contain the data type and the hexadecimal address of the variable they reference; for example, here is a reference to a scalar variable: *SCALAR(0xb057c)*. Unlike C, Perl keeps track of managing memory and of reference counts, and when there are no more references to the data, then Perl will automatically destroy the data. But, as mentioned earlier, because both references and pointers do point to something, the terms are often used interchangeably.

When you create a Perl reference, it is stored in a scalar variable. Now the big question is, "What's the point? Why do we need references?" There are three good reasons to use references:

- To pass arguments by reference to subroutines
- To create complex data structures, such as a hash of hashes, an array of arrays, a hash consisting of nested hashes, arrays, subroutines, and so forth
- To create Perl objects, as shown in the next chapter

Perl has two types of references: hard references and symbolic references. The hard references were introduced with Perl 5. Before hard references, typeglob aliases were used, but were of limited usefulness, other than for manipulating the internal symbol table (see Section 13.1.4, "The Symbol Table," in Chapter 13, "Modularize It, Package It, and Send It to the Library!"). A symbolic reference is when a variable holds the name of another variable and is also of limited use (*http://perlmaven.com/symbolic-reference-in-perl*). Although this chapter focuses on hard references, we will include a discussion of symbolic references and typeglobs at the end of the chapter.

12.1.1   Hard References

A **hard reference** is a scalar that holds the address of another variable or subroutine. It is an indirect way to access a variable. Perl references not only contain the hexadecimal address, but the data type:

```
ARRAY(0x7f9241004ee8)
```

The reference can point to (reference) a scalar, an array, a hash, a subroutine, a typeglob, another reference, and so forth.

The Backslash Operator.   The backslash unary operator is used to create a reference, similar to the *&* used in *C* to get the "address of." In the following example, *$p* is a scalar that is assigned a reference to *$x*.

```
$x = "Tom";
$p = \$x;    # $p gets the memory address of $x
```

Examples of hard references from the Perl *man* page *perlref* include the following:

```
$scalarref = \$foo;         # reference to scalar $foo
$arrayref  = \@ARGV;        # reference to array @ARGV
$hashref   = \%ENV;         # reference to hash %ENV
$coderef   = \&handler;     # reference to subroutine handler
$globref   = \*STDOUT;      # reference to typeglob STDOUT
$reftoref  = \$scalarref;   # reference to another reference
                             (pointer to pointer, ugh)
```

Dereferencing the Pointer.   If you print the value of a reference, you will see a data type and a hexadecimal address.

```
@list = qw(Tom Dick Harry);
$ref = \@list;  # $ref contains the data type and memory address of @list
```

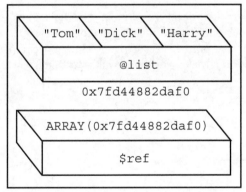

Figure 12.1   *$ref* contains the address of *@list*.

If you want to go to the address that *$ref* points to (that is, the address of *@list*), and get the values stored there, you would say:

```
print @{$ref}    # prints Tom Dick and Harry
```

This is called **dereferencing the pointer**. Notice the *$ref* (the address) is prepended with the @ sign. That tells Perl to get the array values from *@list*. (Although the curly braces aren't necessary in this example, they will be later on in more complex examples.) The first is the dollar sign, because the reference itself is a scalar, *$ref*, and then preceding that goes the sigil, representing the type of data it references. In the following examples, we will get into much more detail about how to use references.

EXAMPLE 12.1

```
(The Script)
    use warnings;
1   my $num=5;
2   my $p = \$num;        # $p is assigned the address of $num
3   print 'The address assigned $p is ', $p, "\n";
4   print "The value stored at that address is ${$p}\n"; # dereference

(Output)
3   The address assigned $p is SCALAR(0xb057c)
4   The value stored at that address is 5
```

EXPLANATION

1   The scalar *$num* is assigned the value 5.

2   The scalar *$p* is a reference and assigned the address of *$num*. This is the function of the backslash operator.

3   The value in *$p* is printed. Along with an address, Perl also tells you the data type is *SCALAR*.

4   To dereference *$p*, another dollar sign is prepended to *$p*. This dollar sign tells Perl that you are looking for the value of the scalar that *$p* references; that is, *$num*. The curly braces are optional, but a good practice because later, with more complex references, they will be necessary when retrieving or setting values with references.

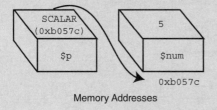

Memory Addresses

EXAMPLE 12.2

```
    use warnings;
    use strict;
1   my @toys = qw( Barbie Elmo Thomas Barney );
2   my $num = @toys;
3   my %games=("Nintendo"  => "Wii",
               "Sony"      => "PlayStation 4",
               "Microsoft" => "XBox One",
           );
```

EXAMPLE 12.2 (CONTINUED)

```
 4  my $ref1 = \$num;   # Create references
 5  my $ref2 = \@toys;
 6  my $ref3 = \%games;

 7  print "There are ${$ref1} toys.\n";  # dereference $ref1
 8  print "They are: ",join(",",@{$ref2}), ".\n";
 9  print "Jessica's favorite toy is $ref2->[0].\n";
10  print "Willie's favorite toy is $ref2->[2].\n";

11  while((my($key, my $value))=each(%$ref3)){
        print "$key=>$value\n";
    }
12  print "They waited in line for a $ref3->{'Nintendo'}\n";
```

(Output)
```
There are 4 toys.
They are: Barbie,Elmo,Thomas,Barney.
Jessica's favorite toy is Barbie.
Willie's favorite toy is Thomas.
Microsoft => XBox One
Sony => PlayStation 4
Nintendo => Wii
They waited in line for a Wii
```

EXPLANATION

1   A list is assigned to the array @*toys*.

2   The array @*toys* is assigned to the scalar variable $*num*, returning the number of elements in the array.

3   The hash %*games* is assigned key/value pairs.

4   $*ref1* is a reference. It is assigned the address of the scalar $*num* by using the backslash operator.

5   $*ref2* is also a reference. It contains the address of the array @*toys*.

6   The reference $*ref3* is assigned the address of the hash %*games*.

7   The reference is dereferenced, meaning: Go to the address that $*ref1* is pointing to and print the value of the scalar stored there.

8   The reference is again dereferenced, meaning: Go to the address that $*ref2* is pointing to, get the array, and print it.

9   The -> arrow operator is used to dereference $*ref2* and get the first element of the array. (You could also write this as $$*ref2[0]*.)

10 Again, the -> arrow operator is used to dereference the pointer and retrieve the third element of the array.

11 The *each* function is used to retrieve the keys and values from the hash via its reference. To dereference a hash, the % sign precedes the reference variable.

12 The -> arrow operator is used to dereference $*ref3* and get the value of the hash where the key is *Nintendo*. (You could also write this as $$*ref3{"Nintendo"}*.)

12.1.2   References and Anonymous Variables

It is not necessary to name a variable to create a reference to it. If an array, hash, or subroutine has no name, it is called **anonymous**. If, for example, an array has no name and its data is assigned to a reference variable, you can use the reference to assign and fetch data from the anonymous array.

Use the **arrow operator** (->), called an **infix operator**, to dereference a reference to anonymous arrays, hashes, and subroutines. Although not really necessary, the arrow operator makes the program easier to read.

Anonymous Arrays.   Enclose anonymous array elements in square brackets (*[ ]*). These square brackets are not to be confused with the square brackets used to subscript an array. They represent the address of an unnamed array. The brackets will not be interpolated if enclosed within quotes. Use the arrow (infix) operator to get the individual elements of the array.

EXAMPLE 12.3

```
(The Script)
   use warnings;
   use strict;
1  my $arrayref = [ 'Woody', 'Buzz', 'Bo', 'Mr. Potato Head' ];
2  print "The value of the reference, \$arrayref is ",
                                  $arrayref, "\n";
   # All of these examples dereference $arrayref
3  print "$arrayref->[3]", "\n";  # Preferred method for derefencing
4  print $$arrayref[3], "\n";  # Dereferencing in alternate way
5  print ${$arrayref}[3], "\n";
6  print "@{$arrayref}", "\n";

(Output)
2  The value of the reference, $arrayref is ARRAY(0x8a6f134)
3  Mr. Potato Head
4  Mr. Potato Head
5  Mr. Potato Head
6  Woody Buzz Bo Mr. Potato Head
```

EXPLANATION

1   The anonymous array is assigned to the array reference *$arrayref*.

2   The array reference contains the data type and the hexadecimal address of the anonymous array.

3   The fourth element of the array is printed. The reference, *$arrayref*, is followed by the arrow operator pointing to the index value that will be retrieved. This is the preferred method for dereferencing.

4   The arrow operator is not needed here. Instead, the two methods in lines 4 and 5 can also access the element.

6   The entire array is printed after dereferencing the pointer. Curly braces are required in more complicated structures. It's a good idea to get used to them now.

Anonymous Hashes. An **anonymous hash** is a hash without a name. Create a reference to it by using curly braces (*{}*). You can mix array and hash composers to produce complex data types. These braces are not the same braces that are used when subscripting a hash. The anonymous hash is assigned to a scalar reference.

EXAMPLE 12.4

```
(The Script)
    use warnings;
    use strict;
1   my $hashref = { "Name"=>"Woody",
                    "Type"=>"Cowboy"
                  };
2   print $hashref->{"Name"}, "\n\n";
3   print keys %$hashref, "\n";
4   print values %$hashref, "\n";

(Output)
2   Woody

3   NameType
4   WoodyCowboy
```

EXPLANATION

1 The anonymous hash contains a set of key/value pairs enclosed in curly braces. The anonymous hash is assigned to the reference *$hashref*.
2 The arrow operator with *$hashref* is used to dereference the hash. The key *Name* is associated with the value *Woody*.
3 The *keys* function returns all the keys in the anonymous hash via the reference.
4 The *values* function returns all the values in the anonymous hash via the reference.

12.1.3 Nested Data Structures

The ability to create references to anonymous data structures lends itself to more complex types. For example, you can have hashes nested in hashes, or arrays of hashes, or arrays of arrays, and so forth.

Just as with simpler references, you dereference the anonymous data structures by prepending the reference with the correct funny symbol (sigil) that represents its data type. For example, if *$p* is a pointer to a scalar, you can write *$$p* to dereference the scalar reference, and if *$p* is a pointer to an array, you can write *@$p* to dereference the array reference or *$$p[0]* to get the first element of the array. You can also dereference a reference by treating it as a block. You could write *$$p[0]* as *${$p}[0]* or *@{p}[0..3]*. Sometimes, you use the braces to prevent ambiguity, and sometimes they are necessary so that the funny character dereferences the correct part of the structure.

Using _Data::Dumper_. Now that we are getting ready to create more complex data structures with Perl references, this is a good time to take a moment to talk about the _Data::Dumper_ module. This module, found in the standard Perl library, makes it easy for you to see the contents of nested hashes, arrays, and combinations of these.

EXAMPLE 12.5

```
1   use Data::Dumper;
    use warnings;
    use strict;
2   my %student = ( "Name"=>"Tom Jones",
                    "Subject"=>"Algebra",
                    "Major"=>"Math",
                  );

3   my $ref = \%student;  # A reference to a hash

4   print Dumper $ref;  # The Dumper function dumps out the hash

5   $Data::Dumper::Varname="student";  # Varname is a user-defined value
6   print Dumper \%student;  # Dumper requires a reference

(Output)
4 $VAR1 = {
            'Subject' => 'Algebra',
            'Major' => 'Math',
            'Name' => 'Tom Jones'
          };
6 $student1 = {
                'Subject' => 'Algebra',
                'Major' => 'Math',
                'Name' => 'Tom Jones'
              };
```

EXPLANATION

1   This loads the _Data::Dumper_ module into the program's memory.
2   Now we create a simple hash.
3   The address of the hash is assigned to _$red_, a reference.
4   The _Dumper_ function from the _Data::Dumper_ module takes a pointer and dumps out a string displaying the structure of the hash.
5   There are different ways to change the appearance of the data structure; for example, you can change the _$VAR1_ variable to another name, change the amount of indentation, and so forth. Here, we change _$Varname_ to _student_ to clarify what data structure we are displaying.
6   The output of _Dumper_ now shows the hash with its name _student_. The _1_ appended to the student name means that we only have one of these students defined.

Array of Lists. An array may contain another list or set of lists, most commonly used to create a multidimensional array. Each row in square brackets is reference to an anonymous array.

EXAMPLE 12.6

```
1  use feature 'say';
   use warnings;
   use strict;
2  use Data::Dumper;
3  $Data::Dumper::Indent = 0;
4   my @matrix = ( [ 1,3,4 ],
                   [ 4,5,6 ],
                   [ 10,12,14 ],
                 );

5  say @matrix;  # @matrix is an array of references
6  say $matrix[0];  # reference to the first row
7  say "@{$matrix[0]}";  # get values in first row
8  say $matrix[0]->[0];  # get first value in first row
9  say $matrix[0][0];  # same as line 6
10 say Dumper \@matrix;

(Output)
5  ARRAY(0x7f7f72004ee8)ARRAY(0x7f7f7202d388)ARRAY(0x7f7f7202d4d8)
6  ARRAY(0x7f7f72004ee8)
7  1 3 4
8  1
9  1
10 $VAR1 = [[1,3,4],[4,5,6],[10,12,14]];
```

1 The *feature* module allows you to use the *say* function the same as the *print* function, except it puts a newline at the end of the output string and may save a little time.

2 We'll use the *Data::Dumper* module to pretty-print the array of arrays.

3 By setting the indent value for *Data::Dumper*, the output will display the matrix as one row, rather than adding newlines after each row. The default indent value is 1.

4 *@matrix* is a named array, consisting of three elements, references to three arrays; that is, this is an array of array references.

5 The three references are printed.

6 The reference to the first row is printed.

7 The @ sign is used to dereference the first row. The curly braces are used to block *$matrix[0]*, and are not necessary in this example, but will be in more complex expressions.

8 The infix arrow operator is used to dereference and access the first row of values.

9 When two index values are adjacent to each other, you may omit the infix arrow operator.

10 The *Dumper* function takes a reference to *@matrix* and pretty-prints the values.

A Reference to a List of Lists

In the following example, a reference points to an anonymous list of lists. Notice that in this example, *$matrix* is a reference to an anonymous array in square brackets, whereas in the previous example, *@matrix* is a named array with parentheses to contain its values. This distinction is important as it is a common error to use *[ ]* when one should use *( )*, and vice versa.

EXAMPLE 12.7

```
(The Script)
    use warnings;
    use strict;
    # A reference to a two-dimensional array
1   my $matrix = [
                    [ 0, 2, 4 ],
                    [ 4, 1, 32 ],
                    [ 12, 15, 17 ]
                 ] ;

2   print "Row 3 column 2 is $matrix->[2]->[1].\n";

3   print "Dereferencing with two loops.\n";
4   for(my $x=0; $x<3; $x++){
5      for(my $y=0;$y<3;$y++){
6         print "$matrix->[$x]->[$y] ";
       }
       print "\n";
    }
    print "\n";
7   print "Dereferencing with one loop.\n";
8   for(my $i=0; $i < 3; $i++){
9      print "@{$matrix->[$i]}\n";
    }

(Output)
2   Row 3 column 2 is 15.
3   Dereferencing with two loops.
6   0 2 4
    4 1 32
    12 15 17

7   Dereferencing with one loop.
9   0 2 4
    4 1 32
    12 15 17
```

EXPLANATION

1   The reference (pointer) *$matrix* is assigned an anonymous array of three anonymous arrays; that is, a two-dimensional array (list of lists).

2   The arrow operator is used to access the first element of the array. An arrow is implied between adjacent subscript brackets and is not needed. It could have been written as *$matrix->[2][1]*.

4   The outer *for* loop is entered. This will iterate through the rows of the array.

5   The inner *for* loop is entered. This loop iterates through the columns of the array.

6   Each element of the two-dimensional array is printed via the reference (pointer).

8   This time, only one *for* loop is used to print out the contents of the matrix.

9   The block format is used to dereference the reference. All elements of each list are printed.

Array of Hashes.   A list may contain a hash or references to hashes. In Example 12.8, a reference is assigned an anonymous array containing two anonymous hash references.

EXAMPLE 12.8

```
    use Data::Dumper;
    use warnings;
    use strict;
1   my $petref = [    {  "name"  => "Rover",
                         "type"  => "dog",
                         "owner" => "Mr. Jones",
                      },
2                     {  "name"  => "Sylvester",
                         "type"  => "cat",
                         "owner" => "Mrs. Black",
                      }
3                 ];

4   print "The first pet's name is $petref->[0]->{name}.\n";
5   print "Printing an array of hashes.\n";

6   for my $i (0..2){
7      foreach my $key (keys %{$petref->[$i]}  ){
8          print "$key -- $petref->[$i]->{$key}\n";
       }
       print "\n";
    }
    print "Adding a hash to the array.\n";
9   push @{$petref},{ "owner"=>"Mrs. Crow",
                      "name"=>"Tweety",
                      "type"=>"bird",
                    };

10  print Dumper $petref;
```

EXAMPLE 12.8 (CONTINUED)

```
(Output)
4   The first pet's name is Rover.
    Printing an array of hashes.
7   owner -- Mr. Jones
    name -- Rover
    type -- dog

    owner -- Mrs. Black
    name -- Sylvester
    type -- cat


    Adding a hash to the array.
    $VAR1 = [
             {
               'owner' => 'Mr. Jones',
               'name' => 'Rover',
               'type' => 'dog'
             },
             {
               'owner' => 'Mrs. Black',
               'name' => 'Sylvester',
               'type' => 'cat'
             },
             {
               'owner' => 'Mrs. Crow',
               'name' => 'Tweety',
               'type' => 'bird'
             }
           ];
```

EXPLANATION

1   The reference $petref$ is assigned the address of an anonymous array containing two anonymous hash references.

2   This is the second list element, an anonymous hash reference with its key/value pairs.

3   This is the closing square bracket for the anonymous array.

4   The reference $petref$ is used to dereference the list reference, first by selecting the zeroth element of the array and, with the arrow operator, selecting the key in the hash. The value associated with the key *name* is displayed.

6   The *for* loop is entered to loop through the list with i representing the index value in the array. Each element of the array is an anonymous hash.

7, 8   The *foreach* loop is entered. It loops through each of the keys, *name, type, owner*, from the anonymous hash. Each time through the loop, the key, key, and its value, $petref->[\$i]->\{\$key\}$, are printed.

9   A new anonymous hash reference is pushed onto the end of the array, @{$petref}, with the built-in *push* function.

10   The *Dumper* function from the *Data::Dumper* module displays the array of hashes.

Hash of Hashes.   A hash may contain another hash or a set of hash references. In Example 12.9, a reference is assigned an anonymous hash reference consisting of two keys, each of which is associated with a value that happens to be another hash reference (consisting of its own key/value pairs).

EXAMPLE 12.9

```
      use Data::Dumper;
      use strict;
      use warnings;
      # Reference to a hash containing anonymous hashes.
1   my $hashref = {
2              Math=>{                      # key
                      "Anna"=>100,
                      "Hao"=>95,     # values
                      "Rita"=>85,
                     },
3              Science=>{                   # key
                      "Sam"=>78,
                      "Lou"=>100,    # values
                      "Vijay"=>98,
                     },
4              };

5   print "Anna got $hashref->{'Math'}->{'Anna'} on the Math test.\n";
6   $hashref->{'Science'}->{'Lou'}=90;
7   print "Lou's grade was changed to $hashref->{'Science'}->{'Lou'}.\n";
8   print "The nested hash of Math students and grades is: ";
9   print %{$hashref->{'Math'}}, "\n";   # Prints the nested hash, Math

10  foreach my $key (keys %{$hashref}){
11     print "Outer key: $key \n";
12     foreach my $nkey (keys %{$hashref->{$key}}){
13        printf "\tInner key: %-5s -- Value: %-8d\n",
               $nkey, $hashref->{$key}->{$nkey};
       }
    }
    print "-" x 40, "\n";
14  print Dumper $hashref;   # Let Data::Dumper display the structure
```

(Output)
```
5   Anna got 100 on the Math test.
7   Lou's grade was changed to 90.
8   The nested hash of Math students and grades is: Rita85Hao95Anna100
11  Outer key: Science
13  Inner key: Lou   -- Value: 90
    Inner key: Sam   -- Value: 78
    Inner key: Vijay -- Value: 98
11  Outer key: Math
```

EXAMPLE 12.9 (CONTINUED)

```
13  Inner key: Rita  -- Value: 85
    Inner key: Hao   -- Value: 95
    Inner key: Anna  -- Value: 100
    Anna got 100 on the Math test.

    ------------------------------------------------

14   $VAR1 = {
            'Science' => {
                            'Vijay' => 98,
                            'Lou' => 90,
                            'Sam' => 78
                         },
            'Math' => {
                        'Rita' => 85,
                        'Hao' => 95,
                        'Anna' => 100
                      }
         };
```

EXPLANATION

1   The anonymous hash is defined. It consists of two hash keys, *Math* and *Science*, whose values are themselves a hash (key/value pair). The address of the hash is assigned to *$hashref*. *$hashref* is a reference.

2   *Math* is the key for its value, a nested hash reference.

3   *Science* is the key for its value, also a nested hash reference.

4   This is the closing curly brace of the anonymous hash reference.

5   To access Anna's grade, first the key *Math* is dereferenced, followed by the arrow operator and the nested key *Anna*. The second arrow is not necessary but may make the construct easier to follow. In fact, you don't need to use the arrow operator at all. This could have been written as *$$hashref{Math}{Anna}*. However, just because you can, doesn't mean you should!

6   Using the *$hashref* reference, you can also change or add new values to the hash. Lou's grade is changed.

7   The new grade is printed by dereferencing *$hashref*.

8, 9   The nested hash *Math* is printed by enclosing the reference *$hashref->{Math}* in curly braces prepended by a %. The % represents the unnamed hash, both keys and values.

10   The *foreach* loop iterates through the list (produced by the *keys* function) of outer keys in the anonymous hash.

11   Each of the outer keys is printed.

12   Since each of the outer keys is associated with a value that happens to be another hash, the reference *$hashref* is dereferenced by placing %{$hashref->{$key}} in a block prepended by a percent sign. The second *foreach* loop gets a list of all the inner keys and loops through them using *$nkey* first as *Math* and the next time as *Science*.

13   The nested keys and their associated values are printed.

14   *Data::Dumper* makes it a lot easier to see what your complex structure looks like; very helpful for debugging.

12.1.4 More Nested Structures

A hash may contain nested hash keys associated with lists of values. In Example 12.10, a named hash has two keys whose values are references to another set of nested key/value pairs. And the values for the nested keys are references to arrays. Argh!

In Example 12.11, a reference is assigned the address of an anonymous hash (has no name). It also has two keys whose values are another set of key/value pairs.

The only difference between Example 12.10 and Example 12.11 is that in Example 12.10 the definition of a <u>named</u> hash, *%profession*, is enclosed in parentheses, and consists of nested key/value pairs; in Example 12.11, a reference to a nameless hash is defined and enclosed in curly braces, not parentheses. Also, when extracting the values, the syntax is different when using a named hash versus a reference to an unnamed hash. When using these nested structures, the syntax can get confusing. Use *Data::Dumper* to help you see what kind of a monster you have created!

EXAMPLE 12.10

```
(The Script)
   use Data::Dumper;
   use strict;
   use warnings;
   # A named hash is assigned nested hash keys and
   # anonymous arrays of values
1  my %profession=("Teacher"=>{"Subjects"=>[ qw(Science Math  English)]},
                   "Musician"=>{"Instruments"=>[ qw(piano flute harp)]},
                 );
                   # Teacher and Musician are keys.
                   # The values consist of nested hashes.
2  print $profession{"Teacher"}->{"Subjects"}->[0],"\n";
3  print "@{$profession{'Musician'}->{'Instruments'}}\n";
4  print Dumper \%profession;

(Output)
2 Science
3 piano flute harp


4 $VAR1 = {
          'Teacher' => {
                         'Subjects' => [
                                         'Science',
                                         'Math',
                                         'English'
                                       ]
                       },
```

EXAMPLE 12.10 (CONTINUED)

```
        'Musician' => {
                  'Instruments' => [
                                   'piano',
                                   'flute',
                                   'harp'
                                 ]
                   }
        };
```

EXPLANATION

1   The <u>named hash</u> *%profession* consists of two keys, *Teacher* and *Musician*. The value for the *Teacher* is a reference to another set of nested key/value pairs, *Subjects* being the key, associated with a reference to a list of values: *Science*, *Math*, and *English*. The key *Musician* also consists of an anonymous hash reference with a key, *Instruments*, associated with an anonymous array of values: *piano*, *flute*, and *harp*.

2   To access the key/value pairs of the hash *%profession*, we key into the hash as we always do with named hashes. Then to access the values associated with the keys, which are references, we start using the arrow operator to get to the list of the *Teacher's Subjects*. The final arrow refers to the first element of the list of values associated with *Subjects*, which is *Science*.

3   To get all the *Subjects* for the *Musician*, we must first use the @ symbol to indicate we want a list, followed by a block (required) consisting of the hash ($*profession*), the key (*Subjects*), and its associated values, which just happen to consist of another set of nested keys and values. To access the values, each key is separated with the arrow operator. The curly braces enclosing the entire structure allow you to dereference the whole block as an array.

4   The *Dumper* function requires a reference, \%*profession*.

EXAMPLE 12.11

```
(The Script)
   use warnings;
   use strict;
   use Data::Dumper;
   # A reference to a hash is assigned nested hash keys and
   # anonymous arrays of values
1   my $hashref = { "Teacher"=>{"Subjects"=>[ qw(Science Math English)]},
                    "Musician"=>{"Instruments"=>[ qw(piano flute harp)]},
                  };
                    # Teacher and Musician are keys.
                    # The values consist of nested hashes.
2   print $hashref->{"Teacher"}->{"Subjects"}->[0],"\n";
3   print "@{$hashref->{'Musician'}->{'Instruments'}}\n";
4   print Dumper $hashref;
```

EXAMPLE 12.11 (CONTINUED)

```
(Output)
2  Science
4  piano flute harp

4  $VAR1 = {
          'Teacher' => {
                         'Subjects' => [
                                         'Science',
                                         'Math',
                                         'English'
                                       ]
                       },
          'Musician' => {
                          'Instruments' => [
                                             'piano',
                                             'flute',
                                             'harp'
                                           ]
                        }
        };
```

EXPLANATION

1   The reference $hashref is assigned an anonymous hash consisting of two keys, *Teacher* and *Musician*. Notice that the entire hash structure is enclosed in curly braces rather than parentheses. That means $hashref is getting the address of this set of key/value pairs. The rest of this example is just like Example 12.10.

2   To dereference $hashref, the arrow operator is used to get to the first key, *Teacher* or *Musician*, and then arrows will be used to separate the remaining nested keys/value pairs. The final arrow refers to the first element of the array of values associated with *Subjects*, which is *Science*.

3   To get all the values from the anonymous array associated with the key, the @ symbol precedes a block consisting of the reference and its nested keys, each key separated with the arrow operator.

4   The *Dumper* function requires a reference, $hashref.

12.1.5   References and Subroutines

Anonymous Subroutines.   A reference to an anonymous subroutine is created by using the keyword *sub* without a subroutine name. The expression is terminated with a semicolon. For more on using anonymous subroutines, see Section 14.3.1, "What Is a Closure?"

EXAMPLE 12.12

```
(The Script)
1   my $subref = sub { print @_ ; };
2   $subref->('a','b','c');
    print "\n";

(Output)
1   abc
```

EXPLANATION

1   The scalar *$subref* is assigned a reference to an anonymous subroutine. The only func-
    tion of the subroutine is to print its arguments stored in the @_ array.
2   The subroutine is called via its reference and passed three arguments.

Subroutines and Passing by Reference. When passing arguments to subroutines,
they are sent to the subroutine and stored in the @_ array. If you have a number of
arguments—say an array, a scalar, and another array—the arguments are all flattened out
onto the @_ array. It would be hard to tell where one argument ended and the other began
unless you also passed along the size of each of the arrays, and then the size would be
pushed onto the @_ array and you would have to get that to determine where the first
array ended, and so on. The @_ could also be quite large if you are passing a 1,000-element
array. So, the easiest and most efficient way to pass arguments is by reference, as shown in
Example 12.13.

EXAMPLE 12.13

```
(The Script)
    use strict;
    use warnings;
1   my @toys = qw(Buzzlightyear  Woody  Bo);
2   my $num = @toys;  # Number of elements in @toys is assigned to $num
3   gifts( \$num, \@toys );    # Passing by reference

4   sub gifts {
5       my($n, $t) = @_;   # Copy references to $n and $t
6       print "There are $$n gifts: ";
7       print "@$t\n";
8       push(@{$t}, 'Janey', 'Slinky');
    }
9   print "The original array was changed to: @toys\n";

(Output)
6,7 There are 3 gifts: Buzzlightyear Woody Bo
9    The original array was changed to: Buzzlightyear Woody Bo Janey Slinky
```

EXPLANATION

1   The array @*toys* is assigned three values.

2   The scalar $*num*$ is assigned the number of elements in the @*toys* array. (Remember, a scalar contains only one value, so when you assign an array to a scalar, the number of elements in the array is assigned to the scalar.)

3   The subroutine *gifts* is called with two references as parameters.

4   The subroutine is entered.

5   The @_ array contains the two references. The values of the references are copied into two lexical variables, $*n* and $*t*.

6   The reference to the scalar is dereferenced. It points to the scalar $*n*.

7   The reference to the array is dereferenced. It references the array @*toys*.

8   The *push* function adds two new elements to the array referenced by $*t*.

9   After exiting the subroutine, @*toys* is printed with its new values.

EXAMPLE 12.14

```
(The Script)
    use strict;
    use warnings;
    # This script demonstrates the use of references
    # to pass arrays. Instead of passing the entire
    # array, a reference is passed.
    # The value of the last expression is returned.

1   my @list1=(1 .. 100);
2   my @list2=(5, 10, 15, 20);
3   print "The total is : ",  addemup( \@list1, \@list2) , ".\n";
            # Two references are passed
4   sub addemup{
5      my( $arr1, $arr2) = @_;
            # @_ contains two references
6      my $total;
7      print $arr1, "\n" ;
8      print $arr2, "\n";

9      foreach my $num ( @{$arr1}, @{$arr2} ){
10        $total+=$num;
       }

11     return $total; # The expression is evaluated and returned
    }

(Output)
7   ARRAY(0x8a62d68)
8   ARRAY(0x8a60f2c)
3   The total is:  5100.
```

EXPLANATION

1   The array @*list1* is assigned a list of numbers between *1* and *100*.
2   The array @*list2* is assigned the list of numbers *5, 10, 15,* and *20*.
3   The *addemup* subroutine is called. Two arguments are passed. The backslash preceding each of the arrays causes references to be passed.
4   The subroutine *addemup* is declared and defined.
5   The references are passed to the @_ array and assigned to *my* variables $*arr1* and $*arr2*, respectively.
6   The *my* variable $*total* is declared.
7, 8   The address or values of the references are printed.
9   The *foreach* loop is entered. @$*arr1* and @$*arr2* dereference the references, creating a list of array elements to be processed, one at a time.
10   Each time through the loop, $*total* accumulates the sum of $*total* + $*num*.
11   The sum is returned to where the subroutine was called on line 3. Since the subroutine was called as an argument to the *print* function, the results will be printed after they are returned from the subroutine.

12.1.6 The *ref* Function

The *ref* function is used to test for the existence of a reference. It returns a non-empty string if its argument is a reference and with no argument, $_ is used. The string returned is the type of data the reference points to; for example, *SCALAR* is returned if the reference points to a scalar, and *ARRAY* is returned if it points to an array. If the argument is not a reference, the empty string is returned. Table 12.1 lists the values returned by the *ref* function.

Table 12.1   Return Values* from the *ref* Function

What Is Returned	Meaning
REF	Reference to reference
SCALAR	Reference to scalar
ARRAY	Reference to array
HASH	Reference to hash
CODE	Reference to subroutine
GLOB	Reference to typeglob

* For a complete list, see *perldoc -f ref*.

EXAMPLE 12.15

```
(The Script)
   use warnings;
   use strict;
1  sub gifts;       # Forward declaration
2  my $num = 5;
3  my $junk = "xxx";
4  my @toys = qw/Budlightyear Woody Thomas/ ;
5  gifts( \$num, \@toys, $junk );
6  sub gifts {
7     my( $n, $t, $j) = @_;
8     print "\$n is a reference.\n" if ref($n);
       print "\$t is a reference.\n" if ref($t);
9     print "\$j is a not a reference.\n" if ref($j);
10    printf "\$n is a reference to a %s.\n", ref($n);
11    printf "\$t is a reference to an %s.\n", ref($t);
   }

(Output)
8  $n is a reference.
   $t is a reference.
9
10 $n is a reference to a SCALAR.
11 $t is a reference to an ARRAY.
```

EXPLANATION

1   The subroutine *gifts* is a forward declaration, allowing Perl to know it is a subroutine defined somewhere in the program. You will not need parentheses to call the subroutine if it is declared before it is defined.

2   The scalar *$num* is assigned 5.

3   The scalar *$junk* is assigned the string *xxx*.

4   The array *@toys* is assigned a list.

5   The subroutine *gifts* is called. The first two variables are passed as references by preceding them with a backslash. The last variable, *$junk*, is not passed as a reference.

6   The subroutine *gifts* is defined.

7   The values assigned to the @_ array, in this case, two references (addresses) and one nonreference, will be assigned to *$n*, *$t*, and *$j*, respectively.

8   The *ref* function is called with a reference, *$n*, as its argument. The line will be printed only if the variable *$n* is a reference.

9   *$j* is not a reference. The return value for the *ref* function is null.

10 The *printf* function prints the value of the data type returned from *ref*, a scalar.

11 The *printf* function prints the value of the data type returned from *ref*, an array.

12.1.7   Symbolic References

A **hard reference** is a scalar variable that holds the address of another type of data. This chapter focused on hard references. This is an example of the value of a hard reference:

ARRAY(0x7f9241004ee8)

A **symbolic reference** names another variable rather than just pointing to a value; that is, it doesn't contain the data type and address. Their use is discouraged because they cannot be lexically scoped, and will not get past *strict* if you have it turned on. You would see something like this: *Global symbol "$animal" requires explicit package name at symbolicref line 3.*

Example 12.16 demonstrates a symbolic reference where the value of one variable references the name of another variable. For more on symbolic references, see *http://perlmaven.com/symbolic-reference-in-perl*.

EXAMPLE 12.16

```
     # Program using symbolic references
     use feature qw(say);
1    $animal="dog";
2    $dog="Lady";
3    say "Your dog is called ${$animal}";   # Symbolic reference
4    ${$animal}='Lassie';";
5    say "Why don't you call her ${$animal}?";

     # Now create symbolic references for an array, hash, and subroutine

6    @letters = ('a' .. 'z');  # Create an array
7    %capital = {"Maine"=>"Portland",
                 "California"=>"Sacramento",
                 "Montana"=>"Helena",
                };
8    sub greetme { print "hello\n";}
9    $refarray = "letters";  # Create symbolic references
10   $refhash = "capital";
11   $refsub = "greetme";

12   say "The array: @$refarray";    # Get the values in the array
13   say "The first element in the array: $$refarray[0]";
                                     # Get the first value in the array
14   say "Call to greetme(): ", &$refsub; # Call to subroutine greetme

(Output)
3    Your dog is called Lady
5    Why don't you call her Lassie?
12   The array: a b c d e f g h i j k l m n o p q r s t u v w x y z
13   The first element in the array: a
14   Call to greetme(): hello
```

EXPLANATION

1   The scalar $animal is assigned the value *"dog"*. The name *animal* is stored in the symbol table along with a reference to its value *dog*.

2   The scalar $*dog* is assigned the string *"Lady"*.

3   The variable ${$animal} evaluates to *Lady*. This is a symbolic reference. $animal, one variable, is evaluated to *dog*. The first dollar sign causes *dog* to become $*dog*, and references its underlying value, *"Lady"*. One variable has referenced another.

4   $animal will be evaluated to its value, *dog*. The dollar sign, prepended to the result of the evaluation leaves $*dog*="Lassie" as the statement.

5   The value of ${$animal}; that is, $*dog* is *Lassie*, is printed.

6–8   Now we will define an array, a hash, and a subroutine.

9–11   The symbolic references are given the names of variables.

12   By preceding the symbolic reference with an @ sign, Perl will retrieve the values stored in the array @*letters*.

13   Now we get the first element in @*letters* using the symbolic reference.

14   The subroutine is called using the symbolic reference. This is one of the rare times you will use & to call a subroutine.

EXAMPLE 12.17

```
    use feature qw(say);
1   $perm1="readonly";
    $perm2="read/write";
    $perm3="execute";

2   foreach $n (1..3){
3      $attr = 'perm' . $n;
4      say "$attr is ${$attr}";
    }
```

(Output)
3 *perm1 is readonly*
  perm2 is read/write
  perm3 is execute

EXPLANATION

1   Here is a case where the variables are numbered. (This is a technique used in Shell programming for dealing with numbered files, such as *foo1, foo2,* and *foo3*. Here, it would be much better to use a hash or an array since *strict* will complain. Symbolic references cannot be lexically scoped.)

2   The *foreach* loop will iterate through the numbers 1, 2, 3.

3   The value of the number, $n, is appended to the string *perm* and then assigned to the variable $attr. The value of $attr is the name of variable *perm1* (first time through the loop) and when used as a symbolic reference, ${$attr} evaluates to the string *"readonly"* that was assigned to $*perm1* on line 1. The next time through the loop, $attr will be *perm2*, and so forth.

The *strict* Pragma.   To protect yourself from inadvertently using symbolic references in a program, use the *strict* pragma with the *refs* argument. This restricts the use of symbolic references in your program. Here, we re-execute the previous example using the *strict* pragma.

EXAMPLE 12.18

```
    # Program using symbolic references
1   use strict "refs";
2   $animal="dog";
3   $dog="Lady";
4   print "Your dog is called ${$animal}\n";
5   eval "\$$animal='Lassie';";
6   print "Why don't you call her ${$animal}?\n";
```

(Output)
Can't use string ("dog") as a SCALAR ref while "strict refs" in use at symbolic.plx line 4.

EXPLANATION

1   The *strict* pragma ensures that the program uses only hard references and, if it doesn't, will abort during compilation and print an error message, as shown in the output of this script.

4   The program exited with an error at this point because of the first use of a symbolic reference, *${dog}*. This line also includes a symbolic reference but is never reached; the program had already aborted because *strict* caught it.

12.1.8 Typeglobs (Aliases)

Typeglobs are an internal type that Perl uses to create a symbol table, containing the namespace entries for a package; for example, the package we have been working in for all the examples thus far is called *main* and provides a namespace for all of its identifiers (except those preceded by the *my* operator). This namespace is created as a hash using typeglobs. We will discuss symbol tables and typeglobs in Chapter 13, "Modularize It, Package It, and Send It to the Library!"

Before Perl 5, typeglobs were used to create aliases, mainly for the purpose of passing arrays and hashes to functions by reference, but now that we have hard references, they are seldom used for that purpose.

Typeglobs are identifier names preceded by an *. They are a type of reference or alias. You can think of a typeglob as a way for Perl to glob onto data types; for example, *x is a typeglob. You could say it globs onto all data types named x, such as @x, %x, $x, sub x, and so on. Be careful not to confuse this with the *glob* function used with the shell globbing metacharacters such as the *, ?, and [ ] and used in filename expansion; see Section 16.3.5, Globbing (Filename Expansion and Wildcards)."

EXAMPLE   12.19

```
     use feature qw(say);
 1   $x = 54;
 2   @x = ('a'..'c');
 3   %x = ( "Name"=>"Joe",
            "Id" => "XY123",
          );
 4   sub x  { return "hello";}

 5   *alias = *x;  # *alias represents any type 'x'

 6   say "\$x is $alias";  # Represents scalar $x
 7   say "\@x is @alias";  # Represents array @x
 8   say "\%x is %alias";  # Representss hash %x
 9   say "sub x is ", alias();  # Represents subroutine x

(Output)
$x is 54
@x is a b c
%x is %alias
sub x is hello
```

EXPLANATION

1–3   The variables x, @x, and %x are all of the same name and assigned their respective values.

4   The subroutine x is defined.

5   *alias* is a typeglob. It is an alias for all data types called x; that is, the * globs onto all types called x.

6   By preceding the typeglob *alias* with the sigil of the datatype, we are able to reference the correct type. Here, by using $alias, we are really referencing x.

7, 8   By preceding the typeglob *alias* with the @, we are referencing the array, @x, and by preceding it with a %, we are referencing the hash %x.

9   Now we call the function *sub x*, using the alias.

Another example of a typeglob is found in modern Perl when you create a lexical filehandle as we did in Chapter 10, "Getting a Handle on Files." As you can see in the output of the following example, the filehandle is stored as a GLOB at some address, making it a type of reference.

```
open($fh, "<", "datebook") or die $!
print $fh;
GLOB(0x7fd6c2004ee8)
```

Example 12.20 illustrates how typeglobs were used in the early days of Perl to pass arguments to subroutines as aliases. For an excellent discussion on typeglobs, see Chapter 3 of *Advanced Perl Programming, First Edition* by Sriram Srinivasan (O'Reilly, 1998).

EXAMPLE 12.20

```
   use warnings;
   our @m = (1..100);
   our @n = (2..29);

1  print addem(*m,*n);  # Pass two typeglobs

   sub addem{
2     local(*list1, *list2)=@_;  # Receive typeglobs in @_
      $sum = 0;
3     foreach $n (@list1,@list2){
         $sum += $n;
      }
      return $sum;
   }
```

EXPLANATION

1   The typeglobs *m and *n are passed to the function *addem()*. They are aliases for any type called *m* or *n*; that is, @m, @n, %m, %n, $m, $n, and so forth.

2   The *local* operator is used to create dynamically scoped local variables. (Since type-globs are being passed, they cannot be preceded by *my* to make them local because they are considered to be package variables.) When the typeglobs are assigned to *list1* and *list2*, they are local typeglobs referencing the same values as *m and *n, respectively. The *strict* pragma does not allow typeglobs unless, before using them, you use:

```
no strict "refs";
```

3   To get access to the original arrays referenced by the typeglobs, the * is replaced by the @ for an array, followed by the name *list1* or *list2*. This means that the symbol @*list1* references the original array called @m and @*list2* references the original array, @n. The *foreach* loop iterates through each element of both arrays summing all the numbers. The total will be returned.

Filehandle References and Typeglobs.   One of the only ways to pass a bareword filehandle to a subroutine is by reference. You can use a typeglob to create an alias for the filehandle and then use the backslash to create a reference to the typeglob. Wow.

If you are using the modern lexical filehandles, such as $*fh*, which is really just a reference to a typeglob, you don't need to use typeglobs at all. But if you are using the older style of creating filehandles with barewords or *STDIN*, *STDOUT*, *STDERR*, and the like, then you can use a typeglob to create a symbolic reference.

EXAMPLE 12.21

```
(The Script)
    #!/bin/perl
    # Using UNIX
    # use strict;
    use warnings;

1   open(README, "/etc/passwd") || die;

2   readit(\*README);       # Reference to a typeglob

3   sub readit {
4      my ($passwd)=@_;
5      print "\$passwd is a $passwd.\n";
6      while(<$passwd>){
7      print;
       }
    }

9   seek(README,0,0) || die "seek: $!\n";
                      # Reset back to begining of job


(Output)
5   $passwd is a GLOB(0xb0594).
7   root:x:0:1:Super-User:/:/usr/bin/csh
    daemon:x:1:1::/:
    bin:x:2:2::/usr/bin:
    sys:x:3:3::/:
    adm:x:4:4:Admin:/var/adm:
    lp:x:71:8:Line Printer Admin:/usr/spool/lp:
    smtp:x:0:0:Mail Daemon User:/:
    uucp:x:5:5:uucp Admin:/usr/lib/uucp:
    nuucp:x:9:9:uucp Admin:/var/spool/uucppublic:/usr/lib/uucp/uucico
    listen:x:37:4:Network Admin:/usr/net/nls:
    nobody:x:60001:60001:Nobody:/:
    noaccess:x:60002:60002:No Access User:/:
    nobody4:x:65534:65534:SunOS 4.x Nobody:/:
    ellie:x:9496:40:Ellie Quigley:/home/ellie:/usr/bin/csh
9   seek: Bad file number
```

EXPLANATION

1   The */etc/passwd* file is attached to the *README* filehandle and opened for reading.
2   The *readit* subroutine is called. The filehandle is passed by creating a reference to a typeglob. First, the filehandle symbol is globbed with the asterisk. Then, the reference to the typeglob is created by prefixing the typeglob with a backslash.
3   The *readit* subroutine is defined.
4   The @_ variable contains the reference. It is assigned to a local scalar variable called *$passwd*. *$passwd* is a reference to the filehandle.

EXPLANATION (CONTINUED)

5   The reference $passwd, when printed, shows that it contains the address of a typeglob (alias).

6, 7   The expression in the *while* loop causes a line to be read from the */etc/passwd* file and assigned to the $_ variable. The line is printed to the screen. The loop will continue until all the lines have been read and printed.

9   The *seek* function resets the read pointer for this file back to the beginning of the file.

12.2 What You Should Know

1. What is the difference between a symbolic and a hard reference?

2. What is a typeglob?

3. How do you create a reference to a hash?

4. How can you tell an anonymous array from a named array?

5. How do you dereference $ref where $ref = { 'Name' => "John"; }?

6. How do you dereference $p where $p = \$x;?

7. What is meant by a nested hash?

8. How do you create a two-dimensional array?

9. What is the advantage of passing by reference?

10. What is the purpose of the *ref* function?

11. How would you create an array of hashes using a reference?

12.3 What's Next?

Next, we will expand your horizons and go from the "introverted" Perl programmer to the "extroverted" programmer. Instead of writing stand-alone scripts, you will start learning how to use the libraries and modules already provided by Perl. You will explore CPAN and learn how to download and use modules that other programmers have written.

You will understand packages and namespaces and how to export and import symbols, how to use the standard Perl library, and how to create your own. You will learn how to create procedural modules and how to store and use them.

EXERCISE 12
It's Not Polite to Point!

1. Rewrite *tripper* (from Chapter 11) to take two references as arguments and copy the arguments from the @_ in the subroutine into two *my* variables.

2. Create a hash **named** *employees* with the following three keys:

   Name
   Ssn
   Salary

3. The values will be assigned as undefined (*undef* is a built-in Perl function). For example: *Name => undef,*

   a. Create a reference to the hash.

   b. Assign values to each of the keys using the reference.

   c. Print the keys and values of the hash using the built-in *each* function and the reference.

   d. Print the value of the reference; in other words, what the reference variable contains, not what it points to.

4. Rewrite the exercise so the hash is anonymous, and assign the anonymous hash to a reference. Delete one of the keys from the hash using the reference (use the *delete* function).

5. Write a program that will contain the following structure:

```
$student = {   Name    => undef,
               SSN     => undef,
               Friends => [],
               Grades  => {   Science => [],
               Math    => [],
               English => [],
                             }
           };
```

   Use the reference to assign and display output resembling the following:

```
Name is John Smith.
Social Security number is 510-23-1232.
Friends are Tom, Bert, Nick.
Grades are:
            Science--100, 83, 77
            Math--90, 89, 85
            English--76, 77, 65
```

6. Write a program that contains a reference to an anonymous subroutine. Call the subroutine passing the hash you created in Exercise 4. The subroutine will display the hash sorted by keys.

chapter

13

Modularize It, Package It, and Send It to the Library!

Upon finishing this chapter, you should have a good understanding of how to read and create a Perl procedural style module similar to this one found at *http://www.perlmonks.org*.

```
package MyModule;
    # filename is myModule.pm
use strict;
use warnings;
use Exporter;
use vars qw($VERSION @ISA @EXPORT @EXPORT_OK %EXPORT_TAGS);

$VERSION      = 1.00;
@ISA          = qw(Exporter);
@EXPORT       = ();
@EXPORT_OK    = qw(func1 func2);
%EXPORT_TAGS  = ( DEFAULT => [qw(&func1)],
                  Both    => [qw(&func1 &func2)]);

sub func1  { return reverse @_  }
sub func2  { return map{ uc }@_ }

1;
```

13.1 Before Getting Started

In the following sections, we discuss packages, namespaces, and modules found in the standard Perl library and how to use them. Many of today's modules use an object-oriented approach to programming, discussed in Chapter 14, "Bless Those Things! (Object-Oriented Perl)," which will include such terms as classes, objects, and methods. This chapter will focus on procedural, function-oriented modules and libraries and how to use and create them. We will also show you how to install modules from the Standard Perl Library and the Comprehensive Perl Archive Network (CPAN). You will learn how to use the *cpan* shell, PPM (the Perl Program Manager), PerlBrew, and *cpanm* to assist you in the retrieval of CPAN modules.

13.1.1   An Analogy

Two boys each have a box of Lego® building blocks. One set of Lego blocks will build a toy boat, the other a toy plane. The boys open their boxes and throw the contents on the floor, mixing them together. The Lego blocks are different shapes and colors. There are yellow square pieces, red triangular pieces, and blue rectangular pieces from both boxes, but now they are mixed up so it is difficult to tell which Lego blocks should be used to build the toy boat or the toy plane. If the pieces had been kept in their separate boxes, this confusion never would have happened.

In Perl, the separate boxes are called **packages**, and the Lego blocks are called **symbols** (that is, names for identifiers such as variables, subroutines, and constants). Keeping symbols in their own private packages makes it possible to include library modules and routines in your program without causing a conflict between what you named your variables and what they are named in the module or library file you have included.

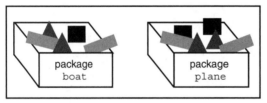

Figure 13.1   Packages are a separate namespace for holding symbols in Perl.

13.1.2   What Is a Package?

The bundling of data and functions into a separate namespace is termed **encapsulation**, and in object-oriented languages like *C++* or *Java*, it is called a **class**. The separate namespace is termed a Perl **package** and offers a way to prevent the variables in one package from stomping on those in another. A separate namespace means that Perl has a separate symbol table for the identifiers in a named package unless they are *my*, *our*, or *state* variables. By default, the current package is called package *main*. All the example scripts up to this point are in package *main*. It is now time to see how the package mechanism works in order to use and create libraries.

The scope of the package is from the declaration of the package to the end of the file, end of the innermost enclosing block, or until another package is declared. Normally, a package is of file scope. The following example shows you how to declare a package. The special *__PACKAGE__* literal displays the current package name:

EXAMPLE 13.1

```
1  package Dog;  # Declaration of a package called Dog
2  print "This is package ", __PACKAGE__, "\n";

3  package Cat;  # Declaration of a package called Cat
4  print "This is package ", __PACKAGE__, "\n";

(Output)
2  This is package Dog
4  This is package Cat
```

EXPLANATION

1   The *Dog* package is declared and is in scope until the end of the block, *eval*, or file where it is defined, or until another package is declared. Normally, there is one package per file. This package is visible until line 3 when another package, *Cat*, is declared.
2   The special literal contains the name of the current package.
3   Another package is declared. The *Cat* package is visible from here to the end of the file.

Referencing Package Variables and Subroutines from Another Package.

Although we have been using the term **global** throughout this text to describe the scope (visibility) of variables and to differentiate them from private, lexically scoped variables (*my* or *state* variables), keep in mind that global variables are technically just **package** variables. They live in a package and are in the namespace for that package, whereas lexical variables have no concept of a package and live in their own little world (that is, a private scratchpad that is created for the current scope and cleared when they go out of scope). When you have *strict* turned on, you are restricted from using package variables unless you fully qualify their names. The names of subroutines, however, are in the global namespace, and are not restricted.

To reference a package variable in another package, prefix the package name by the sigil (funny character) representing the data type of the variable, followed by two colons and the variable name;[1] for example, if the package name is *Dog* and another package needs to access the package variables in *Dog*, you might see the following:

```
$Dog::name
@Dog::treats
$Dog::treats[1]
```

---

1. In ancient Perl 4, and still valid, an apostrophe was used instead of the double colon, that is, *$Dog'name*. The apostrophe is still acceptable in Perl 5 scripts as of version 5.003.

The double colons are reminiscent of the *C++* scope resolution operator. When referring back to the *main* package from another package, you can omit the name of the package. Instead of *$main::friend*, you could say *$::friend*. To reference a subroutine in another package where, for example, the package name is *Dog*, a call to a subroutine from another package might be as follows:

```
Dog::play("catch")
Dog::sit()
```

In the following example, you will see package declarations within the same file, their scope, and how to switch from one package to the other.

EXAMPLE 13.2

```
1   package Dog;  # Package declaration
2   our $name="Lassie";   # Package variable
3   my $gender="female";  # Lexical private variable
4   @treats=("rawhide", "pork bone", "bacon twists", "milkbone" );
5   sub play{
       my $dogname = shift;
       print "$dogname catches a tennis ball.\n";
    }

6   package Cat;  # Package declaration

7   $name = "Skiddy";
8   print "Treats are: @treats\n";  # Not defined in this package
9   print "$name says hello to $Dog::name.\n";
10  print "$Dog::name is a $Dog::gender.\n";
11  print "$name prefers chicken flavored Temptations\n";
12  print "$Dog::name loves ",join(", ",@Dog::treats),
         " but prefers $Dog::treats[0]\n";
13  Dog::play($name);  # Call function in package Dog

(Output)
8   Treats are:
9   Skiddy says hello to Lassie.
10  Lassie is a .
11  Skiddy prefers chicken flavored Temptations
12  Lassie loves rawhide, pork bone, bacon twists, milkbone but prefers
    rawhide
13  Skiddy catches a tennis ball.
```

EXPLANATION

1   This is a package declaration. The *Dog* package is in scope until the end of the file or until another package is declared.

2   This package variable belongs to package *Dog*. It is available until the *Dog* package goes out of scope.

3   The *my* variable, *$gender*, is not a package variable. It is lexically scoped and will be visible until the end of the program.

4   Another package variable, called *@treats*, is defined for package *Dog*.

5   The *sub play*, is in package *Dog*. You can't use the *my* operator with a named subroutine.

6   Now we switch to package *Cat*. This package is in scope until the end of the program.

7   *$name* is a package variable for the *package Cat*.

8   *@treats* is not defined in this package. Nothing prints.

9   The variable, *$name*, for this package evaluates to *"Skiddy"*. To retrieve the value of *$name* in the *Dog* package, the package name is included. Note the $ sigil for the scalar precedes the package name: *$Dog::name*.

10 *$Dog::name* is accessible from the *Cat* package since it is a package variable, but *$Dog::gender* is not a package variable and cannot be retrieved by using the package name. It was defined in the *Dog* package as a *my* variable and is not associated with any package.

11 This line demonstrates how to get an array and its elements in another package.

13 Function names are always in the namespace of the package where they are defined and can be called by preceding the function name with the package name and ::. It is much more common to call functions from another package than to directly access variables from another package. This will all become clear as we move on. (Note that in this example, we pass the name of the cat as an argument to the dog's function, *play()*. Now we have a cat who likes to catch tennis balls!)

13.1.3   What Is a Module?

Perl 5 extends the notion of packages to that of **modules**. A module is a package that is usually defined in a library and is reusable. Modules are more complex than simple packages. They have the capability to export symbols to other packages and to work with classes and methods. A module is a package stored in a file, where the basename of the file is given the package name appended with a *.pm* extension. For example, a file named *House.pm* that serves as a module will contain a package declared as *package House*. The *use* function takes the package name as its argument and loads the module into your script(for example, *use House;*).

13.1.4 The Symbol Table

To compile a program, the compiler must keep track of the names of all the package identifiers (for example, variables, filehandles, directory handles, formats, and subroutines). Perl stores the names of these symbols as keys in a hash table for each package. The name of the hash is the same name as the package followed by two colons; for example, the name of the symbol table for *main* is *%main::* or *simply %::* and the symbol table for package *Dog* is *%Dog::*. The values associated with the hash keys are the corresponding typeglob values, known as aliases. (We discussed typeglobs in Chapter 12, "Does This Job Require a Reference?") The typeglob "globs" onto all "types" that could be represented by the name of the symbol. Perl actually creates separate internal pointers for each of the values represented by the same name (see Figure 13.2).

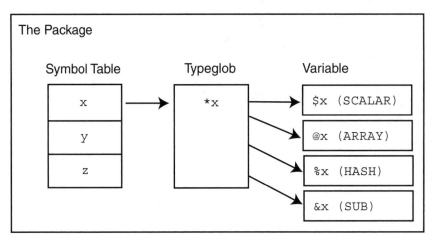

Figure 13.2 Each symbol is assigned a typeglob, *x, which represents all types named *x*.

Each package has its own symbol table (see Figure 13.3). Any time you use the package declaration, you switch to the symbol table for that package.

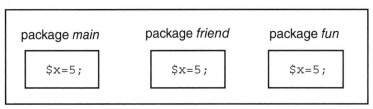

Figure 13.3 Each package has its own namespace (symbol table). Each package has its own *$x*.

A variable assigned using the *local* operator can be accessed in another package by using a double colon :: to qualify it by package name. It is still within scope and accessible from the main symbol table.

As discussed in earlier chapters, there are package (also called global) variables and lexical variables. The lexical variables declared by using the *my* (and *state*) operator are not accessible outside their own packages (unless using references to objects; see Chapter 14, "Bless Those Things! (Object-Oriented Perl)"). They are <u>not</u> stored in a package symbol table but are stored in a private scratch pad created for the scope in which they are defined. In fact, a subroutine containing a *my* variable is given a separate scratch pad for that variable each time the subroutine is called. When we use *my* variables, they cannot be accessed via the package symbol table, because they aren't there!

The *our* variables are also lexical (that is, visible from the current scope), but they are not stored on a scratch pad like the *my* and *state* variables. The name of the *our* variable is associated with a package and can be found on the global symbol table. If you need a global variable and use *our* variables, *strict* will not complain.

In the following example, you will notice that the *main* package stores not only symbols that are provided by the program, but also other symbols, such as *STDIN, STDOUT, STDERR, ARGV, ARGVOUT, ENV,* and *SIG*. These symbols and special variables, such as $_ and $!, are forced into package *main*. If not in the main package, only identifiers starting with letters or an underscore are stored in a package's symbol table. The next example displays the contents of the symbol table for the *main* package.

EXAMPLE 13.3

```
(The Script)
    use feature 'state';
    #use strict;
    #use warnings;
1   state $persist = 1;  # lexical private
2   my $money;  # lexical private
3   our(@friends, %family, $dog);
4   $name="Joe";  # package variable
    # Print the symbol table for main
5   while(($key, $val) = each %main::){  # Dump the main symbol table
       printf "%-15s\t=>\t%-s\n", $key, $val;
    }

(Output)
version::          =>    *main::version::
/                 =>    *main::/
                  =>    *main::
stderr            =>    *main::stderr
_<perl.c          =>    *main::_<perl.c
friends           =>    *main::friends
'                 =>    *main::,
_<symboltable     =>    *main::_<symboltable
2                 =>    *main::2
_<mro.c           =>    *main::_<mro.c
key               =>    *main::key
utf8::            =>    *main::utf8::
1                 =>    *main::1
"                 =>    *main::"
```

EXAMPLE 13.3 (CONTINUED)

```
ARNING_BITS        =>    *main::ARNING_BITS
re::               =>    *main::re::
CORE::             =>    *main::CORE::
DynaLoader::       =>    *main::DynaLoader::
mro::              =>    *main::mro::
stdout             =>    *main::stdout
                   =>    *main::
stdin              =>    *main::stdin
ARGV               =>    *main::ARGV
INC                =>    *main::INC
name               =>    *main::name
ENV                =>    *main::ENV
Regexp::           =>    *main::Regexp::
UNIVERSAL::        =>    *main::UNIVERSAL::
family             =>    *main::family
_<perlio.c         =>    *main::_<perlio.c
E_TRIE_MAXBUF      =>    *main::E_TRIE_MAXBUF
main::             =>    *main::main::
Carp::             =>    *main::Carp::
_<perlmain.c       =>    *main::_<perlmain.c
PerlIO::           =>    *main::PerlIO::
0                  =>    *main::0
_<universal.c      =>    *main::_<universal.c
BEGIN              =>    *main::BEGIN
                   =>    *main::
@                  =>    *main::@
feature::          =>    *main::feature::
STDOUT             =>    *main::STDOUT
IO::               =>    *main::IO::
val                =>    *main::val
                   =>    *main::
                   =>    *main::
_                  =>    *main::_
Exporter::         =>    *main::Exporter::
STDERR             =>    *main::STDERR
Internals::        =>    *main::Internals::
dog                =>    *main::dog
STDIN              =>    *main::STDIN
warnings::         =>    *main::warnings::
```

EXPLANATION

1   The lexical *state* variable is declared. It is not on the global symbol table. To see an example how *state* variables are used, see Chapter 11, "How do Subroutines Function?"

2   The lexical *my* variable is declared and is not on the symbol table.

3   Global *our* variables are declared. They are on the symbol table and available to other packages. They will not be flagged as global variables when the *strict* pragma is turned on.

4   *$name* is a global package variable and found on the symbol table, accessible by this and other packages.

5   Now we will loop through the symbol table for *%main::*. The key is the name of the identifier, and the value is the corresponding *typeglob* value. The typeglob is an alias for any type of that name; for example, **main::friends* is an alias for *@friends*, *$friends*, *%friends*, *sub friends*, and so forth.

EXAMPLE 13.4

(The Script)

```
1   package A;   # Package declaration
    use 5.010;
    #use strict;
    #use warnings;
2   sub count{
3      state $n = 1;
4      $n++;
       return $n;
    }

5   say count;
6   say count;
7   say count;
8   my $money=50000;  # lexical, not a package variable
9   our @friends=qw(tom dick harry);
10  $name="Joe";   # package

11  package B;  # Declare a new package

    # Let's see what we can get from the A:: package
12  say "My money is: $A::money";  # Not a package variable
13  say "The state variable is not package variable $A::n.";
14  say "Your name is $A::name";
15  say "Call function in A package: ", A::count();
16  say "You can see your friends:@A::friends ";
17  say "and like this  @friends";  # lexical scope
18  say "I am in scope: $money";
```

(Output)

```
5   2 6  37  4
12  My money is:
13  The state variable is not package variable .
14  Your name is Joe
15  Call function in A package: 5
16  You can see your friends:tom dick harry
17  and like this  tom dick harry
18  I am in scope: 50000
```

EXPLANATION

1	This is a declaration for package *A*. It will have its own namespace called *%A::*
2	A subroutine, *count*, is defined.
3	A *state* variable, *$n*, is declared and initialized. This is just like a *my* variable in that it is lexically scoped, except it will never be reinitialized and will retain its value from one call of the function to the next. The variable will go out of scope when the function block ends. It is not in the symbol table for this package and can only be accessed when the function is called.
4	Every time the function is called, the value of *$n* is increased by one.
5–7	The *count* function is global in scope for package A. Its name is on the symbol table and it is available to other packages. It is called three times.
8	*$money* is declared as a lexically scoped *my* variable. It is given its own private scratch pad and visible from the point of declaration until the end of the block or file. It is not on the symbol table.
9	*@friends* is declared as an *our* variable. It is global for the package and is found on the symbol table. It is just like *my* and *state* variables in that it is lexically scoped but isn't allocated a private scratch pad. Its value is not printed.
10	*$name* is a global package variable for package *A*.
11	Package *B* is declared. We now switch from package *A* to package *B*. Each package has its own symbol table. From this point on until the program ends or unless another package is declared, the *B* package is in scope.
12	To access the variable *$money* in package *A*, first the dollar sign is prepended to the package name to indicate that the type of the variable is a scalar, followed by the name of the package, *A*, two colons, and the variable name, *money*. This allows you to switch namespaces from within this package. But *$money* is a *my* variable, **not a package variable**, and therefore is not associated with the symbol table for package *A*.
13	The *state* variable *$n* is like the *my* variable in that it is not associated with a symbol table and cannot be accessed from package *A*'s symbol table.
14	The global package variable, *$name*, is available to this package by qualifying its name with *A::* since it is on the symbol table for package *A*.
15	The subroutine, *count*, is also global and was defined in package *A*. We can call the subroutine by qualifying its name as *A::count()*. We have access to the state variable within the subroutine and, as you can see, the count has gone up to 5.
16, 17	*@friends* was declared in package *A* as an *our* variable. It is a package variable and can be accessed in two ways: by fully qualifying its name with the package name, or, in this example, because it is in file scope, it can be accessed as on line 17.
18	*$money* variable was declared in package *A* as a lexically scoped *my* variable. It is still in scope, but cannot be accessed as *$A::money* because it isn't in *A*'s symbol table. It isn't associated with any package.

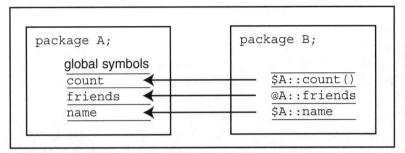

Figure 13.4 Accessing package variables.

13.2 The Standard Perl Library

The Perl distribution comes with a number of standard Perl library functions and packages. The Perl 4 library routines are procedural programs and their names end in a *.pl* extension. The Perl 5 modules end with a *.pm* extension. In Perl 5, the *.pm* files are called **modules**. The *.pm* files are modules written in two programming styles: procedural and object-oriented. The module filenames start with a capital letter. The *.pm* filenames starting with a lowercase letter are a special type of module, called a pragma. A **pragma** is a module that tells the compiler that certain conditions must be checked in a Perl program before it can run. Files that have no extension at all are subdirectories. They contain common modules that are divided into several *.pm* files; for example, the *Math* subdirectory contains *BigFloat.pm*, *BigInt.pm*, *Complex.pm*, and *Trig.pm*.

The following is a sample listing from the standard Perl 5.18 library:[2]

ActivePerl	*Bit*	*Compress*	*Data*	*Errno.pm*
ActivePerl.pm	*Bundle*	*Config*	*Date*	*Eval*
ActiveState	*CGI*	*Config.pm*	*Devel*	*Exception*
Algorithm	*CGI.pm*	*Config.pod*	*Digest*	*Exporter*
AnyDBM_File.pm	*CORE*	*Config_git.pl*	*Digest.pm*	*Exporter.pm*
App	*CORE.pod*	*Config_heavy.pl*	*DirHandle.pm*	*ExtUtils*
Archive	*CPAN*	*Cwd.pm*	*Dist*	*Fatal.pm*
Attribute	*CPAN.pm*	*DB.pm*	*Dumpvalue.pm*	*Fcntl.pm*
AutoLoader.pm	*CPANPLUS*	*DBD*	*DynaLoader.pm*	*File*
AutoSplit.pm	*CPANPLUS.pm*	*DBI*	*Email*	*FileCache.pm*
B	*Carp*	*DBI.pm*	*Encode*	*FileHandle.pm*
B.pm	*Carp.pm*	*DBM_Filter*	*Encode.pm*	*Filter*
BSD	*Class*	*DBM_Filter.pm*	*English.pm*	*FindBin.pm*
Benchmark.pm	*Clone.pm*	*DB_File.pm*	*Env.pm*	*GD*

---

2. The pathname to the standard Perl library is determined at the time Perl is installed. This can be assigned either a default value or a pathname designated by the person installing Perl.

GD.pm	O.pm	Symbol.pm	autodie	mro.pm
Getopt	Object	Sys	autodie.pm	mylib.pm
HTML	Opcode.pm	TAP	autouse.pm	newgetopt.pl
HTTP	POSIX.pm	Task	base.pm	oose.pm
Hash	POSIX.pod	Tcl	benchmark.pl	open.pm
I18N	PPI	Tcl.pm	bigint.pm	ops.pm
IO	PPI.pm	Term	bignum.pm	overload
IO.pm	PPIx	Test	bigrat.pm	overload.pm
IPC	PPM	Test.pm	blib.pm	overloading.pm
JSON	Package	Text	bytes.pm	parent.pm
JSON.pm	Params	Thread	bytes_heavy.pl	perl5db.pl
LWP	Parse	Thread.pm	charnames.pm	perlfaq.pm
LWP.pm	Perl	Tie	constant.pm	perllocal.pod
List	PerlIO	Time	dbixs_rev.pl	pods
Locale	PerlIO.pm	Tkx	deprecate.pm	re.pm
Log	Pod	Tkx.pm	diagnostics.pm	sigtrap.pm
MIME	Readonly	Try	dumpvar.pl	sort.pm
MLDBM	Readonly.pm	UNIVERSAL.pm	encoding	strict.pm
MLDBM.pm	SDBM_File.pm	URI	encoding.pm	subs.pm
MRO	SQL	URI.pm	feature.pm	threads
Mac	Safe.pm	Unicode	fields.pm	threads.pm
Math	Scalar	User	filetest.pm	unicore
Memoize	Scope	WWW	if.pm	utf8.pm
Memoize.pm	Search	Win32	inc	utf8_heavy.pl
Module	SelectSaver.pm	XML	integer.pm	vars.pm
Moose	SelfLoader.pm	XSLoader.pm	less.pm	version
Moose.pm	Shell	YAML	lib.pm	version.pm
Mozilla	Shell.pm	_charnames.pm	locale.pm	version.pod
NDBM_File.pm	Socket.pm	arybase.pm	lwpcook.pod	vmsish.pm
NEXT.pm	Storable.pm	attributes.pm	lwptut.pod	warnings
Net	Sub	auto	metaclass.pm	warnings.pm

13.2.1   The *@INC* Array

The special array *@INC* contains the directory path to where the library modules are located and is set when Perl is installed. To include directories not in the @INC array, you can use the *-I* switch[3] at the command line, or set the *PERL5LIB* environment variable to the full pathname. Normally, this variable is set in one of your shell initialization files, either *.login* or *.profile* if using UNIX.

---

3. See Table A.18 in Appendix A for a description of the *-I* switch.

EXAMPLE 13.5

```
1  $ perl -V
   < Look at the bottom of the output on your screen for
     the @INC array >

   Compiled at Sep 20 2013 20:14:50
     @INC:
   /Users/eleanorquigley/Library/ActivePerl-5.18/lib
   /usr/local/ActivePerl-5.18/site/lib
   /usr/local/ActivePerl-5.18/lib

2  $ perl -le 'print for @INC'
```

EXPLANATION

1   Perl with the -V option displays version, configuration, and library information. At the Mac/UNIX command-line prompt, the @*INC* array is printed. The first element in the path is the full path to the standard Perl library for version 5.18.

Those pathnames with the word *site* or *linux* (*solaris* if you are using Solaris UNIX) are for site-specific library routines and modules, and the final dot represents the current working directory.

The blank line needs to be deleted. The final dot is important. Any libraries stored in the current working directory (folder) will be included when Perl searches for these files.

2   This is another way to view the library directories listed in the @*INC* array. (The $ is the shell prompt.)

Setting the *PERL5LIB* Environment Variable.   If you are using UNIX/Linux operating systems, to add new path elements to the @*INC* array, you can set the *PERL5LIB* environment variable in your startup initialization files.

In *.login* for the *C* and *TC* shells:

```
setenv PERL5LIB "directory path"
```

In *.profile* for the *Bourne*, *Korn*, and *Bash* shells:

```
PERL5LIB="directory path"; export PERL5LIB
```

If you are using Windows, go to the the command window and type:

```
set PERL5LIB = c:\path\to\directory
```

Or go to the *Start* menu, then to *Settings*, then *Advanced System Properties*, then *Environment Variables*, and finally *New*.

To give your own library routines precedence over those listed in the @*INC* array, you can put the following line in your program:

```
BEGIN{ unshift(@INC,"."); }
```

Unshift causes the dot to be prepended to the *@INC* array, making your present working directory the first element in the search path. If your library is in a different directory, use its full pathname rather than the dot. (Note the *BEGIN* code block is executed as soon as possible, even before the rest of the containing file is parsed, ensuring that the *@INC* array is updated at compile time.)

The *lib* Pragma.   The *lib* pragma is used to update the *@INC* array at compile time. This is necessary when you *use* a module that is not found in the standard *@INC* locations. This is the same as *BEGIN{ unshift @INC, 'directory list');};* .

```
use lib (directory list);
use lib ('C:\bin\perl\bin\junk');
```

When the *lib* module is first loaded, it records the current value of *@INC* in an array *@lib::ORIG_INC*. To restore *@INC* to its original value, you can use *@INC = @lib::ORIG_INC;*. When using one of the modules (those files ending in *.pm*) provided in the standard Perl library, you must first make sure the *@INC* array contains the full pathname to your library distribution and that you include the *use* function with the module name.

If you are trying to find out how a particular module works, you can use the *perldoc* command to get the documentation. (The *perldoc* command does not work for older *.pl* files from the library.) For example, if you want to know about the *Moose.pm* module, type at the command line:

```
perldoc Moose
```

and the documentation for the *Moose.pm* module will be displayed. If you type:

```
perldoc lib
```

the documentation for the *lib.pm* pragma is displayed.

13.2.2   Packages and *.pm* Files

Most of the library routines found in the standard Perl library ending in *.pl* were written in the Perl 4 days and have been deprecated. They consisted of subroutines contained within a package or packages declared within a subroutine. The library files are still available in older versions of Perl, but have largely been replaced with modules or *.pm* files. In order to include and execute routines from the standard Perl library (such as the recently deprecated *.pl* files) or Perl code from any other script, use the *require* or *use* functions, similar to the C *#include* statement. For an up-to-date list of modules, go to *http://perldoc. perl.org/perlmodlib.html*.

The *require* Function. The *require* function checks to see if the library has already been included, unlike the *eval* and the *do* functions, which are older methods for including files. Without an argument, the value of the $_ variable is included. If the @INC array does not have the correct path to the library, the *require* will fail with a message such as the following:

Can't locate pwd.pl in @INC at package line 3.

The *require* function loads files into the program during runtime. To request a particular version of a library module, use:

```
require 5.010
require 5.6.1
```

FORMAT

```
require VERSION
require Expr
require
```

If the file being required is not a module, you would quote the file being loaded, like so:

```
require "myfile.pl";
```

If the file is a module, it is required without quotes. For example, the *Exporter.pm* module would be required as follows:

```
require Exporter;
```

The *use* Function (Modules and Pragmas). The *use* function allows Perl modules and pragmas to be imported into your program at **compile** time. The *use* function will not import a module if the module's filename does not have the *.pm* extension. The *require* function does the same thing but does not do imports and loads the module at **runtime**.

A **module** is a file in a library that behaves according to certain set of conventions. The modules in the standard Perl library are suffixed with the *.pm* extension. They can also be found in subdirectories. For example, the module *Bigfloat* is found in the file *BigFloat.pm*, which is found in a subdirectory called *Math*. To use a module found in a subdirectory, the directory name is followed by two colons and the name of the module, such as *Math::Bigfloat.pm*. (Although using the two colons makes it appear that *Bigfloat.pm* is in a package called *Math*, in this context the two colons are used to separate the *Math* directory/folder from the module. The colon then will be translated to a forward slash for UNIX-type operating systems and a backslash for Windows sytsems.)

A **pragma**, spelled in lowercase letters, is a directive to the compiler that your program should behave in a certain way and, if it doesn't, the program will respond accordingly; for example, *warnings* will issue warnings, *strict* will cause the program to abort, and so forth. Some common pragmas are *lib, utf8,featurestrict, subs*, and *diagnostics*. For a list of modules and pragmas, see Tables A.4 and A.5 in Appendix A, "Perl Built-ins, Pragmas, Modules, and the Debugger."

In object-oriented terminology, subroutines are called methods. If you receive diagnostics using the term *method*, for now just think of methods as glorified subroutines. Many of the modules in the library use object-oriented Perl. The modules discussed in this chapter do not require any understanding of objects. For a complete discussion on how to use the object-oriented modules, see Chapter 14, "Bless Those Things! (Object-Oriented Perl)."

FORMAT

```
use Module;
use Module ( list );
use Directory::Module;use pragma (list);
no pragma;
```

If you try to use a module that doesn't exist, you may get a display of errors that looks like the following:

```
Can't locate SomeModule.pm in @INC (@INC contains: /Library/Perl/5.16/
darwin-thread-multi-2level  /Library/Perl/5.16  /Network/Library/Perl/5.16/
darwin-thread-multi-2level    /Network/Library/Perl/5.16    /Library/Perl/
Updates/5.16.2/darwin-thread-multi-2level  /Library/Perl/Updates/5.16.2  /
System/Library/Perl/5.16/darwin-thread-multi-2level        /System/Library/
Perl/5.16   /System/Library/Perl/Extras/5.16/darwin-thread-multi-2level   /
System/Library/Perl/Extras/5.16 .) at usetest line 1.
BEGIN failed--compilation aborted at usetest line 1.
```

Using Perl to Include Your Own Library. The following example shows you how to create your own library functions and include them in a Perl script with the *use* function. When including user-defined routines or adding routines to a library, make sure to include *1;* (a nonzero value) as the last line of the routine. If you do not return a true value as the last line of your library file, this is the type of error you will get from the *require* function:

*Average.pm **did not return a true value** at user.plx line 3.*

EXAMPLE 13.6

```
(The midterms Script)
    # Program name: midterms
    # This program will call a subroutine from another file
    use strict;
    use warnings;
1   use lib qw(/home/ellie/perl/mylib);
2   use Average;
```

EXAMPLE 13.6 (CONTINUED)

```
        print "Enter your midterm scores.\n";
        my @scores=split(' ', <STDIN>);
3       printf "The average is %.1f.\n", Average::ave(\@scores);
        # The ave subroutine is found in a file called Average.pm
    -----------------------------------------------------------
4   $ cd mylib          # Directory where library is located
    -----------------------------------------------------------

    (The Script)
5   $ cat Average.pm    # File where subroutine is defined
6   package Average;     # Declare a package
    use strict;
    use warnings;
    # Average a list of grades
7   sub ave {
8       my $graderef = shift @_;  # Shift off the reference
        my $num_of_grades = @{$graderef};  # Get the size of the list
        my $total;
        foreach my $grade ( @{$graderef} ){
            $total += $grade;
        }
9       return $total/$num_of_grades;  # What gets returned
    }
10  1;   # Make sure the last statement returns true
        # or use will not succeed!
```

EXPLANATION

1   The *use lib* pragma prepends the *@INC* array with the pathname to your personal directory, *mylib*.

2   The *use* function first checks the *@INC* array to get a listing of all directories in which it will search for the *.pm* file and if it is found, includes the Perl file *Average.pm*.

3   The *ave* function is called with one argument, a reference to an array, and returns a value to be stored in the scalar *$average*. Since the subroutine *ave()* is defined in a package called *Average* in another module, the package name (and two colons) must precede the call to *ave()*. If not, Perl will try to find *ave()* in *main*, the current package.

4   Now we cd to the directory where the module is located.

5   The UNIX *cat* command displays the contents of the module, *Average.pm*. (Use the *type* command for MS-DOS rather than *cat*.)

6   The package *Average* is declared.

7   The subroutine, *ave()*, in this package is defined. Remember, subroutine names are global; meaning they are stored on the symbol table for the package and accessible in another package with the *::* syntax.

8   A reference to the array of grades is sent to the function, shifted off the *@_* array, and assigned to a local reference, *$graderef*.

9   The average is calculated and returned to the caller.

10 Without the *1;* as the last statement in the module, Perl will not load the module and will complain that it "did not return a true value."

13.2.3   Exporting and Importing

In the export/import business, someone exports his goods and someone is waiting on the other side to import them. Let's say a wine maker in California has four great-tasting wines in his cellar, and he decides to export three of the wines to buyers but keep the best ones for himself. So he creates an export list and tacks it to the wall of his cellar, and, when the buyer comes, the buyer selects only those wines on the export list. The buyer is the importer. There's nothing preventing the importer from taking all four of the wines, but if he follows the guidelines of the export list, he will take only those listed.

When you use a Perl module from the library with the *use Module*, you are like the buyer. You import symbols (for subroutines, variables, arrays, and so forth) from the export list provided by the module and magically add them to your own symbol table. When you are the user of a module, you can import what's on the module's export list by default, you can ask for specific symbols from the list, import a whole collection of symbols, or you can even exclude some or all of the symbols on the list. The business of exporting and importing is really just a way of getting symbols into the namespace of your program package so you get what you need and don't have to fully qualify all the imported names with the module package name and two colons, such as *Module::fun1*. List what you import after the *use* directive, such as *use Module qw(fun1 fun2);*.

The *Exporter.pm* Module. The *Exporter.pm* module found in the standard Perl library (called "Perl core") supplies the necessary semantics for modules to be able to export symbols. It implements a method that allows a module to export identifiers such as function names and variables to its users' namespaces. As we discussed earlier, symbols are stored on the symbol table for a package as the keys of a hash with corresponding typeglobs. The import routine in a module creates an alias for the symbol that is being taken from one package and used in another. (See Example 13.11 to see a simple example of an import routine for a module.)

The *Exporter.pm* module, then, implements an import routine for a module. For example, if you create a module called *Checking.pm*, and you want the user of your module to be able to directly call the subroutines *deposit* and *withdraw* (without qualifying their names: *Checking::deposit* and *Checking::withdraw*), you can use the *Exporter.pm* module to do the job. The *Exporter.pm* module allows the user of a module to get access to symbols from the exporting module. This may sound strange that the *Exporter.pm* module has an import routine. It simply means that when you "use" a module, you will automatically be able to import (get access to) symbols from the module you are using. Although you can write your own import function, many modules use *Exporter.pm* because it provides a highly flexible interface and is easy to use.

Perl automatically calls the import method when processing a *use* statement for a module. Modules and *use* are documented in *perlfunc* and *perlmod*. Understanding the concept of modules and how the *use* statement operates is important to understanding the *Exporter*.[4] The *Exporter.pm* module is an object-oriented module that functions as a class. Other modules inherit from the *Exporter* class the capability to export symbols. (See

---

4. For details, see *http://perldoc.perl.org/Exporter.html#Declaring-%40EXPORT_OK-and-Friends.*

Chapter 14, "Bless Those Things! (Object-Oriented Perl)," for more on object-oriented programs.) You must list inherited classes in the *@ISA* array, but instead of directly using *@ISA*, you can list inherited classes as arguments to the *parent* or *base* modules.

```
our @ISA=qw(Exporter);
require Exporter;5
```

or as of Perl 5.8.3, you can skip the *@ISA* and use:

```
use Exporter qw(import);
```

which will not include a number of helper methods that you probably don't need or want.

In addition to loading the *Exporter.pm* module and defining the *@ISA* array, your module must list the symbols (normally the names of subroutines) that you want to export.

@EXPORT lists

If the names are listed in the *@EXPORT* array, they are by default installed into the namespace of the program using the module; if the names are listed on the *@EXPORT_OK* array, they are added to the user's namespace only if requested. The *@EXPORT_FAIL* array lists those symbols that cannot be exported. If there are a number of symbols, the *%EXPORT_TAGS* hash allows you to represent them as a collection with one name where the key is a reference to an array consisting of a whole list of symbols.

If a module is imported with *use* and parentheses are added to the module name, as in *use Module()*, none of the symbols are imported. Table 13.1 describes the exporting modules and the users of the modules.

Table 13.1 Importing and Exporting Symbols

The Exporting Module	*What It Means*
package SomeModule;	Package declaration.
require or *use Exporter;*	Use the *Exporter.pm* module to export symbols from package to package.
our @ISA = qw(Exporter);	*@ISA* contains the names of base classes needed to do the exporting.
use base qw(Exporter);	In one step, updates *@ISA* and loads listed modules.
our @EXPORT = qw($x @y z);	Symbols in this list are automatically exported to the user of this module.
our @EXPORT_OK = qw(fun b c);	Symbols in this list are exported only if requested by the user of this module.
our @EXPORT_FAIL=qw(fun3 e);	These symbols are not to be exported.*

our %EXPORT_TAGS= (
  'group1' => [qw(x y z)],
  'group2' => [qw($l @m %o)]
);
	The key *'group1'* represents the symbols *x, y,* and *z* (function names), collectively; *'group2'* represents the symbols *$m, @n,* and *%o,* collectively. You must use *@EXPORT_OK* and list symbols with *%EXPORT_TAGS*.

(continued)

---

5. Note that the Exporter module is not enclosed in double quotes when used as an argument to require and that .pm is missing. This tells the compiler two things: if, for example, the module is *Math::BigFloat*, that will be translated to *Math/BigFloat*, and if there are indirect method calls within the module, they will be treated as object-oriented method calls, not ordinary subroutine calls.

Table 13.1   Importing and Exporting Symbols (continued)

The Importing Module	*What It Means*
use SomeModule;	*SomeModule* is loaded.
use SomeModule qw(fun2);	*SomeModule* is loaded; *fun2* is imported.
use SomeModule();	*SomeModule* is loaded, no symbols are imported.
use SomeModule qw(:group1 !:group2);	*SomeModule* imports symbols from *group1* (See *%EXPORT_TAGS* hash, above) but not symbols from *group2*.
use SomeModule qw(:group1 !fun2);	*SomeModule* imports symbols from *group1*, not the symbol *fun2*.
use SomeModule qw(/^fu/);	*SomeModule* imports symbols whose names start with *fu*.

SomeModule.pm	*User of the Module*
package SomeModule	*use SomeModule;*
use Exporter;	*x();*
our @ISA = qw(Exporter);	*y();*
our @EXPORT=qw(x y z);	*x(); y(); z(); # functions/variables automatically imported from the @EXPORT array*
sub x{ }	*SomeModule::d(); # d isn't on the @EXPORT list; its name must be fully qualified*
sub y { }	
sub z { }	
sub d { }	
1;	
package SomeModule	*use SomeModule qw(x z); # must ask for symbols or they won't be imported*
use Exporter;	*x();*
our @ISA = qw(Exporter);	*z();*
our @EXPORT_OK=qw(x y z d); *our %EXPORT_TAGS = ("standard" => [qw(x y z d)]);*	*use SomeModule (:standard); # import all symbols labeled :standard*
sub x { }	*x(); y(); z(); d() # All symbols available listed in @EXPORT_OK and in # %EXPORT_TAGS*
sub y { }	
sub z{ }	
sub d { }	
1;	

*   Variables have the funny symbol preceding their name; subroutines don't have a funny symbol. *x*, *y*, and *z* refer to subroutines with those names.

13.2.4 Finding Modules and Documentation from the Standard Perl Library

When you are ready to start using Perl modules from the standard Perl library, you can use the built-in *perldoc* command to retrieve the documentation from Perl 5 modules that were formatted with special *pod* directives (see Chapter 14, "Bless Those Things! (Object-Oriented Perl)," for details on this type of formatting). The following example was taken from the *Carp.pm* module in the standard Perl library.

EXAMPLE 13.7

```
(At the Command line prompt for both Windows and Unix)
$ perldoc Carp
System::Library::Perl:User6Contributed
PerSystem::Library::Perl::5.16::Carp(3)


NAME
    Carp - alternative warn and die for modules

SYNOPSIS
      use Carp;

      # warn user (from perspective of caller)
      carp "string trimmed to 80 chars";

      # die of errors (from perspective of caller)
      croak "We're outta here!";

      # die of errors with stack backtrace
      confess "not implemented";

      # cluck not exported by default
      use Carp qw(cluck);
      cluck "This is how we got here!";

DESCRIPTION
      The Carp routines are useful in your own modules because they act like
    die() or warn(), but with a message which is more likely to be useful
    to a user of your module.  In the case of cluck, confess, and longmess
    that context is a summary of every call in the call-stack.  For a shorter
    message you can use "carp" or "croak" which report the error as being from
    where your module was called.  There is no guarantee that that is where
    the error was, but it is a good educated guess.
      You can also alter the way the output and logic of "Carp" works, by
    changing some global variables in the "Carp" namespace. See the section on
    "GLOBAL VARIABLES" below.
```

Viewing the Contents of the *Carp.pm* Module.   If you type at the command line *perl -V*, at the bottom of the output, you will find a list of pathnames stored in the *@INC* array where Perl searches for modules when you *use* or *require* them. For Windows, the path to the standard library is normally a simple path such as *C:/Perl64/lib*, but for UNIX systems, there are often many more choices. When viewing the output of *perl -V*, look for the System library, simplest path. The following list comes from UNIX/Mac:

```
$ perl -V
@INC:
    /Library/Perl/5.16/darwin-thread-multi-2level
    /Library/Perl/5.16
    /Network/Library/Perl/5.16/darwin-thread-multi-2level
    /Network/Library/Perl/5.16
    /Library/Perl/Updates/5.16.2
    /System/Library/Perl/5.16/darwin-thread-multi-2level
    /System/Library/Perl/5.16
    /System/Library/Perl/Extras/5.16/darwin-thread-multi-2level
    /System/Library/Perl/Extras/5.16
```

A simple way to find the library for a module is to use the *-l* switch at the command line with the name of the module:

```
$ perldoc -l Carp
/Applications/XAMPP/xamppfiles/lib/perl5/5.16.3/Carp.pm
```

After *cd*'ing to the standard Perl library, you can list all the modules there. In the following example, we will look at the contents of the *Carp.pm* module.

EXAMPLE 13.8

```
(The Carp.pm module from the Standard Perl Library)[1]
1  package Carp;
   < Some documentation not included here >

   our $VERSION = '1.26';

   our $MaxEvalLen = 0;
   our $Verbose    = 0;
   our $CarpLevel  = 0;
   our $MaxArgLen  = 64;   # How much of each argument to print. 0 = all.
   our $MaxArgNums = 8;    # How many arguments to print. 0 = all.

2  require Exporter;
3  our @ISA = ('Exporter');
4  our @EXPORT      = qw(confess croak carp);
5  our @EXPORT_OK   = qw(cluck verbose longmess shortmess);
6  our @EXPORT_FAIL = qw(verbose);     # hook to enable verbose mode
```

EXAMPLE 13.8 (CONTINUED)

```perl
# The members of %Internal are packages that are internal to perl.
# Carp will not report errors from within these packages if it
# can.  The members of %CarpInternal are internal to Perl's warning
# system.  Carp will not report errors from within these packages
# either, and will not report calls *to* these packages for carp and
# croak.  They replace $CarpLevel, which is deprecated.    The
# $Max(EvalLen|(Arg(Len|Nums)) variables are used to specify how the eval
# text and function arguments should be formatted when printed.

our %CarpInternal;
our %Internal;

# disable these by default, so they can live w/o require Carp

    <continues here>

# if the caller specifies verbose usage ("perl -MCarp=verbose script.pl")
# then the following method will be called by the Exporter which knows
# to do this thanks to @EXPORT_FAIL, above.  $_[1] will contain the word
# 'verbose'.

sub export_fail { shift; $Verbose = shift if $_[0] eq 'verbose'; @_ }

sub _cgc {
    no strict 'refs';
    return \&{"CORE::GLOBAL::caller"} if defined
&{"CORE::GLOBAL::caller"};
    return;
}

sub longmess {
    # Icky backward compatibility wrapper. :-(
    #
    # The story is that the original implementation hard-coded the
    # number of call levels to go back, so calls to longmess were off
    # by one.  Other code began calling longmess and expecting this
    # behaviour, so the replacement has to emulate that behaviour.
    my $cgc = _cgc();
    my $call_pack = $cgc ? $cgc->() : caller();
    if ( $Internal{$call_pack} or $CarpInternal{$call_pack} ) {
        return longmess_heavy(@_);
    }
    else {
        local $CarpLevel = $CarpLevel + 1;
        return longmess_heavy(@_);
    }
}
```

EXAMPLE 13.8 (CONTINUED)

```
our @CARP_NOT;

sub shortmess {
    my $cgc = _cgc();

    # Icky backward compatibility wrapper. :-(
    local @CARP_NOT = $cgc ? $cgc->() : caller();
    shortmess_heavy(@_);
}

7   sub croak   { die shortmess @_ }
    sub confess { die longmess @_ }
    sub carp    { warn shortmess @_ }
    sub cluck   { warn longmess @_ }

        < Continues here >
```

EXPLANATION

1   This is the package declaration. The package is named after the file it resides in, which is *Carp.pm, version 1.26.* (The functions *carp, croak,* and *confess* generate error messages, such as *die* and *warn.* The difference is that with *carp* and *croak*, the error is reported at the line in the calling routine where the error was invoked, whereas *confess* prints out the stack backtrace showing the chain of subroutines that was involved in generating the error. It prints its message at the line where it was invoked.)

2, 3 The *Exporter.pm* module is *required* to implement its import routine that make subroutines and variables available to the namespace of users of this module. The *@ISA* array contains the names of the *Exporter.pm* module, which allows the necessary methods from Exporter to be inherited by the user of this module. (See *@ISA* in Section 14.4, "Inheritance.")

4   The *@EXPORT* array lists the subroutines *confess, croak,* and *carp,* that will be exported to the namespace of a program using this module whether the owner of the namespace wants them or not. (The process of putting unwanted symbols in another's namespace is called namespace pollution.)

5   To prevent namespace pollution, Perl provides the *@EXPORT_OK* array, which is assigned a list of variables and subroutines (*cluck, verbose, longmess,* and *shortmess*) that will be exported only by demand of the user; that is, if he doesn't ask for them, he won't get them.

6   The *@EXPORT_FAIL* array lists symbols that cannot be exported.

7   The subroutines that appear on the *EXPORT* lists are defined here.

13.2.5 How to "Use" a Module from the Standard Perl Library

The following example demonstrates how to use the *Carp.pm* module from the standard Perl library. The first step in using a module is to read the documentation. Use the *perldoc* command to do this.

The *use* directive makes sure the requested module is loaded at compile time. If there is a list following the module name, that list represents symbols that will be exported from the module to be used (imported) in your program. In the *Carp.pm* module, one of the functions is called *croak*. If requested, the user can call the *croak* function without fully qualifying the symbol name with the :: syntax (*Carp::croak*).

EXAMPLE 13.9

```
(Using the Carp.pm module from the Standard Perl Library in a Script)
1  use Carp;  # import croak, confess, carp
2  use Carp qw(cluck);  # import cluck

   my ($miles, $gas);
   START:{
       print "How many miles did you drive? ";
       chomp($miles=<STDIN>);
       print "How many gallons of gas did you use? ";
       chomp($gallons=<STDIN>);
3      if( $miles !~ /^\d*\.?\d+$/ or $gallons !~ /^\d*\.?\d+$/){
4          cluck "Miles and gallons must be numbers";
           redo START;
       }
   }
5  my $mpg = mileage($miles, $gallons);
   printf "Your average miles per gallon was %.1f\n", $mpg;

   sub mileage {
       my ($miles, $gallons) = @_;
6      check($gallons);
       return ($miles / $gallons);
   }

   sub check{
       my $gas = shift;
7      croak "Illegal value for division" if $gas == 0;
   }
```

EXAMPLE 13.9 (CONTINUED)

```
(Output)
   How many miles did you drive? 100
   How many gallons of gas did you use? I dunno
4  Miles and gallons must be numbers at croak.plx line 11, <STDIN> line 2.
   How many miles did you drive? 100
   How many gallons of gas did you use? 0
6  Illegal value for division at croak.plx line 26, <STDIN> line 4.
   main::check(0) called at croak.plx line 20
   main::mileage(100, 0) called at croak.plx line 15
```

EXPLANATION

1   The *Carp* module is used in (loaded into) the current package, *main*. The module's *@EXPORT* list includes *confess*, *croak*, and *carp*. The user of the module will automatically import these subroutine names unless otherwise specified.

2   The module user must request the *cluck* subroutine as it is listed in *Carp*'s *@EXPORT_ OK* array. If not listed here, Perl would send a syntax error including (*Do you need to predeclare cluck?*).

3   The user input is checked for a numeric value.

4   If one of the input values is not a number, *cluck* will send a warning, but not cause the program to exit.

5   The user-defined *mileage* function is called with two arguments.

6   This function is used to check that value of *$gallons* is not zero. It is here just to demonstrate how the *croak* method reports the error from where the function was called.

7   The *croak* function is called with an error message. The *croak* function was imported from the *Carp* module. The program will die if the value of *$gas* is *0*. The error message reports the line where the program died, as well as the name of the package, subroutine name, and the number of the line where the subroutine was invoked.

13.2.6   Using Perl to Create Your Own Module

The following example illustrates how you can create a module in a separate *.pm* file and use the module in another program. Although this module itself looks like any other package, it additionally includes the *Exporter* module, and *@EXPORT*, *@EXPORT_OK*, and *%EXPORT_TAGS* in order to list and export symbols. When exporting lists, try not to export the names of Perl's built-in functions. In the following example, the function is called *nap* rather than *sleep*. If your function is named *sleep*, the built-in *sleep* function would be overridden by your function, which could have unexpected consequences for an unwary user. For guidelines on module creation, see *perlmodlib*. To see a skeletal module to create extensions and modules for CPAN, see *Module::Starter* or *Dist::Zilla*. Both are located at *perldoc.perl.org* or by using the *perldoc* command.

There are a number of sites that discuss style guides on the naming of modules. See "The Naming of Modules" at *https://pause.perl.org/*. Also check *perldoc.perl.org/perlmodstyle.html*.

When naming modules, think about who will be using your module and give it context. Just because you know what it does, others won't. Good documentation is also an important part of module creation. We cover documentation in Section 14.5, " Plain Old Documentation—Documenting a Module." The following example is a function-oriented module that utilizes the *Exporter.pm* module to export variable and subroutine names to the user of the module. Both the module and its user are shown here.

EXAMPLE 13.10

```
(The MyPet/Cat.pm Module)
1   package MyPet::Cat;
    use strict;
    use warnings;
    our $VERSION="0.01";  # The version number for the Cat.pm module
2   use Exporter qw(import); # Simplified import
3   #require Exporter;
    #our @ISA=qw(Exporter);
4   our @EXPORT=qw(eat); # Default is to eat
5   our @EXPORT_OK=qw(speak nap play); # Exported on demand
6   our %EXPORT_TAGS = ('all'=>[ qw(speak nap play eat)]);
                                  # Export a collection

    sub name{  # Not on the export lists
        my $name = shift;
        return $name;
    }
7   sub speak{
        return "Meowwww\n";
    }

8   sub eat{
        return "likes fish\n";
    }
     sub nap {
        return "ZZZzzzzz\n";
    }

     sub play {
        return "catch a mouse!\n";
    }
9   1;
```

EXAMPLE 13.10 (CONTINUED)

```
   -------------------------------------------------------------
10 use MyPet::Cat qw(:all);
11 use MyPet::Cat;
12 my $petname = MyPet::Cat::name("Sneaky");
13 print "$petname ", eat();
14 print "$petname likes to ", play();
      print nap();
      print speak;


(Output)
Sneaky likes fish
Sneaky likes to catch a mouse!
ZZZzzzzz
Meowwww
```

EXPLANATION

1   The file is called *MyPet::Cat.pm*. It contains a package of the same name without the extension.

2   The *Exporter* module allows this module to export functions to a user's namespace using its standard import method.

3   This is typically the way *Exporter* is loaded using the *@ISA* array and inheritance. (See Section 14.4, "Inheritance," for more on object-oriented inheritance.)

4   The *@EXPORT* array lists variables and subroutines that will export by default into the user's namespace.

5   The *@EXPORT_OK* array lists variables and subroutines that can export if the user of the module requests them in his *use* statement. If he doesn't ask, he won't get them.

6   The *%EXPORT_TAGS* hash is a convenient way to bundle up the variables and subroutines in the *@EXPORT_OK* array and give them one name, the key in the hash. In this example, *'all'* is the key and will serve as a label for those names listed as values (that is, *speak*, *nap*, and *play*). The name listed in the *%EXPORT_TAGS* hash must also be listed in either the *@EXPORT_OK* or the *@EXPORT* array as well.

7   The user must request the *speak* subroutine since it is listed in the *@EXPORT_OK* array.

8   The *eat* subroutine is exported to the user's namespace by default.

9   A module must return a *true* value or the *use* will fail.

10 The *use* directive will import a list of symbols labeled *:all*, created in the *%EXPORT_TAGS* hash on line 6.

11 The *use* directive will also import the *eat* function listed in the *@EXPORT* array on line 4. Symbols listed in the *@EXPORT* array are imported by default with *use*.

12 The pet's name must be fully qualified as it is not imported (that is, not on any of the export lists).

13, 14 The *eat* and *play* functions are now available to the user from the *Cat.pm* module without qualifying their names.

Creating an Import Method Without *Exporter*. The following module implements its own import function that is somewhat limited in what it can do, but demonstrates how importing works. Note the use of a typeglob and a reference to manipulate the symbol table of the caller of this import function (that is, the user of *MyPet::Dog.pm*).

EXAMPLE 13.11

```
1   package MyPet::Dog;
    use strict;
    use warnings;
2   sub import{
3     no strict 'refs';  # Allow typeglobs
4     my $pkg=caller 0;  # Get the name of the calling package
5     foreach my $sym(qw(speak eat nap)){
6       *{"${pkg}::$sym"} = \&$sym;  # put a reference to the symbol
                                       # on the user's symbol table
      }
    }
    sub name{  # Not exported
      my $name = shift;
      return $name;
    }
    sub speak{
      return "BowWow";
    }

    sub eat{
      return "likes steak";
    }

    sub nap {
      return "ZZZzzzzz\n";
    }

    1;

---------------------------------------------------
(Module user)
1   use MyPet::Dog;  # use will call Module's import function
2   $dogname = MyPet::Dog::name("Rover");
3   print "$dogname says ", speak(), "\n";
4   print "$dogname ", eat(), "\n";
    print nap();

(Output)
Rover says BowWow
Rover likes steak
ZZZzzzzz
```

EXPLANATION

1   The *Dog.pm* module is in a directory called *MyPet*.
2   This is a user-defined **import** function that will be automatically called when the user of this module says *use MyPet::Dog;*.
3   Turning off *'refs'* for *strict* allows the program to use symbolic references; in this case, symbolic refs to typeglobs to manipulate the symbol table.
4   Perl's built-in *caller* function, with an argument *0*, returns the name of the package where this *import()* was called.
5   Each symbol in the *foreach* list (*speak, eat,* and *nap*) will be exported by this import routine to the caller's namespace.
6   Here's where we manipulate the user's symbol table. A reference to each of the symbols in the list is assigned to the user's package symbol table via a typeglob.

13.3 Modules from CPAN

You may want to use a module that has already been created by another programmer and stored somewhere other than in your library files. The best resource to start with is CPAN (the Comprehensive Perl Archive Network) a central repository for a collection of thousands of Perl modules. To find the CPAN mirror closest to you, go to *http://www.perl.com/CPAN*.

Perl modules that depend on each other are bundled together by name, author, and category. You can find these modules under the CPAN *modules* directory or by using the CPAN search engine at *http://metacpan.org*. If you need to install these modules, the CPAN documentation gives you easy-to-follow instructions. The home page for CPAN is shown in Figure 13.5.

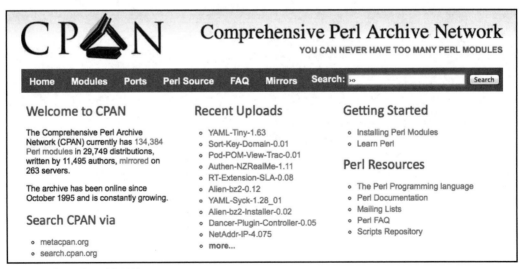

Figure 13.5 The CPAN homepage.

ActivePerl, available for the Linux, Solaris, Mac OS, and Windows operating systems, contains the Perl Package Manager (PPM, for installing packages of CPAN modules) and complete online help (see Figure 13.6). PPM allows you to access package repositories and install new packages or update old ones you already have with relative ease.

Go to *www.activestate.com* to access the ActiveState Package repository.

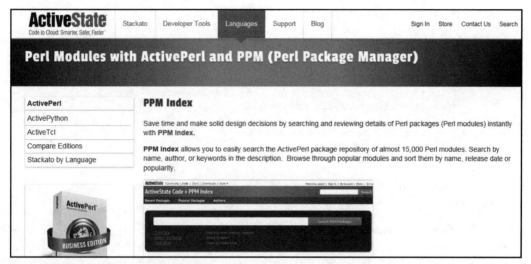

Figure 13.6   Perl Package Manager.

An excellent resource for installing modules for all major operating systems is found at *http://perlmaven.com/how-to-install-a-perl-module-from-cpan*.

13.3.1   The *CPAN.pm* Module

The *CPAN.pm* module allows you to query, download, and build Perl modules from CPAN sites. It runs in both interactive and batch mode and is designed to automate the installation of Perl modules and extensions. The modules are fetched from one or more of the mirrored CPAN sites and unpacked in a dedicated directory. To learn more about this module, type the following at your system command line to see the output that follows:

```
$ perldoc cpan

CPAN(1)      User Contributed Perl Documentation           CPAN(1)

NAME
    cpan - easily interact with CPAN from the command line

SYNOPSIS
    # with arguments and no switches, installs specified modules
    cpan module_name [ module_name ... ]
```

```
# with switches, installs modules with extra behavior
cpan [-cfgimt] module_name [ module_name ... ]

# with just the dot, install from the distribution in the
# current directory
cpan .

# without arguments, starts CPAN.pm shell
cpan

# dump the configuration
cpan -J

# load a different configuration to install Module::Foo
cpan -j some/other/file Module::Foo

# without arguments, but some switches
cpan [-ahrvACDlLO]
```

DESCRIPTION
This script provides a command interface (not a shell) to CPAN. At the moment it uses CPAN.pm to do the work, but it is not a one-shot command

Retrieving a Module from CPAN with the *cpan* Shell.   The following example shows how to install a module from CPAN using the *cpan* shell, which comes with your distribution of Perl. It is a very verbose process and may take some time.

The help command, *h*, gives you a list of all *cpan*'s available commands. The main commands you will use are *get*, *make*, *test*, and *install*. Although *install* will do all four, you may want to do them one at a time so that if there is an error, you can see exactly what happened. The *clean* command is helpful if you want to start over again. You quit with *q*.

EXAMPLE 13.12

```
# perl -MCPAN -e shell

    cpan shell -- CPAN exploration and modules installation (v1.7602)
    ReadLine support enabled

    cpan> h

    Display Information
    command  argument        description
    a,b,d,m  WORD or /REGEXP/ about authors, bundles, distributions,
modules
    i        WORD or /REGEXP/ about anything of above
    r        NONE            reinstall recommendations
    ls       AUTHOR          about files in the author's directory
```

EXAMPLE 13.12 (CONTINUED)

```
    Download, Test, Make, Install...
    get                      download
    make                     make (implies get)
    test      MODULES,       make test (implies make)
    install   DISTS, BUNDLES make install (implies test)
    clean                    make clean
    look                     open subshell in these dists' directories
    readme                   display these dists' README files


    Other
    h,?           display this menu     ! perl-code   eval a perl command
    o conf [opt]  set and query options q             quit the cpan shell
    reload cpan   load CPAN.pm again     reload index  load newer indices
    autobundle    Snapshot               force cmd     unconditionally do
cmd


    cpan> install Mail::Sendmail
Reading '/Users/eleanorquigley/.cpan/Metadata'
  Database was generated on Tue, 20 May 2014 21:29:02 GMT
Fetching with LWP:
http://httpupdate23.cpanel.net/CPAN/authors/01mailrc.txt.gz
Reading '/Users/eleanorquigley/.cpan/sources/authors/01mailrc.txt.gz'
..............................................................................
...DONE
Fetching with LWP:
http://httpupdate23.cpanel.net/CPAN/modules/02packages.details.txt.gz
<continues installing here>
```

13.3.2   Using Perl Program Manager

Although not officially supported by the Perl community, PPM is a program manager that comes with ActivePerl (*www.activestate.com*). It is very easy to use and runs on Linux, Windows, and Mac OS. It comes in both a GUI and command-line interface. When the PPM is activated, it brings up a window with all the currently installed packages. You can search for specific modules and install, upgrade, and remove modules using this graphical interface. For everyday use, this is much easier than using CPAN. (See *youtube.com* for Perl Tutorial 67, Perl Package Manager PPM: Install Modules with PPM.)

The steps for getting a Module using PPM:

1. Type **ppm** at your command-line prompt. A PPM GUI will display (see Figures 13.7 and 13.8).

2. Type the module name you need in the Search window (see Figure 13.9).

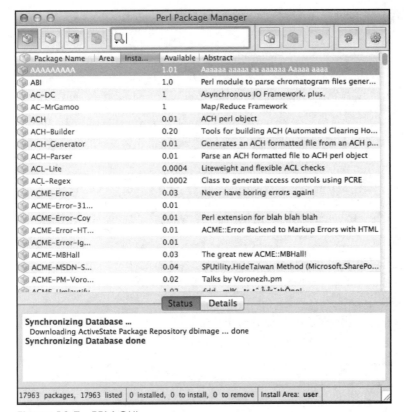

Figure 13.7   PPM GUI.

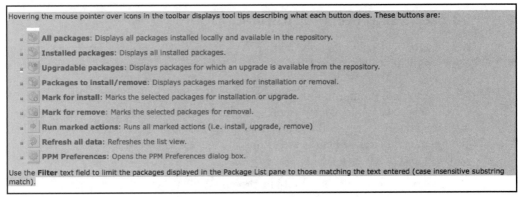

Figure 13.8   What the icons mean in the PPM window (ActiveState's documentation).

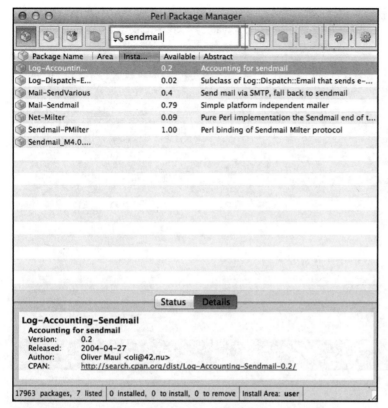

Figure 13.9 Searching for a Perl module to Send Mail.

3. In the left-hand icon, view all packages. (When you move your mouse over an icon, you will see its function.)

4. When your module is highlighted in the main window, go to the right-hand icon (after the search window) and click the icon "Mark for install."

5. When you're ready, click the right-arrow icon "Run marked actions" or press <CTRL>+<ENTER> to install the module, and voila! That's it.

13.4 Using Perlbrew and CPAN Minus

When trying to manage different Perl installations or having issues when downloading modules from CPAN, UNIX users (use PPM with Activestate for Windows users) may want to consider an indispensable and simple tool called Perlbrew (see Figure 13.10).

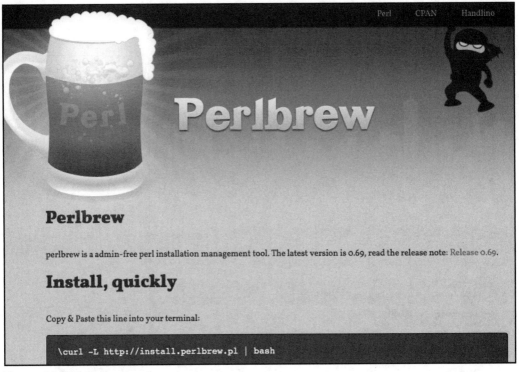

Figure 13.10   Perlbrew.

Perlbrew allows you to manage multiple Perl installations in your home directory. To get some good information on how to manage different Perl versions, see *http://www.dagolden. com/index.php/2134/how-i-manage-new-perls-with-perlbrew/*.

Perlbrew also makes it easy to upgrade, download, and install new versions of Perl by simply typing:

```
perlbrew install perl-5.20.0
perlbrew switch perl-5.20.0
```

If you find working at the standard CPAN shell a little daunting with all its messages and such, you can use a simpler, minimal version of CPAN called CPAN Minus. This is installed by Perlbrew as an executable command called *cpanm*, a stand-alone script used only for installing CPAN modules; that is, it can get, unpack, build, and install Perl modules and that's it. If you don't find *cpanm*, but have Perlbrew, just execute the following command at your prompt:

```
perlbrew install-cpanm
```

If you don't get it from Perlbrew, you can find it at *cpanmin.us*, *github.com* or *metacpan. org* and install it that way.

Once you have installed *cpanm*, you can install a module by its name simply by running the *cpanm* command at your shell prompt:

```
# cpanm ModuleName # logged in as root
$ cpanm --sudo ModuleName # if you want to install the module system-wide
and are not logged in as root.)
```

And that's it! You may need to enter a password if you are not running as root, but otherwise, *cpanm* will get the module and its dependencies without all the verbose output that you get from *cpan*. In the following example, we use *cpanm* to retrieve a module from *cpan* called *Data::Dumper::Perltidy*, which does as its name suggests and makes the output of *Data::Dumper* neat and tidy.

EXAMPLE 13.13

```
$ sh-3.2
# cpanm Data::Dumper::Perltidy
--> Working on Data::Dumper::Perltidy
Fetching http://www.cpan.org/authors/id/J/JM/JMCNAMARA/Data-Dumper-
Perltidy-0.03.tar.gz ... OK
Configuring Data-Dumper-Perltidy-0.03 ... OK
==> Found dependencies: Perl::Tidy
--> Working on Perl::Tidy
Fetching http://www.cpan.org/authors/id/S/SH/SHANCOCK/Perl-Tidy-
20140328.tar.gz ... OK
Configuring Perl-Tidy-20140328 ... OK
Building and testing Perl-Tidy-20140328 ... OK
Successfully installed Perl-Tidy-20140328
Building and testing Data-Dumper-Perltidy-0.03 ... OK
Successfully installed Data-Dumper-Perltidy-0.03
distributions installed


-----------------------------------------------------------------


$ su root
Now let's see if the new module shows up with the perldoc command.
sh-3.2# perldoc Data::Dumper::Perltidy

Library::Perl::5.16::DUser:ContrLibrary::Perl::5.16::Data::Dumper::Perlti
dy(3)


NAME
    Data::Dumper::Perltidy - Dump and pretty print Perl data structures.
```

EXAMPLE 13.13 (CONTINUED)

SYNOPSIS

 To use *"Data::Dumper::Perltidy::Dumper()"* to stringify and pretty print
a Perl data structure:

        use Data::Dumper::Perltidy;

        . . .

        print Dumper $some_data_structure;

DESCRIPTION

 "Data::Dumper::Perltidy" encapsulates both *"Data::Dumper"* and
"Perl::Tidy" to provide a function that stringifies a Perl data
structure in a pretty printed format. See the documentation for
 Data::Dumper and Perl::Tidy for further information

<continues here>

13.5 What You Should Know

1. What is the default package in a Perl program?

2. What is the symbol table?

3. How can you view the symbol table?

4. What is the *@INC* array?

5. What is the *lib* pragma?

6. What is the *base.pm* module used for?

7. What is meant by a fully qualified name when using a variable from another package?

8. What is the *PERL5LIB* environment variable for?

9. When should you use *require*?

10. How does *require* differ from *use*?

11. What is the *Exporter* module?

12. What is the *@EXPORT_OK* array? The *%EXPORT_TAGS* hash?

13. What is the meaning of putting an *1* at the end of a *.pl* or *.pm* file?

14. How do you update the *@INC* array?

15. How do you access subroutines from another package?

16. How do you keep variables private?

17. What are some utilities useful for installing modules from CPAN?

13.6 What's Next?

We have devoted this chapter to modules containing procedural style functions, how to create and use the modules, whether you get them from a library or you create them yourself. The next chapter will show you how to use and create object-oriented modules and how to document both styles.

EXERCISE 13
I Hid All My Perls in a Package

1. Write a script called *myATM*. It will contain two packages: *Checking* and *main*. Later, this file will be broken into a user file and a module file.

2. In the *myATM* script, declare a package called *Checking*. It will contain a lexical *my* variable called *balance* set to *0*. It will initially contain three subroutines:

   a. *get_balance*

   b. *deposit*

   c. *withdraw*

3. In package *main* (in the same file), create a *here document* that will produce the following output:

   1. Deposit

   2. Withdraw

   3. Current Balance

   4. Exit

   a. Ask the user to select one of the menu items. Until he selects number 4, the program will go into a loop to redisplay the menu and wait for the user to select another transaction.

   b. The subroutines will be called in the *main* package by qualifying the *Checking* package name with double colons.

   c. If the user chooses number 4, before the program exits, print today's date and the current balance to a file called *register*.

   d. Can you print the value of the balance without calling the *get_balance* subroutine from the user script?

4. Rewrite the *Checking* package so it gets the balance from the file *register* if the file exists; otherwise, it will start at a zero balance. Each time the program exits, save the current balance and the time and date in the *register* file.

5. Move the *Checking* package from the *myATM* script into a file called *Checking.pm*. Now move the *Checking.pm* module into a directory called *myModules*. Update the *@INC* array in the *myATM* script that will *use* the module. Use the *Checking* module in the *myATM* script.

6. Examine the following code:

```
package Checking;
use base qw(Exporter);
our @EXPORT_OK = qw(deposit withdraw get_balance startup onexit );
our %EXPORT_TAGS = ("transactions" =>
   [ qw(deposit withdraw get_balance startup onexit) ] );
```

   a. How would the user import the symbols from this module?

   b. Can you implement the Exporter module in your *Checking.pm* module?

chapter

14

Bless Those Things!
(Object-Oriented Perl)

14.1 The OOP Paradigm

By the end of this chapter, you will be able to read and write the following code:

```
use Cirle::Area;
use base qw(Shape);
$c1 = Circle::Area->new();
$c2 = Circle::Area->new();

$c1->setRadius(5);
$c1->setArea();
$c2->setRadius(12);
$c2->setArea();

print $c1->getArea();
```

14.1.1   What Are Objects?

Objects are things we deal with every day. Most programming languages, such as *Java* and *C++*, also deal with objects, and those languages are called OOP (Object-Oriented Programming) languages. OOP is a way of organizing a program to solve problems in terms of real-world objects. Early Perl (Perl 4) did not support OOP, but with the advent of Perl 5, the big addition was the ability to do object-oriented programming.

Today, many programmers prefer to use a module called Moose to simplify Perl OOP. We'll get into Moose later, but to start, this chapter will demonstrate the traditional Perl style.

OOP is not for everyone and not necessarily the best solution to your problem. Not every program lends itself to using OOP, but as the programs get larger and more complex, involve the reuse of code, perform multiple operations on related data, or are shared by multiple programmers, the OOP approach can prove to be more efficient. See the Perl documentation (*http://perldoc.perl.org/perlootut.html*) for a complete discussion on why you might use the OOP paradigm.

OOP provides a way to organize a collection of data into a single unit. For example, languages such as *C++* and *Java,* bundle up data into a variable and call it an **object**. When learning about objects, they are often compared to real-world things, such as a cat, a computer, or an employee. A cat, a computer, and an employee are nouns.

Next, we have adjectives that describe the nouns. For example, "the cat is black and sneaky," "the computer is portable and fast," or "the employee is called John." In OOP languages, the adjectives that describe the objects are called **properties** or **attributes**.

We also have verbs that describe what the objects can do or what can be done to them. These verbs are called **methods**. For example, "the cat eats and sleeps," "the computer boots or crashes," or "the employee works." Perl methods are just special subroutines.

The object's data is normally kept **private**. Messages are sent to the object through its methods. The methods are normally **public**. The only way that a user of the program should access the data is through these public methods. The idea of hiding data and using methods to interact with the data is known as **data encapsulation**, a fundamental principal of all object-oriented programing. If you have an object called *account*, the methods to manipultate it might be *view()*, *withdraw()*, *deposit()*, and so forth. The account details are kept private, and the only way to access it are through the public methods, similar to putting an ATM card in the bank machine. You access your money through the menus provided for you, but you can't directly take it from the machine.

14.1.2   What Is a Class?

In OOP languages, the data and the methods are packaged up into a data structure called a **class**. It contains a collection of properties to describe an object and functions, called **methods**, to determine its behavior, but by itself, a class is merely a template or a blueprint that defines what an object looks like and what it can do. A class represents a group of similar objects, such as a class of employees, a class of cars, or a class of computers.

Encapsulation and information hiding are closely related terms you will hear often in the OOP world. When combining the properties and methods of an object within a class, the details can be hidden from the user, or **encapsulated** within the class. The user of the class should only access the data through functions or methods provided by the class. Perl has no specific keywords for *private* or *public* as found in languages such as *C++* and *Java*.

The object in a class is a concrete person, place, or thing. Like a blueprint, a class gives an object form, and as with a blueprint, you can use it to build many objects of the same class. For example, an object in an *Employee* class might be described to have a *name*, *address*, and *phone number*. There may be one *employee* object or many more, but they all have a *name*, an *address*, and a *phone number* as defined by the *Employee* class. Although the object can later change its values, it still belongs to the same class. Classes can also be extended to create more refined classes. From a *Computer* class, for example, you could create a *Laptop* class or a *SmartPhone* class, allowing you to reuse functionality already built into the *Computer* class. This ability to extend a class is called **inheritance**.

In Perl, a package will function as a class when using the object-oriented approach. This is not really a new idea for Perl, since data is already encapsulated in packages. Recall from our short discussion of packages that a package gives a sense of privacy to your program. Each package has its own symbol table, a hash that contains all the global names (not *my* variables) in the "current" package. This makes it possible to create variables and subroutines that have their own namespace within a package. The idea of hiding data in packages, then, is inherently part of Perl, and as stated earlier, also happens to be one of the basic tenets of object-oriented programming.

By putting a package in a separate file containing subroutines, we created a Perl module in the last chapter. It was a procedural or top-down style of programming in that the focus of the program was on how the subroutines were to act on the data provided to them, whereas in this chapter we will build an object-oriented module in the same fashion but where the focus is on the data or object. Special features introduced in Perl 5 give you the ability to model your programs with the object-oriented way of abstract thinking. You can think of procedural languages as action-oriented and OO languages as object-oriented.

Tom Christianson, discussing Perl and objects on his Web page "Easy Perl5 Object Intro," says that people tend to shy away from highly convenient Perl 5 modules because some of them deal with objects. Unfortunately, some problems very much lend themselves to objects. Christianson says that people shouldn't be scared by this, because merely knowing enough object-oriented programming to use someone else's modules is not nearly as difficult as actually designing and implementing one yourself.[1] Even if you are not interested in writing programs that take advantage of the OOP features of Perl but still need to use Perl modules that do utilize objects, reading through this chapter should greatly enhance your understanding of how these modules work.

14.1.3 Some Object-Oriented Lingo

Object-oriented programming is a huge subject. Thousands of books have been written on its design and methodology. Many programmers of the 1990s moved away from traditional top-down structured programming and toward object-oriented programming languages for building complex software. This is not a book on object-oriented design or programming. However, there are some basic key words associated with OOP that should be mentioned before tackling Perl's OOP features. They are listed in Table 14.1.

---

1. Go to *http://perl.com/doc/FMTEYEWTK/easy_objects.html* to see Tom Christianson's Web page.

Table 14.1   OOP Terminology

Term	Perl Meaning
Data encapsulation	Hiding data and subroutines from the user, as in a package
Inheritance	The reuse of code, usually from a library where a package inherits from other packages
Polymorphism	Literally "many forms" and specifically, the ability to extend the functionality of a class
Object	A referenced type that knows what class it belongs to; an instance of a class
Method	A special subroutine that manipulates objects
Class	A package that defines the structure of the data and methods
Constructor	A method that creates and initializes an object
Destructor	A method that destroys an object
Setters/Getters	Methods that store data in an object or fetch data from an object

14.2 Perl Classes, Objects, and Methods— Relating to the Real World

As previously mentioned, OOP is a way of organizing a program to solve problems in terms of real-world objects. For example, suppose you want to build a house. First, you would buy a piece of property located at a specific address. Then you would hire an architect to create the blueprint and design the house. You would decide on the style, how many rooms, doors, windows, and so on. After you design the house, you will hire a contractor to build the house. Once it's built, and you have access to your new house, you can go inside, paint it, clean it, furnish it, remove trash, landscape it, whatever.

Since you now have the blueprints, you could, in the future, find another piece of property and build another house at a new address just like your first house. However, this time you could paint it a different color, change the landscaping, and so forth. In fact, you could build a whole development with houses like yours from the same design, each house identified by its unique address.

In an object-oriented language, the house would be the object, a noun. The style or number of rooms would be the properties that describe the object, like adjectives. The verbs, such as paint the house, clean the house, or show the house, would describe the behaviors for the object. The class would be the blueprint produced by the architect.

All of this will become clearer as we examine a number of examples and discuss how Perl creates, manipulates, and destroys objects.

14.2.1 The Steps

This chapter will discuss a number of topics in detail. For the big picture, the following steps are necessary to create the new data type, called an object, and define what it can do:

1. Determine what your object (noun) is and what it is supposed to accomplish (design) and put it in a class; for example, it could be a house, employee, circle, database handle, file, or so forth.
2. Create the new object (reference to scalar, array, hash, subroutine, and so on) in a package, called a class. Give it a unique identity (constructor).
3. Describe the object by giving it properties, also called attributes (adjectives). (Defining attributes can be done when the object is created or later on in the program.)
4. Bless the object into the class (make the data type an object), and make an association between the object and the class.
5. Define the instance/access methods (subroutines) to create behaviors for the object that describe what the object can do or what can be done to it (verbs).

After defining the class, including the object and its methods, we need to define the user interface, as follows:

1. Use the class; i.e., load the class into the progam's memory.
2. Create an instance of the class (call the constructor method).
3. Manipulate the object (call access methods).

And finally we can:

1. Reuse the class (inheritance).
2. Destroy the object (remove the object from memory).

14.2.2 A Complete Object-Oriented Perl Program

Before getting into the details, let's look at a complete object-oriented Perl script and then break it down, step by step, as the chapter progresses. By the end of this chapter, come back to this example, and any part that confuses you now, should be cleared up. In fact, this example will probably look trivial and you may have suggestions on how to improve it. For now, this is a good template to start with. Note that the class definition and the user interface are all in one file. Later, we will separate them into two parts with the class in one file (a module), and the user of the module in another (the driver program); specifically, we will create a *House.pm* module, with the user interface as the driver program.

EXAMPLE 14.1

```perl
package House;  # House class
use warnings;
use strict;
sub new{  # The constructor method
   my $class=shift;
   my $house_obj={  "Owner"=>"Planet Bank",  # Properties/attributes
                    "Color"=>"Beige",
                    "Payment"=>undef,
                 };
   return bless($house_obj, $class); # The blessing creates the object
}

sub set_owner{  # Instance/Access methods
   my $self=shift;
}
sub set_color{
   my $self=shift;
   $self->{"Color"}=shift;
}
sub set_payment{
   my $self=shift;
   my $payment=shift;
   $self->{"Payment"}=$payment unless $payment < 0;;
}
sub get_owner{  # Retrieve data from the object
   my $self=shift;
   return $self->{Owner};
}

#----------End of Class definition-----------------------------------

# User of the Class
use Data::Dumper;  # We'll look at the structure of the object

my $house1=House->new();   # Make a new house object and get back
                           # its address
my $house2=House->new();   # Make another house object
$house2->set_owner("Mr. T"); # Change the default owner of the
                             # second house
$house2->set_payment("2000");# Set the payment of the second house
print "The owner of my first house is ", $house1->get_owner(),"\n";
         # Retrieve data from the first house.

print Dumper($house1,$house2);  # Look at the content of the
                                # house objects
```

EXAMPLE 14.1 (CONTINUED)

```
(Output)
The owner of my first house is Planet Bank
$VAR1 = bless( {
                 'Owner' => 'Planet Bank',
                 'Payment' => undef,
                 'Color' => 'Beige'
               }, 'House' );
$VAR2 = bless( {
                 'Owner' => 'Mr. T',
                 'Payment' => 2000,
                 'Color' => 'Beige'
               }, 'House' );
}
```

A Perl Package Is a Class.   A Perl package serves as a class. There is no reserved word called *class*, but with object-oriented Perl, a package is often called a class. A class is normally stored in a *.pm* module, and the class name is the same as the module (minus the *.pm* extension). If you want to distinguish between the two terms, a class is a package containing special subroutines called methods that create and manipulate an object. A Perl class normally consists of the following:

1. The data that describes the object.
2. A constructor method that creates the object with a *bless* function.
3. Special subroutines, called "methods," that know how to create, access, manipulate, and destroy the object.

There are no special Perl keywords such as *private, public,* or *protected* as in other object-oriented languages. Perl's package mechanism makes up the class where the data and subroutines, called methods, are stored. The *my* function keeps variables lexically scoped, and the *bless* function guarantees that when the object is created, it will know to which class it belongs. In summary, the object is a reference to an anonymous hash, array, scalar, or subroutine and is manipulated by special functions called methods that get access to the object via the reference.

A Perl Class.   Since a class is really just a package, it has its own symbol table, and the global data or routines in one class can be accessed in another.

Unlike other languages, Perl does not strictly monitor public/private borders within its modules.[2] To keep data private, there are several techniques that can be used (see Section 14.3, "Anonymous Subroutines, Closures, and Privacy," later in this chapter).

---

2. Wall, L., and Schwartz, R. L., *Programming Perl*, 2nd ed., O'Reilly & Associates: Sebastopol, CA, 1998, p. 287.

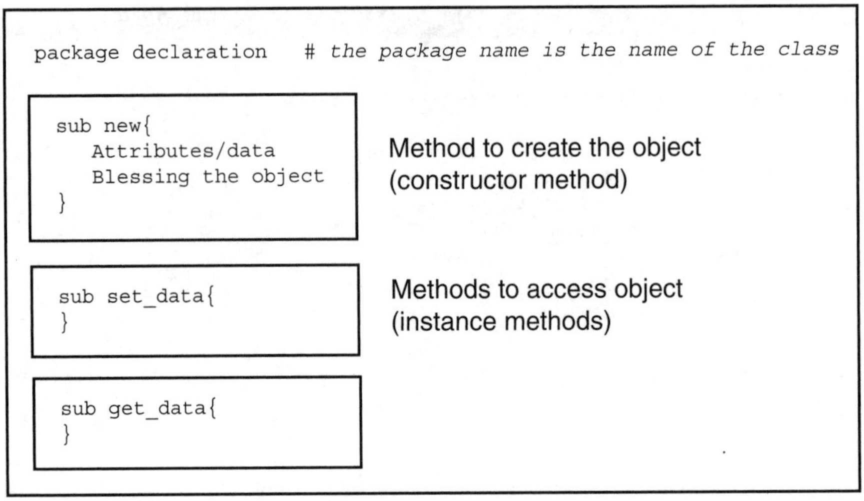

```
package declaration   # the package name is the name of the class

  sub new{
     Attributes/data              Method to create the object
     Blessing the object          (constructor method)
  }


  sub set_data{                   Methods to access object
  }                               (instance methods)


  sub get_data{
  }
```

Figure 14.1   What makes up a class?

14.2.3 Perl Objects

References.   To begin with, an object in Perl is created by using a reference. You may want to review Chapter 12, "Does This Job Require a Reference?" if you are not clear about how to use references. Briefly, a reference is a scalar that holds the address of some variable. A reference might also point to a data type that has no name, called an **anonymous variable**. For example, here is a reference, called $ref, to an anonymous hash consisting of two key/value pairs:

```
my $ref={"Owner"=>"Tom", "Price"=>"25000"};
```

To access a value in the anonymous hash, the reference (pointer) $ref can be dereferenced by using the arrow operator, as follows:

```
$ref->{"Owner"}
```

To make a Perl object, first a reference is created. The reference is often to an anonymous hash (although it could be assigned the address of an array or scalar or even a subroutine). The hash will contain the data members and properties of the object.

The Blessing.   The memory address referenced (called a **referent**), must be "blessed" in order to transform it into a Perl object; in other words, the referent must know what package it belongs to. This is done by creating the reference and then blessing (the thing it references) into a package. Think of the blessing as creating a new data type, an object.

```
my $ref={Owner=>"Tom", Price=>250000};  # Properties Owner, Price
bless($ref, "House");  # Tag the reference as belonging to a House
return $ref;  # A reference to the object is returned to the caller
```

The *bless* function takes one or two arguments. The first argument is <u>always</u> a reference, and the second optional argument is the name of the class (package). The *bless* function tags the thing being referenced (called a referent). It creates an internal pointer to track what package the thing (object) belongs to. The object is the thing (usually a hash) that was blessed into the class (package). If the package is not listed as the second argument, the *bless* function assumes the current package.

The *bless* function returns a reference to the blessed object. In the Figure 14.2, the address of the object is displayed before the blessing and after the blessing. Notice that after the blessing, the address is tagged with the name of the class, in this example *House*.

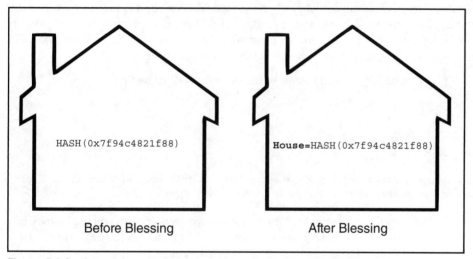

Figure 14.2 An address before and after the blessing.

Since the blessing associates the object with a particular package (class), Perl will always know to what package the object belongs, eliminating the need to use the :: syntax we used in the procedural modules. An object can be blessed into one class and then *reblessed* into another and then another, and so on, but an object can belong to only one class at a time. Once an object has been blessed, you don't have to export symbols with the @EXPORT_OK or @EXPORT arrays. In fact, as a general rule, if the module is trying to be object-oriented, then export nothing.

14.2.4   Methods Are Perl Subroutines

Definition.   A **method** is a subroutine that works with objects. For example, it is used to create an object, store or modify data in an object, retrieve data from the object, and so on. It is a special subroutine that belongs to a class, and its first argument will be one of the following:

1. A class (package) name
2. A reference to an object

This first argument is sent by Perl implicitly. Even though you may call a method without any arguments, Perl will automatically send one; either a package name or object reference. Otherwise, it looks like any other subroutine. In Example 14.1, we created two house objects. The method to create the objects was called *new* (although it could be called anything) and as you can see next, when the method is called, it is preceded by the class name, *House*, followed by an arrow, *House->new()*. Perl will automatically send what is on the left-hand side of the arrow to the method. So in this case, the *new()* method will automatically get one argument, which is *House*, the class name.

   1. Perl implicitly sends the name of the class to the *new()* method.

```
$house1 = House->new(); # Make a new house object and get back its address
$house2 = House->new(); # Make another house object
```

> Although the parameter list for the *new* method is empty, Perl will implicitly send what is on the left-hand side of the arrow to the method; in this case, *House* (the name of the class) is sent to *new()* as its first argument.

   2. Perl sends a reference to the second house, *$house2*, to the *set_owner()* method.

```
$house2->set_owner("Mr. T"); # Perl sends the address of the second
                             # house as the first argument to set_owner()
                             # and "Mr. T" as the second argument
```

The first argument in the *set_owner()* method appears to be *"Mr. T"* but it's not. The first argument in this method is a reference to the second house object, *$house2*. Notice this time, the reference is on the left-hand side of the arrow rather than the class name. Perl will implicitly send the reference as the first argument to this method, and *"Mr. T"* as the second. In that way, you can be assured that when you set the owner for the second house, Perl will know which address to go to.

Types of Methods.   Now that we've had a brief introduction, let's learn a little more about methods. There are two types of methods: class (or static) methods and instance methods.[3] The class method expects a class name as its first argument, and the instance method expects an object reference as its first argument.

A **class method** is a subroutine that affects the class as a whole; for example, it can create an object or act on a group of objects. It is independent; meaning, it doesn't require an object as its first argument. A counter function to keep track of the number of objects created within a class, can be considered a class method. Another example of a class method is a constructor. In object-oriented programs, a **constructor** is a class method used to create an object and receives the class name as its first argument. In Perl, this method is commonly called *new*, although you can call it anything you like. The creation of the object is often called the **instantiation** of the object, or instance of the class.

Object-oriented programs use **instance methods** (also called access or mutator methods) to control the way the object's data is assigned, modified, and retrieved. You can't use an instance method until you have created the object. Once the reference to the newly created object is returned, the instance method uses that reference, often called $this or $self, to manipulate the object. The instance method automatically receives a reference to the object as its first argument. In that way, it knows which object to manipulate; for example, when invoking a *speak* method, *$dogref->speak()* gets a dog reference and might return "Woof woof," whereas *$catref->speak()* gets a cat reference and might return "Meow." Perl sends the reference for you.

Invoking Methods.   Perl provides a special syntax for invoking methods. Instead of using the *package::function* syntax, methods are invoked in one of two ways: class method invocation or instance method invocation. There are two types of syntax for each method call: object-oriented syntax (shown in all the examples in this chapter) and indirect syntax. If you are using objects, either syntax for these method calls is acceptable, but the object-oriented syntax is less ambiguous. The older way of calling methods with the double colons is not recommended.

Something to remember: a method, unlike an ordinary subroutine, is always sent one argument implicitly, either the name of the class or a reference to the object. If, for example, you call a method with three arguments, four arguments are really sent, the first one being the value found on the left-hand side of the arrow when using the object-oriented style.

Class Method Invocation
Assume the method name is called *new* and the return value, *$ref*, is a pointer to the object.

```
1) $ref = class->new( list of arguments );   # object-oriented syntax
2) $ref = new class ( list of arguments );   # indirect syntax
```

---

3. What you call a method type depends on what book you read. Larry Wall categorizes methods as class methods, instance methods, and dual-nature methods.

If the class is called *House*, Perl translates

```
$ref = House->new();
```

to

```
$ref = House::new(House);
```

Instance Method Invocation

Assume the method name is called *display* and the reference to the object is called *$obj*.

```
1) $obj->display( list of arguments );    # object-oriented syntax
2) display $obj ( list of arguments );    # indirect syntax
```

The example using the arrow operator to invoke a method is called the object-oriented style and is the most commonly used. We will use that style throughout this text; the example without the arrow operator is called the indirect syntax.

When Perl sees one of the preceding methods being invoked, it knows what class the object belongs to, because the object was blessed (an internal pointer is tracking where it is).[4]

If you call either

```
display $ref (arguments...);
```

or

```
$ref->display(arguments...);
```

and *$ref* points to an object in a class called *House*, Perl translates that to

```
House::display($ref, arguments...);
```

Creating the Object with a Constructor.

To create a *House* class, we first create a package. This package is called *House*. In object-oriented lingo, the package will now be called a **class**. A function called a constructor method is used to create the object and give it a memory address so that your program can access it.

The properties, or attributes, describe characteristics of the object, such as its owner, style, size, color, and so forth. In our example, the house properties are *Owner, Color,* and *Payment*. There are a variety of ways to set the properties. Often, the object is described with an anonymous hash, where the key/value pairs are the properties of the object.

In the following example, the class is called *House* and the constructor method is called *new()*. You don't have to name the constructor "new." You can call it whatever fits your situation best. Since we're making a new house, the name "new" seems as fitting as any

---

4. The capability of Perl to call the appropriate module's function is called runtime binding, according to Srinivasan, S., *Advanced Perl Programming,* O'Reilly & Associates: Sebastopol, CA, 1997.

other name; we could have easily used *create()*, *build()*, *startup()*, or *init()*. The job of the constructor is to set up a memory location for the new *House* object; in other words, to get a reference to the object. We can define the actual properties later, but first we need to get the address for the object, just as you have to have an address for a new house before you can build it.

Like any other function, the constructor can receive additional arguments from the caller, and use them as "instance" variables. The next step is to make sure Perl knows that this new address is always associated with its class. The new *house* object is a member of the *House* class, and the *bless* function makes sure Perl knows that. Simply, it converts the ordinary pointer into an object. The piece of memory it points to is stamped: "I'm not a Car, or a Horse, or a Cat. I am a House!"

Example 14.2 illustrates how to define the constructor method, create a reference, and transform it into an object via the *bless* function. At this point in the program, we are only defining the method. Later, we will invoke it.

EXAMPLE 14.2

```
1   package House;    # Name of the class

2   sub new{   # The constructor method

3       my $class=shift @_;  # First argument is the name of the class
4       my $house_obj={ "Owner"=>"Planet Bank", # Default attributes
                        "Color"=>"Beige",
                        "Payment"=>undef,
                      };

5       bless($house_obj, $class);  # Create the object by blessing it
6       return $house_obj;

    # The blessing transforms the ordinary pointer into a pointer to an
    # object. The object now belongs to the House class.
    }
```

EXPLANATION

1   The package *House* is declared. It can be called a class because it contains a method that will bless a reference.

2   The subroutine *new* is called a **constructor** method in OOP lingo. The primary job of a constructor is to create and initialize an object. In Perl, it doesn't really have any special syntax. This is called a class method, since its first argument is the name of the class which is shifted from the @_ array. (See Example 14.4 to see how this method is invoked.) It is a subroutine that blesses a referenced "thing" (object) into a class and returns a reference to it. The subroutine is called a **method** and the "thing" it blessed is an **object**. The package is called a **class**.

EXPLANATION (CONTINUED)

3   The first argument received by this type of subroutine is the name of the package or class, in this case *House*. This is another difference between a method and a subroutine. The first argument of a method is the name of either a class or an object.

4   The reference *$house_obj* is assigned the address of an anonymous hash (object). There are three keys with values. The value of *"Payment"* is assigned *undef,* meaning the values at this time are undefined and will be defined later. These key/value pairs serve as default attributes/properties for the *house* object. You could leave the hash empty and set the properties later; for example, *$house_obj = {};*. They can be set or modified by instance methods defined in Example14.3.

5   The reference, *$house_obj*, is the first argument to the *bless()* function, and the name of the class is the second argument. The blessing does not bless the reference. It blesses the location that the reference points to, called the **referent**. It tags that location with the class name, transforming the ordinary reference into a reference to an object.

6   A reference to the object is returned to the caller.

Creating the Instance Methods. Outside of the constructor method, other methods can be defined. In the object-oriented world, these methods are called public methods, and they are the way you get access to the object, but not until an instance of it exists. They often describe behaviors of the object; meaning, what it can do or what can be done to it. In fact, the methods should be the only way to get access to the object.

For our *house* object, one method to access the house might be to move in, another to clean it, another to display it, and so on. Methods in Perl are just glorified subroutines. In the following example, we add three instance (mutators or setters) methods to the *House* class. These methods, *set_owner()*, *set_color()*, and *set_price()* all assume that an instance of the object has already been created; in other words, you can't own, paint, or make payments on the house if it doesn't exist. **The instance methods always get a reference to the object as their first argument.** Once the method has the address of the object and knows what class it belongs to (blessing), it will go to that address and perform whatever tasks it is programmed to do, such as set values, return values, change the defaults; for example, calculate the mortgage, add a garage, clean the kitchen, tear it down, and so forth.

EXAMPLE 14.3

```
1   package House;    # Name of the class

2   sub new{
       my $class=shift;
       my $house_obj={ "Owner"=>"Planet Bank",    # Default attributes
                       "Color"=>"Beige",
                       "Payment"=>undef,
                     };
       return bless($house_obj, $class);
    }
    #-------------------------------------------------------------------
```

EXAMPLE 14.3 (CONTINUED)

```
      # Create the instance methods that will manipulate the object

      # The setter methods
3     sub set_owner{    # Access or instance methods
4        my ($self, $owner)= @_;
                  # First argument is a pointer to the house object
5        $self->{"Owner"}=$owner;   # Set a new owner
         }
      sub set_color{  # Setter method
         my ($self,$color) = @_;
         # First argument is a pointer to the house object.
         $self->{"Color"}=$color;
      }

      sub set_payment{
         my ($self, $payment) = @_;
         $self->{"Payment"}=$payment;
      }
      # The getter methods
6     sub get_owner{
         my $self=shift;
7        return $self->{"Owner"};
      }
      sub get_color{
         my $self=shift;
         return $self->{"Color"};
      }
      sub get_payment{
        my $self=shift;
        return $self->{"Payment"};
      }
```

EXPLANATION

1   The class is *House*.
2   The constructor is defined with default properties.
3   The instance methods are defined here. This is the *set_owner* method, called a "setter" (mutator). It stores the data in the object.
4   The first argument received by the *set_owner* method is a reference to the object. It is called *$self*. *$self* is commonly used, but the method can be called any valid variable name. The second argument is the value of the *Owner* property for the object. When the method is called by the user, Perl implicitly sends a reference to the object first and then any other arguments sent by the user.
5   A reference to the object is stored in *$self*. The value of the *Owner* property is assigned to the object via this reference.
6   This method is called a "getter." It retrieves (gets) information from the object. The first argument is the address of the object, *$self*.
7   The value of the *Owner* property is retrieved and returned to the user.

Invoking the Methods (User Interaction).   Now that we have created the class and its methods, it is time to invoke the methods. For this example the methods and user interaction will be in one file, but in the next section, there will be two files: a file containing the class module (a *.pm* file), and a separate file for the user interface. Whether defined within one file or more, the class definition is a separate from the main program. In the following example, some of the instance methods have been cut out to reduce the size of the example and to enhance the section where the user comes in.

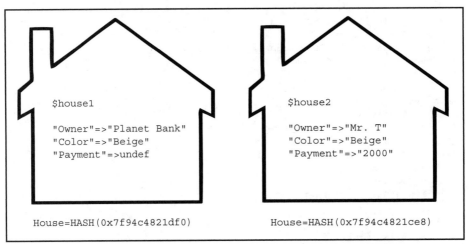

Figure 14.3 Two houses with different addresses.

EXAMPLE 14.4

```
# The Class Definition Outside the Main Part of the Program
  use strict;
  use warnings;
1 package House;    # Name of the class
2 sub new{
     my $class=shift;
     my $house_obj={ "Owner"=>"Planet Bank", # Default attributes
                     "Color"=>"Beige",
                     "Payment"=>undef,
                   };
     return bless($house_obj, $class);
  }
#----------------------------------------------------------------------
  # Create the functions/methods that will manipulate the object
3 sub set_owner{   # Access or instance methods
     my $self=shift;
     # First argument is a pointer to the house object
     $self->{"Owner"}=shift;   # Now set a new owner.
  }
```

EXAMPLE 14.4 (CONTINUED)

```
    sub set_color{
       my $self=shift;
       # First argument is a pointer to the house object.
       $self->{"Color"}=shift;
    }

    sub set_payment{
       my $self=shift;
       $self->{"Payment"}=shift;
    }

4   sub get_owner{
       my $self=shift;
       return $self->{Owner};
    }

#--------------------------------------------------------
#   Now we enter the main part or user part of the program
    use Data::Dumper;  # Dump out both objects to display contents

5   my $house1 = House->new(); # Call constructor to create
                               # a new house object

6   my $house2=House->new(); # Create another house object

7   $house2->set_owner("Mr. T"); # Call access method for the second house

    $house2->set_payment("2000");

8   print "The owner of my first house is ",$house1->get_owner(),"\n";

9   print Dumper($house1,$house2);  # Take a look at the two instances

(Output)
The owner of my first house is Planet Bank
$VAR1 = bless( {
                 'Owner' => 'Planet Bank',
                 'Payment' => undef,
                 'Color' => 'Beige'
               }, 'House' );
$VAR2 = bless( {
                 'Owner' => 'Mr. T',
                 'Payment' => '2000',
                 'Color' => 'Beige'
               }, 'House' );
```

EXPLANATION

1   The *House* class is declared.

2   This is the constructor method that gives us the reference to our new house and blesses it into the class; meaning, it creates an instance of the *House* class.

3   Now the instance methods are defined in order to set values or retrieve values from a house object.

4   This is a "getter" method designed to retrieve data from house objects.

5   Now the user is ready to create more house objects. This is a call to the *new()* constructor method. The first argument is on the left-hand side of the arrow; this is the name of the class. A reference to a blessed house object is returned and assigned to *$house1*.

6   Another house object, *$house2*, is created and its reference returned.

7   Once we have an instance of the object, we can go to that address and set values. The instance method, *set_owner()*, implicitly gets *$house2* as its first argument, that is what is on the left-hand side of the arrow. Getting the address of the second house as its first argument ensures that Perl sets data at the correct location. The second argument, *"Mr. T"*, is supplied by the user. This will override the default value set in the constructor, *"Planet Bank"*.

8   Now we retrieve the value of the owner for the first house with the *get_owner()* method.

9   The *Data::Dumper* function displays the values of both houses. (You could save this data in a file and reconstruct the objects with it.) If you set *$Data::Dumper::Terse=1*, the *$VAR1* and *$VAR2* variables will be omitted in the display. For serialization of the objects, see *http://perl.find-info.ru/perl/025/advperl2-chp-4-sect-2.html*.

14.2.5 Creating an Object-Oriented Module

In the last example, all of the code was contained within a single package in a single file. Now it's time to create a module.

Figure 14.4 illustrates the layout of a simple object-oriented module and the user interface. The *.pm* file where the class is defined is a module. In this example, the *.pm* file is *House.pm*. The file consists of one package declaration. The package will be called a *class*; so, this is the *House* class. Normally the class name is the same as the module name minus the *.pm* extension. The class consists of subroutines, now called *methods*, as shown in the previous example. The first method in the sample program is called *new*, a constructor method. It is the method that will define and create (construct) the object. When a user of this module calls the method *new*, he will get back a reference to the newly blessed *House* object (the address of the house). The instance methods store and fetch the data from the object. Once the user has a reference to the object, it will be used to call the instance methods.

Another little detail: when the class is separated from the user interface, as in the procedural modules we created in Chapter 13, "Modularize It, Package It, and Send It to the Library!" it <u>must return a true value</u> by placing a *1;* at the end of the module.

The user of the module, must designate the module to be included with the *use Module* directive, also discussed in Chapter 13.

There are many ways the module can be designed. This is just one simple approach.

The Module Filename: *House.pm*

```perl
package House;  # House is the class
# The package name normally matches the filename minus the .pm extension
sub new{                        # Constructor method
   my $class = shift;           # First argument is the name of the class
   my $house_obj = { };         # Create the reference/pointer.
   bless($house_obj, $class);   # Bless the referent; Create an object
   return $house_obj;           # Return a reference to the object
}

sub set_owner{                  # Access/instance method
   my $self = shift;            # First argument is a reference to the object
   $self->{"Owner"}=shift;      # Sometimes called a "setter" method
}
sub get_owner{                  # Access/instance method
   my $self = shift;            # First argument is a reference to the object
   return $self->{"Owner"};     # Sometimes called a "getter" method
}
1;   # Must return a true value, or module won't load
```

The user of the Class; the Perl script, *myHouse.plx*

```perl
use House;  # Tell Perl to load House.pm

my $house1 = House->new();    # Call class constructor.
                              # Get back a reference to a new house. Perl sends
                              # the name of the class as its first argument
my $house2 = House->new();    # Create another house object

$house1->set_owner("B of A"); # Call access method;
                              # Perl sends the address of the first house
                              # object, to method set_owner()

print "The owner of the first house is ", $house1->get_owner, "\n";
    # Perl gets the object's data with the get_owner access method
```

Figure 14.4   A simple object-oriented module.

Passing Arguments to Methods.   Instance variables are used to initialize the object when it is created. In this way, each time the object is created, it can be customized. The properties that describe the object may be passed as arguments to the constructor method and assigned to instance variables. They are called **instance variables** because they come into existence when the object is created, or instantiated. Either an anonymous hash or an anonymous array is commonly used to hold the instance variables. In the following example, the object "has a" or "contains a" owner and a price.

EXAMPLE 14.5

```
(The Module: House.pm)
1   package House;
2   sub new{          # Constructor  method
3       my $class = shift;
4       my ($owner, $price) = @_;        # Instance variables
5       my $ref={"Owner"=>$owner,        # Instance variables to
                "Price"=>$price,         # initialize the object
            };
6       bless($ref, $class);
            return $ref;
    }
7   sub display_object {      # An instance method
        my $self = shift;        # A reference to the object is received
8       foreach $key (keys %$self){
            print "$key: $self->{$key} \n";                    }
        }
    }
    1;


- - - - - - - - - - - - - - - - - - - - - - - - - - - - - - - - - - - - - - - - - - - - - - - - - - -


(The Script)

    # User of the class; another program
9   use House;

    # my $house1 = new House("Tom Savage", 250000);
    # Invoking constructor--two ways.
10  my $house1 = House->new("Tom Savage", 250000);
11  my $house2 = House->new("Devin Quigley", 55000);
    # Two objects have been created
12  $house1->display_object();
13  $house2->display_object();
14  print "$house1, $house2\n";

(Output)
12  Owner: Tom Savage
    Price: 250000
13  Owner: Devin Quigley
    Price: 55000
14  House=HASH(0x9d450), House=HASH(0xa454c)
```

EXPLANATION

1   The package *House* is declared. (At this point, the program has not provided any instructions describing what this class does or how to use it. Documentation explaining how to use a class is called the public interface. See Section 14.5, " Plain Old Documentation—Documenting a Module," for instructions on how to document your modules the Perl way.)

2   The class method *new* is defined as a constructor.

3   The first argument to the class method is the name of the class (package).

4   The "instance variables" are created from the remainder of the @_ array.

5   The address of an anonymous hash is assigned to the reference *$ref*. The keys are hard coded and the values are supplied from the instance variables.

6   The "thing" the reference *$ref* points to is blessed into the class and becomes the new object.

7   The value of the reference *$ref* will be returned when the method is called. The subroutine *display_object* is an instance method. It is defined in this class.
    The first argument to the instance method is the reference to the object.

8   The *foreach* loop is used with the *keys* function to get the keys from the hash (object) referenced by *$self*, and in the block of the loop to print both keys and values.

9   The user of the class loads *House.pm* into his namespace.

10   The *new* method is called with three arguments, *House*, *Tom Savage*, and *250000*. The first argument is the name of the class. You don't see it, but Perl implictly sends it to the constructor. The next two arguments are sent explicitly by the user of the class. The only requirement here is that the *Owner* value is the first argument and the *Price* value is the second argument. There is no error checking. The example simply shows how to pass arguments to a constructor. A reference to a new *House* object is returned and assigned to *$house1*, a reference to a hash.

11   The *new* method is called again with different arguments, *Devin Quigley* and *55000*. The value returned to *$house2* is a reference to another object. The *new* method has been used to create two *House* objects. You can create as many objects as you want. They will all have unique addresses, as shown in the output at line 14. Since the objects were blessed in the constructor, Perl knows that the objects are in the *House* class.

12   The instance method is called to display the data for the object referenced by *$house1*.

13   The instance method is called again but to display the data of the object referenced by *$house2*.

14   The addresses of the two objects are printed. You can see that the addresses have been tagged as belonging to the *House* class.

Passing Parameters to Instance Methods.   The first argument to an instance method is always a reference to the object. In the called method, this value is typically shifted from the @_ array and stored in a variable called *$self* or *$this*, although it doesn't matter what you call the variable. The remaining arguments are then processed as they are in any regular subroutine.

The following example demonstrates an instance method that is sent additional arguments when called.

EXAMPLE 14.6

```
    #!/bin/perl
    # Program to demonstrate passing arguments to an instance method.
    # In this example, a pointer to an array is passed.
1   package House;  # Class
    use warnings;
2   sub new{   # Constructor
       my $class = shift;
       my $ref={}; # Define properties later
       return bless ($ref, $class);
    }

3   sub set_props{  # Instance methods
4       my $object = shift;  # Pointer to object
5       my $val_ptr=shift;    # Receive another pointer
6       my ($owner,$price,$style)=@{$val_ptr};  # Create a slice
7       $object->{"Owner"}=$owner;
        $object->{"Price"}=$price;
        $object->{"Style"}=$style
    }
8   sub get_owner{
       my $self=shift;
       return $self->{"Owner"};
    }
    sub get_price{
       my $self=shift;
       return $self->{"Price"};
    }
    sub get_address{
       my $self=shift;
       return $self->{"Address"};
    }

9   sub display_props{
       my $self = shift;
10     print "Properties for the ",ref($self), " are:\n";
11     foreach $key (keys %{$self})){ # Dereference hash ref
               printf "%-10s%-10s\n",$key,$value;2
    }
    1; # Don't forget this!
------------------------------------------------------------------------

(The Script)
12 use House;
   use warnings;
   use strict;
```

EXAMPLE   14.6 (CONTINUED)

```
13 my $h1=House->new();
14 my $h1->set_props([ "Unity Bank", "150000", "12 Main St."]);
                 # Pass reference
   $h1->display_props();

   $h2=House->new();
15 $h2->set_props([ "Pierre Dupont", "150000","Pacific Ridge" ]);
   $h2->display_props();

(Output)
Owner      Unity Bank
Address    12 Main St.
Price      150000
Owner      Pierre Dupont
Address    10 Pacific Ridge
Price      1500000
```

EXPLANATION

1   The *House* class is declared.

2   The *new* method is a constructor. The object is an empty anonymous hash. The key/
    value pairs, the **properties**, or **attributes**, of the object will be assigned later. The
    object, referenced by *$ref*, is blessed into the *House* class.

3   The instance method *set_props* is defined.

4   The first argument is a reference to a *House* object. It is shifted from the @_ array and
    assigned to *$object*. The name of the reference could be *$this* or *$self*. It doesn't matter.

5   The second argument is a shifted from the @_ array. It is a reference to an array.

6   The reference, *$val_ptr*, is dereferenced to get a list of the values passed to this
    method.

7   The values passed to the method are now assigned to the object.

8   The instance methods for retrieving values from the object are defined.

9   The selected values from the hash are printed.

10 The built-in *ref* function, when given an object as its argument, returns the name of
    the class where the object was created.

11 Since the object is a reference to a hash, we dereference it, *%$self*, to get to its key/
    value pairs. The user of the class then loads the module into his program.

13 A call to the constructor *new()* returns a newly blessed house.

14 The instance method, *set_props()*, is provided with arguments. The first implicit one
    is a reference to the object (what is on the left-hand side of the arrow). The second
    argument is a reference to an anonymous array (square brackets) containing a list of
    values that will be set as properties for the object.

15 The instance method, *set_props()*, for the second house is given a reference to a list of
    values.

Named Parameters and Data Checking.   All of the examples so far have used a *House* object. In the next example, we will create an *Employee* object. The *Employee* constructor will take parameters to be used as properties of an employee. If a constructor method is expecting a name, address, and salary to be passed in that order, it would be a problem if the arguments were sent in the wrong order, causing the address to be assigned to the name, or the name to the salary, and so on. One way to prevent that would be to pass arguments as a hash when calling methods. In this way when received by the method as parameters, they will be in the form of key/value pairs. (Of course, spelling the expected keys incorrectly could be a problem.) The following example demonstrates how to use named parameters.

EXAMPLE 14.7

```
      # User of Employee.pm--See Example 14.8 for module
1   use Employee;
2   use warnings;
    use strict;
3   my($name, $extension, $address, $basepay, $employee); # Declare
                                                           # my variables

4   print "Enter the employee's name. ";
    chomp($name=<STDIN>);
    print "Enter the employee's phone extension. ";
    chomp($extension=<STDIN>);
    print "Enter the employee's address. ";
    chomp($address=<STDIN>);
    print "Enter the employee's basepay. ";
    chomp($basepay=<STDIN>);

    # Passing arguments as a hash
5   $employee = Employee->new( "_Name"=>$name,
                               "_Address"=>$address,
                               "_Extension"=>$extension,
                               "_PayCheck"=>$basepay,
                             );
    print "\nThe statistics for $name are: \n";

6   $employee->get_stats;

(Output)
Enter the employee's name. Daniel Savage
Enter the employee's phone extension. 2534
Enter the employee's address. 999 Mission Ave, Somewhere, CA
Enter the employee's basepay. 2200

The statistics for Daniel Savage are:
Address = 999 Mission Ave, Somewhere, CA
PayCheck = 2200
IdNum = Employee Id not provided!
Extension = 2534
Name = Daniel Savage
```

EXPLANATION

1 The *Employee.pm* module will be used by this program.

2 *warnings* will be issued for possible errors, and the *strict* pragma will track global and undefined variables, barewords, and so forth.

3 A list of lexical private variables is created.

4 The user of the program will be asked for the information that will be passed to the *Employee* module.

5 The constructor is called to pass arguments as key/value pairs; that is, a hash is passed to the constructor in the *Employee* module. A reference to the object is returned and assigned to *$employee*.

6 The instance method *get_stats* is called to display the employee's attributes.

In the next example, let's see how the module handles it's named parameters.

EXAMPLE 14.8

```
   # Module Employee.pm--See Example 14.7 to use this module.
1  package Employee;
2  use Carp;
3  sub new {
4     my $class = shift;
5     my(%params)=@_;    # Receiving the hash that was passed
6     my $ref={
7        "_Name"=>$params{"_Name"} || croak("No name assigned"),
          "_Extension"=>$params{"_Extension"},
8        "_Address"=>$params{"_Address"},
          "_PayCheck"=>$params{"_PayCheck"} ||
          croak("No pay assigned"),
9        ((defined $params{"_IdNum"})?("_IdNum"=>$params{"_IdNum"}):
             croak "Employee's id was not provided!\n"
          )),
       };
10 return bless($ref,$class);
   }
11 sub get_stats{
12    my $self=shift;
13    foreach my $key (keys %params, %$self){
          print $key, " = ", $self->{$key}, "\n";
       }
       print "\n";
   }
   1;
```

EXPLANATION

1   The class *Employee* is declared.
2   The *Carp* module from the standard Perl library is used to handle error messages. Instead of using the built-in *die* function, we can use the *croak* method from the *Carp* module to exit when there is an error, with a little more detail on what caused the error.
3   The constructor method *new* is defined.
4   The first argument to the constructor method is the name of the class. It is shifted from the @_ array and assigned to *$class*.
5   The rest of the arguments in the @_ array are assigned to the hash *%params*. They were sent to the constructor as a set of key/value pairs in the @_.
6   A reference, *$ref*, is assigned the address of an anonymous hash.
7   The key *Name* is assigned a value, retrieved from the *%params* hash. Error checking is done here. If a corresponding value for the key *Name* is not provided, the *croak* function will be executed, letting the user know that he did not assign a value to the *Name*, and the program will exit.
8   The *Address* property is assigned by getting its value from the *%params* hash.
9   This is an example of how you can make sure the user of the module passed the expected arguments. The conditional statement reads: If the *%params* has a key called *IdNum* defined, then get its value and assign it to *IdNum*; otherwise, when the program runs, tell the user he forgot to include this parameter. In the examples using *croak*, the program will die if the user doesn't provide input when asked for it, whereas in this form of checking, the program will continue to run.
10 After assigning properties, a reference to the object is blessed into the class and returned to the caller.
11 The instance method *get_stats* is defined.
12 The first argument is shifted from the @_ array and assigned to *$self*. It is a pointer to the object.
13 The *foreach* loop is entered. The built-in *keys* function extracts all the keys from the object. The keys and values are printed on the next line.

14.2.6 Polymorphism and Runtime Binding

Webster's Dictionary defines polymorphism as follows:

> polymorphism: *n.* 1. the state or condition of being polymorphous.[5]

There, that should clear things up! Here's another definition from Webopedia.com:

> Generally, the ability to appear in many forms. In object-oriented programming, polymorphism refers to a programming language's ability to process objects differently depending on their data type or class.

---

5. *Webster's Encyclopedic Unabridged Dictionary of the English Language*, Random House Value Publishing: Avenel, NJ, 1996, p. 1500.

Polymorphism can be described in many ways, and it's a word that is inherently part of the object-oriented lingo, meaning the name of a method can have many behaviors. You can define a method with the same name in different classes and when you call the method, it will do the right thing; or you could say when the reference to the object invokes the method, it will go to the class where the object belongs.

Let's move on to a new example. Let's start with three modules, *BasketballPlayer.pm*, *Director.pm*, and *Rifleman.pm*, each of which have a *shoot()* method. The driver, or user, program will use all three modules. A blessed reference to each of the objects is returned when its respective class constructors are called. When the instance methods are called, recall that Perl sends that object's reference as the first argument so that Perl knows which method to call and to which class it belongs, even though the methods have the same name. Perl determines which class the invoking object belongs to and looks in that class (package) for the method being called. The ability to call the right method demonstrates polymorphism.

When you call a function or method in a program, the method call must be associated with or bound to the definition for that method. This happens either at compile time or runtime. Runtime or dynamic binding allows the program to defer calling the correct method until the program is running; meaning, once it knows what object (reference) will be sent to the method. Along with polymorphism and runtime binding, the program can tie the correct method to its associated class without using *if* statements to determine which method to call. This provides a great deal of flexibility and is necessary for inheritance to work properly.

To take advantage of polymorphism and runtime binding, the object-oriented syntax must be used rather than the :: syntax. Let's say you have two classes, *Director* and *Rifleman*, and both classes contain an instance method called *shoot*, you can write *$object->shoot()*, and Perl will know which class the object belongs to because the first argument sent to the *shoot()* method will be a reference to the object. (It determined the correct class at compile time during the blessing.) In this way, the *Director* will not shoot bullets at his cast, and the *Rifleman* will not try to shoot movies on the rifle range. It is also possible to add another class, such as a *BasketballPlayer* class, with a different *shoot()* method and be sure that the appropriate method will be called for that class. Without runtime binding and polymorphism, the correct class would be determined based on the outcome of some condition, as shown here:

```
if ( ref($object1) eq "Director") {
       Director::shoot($object1);
elsif ( ref($object2) eq "Rifleman" ){
       Rifleman::shoot($object2);
else{
       BasketballPlayer::shoot($object3);
}
```

And what if you sent the *shoot()* method the wrong object? With the object-oriented syntax, a reference to the object is implicitly passed to the method. Since Perl sends the object to the instance method as its first argument and the object has been blessed into the proper class, Perl can implement polymorphism and do the right thing! Assume that, as in the following example, $object1 was created as an object in the *Director* class, $object2 as an object in the *Rifleman* class, and $object3 as an object in the *BasketballPlayer* class.

EXAMPLE 14.9

```
$object1->shoot;        evaluates to   Director::shoot($object1);
$object2->shoot;        evaluates to   Rifleman::shoot($object2);
$object3->shoot;        evaluates to   BasketballPlayer::shoot($object3);
```

The following example demonstrates polymorphism. There are three classes. Each class has a constructor method (not all with the same name), and each class has an instance method, all called *shoot()*.

The user program includes all three modules and creates instances of each of the classes. Each time the *shoot()* method is called, Perl sends a reference to its object. Since the *shoot()* method will receive a blessed reference to the object that called it, there is no confusion as to which method the object belongs to. Perl just goes to the address for that object of that class and calls the method.

EXAMPLE 14.10

```
      #----------File: BasketballPlayer.pm
1   package BasketballPlayer;  # Class
    sub new{
        my $class = shift;
        my ($name, $team, $position)=@_;
        my $player={
          "Name"=>$name,
          "Team"=>$team,
          "Position"=>$position,
        };
        return bless($player, $class);
    }
2   sub shoot {  # Instance method for the basketball player
        my $self = shift;
        print "$self->{'Name'} was a $self->{'Position'}
          and shot baskets for the $self->{Team}.\n";
    }
    1;
      #----------------File: Director.pm
3   package Director;  # Class
    sub new{
        my $class = shift;
        my $info_ptr=shift;
        my $director={
          "Name"=>$info_ptr->{"Name"},
          "Movie"=>$info_ptr->{"Movie"},
          "Type"=>$info_ptr->{"Type"},
        };       return bless($director, $class);
    }
```

EXAMPLE 14.10 (CONTINUED)

```
4   sub shoot{  # Instance method for the director
       my $self = shift;
       print "$self->{'Name'} is shooting the movie $self->{'Movie'}.\n";
    }
    1;
    #---------------File: Rifleman.pm
5   package Rifleman;  # Class
    sub init{
       my $class = shift;
       my ($name, $shooting_range)=@_;
       my $rifleman={
           "Name"=>$name,
           "Range"=>$shooting_range,
       };
       return bless($rifleman, $class);
    }
6   sub shoot{  # Instance method for the rifleman
       my $self = shift;
       print "$self->{'Name'} went to the $self->{'Range'} range to shoot
           target    s.\n";
    }
    1;
    ------------------File: user.plx-----------------------
7   use BasketballPlayer
    use Director;
    use Rifleman;
    use feature qw(say);

    # Create instances of each class
8   $ballplayer=BasketballPlayer->new("Wilt Chamberlain",
                                      "Boston Globe Trotters",
                                      "center");
9   $movie_director=Director->new( {"Name"=>"Steve McQueen",
                                      "Movie"=>"12 Years A Slave",
                                      "Type"=>"Historical Drama"}
                                   );
10  $gunman=Rifleman->init("Lucas McCain", "North Fork Range");
11  say "The basketball player is a ", ref $ballplayer;
12  say "The director is a ", ref $movie_director;
13  say "The rifleman is a ", ref $gunman;
14  $ballplayer->shoot();  # polymorphism
15  $movie_director->shoot();
16  $gunman->shoot();
```

(Output)
11 *The basketball player is a BasketballPlayer*
12 *The director is a Director*
13 *The rifleman is a Rifleman*
14 *Wilt Chamberlain was a center and shot baskets for the Boston Globe*
   Trotters.
15 *Steve McQueen is shooting the movie 12 Years A Slave.*
16 *Lucas McCain went to the North Fork Range range to shoot targets.*

EXPLANATION

1   This is the *BasketballPlayer* class, containing its own constructor and instance variables.

2   This is the *shoot()* instance method for the *BasketballPlayer* class.

3   Now we are in the *Director* class, which has its own constructor method called *new()* and instance variables.

4   The *Director* class has defined its own *shoot()* method.

5   The class called *Rifleman* has defined a constructor called *init()* with instance variables pertaining to a rifleman.

6   The *Rifleman* class has also defined a *shoot()* method.

7   The driver/user program uses all three classes, the *BasketballPlayer*, the *Director*, and the *Rifleman*.

8   A call to the *BasketballPlayer* constructor returns a reference to a new *BasketballPlayer* object.

9   A call to the *Director* constructor returns a reference to a new *Director* object.

10 And a call to the *Rifleman* constructor returns a reference to a new *Rifleman* object.

11 The Perl built-in *ref* function, when given an object as its argument, will return the class name of the object rather than its data type. For an unblessed reference, the return value would have been *HASH*. You can see that the address contains the name of the class.

14–16 Polymorphism is demonstrated when all three objects make a call to their respective *shoot()* methods. Because Perl sends the blessed reference to the method as its first argument, Perl knows what class to go to, as you can see here. The references for the blessed objects are:

BasketballPlayer=HASH(0x7ff98a004ff0),
Director=HASH(0x7ff98a033128),
Rifleman=HASH(0x7ff98a02d4d8)

14.2.7 Destructors and Garbage Collection

Perl keeps track of the number of references to an object, and when the count reaches *0*, the object is automatically destroyed. If a reference goes out of scope or your program exits, Perl handles the garbage collection by destroying every object associated with a reference and deallocating any memory that was used. So, you don't have to worry about cleaning up memory.[6] However, you can define a *DESTROY* method in your program to get control of the object just before it goes away.

---

6. If you use self-referencing data structures, you will be responsible for destroying those references.

EXAMPLE 14.11

```
(The Class)
1   package Employee;
    sub new{
        my $class = shift;
        my $name = shift;
        my $ref={"Name"=>$name};
        bless($ref, $class);
        return $ref;
    }

2   sub DESTROY{
        my $self = shift;
3       print "Employee $self->{Name} is being destroyed.\n";
    }

    1;
    -----------------------------------------------------------------

(The Script)
    # User of the class
4   use Employee;
5   my $emp1 = Employee->new("1: Daniel");
6   { my $emp2 = Employee->new("2: Tom");   # Lexical scoping
7     print "I'm being destroyed.\n";
    }
8   my $emp3 = Employee->new("3: Jenny");   # Create the object

(Output)
7   I'm being destroyed.
6   Employee 2: Tom is being destroyed.
5   Employee 1: Daniel is being destroyed.
8   Employee 3: Jenny is being destroyed.
```

EXPLANATION

1   The *Employee* class is declared and its constructor method defined.
2   When an *Employee* object is no longer in scope, the *DESTROY* method is called and this line is printed. The object on line 6 is defined within a block. It goes out of scope when the block exits. The other objects go out of scope when the program ends.
3   Each time an object goes out of scope, this line is printed.
4   The *Employee* module will be used.
5   A new *Employee* object, referenced by *$emp1*, is being created by calling the constructor method and passing the name as *"1: Daniel"*.
6   Another *Employee* object is created within a block. The object is assigned a name value of *"2: Tom"*. Since it is a *my* variable, it is lexically scoped, meaning the object will go out of scope when the block is exited, at which time the *DESTROY* method will be called and remove it from memory.

7   This line is printed just before the object ("2: Tom") goes out of scope. Then DESTROY is called. The Employee objects are assigned key/value pairs.

8   The last object is created ("3: Jenny") and this is the last one to be destroyed when the program ends.

14.3 Anonymous Subroutines, Closures, and Privacy

One of the problems with the object-oriented examples we have used thus far is that a user can manipulate the object directly once he gets a reference to it. Even if he is supposed to use the methods provided by the module, there is nothing to stop him from accessing the object's data directly, since Perl does not specifically provide a private section for the class data. But for those who feel this lack of guaranteed privacy is an affront to the object-oriented approach, Perl provides several solutions. One of them is the use of closures.

14.3.1   What Is a Closure?

Larry Wall describes **closures** as just anonymous subroutines with an attitude.[7] Barrie Slaymaker calls closures "inside-out objects," in that objects are data that have some subroutines attached to them, whereas closures are subroutines that have some data attached to them.

A closure is a subroutine that has access to *my* (lexical) variables even if it is called from outside the block where the variables were defined and it seems as though those variables should no longer be in scope. The subroutine clings to the lexical variables it references. Each time the subroutine is called via its reference, the same lexical variables are used. The lexical variables stay in scope until they are no longer being referenced.

```
(The Script)
1   my $name="Tommy";

2   {  my $name = "Grandfather";  # Lexical variables
3      my $age = 86;
4      $ref = sub{ return "$name is $age.\n"; }  # Anonymous subroutine
    }
5   print "$name is back\n";
6   print $ref->();  # Call to subroutine outside the block
                  # Could also call subroutine with this syntax: &{$ref};
```

7. Wall, L., Christianson, T., and Orwant, J., *Programming Perl, 3rd ed.*, O'Reilly & Associates: Sebastopol, CA, 2000, p. 262.

EXAMPLE 14.12 (CONTINUED)

```
(Output)
5   Tommy is back.
6   Grandfather is 86.
```

EXPLANATION

1   The lexical variable *$name* is assigned *Tommy*. The variable is visible from here to the end of the file.

2   A block is entered. A new lexical variable, *$name*, is assigned *Grandfather*. It is visible from here to the end of its block.

3   Another lexical variable, *$age*, is defined. It is visible from here to the end of the enclosing block.

4   An anonymous subroutine is defined within the same block as the two lexical variables (*my* variables), *$name* and *$age*. The address of the subroutine is assigned to *$ref*. The subroutine has access to those variables even if it is called from outside the block. The subroutine is called a closure because the variables referenced within the subroutine are enclosed there until they are no longer needed.

5   The value of *$name*, *Tommy*, is now visible.

6   The anonymous subroutine is called via the pointer *$ref*. The lexical variables are still available even though they appear to be out of scope. They remain in scope because the reference still needs access to them. Perl doesn't clean up the variables until they are no longer referenced.

EXAMPLE 14.13

```
(The Script)
    # Closure
1   sub paint {
2       my $color = shift;      # @_ array is shifted
3       my $ref = sub {         # Pointer to an anonymous subroutine
4           my $object=shift;
5           print "Paint the $object $color.\n"; # $color still in scope
        };
6       return $ref;     # Returns a pointer (closure)
    }

7   my $p1=paint("red"); # $p1 is a pointer to anonymous subroutine
    my $p2=paint("blue");
8   $p1->("flower");  # Call to anonymous subroutine
9   $p2->("sky");
10  use Data::Dumper;
    $Data::Dumper::Deparse=1;

11  print Dumper $p1, $p2;
```

EXAMPLE   14.13 (CONTINUED)

```
(Output)
5   Paint the flower red.
5   Paint the sky blue.
      < Data::Dumper Output>
10  $VAR1 = sub {
        my $object = shift();
        print "Paint the $object $color.\n";
    };
    $VAR2 = sub {
        my $object = shift();
        print "Paint the $object $color.\n";
    };
```

EXPLANATION

1   The *paint()* subroutine is defined.

2   The lexical scalar *$color* is assigned the value shifted from the @_ array.

3   The value in *$ref* is assigned an anonymous subroutine.

4   The anonymous subroutine takes one argument from the @_ array. In this example, the value of *$object* will be *"flower"* the first time this subroutine is called, and *"sky"* the next time.

5   Here is where we see a closure in action. The lexical variable *$color* is still in scope. The lexical variable *$color* doesn't go out of scope even after the subroutine called *paint()* is called and exited, because the anonymous subroutine still needs it. *$color* is still available here even though the *paint()* function was called and exited.

6   The *paint()* subroutine returns a reference to the anonymous subroutine. The reference looks like this: *(CODE(0x100804ee8))*. The reference forms the closure; it keeps the lexical variables, in this case *$color*, around until no longer being referenced.

7   The *paint()* subroutine is called twice with different arguments. Each time *paint()* is called, Perl creates a new lexical scalar, *$color*, with its own value. The *$color* variable gets wrapped up in the closure that is returned. So *$p1* encloses one *$color*, which is initialized to *"red"*, and *$p2* encloses a totally different *$color*, initialized to *"blue"*. You can see that these variables get their own addresses, by printing \$color each time the function *paint()* is called to produce:

   SCALAR(0x7f947382db80)
   SCALAR(0x7f947382d4c0)

8, 9   *$p1* and *$p2* are references to the anonymous subroutine defined on line 3. They have formed a "closure" around the variable *$color* defined in *paint()* and will have access to their own copy of that variable until it is no longer being referenced.

10   We can use *Data::Dumper* to display the values of the code references, but unless we set the *$Data::Dumper::Deparse* variable to 1, the contents of an anonymous subroutine will be printed as *DUMMY*. *Data::Dumper* displays the contents of the anonymous subroutine.

14.3.2 Closures and Objects

Closures provide a way to encapsulate the object's data and thereby prevent the user from directly accessing the object. This can be done by defining the constructor with the object's data and an anonymous subroutine that will act as the closure. The anonymous subroutine will be the only way to set and get data for the object. Instead of blessing the data (for example, anonymous hash into the class), the anonymous subroutine will be blessed. The reference to the anonymous subroutine will be returned and serve as the only way to access the private data defined in the constructor. The blessed anonymous subroutine will have access to the object's data because it was declared within the same lexical scope. It encapsulates the data with the subroutine; thus, it forms a closure. As long as the anonymous subroutine refers to the object's data, the data will be accessible.

Example 14.14 demonstrates how to use a closure to encapsulate the data for an object by following these steps:

1. A constructor method is defined for a *Student* class. The constructor will define an empty anonymous hash that will be used to set properties for each new *Student* object, a global class variable to keep track of the number of students, and an anonymous subroutine to encapsulate the data to be assigned to and retrieved from the object. The blessing will return a pointer to the anonymous subroutine.
2. The instance methods will be defined for the object for setting and getting the data. Instead of getting back a pointer to the object's data, these methods will get back a pointer to the anonymous subroutine. The only way they can access the data is by calling this anonymous subroutine with the appropriate arguments.
3. A destructor method will be defined to display each *Student* object as it is being destroyed.

EXAMPLE 14.14

```
# File is House.pm

   package House;

1  my @props=qw(Owner Color Price);  # Define property keys

2  sub new{
      my ($class)=shift;
      my @values=@_;    # Values for properties
      my %data;         # Will store properties
3     @data{@props}=@values;  # Create the hash with keys and values

4     my $access_ptr = sub{  # Anonymous subroutine
         print "Caller is ",(caller)[0],"\n";
5        my($access_type, $key, $value) = @_;
                          # Determines if setting or getting data
6        die "Direct access not allowed" if caller() ne "House";
```

EXAMPLE 14.14 (CONTINUED)

```
 7          if ($access_type eq "set" && $key eq "Price"){
                die "Can't change Price\n";
            }
 8          if ($access_type eq "set"){
                $data{$key}=$value;  # Closure, %data still available here
            }
 9          if ($access_type eq "get"){
                return $data{$key};
            }
        };
10      return bless( $access_ptr, $class);  # Bless anonymous sub
    } # End new

11 sub set {
        my ($self, $key, $value)= @_;
        $self->("set", $key, $value);
    }
12 sub get {
        my ($self, $key)= @_;
        $self->("get",$key);
    }

    1;
```

EXPLANATION

1   The *House* class objects will have the properties, *Owner, Color,* and *Price,* assigned to the array *@props.*

2   The constructor will be used to create and bless the object. First the properties are set in a hash, the values supplied by the user.

3   The key/value pairs (properties) are assigned to the hash *%data.* This is an example of a hash slice.

4   The variable *$access_ref* is assigned a reference to an anonymous subroutine to serve as a closure. This subroutine will be blessed into the class and will be used to set and get the data for *House* objects. The user will use the reference to get access to the object's data which is encapsulated within the function. The closure will allow access to the properties in *%data* even though it appears that *%data* should be out of scope.

5   The subroutine takes three arguments: the access type (which is *"set"* or *"get"*), a key for the object, and a value for the object.

6   The Perl built-in function *caller()* returns the name of the package (class) from where the function was called. If the caller is trying to call this method from a package other than *House,* the error will be printed and the program will die. This will become clear later. For now, you cannot access the object's data directly from the user program. You must access the data through methods defined by the class.

7   If the access type is *"set"* and the key to the object is *"Price",* then the user is not allowed to change the *Price* value and the program will die with the message.

EXPLANATION (CONTINUED)

8   If the access type is *"set"*, the value will be set for the object.

9   If the access type is *"get"*, the value for the object will be retrieved.

10   The blessing returns a blessed reference to an anonymous subroutine to the user. In the previous examples, a blessed *HASH* was returned.

11   This is the *set* method that will be called by the user. It serves as a wrapper function in that it doesn't set the data itself, but makes it possible for the user to get access to the function that does. The first argument coming in is a reference to the anonymous subroutine, not a reference to a hash, array, scalar, but a reference to a subroutine! The second argument is a key for the object, and finally a value for the object. $self$, then, is a reference to the anonymous subroutine that was blessed into the class on line 10, and when called, allows access to the object's data.

12   The *get* method is similar to the *set* method in that it allows access to the object's data by using the $self$ to call the anonymous subroutine that gets the data.

EXAMPLE 14.15

```
    # User of the House Module
1   use House;  # Load the House module

2   my $obj1 = House->new("John","red","10000");
    my $obj2 = House->new("Alice","green","20000");

3   print "The owner of the first house is ", $obj1->get("Owner"),"\n";
    print "The owner of the second house is ", $obj2->get("Owner"),"\n";

4   $obj1->set("Owner"=>"Mary");
    $obj1->set("Style"=>"ranch");
    print "After reset for Alice:\n";
5   print "Alice sold her house to ", $obj1->get("Owner"),"\n";
6   #$obj1->set("Price"=>"50");   # Can't change price
7   #$ obj1->("set","Owner"=>"Bank");  # Direct access not allowed

(Ouput)
3   The owner of the first house is John
    The owner of the second house is Alice
5   After reset for Alice:
6   Alice sold her house to Mary
```

EXPLANATION

1   Load the *House* module.

2   Make two house objects and pass arguments to the constructor for each house. (The object for each house is a reference to a blessed anonymous subroutine.)

3   Use the *get()* method to print the owner for the first and second house. A reference to the house object is passed as the first argument. The second argument is the key *"Owner"*. Its value is retrieved. (See line 9 in *House.pm*.)

4   The *set()* method in *House.pm* is called and sent a hash with a key and a value. (See line 11 in *House.pm*.)

5   This line shows that the owner was reset by calling *$obj1->get("Owner")*.

6   User cannot change the *Price* to $50.00. See line 7 in the *House.pm* module. This ro-gram will die if you try to reset the price.

7   This is an attempt by the user to access the data directly by using the reference, *$obj1*, without calling the *set()* method provided by *House.pm*. If he does this, the *caller()* function (line 6 in *House.pm*) will return "main" if he is calling the function from his *main* package, causing an error message and the program to die. If he calls the *set()* method as *$obj1->set('Owner'=>'Bank')* from the *House.pm* module, as he should, the *set()* method will call the anonymous subroutine, and now the *caller()* function will return *House*. Bottom line: if the caller isn't a *House*, die.

14.4 Inheritance

Inheritance means that a new class can inherit methods from an existing class. The new class can then add to or modify existing code in order to customize the class without having to reinvent what has already been done. The principle is that a class may be subdivided into a number of subclasses that all share common features, but each subclass may provide its own additional features, refining what it borrows to a more specific functionality. The idea of this kind of organization is not new. You may have seen it in a biology class when learning about the plant and animal kingdoms and the breakdown of each kingdom, phylum, class, order, family, genus, species, and variety or in procedural programs with the use of functions to combine the common elements of a program into specific tasks.

In object-oriented programming, once a class has been written and debugged, it can be stored in a library and reused by other programmers. The programmer can then add features and capabilities to the existing class without rewriting the whole thing. This is done through inheritance; that is, by deriving a new class from an already existing class. The reuse of software and the increased use of library classes where all this software is stored and organized have contributed to the wide popularity of OOP languages. Let's see how Perl implements inheritance.

14.4.1   The @*ISA* Array and Calling Methods

The classes (packages) listed in the @*ISA* array are the **parent**, or **base**, **classes** of the current class. This is how Perl implements inheritance. The @*ISA* array contains a list of packages (classes) where Perl will search for a method if it can't find it in the current package (class). If the method still isn't found, then Perl searches for an *AUTOLOAD* function and calls that method instead. And if that isn't found, then Perl searches for the last time in a special predefined package called *UNIVERSAL*. The *UNIVERSAL* class is a global base class for all packages, the highest class in the hierarchy of classes.

The *@ISA* array is not searched in a call to a normal subroutine but in a call to a subroutine if it is called with the method invocation syntax.

EXAMPLE 14.16

```perl
#!/bin/perl
# Example of attempting inheritance without updating
# the @ISA array
1  { package Grandpa;
2      $name = "Gramps"; # Global package variable for Grandpa
3      sub greetme {
           print "Hi $Child::name I'm your $name from package Grandpa.\n";
       }
   }
4  { package Parent;
       # This package is empty
   }
5  { package Child;
6      $name = "Baby";
7      print "Hi I'm $name in the Child Package here.\n";
8      Parent->greetme();    # Use method invocation syntax
   }
```

```
(Output)
7  Hi I'm Baby in the Child Package here.
8  Can't locate object method "greetme" via package "Parent" at
   inher2 line 23.
```

EXPLANATION

1   The package *Grandpa* is declared.

2   The global scalar *$name* is assigned *Gramps* in package *Grandpa*.

3   The subroutine *greetme* is defined and when called, the *print* statement will be executed. *$Child::name* refers to the global scalar *$name* in the *Child* package.

4   The package *Parent* is declared. It is empty.

5   The package *Child* is declared. This package will try to call a method from another package. Although objects and methods aren't being used here, the purpose of this example is to show you what happens if you try to inherit a method from a class that this package doesn't know about.

8   Perl can't find the method *greetme* in package *Parent* and prints the error message.

EXAMPLE 14.17

```
#!/bin/perl
# Example of attempting inheritance by updating the @ISA array
1  { package Grandpa;
      $name = "Gramps";
2     sub greetme {
         print "Hi $Child::name I'm your $name from package Grandpa.\n";
      }
   }

3  { package Parent;
4     @ISA=qw(Grandpa);   # Grandpa is a package in the @ISA array.
      # This package is empty.
   }

5  { package Child;
      $name = "Baby";
6     print "Hi I'm $name in the Child Package here.\n";
7     Parent->greetme();    # Parent::greetme() will fail
   }
```

(Output)
6 *Hi I'm Baby in the Child Package here.*
7 *Hi Baby I'm your Gramps from package Grandpa.*

EXPLANATION

1   The package *Grandpa* is declared.
2   The subroutine *greetme* is defined and, when called, the *print* statement will be executed. *$Child::name* refers to the scalar *$name* in the *Child* package.
3   The *Parent* package is declared.
4   The *@ISA* array is assigned the name of the package *Grandpa*. Now if a method is called from this *Child* package and Perl can't find it, it will try the *Grandpa* package listed in the *@ISA* array. If you try to call a normal subroutine without method invocation, Perl won't consult the *@ISA* array, because it uses the *@ISA* array only when methods are being called. Even though the subroutines used here are not technically methods, by calling *greetme* as a class method, Perl will search the *@ISA* array.
5   ·The *Child* package is declared.
6   This line will be printed from the *Child* package.
7   The class method *greetme* is called in the *Parent* package. The *@ISA* array tells Perl to look in the *Grandpa* package if the method isn't in the *Parent* package.

14.4.2   *$AUTOLOAD, sub AUTOLOAD,* and *UNIVERSAL*

If a subroutine (or method) cannot be found in the current package or in the *@ISA* array, the *AUTOLOAD* function will be called. The *$AUTOLOAD* variable is assigned the name of the missing subroutine if it is used with the *AUTOLOAD* function. Arguments passed to the undefined subroutine are stored in the *AUTOLOAD* subroutine's *@_* array. If you assign a function name to the $AUTOLOAD variable, that subroutine will be called if the AUTOLOAD subroutine is provided in place of the missing subroutine. If the $AUTOLOAD variable is used with the AUTOLOAD subroutine, either the method or regular subroutine syntax can be used. If all fails and Perl still can't find the subroutine, a final package (class) called UNIVERSAL is searched for the missing method. The UNIVERSAL class contains three methods that all classes inherit. They are isa(), can(), and VERSION() (see Table 14.2). Type at your command line prompt *perldoc UNIVERSAL* for most recent documentation.

Table 14.2 The *isa()*, *can()*, and *VERSION()* Methods

Method	What It Does	Example
isa()	Returns true if one package inherits from another.	*Salesman->isa("Employee");*
can()	Returns true if a package or any of its base classes contain a specified method.	*Salesman->can("get_data");*
VERSION()	Used to check that the correct modules are loaded for that version number. In the example, Perl calls the UNIVERSAL method *Salesman->VERSION(6.1)*.	*package Salesman;* *use $VERSION=6.1;*

EXAMPLE 14.18

```
1   { package Grandpa;
        $name = "Gramps";
        sub greetme {
2           print "Hi $Child::name I'm your $name from package Grandpa.\n";
        }
    }


3   { package Parent;
4       sub AUTOLOAD{
5           print "$_[0]: $_[1] and $_[2]\n";
6           print "You know us after all!\n";
7           print "The unheard of subroutine is called $AUTOLOAD.\n"
        }
    }
8   { package Child;
        $name = "Baby";
9       print "Hi I'm $name in the Child Package here.\n";
10      Parent->unknown("Mom", "Dad");   # Undefined subroutine
    }

(Output)
2   Hi Baby I'm your Gramps from package Grandpa.
9   Hi I'm Baby in the Child Package here.
5   Parent: Mom and Dad
6   You know us after all!
7   The unheard of subroutine is called Parent::unknown.
```

EXPLANATION

1   The package *Grandpa* is declared. It contains one subroutine.

2   This line is printed from the *Grandpa* package.

3   The package *Parent* is declared.

4   It contains an *AUTOLOAD* subroutine. An undefined subroutine is called on line 10. It has two arguments, *Mom* and *Dad*. If Perl can't find this subroutine in the *Child* package, it will look in the *@ISA* array, and if it is not there, Perl will look for an *AUTOLOAD* function.
    The subroutine *AUTOLOAD* is defined.

5   Since this function was called as a class method, the first argument stored in the *@_* array is the name of the class. The remaining arguments are *Mom* and *Dad*.

6   This line is printed to show that we got here.

7   The *$AUTOLOAD* variable contains the name of the class and the unnamed subroutine.

8   The package *Child* is declared.

9   This line is printed to show in what order the lines are executed.

10 The *Child* package wants to access a method in the *Parent* package. The *Parent* package does not contain a method or subroutine called *unknown*. It does, on the other hand, contain an *AUTOLOAD* subroutine that will be executed because this subroutine can't be found.

EXAMPLE 14.19

```
1   { package Grandpa;
      $name = "Gramps";
2     sub greetme {
          print "Hi $Child::name I'm your $name from package Grandpa.\n";
      }
    }
3   { package Parent;
      # This package is empty
    }
4   { package Child;
      $name = "Baby";
5     print "Hi I'm $name in the Child Package here.\n";
6     Parent->greetme();
    }


7   package UNIVERSAL;
8   sub AUTOLOAD {
9      print "The UNIVERSAL lookup package.\n";
10     Grandpa->greetme();
    }

(Output)
2   Hi I'm Baby in the Child Package here.
9   The UNIVERSAL lookup package.
5   Hi Baby I'm your Gramps from package Grandpa.
```

EXPLANATION

1 The package *Grandpa* is declared.

2 The subroutine *greetme* is defined in this package.

3 The package *Parent* is declared. It is empty.

4 The package *Child* is declared.

5 This line is printed to show the flow of execution in the program.

6 The *greetme* subroutine is called as one of the *Parent* package methods. Since the method could not be found in its own class or in the *@ISA* array, and an *AUTOLOAD* function is not supplied in the *Parent* package, Perl looks for package *UNIVERSAL* as a last resort.

7 This is the built-in base class called *UNIVERSAL* All modules inherit from *UNIVERSAL* which is implicitly on the end of the *@ISA* array.

8 The *AUTOLOAD* function will automatically be called from the *UNIVERSAL* class.

9, 10 Within the *AUTOLOAD* function, the *greetme()* function in the *Grandpa* package will be invoked.

14.4.3 Derived Classes

As already discussed, **inheritance** is when one class can inherit methods from an existing class. The existing class is called the **base**, **parent**, or **superclass**, and the new class that inherits from it is called the **derived**, **child**, or **subclass.** The base class has capabilities that all its derived classes inherit, and the derived class can then go beyond those capabilities.

If a derived class inherits from one base class, it is called **single inheritance.** For example, single inheritance in real life might be that a child inherits his ability to draw from his father. If a derived or subclass inherits from more than one base class, this is called **multiple inheritance**. To continue the analogy, the child inherits his ability to draw from his father and his ability to sing from his mother. In Perl, the derived class inherits methods from its base class and can add and modify these methods when necessary.

The classes are inherited by putting them in the *@ISA* array. In Chapter 13, "Modularize It, Package It, and Send It to the Library!" we looked at modules from the Perl standard library and modules you could create yourself. In order to include a module or pragma into your program, the *use* function was called with the module name (minus the *.pm* extension). The module had the capability of exporting symbols to other packages that might need to use the module. A special module called *Exporter.pm* handled the details for exporting and importing symbols between modules and the symbols were listed in the *@EXPORT* and *@EXPORT_OK* arrays. The *Exporter.pm* module, you may recall, was listed in the *@ISA* array in order to inherit methods necessary for it to do its job. But if a module functions as a class, then its methods can be called without using *Exporter*. Note in the following examples, the class methods and the instance methods are not exported.

The following examples demonstrate inheritance. The user program need not make any reference to the base class, *Employee*. The *Salesman* class and the *Teacher* class are derived from *Employee*. The *Salesman* and *Teacher* class "use" the *Employee* class. Figure 14.5 shows this inheritance hierarchy graphically.

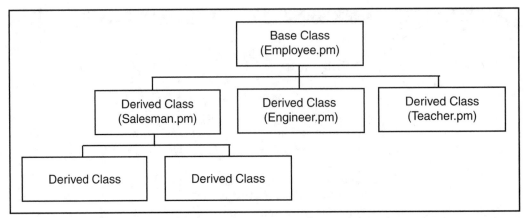

Figure 14.5　Inheritance hierarchy—deriving classes from a base class.

EXAMPLE 14.20

```
    # Module Employee.pm

    # The Base Class
1   package Employee;
    use strict;
    use warnings;
    # Constructor method
2   sub init {
3       my $class = shift;
4       my %info = @_;
5       my $self = { _Name=>$info{"_Name"},
                     _StartDate=>$info{"_StartDate"},
                     _BasePay=>$info{"_BasePay"},
                   };
6       return bless($self, $class);
    }
    # Some instance methods
    sub get_name{
        my $self=shift;
        return $self->{_Name};
    }
     sub get_startdate{
        my $self=shift;
        return $self->{_StartDate};
    }
    sub get_basepay{
        my $self=shift;
        return $self->{_BasePay};
    }
    1;
```

1   *Employee* is the base class in a file called *Employee.pm*.
2   The *init* method is a constructor. It sets properties for all employees.
3   The first argument is the class name from which the method was called.
4   The information being passed in from the caller of this function is a hash of key/value pairs.
5   The values in the *%info* hash are assigned as the employee's properties.
6   The new employee referent is blessed into the class that called this subroutine (its name was passed in as the first argument).

EXAMPLE 14.21

```
1   package Salesman;
    use lib("/usr/local/bin/baseclass");  # Update @INC
    use v5.10.0;
    use feature qw(state say);
2   use base qw(Employee);  # Updates @ISA
    use strict;
    use warnings;
3   sub count_salesman{    # Class method
4       state $counter=0;
        $counter++;
        return $counter;
    }
5   sub new  {  # Constructor for Salesman
        my ($class)= shift;
        my %data=@_;
6       my $emp = $class->init("_Name"=>$data{_Name},
                               "_StartDate"=>$data{_StartDate},
                               "_BasePay"=>$data{_BasePay},
                              )
7       $emp->{"_AnnualSales"}=$data{"_AnnualSales"};
        $emp->{"_Commission"}=$data{"_Commission"};
8       say "This is $emp->{_Name}, salesman #", count_salesman();
        return $emp;
    }
9   sub calculate_pay{
10      my $self=shift;
        my $rate = $self->{"_Commission"};
        my $sales = $self->{"_AnnualSales"};
        my $base = $self->{"_BasePay"},
        my $pay = $sales * $rate + $base;
        return $pay;
    }
11  sub DESTROY{
        my $self=shift
        print "$self->{_Name} is leaving the firm.\n";
    }
    1;
```

EXPLANATION

1 The *Salesman* class is declared in *Salesman.pm*.

2 The *base* module updates the *@ISA* array and loads the *Employee.pm* module. Another way to update *@ISA* is to say:

```
push(@ISA,"Employee");
use Employee;
```

If using version 5.16 and above, you can say:

```
use parent Employee;
```

3, 4 The counter subroutine will keep track of the number of salesmen created. It uses the *state* feature to allow the *$counter* variable to retain its value from one call to the next; meaning, it does not reset the variable to zero each time the function is called. This is a class function as it is specific to the class as a whole and does not take a reference to an object as its first argument.

5 The constructor method for the *Salesman* class is defined.

6 Here we see inheritance being used when calling the *init* method which is defined in the *Employee* class (see *Employee.pm*), not in the current *Salesman* class. When *init* is called, Perl will look in the current *Salesman* class first, and since it is not defined there, will then look in the @ISA array to see if it is listed there. It is. Note that the class name being sent to to the *Employee*'s *init()* function is *Salesman* (meaning, in the *Employee* class the blessing will bless the object into the *Salesman* class, not the *Employee* class). The remaining arguments are the properties for any *Employee*. A blessed reference to a new *Salesaman* object is returned.

7 Now the blessed salesman will get additional properties that further define all salesmen.

8 Each time a new *Salesman* object is created, the *count_salesman* function is called. It is a class function and does not require a reference to the object.

9 An access method, *calculate_pay()*, is defined for the *Salesman*.

10 The first argument is a reference to the object implicitly sent by Perl when the function is called.

11 The *DESTROY* method is called each time an object goes out of scope, usually when the program ends.

EXAMPLE 14.22

```
1  package Teacher;
   use v5.10.0;
   use strict;
   use warnings;
   use feature qw(state say);
2  our @ISA=qw(Employee);
   use Employee;

   my $tracker;
```

EXAMPLE 14.22 (CONTINUED)

```
3   sub count_teacher{    # Class method
        state $counter=0;
        $counter++;
        return $counter;
    }
4   sub new  {  # Constructor for Teacher
        my ($class)= shift;
        my %data=@_;
        my $emp = $class->init("_Name"=>$data{_Name},
5                               "_StartDate"=>$data{_StartDate},
                                "_BasePay"=>$data{_BasePay},
                               );
        $tracker=count_teacher();
        return $emp;
    }
6   sub set_courses{
        my $self=shift;
        my $cptr=shift;
        $self->{"_Courses"}=$cptr;
    }
7   sub get_courses{
        my $self=shift;
        return "@{$self->{'_Courses'}}";
    }

8   END{
        print "$tracker teachers were created.\n";
    }
```

EXPLANATION

1   The *Teacher* class is defined here.
2   In this module, the *@ISA* is updated directly rather than by using the *base.pm* or *parent.pm* pragmas. The name of the base class is listed so that the subclass, *Teacher*, can inherit from it. Not only does the *@ISA* array need to be updated, but the *use* directive must name the base class and load it. This is done automatically when you say *use parent* or *use base*.
3   This class function will track the number of new *Teacher* objects added to the class.
4   The *new()* constructor method for the teacher defines the properties for the teacher as a hash and returns a blessed teacher reference.
5   Like the *Salesman* class described previously, the *Teacher* inherits from the *Employee* class and call its *init()* method. The *init()* constructor in the *Employee* class will then assign the basic properties for an *Employee* and return a blessed *Teacher* object.
6   The teacher object is sent to the *set_courses()* method along with a reference to a list of courses. These courses will be set as a new attribute to the object.
7   The *get_courses()* method will retrieve and send back the list of the teacher's courses by derefencing the pointer, *$self->{Courses}*.

EXPLANATION (CONTINUED)

8   When the program is is ready to exit, the special *END* subroutine prints out the number of *Teacher* objects that were created. This works better than using the *DESTROY* method because the *DESTROY* method would print out the message whenever a teacher object goes out of scope, so that if you had created six teacher objects, the message would print six times.

EXAMPLE 14.23

```perl
    # The Driver (user) Program
1   use Salesman;
2   use Teacher;
    use Data::Dumper;
    use strict;
    use warnings;
3   my $salesguy1=Salesman->new("_Name"=>"Nicky McDonald",
                        "_StartDate"=>"12/12/2010",
                        "_BasePay"=>25000,
                        "_AnnualSales"=>1200,
                        "_Commission"=>.05,
                        );
4   my $pay=$salesguy1->calculate_pay();
    printf "$salesguy1->{_Name} made \$%.2f last year.\n\n", $pay;

5   my $salesguy2=Salesman->new("_Name"=>"Rick Gonzales",
                        "_StartDate"=>"12/12/2010",
                        "_BasePay"=>80000,
                        "_AnnualSales"=>12200,
                        "_Commission"=>.08,
                        );
6   my $pay=$salesguy2->calculate_pay;
    printf "$salesguy2->{_Name} made \$%.2f last year.\n\n", $pay;

7   my $teacher=Teacher->new("_Name"=>"Charles Lee",
                        "_StartDate"=>"08/12/2013",
                        "_BasePay"=>55000,
                        );

8   $teacher->set_courses(["Basic Math", "Algebra", "Calculus"]);
    # Pass ref to Array of courses
    print $teacher->get_name,"\n";        # Inheritance
    print $teacher->get_startdate,"\n";   # Inheritance
    print $teacher->get_basepay,"\n" ;    # Inheritance
    print $teacher->get_courses,"\n";     # Teacher's access method

    $Data::Dumper::Varname="employee";    # Give Dumper a user-defined
                                          # variable name
9   print Dumper($salesguy1, $teacher);   # Dump out data for two objects
```

EXAMPLE 14.23 (CONTINUED)

```
(Output)
    This is Nicky McDonald, salesman #1

    Nicky McDonald made $25060.00 last year.

    This is Rick Gonzales, salesman #2

    Rick Gonzales made $80976.00 last year.

    Charles Lee
    08/12/2013
    55000
    Basic Math Algebra Calculus
    $employee1 = bless( {
                    '_AnnualSales' => 1200,
                    '_BasePay' => 25000,
                    '_Commission' => '0.05',
                    '_StartDate' => '12/12/2010',
                    '_Name' => 'Nicky McDonald'
                }, 'Salesman' );
    $employee2 = bless( {
                    '_BasePay' => 55000,
                    '_StartDate' => '08/12/2013',
                    '_Courses' => [
                                    'Basic Math',
                                    'Algebra',
                                    'Calculus'
                                  ],
                    '_Name' => 'Charles Lee'
                }, 'Teacher' );
    Rick Gonzales is leaving the firm.
    Nicky McDonald is leaving the firm.
        1 teachers were created.
```

EXPLANATION

1 The *Salesman* class is loaded into memory.
2 The *Teacher* class is also loaded into memory.
3 A new *Salesman* object is created with a call to the new constructor. The properties are sent as a hash. In this way the properties can be sent in any order, because both key and value are sent.
4 The *Salesman's* instance/access method, *calculate_pay*, is called and returns the object's pay.
5 Another *Salesman* object is created.
6 Pay for the second *Salesman* object is calculated and returned.
7 A new *Teacher* object is created. Because the classname for a *Teacher* class is the first argument, the *new()* constructor for the *Teacher* is called (polymorphism in action).

8   The teacher's access method, *set_courses()*, is called. Its arguments are the object reference, implicitly sent by Perl, and a reference to an array of courses. These courses will be added as another attribute for the *Teacher*. In the next lines, the values are fetched using the base class methods (inherited) and the *Teacher's* method.

9   The data for two employees, the first salesman and teacher, are displayed by *Data::Dumper*. You can see that each employee was blessed into his respective class.

14.4.4   Multiple Inheritance and Roles with Moose

When a class inherits methods from more than one base, or parent, class, it is called **multiple inheritance**. In Perl, multiple inheritance is accomplished by adding more than one class to the *@ISA* array.

```
package  Child;
our @ISA = qw (Mother Father Teacher);
```

The search is depth-first, meaning that Perl will search for classes in *Mother* and the hierarchy of classes it descends from, then *Father* and the hierarchy of classes it descends from, and finally *Teacher* and all its ancestors. Just as in real life, the hierarchy can get confusing when there are multiple parents on the family tree.

Roles are an alternative to multiple inheritance. Similar to *Java* interfaces, or Smalltalk traits, a role defines a set of methods or attributes for a class that must be implemented by the class and can be shared by other classes. A role itself is not a class. From the Moose manual on describing roles:

A role is *composed* into a class. In practical terms, this means that all of the methods, method modifiers, and attributes defined in a role are added directly to (we sometimes say "flattened into") the class that consumes the role. These attributes and methods then appear as if they were defined in the class itself. A subclass of the consuming class will inherit all of these methods and attributes.

For example, if a *Guard* class and a *Researcher* class are extended from the *Employee* class we created earlier, and these two classes require a method to get a security clearance, you could use multiple inheritance and inherit from both the *Employee* and a *Clearance* class. But inheritance is an "is a" relationship where the derived class is a specialization of the parent class. You can say a *Guard* "is a" *Employee*, but he is not a *Clearance*. It's more that a *Guard* requires a clearance. Not every employee needs a clearance, but some do. Our *Salesman* didn't need one. Creating a role would better satisfy this requirement for those classes that need it. A role allows one class to consist of or consume a role to make it complete. For example, a *Guard* and a *Salesman* inherit from the *Employee* class all those basic requirements of an employee, but the *Guard* class isn't complete until it gets a *Clearance* while the *Salesman* doesn't need one. We can create a role that does the job. Roles are a "does a" relationship, rather than an "is a" relationship.

Since Perl does not implement a built-in way to create roles, there are a number of modules in the Perl library that support them. The most popular is the Moose module, which is an extension of the Perl 5 object system. Try *perldoc Moose* for complete documentation. Examples of using Moose are found in Appendix C, "Introduction to Moose (A Postmodern Object System for Perl 5)." There is also a subset of Moose called Moo that may be better for optimized rapid startup. (See *http://perlmaven.com/videos/oop-with-moo*.) Another watered-down version of Moose is the *Role::Tiny* module described in its documentation "like a nouvelle cuisine portion size slice of Moose."

In the following example, we demonstrate how to create and use a role with *Moose::Role*. In this example, we define a package called *Radius*. The class is a *Shape::Circle*. The *Circle* class will have a *color* property and a *calculate_area* method. In order to get the area of a circle, it must have a radius. If we provide a *setRadius* method in the *Circle*, and then if we want to create a sphere or a cone object, we would still be required to set the radius for those objects. If we put it in an inheritance tree, we could say a *Circle* is a *Shape*, and a *Rectangle* is a *Shape*, but only the *Circle* requires a radius. So with role composition, any object that requires a radius can share the *Radius* role to define the *setRadius* and *getRadius* methods or simply ensure a *setRadius* method is implemented in the module. If it is not, Perl will throw an exception. Using the *Moose::Role* module, we create a role like an ordinary module in a *.pm* file with a package declaration and then assign the attributes and methods that the using module will "consume." Moose roles are not classes and cannot be instantiated. They are simply roles.

EXAMPLE 14.24

```perl
1  package Radius;

2  use Moose::Role;    # Automatically turns on strict and warnings

3  has 'radius' => (   # Attributes and accessors
       is => 'rw',
       isa => 'Int',
       required => 1,
   )
   1;


4  package Shape::Circle;
   use Math::Trig;
5  use Moose;
   with 'Radius';    # Radius is a Role

6  has 'color'=>(   # Define
       is => 'rw',
       isa => 'Str',
       default => 'blue'
   );
```

EXAMPLE 14.24 (CONTINUED)

```
7   sub calculate_area{  # Define method for Circle uses radius
        my $self = shift;
        my $area=$self->{'radius'} ** 2 * pi;
        return $area;
    }

    package main;
    use Data::Dumper;

8   my $c1=Shape::Circle->new('radius' => 6);  # Required argument
9   print Dumper $c1;  # See the new Circle object
10  $c1->radius(3);     # radius is a setter
11  print "The radius is ", $c1->radius;  # radius is a getter
12  printf "The area is %.2f\n ",  $c1->calculate_area;
13  print Dumper $c1;

(Output)
9   $VAR1 = bless( {
                    'color' => 'blue',
                    'radius' => 6
                  }, 'Shape::Circle' );
11  The radius is 3
12  The area is 28.27
13  $VAR1 = bless( {
                    'color' => 'blue',
                    'radius' => 3
                  }, 'Shape::Circle' );
```

EXPLANATION

1   *Radius.pm* serves as a Moose role. It can be used, or "consumed," by any class that requires a radius.

2   *Moose::Role* is an extension of the Moose module. (You may have to download Moose if you are using a version of Perl prior to 5.16.)

3   The *Role* has an attribute called *'radius'* that takes an integer for its value, is readable and writeable (*rw*), and requires that a value for the radius be provided as an argument to the constructor of the "consuming" class. When a class "consumes" a role, it means that all the methods and attributes defined here in this role, are added directly to that class as though the class itself defined them. Moose automatically creates a constructor and setter and getter accessor methods (called *'radius'*) for the consuming class.

4   The *Shape::Circle* class is declared.

5   The *Shape::Circle* class will "consume" the *Radius* role. The *with* function is used to import or compose the role into the current class. Now this class will have the radius attribute that was defined in the *Radius* role.

6   The *Circle* defines a *color* attribute. The *color* is a read/write (*rw*), a string (*Str*) with a default value of *'blue'*.

EXPLANATION (CONTINUED)

7   The *calculate_area* method uses the *radius* attribute (consumed from the role) and the *pi* function from *Math::Trig* to calculate the area of a circle.

8   Moose provides a *new* constructor that creates a blessed object. The user calls *new* with the value for the radius as its argument. This was required by the role when defining the *'radius'* attribute on line 3: *required=>1;*.

9   The the *new* object and its attibutes are displayed by *Dumper*.

10   The radius value is reset to 3. Moose automatically created a setter called *'radius'* when the role was defined.

11   Moose provided a getter method called *'radius'*. This time we use it to get the value of the radius.

12   The *calculate_area* method is called and returns the area of the circle, *$c1;*.

13   *Dumper* displays the *Shape::Circle* object.

14.4.5 Overriding a Parent Method and the *SUPER* Pseudo Class

There are times when two classes may have a method with the same name. If a derived class has a method with the same name as the base class, its method will take precedence over the base method. To override the method in the derived class so you can access the method in the base class, the name of the method must be fully qualified with the class name and two colons. The pseudo class called *SUPER* can also be used by a subclass to call a method in the parent class; for example, *$self->SUPER::setName* would call the method *setName* in the parent class of the current module, and override the *setName* method in the current class. This allows the subclass to wrap or specialize an existing method with its parent method or completely override its own method with the parent's method. (You can also download the *SUPER* module from cpan to control dispatching methods to a superclass.)[8]

EXAMPLE 14.25

```
1    package Employee;   # Base class
     use strict;
     use warnings;
     sub new {           # Employee's constructor is defined
        my $class = shift;
        my %params = @_;
        my $self = { Name=>$params{"Name"},
                     Salary=>$params{"Salary"},
                   };
        bless ($self, $class);
     }
```

---

8. *SUPER* isn't a method. It's a virtual package, documented in *perlobj* under the "Method Invocation" section. It bases itself on the current package, not the package of the object you call it with.

EXAMPLE 14.25 (CONTINUED)

```perl
2  sub display {         # Instance method
      my $self = shift;
      foreach my $key ( @_ ){
3        print "$key: $self->{$key}\n";
      }
4     print "The class using this display method is ", ref($self),"\n";
   }
   1;
   -------------------------------------------------------------------
5  package Salesman;  # Derived class
   use strict;
   use warnings;
6  use base qw(Employee);
7  sub new {              # Constructor in derived Salesman class
      my $class = shift;
      my (%params) = @_;
8     my $self = $class->SUPER::new(%params);   # Call constructor
                                                # in base class
      $self->{Commission} = $params{Commission};
   }
   sub set_salary {
      my $self = shift;
      $self->{Salary}=$self->{Salary} + $self->{Commission};
   }
9  sub display{
      my $self = shift;
      my @args = @_;
      print "Stats for the Salesman\n";
      print "-" x 25, "\n";
10    $self->SUPER::display(@args);  # SUPER references the parent class
   }
   1;
      ----------------------------------------
   # User or Driver Program
11 use Salesman;
   use strict;
   use warnings;
12 my $emp = new Salesman ( "Name", "Tom Savage",
                            "Salary", 50000,   # Call to constructor
                            "Commission", 1500,
                          );
   $emp->set_Salary;  # Call to the access method
13 $emp->display( "Name" , "Salary", "Commission");
                      # Call Salesman's display method

(Output)
9  Stats for the Salesman
   ------------------------
   Name: Tom Savage
   Salary: 51500
   The class using this display method is Salesman
```

EXPLANATION

1   The class *Employee* is declared. It contains a constructor method called *new* and an instance method called *display*.
2   The *display* access method is defined for the *Employee* class.
3   The attributes for the employee are displayed.
4   The *ref* function returns the name of the class of a blessed object.
5   The *Salesman* class is declared.
6   It will inherit from the *Employee* base class. It is a derived class.
7   This is the *Saleman's* constructor.
8   The *SUPER* pseudo class is used to call *new* in the *Employee* class. It sends *Salesman* to the *Employee* class where it will be assigned initial properties and blessed and returned as a new *Salesman*.
9   This is the *display* method for the *Salesman* class.
10   By qualifying the name of the method to be of class *SUPER*, this *display* method will invoke the *display* method in the parent class, *Employee*.
11   This is the driver program. It uses the *Salesman* module.
12   A new *Salesman* object is created, using the pseudo *SUPER* class.
13   The *display* method is called. Since there is a *display* subroutine in the *Salesman* class, it is the one that will be called.

14.5 Plain Old Documentation— Documenting a Module

One of the most important phases in creating a useful class is providing the user with good documentation describing how a module should be used. This is called the **public user interface**. Whether a module is an object-oriented class or a procedural module, there must be some published user interface—the written documentation—available describing how the programmer (client) should use a class (for example, what arguments will be passed to a method). The publicly defined interface should not change, even if something in the class is changed.

Perl 5 introduced *pod* commands as a way to document modules. This is done by interspersing the program with *pod* (Plain Old Documentation) instructions, similar to embedding HTML or *nroff* instructions within the text of a file. Then the program is run through a Perl filtering program, which translates the commands into manual pages in a number of different formats. Wikipedia has excellent documentation on how to use *pod*.[9]

---

9. See *http://en.wikipedia.org/wiki/Plain_Old_Documentation#Example*.

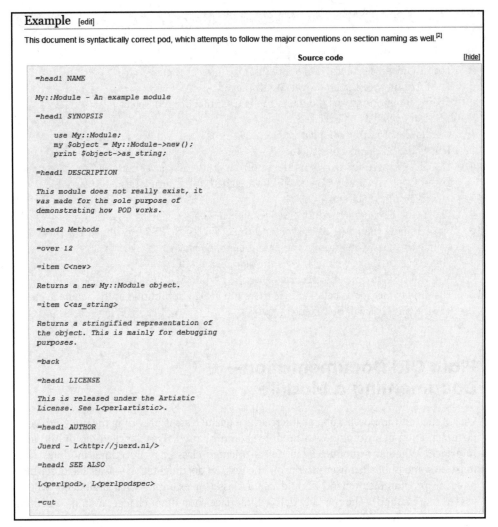

Figure 14.6 The example *pod* at Wikipedia.org.

14.5.1 *pod* Files

If you look in the standard Perl library, you will find that the modules contain documentation explaining what the module is supposed to do and how to use it. (At the command line, type *perldoc perlpod*.) The documentation is either embedded within the program or placed at the end of the program right after the special literal _ _*END*_ _. This documentation is called *pod*, short for Plain Old Documentation. A *pod* file is just an ASCII, utf-8, Unicode text file embedded with special commands that can be translated by one of Perl's special interpreters, *pod2html*, *pod2latex*, *pod2text*, or *pod2man*. The purpose is to create formatted documents that can be represented in a number of ways. The UNIX *man* pages are an example of documentation that has been formatted with *nroff* instructions. It is now easy to embed a set of *pod* formatting instructions in your scripts to provide documentation in any of the four formats: text, HTML, LaTeX, or *nroff*.

The first line of the *pod* documentation starts with an equal sign (=). Each *pod* instruction starting with an equal sign is a formatting instruction for the *pod* translator. **Each formatting instruction must be terminated with a blank line.**

EXAMPLE 14.26

```
(The standard Perl library, under the subdirectory Math.)

=head1 NAME

Math::BigFloat - Arbitrary length float math package

=head1 SYNOPSIS

  use Math::BigFloat;
  $f = Math::BigFloat->new($string);

  $f->fadd(NSTR) return NSTR            addition
  $f->fsub(NSTR) return NSTR            subtraction
  $f->fmul(NSTR) return NSTR            multiplication
  $f->fdiv(NSTR[,SCALE]) returns NSTR   division to SCALE places
  $f->fneg() return NSTR                negation
  $f->fabs() return NSTR                absolute value
  $f->fcmp(NSTR) return CODE            compare undef,<0,=0,>0
  $f->fround(SCALE) return NSTR         round to SCALE digits
  $f->ffround(SCALE) return NSTR        round at SCALEth place
  $f->fnorm() return (NSTR)             normalize
  $f->fsqrt([SCALE]) return NSTR        sqrt to SCALE places

(Here is the documentation found at the end of the BigFloat.pm module in
=head1 DESCRIPTION

All basic math operations are overloaded if you declare your big
floats as

    $float = new Math::BigFloat "2.12312312312312312312312312312312312312";

=over 2

=item number format

canonical strings have the form /[+-]\d+E[+-]\d+/ . Input values can
have inbedded whitespace.
```

EXAMPLE 14.26 (CONTINUED)

```
=item Error returns 'NaN'

An input parameter was "Not a Number" or divide by zero or sqrt of
negative number.

=item Division is computed to

C<max($div_scale,length(dividend)+length(divisor))> digits by default.
Also used for default sqrt scale.

=back

=head1 BUGS

The current version of this module is a preliminary version of the
real thing that is currently (as of perl5.002) under development.

=head1 AUTHOR

Mark Biggar

=cut
```

EXPLANATION

The preceding text is a *pod* file. It consists of lines starting with an equal sign and a *pod* command, then a blank line, and text. Perl provides a special translator program that reads the *pod* file and translates it into a readable file in plain text, HTML format, *nroff* text, or LaTeX. The next section describes how to use the *pod* filter programs to make the translation for you.

14.5.2   *pod* Commands

It's easy to embed *pod* instructions in a text file. Commands are placed at the beginning of a line, starting with =*pod* (or any other *pod* command) and ending with =*cut*. Everything after the first =*pod* instruction to the =*cut* instruction will be ignored by the compiler, just as comments are ignored. The nice thing about using the commands is that they allow you to create bold, italic, or plain text, to indent, to create headings, and more. Table 14.3 contains a list of instructions.

Checking Your pod Commands.   To check that you have correct *pod* instructions in your file, you can use Perl's *podchecker* command. First, to find the path to your modue, type at your prompt:

```
perldoc -l Module.pm
```

and then,

podchecker path/Module.pm

and hope that it displays the following:

path/Module.pm **pod syntax OK.**

Table 14.3 *pod* Commands

Paragraph Commands	*What They Do*
=pod	Marks the start of *pod*, but an equal sign, followed by any *pod* instruction starts the documentation.
=cut	Marks the end of *pod*.
=head1 heading	Creates a level1 heading.
=head2 heading	Creates a level2 heading.
=item *	Starts a bulleted list.
=over N	Moves over *N* number of spaces, usually set to *4*.
=back	Returns indent back to default, no indent.
Formatting Commands	*What They Do*
I<text>	Creates italic text.
B<text>	Creates bold text.
S<text>	Contains text nonbreaking spaces.
C<code>	Contains typed text, literal source code.
L<name>	Creates a link (cross reference) to name.
F<file>	Used for listing filenames.
X<index>	An index entry.
Z<>	A zero-width character.
Filter-Specific Commands	*What They Do*

=for	For HTML-specific commands; e.g., *=for html*
	    <IMG SRC=file.gif>
	    <B>Figure a.>/B>>

	For text-specific commands; e.g., *=for text*

	For *manpage*-specific commands; e.g., *=for man*
	    .ce 3
	    <center next three lines>

14.5.3 How to Use the *pod* Interpreters

The *pod* interpreters come with the Perl distribution and are located in the *bin* directory under the main Perl directory; for example, in */usr/bin/perl5/bin*.

The four interpreters are

- *pod2html* (translate to HTML)
- *pod2text* (translate to plain text)
- *pod2man* (translate to *nroff*, like UNIX *man* pages)
- *pod2latex* (translate to LaTeX)

The easiest way to use the interpreters is to copy the one you want into your own directory. For example:

```
$ cp /usr/bin/perl5/bin/pod2text
```

You may also copy the library routine into your directory:

```
$ cp /usr/bin/perl5/lib/BigFloat.pm
```

Now when you list the contents of the directory, you should have both the *pod* interpreter and the library module.

```
$ ls
BigFloat.pm
pod2text
```

14.5.4 Translating *pod* Documentation into Text

The easiest way to translate the *pod* commands to text for your terminal screen is to use the *perldoc* command that comes with the Perl distribution. It may not be in your search path, but it is usually found in the *bin* directory under *perl*. The following command would display all the documentation for the *BigFloat.pm* module:

```
perldoc Math::BigFloat
```

Another way to translate *pod* directives to text is to let the *pod* interpreter filter through the module and create an output file to save the translated text. If you don't redirect the output to a file, it will simply go to the screen.

```
$ pod2text BigFloat.pm > BigFloat.Text
$ cat BigFloat.Text   (The output file after pod commands have been
                       translated into text.)

NAME
    Math::BigFloat - Arbitrary length float math package

SYNOPSIS
    use Math::BigFloat;
    $f = Math::BigFloat->new($string);
```

```
$f->fadd(NSTR) return NSTR                    addition
$f->fsub(NSTR) return NSTR                    subtraction
$f->fmul(NSTR) return NSTR                    multiplication
$f->fdiv(NSTR[,SCALE])     returns NSTR       division to SCALE places
$f->fneg() return NSTR                        negation
$f->fabs() return NSTR                        absolute value
$f->fcmp(NSTR) return CODE                    compare undef,<0,=0,>0
$f->fround(SCALE) return NSTR                 round to SCALE digits
$f->ffround(SCALE) return NSTR                round at SCALEth place
$f->fnorm() return (NSTR)                     normalize
$f->fsqrt([SCALE]) return NSTR                sqrt to SCALE places
```

DESCRIPTION
    All basic math operations are overloaded if you declare your big
    floats as

```
$float=newMath::BigFloat"2.123123123123123123123123123123123";
```

    number format
    canonical strings have the form /[+-]\d+E[+-]\d+/ . Input
    values can have inbedded whitespace.

Error returns 'NaN'
    An input parameter was "Not a Number" or divide by zero or
    sqrt of negative number.

Division is computed to
    `max($div_scale,length(dividend)+length(divisor))' digits by
    default. Also used for default sqrt scale.

BUGS
    The current version of this module is a preliminary version of
    the real thing that is currently (as of perl5.002) under
    development.

AUTHOR
    Mark Biggar

14.5.5   Translating *pod* Documentation into HTML

To create an HTML document, use the *pod2html* command:

```
$ pod2html BigFloat.pm BigFloat.pm.html
```

The *pod2html* translator will create a file called *BigFloat.pm.html.* Now open your browser
window click on File > Open or <CTRL>+O and get *BigFloat.pm.html* as file protocol in the
URL location box; for example, *<file:///yourdirectory path/BigFloat.pm.html>.*[10]

---

10. If you receive some obscure diagnostic messages, it may be that the documentation for the *.pm* file contains
    links to some other page that cannot be resolved by the *pod* filter.

Figure 14.7   Plain Old Documentation Viewed in a Browser.

14.6 Using Objects from the Perl Library

In Chapter 13, "Modularize It, Package It, and Send It to the Library!" we first looked into the standard Perl library that was provided with this distribution, Perl 5.16. In that library were a number of Perl modules and subdirectories or folders containing additional modules and subdirectories. The examples covered in Chapter 13 dealt with modules that did not require knowledge about Perl's use of objects. Those files utilized standard subroutines, not methods. Now that you know how objects and methods are used in Perl, the following examples will demonstrate how to use those modules that require the OOP methodology.

14.6.1   An Object-Oriented Module from the Standard Perl Library

The following module, *BigFloat*, is an object-oriented module that allows the use of floating-point numbers of arbitrary length. Number strings have the form */[+-]\d*\.?\d*E[+-]\d+/*. When NaN is returned, it means that a non-number was entered as input, that perhaps you tried to divide by zero, or that you tried to take the square root of a negative number. *BigFloat* uses the *overload* module, which allows you to define Perl's built-in operators to methods that will cause the operators to behave in a new way. The operator is the key and the method assigned is the value as you can see in the following example. (See *overload.pm* in the standard Perl library.)

EXAMPLE 14.27

```
(The File: BigFloat.pm)

1   package Math::BigFloat;
2   use Math::BigInt;

    use Exporter;  # Just for use to be happy
    @ISA = (Exporter);
3   use overload
4   '+'   => sub {new Math::BigFloat &fadd},
    '-'   => sub {new Math::BigFloat
            $_[2]? fsub($_[1],${$_[0]}) : fsub(${$_[0]},$_[1])},
    '<=>' => sub {new Math::BigFloat
            $_[2]? fcmp($_[1],${$_[0]}) : fcmp(${$_[0]},$_[1])},
    'cmp' => sub {new Math::BigFloat
            $_[2]? ($_[1] cmp ${$_[0]}) : (${$_[0]} cmp $_[1])},
    '*'   => sub {new Math::BigFloat &fmul},
    '/'   => sub {new Math::BigFloat
            $_[2]? scalar fdiv($_[1],${$_[0]}) :
                scalar fdiv(${$_[0]},$_[1])},
    'neg' => sub {new Math::BigFloat &fneg},
    'abs' => sub {new Math::BigFloat &fabs},
    qw(
        ""   stringify
        0+   numify)    # Order of arguments unsignificant
        ;

5   sub new {
        my ($class) = shift;
        my ($foo) = fnorm(shift);
6       panic("Not a number initialized to Math::BigFloat")
            if $foo eq "NaN";
7       bless \$foo, $class;
    }

    < Methods continue here. Module was too long to put here>
```

EXAMPLE 14.27 (CONTINUED)

```
     # Addition
8    sub fadd {  #(fnum_str, fnum_str) return fnum_str
        local($x,$y) = (fnorm($_[$[]),fnorm($_[$[+1]));
        if ($x eq 'NaN' || $y eq 'NaN') {
          NaN';
        } else {
          local($xm,$xe) = split('E',$x);
          local($ym,$ye) = split('E',$y);
          ($xm,$x e,$ym,$ye) = ($ym,$ye,$xm,$xe) if ($xe < $ye);
          &norm(Math::BigInt::badd($ym,$xm.('0' x ($xe-$ye))),$ye);
        }
     }


     < Methods continue here>


     # divisionbb
     # args are dividend, divisor, scale (optional)
     # result has at most max(scale, length(dividend),
     # length(divisor)) digits
9    sub fdiv    #(fnum_str, fnum_str[,scale]) return fnum_str
     {
        local($x,$y,$scale) = (fnorm($_[$[]),
                               fnorm($_[$[+1]),$_[$[+2]);
        if ($x eq 'NaN' || $y eq 'NaN' || $y eq '+0E+0') {
          'NaN';
        } else {
          local($xm,$xe) = split('E',$x);
          local($ym,$ye) = split('E',$y);
          $scale = $div_scale if (!$scale);
          $scale = length($xm)-1 if (length($xm)-1 > $scale);
          $scale = length($ym)-1 if (length($ym)-1 > $scale);
          $scale = $scale + length($ym) - length($xm);
          &norm(&round(Math::BigInt::bdiv($xm.('0' x $scale),$ym),
                                          $ym),$xe-$ye-$scale);

        }
     }
```

EXPLANATION

1   The *BigFloat* class is declared. The file, *BigFloat.pm* resides in the *Math* subdirectory of the standard Perl library.

2   The *BigFloat* class also needs to use the *BigInt* module.

3   With the *overload* pragma you can change the meaning of the built-in Perl operators. For example, when in *BigFloat*, the + operator is a key and its value an anonymous subroutine that creates an object and calls the *fadd* subroutine.

4   The + operator is overloaded. See previous explanation.

5   This is *BigFloat's* constructor method for creating an object.

6   If the value is not a number, this panic message is printed.
7   The object is blessed into the class.
8   This is the subroutine that performs addition on the object.
9   This is the subroutine that performs division on the object.

14.6.2 Using a Module with Objects from the Standard Perl Library

EXAMPLE 14.28

```perl
1   use warnings;
2   use Math::BigFloat;  # BigFloat.pm is in the Math directory

3   my $number = "000.95671234e-21";
4   my $mathref = Math::BigFloat->new("$number");  # Create the object

5   print "\$mathref is in class ", ref($mathref), "\n";
                  # Where is the object

6   print $mathref->fnorm(), "\n";  # Use methods from the class

7   print "The sum of $mathref + 500 is: ", $mathref->fadd("500"), "\n";
8   print "Division using overloaded operator: ", $mathref / 200.5, "\n";
9   print "Division using fdiv method:", $mathref->fdiv("200.5"), "\n";

10  print "Enter a number ";
    chomp($numstr = <STDIN>);

11  if ( $mathref->fadd($numstr) eq "NaN" ){
        print "You didn't enter a number.\n"};
    }
    # Return value of NaN means the string is not a number,
    # or you divided by zero, or you took the square root
    # of a negative number.

(Output)
5   $mathref is in class Math::BigFloat
6   +95671234E-29
7   The sum of .00000000000000000000095671234 + 500 is:
    +5000000000000000000000000095671234E-29
8   Division using overloaded operator:
    .00000000000000000000004771632618453865336658354114713216957606
9   Division using fdiv method:
    +4771632618453865336658354114713216957606E-63
10  Enter a number hello
11  You didn't enter a number.
```

EXPLANATION

1   Turn on *warnings*.

2   The *use* function loads the module *BigFloat.pm* into the program. Since this module is in a subdirectory of the library called *Math*, that subdirectory is included by prepending its name to the module with two colons.

3   A large number (*e* notation) is assigned to *$number*.

4   Now the methods from the module are utilized. The *BigFloat* constructor is called. A reference to the object is returned and assigned to *$mathref*.

5   The *ref* function returns the name of the class.

6   The *fnorm* method returns the "normal" value of *$number* in signed scientific notation. Leading zeros are stripped off.

7   The *fadd* method adds *500* to the number.

8   In this example, an overloaded operator is used. The / operator is assigned a class method, *fdiv*, to perform the division. See code from *BigFloat.pm* shown in Example 14.26.

9   This time the *fdiv* method is called directly without using overloading to perform the division. The output is slightly different.

10   The user is asked to enter a number.

11   If *NaN* (not a number) is returned from the *fadd* method, the message is printed. This is a way you could check that user input is a valid numeric value.

14.7 What You Should Know

1. What does OOP mean?

2. What is the difference between a package and a class?

3. What is a method?

4. What is the first parameter received by a class method?

5. What function creates an object?

6. What are properties?

7. What is an instance method?

8. Does Perl have a *private* keyword?

9. How do you name a class? Where do you put a class?

10. What is meant by class method invocation?

11. What is polymorphism?

12. What is the *@ISA* array used for?

13. What is a derived class?

14. What is the *SUPER* class?

15. What is a closure?

16. What is a role?

17. What is Moose?

18. How do you document a class?

19. What is a *pod* filter?

20. How is a *pod* directive used?

14.8 What's Next?

Chapter 15, "Perl Connects with MySQL," focuses on using Perl with the MySQL relational database management system, a very popular open-source, fully functional, relational database. You will learn how to issue commands at the MySQL client and then use the DBI module to issue the same commands from a Perl script.

EXERCISE 14
What's the Object of This Lesson?

Part 1—Intro to Objects

1. Write a module called *Rightnow.pm* that contains three methods:

   a. A constructor called *new*.

   b. A method called *set_time* to set the time. Use the *localtime* function.

   c. A method called *print_time* to print the time. This method will take an argument to determine whether the time is printed in military or standard time; for example, *print_time("Military");*

   d. In another Perl script, use the *Rightnow* module to create a *Rightnow* object, and call the *print_time* method to produce output as follows:

   ```
   Time now: 2:48:20 PM

   Time now: 14:48:20
   ```

Part 2—More Objects

1. In a class called *Student*, create an object. The attributes for the *Student* object will be sent as arguments to the constructor method. The *Student* object will have three attributes: the *name* of the student, the student's *major*, and a list of *courses* he is taking. Create an instance method called *show_student* that will display a *Student* object. The user of the module will create two *Student* objects and display each.

2. Add three new attributes to the *Student* object; for example, the student's address, his ID number, his start date, his tuition, like so:

   Address: 140 Kennedy Drive,

   Luxembourg City, Luxembourg

   ID: 123A

   StartDate: 01/10/07

   Tuition: 5400.55

   How will you manage this? If the user has so much information to pass to the constructor, it may be a good time to create an access method called *set_student*. Finally, create three new *Student* objects.

3. Create two new access methods that take arguments. One is called *add_courses* and the other is called *drop_courses*. The user interface will allow the user to add or drop any number of courses by sending a list of parameters to the methods; for example:

   $obj>add_courses(["C++", "Java"]);

4. You will use a "class" function to keep track of the number of new students. Each time you add a student, update the counter. Before exiting the program, print the number of new students. Use the *END* block.

5. From now on, send the data for each student to a file. It should contain a line that looks like this:

   ```
   John Doe:14 Main St:3456IX:Math:Trigonometry,Calculus,French:
   01/01/06:4500
   ```

6. Create another file that keeps track of the number of students. Each time you start your script, read the number from the file. When you add a new student, tell him *Welcome, John D*.

Part 3—Create an Object-Oriented Module

1. Make *Checking.pm* object oriented. The object will be "the balance" and the subroutines will be "methods." The constructor will contain at least two attributes: the *balance* and the *account number*. The account number will be passed to the constructor as an argument. The balance will be retrieved from the register, initially set to 0. When you create the register file, append the account number to the filename. Include the account number, balance, and date in the register file. Use the *Checking* module in the ATM user script you created earlier.

2. Can you make more than one instance of the *Checking* object and keep track of the balance for each account?

Part 4—Using Inheritance

1. Create a *Pet* class with a constructor and one access method. The constructor provides attributes for a generic pet, such as:

   owner

   name

   gender

   a. The access method is called *eat()*. It takes one argument: the type of food a specific pet eats. For example, the dog eats Alpo. The dog will not have an *eat()* method and will inherit from this class.

   b. Create two classes that will inherit from the *Pet* class; for example, a *Dog* and a *Cat* class. They will use the *Pet's* constructor and add new attributes of their own. They will have a *speak()* method, but not an *eat()* method.

2. Now we will create a base class called *Bank.pm* and two modules that use it: *Checking* and *Savings.*

   a. The *Bank.pm* parent class may or may not have a constructor but will contain the *deposit()*, *withdraw()*, and *get_balance()* methods from the *Checking.pm* module.

   b. Remove *deposit()* and *withdraw()* from *Checking.pm*. The program that uses *Checking.pm* will inherit these methods from *Bank.pm* via @ISA.

   c. Create another module called *Savings.pm*.

   d. Both *Checking.pm* and *Savings.pm* will use the *Bank* module and inherit its methods. Each will have its own constructor and attributes. One attribute is the status of the account. It can be "active" or "closed." The *Savings* account accrues compounded daily interest 1% and must start with a minimum balance of $200. The *Checking* account has overdraft protection and charges $35 for each bounced check. It will not allow an overdraft of over $300. It can be opened with a starting balance of $25.

   e. The *Checking.pm* and *Savings.pm* modules will each have its own account numbers and registers.

f. The ATM script will use both modules. The user script will have a main menu allowing the user to select either of the two accounts. After getting a new account object, the user can select from the types of transactions (submenu in your original *Checking.pm* module) for that account and continue transactions until he is ready to quit. When he exits, his account register balance will be updated and he will be asked if he wants to return to the main menu. If he says "yes," he will see the main menu again, and if he says "no," the program will exit, giving him his balance. You will have to uniquely name the register for each account so you can differentiate between savings and checking accounts.

Example: *perl user.pl* (where user input is in bold)

Welcome!

Select an account type:

 1) Checking

 2) Savings

 1

Select a function:

 1) deposit

 2) withdraw

 3) get balance

 4) exit

 1

How much do you want to deposit? 5.00

Select a function:

 1) deposit

 2) withdraw

 3) get balance

 4) exit

 3

Your balance is $30.00

Select a function:

 1) deposit

 2) withdraw

 3) get balance

 4) exit

 2

How much do you want to withdraw? 5.00

Select a function:

1) deposit

2) withdraw

3) get balance

4) exit

3

Your balance is $25.00

Select a function:

1) deposit

2) withdraw

3) get balance

4) exit

4

Return to the main menu? **Y**

Welcome!

Select an account type:

1) Checking

2) Savings

2

Select a function:

1) deposit

2) withdraw

3) get balance

4) exit

3

Your balance is $100.00

Select a function:

1) deposit

2) withdraw

3) get balance

4) exit

1

How much do you want to deposit? **25**

Select a function:

 1) deposit

 2) withdraw

 3) get balance

 4) exit

4

Your balance is 125.00.

Part 5

1. Go to the *pod* directory in the standard Perl library. Look for *perlpod.html*. The file contains Larry Wall's user interface for using *pod* commands to document your Perl programs.

2. Go to your browser and in the Location box, type:

   ```
   file:/<directory-to -your-library-file>/Pod/pod.html
   ```

   Now you have the instructions for creating *pod* documentation.

3. Create a published interface for your *Checking.pm* module. Embed *pod* commands in your *Checking.pm* script explaining how the module should be used. Follow the guidelines of the modules in the library; for example, there should be a NAME, SYNOPSIS, DESCRIPTION, AUTHOR, and so forth. Run the *pod* file through the *pod2html* filter and display the documentation in your browser. Use the *perldoc* command to print your documentation on the terminal screen.

chapter

15

Perl Connects
with MySQL

By the time you finish this chapter, you should be able to read and write the following Perl code:

```
use DBI;
$dbh = DBI->connect('dbi:mysql:sample_db','root','letmein') or die
    "Connection Error: $DBI->errstr\n";
$sql = "select * from teams";
$sth = $dbh->prepare($sql);
$sth->execute  or die "SQL Error: $sth->errstr\n";
while (@row = $sth->fetchrow_array) {
    print "@row\n";
}
$sth->finish;
$dbh->disconnect;
```

15.1 Introduction

The user has filled out a form and submitted it with a list of items he wants to purchase. Information for that user is stored in a database in a table called *customers*. You want to open the database and add the new order directly from your Perl program. And you may want to retrieve all the previous orders and product information for that customer and format the data for a Web page, or use it in an email message, or send it to a spreadsheet, all from your Perl program. This is all possible with Perl and the Perl DBI module, an object-oriented database interface that allows you to connect to any relational database and use Perl methods to perform all the necessary operations for opening and closing the database, as well as send SQL queries to create tables, update and delete them, retrieve and modify records, manage transactions, and display results.

This chapter focuses on using Perl with the MySQL relational database management system, a very popular open-source, fully functional, relational database.[1] You will learn how to issue commands at the MySQL client and then use the DBI module to issue the same commands from a Perl script. Finally, if you are interested in having your Perl DBI script talk to a Web server, you can refer to Appendix E, "Dancing with Perl," where we will tie all of this together by creating a dynamic Web page using both the DBI module with CGI and the new and popular module called Dancer, a fun and easy Web application framework written in Perl.

The subject of databases is huge. This chapter is not an attempt to teach you how to correctly design the structure of a database or the best practices for organizing the data. That would take another book or more, so if you are a complete novice, and have never been exposed to databases and how they work, you might find *Databases Demystified* by Andy Oppel an excellent tutorial for getting started.[2] This chapter will cover the basic concepts and terminology you will need in order to work with the Perl DBI and MySQL.

15.2 What Is a Relational Database?

Until now, we have been storing data in ordinary text files with Perl by creating user-defined filehandles. But text files are limited when you need to efficiently store and manage large amounts of data; for example, to maintain a business such as a hospital, research lab, bank, college, or Web site. A relational database system follows certain standards and has a number of features for storing large collections of data. The data is managed so that retrieving, updating, inserting, and deleting the data is relatively easy and takes the least amount of time. The database management system must store the data so that it maintains its integrity; the data must stay accurate and be protected from being accessed by unauthorized users.

Introduced in the 1970s, the relational model made data manipulation easier and faster for the end users and easier to maintain by the administrator. At the core of this model is the concept of a relation, visually represented as a table in which all data is stored. The data is represented by different types, such as a string, number, date, and so on. Each table is made up of records consisting of horizontal rows and vertical columns or fields, like a two-dimensional array. Tables in the database relate to each other; for example, if you have a database called *school*, it might consist of tables called *student*, *teacher*, *course*, and so forth. The student takes a course from a teacher who teaches one or many courses. The data can be retrieved and manipulated for just the student, teacher, or course, but also joined together based on some common key field. The Structured Query Language (SQL) is used to "talk to" relational databases, making it easy to retrieve, insert, update, and delete data from the tables in the database.

---

1. Although still open source, MySQL was acquired by Oracle in 2010.
2. Oppel, Andrew J., *Databases Demystified*, McGraw-Hill/Osbourne, Emeryville, CA, 2004.

Due to the popularity of relational databases, known as relational database management systems (RDBMS), a number of relational databases are used today, among them Oracle, Sybase, PostgreSQL Informix, SQL server, and MySQL.

15.2.1 Client/Server Databases

Relational databases use a client/server model. Today, MySQL is one of the most popular client/server database systems in the open-source community.

Figure 15.1 shows the model for a client/server architecture. The user goes to the command line and starts the MySQL client to issue MySQL commands. The client makes a request to the MySQL server, which in turn sends a query to the database. The database sends the results of the query back to the server, and the results are displayed in the client's window.

In the second scenario, rather than using the command-line client, a Perl script makes a connection to the database server through a database interface that acts as an interpreter. If a Perl script contains an instruction to connect to a database, in this case MySQL, then once the connection is made and a database selected, the Perl program has access to the database through the MySQL server. The MySQL server receives requests, called **queries**, from the Perl program and sends back information collected from the database.

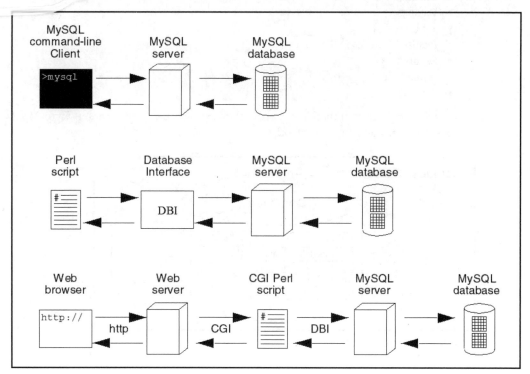

Figure 15.1 The client/server model.

In the third example in the figure, the user requests a page from the browser (the client); an HTTP connection is made to the Web server (Apache, ISS, Nginx, Lighttpd), where the request is received and handled. If the action is to start up a Perl program, the Web server may use the Common Gateway Interface (CGI) to start up the Perl interpreter, and Perl starts processing the information that was sent from the HTTP server to format and send it back to the Web server; or if a request to the database server is made, then the steps to connect, query, and get results from the database are carried out.

Figure 15.1 shows the client/server relationship between the MySQL client and the MySQL server, and the client/server relationship between the Web browser, Web server, Perl program, and the MySQL database server. By the end of this chapter, you will be able to get information sent from a Web browser (client) to a Web server, and from the Web server to a Perl CGI program, which can connect to a database server to retrieve and store information from a MySQL database.

15.2.2 Components of a Relational Database

What makes up a database? The main components of a relational database management system are as follows:

- Database server
- Database
- Tables
- Fields
- Records
- Primary key
- Schema

We will discuss each of these concepts in the next sections of this chapter. Figure 15.2 illustrates their relationship to each other.

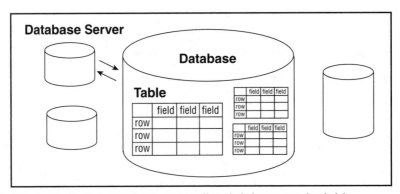

Figure 15.2 The database server, the database, and a table.

The Database Server.   The database server is the actual server process running the databases. It controls the storage of the data, grants access to users, updates and deletes records, and communicates with other servers. The database server is normally on a dedicated host computer, serving and managing multiple clients over a network, but can also be used as a stand-alone server on the local machine to serve a single client; for example, you may be the single client using MySQL on your local machine, often referred to as *localhost*, without any network connection at all. This is probably the best way to learn how to use MySQL.

If you are using MySQL, the server process is the *mysql* service on Windows or the *mysqld* process on Linux/UNIX operating systems. The database server typically follows the client/server model, where the front end is the client (a user sitting at his workstation making database requests and waiting for results), while the back end is the database server that grants access to users, stores and manipulates the data, performs backups, and even talks to other servers. The requests to the database server can also be made from a program that acts on behalf of a user making requests from a Web page or a program.

In this chapter, you will learn how to make requests from the MySQL command line first, and then to connect to the database server from a Perl program using Perl built-in functions to make requests to the MySQL database server, and finally how to make a request from a Web form and send the request to a Perl program and then onto MySQL.

The Database.   A database is a collection of related data elements, usually corresponding to a specific application. A company may have one database for all its HR needs, perhaps another for its sales staff, and a third for e-commerce applications, and so on. Figure 15.3 lists the databases installed on a particular version of MySQL. The databases are listed as *mysql*, *northwind*, *phpmyadmin*, and *test*.

Figure 15.3   MySQL databases.

Tables.   Each database consists of two-dimensional tables identified by unique names. In fact, a relational database stores all of its data in tables, and nothing more. All operations are performed on the table, which can then produce other tables.

One of the first decisions you will make when designing a database is what tables it will contain. A typical database for an organization might consist of tables for customers, orders, and products. All these tables are related to one another in some way. For example, customers have orders and orders have items. Although each table exists on its own, collectively the tables comprise a database. Figure 15.4 lists the tables in a database called *northwind*,[3] a fictional database provided by Microsoft to serve as a model for learning how to manipulate a database. (This database should be on the CD provided with this book.)

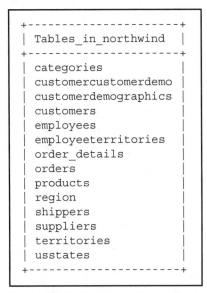

```
+-----------------------+
| Tables_in_northwind   |
+-----------------------+
| categories            |
| customercustomerdemo  |
| customerdemographics  |
| customers             |
| employees             |
| employeeterritories   |
| order_details         |
| orders                |
| products              |
| region                |
| shippers              |
| suppliers             |
| territories           |
| usstates              |
+-----------------------+
```

Figure 15.4 Tables in the *northwind* database.

Records and Fields.   A table has a name and consists of a set of **rows** and **columns**. It resembles a spreadsheet where each row, also called a **record**, consists of vertical columns, also called **fields**. All rows from the same table have the same set of columns. The *shippers* table from the *northwind* database has three columns and three rows (see Figure 15.5).

```
+--------------------------------------------------+
| ShipperID | CompanyName      | Phone             |
+--------------------------------------------------+
|         1 | Speedy Express   | (503) 555-9831    |
|         2 | United Package   | (503) 555-3199    |
|         3 | Federal Shipping | (503) 555-9931    |
+--------------------------------------------------+
```

Figure 15.5 The rows (records) and columns (fields) from the *shippers* table in the *northwind* database.

---

3. The Northwind Traders sample database typically comes as a free sample with Microsoft Access. It is also available at *http://www.geeksengine.com/article/export-access-to-mysql.html*.

There are two basic operations you can perform on a relational table. You can retrieve a subset of its columns and you can retrieve a subset of its rows. Figure 15.6 and Figure 15.7 are samples of the two operations.

```
mysql> select companyname from shippers;
+------------------+
| CompanyName      |
+------------------+
| Speedy Express   |
| United Package   |
| Federal Shipping |
+------------------+
```

Figure 15.6   Retrieving a subset of columns.

```
mysql> select x from shippers where companyname="Federal Shipping";
+------------------------------------------------------+
| ShipperID | CompanyName      | Phone                 |
+------------------------------------------------------+
|         3 | Federal Shipping | (503) 555-9931        |
+------------------------------------------------------+
```

Figure 15.7   Retrieving a subset of rows.

Remember that a relational database manipulates only tables, and the results of all operations are also tables, called **result sets**. The tables are sets, which are themselves sets of rows and columns. The database itself is a set of tables.

You can also perform a number of other operations between two tables, treating them as sets. For example, you can join information from two tables, make Cartesian products of the tables, get the intersection between two tables, add one table to another, and so on. Later, you'll see how to perform operations on tables using the SQL language.

Columns/Fields

Columns are an integral part of a database table. Columns are also known as fields, or **attributes**. Fields describe the data. Each field has a name. For example, the *shippers* table has fields named *ShipperID*, *CompanyName*, and *Phone*. The field also describes the type of data it contains. A data type can be a number, a character, a date, a time stamp, and so on. In Figure 15.8, the *ShipperID* is the name of a field, the data type is an integer, and the shipper's ID will not exceed 11 numbers. There are many data types and sometimes they are specific to a particular database system; for example, MySQL may have different data types available than Oracle. We will learn more about the MySQL data types in the next chapter.

```
+---------------------------------------------------------------------------+
| Field          | Type         | Null | Key | Default | Extra            |
+---------------------------------------------------------------------------+
| ShipperID      | int(11)      |      |PRI  | NULL    | auto_increment   |
| CompanyName    | varchar(40)  |      |     |         |                  |
| Phone          | varchar(24)  | YES  |     | NULL    |                  |
+---------------------------------------------------------------------------+
```

Figure 15.8   Each field has a name and a description of the data that can be stored there.

Rows/Records

A record is a row in the table. It could be a product in the product table, an employee record in the employee table, and so on. Each table in a database contains zero or more records. Figure 15.9 shows us that there are three records in the *shippers* table.

```
+-------------------------------------------------------------+
| ShipperID | CompanyName      | Phone            |
+-------------------------------------------------------------+
|         1 | Speedy Express   | (503) 555-9831   |
|         2 | United Package   | (503) 555-3199   |
|         3 | Federal Shipping | (503) 555-9931   |
+-------------------------------------------------------------+
3 rows in set (0.00 sec)
```

Figure 15.9   There are three records in the *shippers* table.

Primary Key and Indexes

A primary key is a unique identifier for each record. For example, every employee in the United States has a Social Security number, every driver has a driver's license, and every car has a license plate. These identifiers are unique. In the database world, the unique identifier is called a **primary key**. Although it is a good idea to have a primary key, not every table has one. The primary key is determined when the table is created and is more in keeping with a discussion on database design. In Figure 15.10, the *ShipperID* is the primary key for the *shippers* table in the *northwind* database. It is a unique ID that consists of a number that will automatically be incremented every time a new company (record) is added to the list of shippers.

```
+---------------------------------------------------------------------------+
| Field          | Type         | Null | Key | Default | Extra            |
+---------------------------------------------------------------------------+
| ShipperID      | int(11)      |      |PRI  | NULL    | auto_increment   |
| CompanyName    | varchar(40)  |      |     |         |                  |
| Phone          | varchar(24)  | YES  |     | NULL    |                  |
+---------------------------------------------------------------------------+
```

Figure 15.10   The *ShipperID* is the primary key in the *shippers* table.

When searching for a particular record in a table, MySQL must load all the records before it can execute the query. In addition to a primary key, one or more **indexes** are often used to enhance performance for finding rows in tables that are frequently accessed. Indexes are like the indexes in the back of a book that help you find a specific topic more quickly than searching through the entire book page by page. An index, like the index of a book, is a reference to a particular record in a table.

The Database Schema. Designing a very small database isn't difficult, but designing a database for a large Web-based application can be daunting. Database design is both an art and a science and requires an understanding of how the relational model is implemented, a topic beyond the scope of this book. When discussing the design of the database, you will encounter the term **database schema**, which refers to the structure of the database. It describes the design of the database similar to a template, or blueprint; it describes all the tables and how the data will be organized, but does not contain the actual data. Figure 15.11 describes the schema for the tables in the *northwind* database.

Figure 15.11 Database schema.

15.2.3 Talking to the Database with SQL

When Perl output is sent to the browser, the browser understands markup languages, such as HTML or XHTML, and these language tags are embedded in Perl's *print* statements. This output could be displayed as forms, images, stylized text, colors, tables, and so on. Likewise, in order to communicate with the MySQL server, your Perl scripts must speak a language the database will understand. That language is called SQL. **SQL** stands for **Structured Query Language**, the language of choice for most modern multiuser relational databases. It provides the syntax and language constructs needed to talk to relational databases in a standardized, cross-platform, structured way. Just as the English language has a variety of dialects (for example, British, American, Australian), there are many different versions of the SQL language. The version of SQL used by MySQL follows the ANSI (American National Standards Institute) standard, meaning that it must support the major keywords (such as *SELECT*, *UPDATE*, *DELETE*, *INSERT*, *WHERE*, and so on) as defined in the standard. As you can see by the names of these keywords, SQL is the language that makes it possible to manipulate the data in a database.

If you are not familiar with SQL, refer to Appendix B, "SQL Language Tutorial," for a complete guide on how to use the SQL language. There are also a number of very well-written tutorials available on the Internet (see *http://www.w3schools.com/sql/default.asp*, *http://sqlcourse.com/select.html*, or *http://www.1keydata.com/sql/sql.html*).

English-like Grammar.   When you create a SQL statement, it makes a request, or "queries" the database, in the form of a statement, similar to the structure of an English imperative sentence, such as "Select your partner," "Show your stuff," or "Describe that bully." The first word in a SQL statement is an English verb, an action word called a **command**, such as *show*, *use*, *select*, *drop*, and so on. The commands are followed by a list of noun-like words, such as *show databases*, *use datatabase*, or *create databases*. The statement may contain prepositions, such as *in* or *from*; for example, *show tables in database* or *select phones from customer_table*. The language also lets you add conditional clauses to refine your query, such as *select companyname from suppliers where supplierid > 20;*.

When listing multiple items in a query, like English, the items are separated by commas; for example, in the following SQL statement, each field in the list being selected is comma-separated:

```
select companyname, phone, address from suppliers;
```

If the queries get very long and involved, you might want to type them into your favorite editor, because once you have executed a query, the only way to get it back is to use the arrow keys in the MySQL console. By saving the query in an editor, you can cut and paste it back into the MySQL browser or command line without retyping it. But most important, make sure your query makes sense and will not cause havoc on an important database. MySQL provides a *test* database for practice.

Semicolons Terminate SQL Statements.   The semicolon is the standard way to terminate each query statement. Some database systems don't require the semicolon, but MySQL does (exceptions are the *USE* and *QUIT* commands), and if you forget it, you will see a secondary prompt, and execution will go on hold until you add the semicolon.

Naming Conventions.   A database and its tables are easier to read when good naming conventions are used. For example, it makes good sense to make table names plural and field/column names singular. Why? Because a table called *Shippers* normally holds more than one shipper, but the name of the field used to describe each shipper is a single value, such as his *company_name*, *phone*, and so on.

Compound names, such as *company_name*, are usually separated by the underscore, with the first letter of each word capitalized, as in *Company_Name*.

Spaces and dashes are not allowed in any name in the database.

Reserved Words.   All languages have a list of reserved words that have special meaning to the language. Most of these words will be used in this chapter. The SQL reserved words are listed in Table 15.1. (See MySQL documentation for a complete list of all reserved words.)

Table 15.1   SQL Reserved Words

CREATE	GROUP BY	RIGHT JOIN
INSERT	FULL JOIN	DELETE
FROM	LIMIT	SET
ORDER BY	OR	WHERE
CROSS JOIN	ALTER	LEFT JOIN
DROP	SELECT	AND
UPDATE	ON	LIKE
INTO	JOIN	AS

Case Sensitivity.   Database and table names are case sensitive if you are using UNIX, but not if you are using Windows. A convention is to always use lowercase names for databases and their tables.

SQL commands are not case sensitive. For example, the following SQL statements are equally valid:

```
show databases;
SHOW DATABASES;
```

Although SQL commands are not case sensitive, by convention, SQL keywords are capitalized for clarity, whereas only the first letter of the field, table, and database names is capitalized.

```
SELECT * FROM Persons WHERE FirstName='John'
```

When performing pattern matching with the *LIKE* and *NOT LIKE* commands, the pattern being searched for is case sensitive when using MySQL.

The Result Set. A result set is just another table created to hold the results from a SQL query. Most database software systems even allow you to perform operations on the result set with functions, such as *Move-To-First-Record*, *Get-Record-Content*, *Move-To-Next-Record*, and so forth. In the example shown in Figure 15.12, the result set is the table created by asking MySQL to show all the fields in the table called *shippers*.

```
mysql> show fields in shippers;
+-------------+-------------+------+-----+---------+----------------+
| Field       | Type        | Null | Key | Default | Extra          |
+-------------+-------------+------+-----+---------+----------------+
| ShipperID   | int(11)     |      |PRI  | NULL    | auto_increment |
| CompanyName | varchar(40) |      |     |         |                |
| Phone       | varchar(24) | YES  |     | NULL    |                |
+-------------+-------------+------+-----+---------+----------------+
3 rows in set (0.00 sec)
```

Figure 15.12 The result set is just a table produced from a query.

15.3 Getting Started with MySQL

MySQL is an open-source,[4] full-featured relational database management system and has been ported to most platforms, including Linux, Windows, OS/X, HP-UX, AIX, and more. MySQL is portable, fast, reliable, scalable, and easy to use. It is the world's second most widely used relational database management system, said to be installed in more than 10 million computers all over the world, including Antarctica!

There are two versions, one in which you buy a commercial license and one that is free ("free" meaning you can use MySQL in any application as long as you don't copy, modify, or distribute the MySQL software). MySQL supports a number of APIs (application programming interfaces), including Perl, PHP, TCL, Python, *C/C++*, *Java*, and others.

When working with MySQL, a number of like-name terms are used. Table 15.2 is provided to help clarify the use of these terms.

---

4. MySQL is free use for those who are 100 percent GPL. See *http://www.mysql.com/company/legal/licensing/opensource-license.html* for details.

Table 15.2   The Terms in MySQL

Term	Definition
MySQL	The actual software for the database management system
mysqld	The MySQL daemon, or server process
mysql monitor	The monitor where MySQL commands are issued (command-line interpreter)
mysql	The name of the database MySQL uses to manage access privileges
mysqladmin	A MySQL utility program for administrating the database

15.3.1   Installing MySQL

Here, we assume you have installed a database server and it is running. Downloading and installing MySQL is usually a straightforward process. You can get MySQL from the *mysql.com* Web site or use integrated applications, such as XAMPP or WAMP.

XAMPP (for Windows, Linux, Mac OS, and Solaris) is a free, easy-to-install Apache distribution containing MySQL, PHP, and Perl. All you have to do is download, extract, and start it up. For details, go to *http://www.apachefriends.org/en/xampp.html*.

For complete installation instructions, go to *http://dev.mysql.com* (see Figure 15.13).

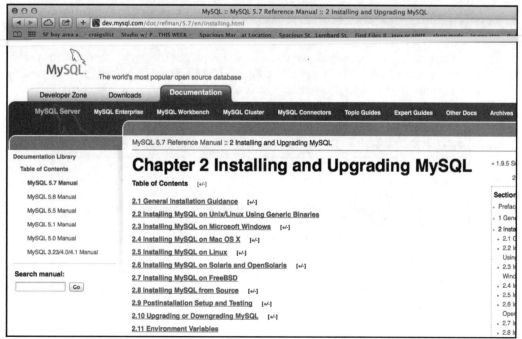

Figure 15.13   The MySQL installation documentation.

15.3.2   Connecting to MySQL

The MySQL database system uses the client/server model described in Section 15.2.1, "Client/Server Databases." You are the client connecting to the database from the command line, a graphical user interface, or from a program. Before connecting to the database from a Perl program, we will first use the the MySQL command-line client. ·

The MySQL command-line client comes with the MySQL installation and is universally available. It is a *mysql* program located in the *bin* folder of your MySQL installation. To run this command-line application, you must start the command-line prompt.

- On Windows, go to the *Start* menu, choose the *Run...* option, and then type *cmd* in the run window.
- On Mac OS X, go to the *Applications* folder in your *Finder* and then navigate to *Utilities*. You will find the *Terminal* application there. You should navigate to the location where you installed MySQL and find the *bin* folder.
- With UNIX, type commands at the shell prompt in a terminal window.

The MySQL client executable is normally located in the *bin* folder.

To connect to a database using this client, you will enter information similar to the following line:

```
mysql --user=root --password=my_password --host=localhost
```

Regardless of the type of client you choose, you may be required to specify the user name and the host machine to which you are connecting. Most configurations expect you to have a password, although if just working by yourself, it is not required. You have the option to specify the default database as well.

Once you are successfully connected, you will get the *mysql>* prompt instead of your standard DOS/UNIX prompt (see Figure 15.14). This means you are now sending commands to the MySQL database server and not to your local computer's operating system.

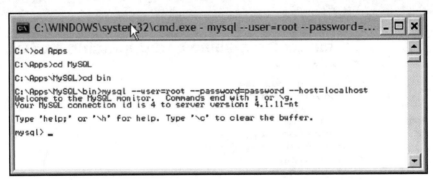

Figure 15.14 The MySQL client.

Editing Keys at the MySQL Console. MySQL supports input-line editing. The up-arrow and down-arrow keys enable you to move up and down through previous input lines, and the left-arrow and right-arrow keys let you move back and forth within a line. The Backspace and Delete keys are used to erase characters from the line and type in new characters at the cursor position. To submit an edited line, press Enter. For UNIX users, MySQL also supports tab completion, allowing you to enter part of a keyword or identifier and complete it using the Tab key.

Setting a Password. When you download MySQL, on some installations, you may be asked to enter a password for user *root*. Even if you are not forced to create a password, it is a good idea to set one to protect the security of your database. To set a password, go to the MySQL console and type the following MySQL command. Replace *'MyNewPassword'* with your password.

```
SET PASSWORD FOR 'root'@'localhost' = PASSWORD('MyNewPassword');
```

After setting the password, you can stop the MySQL server and then restart it in normal mode again. If you run the server as a service, start it from the Windows Services window. If you start the server manually, use whatever command you normally use. You should be able to connect using the new password.

The following example shows how to set the password at the *mysql* prompt.

EXAMPLE 15.1

```
1   $ mysql -u root
    ERROR 1045 (28000): Access denied for user 'root'@'localhost' (using
    password: NO)
    $
    $ mysql -u root -p
    Enter password: ********
    Welcome to the MySQL monitor.  Commands end with ; or \g.
    Your MySQL connection id is 91 to server version: 5.0.21-community-nt

    Type 'help;' or '\h' for help. Type '\c' to clear the buffer.
```

15.3.3 Graphical User Tools

The MySQL Query Browser.   The MySQL Query Browser is a graphical user interface (GUI) client available from *mysql.com* used to connect to the MySQL database server. Once you download it and follow the simple installation wizard, you can start the application from the *Start* menu under Windows.

The MySQL Query Browser then displays a connection dialog box (see Figure 15.15). You must specify the MySQL server where you want to connect, the credentials needed for authorization on that server, which machine that server runs on (and which port it listens to), and the default database (called the **schema**) you will be using. There are also a number of additional options you can specify if necessary.

You must choose a default database in order to issue queries. Although it is possible to choose a default database after connecting to the server, setting the default from the connection dialog can save time on subsequent connections.

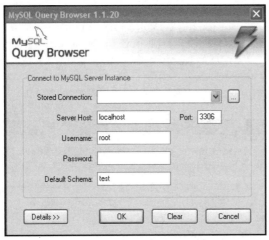

Figure 15.15   The MySQL Query Browser connection dialog box.

The information to enter is very similar to the command-line client: user name, password, and the server host where the database server is running. You can optionally enter the database name and port number (3306 is the default for MySQL) and save the connection information as a bookmark under the Stored Connection section.

By using the familiar tree-like navigation structure on the right-hand side of the application window, you can also navigate the various databases in the MySQL Query Browser (see Figure 15.16).

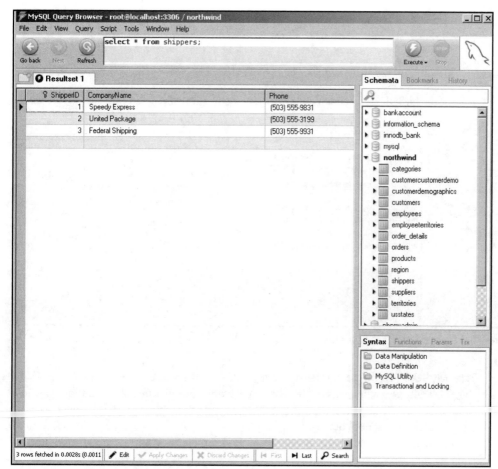

Figure 15.16   The MySQL Query Browser.

The *phpMyAdmin* Tool

The *phpMyAdmin* tool (see Figure 15.17) is written in PHP to handle the administration of MySQL over the Web. It is used to create and drop databases, manipulate tables and fields, execute SQL statements, manage keys on fields, manage privileges, and export data into various formats. You can download it from *http://www.phpmyadmin.net/home_page/index.php*.

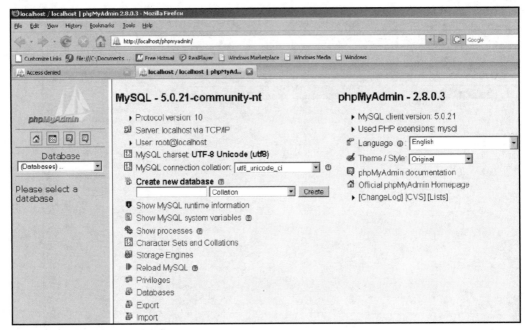

Figure 15.17   The *phpMyAdmin* tool.

The MySQL Privilege System.   With a driver's license, "authentication" is verifying that it is really you who owns the license by checking your picture and expiration date, and "authorization" is validating what type of vehicle you are authorized to drive, such as a car, a large truck, or a school bus.

Similarly, the primary purpose of the MySQL privilege system is to authenticate that the user and password are valid to connect to the specified host, as demonstrated in the previous examples in both the command line and graphical client. The second purpose of the privilege system is to specify what the user, once connected to the database, is authorized to do. For example, some users may only be authorized to select and view the data from a specific table. When MySQL is installed, the MySQL database is created with tables called **grant tables** that define the initial user accounts and privileges. The first account is that of a user named *root*, also called the **superuser**. The superuser can do anything, meaning anyone logging on to the database as root is granted all privileges. Initially, the root account has no password, making it easy for anyone to log on as the superuser. The other types of accounts created are anonymous-user accounts, also without a password. For both the root and anonymous accounts, Windows gets one each and UNIX gets two. Either way, to avoid security problems, the first thing you should do, once the MySQL server starts, is to set a password on the root account and the anonymous accounts.

For administration purposes, you should have root access rights to your server. The *mysqladmin* utility is useful for creating passwords and performing other MySQL administrative tasks. In the next example it is used to set the password for the user *root*.

EXAMPLE 15.2

```
1   $ mysqladmin -u root -h localhost password quigley1

2   $ mysql -uroot -hlocalhost -pquigley1
    Welcome to the MySQL monitor.  Commands end with ; or \g.
    Your MySQL connection id is 29 to server version: 5.0.21 community-nt

    Type 'help;' or '\h' for help. Type '\c' to clear the buffer.
```

EXPLANATION

1   The *mysqladmin* program is used to set the password for user *root* on the localhost. The password is *quigley1*.
2   The user *root* logs into the database server. The -*u* switch is followed by the user or login name (no spaces between -*u* and the user name). This user is logging in as *root*. Similarly, the -*p* switch is followed by the actual password; in this case, *quigley1*. If a password is not provided, you will be prompted to enter one.

15.3.4 Finding the Databases

The database server keeps a list of available databases, which can be displayed as a table by issuing the *show* command at the *mysql* prompt, as shown in the following example. Typically, when you install MySQL, it comes with two databases: *test* and *mysql.test*, which is an empty database used for practicing and testing various features. You normally don't need to have any special permissions to be able work in the *test* database. The *mysql* database is a special database where the MySQL server stores various access permissions. For now, you should not worry about this database unless you need to administer privileges. See the *GRANT* command in the MySQL manual.

EXAMPLE 15.3

```
1   mysql -uroot -pquigley1
    Welcome to the MySQL monitor.  Commands end with ; or \g.
    Your MySQL connection id is 5 to server version: 4.1.11-nt

    Type 'help;' or '\h' for help. Type '\c' to clear the buffer.

2   mysql> show databases;
    +--------------------+
    | Database           |
    +--------------------+
    | information_schema |
    | mysql              |
    | phpmyadmin         |
    | test               |
    +--------------------+
    4 rows in set (0.00 sec)
    mysql>
```

EXPLANATION

2　The *show database* command lists all the databases on this server. Typically, when you install MySQL, you will be given the *mysql* database and the *test* database. The *test* database is just for testing purposes and is empty. The *mysql* database contains all the MySQL server privilege information.

Creating and Dropping a Database.　Creating a database is simple. Designing it is another story and depends on your requirements and the model you will use to organize your data. Even with the smallest database, you will have to create a table. The next section will discuss how to create and drop both databases and tables. Assuming you have been granted permission to create a database, you can do it at the *mysql* command line or with the *mysqladmin* tool as shown in the following example.

EXAMPLE 15.4

```
1   mysql> CREATE database my_sample_db;
    Query OK, 1 row affected (0.00 sec)


2   mysql> USE my_sample_db;
    Database changed


3   mysql> SHOW tables;
    Empty set (0.00 sec)


4   mysql> CREATE table test(
        -> field1 INTEGER,
        -> field2 VARCHAR(50)
        -> );
    Query OK, 0 rows affected (0.36 sec)


5   mysql> SHOW tables;
    +-----------------------+
    | Tables_in_my_sample_db |
    +-----------------------+
    | test                  |
    +-----------------------+
    1 row in set (0.00 sec)


6   mysql> DROP table test;
    Query OK, 0 rows affected (0.11 sec)


7   mysql> DROP database my_sample_db;
    Query OK, 0 rows affected (0.01 sec)
```

EXPLANATION

1. This command creates a database called *my_sample_db*.
2. Just because the database has been created doesn't mean you are in it. To enter the new database, the *use* command is executed.
3. The *show* command lists the tables in the database. This database is empty.
4. A table called *test* is created for the *my_sample_db* database. When a table is created, two columns, *field1* and *field2*, are defined. Each field is assigned the type of data that will be stored there; *field1* will store whole numbers, and *field2* will store a string of up to 50 characters.
5. The *show* command lists all the tables in the database.
6. The *drop table* command destroys a table and its contents.
7. The *drop database* command destroys a database and its contents.

15.3.5 Getting Started with Basic Commands

The examples in this next section illustrate how to issue SQL commands from the MySQL client. These examples do not attempt to cover all the possible SQL statements supported by MySQL but are here to illustrate the basic syntax for creating and dropping databases and tables and how to insert, delete, edit, alter, and select data from the database tables. For a complete description of all that you can do with MySQL, visit the MySQL Documentation page at *http://dev.mysql.com/doc* (see Figure 15.18).

Creating a Database with MySQL. Now we are ready to create a database. This database is called *sample_db*. The *CREATE DATABASE* command creates the database, and the *SHOW DATABASES* statement demonstrates that it is now listed with the other databases. (You can also use the *mysqladmin* command to create and drop databases.)

EXAMPLE 15.5

```
1  mysql> CREATE DATABASE sample_db;
   Query OK, 1 row affected (0.03 sec)

2  mysql> SHOW DATABASES;
   +--------------------+
   | Database           |
   +--------------------+
   | information_schema |
   | mysql              |
   | northwind          |
   | phpmyadmin         |
   | sample_db          |
   | test               |
   +--------------------+
   6 rows in set (0.00 sec)
```

EXPLANATION

1   The *CREATE DATABASE* statement allows you to create a database. Creating a database does not put you in that database. The *USE* statement will let you start working in the database, as shown in the next example.

2   The *SHOW DATABASES* statement lists all the MySQL databases currently available. The *sample_db* database was just created.

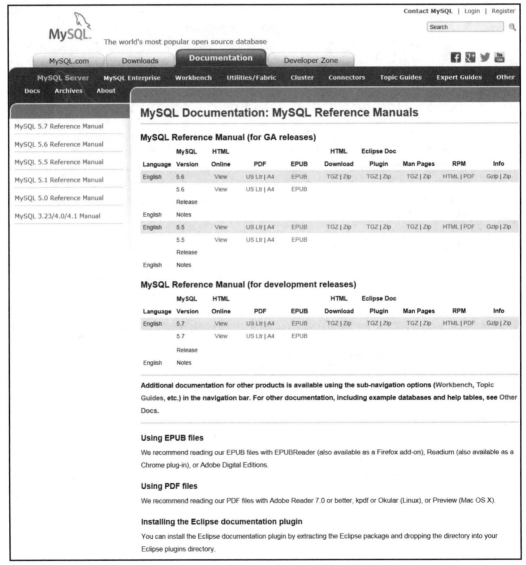

Figure 15.18   MySQL Documentation page.

Selecting a Database with MySQL.   After creating the database, we need to open it so we can use it. This is done with the *USE* statement. We now have a database to work in.

```
mysql> USE sample_db;
Database changed
```

Creating a Table in the Database.   Once the database is created, it is time to create some tables. In a real situation, the relational database will be designed with rules that put logic in the structure of the tables, a process called **normalization** and a topic beyond the scope of this book. In our sample database, we will create one table and put some data in it, just to show you how it is done. The data types define the structure of each field in the table. The *CREATE TABLE* statement defines each field, its name, and its data type.

Data Types.   First, we will have to decide what kind of data will be stored in the table: text, numbers, dates, photos, money, and so on, and what to name the fields (columns) under which the data is stored. MySQL has specific data types to describe all the types of data that can be stored in the database. Most of the MySQL data types are listed in Table 15.3.

Table 15.3   MySQL Data Types

Data Type	Description
Numbers	
TINYINT	Very small numbers; suitable for ages. Can store numbers between 0 and 255 if *UNSIGNED* clause is applied; else the range is between –128 and 127.
SMALLINT	Suitable for numbers between 0 and 65535 (*UNSIGNED*) or –32768 and 32767.
MEDIUM INT	0 to 16777215 with *UNSIGNED* clause or –8388608 and 8388607.
INT	*UNSIGNED* integers fall between 0 and 4294967295 or –2147683648 and 2147683647.
BIGINT	Huge numbers (–9223372036854775808 to 9223372036854775807).
FLOAT	Floating-point numbers (single precision).
DOUBLE	Floating-point numbers (double precision).
DECIMAL	Floating-point numbers represented as strings.

(continued)

Table 15.3 MySQL Data Types (continued)

Data Type	Description
Text	
CHAR(x)	Where x can range from 1 to 255. Holds a fixed-length string (can contain letters, numbers, and special characters). The fixed size is specified in parentheses.
VARCHAR(x)	x ranges from 1 to 255. Holds a variable-length string (can contain letters, numbers, and special characters). The maximum size is specified in parentheses.
TINYTEXT	Small text, case insensitive.
TEXT	Slightly longer text, case insensitive.
MEDIUMTEXT	Medium-size text, case insensitive.
LONGTEXT	Really long text, case insensitive.
Binary	
TINYBLOB	Blob means a Binary Large Object. You should use blobs for case-sensitive searches, maximum length 255, case sensitive.
MEDIUMBLOB	Medium-sized blobs, case sensitive.
LONGBLOB	Really huge blobs, case sensitive.
ENUM	Enumeration data type has fixed values, and the column can take only one value from the given set. The values are placed in parentheses following ENUM declaration. An example is a marital-status column: m_status ENUM("Y", "N")
Dates	
DATE: YYYY-MM-DD	Four-digit year followed by two-digit month and two-digit day; e.g., 20141030.
TIME: hh:mm:ss	Hours:Minutes:Seconds.
DATETIME	YYYY-MM-DD hh:mm:ss (date and time separated by a space character).
TIMESTAMP	YYYYMMDDhhmmss.
YEAR	YYYY (four-digit year); e.g., 2014.

EXAMPLE 15.7

```
1   mysql> CREATE TABLE teams(
        -> name VARCHAR(100) not null,
        -> wins INT unsigned,
        -> losses INT unsigned);
    Query OK, 0 rows affected (0.09 sec)

2   mysql> SHOW TABLES;
    +--------------------+
    | Tables_in_sample_db |
    +--------------------+
    | teams              |
    +--------------------+
    1 row in set (0.00 sec);

3   mysql> DESCRIBE teams;
    +--------+------------------+------+-----+---------+-------+
    | Field  | Type             | Null | Key | Default | Extra |
    +--------+------------------+------+-----+---------+-------+
    | name   | varchar(100)     | NO   |     |         |       |
    | wins   | int(10) unsigned | YES  |     | NULL    |       |
    | losses | int(10) unsigned | YES  |     | NULL    |       |
    +--------+------------------+------+-----+---------+-------+
    | teams                     |
    +--------------------+
    1 row in set (0.00 sec)
```

EXPLANATION

1   The *CREATE TABLE* statement creates a table in the database. This table is named teams. It consists of three fields: name, wins, and losses. The name field will consist of a varying string of up to 100 characters; the *wins* and *losses* fields will hold unsigned integers.

2   The *SHOW* command lists the tables in a database. (The *SHOW* command has many forms that provide information about databases, tables, columns, or status information about the server.)

3   The *DESCRIBE* command describes the structure of the table; meaning, the names of the fields and the type of data that can be stored in each field. Note that the *name* field cannot be NULL, and the default value for the *wins* and *losses* is NULL if a value isn't supplied; for example, if a team hasn't played any games, the *wins* and *losses* will be assigned NULL.

Adding Another Table with a Primary Key.   In the next example, we will create another table and add a primary key. A primary key is used to uniquely identify the records in the database. A user's login name, UID, account number, or license plate are examples of unique IDs. A primary key is a unique index where all key columns must be defined as NOT NULL. If they are not explicitly declared as NOT NULL, MySQL declares them so implicitly (and silently). A table can have only one primary key.

EXAMPLE 15.8

```
1   mysql> CREATE TABLE coaches(
        -> id INT NOT NULL AUTO_INCREMENT,
        -> name VARCHAR(75),
        -> team VARCHAR(100),
        -> title VARCHAR(50),
        -> start_date date,
        -> PRIMARY KEY(id));
    Query OK, 0 rows affected (0.38 sec)

2   mysql> DESCRIBE coaches;
    +------------+--------------+------+-----+---------+----------------
    | Field      | Type         | Null | Key | Default | Extra
    +------------+--------------+------+-----+---------+----------------
    | id         | int(11)      | NO   | PRI | NULL    |auto_increment
    | name       | varchar(75)  | YES  |     | NULL    |
    | team       | varchar(100) | YES  |     | NULL    |
    | title      | varchar(50)  | YES  |     | NULL    |
    | start_date | date         | YES  |     | NULL    |
    +------------+--------------+------+-----+---------+----------------
    5 rows in set (0.00 sec)

3   mysql> SHOW TABLES;
    +---------------------+
    | Tables_in_sample_db |
    +---------------------+
    | coaches             |
    | teams               |
    +---------------------+
    2 rows in set (0.00 sec)
```

EXPLANATION

1   The *coach* table is created with the *id* field being assigned a primary key. This is the field that will be used to uniquely identify a specific coach.

2   The structure of the new table shows that the *id* field has a primary key that will be automatically incremented by one by MySQL each time a new coach is added.

3   Now our database has two tables, one called *teams* and one called *coaches*.

Inserting Data into Tables.   The SQL *INSERT* statement adds new records to a table. When you insert data, make sure you provide a value for each field name in the order the data is stored; otherwise, MySQL will send an error message. In the following example, data can be inserted with the *SET* clause where fields are assigned values, or the values can be specified with the *VALUES* list or by simply listing the values for each field in order. See the MySQL documentation for a complete list of ways to add new records to a table.

EXAMPLE 15.9

```
1  mysql> INSERT INTO teams
       -> SET name='Fremont Tigers',
       -> wins=24,
       -> losses=26;
   Query OK, 1 row affected (0.00 sec)

2  mysql> INSERT INTO teams
       -> SET name='Chico Hardhats',
       -> wins=19,
       -> losses=25;
   Query OK, 1 row affected (0.00 sec)

3  mysql> INSERT INTO teams VALUES
       -> ('Bath Warships',32,3);
   Query OK, 1 row affected (0.00 sec)

4  mysql> INSERT INTO teams VALUES
       -> ('Bangor Rams', 22, 24);
   Query OK, 1 row affected (0.00 sec)

5  mysql> SELECT name FROM teams;
   +----------------+
   | name           |
   +----------------+
   | Fremont Tigers |
   | Chico Hardhats |
   | Bath Warships  |
   | Bangor Rams    |
   +----------------+
   4 rows in set (0.00 sec)

6  mysql> INSERT INTO coaches VALUES
       -> (" ",'John Doe','Chico Hardhats','Head Coach', 20021210);
   Query OK, 1 row affected, 1 warning (0.05 sec)
7  mysql>  INSERT INTO coaches VALUES
       -> (" ", 'Jack Mattsone','Chico Hardhats','Offensive Coach' ,
          '20041005');
   Query OK, 1 row affected, 1 warning (0.00 sec)

8  mysql> INSERT INTO coaches(name,team, title,start_date)
       -> VALUES( 'Bud Wilkins', 'Fremont Tigers', 'Head Coach',
                  '19990906');
   Query OK, 1 row affected (0.03 sec)

9  mysql>  INSERT INTO coaches(name, team, title,start_date)
       ->VALUES( 'Joe Hayes', 'Fremont Tigers', 'Defensive Coach',
                 '19980616');
   Query OK, 1 row affected (0.02 seconds)
```

EXPLANATION

1　The fields and values are assigned using the *SET* clause within the *INSERT* statement. For any field not named in the *SET*, MySQL assigns its default value.

2　Again, the fields and values are inserted using the *SET* clause.

3　In this example, the *INSERT* statement contains a *VALUE* list where a value for each field is assigned in the order it was specified when the table was created. To see the order, if you are not sure, use the *DESCRIBE* statement as shown in the previous example.

4　The *VALUES* list is repeated in this example for a new record. Note that the date is inserted in the format *yyyy-mm-dd*.

5　The *SELECT* statement displays the names of all the teams that have been inserted into the table.

6–9　More records are inserted with the *VALUES* list.

Selecting Data from Tables—The *SELECT* Command. One of the most commonly used SQL commands is *SELECT*, mandatory when performing a query. The *SELECT* command is used to retrieve data from a table based on some criteria. It specifies a comma-separated list of fields to be retrieved, and the *FROM* clause specifies the table(s) to be accessed. The results are stored in a result table known as the result set, just a little table itself. The * symbol can be used to represent all of the fields.

Selecting by Columns. In the following examples, data is retrieved for specific columns, each column (field) separated by a comma.

EXAMPLE 15.10

```
1   mysql> SELECT name FROM teams;
    +----------------+
    | name           |
    +----------------+
    | Fremont Tigers |
    | Chico Hardhats |
    | Bath Warships  |
    | Bangor Rams    |
    +----------------+
    4 rows in set (0.00 sec)

2   mysql> SELECT name, wins FROM teams;
    +----------------+------+
    | name           | wins |
    +----------------+------+
    | Bangor Rams    |   22 |
    | Bath Warships  |   32 |
    | Fremont Tigers |   24 |
    | Chico Hardhats |   19 |
    +----------------+------+
    4 rows in set (0.00 sec)
```

EXAMPLE 15.10 (CONTINUED)

```
3   mysql> SELECT id, name, title FROM coaches;
    +----+---------------+-----------------+
    | id | name          | title           |
    +----+---------------+-----------------+
    |  1 | John Doe      | Head Coach      |
    |  2 | Jack Mattsone | Offensive Coach |
    |  3 | Bud Wilkins   | Head Coach      |
    |  4 | Joe Hayes     | Defensive Coach |
    +----+---------------+-----------------+
    4 rows in set (0.00 seconds)
```

EXPLANATION

1   The *SELECT* statement retrieves all values in the *name* field from the *teams* table.
2   The *SELECT* statement retrieves all values in the *name* field and the *wins* field from the table called *teams*. The list of field names are separated with a comma.
3   The *SELECT* statement retrieves all values in the *id* field, the *name* field, and the *title* field from the *coaches* table.

Selecting All Columns.   The * is a wildcard that is used to represent all of the columns in a table.

EXAMPLE 15.11

```
1   mysql> SELECT * FROM teams;
    +----------------+------+--------+
    | name           | wins | losses |
    +----------------+------+--------+
    | Fremont Tigers |   24 |     26 |
    | Chico Hardhats |   19 |     25 |
    | Bath Warships  |   32 |      3 |
    | Bangor Rams    |   22 |     24 |
    +----------------+------+--------+

2   mysql> SELECT * FROM coaches;
    +----+---------------+----------------+-----------------+------------+
    | id | name          | team           | title           | start_date |
    +----+---------------+----------------+-----------------+------------+
    |  1 | John Doe      | Chico Hardhats | Head Coach      | 2002-12-10 |
    |  2 | Jack Mattsone | Chico Hardhats | Offensive Coach | 2004-10-05 |
    |  3 | Bud Wilkins   | Fremont Tigers | Head Coach      | 1999-09-06 |
    |  4 | Joe Hayes     | Fremont Tigers | Defensive Coach | 1998-06-16 |
    +----+---------------+----------------+-----------------+------------+
    4 rows in set (0.00 sec)
```

EXPLANATION

1   The *SELECT* statement retrieves all fields and values from the table called *teams*.
2   The *SELECT* statement retrieves all fields and values from the table called *coaches*.

The *WHERE* Clause. The *WHERE* clause is optional and specifies which data values or rows will be selected based on some condition, called a selection criterion. SQL provides a set of operators to qualify the condition being set (see Table 15.4).

Table 15.4 SQL Operators

Operator	Description	Example
=	Equal to	WHERE country = 'Sweden'
<>, !=	Not equal to*	WHERE country <> 'Sweden'
>	Greater than	WHERE salary > 50000
<	Less than	WHERE salary < 50000
>=	Greater than or equal	
<=	Less than or equal	
IS [NOT] NULL	IS NULL (no value) or NOT NULL	WHERE birth = NULL
BETWEEN	Between an inclusive range	WHERE last_name BETWEEN 'Doe' AND 'Hayes'
LIKE	Search for value like a pattern	WHERE last_name LIKE 'D%'
NOT LIKE	Search for a value not like a pattern	WHERE country NOT LIKE 'Sw%'
!, NOT	logical NOT for negation	WHERE status ! is_married;
||, OR	logical OR	WHERE order_number > 10 || part_number = 80
&&, AND	logical AND	WHERE age > 12 && age < 21
XOR	Exclusive OR	WHERE status = 1 XOR range = 1

* In some versions of SQL, the <> operator may be written as !=.

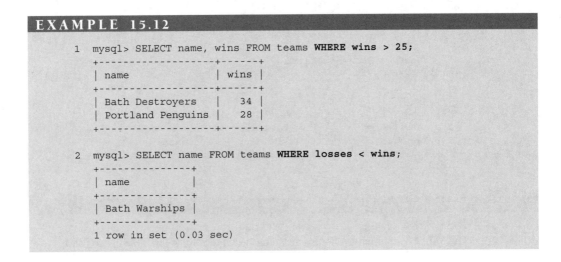

```
E X A M P L E   15.12

1   mysql> SELECT name, wins FROM teams WHERE wins > 25;
    +--------------------+------+
    | name               | wins |
    +--------------------+------+
    | Bath Destroyers    |   34 |
    | Portland Penguins  |   28 |
    +--------------------+------+

2   mysql> SELECT name FROM teams WHERE losses < wins;
    +----------------+
    | name           |
    +----------------+
    | Bath Warships  |
    +----------------+
    1 row in set (0.03 sec)
```

EXAMPLE 15.12 (CONTINUED)

```
3  mysql> SELECT name, title FROM coaches WHERE team = 'Chico Hardhats';
   +---------------+-----------------+
   | name          | title           |
   +---------------+-----------------+
   | John Doe      | Head Coach      |
   | Jack Mattsone | Offensive Coach |
   +---------------+-----------------+
   2 rows in set (0.00 sec)

4  mysql> SELECT name FROM coaches WHERE name LIKE 'J%';
   +---------------+
   | name          |
   +---------------+
   | John Doe      |
   | Jack Mattsone |
   | Joe Hayes     |
   +---------------+
   3 rows in set (0.00 sec)

5  mysql> SELECT name FROM teams WHERE wins > 10 && losses < 10;
   +---------------+
   | name          |
   +---------------+
   | Bath Warships |
   +---------------+
   1 row in set (0.00 sec)

6  mysql> SELECT name FROM coaches WHERE id BETWEEN 1 AND 3;
   +---------------+
   | name          |
   +---------------+
   | John Doe      |
   | Jack Mattsone |
   | Bud Wilkins   |
   +---------------+
   3 rows in set (0.00 sec)
```

EXPLANATION

1   The *SELECT* statement retrieves the name of teams from the table called *teams* where the number of wins was greater than 25.

2   The *SELECT* statement retrieves the name of teams from the table called *teams* where the number of losses was less than the number of wins.

3   The *SELECT* statement retrieves the names of coaches and their titles from the table called *coaches* if their team is equal to the string *'Chico Hardhats'*. The string must be quoted in either single or double quotes, and the match must be exact.

EXPLANATION (CONTINUED)

4   The *SELECT* statement retrieves the names of coaches from the table called *coaches* where the coach's name contains a string starting with a *J*. The % sign is a wildcard representing any characters following the *J*.

5   The *SELECT* statement retrieves the name of the team where the number of wins is greater than 10 and the number of losses less than 10. The *&&* is called the logical AND. Both statements must be true or nothing will be selected.

6   The *SELECT* statement retrieves the names of coaches from the table called *coaches* where the ID is between 1 and 3. The *BETWEEN* clause creates a range criteria from which to select.

Sorting Tables.   You can display the output of a query in a particular order by using the *ORDER BY* clause. Rows can be sorted either in ascending (the default) or descending (*DESC*) order where the values being sorted are either strings or numbers. You can limit the output of any query with the *LIMIT* clause.

EXAMPLE 15.13

```
1   mysql> SELECT * FROM teams ORDER BY name;
    +----------------+------+--------+
    | name           | wins | losses |
    +----------------+------+--------+
    | Bangor Rams    |   22 |     24 |
    | Bath Warships  |   32 |      3 |
    | Chico Hardhats |   19 |     25 |
    | Fremont Tigers |   24 |     26 |
    +----------------+------+--------+
    4 rows in set (0.00 sec)

2   mysql> SELECT * FROM teams ORDER BY name DESC;
    +----------------+------+--------+
    | name           | wins | losses |
    +----------------+------+--------+
    | Fremont Tigers |   24 |     26 |
    | Chico Hardhats |   19 |     25 |
    | Bath Warships  |   32 |      3 |
    | Bangor Rams    |   22 |     24 |
    +----------------+------+--------+
    4 rows in set (0.00 sec)

3   mysql> SELECT name, wins FROM teams ORDER BY WINS LIMIT 2;
    +----------------+------+
    | name           | wins |
    +----------------+------+
    | Chico Hardhats |   19 |
    | Bangor Rams    |   22 |
    +----------------+------+
    2 rows in set (0.00 sec)
```

EXPLANATION

1 The *SELECT* statement retrieves all fields from the table called *teams* and sorts the result set by names in ascending order.

2 The *SELECT* statement retrieves all fields from the table called *teams* and sorts the result set by names in descending order.

3 The *SELECT* statement retrieves the names and wins of teams and sorts the number of wins in ascending order, limiting the result set to the top two winners.

Joining Tables. When a database is designed properly, the tables relate to one another based on some criteria; for example, in our database, every team has a name and every coach has a name and a team name. A join allows two or more tables to be combined and return a result set based on the relationships they share. There are different types of join statements (inner joins, cross joins, left joins, and others), but they all follow the basic syntax of a *SELECT* statement with the addition of a *JOIN* clause.

EXAMPLE 15.14

```
1   mysql> SELECT teams.name, coaches.name, teams.wins
           FROM teams, coaches WHERE
           teams.name = coaches.team && coaches.id = 4;
    +----------------+------------+------+
    | name           | name       | wins |
    +----------------+------------+------+
    | Fremont Tigers | Joe Hayes  |   24 |
    +----------------+------------+------+
    1 row in set (0.00 sec)

2   mysql> SELECT teams.name, coaches.name, teams.wins FROM teams,
        -> coaches  WHERE teams.name = coaches.team &&
        -> coaches.title = "Head Coach";
    +----------------+------------+------+
    | name           | name       | wins |
    +----------------+------------+------+
    | Chico Hardhats | John Doe   |   21 |
    | Fremont Tigers | Bud Wilkins|   24 |
    +----------------+------------+------+
    2 rows in set (0.00 sec)

3   mysql> SELECT t.name, c.name, t.wins FROM teams t, coaches c
        -> WHERE t.name = c.team && c.title LIKE "Head%";
    +----------------+------------+------+
    | name           | name       | wins |
    +----------------+------------+------+
    | Chico Hardhats | John Doe   |   21 |
    | Fremont Tigers | Bud Wilkins|   24 |
    +----------------+------------+------+
    2 rows in set (0.00 sec)
```

EXPLANATION

1   The *SELECT* statement will retrieve the team's name, the coach's name, and the number of wins for the team where the team and coach name are the same and the coach's ID is 4. The fields are prepended with the name of the table and a dot to identify the field and table. The join (inner join) means that all unmatched records are discarded. Only the rows that matched the criteria in the *WHERE* clause are displayed in the result set.

2   The *SELECT* statement will retrieve the team's name, the coach's name, and the number of wins for the team where the team and coach name are the same and the coach's title is *Head Coach*. Like the last example, the join (inner join) means only the rows that matched the criteria in the *WHERE* clause are displayed in the result set.

3   The *SELECT* statement will retrieve the team name, the coach name, and the team wins from both the *teams* and *coaches* tables where the team name and the coach name are the same and the coach's title starts with *Head*. The letters *t* and *c* are called aliases for the respective tables, *teams* and *coaches*. Aliases save a lot of typing.

Deleting Rows.   The *DELETE* command allows you to remove rows from a table. The only real difference between *DELETE* and *SELECT* is that the *DELETE* removes records based on some criteria, whereas the *SELECT* retrieves those records and *DELETE* does not take field names.

EXAMPLE 15.15

```
1   mysql> SELECT name FROM teams;
    +----------------+
    | name           |
    +----------------+
    | Fremont Tigers |
    | Chico Hardhats |
    | Bath Warships  |
    | Bangor Rams    |
    +----------------+
    4 rows in set (0.00 sec)

2   mysql> DELETE FROM teams WHERE name = "Bath Warships";
    Query OK, 1 row affected (0.20 sec)

3   mysql> SELECT name FROM teams;
    +----------------+
    | name           |
    +----------------+
    | Fremont Tigers |
    | Chico Hardhats |
    | Bangor Rams    |
    +----------------+
    4 rows in set (0.00 sec)
```

EXPLANATION

1 The *SELECT* statement retrieves all values in the *name* field from the table called *teams*.

2 The *DELETE* statement deletes a row in the *name* field if the name of the team is *Bath Warships*.

3 This *SELECT* statement retrieves all values in the name fields, showing us that the *Bath Warships* team was deleted in the previous *DELETE* statement.

Updating Data in a Table.   The *UPDATE* command is used to edit a table; that is, to modify or change the values in a table. This statement uses the *SET* clause to change the existing value to something else, as shown in the following example.

EXAMPLE 15.16

```
1  mysql> SELECT * FROM teams;
   +-----------------+------+--------+
   | name            | wins | losses |
   +-----------------+------+--------+
   | Fremont Tigers  |   24 |     26 |
   | Chico Hardhats  |   19 |     25 |
   | Bath Warships   |   32 |      3 |
   | Bangor Rams     |   22 |     24 |
   +-----------------+------+--------+
   4 rows in set (0.00 sec)

2  mysql> UPDATE teams SET wins=wins + 2 WHERE name="Chico Hardhats";
   Query OK, 1 row affected (0.02 sec)
   Rows matched: 1  Changed: 1  Warnings: 0

3  mysql> UPDATE teams SET name="Bath Destroyers"
       -> where name="Bath Warships";
   Query OK, 1 row affected (0.13 sec)
   Rows matched: 1  Changed: 1  Warnings: 0

4  mysql> SELECT * FROM teams;
   +-----------------+------+--------+
   | name            | wins | losses |
   +-----------------+------+--------+
   | Fremont Tigers  |   24 |     26 |
   | Chico Hardhats  |   21 |     25 |
   | Bath Destroyers |   32 |      3 |
   | Bangor Rams     |   22 |     24 |
   +-----------------+------+--------+
   4 rows in set (0.00 sec)
```

1   The *SELECT* statement retrieves all rows from the table called *teams*. We will compare this result set with the one on line 3 after the the table is updated.

2   The *UPDATE* statement edits the win field. It adds 2 wins to the wins field for the *Chico Hardhats*.

3   The *UPDATE* statement edits the name field. It causes the *Bath Warships* team to be renamed *Bath Destroyers*.

4   This *SELECT* statement retrieves all values in the *teams* table, showing us that the the *UPDATE* statement changed the team name of the *Bath Warships* and the number of wins for the *Chico Hardhats* was increased by two.

Altering a Table.   The *ALTER TABLE* command allows you to alter the structure of an existing table by adding and dropping columns. The *ALTER* statement has many possible clauses, such as *CHANGE*, *MODIFY*, *RENAME*, *DROP*, and others. Don't confuse *ALTER* with *UPDATE*. Altering a table changes the structure of how the table was described after it was created. You can use it to add primary keys or indexes, change the definition of a column or where it is positioned in the table, and more. Some of these alterations are demonstrated in the following examples.

Adding a Column

Example 15.17 shows how to use *ADD* with the *ALTER TABLE* command to add a column to a table.

EXAMPLE 15.17

```
1   mysql> ALTER TABLE teams ADD captain VARCHAR(100);
    Query OK, 11 rows affected (0.64 sec)
    Records: 11  Duplicates: 0  Warnings:

2   mysql> select * from teams;
    +-----------------------+------+--------+---------+
    | name                  | wins | losses | captain |
    +-----------------------+------+--------+---------+
    | Fremont Tigers        |   24 |     26 | NULL    |
    | Bath Destroyers       |   34 |      3 | NULL    |
    | Chico Hardhats        |   21 |     25 | NULL    |
    | Bangor Rams           |   23 |      5 | NULL    |
    +-----------------------+------+--------+---------+
    4 rows in set (0.01 sec)
```

1   The *ALTER* statement adds a new field called *captain* to the *teams* table. The values in the new field will consist of up to 100 characters.

Dropping a Column

Example 15.18 shows how to use *DROP* with the *ALTER TABLE* command to remove a column from a table.

EXAMPLE 15.18

```
mysql> ALTER TABLE teams DROP captain;
Query OK, 11 rows affected (0.34 sec)
Records: 11  Duplicates: 0  Warnings: 0
```

Adding a Primary Key

In Example 15.19, the *teams* table is altered by making the *name* field a primary key. This means that all new teams must have unique names.

EXAMPLE 15.19

```
1  mysql> ALTER TABLE teams MODIFY name VARCHAR(100) NOT NULL,
    -->   ADD PRIMARY KEY(name);
   Query OK, 10 rows affected (0.06 sec)
   Records: 10  Duplicates: 0  Warnings: 0

2  mysql> DESCRIBE teams;
   +--------+------------------+------+-----+---------+-------+
   | Field  | Type             | Null | Key | Default | Extra |
   +--------+------------------+------+-----+---------+-------+
   | name   | varchar(100)     | NO   | PRI | NULL    |       |
   | wins   | int(10) unsigned | YES  |     | NULL    |       |
   | losses | int(10) unsigned | YES  |     | NULL    |       |
   +--------+------------------+------+-----+---------+-------+
   3 rows in set (0.05 sec)
```

Dropping a Table. To drop a table is relatively simple. Just use the *DROP* command and the name of the table.

EXAMPLE 15.20

```
mysql> DROP TABLE teams;
Query OK, 5 rows affected (0.11 sec)
```

Dropping a Database. To drop a database, use the *DROP DATABASE* command.

EXAMPLE 15.21

```
mysql> DROP DATABASE sample_db;
Query OK, 1 row affected (0.45 sec)
```

15.4 What Is the Perl DBI?

> The DBI is a layer of "glue" between an application and one or more database driver modules.
>
> —Tim Bunce, author of DBI

DBI stands for the **Database Independent Interface**. DBI is an object-oriented module that allows your Perl application to talk to many different types of databases using the same method calls, variables, and conventions. It locates the database driver module (DBD) for a particular database system and dynamically loads the appropriate DBD module. The database driver contains the libraries necessary to talk to a specific database. For example, to connect to a MySQL database, you need to install the DBD-MySQL driver, and in order to talk to an Oracle database, you need the DBD-Oracle driver.

DBI acts as the interface between your Perl script and the database driver modules; meaning, it translates Perl output to code that can be understood by a specific driver whether that driver is Oracle, Sybase, MySQL, or others (see Figure 15.19). You set up the SQL query string and send it via a DBI method to the appropriate database driver, and you get back results that can be managed in your Perl program in the same way no matter what database you are using. For an excellent tutorial by Tim Bunce, the DBI author, see *http://www.slideshare.net/Tim.Bunce/dbi-advanced-tutorial-2007*.

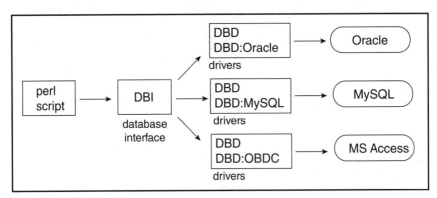

Figure 15.19 The DBI and drivers.

15.4.1 Installing the DBD Driver

Without the DBD-MySQL with PPM. The DBI module has been included in the standard Perl library for most recent versions of Perl, but the DBD-MySQL driver can be retrieved from CPAN for UNIX, Mac, and Linux. (Strawberry for Windows includes the driver.) Instructions for getting the mysql driver for the Mac can be found at *http://bixsolutions.net/forum/thread-8.html*.

A simple way to install DBI or any of the DBD drivers is to use PPM, a package-management utility from ActiveState that simplifies finding, installing, upgrading, and removing Perl modules. To get a complete tutorial on PPM, go to *http://docs.activestate.com/activeperl/5.10/faq/ActivePerl-faq2.html*.

In order to use PPM, first make sure your computer has an Internet connection. You must also have access to a PPM repository, either on a local hard drive, a network, or have access to a mounted ActiveState ActiveDVD. Keep in mind that if your Internet connection is via firewall or proxy, you might need to set the http_proxy environment variable.

Access to the Solaris PPM repository requires an ActivePerl Business Edition license.

To launch PPM you can type the following at the command line:

```
ppm
```

When the Perl Package Manager is initially displayed, it will synchronize the ActiveState repository package list from its database. You can view all the currently installed packages or all the packages in the repository and use the search box to find a module you are looking for. If found, it will be highlighted (see Figure 15.20).

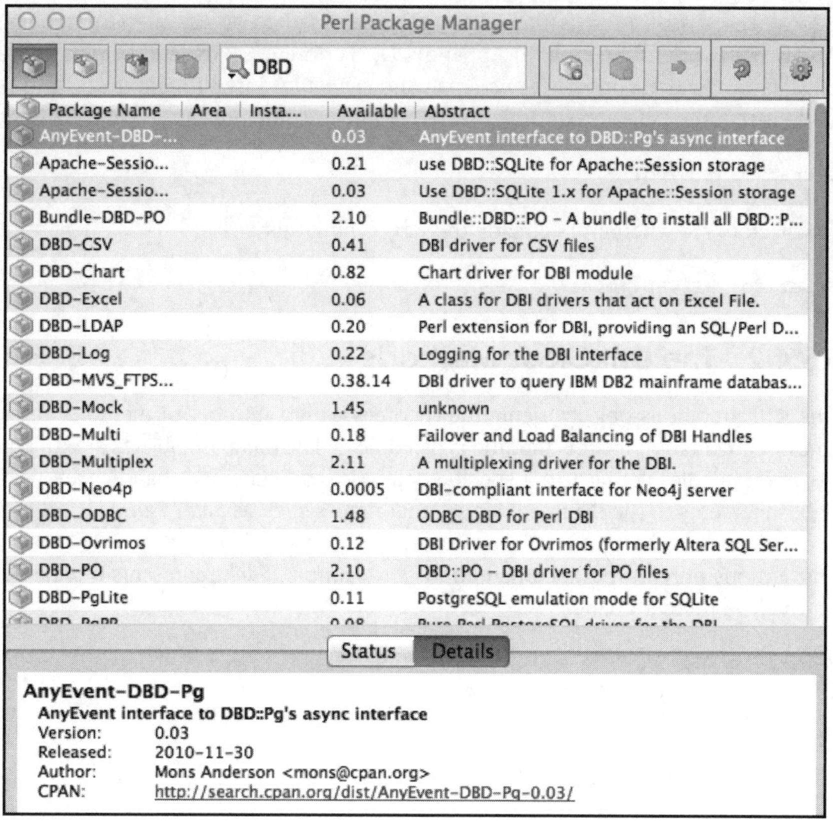

Figure 15.20 Package marked for install.

The small icons in the toolbar at the top of the PPM window indicate what you can do once you have selected a package from the repository. Normally, you select the package, mark it for install, and then click on the green arrow at the right-hand side of the toolbox.

Using PPM with Linux.   If you are using Linux, you can download Perl 5.18.2 from ActiveState as an *rpm* (RedHat Package Manager) file or as a tarfile. The instructions for downloading ActivePerl are found at *http://www.activestate.com/activeperl*. Then run the *install.sh* shell script found in the *perl* directory. After you run the install script, set your *PATH* to the *perl* directory. Then you can use the PPM program to install modules from CPAN just as you would with Windows. This is by far easier than using CPAN with all its questions and issues.

You need to be connected to the Internet to install the required packages. To see the installed packages, type the following:

```
\rpm -i Active-State.....rpm
sh install.sh
```

Installing the DBD::mysql Driver from CPAN.   The primary tool used to maintain a local Perl distribution is the CPAN module, used to access the Comprehensive Perl Archive Network, aka CPAN. In Appendix D, "Perlbrew, CPAN, and cpanm," you will find detailed instructions on how to use *cpan* and *cpanm* for installing modules.

To install the DBD-mysql driver, at the command-line prompt, type the following:

```
$ cpan DBD::mysql
```

Or check to see whether it's already there by typing this:

```
$ perldoc -l DBD::mysql
```

15.4.2   The DBI Class Methods

The DBI module is object oriented and comes with a number of methods and variables. The documentation for this module is listed next. The database objects are called **handles**. Database handles connect to a specific database, and statement handles are used to send SQL statements to the database. Notice that names such as $dbi, $sth, $rc,and so forth, are use to describe statement handles, return codes, rows of data, and so on. (These names are conventions only in the documentation; for example, $dbh represents a database handle, and $sth a statement handle.)

```
$ perldoc DBI
 Notation and Conventions
   The following conventions are used in this document:

     $dbh     Database handle object
     $sth     Statement handle object
```

```
    $drh     Driver handle object (rarely seen or used in applications)
    $h       Any of the handle types above ($dbh, $sth, or $drh)
    $rc      General Return Code   (boolean: true=ok, false=error)
    $rv      General Return Value (typically an integer)
    @ary     List of values returned from the database, typically a row of
             data

    $rows    Number of rows processed (if available, else -1)
    $fh      A filehandle
    undef    NULL values are represented by undefined values in Perl
    \%attr   Reference to a hash of attribute values passed to methods
```

Note that Perl will automatically destroy database and statement
handle objects if all references to them are deleted.

NAME
    DBI - Database independent interface for Perl

SYNOPSIS
```
    use DBI;
    @driver_names = DBI->available_drivers;
    @data_sources = DBI->data_sources($driver_name, \%attr);
    $dbh = DBI->connect($data_source, $username, $auth, \%attr);

    $rv  = $dbh->do($statement);
    $rv  = $dbh->do($statement, \%attr);
    $rv  = $dbh->do($statement, \%attr, @bind_values);

    $ary_ref  = $dbh->selectall_arrayref($statement);
    $hash_ref = $dbh->selectall_hashref($statement, $key_field);

    $ary_ref  = $dbh->selectcol_arrayref($statement);
    $ary_ref  = $dbh->selectcol_arrayref($statement, \%attr);

    @row_ary  = $dbh->selectrow_array($statement);
    $ary_ref  = $dbh->selectrow_arrayref($statement);
    $hash_ref = $dbh->selectrow_hashref($statement);

    $sth = $dbh->prepare($statement);
    $sth = $dbh->prepare_cached($statement);

    $rc = $sth->bind_param($p_num, $bind_value);
    $rc = $sth->bind_param($p_num, $bind_value, $bind_type);
    $rc = $sth->bind_param($p_num, $bind_value, \%attr);

    $rv = $sth->execute;
    $rv = $sth->execute(@bind_values);
    $rv = $sth->execute_array(\%attr, ...);

    $rc = $sth->bind_col($col_num, \$col_variable);
    $rc = $sth->bind_columns(@list_of_refs_to_vars_to_bind);
```

```
@row_ary  = $sth->fetchrow_array;
$ary_ref  = $sth->fetchrow_arrayref;
$hash_ref = $sth->fetchrow_hashref;

$ary_ref  = $sth->fetchall_arrayref;
$ary_ref  = $sth->fetchall_arrayref( $slice, $max_rows );

$hash_ref = $sth->fetchall_hashref( $key_field );

$rv   = $sth->rows;

$rc   = $dbh->begin_work;
$rc   = $dbh->commit;
$rc   = $dbh->rollback;

$quoted_string = $dbh->quote($string);

$rc   = $h->err;
$str  = $h->errstr;
$rv   = $h->state;

$rc   = $dbh->disconnect;
```

The synopsis above only lists the major methods and parameters.

15.4.3   How to Use DBI

Once you load the DBI module into your program with the *use DBI* statement, there are only five steps involved: connect to a database, prepare a query, execute the query, get the results, and disconnect.

To connect to MySQL, use the *connect()* method. This method specifies the type of database (MySQL, Oracle, Sybase, CSV files, Informix, and so on), the database name, host name, user, and password with some additional, optional arguments to specify error and transaction handling, and more. It returns a database handle (*$dbh* is used in the manual page, but you can call it any valid scalar name).

Once connected to the MySQL database, you have a database handle (reference to the database object). Now you can send a query by preparing and executing a SQL statement. This can be done by calling the *prepare()* and *execute()* methods or by using the *do()* method. The *prepare()* and *execute()* methods are used for *SELECT* statements, whereas the *do()* method is normally used for SQL statements that don't return a result set, such as the *INSERT*, *UPDATE*, or *DELETE* statements. What is returned from these methods depends on what the query returns. For example, successful *SELECT* queries return a result set (represented as *$sth* in the DBI manual page); successful *INSERT/UPDATE/ DELETE* queries with *do()* return the number of rows affected; and unsuccessful queries return an error or *undef*. Most data is returned to the Perl script as strings, and null values are returned as *undef*.

Once the query has been sent to the database and a result set returned (reference to the result object), you can extract the data with special methods, such as *fetchrow_array()* and *fetchrow_hashref()*. These methods retrieve each record as a Perl array or a Perl hashref, respectively.

Finally, when you are done, the *finish()* method releases the result object returned from the *prepare()* method, and the *disconnect()* method ends the session by disconnecting from the database.

Now we will go through each of these five steps in detail.

15.4.4   Connecting to and Disconnecting from the Database

Once loaded, the DBI module is responsible for loading the appropriate driver for a given database. Then you will work with the database by using the methods provided by the module listed in the output shown from *perldoc* DBI. The first method we will use is the *connect()* method to get a connection to the database, and the last method, *disconnect()*, to break the connection.

The following example shows how to check for available database drivers for DBI.

EXAMPLE 15.22

```
1   use DBI;
2   my @drivers = DBI->available_drivers;
3   print join(", ", @drivers),"\n";

(Output for Windows)
DBM, ExampleP, File, Gofer, Proxy, SQLite, Sponge, mysql
```

The *connect()* Method.   The *connect()* method establishes a connection to the specified database and returns an object called a database handle. You can make multiple connections to the same database or even to different databases in a program by using multiple *connect* statements. The *connect()* method takes several arguments:

```
"dbi:$driver:$database,$port,$username,$password"
```

1. The first argument is the DSN string (Data Source Name), the logical name for the database. Any attributes that define the data source are assigned to the DSN for retrieval by the driver. The DSN contains the name of the DBI module, *dbi*, followed by a colon and the database driver (MySQL, Sybase, Oracle), another colon and the name of the actual database for which the connection will be made, and/or the hostname (default is *localhost*), port, and so on, and is terminated with a semicolon.

2. The next argument to connect is the name of the user.

3. The next argument is the password of the user (optional).

4. And finally, there is a reference to a hash (set of optional attributes for error handling, autocommiting, and so on).

EXAMPLE 15.23

```
1   dbh=DBI->connect("dbi:<RDMS>:<database>","<username>","<password>",
    \%attributes) or die("Couldn't connect");

2   $dbh=DBI->connect('DBI:mysql:sample_db','root','quigley1') or
    die "Can't connect";

3   $dbh=DBI->connect('DBI:mysql:database=sample_db;user=root;
    password=quigley1') or die "Couldn't connect to sample_db"
    . DBI->errstr;

4   $dsn = dbi:mysql:northwind; $username="root"; $password="letmein";
    $dbh = DBI->connect($dsn, $user, $password,
    { PrintError => 0, RaiseError => 1, AutoCommit => 0 });

------------------Using Other Database Systems------------

5   $dbh = DBI->connect('dbi:Oracle:payroll','scott','tiger');
    $dbh = DBI->connect("dbi:Oracle:host=torch.cs.dal.ca;sid=TRCH",
    $user, $passwd);

6   $dbh = DBI->connect('dbi:odbc:MSS_pubs','sa', '12mw_1');
    (MS SQL Server)
```

EXPLANATION

1   The *connect* method will return a database handle. This is the format you use to connect. At minimum, you must have the DSN string, which is the name of the module, *dbi*, the name of the database driver, and the name of the database, represented as *<database>*. The username, hostname, password, and other attributes are optional.

2   We are connecting to the *mysql* database named, *sample_db*; the login is *root*, and the password is *quiqley1*.

3   The arguments to the *connect* method, when given as a single string, should be on one line with no spaces around the arguments.
    DBI->errstr returns the reason why we couldn't connect—"Bad password," for example.

4   This connection will be made to a MySQL database named *northwind*, with a user name *root* and password *letmein*. The attributes are to turn on error.

5   This connection will be made to an Oracle database called *payroll*, with a username of *scott* and a password *tiger*.

6   The data source name of *MSS_pubs* uses the username *sa*, password *12mw_1*, and the ODBC driver.

The *disconnect()* Method. As you may remember from Chapter 10, "Getting a Handle on Files," after we opened a file with a user-defined filehandle, we closed it with the built-in *close* function when finished. Unless lexically scoped, (three-part argument to open) if we forgot to close the file, it would be left up to the operating system to do so when the Perl script exited. The same thing is true with closing a database. After you are finished using the database, it is always a good idea to close the connection with the *disconnect* method. Of course, because the database handle is an object, Perl will automatically remove the reference to it once the program exits or the object goes out of scope. You would use the *disconnect* method, like so:

```
$dbh->disconnect();
```

15.4.5 Preparing a Statement Handle and Fetching Results

The SQL *select* statement is probably the statement used most when querying a database. When preparing a *select* statement for the database, the query is sent as a string argument to the DBI *prepare* method. The query is just as you would type it in the MySQL console but minus the semicolon. The database handle calls the *prepare* method. The database determines how it will execute the query (creates a "plan"), and DBI returns a statement handle containing the details on how the query will be executed. The statement handle (represented as *$sth*) encapsulates individual SQL statements to be executed within the database and calls the *execute* method.

This *execute* method tells the database to perform the SQL statement (execute its "plan") and to return the results back to the program. An *undef* is returned if an error occurs. A successful execute always returns true regardless of the number of rows affected, even if zero rows were affected. The number of statement handles that can be created and executed is basically unlimited.

Even though you have executed the plan, you can't see the results unless you use another DBI method to retrieve it, such as *dump_results()*, *fetchrow_array()*, or *fetch()*.

Select, Execute, and Dump the Results. The DBI *dump_results* method gets all the rows from the statement handle object and prints the results in one simple statement. In the following example, we will connect to the database, prepare the query, execute the query, and print the results.

EXAMPLE 15.24

```
   (The Script)
   use DBI;
1  $dbh=DBI->connect('DBI:mysql:sample_db;user=root;password=quigley1');

2  $sth=$dbh->prepare("SELECT * FROM coaches")
       or die "Can't prepare sql statement" or die . $dbh->errstr;
```

EXAMPLE 15.24 (CONTINUED)

```
3   $sth->execute();
    print qq(\n\tContents of "coaches" table\n) or
        die "Couldn't execute  statement" . $sth->errstr;
4   $sth->dump_results();   # Display results of the execute

5   $sth->finish();
6   $dbh->disconnect();

(Output)
        Contents of "coaches" table
'1', 'John Doe', 'Chico Hardhats', 'Head Coach', '2002-12-10'
'2', 'Jack Mattsone', 'CHardhats', 'Offensive Coach', '2004-10-05'
'3', 'Bud Wilkins', 'Fremont Tigers', 'Head Coach', '1999-09-06'
'4', 'Joe Hayes', 'Fremont Tigers', 'Defensive Coach', '1998-06-16'
'5', 'George Jones', 'Bangor Rams', 'Offensive Coach', '2003-09-03'
'6', 'Jerry O'Connell','Portland Penguins','Head Coach', '2006-02-22'
6 rows
```

EXPLANATION

1 A connection is made to the MySQL database called *sample_db* and a database handle is returned called *$dbh*. It is the object that represents the connection. Now we have access to the database.

2 The *prepare* method is used to prepare the SQL query. It returns a statement handle, an object that encapsulates the query and prepares it for execution. (Note that the SQL statement does NOT end with a semicolon.)

3 The *execute* method causes the query to actually be executed. Now we are ready to retrieve the results of the query.

4 The *dump_results* method is called on the statement handle and prints the results of the query.

Select, Execute, and Fetch a Row As an Array. When the *fetchrow_array()* method is called, the database will return the first row of results as an array, where each field is an element in the array. Each successive call to the *fetchrow_array()* method yields the next row of results, until there are no more results and the call yields a value of *undef*.

In the following example, we will connect to the database, prepare the query, execute the query, and fetch the data with the *fetchrow_array()* method. As in this example, we can use a *while* or *for* loop to fetch all the rows. (An important point to remember is that when the fields are fetched, they are assigned in the order they were listed in the SQL query.)

EXAMPLE 15.25

```
(The Script)
  use DBI;
1 my $dbh=DBI->connect(qq(DBI:mysql:database=sample_db;user=root;
     password=quigley1)) or die "Can't connect". $dbh->errstr;

2 my $sth=$dbh->prepare("SELECT name, wins, losses FROM teams");

3 $sth->execute();
  print "Contents of sample_db, the mysql database.\n\n";

4 while(my @row=$sth->fetchrow_array()){ # Get one row at a time
5    print "name=$row[0]\n";       # Field one
     print "wins=$row[1]\n";       # Field two
     print "losses=$row[2]\n\n";   # Field three
  }
6 print $sth->rows, " rows were retrieved.\n";

7 $sth->finish();
8 $dbh->disconnect();
```

```
(The Output)
Contents of sample_db, the mysql database.

name=Fremont Tigers
wins=24
losses=26

name=Chico Hardhats
wins=19
losses=25

name=Bath Warships
wins=32
losses=3

name=Bangor Rams
wins=22
losses=24

4 rows were retrieved.
```

EXPLANATION

1 The *connect()* method returns a database handle, *$dbh*, an object that references the MySQL database called *sample_db*.
2 A SQL *select* statement is prepared and a statement handle returned, called *$sth*.
3 The query is sent to the database for execution.
4 The *fetchrow_array()* method returns the first row from the database, where fields are elements of the array, called *@row*. To get subsequent rows, a *while* loop is used. The loop ends when there are no more rows.

EXPLANATION (CONTINUED)

5   Each field from a row is assigned to a variable and printed.
6   The *rows()* method returns the number of rows affected by the statement handle.
7   The *finish* method releases the statement handle.
8   The *disconnect* method releases the database handle.

Select, Execute, and Fetch a Row As a Hash.

The *fetchrow_hashref()* method fetches a row from the database table as a hash reference where the keys are the names of the columns and the values are the data stored in that column. The following example is exactly like the previous one, except *fetchrow_arrayref()* is replaced with *fetchrow_hashref()*.

EXAMPLE 15.26

```
      use DBI;
1   my $dbh=DBI->connect(qq(DBI:mysql:database=sample_db;user=root;
         password=quigley1)) or die "Can't connect". DBI->errstr;

2   my $sth=$dbh->prepare("SELECT name, wins, losses FROM teams") ;

3   $sth->execute();

    print "Contents of sample_db, the mysql database.\n\n";

4   while( my $row = $sth->fetchrow_hashref()){
5      print "Name:   $row->{name}\n";
       print "Wins:   $row->{wins}\n";
       print "Losses: $row->{losses}\n\n";
    }
    print $sth->rows, " rows were retrieved";

6   print "There are $count rows in the sample database.\n";
7   $sth->finish();
8   $dbh->disconnect();
```

EXPLANATION

1   The *connect()* method returns a database handle, *$dbh*, an object that references the MySQL database called *sample_db*.
2   A SQL *select* statement is prepared and a statement handle returned, called *$sth*.
3   The query is sent to the database for execution.
4   The *fetch_row_hashref()* method returns the first row from the database as a reference to an anonymous hash consisting of key/value pairs. The key is the name of the field in the table and the value is what is stored there. To get subsequent rows, a *while* loop is used. The loop ends when there are no more rows.
5   Each value from the field, specified as a key, is printed.
7   The *finish* method releases the statement handle.
8   The *disconnect* method releases the database handle.

15.4.6 Getting Error Messages

It is important to know what went wrong when working with DBI. Did the connection fail? Did you prepare the SQL statement correctly? DBI defines several ways to handle errors. You can use automatic error handling with the *PrintError* and *RaiseError* attributes for a specific handle, or you can use diagnostic methods and special DBI variables.

Automatic Error Handling. The DBI module provides automatic error handling when you connect to the database. You can either get warnings every time a DBI method fails, or have the program send a message and abort. The two attributes most often used with the *connect* method are *PrintError* and *RaiseError*.

The *PrintError* Attribute
By default, the *connect()* method sets *PrintError* to on (set to 1) and automatically generates a warning message if any of the DBI methods fail.

The *RaiseError* Attribute
The *RaiseError* attribute can be used to force errors to raise exceptions. It is turned off by default. When set to on, any DBI method that results in an error will cause DBI to die with an error, *$DBI::errstr*. If you turn *RaiseError* on, then you would normally turn *PrintError* off. If *PrintError* is also on, then the *PrintError* is done first. Typically, *RaiseError* is used in conjunction with an *eval* block so that you can catch the exception that's been thrown. If there is a *die*, a compile, or runtime error in the *eval* block, the special variable $@ is set to the error message and set to null if there is not an error. If $@ has been set, then you can handle the error without exiting DBI.

Manual Error Handling. If you want to manually check for errors when a particular method fails, you can use either the error diagnostic methods or the error diagnostic variables provided by the DBI module. This gives you control over each method you call to trap the errors if they occur.

Error Diagnostic Methods
First we will look at two error diagnostic methods, *err()* and *errstr()*. These methods can be invoked against any valid handle, driver, database, or statement. The *err()* method will return the error code associated with the problem that occurred. The error code is a number that differs depending on the database system being used. The *errstr()* method corresponds to the error code number but is a string that contains information as to why the last DBI method call failed. Before another method call, the error messages for a handle are reset, so they should be checked right after a specific handle has produced an error. The diagnostic methods are used as discussed next.

```
$rv  = $h->err();
$str = $h->errstr();
```

Error Diagnostic Variables

The DBI variables *$DBI::err* and *$DBI::errstr*, are class variables and behave similarly to the method described previously, except they have a shorter life span and always refer to the last handle that was used. The *$DBI::err* contains the error number associated with last method that was called, and *$DBI:errstr* contains a string describing the error message associated with the error number in *$DBI::err*. You should generally test the return status of connect and print *$DBI::errstr* if the *connect()* method failed.

EXAMPLE 15.27

```
(The Script)
   use DBI;

   my $dbh=DBI->connect('dbi:mysql:sample_db','root','quigley1',
      {
1         RaiseError => 1,  # Die if there are errors
2         PrintError => 0,  # Warn if there are errors
      }
3  ) or die $DBI::errstr;  # Report why connect failed

4  my $sth=$dbh->prepare("SELECT name, wins, losses FROM teams") or
      die "Can't prepare sql statement" . $dbh->errstr;
   $sth->execute() or die "Can't execute: ". $sth->errstr;
   print "Contents of sample_db, the mysql database.\n\n";
   while(my @val = $sth->fetchrow_array()){
      print "name=$val[0]\n";
      print "wins=$val[1]\n";
      print "losses=$val[2]\n\n";
   }
5  print $sth->rows," rows were retrieved.\n";

   $sth->finish();
   $dbh->disconnect();
```

EXPLANATION

1   Here we turn on the *RaiseError* attribute, which will cause the program to die if there is an error from any DBI method call.

2   The *PrintError* attribute is turned on by default. It sends a warning message if a method fails. It is set to 0 here to turn it off, since *RaiseError* is turned on. You can have both *RaiseError* and *PrintError* turn on or off. If both are turned on, the *PrintError* sends a warning first, and then *RaiseError* prints a message, and the program dies.

3   The *$DBI::errstr* variable will print the reason the connection failed, if it did.

4   This time we use the *errstr* method to report an error that may have occurred if the *prepare* method failed; meaning, the SQL statement was incorrectly prepared.

Examples of Error Messages

The following example shows some common error messages we might receive.

EXAMPLE 15.28

```
1 (Bad Database Name; connect failed)
       DBI connect('ample_db','root',...) failed: Unknown database
'ample_db'at first.dbi line 9

2        Bad Password; connect failed)
   DBI connect('sample_db','root',...) failed: Access denied for user
'root'@'localhost' (using password: YES) at first.dbi line 9

3        Bad SQL Query; execute failed)
DBD::mysql::st execute failed: Unknown column 'win' in 'field list' at
first.dbi line 23.
```

Binding Columns and Fetching Values.   Binding columns is the most efficient way to fetch data. Binding allows you to associate a Perl variable with a field (column) value in the database. When values are fetched, the variables are automatically updated with the retrieved value, making fetching data fast. DBI provides the *bind_columns* method to bind each column to a scalar reference. When the *fetch* method is called, the values from the database are assigned to scalars of the same name rather than to arrays or hashes as seen in the previous examples.

Every time the *fetch* method is called, the scalars will be updated with values from the current row.

(See *bind_col* in the DBI documentation for another way to bind columns.)

EXAMPLE 15.29

```
      use DBI;
      my $driver="DBI:mysql";
      my $database="sample_db";
      my $user="root";
      my $host="localhost";

      my $dbh =
         DBI->connect("$driver:database=$database;host=$host;user=$user")
            or die "Can't connect: " . $DBI->errstr;

1     my $sth=$dbh->prepare("SELECT name, wins, losses FROM teams")
         or die "Can't prepare sql statement" . $dbh->errstr;

2     $sth->execute() or die "Can't prepare sql statement" . $sth->errstr;
```

EXAMPLE 15.29 (CONTINUED)

```
3   my($name, $wins, $losses);    # Scalars references are bound to
                                  # respective columns
4   $sth->bind_columns(\$name,\$wins,\$losses);
    print "\nSelected data for teams.\n\n";
    printf"\t%-20s%-8s%-8s\n","Name","Wins", "Losses";
5   while( $sth->fetch()){
        # Fetch a row and return column values as scalars
        printf "   %-25s%3d%8d\n",$name, $wins, $losses;
    }

    $sth->finish();
    $dbh->disconnect();

(Output)
        Selected data for teams.

    Name                    Wins    Losses
    Bath Warships            34      3
    Berkeley Bombers         12      19
    Denver Daredevils        23      5
    Littleton's Tigers       14      18
    Middlefield Monsters      2      32
    Palo Alto Panthers       24      17
    Portland Penguins        28      14
    San Francisco Fogheads   24      12
    Sunnyvale Seniors        12      24
```

EXPLANATION

1   The SQL *SELECT* statement is prepared and a statement handle returned.
2   The DBI *execute()* method sends the query to the database for execution.
3   Three scalar variables are created that will be bound to each of the three fields listed in the *SELECT* statement.
4   The *bind_columns* method specifies references to scalar variables that will be bound to the individual fields when the result set is retrieved from the database with the *fetch* method. In older versions of DBI, the first argument was specified as *undef* to represent a null field; for example:

    ```
    $sth->bind_columns(undef,\$name,\$wins,\$losses);
    ```

5   The *fetch* method retrieves a row from the result set and assigns each value to the variables named as arguments in the *bind_columns()* method. The name of the team is automatically assigned to *$name*, the number of wins to *$wins*, and the number of losses to *$losses*. Each time through the loop, the next row of column values will be assigned to these variables, and so on, until there is no more data.

15.4.7 The *?* Placeholder and Parameter Binding

Placeholders, represented by a *?*, are used to optimize how queries are handled. Placeholders provide a template for a query and represent values that will be assigned to fields at a later time. They are used primarily with *SELECT*, *INSERT*, *UPDATE*, and *DELETE* statements. Values need to be "bound" to each placeholder before the statement can be executed. There are two ways to bind parameters: in the *execute* statement or with the *bind_params* method.

When a query is prepared by DBI, the database has to plan how it can best handle the query. The statement handle is used to store the prepared plan for the query, called the **execution plan**. Normally, once a query has been executed, the plan is discarded. When placeholders are used, instead of discarding the execution plan, the database accepts the placeholder in a template and makes a plan around it—making the template usable for future queries.

The *?* represents values, such as *name = ?*, where *name* is a field name in the database table and its value will be supplied a value later on. (Remember, the *?* represents a value, not a field name; for example, *? = "John"* is wrong!)

Binding Parameters in the *execute* Statement.   The *execute* method can take arguments representing the values of the placeholders, and those values are replaced in the prepared plan each time the method is called. DBI has to figure out the data type of the value. (Not all databases and DBI drivers support placeholders. See *http://dev.mysql.com/doc/refman/5.7/en/sql-syntax-prepared-statements.html*.)

In the following example, we will use a placeholder to be filled in later as an argument to the *execute* method.

```
      use DBI;
      my $driver="DBI:mysql";
      my $database="sample_db";
      my $user="root";
      my $host="localhost";

      my $dbh =
         DBI->connect("$driver:$database:$host;user=$user;
      password=quigley1")or die "Can't connect: " . DBI->errstr;

1     my $sth=$dbh->prepare("SELECT name, wins, losses FROM teams
         WHERE name = ?") or die "Can't prepare sql statement"
         . DBI->errstr;

      print "Enter the team name: ";
2     chomp($team_name=<STDIN>);
```

EXAMPLE 15.30 (CONTINUED)

```
 3   $sth->execute($team_name);
     # The value of $team_name replaces the ?
     print "\nSelected data for team \"$name\".\n\n";

 4   while(my @val = $sth->fetchrow_array()){
         print "name=$val[0]\n";
         print "wins=$val[1]\n";
         print "losses=$val[2]\n\n";
     }
     $sth->finish();
     $dbh->disconnect();

(Output)
Enter the team name: Chico Hardhats

Selected data for team "Chico Hardhats".

name=Chico Hardhats
wins=18
losses=6
```

EXPLANATION

1 The *SELECT* statement contains a *WHERE* clause with a placeholder *?* for the value that will later be assigned to the *name* field. The statement is prepared and a statement handle returned.
2 The user is asked for a team name, assigned to *$team_name*, later to be used as an argument to the *execute* method.
3 The value of *$team_name* is plugged into the placeholder in the query.
4 The *fetchrow_array()* method retrieves the values for the team that was specified when the query was executed in line 3.

Using Multiple Placeholders

It is also possible to use multiple placeholders to be filled in later in the *execute* method, as shown in the following example.

EXAMPLE 15.31

```
     use DBI;
     my $dbh=DBI->connect("DBI:mysql:host=localhost;user=root;
         password=quigley1;database=sample_db") or die $DBI->errstr;

 1   my $sth=$dbh->prepare("INSERT INTO teams(name, wins, losses)
         VALUES(?,?,?)");
```

EXAMPLE 15.31 (CONTINUED)

```
    # Preset the values in variables
2   my $team_name="Denver Daredevils";  # set values here
    my $wins=18;
    my $losses=5;
3   $sth->execute($team_name, $wins, $losses) or
        die "Can't execute: " . $sth->errstr;
    print "\nData for team table. \n\n";
4   $sth=$dbh->prepare("SELECT * FROM teams");
    $sth->execute();
5   while(my @val = $sth->fetchrow_array()){
        print "name=$val[0]\n";
        print "wins=$val[1]\n";
        print "losses=$val[2]\n\n";
    }

    $sth->finish();
    $dbh->disconnect();
```

EXPLANATION

1 This time, three placeholders act as a template for values that will be filled in at some later time with the SQL *INSERT* statement. Each *?* represents a value for the *name* field, the *wins* field, and the *losses* field, respectively.

2 The scalars are assigned the values that will be sent to the database when the SQL statement is executed.

3 The *execute()* method executes the SQL statement by plugging in the values of these variables where the placeholders are found in the *INSERT* statement.

4 Another SQL statement is prepared to select all the fields in the table so that we can see if the new data was actually inserted.

5 The result set from the previous query is fetched a row at a time and displayed.

Using Placeholders to Insert Multiple Records

We can also use placeholders to represent entire rows (records) to be later inserted into a database, as shown in the following example.

EXAMPLE 15.32

```
    use DBI;
    my $dbh=DBI->connect("DBI:mysql:host=localhost;user=root;
    password=quigley1;database=sample_db") or
        die "Can't connect: ". $DBI->errstr;

    # Using a placeholder. Values will be assigned later

1   my $sth=$dbh->prepare("INSERT INTO teams(name, wins, losses)
        VALUES(?,?,?)") or die "Can't prepare statement: ". $dbh->errstr;
```

EXAMPLE 15.32 (CONTINUED)

```
    # Create a list of new entries
2   my @rows = (
        ['Tampa Terrors', 4, 5],
        ['Arcata Angels', 3 , 4],
        ['Georgetown Giants', 1 ,6],
        ['Juno Juniors', 2, 7],
    );

3   foreach my $row (@rows ){
        $name = $row->[0];
        $wins = $row->[1];
        $losses=$row->[2];
4       $sth->execute($name, $wins, $losses);
    }
    print "\nData for team table. \n\n";
5   $sth=$dbh->prepare("SELECT * FROM teams");
    $sth->execute();
    while(my @row = $sth->fetchrow_array()){
        print "name=$row[0]\n";
        print "wins=$row[1]\n";
        print "losses=$row[2]\n\n";
    }

    $sth->finish();
    $dbh->disconnect();
```

EXPLANATION

1 Again, three placeholders act as a template for values that will be filled in at some later time with the SQL *INSERT* statement. Each *?* represents a value for the *name* field, the *wins* field, and the *losses* field, respectively.

2 An array of rows is created to represent the new records that will later be inserted into the database.

3 Each row from @*row* is broken down into its individual fields and the values assigned to scalars representing the value for each field.

4 The *execute()* method executes the statement by plugging in the values of these variables where the placeholders are found in the *INSERT* statement. This is done for each row of new data until it is all entered. If any of the teams are duplicates, the *execute()* method will fail because the *name* field was earlier assigned to be the primary key.

Binding Parameters and the *bind_param()* Method. Another convenient and efficient way to use placeholders is with the *bind_param()* method. The placeholder tells the database that the value represented by the *?* will be filled in later. The bound parameter is the value that will be filled in to replace the *?* and eliminates sending arguments to the *execute()* method. Make sure that *bind_param* is called **before** the *execute* statement to ensure that the missing value has been filled in.

The *bind_param()* method takes up to three arguments. The first argument represents the position of the parameter in the placeholder; so if the position is 1, then that would be represented by the first *?* (placeholder) to be filled in with a value, and if the position is 2, that would be represented by the second *?*, and so on. The second argument to *bind_param()* is the actual value that will replace the *?*. Last is an optional parameter that hints as to the data type of the replacement value, typically a number or string. The data type for a placeholder cannot be changed after the first *bind_param()* method call. However, it can be left unspecified, in which case it defaults to the previous value.

Two ways to handle the data type are either as an anonymous hash or as a DBI constant, like so:

```
$sth->bind_param(1, $value, { TYPE => SQL_INTEGER });  # Hash
$sth->bind_param(1, $value, SQL_INTEGER);  # DBI Constant
```

EXAMPLE 15.33

```
    use DBI;
    my $driver="DBI:mysql";
    my $database="sample_db";
    my $user="root";
    my $password="quigley1";
    my $host="localhost";

    my $dbh = DBI->connect("$driver:$database:$host","$user",
        "$password") or die "Can't connect: " . $DBI->errstr;

1   my $sth=$dbh->prepare("SELECT name, wins,losses FROM teams
        where name LIKE ? ") or die "Can't prepare sql statement" .
        $dbh->errstr;

2   $sth->bind_param(1, "Ch%");
3   $sth->execute();
4   $sth->dump_results();
    $sth->finish();
    $dbh->disconnect();

(Output)
'Cheyenne Chargers', '6', 14
'Chico Hardhats', '21', '25'
```

EXPLANATION

1   A SQL statement is prepared with a placeholder to serve as a template for the query.
2   The *bind_param()* method takes two arguments: the position of the placeholder and the value (*Ch%*) that will be replace the *?* in the query. Since there is only one parameter, the position is 1. If you had two parameters, the second one would be 2.
3   Since the parameters were bound to the statement with *bind_param*, the *execute* method does not require arguments.
4   The *dump_results* method is used to quickly output the results returned from the database after the query was executed.

15.4.8 Handling Quotes

When strings are sent to a database, they are enclosed in quotes. Strings themselves may also contain quotes, as in the string *"Mrs. O'Donnell"*, and these quotes must be properly escaped when sent to a database. To make things more complicated, different database systems have different rules for handling quotes. The DBI module handles quoting issues with its *quote* method. This method is used with a database handle to convert a string according to rules defined for a specific database and returns the string correctly escaped.

EXAMPLE 15.34

```
    use DBI;
    my $dbh=DBI->connect(qq(DBI:mysql:database=sample_db;user=root;
        password=quigley1)) or die "Can't connect";
1   my $namestring=qq(Jerry O'Connell);
2   $namestring=$dbi->quote($string);
3   print $namestring;
4   my $sth=$dbi->prepare("SELECT * FROM coaches WHERE name = ? ")
        or die "Can't prepare sql statement" . $dbi->errstr;
5   $sth->execute($namestring);
    print qq(\nContents of "coaches" table\n);

6   while(my @val = $sth->fetchrow_array()){
        print "\tid=$val[0]\n";
        print "\tname=$val[1]\n";
        print "\tteam_name=$val[2]\n";
        print "\tteam_name=$val[3]\n";
        print "\tstart_date=$val[4]\n\n";
    }

    $sth->finish();
    $dbh->disconnect();

(Output)
3   'Jerry O\'Connell'
5   Contents of "coaches" table
6   id=6
    name=Jerry O'Connell
    team_name=Portland Penguins
    team_name=Head Coach
    start_date=2006-02-22
```

EXPLANATION

1   A string variable, *$namestring*, is assigned a string of characters containing a single quote.

2   A DBI *quote* method is used to prepare the string for the *mysql* database by enclosing the string in quotes and escaping the single quote with a backslash.

3   This line shows you how the *quote* method prepared the string. Notice the apostrophe in O'Connell is escaped with a backslash.

4   In the *WHERE* clause, the placeholder will be given the quoted string when the *execute* method is called.

5   The *execute* method is called with *$namestring* as its argument. This value will replace the placeholder when making the query on line 3.

6   The table is displayed.

15.4.9 Cached Queries

A **cache** is a temporary storage area where data frequently used can be copied and accessed more quickly. Most database servers utilize a cache to improve the performance of recently seen queries. A SQL statement can be cached rather than destroyed after it is executed. If another query identical to the cached statement is executed, the cached query can be reused. The DBI *prepare_cached* method is used to cache a query. It is just like the *prepare* method, except that it looks to see if the same SQL statement has been previously executed, and if so, gives you the cached statement handle rather than a brand new one. (If you are managing multiple connections, see *Apache::DBI::Cache*.)

EXAMPLE 15.35

```
        use DBI;
        my $driver="DBI:mysql";
        my $database="sample_db";
        my $host="localhost";
        my.$user="root";
        my $password="quigley1";
        my $dbh=DBI->connect("$driver:database=$database;
        host=$host;user=$user;password=$password")or
            die "Can't connect: " . $DBI->errstr;

1   sub get_wins{      # Subroutine to handle database query
2       my($dbh, $team) = @_;
3       my $sth=$dbh->prepare_cached("SELECT wins FROM teams
            WHERE name = ?") or die "Can't prepare sql statement"
            . $dbh->errstr;
4       $sth->execute($team);
        $wins=$sth->fetchrow_array();
5       return $wins;
    }
    STARTOVER: {
6       print "To see how many wins, please enter the team's name. ";
        chomp($team_name=<STDIN>);
```

EXAMPLE 15.35 (CONTINUED)

```
            # Call a function to process database query
7           print "$team_name has won ", get_wins($dbh, $team_name),
               " games.\n";
            print "Do you want to check wins for another team? ";
            chomp($ans = <STDIN>);
8           redo STARTOVER if $ans =~ /^y$|^yes$/i;
        }
        $sth->finish();
        $dbh->disconnect();


(Output)
5   To see how many wins, please enter the team's name. Tampa Terrors
    Tampa Terrors have won 3 games.
7   Do you want to check wins for another team? y
5   To see how many wins, please enter the team's name. San Francisco
    Fogheads
    San Francisco Fogheads have won 24 games.
7   Do you want to check wins for another team? y
5   To see how many wins, please enter the team's name. Chico Hardhats
    Chico Hardhats have won 21 games.
7   Do you want to check wins for another team? n
```

EXPLANATION

1   A user-defined function called *get_wins* will be used to handle the database requests.

2   The @_ contains two values, the database handle and the name of a team in the database.

3   A statement is prepared and for efficiency, it is cached, rather than being destroyed after it is executed. For repeating the same query many times, this is done to make the processing more efficient. Since this function may be called a number of times, the *prepare_cache()* method is used. Other than its name and caching feature, this method is just like the *prepare* method.

4   The query is executed and the name of the team filled in where the *?* appears in the SQL statement.

5   The number of wins for a specified team is retrieved and returned from this function. (The program doesn't test to see if the number of rows returned is zero.)

6   In this main part of the program, a labeled block is entered and the user is asked to select a team.

7   Within the *print* statement, the user-defined function called *get_wins* is called. The database handle and the name of the team selected by the user are passed to the function.

8   If the user wants to see the number of wins for another team, program flow will go back to the beginning of the labeled block and start again.

15.5 Statements That Don't Return Anything

15.5.1 The *do()* Method

The *do()* method is used to prepare and execute nonselect, nonrepeating statements in one step. Statements such as the *UPDATE*, *INSERT*, or *DELETE* are examples of SQL statements that would use the *do* method. These statements change the database but don't return data. Unlike the *prepare* method, *do* doesn't return a statement handle but instead returns a count of the number of rows that were affected or *undef* if the query failed. (A return value of -1 means the number of rows is not known, not applicable, or not available.)

```
$rows_affected = $dbh->do("UPDATE your_table SET foo = foo + 1");
```

The only drawback is performance if you are repeating an operation a number of times with placeholders, as we did in Example 15.35, because then, for each query, the steps of prepare and execute must also be repeated over and over again.

Adding Entries. To add entries to a table in the database, the SQL *INSERT* statement is used in the DBI *do* method. The *do* method will return the number of new entries or *undef* if it fails.

EXAMPLE 15.36

```
    use DBI;
    my $dbh=
    DBI->connect("DBI:mysql:host=localhost;user=root,
        password=quigley1;
        database=sample_db")or $DBI->errstr;
    # Add two new entries
1   $dbh->do("INSERT INTO teams(name,wins,losses)
        VALUES('San Francisco Fogheads', 24,12)");

2   $dbh->do(qq/INSERT INTO teams(name, wins, losses)
        VALUES(?,?,?)/, undef,'Middlefield Monsters', 2, 32);

    $dbh->do(qq/INSERT INTO teams(name, wins, losses)
        VALUES(?,?,?)/,undef,'Littleton's Tigers', 4, 18);

3   $dbh->do("INSERT INTO coaches
        VALUES('','Roger Outback','San Francisco Fogheads',
            'Defensive Coach','2006-03-16'");

    $dbh->disconnect();
```

EXPLANATION

1–3 The DBI *do* method is used to insert values into the *teams* table in the *sample_db* database. The *prepare* and *execute* methods are absent here, because *do* does it all. It returns the number of rows affected. (The *undef* value is used to indicate a SQL NULL field, in this case the primary field.)

Deleting Entries. In the following example, a record is deleted if some condition is true. Since the *delete* method doesn't return a result set, it is called with the DBI *do* method.

EXAMPLE 15.37

```
        use DBI;
        my $driver="DBI:mysql";
        my $database="sample_db";
        my $user="root";
        my $host="localhost";

        my $dbh = DBI->connect("$driver:database=$database;
        host=$host;user=$user") or die "Can't connect: " . $DBI->errstr;

        print "Enter the team name you want to delete: ";
        chomp(my $name=<STDIN>);
1       my $sth=$dbh->prepare('SELECT count(*) from teams WHERE name = ?');
2       $sth->execute($name);
3       print "Number of rows to be deleted: ", $sth->fetchrow_array(), "\n";
        print "Continue? ";
        chomp(my $ans = <STDIN>);
        $ans=lc($ans);
        if ( $ans =~ /y|yes/){
4           my $num=$dbh->do(qq/DELETE from teams WHERE name = ?/,
                undef, $name);
5           print ($num > 1 ?"$num rows deleted.\n":"$num row deleted.\n");
        }
        else {
            die "You have not chosen to delete any entries. Good-bye.\n";
        }
        $sth->finish();
        $dbh->disconnect();

(Output)
Enter the team name you want to delete: Sunnyvale Seniors
Number of rows to be deleted: 1
Continue? y
1 row deleted.
```

EXPLANATION

1   The name of the team to be deleted is assigned to *$team* as input from the user. The SQL statement will query the database with the *count* function to find out how many rows were found matching the selected team name.

2   The *execute()* method will send the query to the database, and the number of rows that matched the name of the team found will be returned.

3   The results of the query are fetched. The user is given the opportunity to remove the entries found. If there aren't any matched teams, there is no point in continuing.

4   The DBI *do()* method is used to prepare and execute the SQL *DELETE* statement.

5   The number of rows deleted returned.

Updating Entries.   To update or edit a database entry, we use the SQL *UPDATE* statement with the DBI *do()* method.

EXAMPLE 15.38

```
      my $driver="DBI:mysql";
      my $database="sample_db";
      my $user="root";
      my $password="quigley1";
      my $host="localhost";

      my $dbi=DBI->connect("$driver:database=$database;host=$host;
          user=$user;password=$password")or die "Can't connect: "
          . $DBI->errstr;

      my $num_of_wins;
      my $num_of_losses;
      my $count;
   1  print "What is the name of the team to update? ";
      chomp(my $team_name=<STDIN>);

      # Show user the table before he tries to update it
   2  my $sth=$dbi->prepare(qq/SELECT * FROM teams
          WHERE name="$team_name"/) or die "Select failed: ". $dbi->errstr;

      $sth->execute or die "Execute failed:".$sth->errstr;

      use DBI;
   3  while((my $name, my $wins, my $losses) = $sth->fetchrow_array()){
   4     $count++;
          print "\nData for $team_name before update:\n"if $count == 1;
          print "\t\twins=$wins\n";
          print "\t\tlosses=$losses\n\n";
      }

   5  if ($count==0){ die "The team you entered doesn't exist.\n";}
   6  print "How many games has $team_name won since the last update?";
      chomp($num_of_wins=<STDIN>);

   7  print "How many games has $team_name lost since the last update? ";
      chomp($num_of_losses=<STDIN>);

   8  $dbi->do(qq/UPDATE teams SET wins=wins+$num_of_wins
         WHERE name = ? /, undef, "$team_name") or
         die "Can't update teams :". $dbi->errstr;

   9  $dbi->do(qq/UPDATE teams SET losses=losses+$num_of_losses
         WHERE name = ? /, undef, "$team_name") or
         die "Can't update teams :". $dbi->errstr;
```

EXAMPLE 15.38 (CONTINUED)

```
      # Show the user the table after it is updated
      print "\nData for $team_name after update:\n";
10   $sth=$dbi->prepare(qq/SELECT * FROM teams
         WHERE name=?/);
      $sth->execute($team_name);
      while((my $name, my $wins, my $losses) = $sth->fetchrow_array()){
         print "\t\twins=$wins\n";
         print "\t\tlosses=$losses\n\n";
      }


      $sth->finish();
      $dbi->disconnect();
```

(Output)
What is the name of the team to update? Chico Hardhats
Data for Chico Hardhats before update:
                    wins=15
                    losses=3
How many games has Chico Hardhats won since the last update? 1
How many games has Chico Hardhats lost since the last update? 2
Data for Chico Hardhats after update:
                    wins=16
                    losses=5

EXPLANATION

1 The user is asked to enter the name of the team in the *teams* table that he will edit.
2 A *SELECT* statement is issued to retrieve selected data in the *teams* table.
3 Before performing the update, the table will be displayed to see it in its current state.
4 The counter will keep track of how many records were returned.
5 If the count is zero, nothing was returned from the *SELECT*, and the program will die with an error message.
6 The user is asked to enter the number of games that have been won since the last update occurred.
7 The user is asked how many games have been lost since the last update.
8 The DBI *do* method is used to prepare and execute the SQL *UPDATE* statement. It returns the number of rows that were affected by the update. This statement will update the *wins* column in the *teams* table.
9 This update is the same as the last one, except it increases the number of losses.
10 After the database table has been updated, this *SELECT* statement is reissued to show the user the table after it was edited.

15.6 Transactions

In the simple example of the *teams* table, if the data is inserted for two teams, and the number of wins and losses for the two teams is accidentally swapped, an update would require both teams be modified, not just one. Suppose you are updating more than one table and the update statements in one table succeed and those in the other fail. A classic example is that you take money out of a savings account in one table and put it in a checking account in another table. The deposit succeeds but the withdrawal fails. The tables are then in an inconsistent state. A transaction is a set of SQL statements that succeed or fail all as a unit. For example, *INSERT*, *UPDATE*, and *DELETE* statements may be executed as a group. If one fails, then none of the statements is executed.

By default, the MySQL client runs with *autocommit* mode enabled. DBI also runs with *autocommit* mode on by default. This means that as soon as you execute any statement that modifies the data in a table, as long as no errors are returned, MySQL immediately commits the statement to the database, and any changes to the affected tables are made permanent.

To use transactions with MySQL, *autocommit* mode must be disabled. We can do that in a Perl script when connecting to the database by setting the hash value of *AutoCommit => 0* as shown in the following example.

In the examples shown so far, when we connected to a database, the hash options available to the *connect()* method for error handling were used, *PrintError* and *RaiseError*. To use transactions, we need to turn off the *AutoCommit* attribute, turn *RaiseErrors* on, and optionally leave *PrintError* on or off (on being the default).

EXAMPLE 15.39

```
1   my $dbh = DBI->connect( 'dbi:mysql:sample_db','root','quigley1',{
        PrintError => 0,
        RaiseError => 1,
2       AutoCommit => 0
    }
```

RaiseError tells DBI to die with the *$DBI::errstr* message if there are errors, and *PrintError* (by default turned on) tells DBI to send a warning with the *$DBI::errstr* message and the program will continue to execute.

15.6.1 Commit and Rollback

Commit means in a transaction that a set of statements will be executed and sent to the database as a group. If all of the statements are successful, the group is committed and the database is modified. If, however, there is an error in any one of the statements in the group, a rollback command is issued, which returns all the tables back to their previous state.

Transactions are often handled in Perl by using an *eval* block to trap errors, then using the *commit()* or *rollback()* methods to finish the transaction.

In the following example, a group of records will be inserted into a table. If an error occurs in the process of adding these entries, the entire process will be rolled back. The error could be because an entry already exists, for example.

EXAMPLE 15.40

```perl
#!/usr/bin/env perl

1   use DBI qw(:sql_types);  # Use DBI constants

2   my $dbh =
3     DBI->connect('dbi:mysql:sample_db;','root','',{RaiseError=>1,
4     AutoCommit=>0}) or die "Connection to sample_db failed:
    $DBI::errstr";
    # Insert new rows
5   my @rows = (
        ['Tampa Terrors', 3, 5],
        ['Los Alamos Lizzards', 12, 3],
        ['Detroit Demons', 22, 0],
        ['Cheyenne Chargers', 6, 0]
    );
6   my $sql = qq{INSERT INTO teams VALUES(?,?,?)};
7   my $sth = $dbh->prepare($sql);
8     foreach $row (@rows){
9        eval{
10           $sth->bind_param(1, $row->[0], SQL_VARCHAR);
             $sth->bind_param(2, $row->[1], SQL_INTEGER);
             $sth->bind_param(3, $row->[3], SQL_INTEGER);
             $sth->execute();
11           $dbh->commit();
         };  # End eval block

12      if($@){   # If error occurred in eval, $@ is set to the error
            warn "Database error: $@\n";
            warn "Rolling back...\n";
13          $dbh->rollback(); # Undo changes if the transaction failed
        }
    } # End loop
    $sth->finish();
    $dbh->disconnect();
```

EXPLANATION

1   Constants representing the values of the SQL standard types are included with the special DBI *:sql_types* tag. The constants are used by the *bind_param* method starting on line 10.

2   Connection to the MySQL database is made.

3   The *RaiseError* attribute is turned on to catch exceptions and die if there is one.

4   The *AutoCommit* attribute is turned off, so that SQL statements are not automatically sent to the database, but must be manually committed.

5   A list of anonymous arrays is created to represent the rows that will be inserted into the table.

6   A SQL statement is created to insert new teams later; the values to be substituted for the *?* placeholders.

7   The SQL statement is prepared. A statement handle is returned.

8   The *foreach* loop is used to iterate through each of the rows that will be added.

9   The *eval* block is entered. If an error occurred, it will be assigned to the special variable, $@. See line 11.

10 The *bind_param()* method binds the first parameter to the first (*?*) placeholder in line 6. The first parameter, *$param->[0]* is *'Tampa Terrors'*, the first time in the loop. It is of type *SQL_VARCHAR*. Next, the second parameter, *param->[1]* is bound to the second placeholder (*?*); the first time through the loop, it represents the number of wins, which is 3.

11 If we got this far, we will commit.

12 If the statement fails, *eval* sets the $@ special variable to the error that occured and will issue a warning that this transaction will be rolled back and will not be committed.

13 If the statement failed, it is rolled back.

15.6.2   Perl DBI, the Web, and the Dancer Framework

Back in the old days, starting in 1993, CGI (Common Gateway Interface) was used to create dynamic Web pages. Writing these pages required configuring the HTTP server (normally Apache), dealing with HTTP headers, requests/responses, as well as environment variables, producing HTML code, understanding HTTP error messages, and more. In the previous edition of this book, a great deal of time was spent explaining how to write these scripts which not only required a considerable understanding of Perl, but also of HTML and HTTP.

When *CGI.pm* was added to the standard Perl library, it provided a solution to simplify writing CGI scripts and handling HTTP requests/responses by adding features for creating forms, file uploads, cookies, and other utilities. However, *CGI.pm* is not simple; it's big and clunky, and to be effective requires a fairly advanced understanding of how the CGI protocol works, not to mention knowing Perl and HTML in depth. The problem was that more often the designer didn't know Perl and the programmer didn't know how to design.

The CGI template system was added to separate the design from the code, make error handling easier, and thus speed up the development process. In fact, although *CGI.pm* has been a standard since 1997, the Perl 5 porters have been discussing a proposal to remove it from the core distribution as of Perl 5.20. (See *http://www.modernperlbooks.com/mt/2013/05/ejecting-cgipm-from-the-perl-core.html.*)

Like it or not, *CGI.pm*, is still a viable way to create Web pages, still part of the Perl core, and according to the Perl 5.20 documentation, "It has the benefit of having developed and refined over 10 years with input from dozens of contributors and being deployed on thousands of Web sites. *CGI.pm* has been included in the Perl distribution since Perl 5.4, and has become a de-facto standard." To speed up the older slower CGI programs, mod_perl and FastCGI provided much better solutions, but moving these from one system to another presented problems.

Enter PSGI and Plack. Like CGI, PSGI (Perl Webserver Gateway Interface) is a specification, an interface between Perl Web servers and Web applications or frameworks, and most modern servers and frameworks already support it. Plack is a Perl module (perldoc plack) and a toolkit for running Web applications and frameworks such as Catalyst and Dancer that are compatible with the PSGI specification (inspired by Python's WSGI and Ruby's Rack). Together, they make developing and deploying Perl Web applications easier, faster, and portable.

Several Perl Web frameworks provide PSGI support including Catalyst, Mason, Dancer, and Mojolicious. This text uses the Dancer framework, which is a simple, yet robust Web application framework for Perl. It is free and open source, written in Perl, and every Dancer application is also a valid Plack applicaton. (See *http://www.perldancer.org.*)

Note to reader: to install and see examples on how to use Dancer, go to Appendix E, "Dancing with Perl."

The following example demonstrates how to use Dancer and DBI to display Perl output on a browser formatted with HTML. It replaces the CGI example from *Perl by Example, Fourth Edition.*

EXAMPLE 15.41

```
(The script)
1  #!/usr/bin/env perl

2  use strict;
3  use warnings;
4  use v5.16;

5  use Dancer;
6  use DBI;

7  set logger => 'console';
   set template => 'template_toolkit';

8  get '/' => sub {
```

EXAMPLE 15.41 (CONTINUED)

```
9    state $html = do { local $/; <DATA> };
10   my $dbh = DBI->connect("DBI:mysql:host=localhost;
        database=sample_db;user=root;password=quigley1")
11      or die "Connection to sample_db failed:  $DBI::errstr";

12   my $sth = $dbh->prepare("SELECT * FROM coaches");
13   $sth->execute();
14   my $rows = $sth->fetchall_arrayref();

15   return (engine 'template')->render( \$html, { rows => $rows } );
16 };

17 dance;

18 __DATA__
   <!DOCTYPE html>

   <html>
       <head>
           <title>Sample Database</title>
           <style>
               body {
                   background: #66ff33;
               }

               table.coaches {
                   border-collapse: collapse;
                   background: white;
               }

               table.coaches, table.coaches tr, table.coaches td {
                   border: 1px;
                   padding: 10px;
               }
           </style>
       </head>
       <body>
           <h1>Contents of the "coaches" Table</h1>

           <table class="coaches">
               <tr>
                   <th>ID</th>
                   <th>Name</th>
                   <th>Team</th>
                   <th>Title</th>
                   <th>Start date</th>
               </tr>
```

EXAMPLE 15.41 (CONTINUED)

```
19                <% FOREACH coach IN rows %>
20                    <tr>
21                        <% FOREACH field IN coach %>
22                            <td><% field %></td>
23                        <% END %>
24                    </tr>
25                <% END %>
            </table>
        </body>
    </html>
```

EXPLANATION

1   The standard *shebang* is used. This ensures that if *perlbrew* is in use, the local Perl is used, instead of the system one. (See Appendix D, "Perlbrew, CPAN, and cpanm," for more information on *perlbrew*.)

2   The script will use *strict* to catch obvious mistakes such as misspelled variable names.

3   The script will use *warnings* to catch less obvious mistakes, such as undefined values being used.

4   The script runs under Perl 5.16 or later.

5   This is a Dancer script. For an introduction to Dancer, see Appendix E, "Dancing with Perl."

6   This is also a DBI script. Dancer can actually be configured to connect to DBI, but we're going to show a manual connection in this script. The *DBI* and *DBD::mysql* modules will be needed. See Appendix D for details on using *cpanm* to install these, if necessary.

7   Dancer is configured here. This can also be done in the *config.yml* shown in the Appendix E. This particular Dancer script does not require any of the extra files created in Appenix E; it runs independently.

8   When the root path '/' is requested, this coderef will run.

9   Perl will read from the DATA filehandle, found at the bottom of this script, and assign what is read to single variable, *$html*. The *do {}* construct simply creates a small block as a single expression, returns the result of the last statement, and assigns the result to *$html*, a *state* variable. (The *state* keyword is like *my*, except if the sub runs again, the previous value is kept, allowing the page to be refreshed without setting and reading from DATA again.) A special Perl variable, *$/*, is the input record separator with the newline being its default; meaning, each line in a file is terminated by the newline character. If set to *undef*, then all the data will be read as a single line and stored in *$html*.

10 DBI is given the DSN to connect to the MySQL database running on *localhost*, with the username *root* and the password *quigley1*. The database *sample_db* is selected as well. The database may also be selected after connection.

EXPLANATION (CONTINUED)

11   If the connection fails, the script dies. *$DBI::errstr* will contain the error message. Now that we have a Dancer application, it may be advisable to respond to the browser with a 500 error.

12   The query *SELECT * FROM coaches* is prepared to select all data from the *coaches* table.

13   The prepared query is executed.

14   The *fetchall_arrayref* method returns a reference to an array for each row of data fetched, assigned to the scalar variable *$rows*. An *arrayref* is appropriate—it will be sent to the template, and as discussed in Appendix E, will send data to the template as references.

15   The template is rendered with the fetched *$rows*. This line is a bit contrived; normally the template would be in a file, and the filename would be used here, simplifying the line. Instead, the template engine is directly sent the template as a ref to the *$html* created earlier.

16   The coderef that handles requests for the root path '/' concludes.

17   Dancer is told that we have finished setting it up, and it is time to dance.

18   The special __DATA__ token defines the end of the script, but also starts an area of freeform text that can be used within the script as a normal filehandle called DATA. Everything following this line is used as the template for the result of the DBI query.

19   After much HTML preamble, a template directive begins a loop over the fetched *$rows*. Each row is stored in the variable *coach*. In the template, variables do not use sigils; meaning, there is not a $ on *rows* or *coaches*. Templates intentionally use a simpler language than Perl.

20   For each *coach* we open a *<tr>* tag, an HTML table row.

21   Another loop begins. Each *coach* is another *arrayref*. The values in the *arrayref* go into *field* and are in the same order as the fields in the database. By specifying the fields explicitly, the risk of the database fields changing can be mitigated, but in this script, we are relying on the table not changing.

22   The value of *field* is output inside a *<td>*, a table cell. As long as the number of fields in the database is as expected, one cell is output per header cell, and the rows match properly. A variable inside *<% %>* is printed by *Template::Toolkit* if nothing else is done with it.

23   The *END* directive closes the *FOREACH* block that is looping over the *field*s in the current *coach*.

24   The *<tr>* tag that represents a single *coach* is closed.

25   The *END* directive closes the *FOREACH* block that is looping over *rows*, putting each one in *coach*. The whole set of lines in between, including the other *FOREACH* loop, is repeated for each *coach* in *rows*. This results in a *<tr>* being output for each *coach*, with as many *<td>*s as there are *field*s, which should be the same number of *<th>*s there are in the *<table>*.

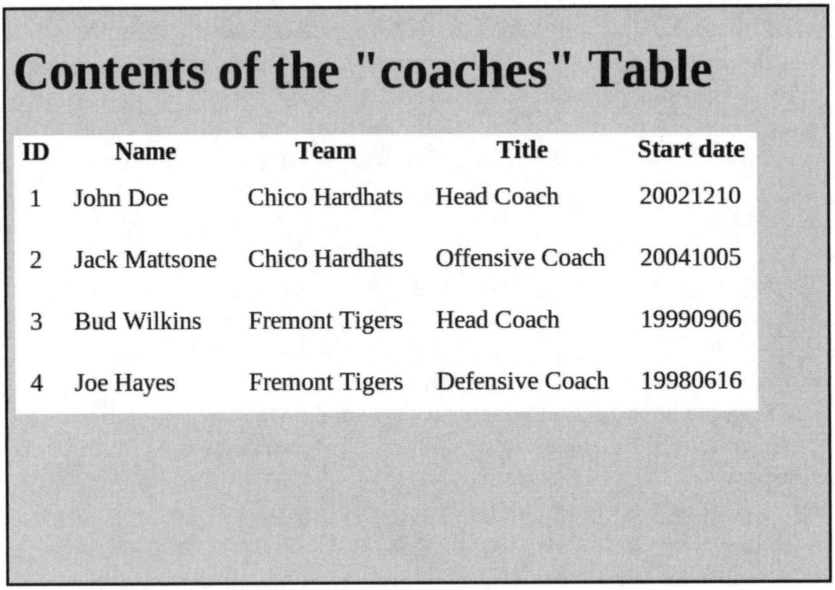

Contents of the "coaches" Table

ID	Name	Team	Title	Start date
1	John Doe	Chico Hardhats	Head Coach	20021210
2	Jack Mattsone	Chico Hardhats	Offensive Coach	20041005
3	Bud Wilkins	Fremont Tigers	Head Coach	19990906
4	Joe Hayes	Fremont Tigers	Defensive Coach	19980616

Figure 15.21   The output from Example 15.41.

15.7 What's Left?

This chapter was provided to introduce you to the MySQL relational database and how to issue SQL statements at the *mysql* client. After you learned the basic queries at the command line, the Perl DBI module was introduced so that you could perform the same *mysql* functions from your Perl scripts. We discussed the most commonly used DBI methods and how to use them for connecting to a database, selecting and retrieving data, updating and removing records, and so on. Finally, if you are interested in creating a dynamic Web page to interact with a user request from a fill-out form and respond with data retrieved from a database, see Appendix E, "Dancing with Perl," where you will learn how to install and use Dancer, a free, open-source Web application framework written in Perl.

Although we have covered the DBI essentials, there is more to be learned. To find detailed documenation of DBI, including methods, variables, constants, functions, and more, the best resource is found at the CPAN repository.

15.8 **What You Should Know**

1. What is a relational database?

2. What is MySQL?

3. Where can you get MySQL?

4. What is the MySQL client?

5. How do you set a password for MySQL?

6. What is the *test* database for?

7. What is the *mysql* database for?

8. What is SQL?

9. What is DBI and how can you get it?

10. What is DBI-MySQL?

11. What is a database handle?

12. What is a statement handle?

13. How does Perl query a database, and where does the result set end up?

14. When you prepare a query for Perl's *prepare* method, is it the same as when you make the query in the MySQL client?

15. How do you retrieve the result set from a Perl program?

16. What is a cached query?

17. What is the purpose of placeholders?

18. How do you know if your database connection was successful?

19. How do you close the database from a Perl script?

20. Who is Tim Bunce?

21. Where can you get a good tutorial on Perl DBI?

15.9 **What's Next?**

The next chapter discusses how Perl scripts can interface with the operating systems by issuing system calls, and Perl functions to work with directories, permissions, ownerships, hard and soft links, rename files, get file statistics, and more. You will learn how to use these functions on both UNIX- and Windows-based systems.

EXERCISE 15
Practicing Queries and Using DBI

Part 1: SQL Lab—Using the *northwind* Database

1. Load the *northwind* database from a script. The *northwind* database is a good sample database used with Microsoft's Access Database but tailored to work with MySQL as well. You will be provided with the *northwind.sql* script for this exercise (on CD), a file containing SQL statements to create and populate the *northwind* database. The file must be located on the client host where you are running *mysql*.

2. To run the script, go to your MySQL console window and type

```
source c:\document\northwind.sql
```

(Notice that there are no quotes around the name of the file and that absolute or relative pathnames can be used.)

Ways to source the SQL script:

```
mysql> SOURCE C:\path\northwind.sql;

mysql> SOURCE ..\path\northwind.sql;

shell> mysql db_name < input_file
```

As the script executes, the results will be displayed on your screen, most of them SQL *insert* statements. If an error occurs, the process will be aborted, and nothing done.

Part 2—Practice SQL Commands

1. After running the *northwind.sql* script, start by typing *use northwind*.

2. Type the following SQL commands and explain what they do.
   a. *SHOW DATABASES;*
   b. *SHOW TABLES FROM NORTHWIND;*
   c. *SHOW FIELDS FROM SHIPPERS;*
   d. *DESCRIBE SHIPPERS;*

3. Use the SQL tutorial, if you need it, to do the following:
   a. Select all rows from the *Shippers* table and display the fields.
   b. Select all rows from the *Employees* table and display only the *FirstName* and *LastName* fields.
   c. Select the *CompanyName* and *Phone* from the *Customers* table only if the *Country* is Italy.
   d. Print in sorted order the *ContactName* and *Country* from the *Customers* table. Sort by *Country*.

e. Select the *ContactName*, *CompanyName*, and *Country* from the *Customers* table where the *Country* begins with either *Po* or *Sw*.

f. Find the total number of products in the *Products* table.

g. Print only the first 10 products from the *Products* table.

h. Select countries from the *Customers* table in alphabetic order with no duplicates.

i. Find all the products between $10 and $20.

j. Insert a new product.

k. Update the products table by adding $5.25 to the unit price of Sir Rodney's Marmalade.

l. Select products below 10 units in stock.

m. Delete the oldest order in the database.

n. Use a SQL function to print the current date and time.

Part 3—Perl/MySQL Lab

Consult the MySQL documentation (*mysql.com*) to get the correct datatypes and functions to help you with this lab. The documentation is excellent.

1. Create a SQL script called *school.sql* that will do the following:

   a. *DROP DATABASE IF EXISTS SCHOOL;*

   b. *CREATE SCHOOL;*

   c. Create a table called *student*. It will consist of the following fields:

   FirstName

   LastName

   Email

   CellPhone

   Major

   GPA

   StartDate

   StudentID (primary key)

2. Use *school* and insert three rows of data into the student table.

3. At the MySQL prompt, execute the *school.sql* script. Use the SQL *describe* statement to see the structure of the *school* database.

4. Select all the rows in the *student* table. If the table has all the columns and data expected, then you are ready to go on to the next part of this lab.

5. In a Perl script, use the DBI module to do the following:

   a. Connect to MySQL and open the *school* database.

   b. Prepare a cached query to select all the rows in the *student* table, sorted by last names, and display all the columns with headings.

6. Create another Perl script so that the user can select the following options from a menu:

   1) Update a record
   2) Delete a record
   3) Insert a new record
   4) Display the table
   5) Exit

   For each of the options in the menu, create a subroutine that will perform the selected task, using MySQL functions. Can you create a CGI program to handle all of this?

   a. Create a loop so that the menu will be redisplayed until the user selects number 5.

   b. Rewrite the program by turning off *AutoCommit* and turning on *RaiseErrors*. Commit all changes to the database when the user chooses *exit*.

Part 4—Back to *Checking.pm*

1. Now you can redesign your original *Checking.pm* module to use the MySQL database, rather than the text file you originally created, to keep track of the balance.

   a. Create the database and the register table at the *mysql* prompt. This register should contain fields that match the text file called *register* you created in the first exercise.

   b. In the Perl module, *Checking.pm*, open the connection to the database. To get the balance, you will select it from the *register* table.

   c. When you call your *exit()* function, insert the last transaction into the database with the new information, using the SQL *INSERT* command.

   d. Create a Perl function that, when called, displays the contents of the register.

chapter

16

Interfacing with the System

When you finish this chapter, you should understand the following program:

```
use Cwd;
use File::Spec;
print cwd, "\n";
my $dir = File::Spec->rootdir;
chdir $dir;
opendir(DIR, $dir) or die $!;
my @files=readdir DIR;
@files = sort {$a cmp$b} @files;
foreach my $file (@files){
    print "$file\n" if -r $file;
}
closedir DIR;
chdir $ENV{HOME};
print cwd, "\n";
```

16.1 System Calls

Those migrating from shell (or batch) programming to Perl often expect that a Perl script is like a shell script—just a sequence of UNIX/Linux (or MS-DOS) commands. However, system utilities are not accessed directly in Perl programs as they are in shell scripts. Of course, to be effective there must be some way in which your Perl program can interface with the operating system. Perl has a set of functions, in fact, that specifically interface with the operating system and are directly related to the UNIX/Linux system calls so often found in C programs. Many of these system calls are supported by Windows. The ones that are generally not supported are found at the end of this chapter.

A **system call** requests some service from the operating system (kernel), such as getting the time of day, creating a new directory, removing a file, creating a new process, terminating a process, and so on. A major group of system calls deals with the creation and termination of processes, how memory is allocated and released, and sending information (such as signals) to processes. Another function of system calls is related to the file system: file creation, reading and writing files, creating and removing directories, creating links, and so forth.[1]

The UNIX[2] system calls are documented in Section 2 of the UNIX manual pages. Perl's system functions are almost identical in syntax and implementation. If a system call fails, it returns a -1 and sets the system's global variable *errno* to a value that contains the reason the error occurred. *C* programs use the *perror* function to obtain system errors stored in *errno*; Perl programs use the special $! variable.

The following Perl functions allow you to perform a variety of calls to the system when you need to manipulate or obtain information about files or processes. If the system call you need is not provided by Perl, you can use Perl's *syscall* function, which takes a UNIX system call as an argument. (See "The *syscall* Function and the *h2ph* Script" in Section 16.3.1.)

In addition to the built-in functions, the standard Perl library comes bundled with a variety of over 200 modules that you can use to perform portable operations on files, directories, processes, networks, and so forth. If you installed ActiveState or Strawberry, you will also find a collection of *Win32* modules in the standard Perl library under *C:\perl64\lib\Win32*.

To read the documentation for any of the modules (filenames with a *.pm* extension) from the standard Perl library, use the Perl built-in *perldoc* function or the UNIX *man* command. ActiveState (Win32) provides online documentation found by clicking the *Start* button, *Programs*, and then *ActiveState*.

EXAMPLE 16.1

```
(At the command line)
1$ perldoc File::Copy
```

EXPLANATION

The *perldoc* function takes a module name as its argument (with or without the *.pm* extension). The documentation for the module will then display in a window (Notepad on Win32 platforms). This example displays part of the documentation for the *Copy.pm* module found in the standard Perl library (see Figure 16.1).

---

1. System calls are direct entries into the kernel, whereas library calls are functions that invoke system calls. Perl's system interface functions are named after their counterpart UNIX system calls in Section 2 of the UNIX manual pages.
2. From now on when referring to UNIX, assume that Linux also applies.

```
perldoc1.1000 - Notepad
File  Edit  Format  Help
NAME
    File::Copy - Copy files or filehandles

SYNOPSIS
        use File::Copy;

        copy("file1","file2");
        copy("Copy.pm",\*STDOUT);'
        move("/dev1/fileA","/dev2/fileB");

        use POSIX;
        use File::Copy cp;

        $n=FileHandle->new("/dev/null","r");
        cp($n,"x");'
```

Figure 16.1 *perldoc* and the *Copy.pm* module.

16.1.1 Directories and Files

When walking through a file system, directories are separated by slashes. UNIX file systems indicate the root directory with a forward slash (/), followed by subdirectories separated by forward slashes where, if a filename is specified, it is the final component of the path. The names of the files and directories are case sensitive, and their names consist of alphanumeric characters and punctuation, excluding whitespace. A period in a filename has no special meaning but can be used to separate the base filename from its extension, such as in *program.c* or *file.bak*. The length of the filename varies from different operating systems, with a minimum of 1 character and on most UNIX-type file systems, up to 255 characters are allowed. Only the root directory can be named / (slash).[3]

The Windows file system in broad use today is mainly NTFS (with Windows 8+ switches up to ReFS, the Resilient File System) and separates the volume name and each of the path elements with a backslash (\) (for example, *C:\Perl64\lib\XML*). The individual components of a path are limited to 260 characters and the path length is limited to approximately 32,000 characters. Files and directory names are not case sensitive, can contain letters and numbers (as well as Unicode and characters in the extended character set (128–255)) that are optionally followed by a period, and a suffix of no more than three characters. The root of the file system is a drive number, such as *C:* or *D:*, rather than only a slash. In networked environments, the universal naming convention (UNC) uses a different convention for separating the components of a path; the drive letter is replaced with two backslashes, as in *\\myserver\dir\dir*.

Backslash Issues. The backslash in Perl scripts is used as an escape or quoting character (\n, \t, \U, \$500, and so forth), so when specifying a Win32 path separator, two backslashes are often needed, unless a particular module allows a single backslash or the pathname is surrounded by single quotes. For example, *C:\Perl\lib\File* should be written "*C:\\Perl\\lib\\File*" or '*C:\Perl\lib\File*'.

---

3. The Mac OS file system (HFS) is also hierarchical and uses colons to separate path components.

The *File::Spec* **Module.**   The *File::Spec* module found in the standard Perl library was designed to portably support operations commonly performed on filenames, such as creating a single path out of a list of path components and applying the correct path delimiter for the appropriate operating system, or splitting up the path into volume, directory, and filename, and so forth. A list of *File::Spec* functions is provided in Table16.1. Since these functions are different for most operating systems, *File::Spec* will choose the appropriate set of routines for the current OS available in separate modules, which includes *File::Spec::UNIX, File::Spec::Mac, File::Spec::OS2, File::Spec::Win32,* and *File::Spec::VMS*.

Table 16.1 *File::Spec* Functions

Function	*What It Does*
abs2rel	Takes a destination path and an optional base path and returns a relative path from the base path to the destination path.
canonpath	No physical check on the file system but a logical cleanup of a path. On UNIX, eliminates successive slashes and successive /.
case_tolerant	Returns a true or false value indicating, respectively, that alphabetic case is or is not significant when comparing file specifications.
catdir	Concatenates two or more directory names to form a complete path ending with a directory and removes the trailing slash from the resulting string.
catfile	Concatenates one or more directory names and a filename to form a complete path ending with a filename.
catpath	Takes volume, directory, and file portions and returns an entire path. In UNIX, *$volume* is ignored, and directory and file are concatenated. A / is inserted if necessary.
curdir	Returns a string representation of the current directory. . on UNIX.
devnull	Returns a string representation of the null device. */dev/null* on UNIX.
file_name_is_absolute	Takes as argument a path and returns true if it is an absolute path.
join	*join* is the same as *catfile*.
no_upwards	Given a list of filenames, strips out those that refer to a parent directory.
path	Takes no argument, returns the environment variable *PATH* as an array.
rel2abs	Converts a relative path to an absolute path.
rootdir	Returns a string representation of the root directory. / on UNIX.
splitpath	Splits a path into volume, directory, and filename portions. On systems with no concept of volume, returns *undef* for volume.
tmpdir	Returns a string representation of the first writable directory from the following list or " " if none is writable.
updir	Returns a string representation of the parent directory. .. on UNIX.

EXAMPLE   16.2

```
   # Use Win32
1  use File::Spec;
2  $pathname=File::Spec->catfile("C:","Perl64","site","bin");
3  print "$pathname\n";

   # Use UNIX
4  @PATH=File::Spec->path();
   print join("\n", @PATH),"\n";


(Output)
3  C:\Perl64\site\bin

4  /Applications/xampp/xamppfiles/bin
   /Users/eleanorquigley/perl5/bin
   /usr/local/ActivePerl-5.16/bin
   /usr/local/bin
   /Users/eleanorquigley/perl5/perlbrew/bin
   /usr/bin
   /bin
   /usr/sbin
   /sbin
   /usr/local/bin
```

EXPLANATION

1   If the operating system is not specified, the *File::Spec* module is loaded for the current operating system, in this case *Windows 8*. It is an object-oriented module but has a function-oriented syntax as well.
2   A scalar, *$pathname*, will contain a path consisting of the arguments passed to the *catfile* method. The *catfile* function will concatenate the list of path elements.
3   The new path is printed with backslashes separating the path components. On UNIX systems, the path would be printed */Perl64/site/lib*.
4   This example was run on Mac OS 10.9 (UNIX). The output is a list of the path elements found in the Shell's *PATH* environment variable (also found in Perl's *%ENV* hash).

16.1.2   Directory and File Attributes

UNIX.   The most common type of file is a regular file. It contains data, an ordered sequence of bytes. The data can be text data or binary data. Information about the file is stored in a system data structure called an **inode**. The information in the inode consists of such attributes as the link count, owner, group, mode, size, last access time, last modification time, and type. The UNIX *ls* command lets you see the inode information for the files in your directory. This information is retrieved by the *stat* system call. Perl's *stat* function also gives you information about the file. It retrieves the device number, inode number, mode, link count, user ID, group ID, size in bytes, time of last access, and so on. (See "The *stat* and *lstat* Functions" in Section 16.1.12.)

A directory is a specific file type maintained by the UNIX kernel. It is composed of a list of filenames. Each filename has a corresponding number that points to the information about the file. The number, called an **inode number**, is a pointer to an inode. The inode contains information about the file as well as a pointer to the location of the file's data blocks on disk. The following functions allow you to manipulate directories, change permissions on files, create links, and so forth.

Directory Entry	
Inode #	Filename

Windows.   Files and directories contain data as well as meta information that describes attributes of a file or directory. The five basic attributes of Win32 files and directories are *ARCHIVE*, *HIDDEN*, *READONLY*, and *SYSTEM*. The attributes of a file or directory are stored in a byte, with the bit value either on or off. Each bit value is added to the file type so that if you have a hidden, readonly directory, the attribute value is 00010011. See Table 16.2.

Table 16.2   Basic File and Directory Attributes

Attribute	Description	Bit Value
ARCHIVE	Set when file content changes	00100000
HIDDEN	A file not shown in a directory listing	00000010
DIRECTORY	A special tag to indicate a folder/directory	00010000
READONLY	A file that cannot be changed	00000001
SYSTEM	Special system files, such as *IO.SYS* and *MS-DOS.SYS*	00000100

To retrieve and set file attributes, use the standard Perl extension *Win32::File*. All of the functions return *FALSE* (*0*) if they fail, unless otherwise noted. The function names are exported into the caller's namespace by request. See Table 16.3.

Table 16.3   *Win32::File* Functions

Function	What It Does
GetAttributes(Filename, ReturnedAttributes)	Gets attributes of a file or directory. *ReturnedAttributes* will be set to the *or*-ed combination of the filename attributes.
SetAttributes(Filename, NewAttributes)	Sets the attributes of a file or directory. *newAttributes* must be an *or*-ed combination of the attributes.

To retrieve file attributes, use *Win32::File::GetAttributes($Path, $Attributes)*, and to set file attributes, use *Win32::File::SetAttributes($Path,$Attributes)*. See Table 16.4. The *Win32::File* also provides a number of constants.

Table 16.4 *Win32::File* Attributes

Attribute	Description
ARCHIVE	Set when file content changes. Used by backup programs.
COMPRESSED	Windows compressed file, not a zip file. Cannot be set by the user.
DIRECTORY	File is a directory. Cannot be set by the user.
HIDDEN	A file not shown in a directory listing.
NORMAL	A normal file. *ARCHIVE, HIDDEN, READONLY*, and *SYSTEM* are not set.
OFFLINE	Data is not available.
READONLY	A file that cannot be changed.
SYSTEM	Special system files, such as *IO.SYS* and *MS-DOS.SYS*, normally invisible.
TEMPORARY	File created by some program.

EXAMPLE 16.3

```
1   use Win32::File;
2   $File='C:\Drivers';
3   Win32::File::GetAttributes($File, $attr) or die;
4   print "The attribute value returned is: $attr.\n";
5   if ( $attr ){
6      if ($attr & READONLY){
          print "File is readonly.\n";
       }
       if ($attr & ARCHIVE){
          print "File is archive.\n";
       }
       if ($attr & HIDDEN){
          print "File is hidden.\n";
       }
       if ($attr & SYSTEM){
          print "File is a system file.\n";
       }
       if ($attr & COMPRESSED){
          print "File is compressed.\n";
       }
       if ($attr & DIRECTORY){
          print "File is a directory.\n";
       }
```

EXAMPLE 16.3 (CONTINUED)

```
        if ($attrib & NORMAL){
            print "File is normal.\n";
        }
        if ($attrib & OFFLINE){
            print "File is offline.\n";
        }
        if ($attrib & TEMPORARY){
            print "File is temporary.\n";
        }
    }
    else{
7        print Win32::FormatMessage(Win32::GetLastError),"\n";
    }
```

```
(Output)
4  The attribute value returned is 18. (00010010)
   File is hidden.
   File is a directory.
```

EXPLANATION

1   The *Win32::File* module is loaded.

2   The folder *Drivers* on the *C:* drive is assigned to *$File*.

3   The *GetAttributes* function is called with two arguments: the first is the name of the file, and the second is the bitwise *or*-ed value of the attribute constants, *READONLY, HIDDEN,* and so on. This value is filled in by the function *GetAttributes.* Note the *GetAttributes* function is called with a fully qualified package name. That is because it is listed in *@EXPORT_OK* in the *Win32::File* module and must be either specifically requested by the user or given a fully qualified name. If specifically requested, all of the constants would have to be listed as well or they will not be switched to the user's namespace.

4   The value of the *or*-ed attributes is printed. If the value is *0*, something is wrong, and an error will be formatted and printed from line 7. (In this example, *(00010010)* is not produced by the program, but is here to show 18 in binary.)

5   If one of the attributes for a file or directory is present, the following tests will show which ones were returned describing the file or directory.

6   By bitwise *AND*ing the value of *$attr* with the value of a constant (in this case, *READONLY*), if the resulting value is true (nonzero), the file is read-only.

7   This function will produce a human-readable error message coming from the last error reported by Windows.

16.1.3 Finding Directories and Files

The *File::Find* module lets you traverse a file system tree for specified files or directories based on some criteria, like the UNIX *find* command or the Perl *find2perl* translator.

FORMAT

```
use File::Find;
find(\&wanted, '/dir1', '/dir2');
sub wanted { ... }
```

The first argument to *find()* is either a hash reference describing the operations to be performed for each file or a reference to a subroutine. Type *perldoc File::Find* for details. The *wanted()* function does whatever verification you want for the file. *$File::Find::dir* contains the current directory name, and *$_* is assigned the current filename within that directory. *$File::Find::name* contains the complete pathname to the file. You are *chdir()*ed to *$File::Find::dir* when the function is called, unless *no_chdir* was specified. The first argument to *find()* is either a hash reference describing the operations to be performed for each file or a code reference. See Table 16.5.

Table 16.5 Hash Reference Keys for *Find::File*

Key	Value
bydepth	Reports directory name after all entries have been reported.
follow	Follows symbolic links.
follow_fast	Similar to *follow* but may report files more than once.
follow_skip	Processes files (but not directories and symbolic links) only once.
no_chdir	Doesn't *chdir* to each directory as it recurses.
untaint	If *-T* (taint mode) is turned on, won't *cd* to directories that are tainted.
untaint_pattern	This should be set using the *qr* quoting operator. The default is set to $qr\|^([-+@\w./]+)\$\|$.
untaint_skip	If set, directories (subtrees) that fail the *untaint_pattern* are skipped. The default is to *die* in such a case.
wanted	Used to specify the *wanted* function.

EXAMPLE 16.4

```
(UNIX)
1   use File::Find;
2   find(\&wanted, '/httpd', '/ellie/testing' );

3   sub wanted{
        -d $_ && print "$File::Find::name\n";
    }

(Output)
/httpd
/httpd/php
/httpd/Icons
/httpd/Cgi-Win
/httpd/HtDocs
/httpd/HtDocs/docs
/httpd/HtDocs/docs/images
/httpd/Cgi-Bin
/httpd/Logs
/ellie/testing
/ellie/testing/Exten.dir
/ellie/testing/extension
/ellie/testing/mailstuff
/ellie/testing/mailstuff/mailstuff
/ellie/testing/OBJECTS
/ellie/testing/OBJECTS/polymorph
```

EXPLANATION

1   The *File::Find* module is loaded from the standard Perl library.
2   The first argument to *find()* is a reference to a subroutine called *wanted*, followed by two directories to be searched.
3   The *wanted* function will check that each name is a directory (*-d*) and list the full pathname of all subdirectories found. *$_* is assigned the name of the current directory in the search.

EXAMPLE 16.5

```
(Windows)
1   use File::Find;
2   use Win32::File;
    # Works on both FAT and NTFS file systems.
3   &File::Find::find('\&wanted,C:\httpd', 'C:\ellie\testing');
4   sub wanted{
5       (Win32::File::GetAttributes($_,$attr)) &&
        ($attr & DIRECTORY) &&
        print "$File::Find::name\n";
    }
```

EXAMPLE   16.5 (CONTINUED)

```
(Output)
C:\httpd
C:\httpd/php
C:\httpd/Icons
C:\httpd/Cgi-Win
C:\httpd/HtDocs
C:\httpd/HtDocs/docs
C:\httpd/HtDocs/docs/images
C:\httpd/Cgi-Bin
C:\httpd/Logs
C:\ellie\testing
C:\ellie\testing/Exten.dir
C:\ellie\testing/extension
C:\ellie\testing/mailstuff
C:\ellie\testing/mailstuff/mailstuff
C:\ellie\testing/OBJECTS
C:\ellie\testing/OBJECTS/polymorph
```

EXPLANATION

1   The *File::Find* module is loaded from the standard Perl library.
2   The *Win32::File* module is loaded from the standard Perl library, from the site-specific directory for Win32 systems. It is used to retrieve file or directory attributes.
3   The first argument to *find()* is a reference to a subroutine called *wanted*, followed by two directories to be found.
4   The *wanted* function is defined.
5   The *wanted* function will check that each name is a directory by calling the *Get-Attributes* function (*Win32::File::GetAttributes*) and will list the full pathname of all subdirectories found. *$_* is assigned the name of the current file in the search.

16.1.4   Creating a Directory—The *mkdir* Function

UNIX.   The *mkdir* function creates a new, empty directory with the specified permissions (mode). The permissions are set as an octal number. The entries for the . and .. directories are automatically created. The *mkdir* function returns *1* if successful and *0* if not. If *mkdir* fails, the system error is stored in Perl's *$!* variable.

Windows.   If creating a directory at the MS-DOS prompt, the permission mask has no effect. Permissions on Win32 don't use the same mechanism as UNIX. For files on FAT partitions, you don't have to set permissions explicitly on a file. All files are available to all users, and the directory is created with all permissions turned on for everyone.

FORMAT

```
mkdir(FILENAME, MODE);    (UNIX)
mkdir(FILENAME);          (Windows)
```

EXAMPLE 16.6

```
    (In Script)
1   mkdir("joker", 0755);    # UNIX

    (The Command Line)
2   $ ls -ld joker
    drwxr-xr-x  2 ellie           512 Mar  7 13:43 joker

3   (In Script)
    mkdir("joker");          # Windows
    (The Command line)
    $ dir
    06/24/2014 06:45 PM    <DIR>        joker
```

EXPLANATION

1   The first argument to the *mkdir* function is the name of the directory. The second argument specifies the **mode**, or permissions, of the file. The permissions, *0755*, specify that the file will have read, write, and execute permission for the owner; read and execute for the group; and read and execute for the others. (Remember that without execute permission, you cannot access a directory.)

2   The *ls -ld* command prints a long listing of the directory file with information about the file, the inode information. The leading *d* is for directory, and the permissions are *rwxr-xr-x*.

3   On Win32 systems, the directory is created with all permissions turned on for everyone.

EXAMPLE 16.7

```
    # This script is called "makeit"
1   die "$0 <directory name> " unless @ARGV;
2   mkdir ($ARGV[0], 0755 ) || die "mkdir: $ARGV[0]: $!\n";

(At The Command Line)
    $ makeit
1   makeit <directory name> at makeit line 3.
    $ makeit joker
2   makeit: joker: File exists
    $ makeit cabinet
    $ ls -d cabinet
    cabinet
```

1   If the user doesn't provide a directory name as an argument to the script, the *die* function prints an error message and the script exits.
2   Unless the directory already exists, it will be created.

16.1.5 Removing a Directory—The *rmdir* Function

The *rmdir* function removes a directory, but only if it is empty.

FORMAT

```
rmdir(DIRECTORY);
rmdir DIRECTORY;
```

EXAMPLE 16.8

```
(At the Command Line)
1   rmdir("joker") || die qq(joke: $!\n)'      # UNIX
    joker: Directory not empty
2   $ perl -e 'rmdir("joke") || die qq(joke: $!\n)'
    joke: No such file or directory
3   $ perl -e "rmdir(joke" || die qq(joke: $!\n);"    # Windows
    joke: No such file or directory
```

EXPLANATION

1   The directory *joker* contains files. You cannot remove it unless it is empty. The *$!* variable contains the system error *Directory not empty*.
2   The directory *joker* does not exist; therefore, you cannot remove it. The system error is stored in *$!*.
3   On Win32 systems, *rmdir* works the same way. You just have watch the quotes if you are doing this at the MS-DOS *cmd* prompt. The directory *joke* is not removed, because it doesn't exist.

16.1.6 Changing Directories—The *chdir* Function

Each process has its own present working directory. When resolving relative path references, this is the starting place for the search path. If the calling process (for example, your Perl script) changes the directory, it is changed only for that process, not the process that invoked it (normally the shell). When the Perl program exits, the shell returns to the same working directory it started with.

The *chdir* function changes the current working directory. Without an argument, the directory is changed to the user's home directory. The function returns *1* if successful and *0* if not. The system error code is stored in Perl's *$!* variable.[4]

FORMAT

```
chdir (EXPR);
chdir EXPR;
chdir;
```

EXAMPLE 16.9

```
   use warnings;
1  use Cwd;
2  use File::Spec;
3  print cwd, "\n";
4  my $dir = File::Spec->rootdir;
5  chdir $dir;
6  print cwd, "\n";
```

(Output)
 /Users/eleanorquigley/perl
 /

EXPLANATION

1   The *Cwd* module gets the pathname for the current working directory. It behaves the same for both UNIX and Windows.

2   The *File::Spec* module is used to perform operations on filenames.

3   The *cwd* function from the *Cwd* module prints the current working directory without the newline.

4   The *File::Spec* method *rootdir* returns the value of the system root directory. (This will be a backslash on Win32 systems.)

5   The directory is changed to *root* directory. Since the Perl program is a separate process invoked by the shell, when Perl changes the present working directory, the directory is changed only while the Perl process is in execution. When Perl exits, the directory in the parent process (shell) is unchanged.

6   The present working directory is printed. It is root while we're in this script.

16.1.7   Accessing a Directory via the Directory Filehandle

The following Perl directory functions are modeled after the UNIX system calls sharing the same name. Although the traditional UNIX directory contained a 2-byte inode number and a 14-byte filename, not all UNIX systems have the same format. The directory functions allow you to access the directory regardless of its internal structure. The directory functions

---

4.   *chdir* is a system call provided with Perl for changing directories. The *cd* command used at the command line is a shell built-in and cannot be used directly in a Perl script.

work the same way with Windows. Figure 16.2 illustrates the directory structure for a typical UNIX system where each file is given an identifying inode number.

Inode	Filename
10	.
22	. .
32	memo
45	mbox
23	notes
12	src

Figure 16.2   A UNIX directory.

The *opendir* Function.   The *opendir* function opens a named directory and attaches it to the directory filehandle. This filehandle has its own namespace, separate from the other types of filehandles used for opening files and filters. The *opendir* function initializes the directory for processing by the related functions *readdir()*, *telldir()*, *seekdir()*, *rewinddir()*, and *closedir()*. The function returns 1 if successful.

FORMAT

```
opendir(DIRHANDLE, EXPR)
opendir(my $dir, EXPR)
```

EXAMPLE 16.10

```
1   opendir(DIR, "joker");
2   opendir(my $dirhandle, "joker");
```

EXPLANATION

1   The file *joker* is attached to the directory filehandle, *DIR*, and is opened for reading. The directory *joker* must exist and must be a directory.
2   The modern way to specify the directory handle is to use a lexically scoped variable.

The *readdir* Function.   Anyone who has read permission on the directory can read it; meaning, view its contents. You can't write to the directory itself even if you have write permission. The write permission on a directory means that you can create and remove files from within the directory, not alter the directory data structure itself.

When we speak about reading a directory with the *readdir* function, we are talking about looking at the contents of the directory structure maintained by the system. If the *opendir* function opened the directory, in a scalar context, *readdir* returns the **next** directory entry. In an array context, it returns the rest of the entries in the directory.

FORMAT

```
readdir(DIRHANDLE);
readdir DIRHANDLE;
```

The *closedir* Function.   The *closedir* function closes the directory that was opened by the *opendir* function.

FORMAT

```
closedir (DIRHANDLE);
closedir DIRHANDLE;
```

EXAMPLE 16.11

```
(The Script)
    use warnings;
1   opendir(DIR, "..") || die "Can't open: $!\n";
                          # Open parent directory
2   my @parentfiles=readdir(DIR);
                          # Gets a list of the directory contents
3   closedir(DIR);        # Closes the  filehandle
4   foreach my $file ( @parentfiles )
                          # Prints each element of the array
       { print "$file\n";}


(Output)
.
..
filea
fileb
filec
.sh_history
stories
```

EXPLANATION

1   The *opendir* function opens the directory structure and assigns it to *DIR*, the directory filehandle. The .. (parent) directory is opened for reading.
2   The *readdir* function assigns all the rest of the entries in the directory to the array *@parentfiles*.
3   The *closedir* function closes the directory.
4   The files are printed in the order in which they are stored in the directory structure. This may not be the order that the *ls* command prints out the files.

The *telldir* Function.   The *telldir* function returns the current position of the *readdir()* routines on the directory filehandle. The value returned by *telldir* may be given to *seekdir()* to access a particular location in a directory.

FORMAT

```
telldir(DIRHANDLE);
```

The *rewinddir* Function.   The *rewinddir* function sets the position of *DIRHANDLE* back to the beginning of the directory opened by *opendir*. It is not supported on all machines.

FORMAT

```
rewinddir(DIRHANDLE);
rewinddir DIRHANDLE;
```

The *seekdir* Function.   The *seekdir* sets the current position for *readdir()* on the directory filehandle. The position is set by the value returned by *telldir()*.

FORMAT

```
seekdir(DIRHANDLE, POS);
```

EXAMPLE 16.12

```
(The Script)
1   opendir(DIR, ".");  # Opens the current directory
2   while( $myfile=readdir(DIR) ){
3       $spot=telldir(DIR);
4       if ( "$myfile" eq ".login" ) {
            print "$myfile\n";
            last;
        }
    }
5   rewinddir(DIR);
6   seekdir(DIR, $spot);
7   $myfile=readdir(DIR);
    print "$myfile\n";

(Output)
.login
.cshrc
```

EXPLANATION

1   The *opendir* function opens the present working directory for reading.
2   The *while* statement is executed, and the *readdir* function returns the next directory entry from the directory filehandle and assigns the file to the scalar *$myfile*.
3   After the *readdir* function reads a filename, the *telldir* function marks the location of that read and stores the location in the scalar *$spot*.
4   When the *.login* file is read, the loop is exited.
5   The *rewinddir* function resets the position of the *DIR* filehandle to the beginning of the directory structure.
6   The *seekdir* function uses the results of the *telldir* function to set the current position for the *readdir* function on the *DIR* filehandle.
7   The **next** directory entry is read by the *readdir* function and assigned to the scalar *$myfile*.

16.1.8   Permissions and Ownership

UNIX.   There is one owner for every UNIX file. The one benefit the owner has over everyone else is the ability to change the permissions on the file, thus controlling who can do what to the file. A group may have a number of members, and the owner of the file may change the group permissions on a file so that the group will enjoy special privileges.

Every UNIX file has a set of permissions associated with it to control who can read, write, or execute the file. There are a total of nine bits that constitute the permissions on a file. The first three bits control the permissions of the owner of the file, the second set controls the permissions of the group, and the last set controls every one else. The permissions are stored in the mode field of the file's inode.

Windows.   Win32 systems do not handle file permissions the way UNIX does. Files are created with read and write turned on for everyone. Files and folders inherit attributes that you can set. By clicking the mouse on a file icon and selecting *Properties*, you can, in a limited way, select permission attributes, such as *Archive*, *Read-only*, and *Hidden* (see Figure 16.3).

If your platform is Win32, you can set file and folder permissions only on drives formatted to use NTFS.[5] To change permissions, you must be the owner or have been granted permission to do so by the owner. If you are using NTFS, go to File Explorer (formerly Windows Explorer) and locate the file or folder for which you want to set permissions. Right-click the file or folder, click *Properties*, and then click the *Security* tab. You will be able to allow, deny, or remove permissions from the group or user.

See the *Win32::FileSecurity* module in the Perl Resource Kit for Win32 if you need to maintain file permissions. To retrieve file permissions from a file or directory, use the *Win32::FileSecurity::Get($Path, \%Perms)* extension, where *$Path* is the relative or absolute

---

5. NTFS is an advanced file system designed for Windows NT.

path to the file or directory for which you are seeking permissions, and \%*Perms* is a reference to a hash containing keys representing the user or group and corresponding values representing the permission mask. See Table 16.6.

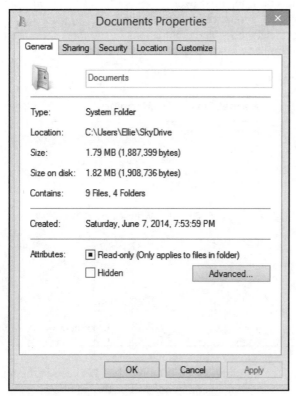

Figure 16.3 File attributes (Windows).

Table 16.6 Win32 Extensions to Manage Files and Directories

Extension	What It Does
Win32::File	Standard module for retrieving and setting file attributes
Win32::File::GetAtributes(path,attribute)	Retrieves file attributes
Win32::File::SetAttributes(path,attribute)	Sets file attributes
Win32::AdminMisc::GetFileInfo	Retrieves file information fields: CompanyName, FileVersion, InternalName, LegalCopyright, OriginalFileName, ProductName, ProductVersion, LangID, and Language

The *chmod* Function (UNIX).

The *chmod* function changes permissions on a list of files. The user must own the files to change permissions on them. The files must be quoted strings. The first element of the list is the numeric octal value for the new mode. (Today, the binary/octal notation has been replaced by a more convenient mnemonic method for changing permissions. Perl does not use the new method.)

Table 16.7 illustrates the eight possible combinations of numbers used for changing permissions if you are not familiar with this method.

Table 16.7 Permission Modes

Octal	Binary	Permissions	Meaning
0	000	none	All turned off
1	001	--x	Execute
2	010	-w-	Write
3	011	-wx	Write, execute
4	100	r--	Read
5	101	r-x	Read, execute
6	110	rw-	Read, write
7	111	rwx	Read, write, execute

Make sure the first digit is a *0* to indicate an octal number. Do not use the mnemonic mode (for example, *+rx*), because all the permissions will be turned off.

The *chmod* Function (Windows).

ActivePerl supports a limited version of the *chmod* function. However, you can only use it for giving the owner read/write access. (The *group* and *other* bits are ignored.)

The *chmod* function returns the number of files that were changed.

FORMAT

```
chmod(LIST);
chmod LIST;
```

EXAMPLE 16.13

```
(UNIX)
1  $ perl -e '$count=chmod 0755, "foo.p", "boo.p" ;print "$count
       files changed.\n"'
2  2 files changed.
3  $ ls -l foo.p boo.p
   -rwxr-xr-x  1 ellie    0 Mar  7 12:52 boo.p*
   -rwxr-xr-x  1 ellie    0 Mar  7 12:52 foo.p*
```

EXPLANATION

1   The first argument is the octal value *0755*. It turns on *rwx* for the user, *r* and *x* for the group and others. The next two arguments, *foo.p* and *boo.p*, are the files affected by the change. The scalar *$count* contains the number of files that were changed.
2   The value of *$count* is 2 because both files were changed to *0755*.
3   The output of the UNIX *ls -l* command is printed, demonstrating that the permissions on files *foo.p* and *boo.p* have been changed to *0755*.

The *chown* Function (UNIX).   The *chown* function changes the owner and group of a list of files. Only the owner or superuser can invoke it.[6] The first two elements of the list must be a numerical *uid* and *gid*. Each authorized UNIX user is assigned a *uid* (user identification number) and a *gid* (group identification number) in the password file.[7] The function returns the number of files successfully changed.

FORMAT

```
chown(LIST);
chown LIST;
```

EXAMPLE 16.14

```
(The Script)
1  $ uid=9496;
2  $ gid=40;
3  $number=chown($uid, $gid, 'foo.p', 'boo.p');
4  print "The number of files changed is $number\.n";

(Output)
4  The number of files changed is 2.
```

EXPLANATION

1   The user identification number *9496* is assigned.
2   The group identification number *40* is assigned.
3   The *chown* function changes the ownership on files *foo.p* and *boo.p* and returns the number of files changed.

---

6. On BSD UNIX and some POSIX-based UNIX, only the superuser can change ownership.
7. To get the *uid* or *gid* for a user, use the *getpwnam* or *getpwuid* functions.

The *umask* Function (UNIX).   When a file is created, it has a certain set of permissions by default. The permissions are determined by what is called the **system mask**. On most systems, this mask is *022* and is set by the login program.[8] A directory has *777* by default (*rwxrwxrwx*), and a file has *666* by default (*rw-rw-rw*). Use the *umask* function to remove or subtract permissions from the existing mask.

To take *write* permission away from the "others" permission set, the *umask* value is subtracted from the maximum permissions allowed per directory or file:

777 (directory)	666 (file)
– 002 (umask value)	– 002 (umask value)
775	664

The *umask* function sets the *umask* for this process and returns the old one. Without an argument, the *umask* function returns the current setting.

FORMAT

```
umask(EXPR)
umask EXPR
umask
```

EXAMPLE 16.15

```
1   $ perl -e 'printf("The umask is %o.\n", umask);'
    The umask is 22.
2   $ perl -e 'umask 027; printf("The new mask is %3o.\n", umask);'
    The new mask is 027.
```

EXPLANATION

1   The *umask* function without an argument prints the current *umask* value.
2   The *umask* function resets the mask to octal *027*.

16.1.9   Hard and Soft Links

UNIX.   When you create a file, it has one **hard** link; that is, one entry in the directory. You can create additional links to the file, which are really just different names for the same file. The kernel keeps track of how many links a file has in the file's inode. As long as there is a link to the file, its data blocks will not be released to the system. The advantage to having a file with multiple names is that there is only one set of data, or master file, and that file can be accessed by a number of different names. A hard link cannot span file systems and must exist at link-creation time.

---

8. The user can also set the *umask* in the *.profile* (*sh* or *ksh*) or *.cshrc* (*csh*) initialization files.

A soft link is also called a **symbolic** link and sometimes a **symlink**. A symbolic link is really just a very small file (it has permissions, ownership, size, and so forth). All it contains is the **name** of another file. When accessing a file that has a symbolic link, the kernel is pointed to the name of the file contained in the symbolic link. For example, a link from *thisfile* to */usr/bin/joking/otherfile* links the name *thisfile* to */usr/bin/joking/otherfile*. When *thisfile* is opened, *otherfile* is the file really accessed. Symbolic links can refer to files that do or don't exist and can span file systems and even different computers. They can also point to other symbolic links.[9]

Windows. The Win32 system introduced **shortcuts**, special binary files with a *.lnk* extension. A shortcut is similar to a UNIX symlink, but it is processed by a particular application rather than by the system and is an alias for a file or directory. Shortcuts are icons with a little arrow in a white box in the left corner (see Figure 16.4).

If you are using Windows 8, see "How to create software shortcut methods in the desktop mode of Windows 8" at *http://support.microsoft.com/kb/2820848/en-gb*.

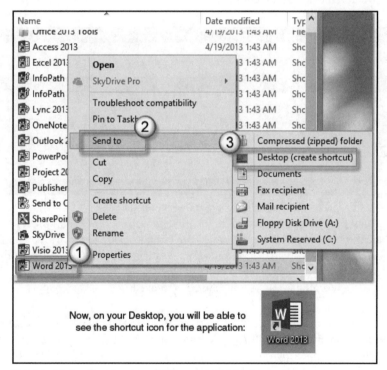

Figure 16.4 Shortcuts and the *.lnk* extension.

---

9. Symbolic links originated in BSD and are supported under many ATT systems. They may not be supported on your system.

See the *Win32::Shortcut* module to create, load, retrieve, save, and modify shortcut properties from a Perl script. To give you a sample of how to use the *Win32::Shortcut* module, the following example is just one of several from the Perl documentation:

```
use Win32::Shortcut;

$LINK = Win32::Shortcut->new();
$LINK->{'Path'} = "C:\\Directory\\Target.exe";
$LINK->{'Description'} = "Target executable";
$LINK->Save("Target.lnk");
$LINK->Close();
```

The *link* and *unlink* Functions (UNIX). The *link* function creates a hard link (that is, two files that have the same name) on UNIX systems. The first argument to the *link* function is the name of an existing file; the second argument is the name of the new file, which cannot already exist. Only the superuser can create a link that points to a directory. Use *rmdir* when removing a directory.

FORMAT

```
link(OLDFILENAME, NEWFILENAME);
```

EXAMPLE 16.16

```
(UNIX)
1  $ perl -e 'link("dodo", "newdodo");'
2  $ ls -li dodo newdodo
   142726 -rw-r--r--  2 ellie        0 Mar  7 13:46 dodo
   142726 -rw-r--r--  2 ellie        0 Mar  7 13:46 newdodo
```

EXPLANATION

1 The old file *dodo* is given an alternative name, *newdodo*.
2 The i option to the *ls* command gives the inode number of the file. If the inode numbers are the same, the files are the same. The old file, *dodo*, started with one link. The link count is now two. Since *dodo* and *newdodo* are linked, they are the same file, and changing one will then change the other. If one link is removed, the other still exists. To remove a file, all hard links to it must be removed.

The *unlink* function deletes a list of files on both UNIX and Windows systems (like the UNIX *rm* command or the MS-DOS *del* command). If the file has more than one link, the link count is dropped by one. The function returns the number of files successfully deleted. To remove a directory, use the *rmdir* function, since only the superuser can unlink a directory with the *unlink* function.

FORMAT

```
unlink (LIST);
unlink  LIST;
```

EXAMPLE 16.17

```
(The Script)
1  unlink('a','b','c') || die "remove: $!\n";
2  $count=unlink <*.c>;
   print "The number of files removed was $count\n";
```

EXPLANATION

1   The files *a*, *b*, and *c* are removed.
2   Any files ending in .*c* (*C* source files) are removed. The number of files removed is stored in the scalar *$count*.

The *symlink* and *readlink* Functions (UNIX).   The *symlink* function creates a symbolic link. The symbolic link file is the name of the file that is accessed if the old filename is referenced.

FORMAT

```
symlink(OLDFILE, NEWFILE)
```

EXAMPLE 16.18

```
1  $ perl -e 'symlink("/home/jody/test/old", "new");'
2  $ ls -ld new
   rwxrwxrwx  1 ellie   8 Feb 21 17:32 new  -> /home/jody/test/old
```

EXPLANATION

1   The *symlink* function creates a new filename, *new*, linked to the old filename, */home/jody/test/old*.
2   The *ls -ld* command lists the symbolically linked file. The symbol -> points to the new filename. The *l* preceding the permissions also indicates a symbolic link file.

The *readlink* function returns the value of the symbolic link and is undefined if the file is not a symbolic link.

FORMAT

```
readlink(SYMBOLIC_LINK);
readlink SYMBOLIC_LINK;
```

EXAMPLE 16.19

```
1   $ perl -e 'print readlink("new")';
    /home/jody/test/old
```

1   The file *new* is a symbolic link. It points to */home/jody/test/old*, the value returned by the *readlink* function.

16.1.10   Renaming Files

The *rename* Function (UNIX and Windows).   The *rename* function changes the name of the file, like the UNIX *mv* command. The effect is to create a new link to an existing file and then delete the existing file. The *rename* function returns *1* for success and returns *0* for failure. This function does not work across file system boundaries. If a file with the new name already exists, its contents will be destroyed.

```
rename(OLDFILENAME, NEWFILENAME);
```

EXAMPLE 16.20

```
1   rename ("tmp", "datafile");
```

1   The file *tmp* is renamed *datafile*. If *datafile* already exists, its contents are destroyed.

16.1.11   Changing Access and Modification Times

The *utime* Function.   The *utime* function changes the access and modification times on each file in a list of files, like the UNIX *touch* command. The first two elements of the list must be the numerical access and modification times, in that order. The *time* function feeds the current time to the *utime* function. The function returns the number of files successfully changed. The inode modification time of each file in the list is set to the current time.

```
utime (LIST);
utime LIST;
```

EXAMPLE 16.21

```
(The Script--UNIX)
   use warnings;
1  print "What file will you touch (create or change time stamp)? ";
   chomp(my $myfile=<STDIN>);
2  my $now=time;  # This example makes the file if it doesn't exist
3  utime($now, $now, $myfile) || open(my $tmp,">>","$myfile");


(The Command Line)
$  ls -l brandnewfile
   brandnewfile: No such file or directory

$ perl update.pl
1  What file will you touch (create or update time stamp) ? brandnewfile


$  ls -l brandnewfile
2  -rw-r--r-- 1  ellie   0 Mar   6  17:13 brandnewfile
```

EXPLANATION

1   The user will enter the name of a file either to update the access and modification times or, if the file does not exist, to create it.
2   The variable *$now* is set to the return value of the *time* function, the number of non-leap seconds since January 1, 1970, UTC.
3   The first argument to *$now* is the access time, the second argument is the modification time, and the third argument is the file affected. If the *utime* function fails because the file does not exist, the *open* function will create the file, using *TMP* as the filehandle, emulating the UNIX *touch* command.

16.1.12 File Statistics

The information for a file is stored in a data structure called an **inode**, maintained by the kernel. For UNIX users, much of this information is retrieved with the *ls* command. In C and Perl programs, this information may be retrieved directly from the inode with the *stat* function. See the *File::stat* module, which creates a user interface for the *stat* function. Although the emphasis here is UNIX, the *stat* function also works with Win32 systems.

The *stat* and *lstat* Functions. The *stat* function returns a 13-element array containing statistics retrieved from the file's inode. The last two fields, dealing with blocks, are defined only on BSD UNIX systems.[10]

The *lstat* function is like the *stat* function, but if the file is a symbolic link, *lstat* returns information about the link itself rather than about the file it references. If your system does not support symbolic links, a normal *stat* is done.

---

10. Wall, L., Christianson, T., and Orwant, J., *Programming Perl,* 3rd ed., O'Reilly & Associates: (2000), p. 188.

The special *underscore* filehandle is used to provide *stat* information from the file most previously *stat*-ed. The 13-element array returned contains the following elements stored in the *stat* structure. (The order is a little different from the UNIX system call *stat*.)

1. Device number
2. Inode number
3. Mode
4. Link count
5. User ID
6. Group ID
7. For a special file, the device number of the device it refers to
8. Size in bytes, for regular files
9. Time of last access
10. Time of the last modification
11. Time of last file status change
12. Preferred I/O block size for file system
13. Actual number of 512-byte blocks allocated

FORMAT

```
stat FILEHANDLE;
stat(EXPR);
```

EXAMPLE 16.22

```
(UNIX)
   use warnings;
1  open(my $myfile, "<","perl1") || die "Can't open: $!\n";
2  @statistics=stat($myfile);
3  print "@statistics\n";
   close $myfile;

4  my @stats=stat("perl1");
5  printf("The inode number is %d and the uid is %d.\n",
          $stats[1], $stats[4]);
6  print "The file has read and write permissions.\n",
       if -r _ && -w _;

(Output)
3  1819 142441 33261 1 9496 40 -21335 75 761965998 727296409 8192 2
5  The inode number is 142441 and the uid is 9496.
6  The file has read and write permissions.
```

EXPLANATION

1   The file *perl1* is opened via the filehandle expression, *$myfile*.
2   The *stat* function retrieves information from the file's inode and returns that information to a 13-element array, *@statistics*.

EXPLANATION (CONTINUED)

3   The 13-element array is printed. The last two elements of the array are the block size
    and the number of blocks in 512-byte blocks. The size and number of blocks may dif-
    fer because unallocated blocks are not counted in the number of blocks. The negative
    number is an NIS device number.

4   This time, the *stat* function takes the filename as its argument, rather than the
    filehandle.

5   The second and fifth elements of the array are printed.

6   The special underscore _ filehandle is used to retrieve the current file statistics from
    the previous *stat* call. The file *perl1* was *stat*-ed last. The file test operators, *-r* and *-w*,
    use the current *stat* information of *perl1* to check for read and write access on the file.

EXAMPLE 16.23

```
(Windows)
    # Since UNIX and Windows treat files differently,
    # some of the fields here are
    # blank or values returned are not meaningful
    use warnings;
1   my @stats = stat("C:\\ellie\\testing");
2   print "Device: $stats[0]\n";
3   print "Inode #: $stats[1]\n";
4   print "File mode: $stats[2]\n";
5   print "# Hard links: $stats[3]\n";
6   print "Owner ID: $stats[4]\n";
7   print "Group ID: $stats[5]\n";
8   print "Device ID: $stats[6]\n";
9   print "Total size: $stats[7]\n";
10  print "Last access time: $stats[8]\n";
11  print "Last modify time: $stats[9]\n";
12  print "Last change inode time: $stats[10]\n";
13  print "Block size: $stats[11]\n";
14  print "Number of blocks: $stats[12]\n";

(Output)
2   Device: 2
3   Inode #: 0
4   File mode: 16895
5   # Hard links: 1
6   Owner ID: 0
7   Group ID: 0
8   Device ID: 2
9   Total size: 0
10  Last access time: 981360000
11  Last modify time: 977267374
12  Last change inode time: 977267372
13  Block size:
14  Number of blocks:
```

16.1.13 Packing and Unpacking Data

Remember the *printf* and *sprintf* functions? They were used to format their arguments as floating-point numbers, decimal numbers, strings, and so forth. The *pack* and *unpack* functions take this formatting a step further. Both functions act on strings that can be represented as bits, bytes, integers, long integers, floating-point numbers, and so forth, but *pack* can also act on general data as well as strings. The format type tells both *pack* and *unpack* how to handle these strings.

The *pack* and *unpack* functions have a number of uses. These functions are used to pack a list into a binary structure and then expand the packed values back into a list. When working with files, you can use these functions to create uuencode files, relational databases, Unicode strings, and binary files.

When working with files, not all files are text files. Some files, for example, may be packed into a binary format to save space, store images, and so forth. These files are not readable as is the text on this page. You can use the *pack* and *unpack* functions to convert the lines in a file from one format to another. The *pack* function converts a list into a scalar value that may be stored in machine memory. The template shown in Table 16.8 is used to specify the type of character and how many characters will be formatted. For example, the string *c4*, or *cccc*, packs a list into 4 unsigned characters, and *a14* packs a list into a 14-byte ASCII string, null padded. The asterisk (as in *H**) is a repeating character representing all characters until the end of the string. The *unpack* function converts a binary formatted string into a list. The opposite of *pack* puts a string back into Perl format.

Table 16.8 The Template *pack* and *unpack*—Types and Values

Template	Description
a	An ASCII string (null padded)
A	An ASCII string (space padded)
b	A bit string (low-to-high order, like *vec*)
B	A bit string (high-to-low order)
c	A signed *char* value
C	An unsigned *char* value
d	A double-precision float in the native format
f	A single-precision float in the native format
h	A hexadecimal string (low nybble first, to high)
H	A hexadecimal string (high nybble first)
i	A signed integer
I	An unsigned integer
l	A signed long value
L	An unsigned long value

(continued)

Table 16.8   The Template *pack* and *unpack*—Types and Values (continued)

Template	Description
n	A short in "network" (big-endian) order
N	A long in "network" (big-endian) order
p	A pointer to a null-terminated string
P	A pointer to a structure (fixed-length string)
q	A signed 64-bit value
Q	An unsigned 64-bit value
s	A signed short value (16-bit)
S	An unsigned short value (16-bit)
u	A uuencoded string
v	A short in "VAX" (little-endian) order
V	A long in "VAX" (little-endian) order
w	A BER compressed unsigned integer in base 128, high bit first
x	A null byte
X	Back up a byte
@	Null fill to absolute position

FORMAT

```
$string=pack(Template, @list );
@list = unpack(Template, $string );
```

EXAMPLE 16.24

```
(The Script)
1  $bytes=pack("c5", 80,101,114, 108, 012);   # 5 ASCII characters
2  print "$bytes";

(Output)
Perl
```

EXPLANATION

1   The first element in the list, the template (see Table 16.8), is composed of the type and the number of values to be packed; in this example, four signed characters. The rest of the list consists of the decimal values for characters *P*, *e*, *r*, and *l* and the octal value for the newline. This list is packed into a binary structure. The string containing the packed structure is returned and stored in *$bytes*. (See your ASCII table.)

2   The 5-byte character string is printed.

EXAMPLE 16.25

```
(Script)
1  $string=pack("A15A3", "hey","you");   # ASCII string, space padded
2  print $string;

(Output)
2  hey             you
```

EXPLANATION

1   Two strings, *hey* and *you*, are packed into a structure using the template *A15A3*. *A15* will convert the string *hey* into a space-padded ASCII string consisting of 15 characters. *A3* converts the string *you* into a 3-character space-padded string.

2   The strings are printed according to the *pack* formatting template. They are left justified.

EXAMPLE 16.26

```
(The Script)

   # Program to uuencode a file and then uudecode it
   use warnings;
1  open(my $pw, "<", "/etc/passwd") || die "Can't open: $!\n";
2  open(my $coded, ">","codedpw") || die "Can't open: $!\n";

3  while(<$pw>){
4     $uuline=pack("u*", $_);   # uuencoded string
5     print $coded $uuline;
   }
   close $pw;
   close $coded;

6  open($uupw, "<", "codedpw") || die "Can't open: $!\n";
   while(<$uupw>){
7     print;
   }
   close $uupw;
   print "\n\n";

8  open($decode,"<", "codedpw") || die;
9  while(<$decode>){
10    @decodeline = unpack("u*", $_);
11    print "@decodeline";
   }

(Output)
7  E<F]O=#IX.C`Z,3I3=7!E<BU5<V5R.B\Z+W5S<B]B:6X08W-H"@``
   19&%E;6]N.G@@Z,3HQ.CHO.@H`
   58FEN.G@@Z,CHR.CHO=7-R+V)I;CH*
   .<WES.G@@Z,SHS.CHO.@H`
```

EXAMPLE 16.26 (CONTINUED)

```
:861M.G@Z-#HT.D%D;6EN.B]V87(O861M.@H`
L;'`Z>#HW,3HX.DQI;F4@4')I;G1E<B!!9&UI;CHO=7-R+W-P;V]L+VQP.@H`
?<VUT<#IX.C`Z,#I-86EL($1A96UO;B!5<V5R.B\Z"@!!R
E=75C<#IX.C4Z-3IU=6-P($$D;6EN.B]U<W(O;&EB+W5U8W`:"#@!!L
M;G5U8W`Z>#HY.CDZ=75C<<"!!9&UI;CHF%R>+W-P;V]L+W5U8W!P=6)L:6,O=7-R+VQI8B]U=6-P+W5U8VEC;PH`
P;V]L+W5U8W`!P>#HY.CDZ=75C<`:6,Z,56
5+W5S<B!]L;C6(O=75C<"]U=6-P+W5U8VEC;PH`
J;&ES=&5N.&5N.G@@Z,S<Z-#I.971W;W)K(%!9&UI;CHv.O;F5T+VYL<SH`
?;F]B;V1Y.G@@Z-C`P,#$Z-C`P,#$Z3F]B;V1Y.B]:2@CA`O
I;F]A8V-E<W,Z>#HV,#`P,C`Z-C`P,#(Z3F\@06-C97-S(%5S97(Z+SH`R!!9&UI;Ch>@H`
J;F]B;V1Y-#HV-34S-#HV-34S-#I3=6Y/4R`T+G@@@@Z3F]B;V1Y.B]:2@3(#0N>"!.;V)O9'D@@:+R\*
M96QL:64Z>#HY-#DV.C0W
#DV.C0P.D5L;&EE(%%U:6=L97D@@Z+VAO;64O96QL:64@@Z+W5S<B]B:6XO8W-H
*<B]B:6X@@:-6X08W-H"@!C
```

11 `root:x:0:1:Super-User:/:/usr/bin/csh`
   `daemon:x:1:1::/:`
   `bin:x:2:2::/usr/bin:`
   `sys:x:3:3::/:`
   `adm:x:4:4:Admin:/var/adm:`
   `lp:x:71:8:Line Printer Admin:/usr/spool/lp:`
   `smtp:x:0:0:Mail Daemon User:/:`
   `uucp:x:5:5:uucp Admin:/usr/lib/uucp:`
   `nuucp:x:9:9:uucp Admin:/var/spool/uucppublic:/usr/lib/uucp/uucico`
   `listen:x:37:4:Network Admin:/usr/net/nls:`
   `nobody:x:60001:60001:Nobody:/:`
   `noaccess:x:60002:60002:No Access User:/:`
   `nobody4:x:65534:65534:SunOS 4.x Nobody:/:`
   `ellie:x:9496:40:Ellie Quigley:/home/ellie:/usr/bin/csh`

EXPLANATION

1 The local *passwd* file is opened for reading.
2 Another file, called *codepw*, is opened for writing.
3 Each line of the filehandle is read into $_ until the end of file is reached.
4 The *pack* function uuencodes the line ($_) and assigns the coded line to the scalar *$uuline*. uuencode used to be used to convert a binary file into an encoded representation that can be sent using e-mail.
5 The uuencoded string is sent to the filehandle.
6 The file containing the uuencoded text is opened for reading.
7 Each line of uuencoded text is printed.
8 The uuencoded file is opened for reading.
10 Each line of the file is read from the filehandle and stored in $_. The *unpack* function converts the uuencoded string back into its original form and assigns it to *@decodeline*.
11 The uudecoded line is printed.

EXAMPLE 16.27

```
(The Script)
   use warnings
1  $ints=pack("i3", 5,-10,15);      # pack into binary structure
2  open(my $bin, "+>", "binary" ) || die;
3  print $bin $ints;
4  seek($bin, 0,0) || die;
   while(<$bin>){
5     ($n1,$n2,$n3)=unpack("i3", $_ );
6     print "$n1 $n2 $n3\n";
   }


(Output)
6  5 -10 15
```

EXPLANATION

1   The three integers *5*, *-10*, and *15* are packed into three signed integers. The value returned is a binary structure assigned to *$ints*.

2   The *BINARY* filehandle is opened for reading and writing.

3   The packed integers are sent to the file. This file is compressed and totally unreadable. To read it, you must convert it back into an ASCII format. This is done with *unpack*.

4   The *seek* function puts the file pointer back at the top of the file at byte position *0*.

5   We're reading from the file one line at a time. Each line, stored in *$_*, is unpacked and returned to its original list of values.

6   The original list values are printed.

EXAMPLE 16.28

```
(The Script)
   use warnings;
   my $str="0x123456789ABCDE ellie...";
1     print "$str\n";

   my $bytes=unpack("H*",$str);    # hex string (regular order)
2     print "$bytes\n";

   my $str2 = pack("H*", $bytes);
3     print "$str2\n";

   $bytes = unpack("h*",$str);     # hex string (reversed order)
4     print "$bytes\n";

   my $str1 = pack("h*", $bytes);
5     print"$str1\n";
```

EXAMPLE 16.28 (CONTINUED)

```
(Output)
1   0x123456789ABCDE ellie...
2   3078313233334353637383941424344 4520656c6c69652e2e2e
3   0x123456789ABCDE ellie...
4   03871323334353637383931424344 4540256c6c69656e2e2e2
5   0x123456789ABCDE ellie...
```

EXPLANATION

1   The string contains a hexadecimal number and some text.

2   The h and H fields pack a string that many nybbles (4-bit groups, representable as hexadecimal digits, 0-9a-f) long. Each byte of the input field of pack() generates 4 bits of the result. The asterisk * represents all characters in the string. The variable *$bytes* consists of a hexadecimal string in regular hex order, where each character in the original string is represented by two hexadecimal numbers. For example, *ellie* is represented as *65 6c 6c 69 65*, and the three dots are *e2 e2 e2*. (For futher discussion on this, see *http://stackoverflow.com/questions/3857499/when-would-you-use-unpackh-or-packh.*)

3   H* fields are the way bytes are normally converted to and from hexadecimal (high nybble first).

4   The hex string is converted back into bytes .

16.2 Processes

Your Perl script is a program that resides on disk. When the program is placed in memory and starts execution, it is called a **process**. Each process has a number of attributes that are inherited from its parent, the **calling process**. Perl has a number of functions that will allow you to retrieve the information about the process. Before examining these functions, a short discussion about processes may help you to understand (or recall) the purpose of some of Perl's system calls.

16.2.1 UNIX Processes

Every process has a unique process ID, a positive integer called the ***pid***. Every process has a **parent** except process 0, the swapper. The first process *init*, *pid 1*, is the ancestor of all future processes, called **descendants**, or more commonly, **child** processes.

In Figure 16.5, the Perl process is a descendant of the UNIX shell (*sh*). The first process is pid#1, called *init*. The *init* process spawns *getty*, which execs *login* and *login* execs *sh*, the shell program. From the shell program, the Perl process is spawned; that is, the shell is Perl's parent.

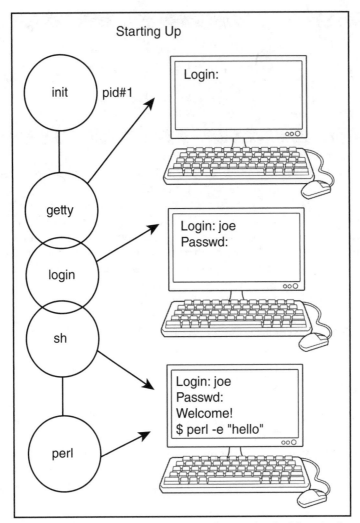

Figure 16.5 The Perl process as a descendant of the shell.

Each process also belongs to a **process group**, a collection of one or more processes used for job control and signal handling. Each process group also has a unique *pid* and a process leader. When you log on, the process group leader may be your login shell. Any process created from your shell will be a member of this process group. The terminal opened by the process group leader is called the **controlling terminal**, and any processes it spawns inherit it. Any signals sent to the process will be sent to all processes in the group. That is why, when you press <CTRL>+C, the process you are running and any of its children will terminate. Perl provides functions to obtain the process group ID and to set the process group.

When a process is created, it is assigned four numbers indicating who owns the process. They are the real and effective user ID, and the real and effective group ID. The user ID, called the real *uid*, is a positive integer that is associated with your login name. The real *uid* is the third field in the */etc/passwd* file. When you log on, the first process created is called the *login* shell, and it is assigned the user ID. Any processes spawned from the shell also inherit this *uid*. Any process running with the *uid* of zero is called a **root**, or **superuser**, process with special privileges.

There is also a group ID number, called the real *gid*, which associates a group with your login name. The default *gid* is the fourth field in the password file, and it is also inherited by any child process. The system administrator can allow users to become members of other groups by assigning entries in the */etc/group* file.

The following is an entry from the *passwd* file, illustrating how the *uid* and *gid* values are stored (fields are separated by colons).

EXAMPLE 16.29

```
(Entry from /etc/passwd)
    john:aYD17IsSjBMyGg:9495:41:John Doe:/home/dolphin/john:/bin/ksh
```

EXPLANATION

(The Fields)
1   login name
2   encrypted password
3   uid
4   gid
5   gcos (Comment field)
6   home directory
7   login shell

The **effective *uid* (*euid*)** and **effective *guid* (*guid*)** of a process are normally set to the same number as the real *uid* and real *gid* of the user who is running the process. UNIX determines what permissions are available to a process by the effective *uid* and *gid*. If the *euid* or *guid* of a file is changed to that of another owner, when you execute a program, you essentially become that owner and get his access permissions. Programs in which the effective *uid* or effective *gid* have been set are called **set user ID** programs, or *setuid* programs. When you change your password, the */bin/passwd* program has a *setuid* to *root*, giving you the privilege to change your password in the *passwd* file, which is owned by *root*.

16.2.2 Win32 Processes

The process model for Windows differs from UNIX systems, and since Perl was originally designed for UNIX, a number of library routines were added to the standard Perl library to accommodate the Windows world. The Win32 directory (*C:/Perl/lib/Win32*) is a Windows-specific directory that comes with Windows versions of Perl and contains a number of modules for creating, suspending, resuming, and killing processes. The *Win32::Process* module contains a number of functions to manipulate processes. Here is a listing from the Win32 directory:

AuthenticateUser.pm	Internet.pm	Registry.pm
ChangeNotify.pm	Mutex.pm	Semaphore.pm
Client.pl	NetAdmin.pm	Server.pl
Clipboard.pm	NetResource.pm	Service.pm
Console.pm	ODBC.pm	Shortcut.pm
Event.pm	OLE	Sound.pm
EventLog.pm	OLE.pm	Test.pl
File.pm	PerfLib.pm	TieRegistry.pm
FileSecurity.pm	Pipe.pm	WinError.pm
IPC.pm	Process.pm	test-async.pl

16.2.3 The Environment (UNIX and Windows)

When you log on, your shell program inherits a set of environment variables initialized by either the login program or one of shell's startup files (*.profile* or *.login*). These variables contain useful information about the process, such as the search path, the home directory, the user name, and the terminal type. The information in environment variables, once set and exported, is inherited by any child processes that are spawned from the process (parent) in which they were initialized. The shell process will pass the environment information on to your Perl program.

The special *%ENV* hash contains the environment settings. If you change the value of an environment setting in your Perl script, it is set for this process and any of its children. The environment variables in the parent process, normally the shell, will remain untouched.

EXAMPLE 16.30

```
(The Script)
(UNIX)
    use warnings;
1   foreach my $key (keys(%ENV)){
2       print "$key\n";
    }
3   print "Your login name is $ENV{'LOGNAME'}\n";
4   my $pwd = $ENV{'PWD'};
    print "The present working directory is $pwd\n";

(Output)
2   OPENWINHOME
    MANPATH
    FONTPATH
    LOGNAME
    USER
    TERMCAP
    TERM
```

EXAMPLE 16.30 (CONTINUED)

```
      SHELL
      PWD
      HOME
      PATH
      WINDOW_PARENT
      WMGR_ENV_PLACEHOLDER
   3  Your login name is ellie
   4  The present working directory is /home/jody/ellie
```

EXPLANATION

1 The *keys* function is used to get all the currently set environment variables from the %ENV array. These variables were inherited from the parent process, the shell.

2 Each environment variable is printed.

3 The value of *LOGNAME*, the user name, is printed.

4 The value of *PWD*, the present working directory, is assigned to *$pwd* and printed.

EXAMPLE 16.31

```
(Windows)
1  while(($key,$value)=each(%ENV)){
       print "$key $value\n" if $key =~ /^P/;
   }


(Output)
PROGRAMFILES C:\Program Files (x86)
PROGRAMW6432 C:\Program Files
PATHEXT .COM;.EXE;.BAT;.CMD;.VBS;.VBE;.JS;.JSE;.WSF;.WSH;.MSC
PROMPT $P$G
PATH C:\WINDOWS\system32;C:\WINDOWS;C:\WINDOWS\System32\Wbem;C:\WINDOWS\
System32
\WindowsPowerShell\v1.0\;C:\Program Files\Intel\WiFi\bin\;C:\Program
Files\Commo
n Files\Intel\WirelessCommon\;C:\Strawberry\perl\bin;C:\Strawberry\perl\
site\bin
;C:\Strawberry\c\bin;
PROCESSOR_ARCHITEW6432 AMD64
PROGRAMDATA C:\ProgramData
PROCESSOR_ARCHITECTURE x86
PSMODULEPATH C:\WINDOWS\system32\WindowsPowerShell\v1.0\Modules\
PROCESSOR_REVISION 4501
PROCESSOR_LEVEL 6
PUBLIC C:\Users\Public
PROCESSOR_IDENTIFIER Intel64 Family 6 Model 69 Stepping 1, GenuineIntel
PROGRAMFILES(X86) C:\Program Files (x86)
```

EXPLANATION

1 The *each* function is used to get all the currently set environment variables from the %ENV array. These variables were inherited from the parent process, the MS-DOS shell. This display is a partial list.

16.2.4   Processes and Filehandles

As discussed in Chapter 10, "Getting a Handle on Files," processes can be opened in Perl via either an input or output filehandle. For example, if you want to see all the currently running processes on your machine, you could create a filehandle for the UNIX *ps* command. (See Chapter 10 for details. See also "The *system* Function" in Section 16.3.4.)

EXAMPLE   16.32

```
(The Script)
   # UNIX ps command
1  open(PROC, "ps -aux  |" ) || die "$!\n";  # Check your UNIX man pages
         # for ps options. If running on MacOS, use ps -ef
2  print STDOUT <PROC>;

(Output)
2  ellie  3825  6.4  4.5  212   464 p5  R 12:18   0:00 ps -aux
   root      1  0.0  0.0   52     0 ?  IW Feb 5   0:02 /sbin/init
   root     51 10.0  0.0   52     0 ?  IW Feb 5   0:02 portmap
   root      2 10.0  0.0   52     0 ?   D Feb 5   0:02 pagedaemon
   root     90 10.0  0.0   52     0 ?  IW Feb 5   0:02 rpc.statd


<more processes here>


ellie 1383  0.8  8.4  360   876 p4  S Dec 26 11:34 /usr/local/OW3/bin/xview
ellie  173  0.8 13.4 1932 1392 co  S Dec 20389:19 /usr/local/OW3/bin/xnews
ellie  164  0.0  0.0  100     0 co IW Dec 20  0:00 -c


<some of the output was cut to save space>


ellie 3822  0.0  0.0    0     0 p5  Z Dec 20  0:00 <defunct>
ellie 3823  0.0  1.1   28   112 p5  S 12:18   0:00 sh -c ps -aux | grep '^'
ellie 3821  0.0  5.6  144   580 p5  S 12:18   0:00 /bin/perl checkon ellie
ellie 3824  0.0  1.8   32   192 p5  S 12:18   0:00 grep ^ellie
```

EXPLANATION

1   The *PROC* filehandle is a pipe. The output from the Linux *ps* command is piped to Perl via the *PROC* filehandle.
2   The contents of the filter are printed to *STDOUT*.

Login Information—The *getlogin* Function. The *getlogin* function returns the current login from */etc/utmp*. If the empty string is returned from *getlogin*, use *getpwuid*. The *getpwuid* function takes the *uid* of the user as an argument and returns an entry from the password file associated with that *uid*.

The $< variable evaluates to the real *uid* of this process.

FORMAT

```
getlogin;
```

EXAMPLE 16.33

```
(The Script)
1  my $loginname=getlogin || (getpwuid($<))[0]|| die "Not a user here!!";
2  print "Your loginname is $loginname.\n";

(Output)
2  Your loginname is john.
```

EXPLANATION

1   The *getlogin* function returns the login name from */etc/utmp* and, if that fails, retrieves it from the password file with the *getpwuid* function. The $< variable contains the real *uid* of this process.
2   The scalar *$loginname* contains the user's login name, the first entry of the password file.

Special Process Variables (*pid, uid, euid, gid, egid*). Perl provides some special variables that store information about the Perl process executing your script. If you want to make your program more readable, you can use the *English* module in the standard Perl library to represent these variables in English.

- $$ The process ID of the Perl program running this script
- $<   The real *uid* of this process
- $>   The effective *uid* of this process
- $(The real *gid* of this process
- $)   The effective *gid* of this process

The Parent Process ID—The *getppid* Function and the *$$* Variable. Each process on the system is identified by its process identification number (*pid*), a positive integer. The special variable $$ holds the value of the *pid* for this process. This variable is also used by the shell to hold the process ID number of the current process.

The *getppid* function returns the process ID of the parent process.

EXAMPLE 16.34

```
(The Script)
1  print "The pid of this process is $$\n";
2  print "The parent pid of this process is ", getppid,"\n";

(Output)
1  The pid of this process is 3304
2  The parent pid of this process is 2340

(At the Command Line)
3  $ echo $$
   2340
```

EXPLANATION

1   The process identification number (*pid*) for this process, this Perl script, is printed.
2   The process that spawned this process is the parent process, in this case the shell. The parent's *pid* is called the *ppid*.
3   After the Perl script exits, the $$ is used to print the *pid* of the shell. The *ppid* for the Perl script was *2340*; the value of its parent's *pid*, that of the shell.

The Process Group ID—The *pgrp* Function.   The *pgrp* function returns the current group process for a specified *pid*. Without an argument or with an argument of *0*, the process group ID of the current process is returned.

FORMAT

```
getpgrp(PID);
getpgrp PID;
getpgrp;
```

EXAMPLE 16.35

```
(The Script)
1  print "The pid of the Perl program running this script is ", $$;
2  printf "The ppid, parent's pid (Shell) , is %d\n", getppid;
3  printf "The process group's pid is %d\n", getpgrp(0);

(Output)
1  The pid of the Perl program running this script is 6671
2  The ppid, parent's pid (Shell), is 6344
3  The process group's pid is 6671
```

16.2.5 Process Priorities and Niceness

The kernel maintains the scheduling priority selected for each process. Most interactive and short-running jobs are favored with a higher priority. The UNIX *nice* command allows you to modify the scheduling priority of processes. On moderately or heavily loaded systems, it may be to your advantage to make CPU-intensive jobs run slower so that jobs needing higher priority get faster access to the CPU. Those jobs that don't hog the processor are called *nice*.

The *nice* value is used in calculating the priority of a process. A process with a positive *nice* value runs at a low priority, meaning that it receives less than its share of the CPU time. A process with a negative *nice* value runs at a high priority, receiving more than its share of the processor. The *nice* values range from *-20* to *19*. Most processes run at priority zero, balancing their access to the CPU. (Only the superuser can set negative *nice* values.)

The following functions, *getpriority* and *setpriority*, are named for the corresponding system calls, found in Section 2 of the UNIX *man* pages.

The *getpriority* Function. The *getpriority* function returns the current priority (*nice* value) for a process, a process group, or a user. Not all systems support this function. If not implemented, *getpriority* produces a fatal error. WHICH is one of three values: 0 for the process priority, 1 for the process group priority, and 2 for the user priority. WHO is interpreted relative to the process identifier for the process priority, process group priority, or user priority. A value of zero represents the current process, process group, or user.

FORMAT

```
getpriority(WHICH, WHO);
```

EXAMPLE 16.36

```
(The Script)
1  $niceval = getpriority( 0,0);
2  print "The priority, nice value, for this process is $niceval\n";

(Output)
2  The priority, nice value, for this process is 0.
```

EXPLANATION

1   The *getpriority* function will return the *nice* value for the current process.
2   The *nice* value for this process is zero. This gives the process no special favor when taking its share of time from the CPU.

The *setpriority* Function (*nice*). The *setpriority* function sets the current priority (*nice* value) for a process, a process group, or a user. It modifies the scheduling priority for processes. If the *setpriority* system call is not implemented on your system, *setpriority* will throw an error.

WHICH is one of three values: *0* for the process priority, *1* for the process group priority, and *2* for the user priority. *WHO* is interpreted relative to the process identifier for the process priority, process group priority, or user priority. A value of zero represents the current process, process group, or user. *NICEVALUE* is the *nice* value. A low *nice* value raises the priority of the process and a high *nice* value decreases the priority of the process. (Confusing!)

Unless you have superuser privileges, you cannot use a negative *nice* value. Doing so will not change the current *nice* value.

FORMAT

```
setpriority(WHICH, WHO, NICEVALUE);
```

EXAMPLE 16.37

```
(The Script)
1   $niceval = getpriority(0,0);
2   print "The nice value for this process is $niceval.\n";
3   setpriority(0,0, ( $niceval + 5 ));
4   print "The nice value for this process is now", getpriority(0,0);


(Output)
2   The nice value for this process is 0.
4   The nice value for this process is now 5.
```

EXPLANATION

1   The *getpriority* function will return the *nice* value for the current process.
2   The *nice* value is printed.
3   The *setpriority* function adds 5 to the *nice* value of the current process. The process will have a lower priority. It is being "nice."
4   The new *nice* value returned by the *getpriority* function is 5.

16.2.6   Password Information

UNIX.   The following functions iterate through the */etc/passwd* file and retrieve information from that file into an array. These functions are named for the same functions found in the system library (see Section 3 of the UNIX manual) and perform the same tasks. If you are interested in obtaining information about the */etc/group* file, the Perl functions *getgrent*, *getgrgid*, and *getgrnam* all return a four-element array with information about group entries. A description of these functions is in the UNIX manual pages. Here is an example of an */etc/passwd* file:

```
root:YhTLR4heBdxfw:0:1:Operator:/:/bin/csh
nobody:*:65534:65534::/:
sys:*:2:2::/:/bin/csh
bin:*:3:3::/bin
```

```
uucp:*:4:8::/var/spool/uucppublic:
news:*:6:6::/var/spool/news:/bin/csh
sync::1:1::/:/bin/sync
ellie:aVD17TSsBMfYg:9496:40:Ellie Shellie:/home/jody/ellie:/bin/ksh
```

Windows. Windows stores information about users in a binary database called *SAM* (Security Accounts Manager), part of the Registry. Because the data is stored in binary format, normal Perl read operations won't work. It is better to use the Win32 extensions to get user information. *Win32::NetAdmin* is bundled with ActiveState under *\perl\site\lib\ win32*. (See Table 16-9.) You can manipulate a user account with two functions of this module: *UserGetAttributes* and *UserSetAttributes*.

The Win 32 *net.exe* command also displays information about the user and the system.

EXAMPLE 16.38

```
1   C:\ net help
    The syntax of this command is:

    NET HELP command
      -or-
    NET command /HELP


    Commands available are:

    NET ACCOUNTS              NET HELP            NET SHARE
    NET COMPUTER              NET HC:\ELPMSG      NET START
    NET CONFIG                NET LOCALGROUP      NET STATISTICS
    NET CONFIG SERVER         NET NAME            NET STOP
    NET CONFIG WORKSTATION    NET PAUSE           NET TIME
    NET CONTINUE              NET PRINT           NET USE
    NET FILE                  NET SEND            NET USER
    NET GROUP                 NET SESSION         NET VIEW

    NET HELP SERVICES lists the network services you can start.
    NET HELP SYNTAX explains how to read NET HELP syntax lines.
    NET HELP command | MORE displays Help one screen at a time.


2   C:\ net user

    User accounts for \\HOMEBOUND

    -----------------------------------------------------------------

    Administrator          Ellie Quigley            Guest
    The command completed successfully.
```

Table 16.9   *Win32::NetAdmin* Extensions

Win32::NetAdmin::UserGetAttributes(*$Machine,*

  $UserName,

  $Password,

  $PasswordAge,

  $Privilege,

  $Homedir,

  $Comment,

  $Flags,

  $ScriptPath);

Win32::NetAdmin::UserSetAttributes(*$Machine,*

  $UserName,

  $Password,

  $PasswordAge,

  $Privilege,

  $Homedir,

  $Comment,

  $Flags,

  $ScriptPath);

EXAMPLE 16.39

```
1  use Win32::NetAdmin qw(GetUsers UserGetAttributes) ;
2  GetUsers("", FILTER_NORMAL_ACCOUNT,\%hash)or die;
3  foreach $key(sort keys %hash){
     print "$key\n";
   }

(Output)
Administrator
Ellie Quigley
Guest
```

You cannot transfer encrypted passwords from UNIX to Win32 systems, and vice versa. They are cryptologically incompatible. To manage passwords, use the *Win32::AdminMisc* or the *Win32::NetAdmin* module extension. See Table 16.10.

Table 16.10 Win32 Password Extensions

Win32::AdminMisc::UserCheckPassword($Machine, $User, $Password)

Win32::AdminMisc::SetPassword($Machine | $Domain), $User, $NewPassword);

Win32::AdminMisc::UserChangePassword($Machine | $Domain), $User, $OldPassword, $NewPassword);

Win32::NetAdmin::UserChangePassword(($Machine | $Domain), $User, $OldPassword, $NewPassword);

For Windows users, the following functions for obtaining group and user information have not been implemented:

```
endgrent(), endpwent(), getgrent(), getgrgid(), getgrnam(),
getpwent(), getpwnam(), getpwuid(), setgrent(), setpwent()
```

At your prompt, type *perldoc perlport* to help with portability issues between different operating systems.

Getting a Password Entry (UNIX)—The *getpwent* Function. The *getpwent* function retrieves information from the */etc/passwd* file. The return value from *getpwent* is a nine-element array consisting of:

1. Login name
2. Encrypted password
3. User ID
4. Group ID
5. Quota
6. Comment
7. Gcos (user information)
8. Home directory
9. Login shell

FORMAT

```
($name, $passwd, $uid, $gid, $quota, $comment, $gcos, $dir,
     $shell )=getpwent;
```

EXAMPLE 16.40

```
(The Script)
1   while( @info=getpwent) {
2      print "$info[0] \n" if $info[1] =~ /\*/;
    }
```

EXAMPLE 16.40 (CONTINUED)

```
(Output)
2  nobody
   daemon
   sys
   bin
   uucp
```

EXPLANATION

1   The *getpwent* function gets a line from the */etc/passwd* file and stores it in the array @*info*. The loop continues until *getpwent* cannot read another entry from */etc/passwd*.
2   If the second element of the array contains at least one star (*), the first element, the user name, is printed.

Getting a Password Entry by Username—The *getpwnam* Function.   The *getpwnam* function takes the user name as an argument and returns a nine-element array corresponding to that user's name field in the */etc/passwd* file.

FORMAT

```
getpwnam(loginname);
```

EXAMPLE 16.41

```
(The Script)
   use warnings;
1  foreach $name ( "root", "bin", "ellie" ){
2      if (($login, $passwd, $uid)=getpwnam($name)){
3          print "$login--$uid\n";
       }
   }

(Output)
3  root--0
   ellie--9496
   bin--3
```

EXPLANATION

1   The *foreach* loop contains login names in its list, each to be processed in turn.
2   The *getpwnam* function retrieves information from */etc/passwd* and stores the first three fields of information in the array elements *$login*, *$passwd*, and *$uid*, respectively.
3   The *login* name and the *uid* are printed.

Getting a Password Entry by *uid*—**The** *getpwuid* **Function.** The *getpwuid* function takes a numeric user ID (*uid*) as an argument and returns a nine-element array corresponding to that user's *uid* entry in the */etc/passwd* file.

FORMAT

```
getpwuid(UID)
```

EXAMPLE 16.42

```
(The Script)
   use warnings;
1  foreach my $num ( 1 .. 10 ){
2     if (($login, $passwd, $uid)=getpwuid($num)){
3        print "$login--$uid\n";}
   }

(Output)
3  daemon--1
   sys--2
   bin--3
   uucp--4
   news--6
   ingres--7
   audit--9
```

EXPLANATION

1   The *foreach* loop contains a range of *uid* numbers from *1* to *10* in its list, each to be processed in turn.

2   The *getpwuid* function retrieves information from */etc/passwd* and stores the first three fields of information in the array elements *$login*, *$passwd*, and *$uid*, respectively.

3   The *login* name and its corresponding *uid* are printed.

16.2.7 Time and Processes

When working in a computer environment, programs often need to obtain and manipulate the current date and time. UNIX systems maintain two types of time values: calendar time and process time.

The calendar time counts the number of seconds since 00:00:00 January 1, 1970, UTC (Coordinated Universal Time, which is a new name for Greenwich Mean Time, although UTC does not adjust for leap seconds).

The process time, also called CPU time, measures the resources a process utilizes in clock time, user CPU time, and system CPU time. The CPU time is measured in clock ticks per second.

Perl has a number of time functions that interface with the system to retrieve time information.

If you want a list of CPAN modules for manipulating dates and times, go online to *http://www.techrepublic.com/article/manipulate-dates-and-time-with-these-10-perl-cpan-modules*. There, you'll get a list of 10 popular modules, a full description, and a link to the download page. The modules include:

- *Date::Manip*
- *DateTime*
- *Time::Format*
- *Time::Interval*
- *Date::Convert*
- *Benchmark*
- *Time::Normalize*
- *Regexp::Common::time*
- *MySQL::DateFormat*
- *Net::Time*

Since Perl 5.10, the **Time::Piece** module was added to the standard library to simplify the handling of date and time, discussed next.

The *Time::Piece* Module. The *Time::Piece* module is available in the standard Perl library (since version 5.10) to replace the *localtime* and *gmtime* functions. It provides a built-in constructor to create a date/time object and methods to get the current date and time, the weekday, year, month, and so forth. It also provides support for working with different locales, doing comparisons and calculations on dates and times, and methods for parsing and formatting the time and date. For full documentation, type at your prompt:

```
perldoc Time::Piece
```

EXAMPLE 16.43

```
(The Script)
    use warnings;
1   use Time::Piece;
    use feature qw(say);
2   my $t = localtime; # Create a time object
3   say "The time is $t.";
4   say "The year is ", $t->year, ".";
5   say "The month is ", $t->fullmonth, ".";
6   say "The day is ", $t->fullday, ".";

7   say $t->strftime("%A, %B %d, %Y");

8   say "Six months from now: ",$t->add_months(6);
9   say "Five years from now: ",$t->add_years(5);
10  my @days = qw( Dimanche Lundi Merdi Mercredi Jeudi Vendredi Samedi );
11  my $french_day = localtime->day(@days);
12  say "French for ",$t->fullday," is $french_day.";
```

EXAMPLE 16.43 (CONTINUED)

```
(Output)
3   The time is Tue Jul 22 12:46:50 2014.
4   The year is 2014.
5   The month is July.
6   The day is Tuesday.
7   Tuesday, July 22, 2014
8   Six months from now: Thu Jan 22 13:25:53 2015
9   Five years from now: Mon Jul 22 13:25:53 2019
12  French for Tuesday is Merdi.
```

EXPLANATION

1   The *Time::Piece* module is imported to create an object-oriented implementation of the *localtime* and *gmtime* built-in functions.

2   When *localtime* is used in a scalar context with *Time::Piece*, a time object is returned rather than a string. Once you get a time object, then you can use the methods provided by the module to manipulate the time.

3   Printing the object itself stringifies it to give the date/time values as in *localtime* and *gmtime*.

4–6   Some of the *Time::Piece* methods provided for the object are used in these examples.

7   The *Time::Piece* module has its own version of the POSIX *strftime* and *strptime* function and is used to format the time in a variety of ways.

8   The *add_months* method allows you to add months to the current month. You can also specify a negative number to subtract months.

9   The *add_years* method allows you to add or subtract years from the current year.

10 A locale is a set of data that categorizes how different parts of the world deal with their numbers, alphabets, money, time/date, and so forth. This example comes from the Perl documentation to show you how to work with times and dates without installing or using locales. See *perldoc.perl.org/perllocale* for recent documentation on working with locales. The array *@days* contains a list of the days of the week in French.

11 Now using *localtime* as a *Time::Piece* object, the *days* method will extract from the list of days the current day, based on the index value of the day name.

12 Now using the *fullday* method and the variable *$french_day*, we can print the day of the week in both English and in French.

The *times* Function. The built-in *times* function returns a four-element array consisting of the CPU time for a process, measured as follows:

- User time—Time spent executing user's code
- System time—Time spent executing system calls
- Children's user time—Time spent executing all terminated child processes
- Children's system time—Time spent executing system calls for all terminated child processes

FORMAT

```
($user, $system, $cuser, $csystem) = times;
```

EXAMPLE 16.44

```
(The Script)
    use warnings;
1   printf "User time in this program %2.3f seconds\n", (times)[0];
2   printf "System time in this program %2.3f seconds\n", (times)[1];

(Output)
1   User time in this program 0.217 seconds
2   System time in this program 0.600 seconds
```

EXPLANATION

1   The *times* function returns a four-element array and the first element is printed, the user time.
2   The *times* function returns a four-element array and the second element is printed, the system time.

The *time* Function (UNIX and Windows).   The *time* function returns the number of nonleap seconds since January 1, 1970, UTC. Its return value is used with the *gmtime* and *localtime* functions to put the time in a human-readable format. The *stat* and *utime* functions also use the *time* functions when comparing file modification and access times.

The *gmtime* Function.   The *gmtime* function converts the return value of the *time* function to a nine-element array consisting of the numeric values for the GMT. If you are a C programmer, you will recognize that these values are taken directly from the *tm structure* found in the header file */usr/include/time.h*. See Table 16.11.

FORMAT

```
gmtime(EXPR);
gmtime EXPR;
($sec, $min, $hour, $monthday, $month, $year, $weekday,
      $yearday, $isdaylight)=gmtime;
```

Table 16.11 Return Values for the *gmtime* Function

List Element	Meaning
$sec	Seconds after the minute: [0, 59]
$min	Minutes after the hour: [0, 59]
$hour	Hour since midnight: [0, 23]
$monthday	Day of the month: [1, 31]
$month	Months since January: [0, 11]
$year	Years since 1900
$weekday	Days since Sunday: [0, 6]
yearday	Days since January 1: [0, 365]
isdaylight	Flag for daylight savings time

EXAMPLE 16.45

```
(The Script)
   use warnings;
1  my ($sec, $min, $hour, $monthday, $month, $year, $weekday, $yearday,
      $isdaylight) = gmtime;
2  print "The weekday is $weekday and the month is $month.\n";
3  printf "The time in California since midnight is %02d:%02d\n",
      $hour,$min;
4  print "The Coordinated Univeral Time is $hour:$min
      since midnight\n";
5  print "Daylight saving is in effect.\n" if $isdaylight;

(Output)
2  The weekday is 2 and the month is 6.
3  The time in California since midnight is 20:35.
4  The Coordinated Univeral Time is 3:35 since midnight.
5  <no output>
```

EXPLANATION

1   The *gmtime* function returns an array, as defined in Table 16.11.
2   The weekday and the month are printed for Coordinated Universal Time.
3   The time in California is formatted and printed with the *printf* function. (See the *strftime* function in Perl's POSIX module or *Time::Piece* for formatting dates and times.)
4   The Coordinated Universal Time is printed.
5   If daylight savings is in effect, the value of *$isdaylight* is set to nonzero. Daylight saving time is not in effect, so nothing prints.

The *localtime* Function. The *localtime* function converts the UTC to a nine-element array with the local time zone.

FORMAT

```
localtime(EXPR);
localtime EXPR;
($sec, $min, $hour, $mday, $mon, $year, $wday, $yday,
    $isdst)=localtime(time);
```

EXAMPLE 16.46

```
(At the Command Line)
1  $ perl -e "print scalar (localtime);"
   Wed Jun 25 15:26:16 2014


(In Script)
2  $localtime=localtime;
   print $localtime;
```

EXPLANATION

1   If the *localtime* function is used in scalar context, its return value is output similar to the UNIX/Win32 *date* command. The *scalar* function forces scalar context.

2   The return value of *localtime* is assigned to a scalar.

EXAMPLE 16.47

```
(The Script)
   use warnings;
1  my ($sec, $min, $hour, $mday, $mon, $year, $wday, $yday, $isdst)=
       localtime(time);
2  my   %weekday=(
      "0"=>"Sunday",
      "1"=>"Monday",
      "2"=>"Tuesday",
      "3"=>"Wednesday",
      "4"=>"Thursday",
      "5"=>"Friday",
      "6"=>"Saturday",
   );
   if ( $hour > 12 ){
3      print "The hour is ", $hour - 12 ," o'clock.\n";
   }
   else {
       print "The hour is $hour o'clock.\n";
   }
4  print qq/Today is $weekday{"$wday"}.\n/;  # day starts at zero
5  print "It is ",$mon + 1, "/$mday/" , 1900+$year,".\n";
6  print "The isdst is $isdst.\n";
```

EXAMPLE 16.47 (CONTINUED)

```
(Output)
3   The hour is 1 o'clock.
4   Today is Wednesday.
5   It is 6/25/2014.
6   The isdst is 1.
```

EXPLANATION

1   The *localtime* function converts the return of the time function to the local time.
2   A hash, *%weekday*, associates a number of the weekday with the string for the day of the week.
3   The hour and the minutes are printed.
4   The scalar *$wday* returned from the *localtime* function represents the number of the weekday starting at 0. It is used to key into the hash *%weekday* to get the value of the string *Wednesday*.
5   The month, day of the month, and year are printed.
6   The *$isdt* element of the array prints *1* if daylight savings is in effect, and *0* if not.

16.2.8 Process Creation UNIX

What happens when your Perl program starts executing? Here is a brief sketch of what goes on. Normally, the Perl program is executed from the shell command line. You type the name of your script (and its arguments) and then press the ENTER key. At that point, the shell starts working. It first creates (*forks*) a new process called the **child process**. The child is essentially a copy of the shell that created it. There are now two processes running, the parent and child shells.

After the child process is created, the parent shell normally sleeps (*waits*) while its child process gets everything ready for your Perl program; that is, it handles redirection (if necessary), pipes, background processing, and so forth. When the child shell has completed its tasks, it then executes (*execs*) your Perl program in place of itself. When the Perl process completes, it exits (*exits*), and its exit status is returned to the waiting parent process, the shell. The shell wakes up, and a prompt appears on the screen. If you type in a UNIX command, this whole process is repeated.

It's conceivable that your Perl program may want to start up a child process to handle a specific task; for example, a database application or a client/server program.

The *fork* Function. You use the *fork* function to create processes on UNIX systems. The *fork* function is called once and returns twice. It creates a duplicate of the parent (calling) process. The new process is called the child process. The child process inherits its environment, open files, real and user IDs, masks, current working directory, signals, and so on. Both processes, parent and child, execute the same code, starting with the instruction right after the *fork* function call.

The *fork* function lets you differentiate between the parent and child because it returns a different value to each process. It returns 0 to the child process and the *pid* of the child to the parent process. It is not guaranteed which process will execute first after the call to the *fork* function.

Normally, the *wait, exec*, and *exit* functions work in conjunction with the *fork* function so that you can control what both the parent and the child are doing. The parent, for example, waits for the child to finish performing some task, and after the child exits, the parent resumes where it left off.

Figure 16.6 illustrates how the UNIX shell uses the *fork* system call to create a new process. After you type the name of your Perl program at the shell prompt, the shell forks, creating a copy of itself called the child process. The parent shell sleeps (*waits*). The child shell executes (*execs*) the Perl process in its place. The child never returns. Note that *ENV* variables, standard input, output, and standard error are inherited. When the Perl program completes, it exits and the parent shell wakes up. The shell prompt reappears on your screen. The Perl program could use the *fork* function to spawn off another application program.

FORMAT

```
fork;
```

EXAMPLE 16.48

```
(The Script)
1   $return_val=fork;
2   if ( $return_val == 0 ){
        print "This is the child process; return value
                is $return_val.\n";
    }
3   elsif ( defined $return_val ){
        print "This is the parent process; return value
                is $return_val.\n";
    }
    else{
4       die "fork error: $!\n";
    }

(Output)
2   This is the child process; return value is 0.
3   This is the parent process; return value is 3512.
```

EXPLANATION

1   The *fork* function is called to create a copy of this process.
2   The return value is checked. If the return value is 0, the child's code is in execution.
3   If the return value is nonzero, the parent process is executing.
4   This statement is executed if the *fork* function fails. It might fail if the process table is full (that is, if the system has reached its maximum number of allowed processes).

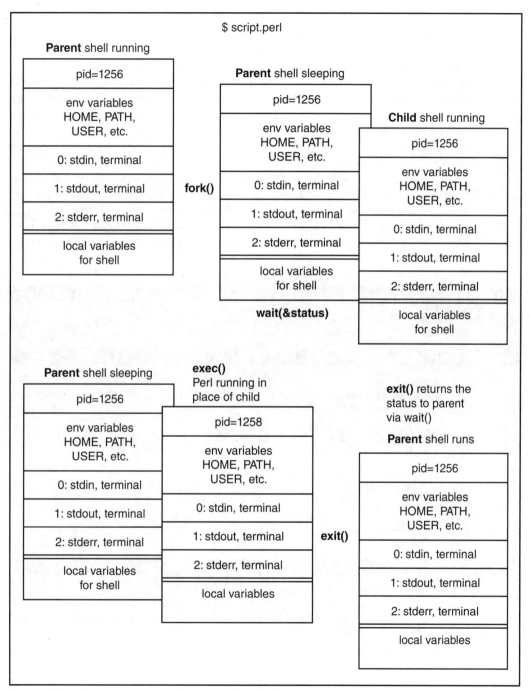

Figure 16.6 Perl process creation from the shell.

The *exec* Function.   While *fork* creates a brand new process, the *exec* function initiates a new program in place of the currently running program. Normally, the *exec* function is called after *fork*. Perl inherits attributes from the shell, and a process that is executed from within Perl also inherits Perl's attributes, such as *pid*, *gid*, *uid*, signals, directories, and so forth. If, then, the *exec* function is called directly (no *fork*) from within a Perl script, the new program executes in place of the currently running Perl program. When that program completes, you do not return to your Perl program. Since *exec* does not flush the output buffer, the $| variable needs to be set to ensure command buffering.

The filehandles *STDIN*, *STDOUT*, and *STDERR* remain open following a call to the *exec* function.

At the system level, there are six different *exec* functions used to initiate new programs. Perl calls the *C* library function *execvp* if more than one argument is passed to the *exec* function. The arguments are the name of the program to execute and any other arguments that will be passed to that program. If a single scalar is passed to the *exec* function and it contains any shell metacharacters, the shell command */bin/sh -c* is passed the command for interpretation.

FORMAT

```
exec(UNIX/Windows COMMAND);
exec UNIX/Windows COMMAND;
```

EXAMPLE 16.49

```
(The Script)
1   exec 'echo hi there you!';
2   print "hello";

(Output)
1   hi there you

(The Script)
1   exec 'ls *.c';
2   print "hello.";

(Output)
file1.c file2.c file3.c
```

EXPLANATION

1   In both examples, the *exec* function will execute the UNIX command.
2   In both examples, the *print* statement will not be executed, because *exec* never returns. The UNIX commands were executed **in place** of the Perl program.

The *wait* and *waitpid* Functions. The *wait* function waits for a child process to finish execution. After a *fork* call, both processes, parent and child, execute. The *wait* function forces the parent to wait until its child is finished and returns the *pid* of the child process to the parent. If there are no child processes, *wait* returns a *-1*.[11]

FORMAT

```
wait;
```

EXAMPLE 16.50

```
(The Script)
   use warnings;
1  $return_val=fork;
2  if ( $return_val == 0 ){        # In child
      print "This is the child process; return value
          is $return_val.\n";
3     exec "/bin/date" || die "exec failed: $!\n";
   }
4  elsif ( defined $return_val ){   # In parent
      print "This is the parent process; return value is $pid.\n";
5     $pid = wait;
      print "Back in parent process.\n";
      print "The deceased child's pid is $pid.\n";
   }
   else{
6     die "fork error: $!\n";
   }

(Output)
4  This is the parent process; return value is 3530.
2  This is the child process; return value is 0.
3  Fri May 30 23:57:18 PST 2014.
5  Back in the parent process.
   The deceased child's pid is 3530.
```

EXPLANATION

1 The *fork* function creates a copy of the current process. Now there are two processes running, the parent Perl process and the child Perl process. They are both executing the code directly following the *fork* call. The return value is assigned *0* in the child and the *pid* of the child in the parent.

2 If in the child process, the *if* statement block is executed.

3 The *exec* function executes the UNIX *date* command and does not return.

4 If in the parent process, the *elsif* statement block is executed. The value of $return_val is the *pid* of the child process.

---

11. The *waitpid* function also waits for a child process to finish execution, but it can specify which child it will wait for, and it has special flags that control blocking.

EXPLANATION (continued)

5   The *wait* function is called by the parent, which waits for the child to finish. The *pid* of the deceased child is returned.

6   If the *fork* failed (no more processes?), the *die* function will print the error message and the program will exit.

The *exit* Function.   The *exit* function causes the program to exit. It can be given an integer argument ranging from values between 0 and 255. The exit value is returned to the parent process via the *wait* function call. By convention, UNIX programs exiting with a zero status are successful, and those exiting with nonzero failed in some way. (Of course, the criteria for success for one programmer may not be the same as those for another.)

FORMAT

```
exit (Integer);
exit Integer;
```

EXAMPLE 16.51

```
(The Script)
   # The name of the script is args.pl
1  exit 12 if $#ARGV == 0;


(Output)
1  $ args.pl
2  $ echo $?
   12
```

EXPLANATION

1   The script is missing an argument.

2   The shell's *$?* variable contains the exit status of the Perl program. If using *C* shell, the exit status is stored in *$status*.

16.2.9   Process Creation Win32

You can use the *system* and *exec* functions and backquotes on Win32 systems just the same as you would with UNIX.

The *start* Command.   The Perl *system* function is used by both Windows and UNIX to start an operating system command. The *system* function executes a program and doesn't return until that program finishes. If the Windows *start* command is given as an argument to the Perl *system* function, a new application will run, and your script will also continue to run.

EXAMPLE 16.52

```
    use warnings;
1   $return_value = system ('start "C:\Program Files/Internet
        Explorer/iexplore.exe"');
2   print "Program continues; Explorer is running.\n";
3   print "The return_value from system is $return_value.\n";

(Output)
2   Program continues; Explorer is running.
3   The return_value from system is 0.
```

EXPLANATION

1   The Perl *system* function starts a new process. It behaves like the *exec* function, except that a fork is done first and the parent process waits for the child process to exit. By using the Win32 *start* command, you can start a new process and the Perl script will continue to run rather than waiting for the new process to complete. If the process starts up successfully, a return value of *0* is returned by the *system* function.
2   Internet Explorer has started up and will continue to run until its window is closed.
3   The return value from the *system* function is printed.

The *Win32::Spawn* Function.   The *Win32::Spawn* function behaves like the *system* function and the Windows *Start* command.

FORMAT

```
use Win32;
Win32::Spawn($ProgramName, $CommandLine,$ProcessID);
```

EXAMPLE 16.53

```
1   use warnings;
2   use Win32;
3   $|=1;
4   $Application="C:/mksnt/date.exe";
5   $CommandLine="date +%D";
6   $status=Win32::Spawn($Application, $CommandLine, $ProcessID);
7   if ($status != 0){
8       print "pid is $ProcessID.\n";
    }
    else{
9       print "Didn't spawn $Application.\n";
10      print Win32::FormatMessage(Win32::GetLastError);
    }

(Output)
8 pid is 448.
06/01/14
```

EXPLANATION

1   The *warnings* pragma will send syntactic warnings, unitialized values, and so forth, to help with possible problems that may occur in the program.

2   The *Win32* module is loaded from the standard Perl library; that is a core module. It contains a number of useful modules for Windows programmers to handle servers, clients, registries, events, network administration, processes, and more.

3   The special scalar *$|* is assigned the value *1*. It ensures that the output buffers will be flushed immediately when the *print* function is used. (Type at your prompt, for UNIX or Windows, *perldoc Win32*.)

4   The application is the MSK toolkit,* found on the *C:* drive. This toolkit contains *.exe* files that emulate UNIX commands. The *date.exe* file produces today's date.

5   The command line consists of any arguments that will be passed to the application.

6   The *Win32::Spawn* function is called with three arguments. Two of them have been given values, but *$ProcessID* is not known. It will be given a value after the application is started.

7   If the status returned from the *Win32::Spawn* function is not *0*, the process ID number will be printed.

8   The process ID number is *448*.

9   *Didn't spawn C:/mksnt/date.exe.* is displayed if the *.exe* file doesn't exist.

10 If the process couldn't be started because the application doesn't exist, the *GetLastError* function prints:

The system cannot find the file specified.
Program continues to run....

This is a Windows-generated error caused when the operating system failed to start the program. The *FormatMessage* function creates a readable printout of the error.

---

* MSK Toolkit for Windows NT and Windows 95 Release 6.1, Mortice Kern Systems Inc.

The *Win32::Process* Module.   Another extension you can use to launch Windows applications is the object-oriented *Win32::Process* module. It provides a number of methods to create and manage processes. You can suspend, resume, and kill processes with this module. See Table 16.12.

Table 16.12   *Win32::Process* Methods

Method	What It Does
Create($Obj, $AppName, $CommandLine, $Inherit, $CreateFlags, $InitialDir);	Creates the process object
$Obj->GetExitCode($ExitCode);	Gets the exit code of the process
$Obj->GetPriorityClass($Class);	Gets the process priority class

(continued)

Table 16.12 *Win32::Process* Methods (continued)

Method	What It Does
$ProcessObj->GetProcessID()	Returns the process ID
$Obj->Kill($ExitCode);	Kills the process with exit code
$Obj->Resume();	Resumes a suspended process
$Obj->SetPriorityClass($Class);	Sets the process affinity mask (NT)
$Obj->Suspend();	Suspends the process
$Obj->Wait($Timeout);	Waits for the process to die

EXAMPLE 16.54

```
1   use Win32::Process;
2   use Win32;
3   sub ErrorReport{
        print Win32::FormatMessage( Win32::GetLastError );
    }

4   Win32::Process::Create($ProcessObj,
        "C:\\windows\\notepad.exe", "notepad myfile.txt", 0,
        NORMAL_PRIORITY_CLASS, ".") || die ErrorReport;
    print "Notepad has started\n";
5   print "The exit code is:
        ",$ProcessObj->GetExitCode($ExitCode),"\n";
```

(Output)
Notepad has started
The exit code is: 1

EXPLANATION

1   The *Win32::Process* module is loaded. It is used to launch Windows applications.
2   The Win32 module is loaded.
3   The *ErrorReport* function will send a formatted error message for the last system error that occurred, if there was one.
4   The *Create* function creates a process. The first argument, *$ProcessObj,* is a container for the process object, followed by the full pathname of the application, command-line arguments, and required flags.
5   The exit code of the process is returned.

16.3 Other Ways to Interface with the Operating System

If the system functions are still not enough, Perl offers a number of alternative ways to deal with the operating system. You can use the *syscall* function, command substitution, the *system* function, and the *here document* to get system information.

16.3.1   The *syscall* Function and the *h2ph* Script

The *syscall* function calls a specified system call with its arguments. If the *C* system call is not implemented, a fatal error is returned. The first argument is the name of the system call, preceded by *&SYS_*. The remaining arguments are the actual parameters that are required by the real system call. If the argument is numeric, it is passed as a *C* integer. If not, the pointer to the string value is passed. You may have to coerce a number to an integer by adding *0* to it if it is not a literal and cannot be interpreted by context.

Before using the *syscall* function, you should run a script called *h2ph* (*h2ph.bat* on Windows) that comes with the Perl distribution (*http://perldoc.perl.org/h2ph.html*). At the bottom of the *h2ph* script (after *__END__*) are the manual pages for *h2ph*, including an explanation on how to run the script. This script converts the proper *C* header files to the corresponding Perl header files. You must add these files to the Perl library if you are using functions that require them. All the files created have the *.ph* extension. After running the *h2ph* script, make sure that the *@INC* array in your program includes the path to these library functions.[12]

FORMAT

```
syscall (&SYS_NAME, LIST);
```

EXAMPLE 16.55

```
(UNIX: At the Command Line)
1   $ cd /usr/include; /usr/local/bin/perl/h2ph  *  sys/*

(In Script)
    #!/bin/perl
    # The name of the script is args.p
2   push(@INC, "/usr/local/lib");
3   require "syscall.ph";
4   $bytes=syscall(&SYS_getpagesize);
5   printf "The pagesize for this Sparc Sun Workstation is %d
        bytes \n",$bytes;

(Output)
5   The pagesize for this Sparc Sun Workstation is 4096 bytes.
```

---

12. See also the *h2xs* script that comes with the Perl 5 distribution, for building a Perl extension from any C header file.

1   *h2ph* is executed so that the necessary *C* header files are converted to Perl header files. The files created will be placed in */usr/local/lib* and end with a *.ph* extension.
2   The directory containing the *.ph* files is pushed onto the *@INC* array.
3   The file *syscall.ph* is required for using *C* system calls.
4   The Perl *syscall* function will call the *getpagesize* system call. The prefix *&SYS_* is necessary Perl syntax. It must be prepended to the real system call name.
5   The page size for this Sun4c is *4,096* bytes.

16.3.2   Command Substitution—The Backquotes

Although we have already discussed command substitution and backquotes in Chapter 5, "What's in a Name?" a quick review might be in order here because command substitution is yet another way for Perl to interface with operating system commands.

Backquotes are used by the UNIX/Linux shells (not Windows) to perform command substitution and are implemented in Perl scripts pretty much the same way. For example, the command line *echo The present working directory is `pwd`* will cause the command in backquotes to be executed and its results substituted into the string. **Like** the UNIX/Linux shell, enclosing a command in backquotes causes it to execute. **Unlike** the shell, if double quotes surround the backquoted string, command substitution will **not** occur. The output resulting from executing the command is saved in a scalar variable.

```
(The Script)
   use warnings;
1  print "The hour is ",`date`;

2  my @d=`date`;
3  print $d[0];

4  @d=split(/ /,`date`);
5  print "$d[0]\n";
6  my $machine=`uname -n`;
7  print "$machine\n";

(Output)
1  The hour is Sat May 31 20:47:17 PDT 2014
3  Sat Sat 31 20:59:11 PDT 2014
5  Sat
7  dolphin
```

EXPLANATION

1 The UNIX *date* command is enclosed in backquotes. It is executed and appended to the string *The hour is*.
2 The array *@d* is set to the output of the *date* command. The output is stored as a single string in the first element of the array.
3 *$d[0]* is the entire date/time string.
4 The *split* command creates a list from the output returned from the *date* command.
5 Now the first element of the array is the first word in the list, *Sat*.
6 The scalar *$machine* is assigned the value of the UNIX command, *uname -n*, which contains the name of the host machine (*hostname* on BSD/Linux).
7 The name of the host machine is printed.

16.3.3 The *Shell.pm* Module

This module lets you use UNIX commands that you normally type at the shell prompt in a Perl script. The commands are treated like Perl subroutines. Arguments and options are passed to the commands as a list of strings. As of Perl 5.16, this core module has been removed and can be found at CPAN.

EXAMPLE 16.57

```
(The Script)
    use warnings;
1   use Shell qw(pwd ls date);     # Shell commands listed
2   print "Today is ", date();
3   print "The time is ", date("+%T");
4   print "The present working directory is ", pwd;
5   my $list=ls( "-aF");
6   print $list;

(Output)
2   Today is Tue May 29 13:41:56 PDT 2014
3   The time is 13:41:57
4   The present working is /home/ellie/sockets
6   ./
    ../
    sh.test*
    shellstuff
    timeclient*
    timeclient5*
    timeserver*
    timeserver5*
```

EXPLANATION

1 The *Shell.pm* module will be used in this program. The three UNIX shell commands *pwd*, *ls*, and *date* will be treated as ordinary Perl subroutines.
2 The *date* command is executed as a subroutine. This is an alternative to using backquotes.
3 Arguments passed to the *date* command are strings enclosed in quotes.
4 The *pwd* command is executed.
5 The output of the *ls* command is assigned to scalar *$list*. The argument is passed to the function as a single string.
6 The output of *ls -aF* is a list of files in the present working directory. The *-a* switch includes the dot files, and the *F* causes the executable scripts to be marked with an asterisk (*) and the directories with a /.

16.3.4 The *system* Function

Like its *C* counterpart, the *system* function takes a system command as its argument, sends the command to the system shell for interpretation, and returns control back to the calling program, your script. This is just like the *exec* functions, except that a *fork* is done first, so that control is returned to the Perl script. Because it does not flush the output buffer, the special Perl variable *$|* is set to *1* to force the buffer to flush after *print* or *write* statements.[13]

FORMAT

```
system("system command");
system "system command";
```

EXAMPLE 16.58

```
(UNIX: The Command Line)
1   system("cal 1 2015");
    print "Happy New  Year!\n";'

(Output)
        January 2015
    Su Mo Tu We Th Fr Sa
                   1  2  3
     4  5  6  7  8  9 10
    11 12 13 14 15 16 17
    18 19 20 21 22 23 24
    25 26 27 28 29 30
        Happy New Year!

(Windows)
2   system("notepad.exe");
```

---

13. A fork is done, the script waits for the command to be executed, and control is then returned to the script.

EXPLANATION

1   The *system* function executes the UNIX *cal* command to print out the calendar for the month of January 2015.

2   The *system* function executes the Windows *notebook.exe* command and starts up a session of Notepad.

EXAMPLE 16.59

```
(The Script)
1   print "Hello there\n";
2   print "The name of this machine is ";
3   system ("uname -n");        # Buffer is not flushed
4   print "The time is ", `date`;


(Output)
1   Hello there
3   jody
2,4 The name of this machine is The time is Tue May 29 13:39:35 PDT 2007
```

EXPLANATION

1   The first *print* statement is executed as expected.

2   Since Perl depends on the default I/O buffering mechanism, the buffer may not be flushed immediately after the *print* statement; the results of the *system* function, executed by the shell, are printed first.

3   The *system* function causes the shell to execute the UNIX command *uname -n*.

4   This *print* statement is printed directly after the *print* statement in line 2.

EXAMPLE 16.60

```
(The Script)
    use warnings;
1   $|=1;       # Set special variable to flush the output buffer
2   print "Hello there\n";
3   print "The name of this machine is ";
    system ("uname -n");
4   print "The time is ", `date`;


(Output)
2   Hello there
3   The name of this machine is jody
4   The time is Mon Jan 26 13:43:54 PST 2015
```

EXPLANATION

1   The $| special variable, when set to nonzero, forces the output buffer to flush after every *write* or *print*.

16.3.5   Globbing (Filename Expansion and Wildcards)

If you have worked at the UNIX or MS-DOS command line, you have been introduced to the shell metacharacters used to expand filenames. The asterisk (*) is used to match all characters in a filename, the question mark (?) to match one character in a filename, and brackets ([ ]) to match one of a set of characters in a filename. The process of expanding these shell metacharacters to a filename is called **globbing**.

Perl supports globbing if the filenames are placed within angle brackets, the read operators. However, today you should use the built-in *glob* function, shown next. The following example is here so that if you encounter older code, you will understand what is going on.

EXAMPLE 16.61

```
(The Script)
    use warnings;
1   @myfiles=<*.[1-5]>;
2   print "@myfiles\n";
3   foreach $file ( <p??l[1-5]*>){
4       print "$file\n" if -T $file;
    }

(Output)
2   exer.3 exer.4 exer.5 fileter.1 format.1 format.2 format.3 perl.4
    perl.4.1
4   perl1
    perl2
    perl3
    perl4
    perl4.1
    perl5
```

EXPLANATION

1   In an array context, after the globbing is performed, a list of all the matched files is returned to the array *@myfiles*. The list consists of any files that start with zero or more of any character, followed by a period, and ending with a number between *1* and *5*.
2   The list of matched files is printed.
3   The *foreach* loop is entered. Each time through the loop, the scalar *$file* is set to the next file that is successfully globbed; that is, any file starting with a *p*, followed by any two characters, followed by an *l*, followed by a number between *1* and *5*, and ending in zero or more of any character.
4   If the file is a text file (-*T*), its name is printed.

The *glob* Function.   The builtin *glob* function does the same thing as the <*> operator and is the function you should use when globbing filenames. It expands the filename metacharacters just as the shell does and returns the expanded filenames.

EXAMPLE 16.62

```
(Command Line)
1   $ perl -e 'while(glob("p???[1-5]")) {print "$_\n";}'
    perl1
    perl2
    perl3
    perl4
    perl5


(In Script)
2   while ( glob("p???[1-5]")){
3       print "$_\n";
    }


(Output)
3   perl1
    perl2
    perl3
    perl4
    perl5
```

EXPLANATION

1   At the command line, the *glob* function will "glob" onto any files in the current work-ing directory whose name begins with a *p*, followed by any three characters (*???*), followed by any number between *1* and *5* (*[1-5]*). Each filename that matches the expression is assigned to $_ and then printed.

2   This time, *glob* is being used in a script. The behavior is the same as in the first example.

3   The expanded filenames are printed.

16.4 Error Handling

There are a number of occasions when a system call can fail; for example, when you try to open a file that doesn't exist or remove a directory when it still contains files or when you try to read from a file for which you do not have read permission. Although we have used the *die* function in earlier examples, now we will go into more detail about error handling and functions you can use to handle errors. The functions are the *die* function, the *warn* function, and the *eval* function.

- Use the *die* function to quit the Perl script if a command or filehandle fails.
- The *warn* function is like the *die* function, but it does not exit the script.
- The *eval* function has multiple uses, but it is used primarily for exception handling.

You may remember that the *short-circuit* operators, *&&* and *||*, evaluate the operands on the left and then evaluate the operands on the right. If the operand to the left of the *&&* is *true*, the right-hand side is evaluated. If the operand to the left of the *||* is *false*, the right-hand side is evaluated.

16.4.1 The *Carp* Module

There are many ways to *die*. Perl 5's *Carp* module extends the functionality of *die* and *warn*.

The *die* Function.   If a system call fails, the *die* function prints a string to *STDERR* and exits with the current value of *$!*. The *$!* variable yields the current value of *errno*, the UNIX global variable containing a number indicating a system error. The only time that *errno* is updated is when a system call **fails**. When a system call fails, a code number is assigned to *errno* to indicate the type of error. If the newline is omitted in the string, the message is printed with its line number. (See */usr/include/sys* for a complete list.)

Here is an example from */usr/include/sys/errno.h*:

```
#define EPERM      1    /* Not owner */
#define ENOENT     2    /* No such file or directory */
#define ESRCH      3    /* No such process */
#define EINTR      4    /* Interrupted system call */
#define EIO        5    /* I/O error */
...
```

Win32 error codes differ from UNIX error codes, making it impossible to rely on the value returned in *$!*. There are a number of Win32 extensions that provide their own error functions to give more meaningful results. See the documentation for *Win32::GetLastError* in the standard Perl library included with ActiveState.

FORMAT

```
die(LIST)
die LIST
die
```

EXAMPLE 16.63

```
(In Script)
1 die "Can't cd to junk: $!\n" unless chdir "/usr/bin/junk";

(Output)
1 Can't cd to junk: No such file or directory
```

EXPLANATION

1   The *chdir* failed. The *$!* contains the error message from *errno*. The newline causes the string after the *die* function to be printed with the value of the *$!* variable.

EXAMPLE 16.64

```
(In Script)
1  chdir '/plop' or die "Stopped";

(Output)
1  Stopped at croak.perl line 4.
```

EXPLANATION

1   This example produces the same output as the previous example, but using a different syntax. If *chdir* fails, the *die* function to the right of *or* is executed.

The *warn* Function.   The *warn* function is just like the *die* function except that the program continues to run. If the *die* function is called in an *eval* block, the argument string given to *die* will be assigned to the special variable *$@*. After a *die*, this variable can pass as an argument to *warn* and the output sent to *STDERR*. (See Section 16.4.2, "The *eval* Function.")

16.4.2   The *eval* Function

Use the *eval* function for exception handling; that is, catching errors. The block following *eval* is treated and parsed like a separate Perl program, except that all variable settings and subroutine and format definitions remain after *eval* is finished.

The value returned from the *eval* function is that of the last expression evaluated. If there is a compile or runtime error or the *die* statement is executed, an undefined value is returned, and a special variable, *$@*, is set to the error message. If there is no error, *$@* is a null string.

Example 16.65 shows an example of evaluating Perl expressions using *eval*.

EXAMPLE 16.65

```
(The Script)
   use warnings;
   # The eval function will evaluate each line you type
   # and return the result. It's as though you are
   # running a little independent Perl script.
   # Script name: plsh
   my $result;
1  print "> ";        # Print the prompt
2  while(<STDIN>){
3     $result=eval ;  # eval evaluates the expression $_
4     warn $@ if $@;  # If an error occurs, it will be assigned to $@
5     print "$result\n" if $result;
6     print "> ";     # Print the prompt
   }
```

EXAMPLE 16.65 (CONTINUED)

```
(Output)
(The Command line)
   $ plsh
2  > hello
5  hello
2  > bye
5  bye
2  > 5 + 4
5  9
2  > 8 / 3
5  2.66666666666667
2  > 5 / 0
4  Illegal division by zero at (eval 5) line 3, <STDIN> line 5.
   > "Oh I see
   Can't find string terminator '"' anywhere before EOF at (eval 6)
      line 1,   <STDIN> line
   > exit
```

EXPLANATION

1   This line prints a prompt for the user. This program is like a little Perl shell. It can help you evaluate an expression before putting it in a program, especially if you're not sure how Perl will handle it.

2   The *while* loop is entered. Each time the loop is entered, it will read a line of input from the user and assign it to $_.

3   The *eval* function, without an argument, will evaluate the expression in $_ and assign the result of the evaluation to *$result*.

4   If the *eval* finds a syntax error or a system error results from the evaluation of the expression, the error message returned will be assigned to the $@ variable. If there is no error, the $@ variable is assigned a null string.

5   If the expression was successfully evaluated, the result will be printed.

6   The prompt is displayed and the loop reentered.

Next, we will see how to use eval to catch errors in a program.

EXAMPLE 16.66

```
(In Script)
   #!/bin/perl
   print "Give me a number.";
   chop($a=<STDIN>);
   print "Give me a divisor.";
   chop($b=<STDIN>);
1  eval{ die unless $answer = $a/$b ; };
2  warn $@ if $@;
3  printf "Division of %.2f by %.2f is %.2f.\n",$a,$b,
         $answer if $answer ;
4  print "I'm here now. Good-day!\n";
```

EXAMPLE 16.66 (CONTINUED)

```
(Output)
    Give me a number.45
    Give me a divisor.6
3   Division of 45.00 by 6.00 is 7.50.
4   I'm here now. Good-day!

(Output)
    Give me a number.5
    Give me a divisor.0
2   Illegal division by zero at ./eval.p line 8, <STDIN> line 2.
4   I'm here now. Good-day!
```

EXPLANATION

1   The *eval* function will evaluate the division (*$a/$b*) and store the result in *$answer*. Note that *$answer* is first used inside the *eval* function. It remains after *eval* is finished.

2   If all went well, and the division was completed, this line is ignored. If there was an error (for example, division by zero), the *$@* variable is set to the system error. The *warn* function then prints the message to *STDERR*, and the program resumes. If the *die* function is called in an *eval* block, the program does not exit but continues execution after the *eval* block exits.

3   The result of the division is printed, if successful.

4   This line is printed just to show you that the program continued execution even after a failure, since the *warn* function does not cause the script to exit.

The next example shows how to use the *eval* function with a *here document*.

EXAMPLE 16.67

```
(The Script)
    #!/bin/perl
1   eval<<"EOF";
2      chdir "joker" || die "Can't cd: $!\n";
3   EOF
4   print "The error message from die: $@";
5   print "Program $0 still in progress.\n";

(Output)
4   The error message from die: Can't cd: no such file or directory
5   Program ./eval4.p still in progress.
```

EXPLANATION

1   The *here document* is like a special form of quoting. The *eval* function will get everything between the first *EOF* and the terminating *EOF*.

2   If the *chdir* function fails, the *die* function is called, and the program resumes after the last *EOF* of the *here document*.

3   EOF terminates the *here document*.
4   The error message from the *die* function is stored in the $@ variable.
5   The program continues.

16.5 Signals and the *%SIG* Hash

A signal sends a message to a process and normally causes the process to terminate, usually due to some unexpected event, such as illegal division by zero, a segmentation violation, a bus error, or a power failure. The UNIX kernel also uses signals as timers; for example, to send an alarm signal to a process. The user sends signals when he hits the BREAK, DELETE, QUIT, or STOP keys.

The kernel recognizes 31 different signals, listed in */usr/include/signal.h*. You can get a list of signals by simply typing *kill -l* at the UNIX prompt (see Table 6.13).

Table 6.13 Signals (BSD) *

Name	Number	Default	Description
SIGHUP	1	Terminate	Hangup
SIGINT	2	Interrupt	Interrupt
SIGQUIT	3	Terminate	Quit/produces core file
SIGILL	4	Terminate	Terminate

* This is a partial listing of the signals.

16.5.1 Catching Signals

Signals are asynchronous events; that is, the process doesn't know when a signal will arrive. Programmatically, you can ignore certain signals coming into your process or set up a signal handler to execute a subroutine when the signal arrives. In Perl scripts, any signals you specifically want to handle are set in the *%SIG* hash. If a signal is ignored, it will be ignored after *fork* or *exec* function calls.

A signal may be ignored or handled for a segment of your program and then reset to its default behavior. See *http://perldoc.perl.org/perlvar.html* for more examples.

FORMAT

```
$SIG{'signal'};
```

Interfacing with the System

EXAMPLE 16.68

```
(The Script)
   use warnings;
1  sub handler{  # user-defined signal handling function
2     my $sig = shift;     # First argument is signal name
3     print "Caught SIG$sig--shutting down\n";
4     exit(1);
   }
5  $SIG{'INT'} = 'handler';  # Catch <Ctrl>-C
6  $SIG{'HUP'}='IGNORE';
7  print "Here I am!\n";
   sleep(10);
8  $SIG{'INT'}='DEFAULT';³
```

```
(Output)
7  Here I am
      < Ctrl+C is pressed while the process sleeps >
3  Caught SIGINT--shutting down
```

EXPLANATION

1   The user-defined subroutine called *handler* is defined.
2   The first argument, the signal name, is shifted from the @_ and assigned to the scalar $*sig*.
3   If the signal arrives, the handler routine is executed and this statement is printed. Use this function to close or clean up files, or take care of any housekeeping required in case the program is suddenly aborted.
4   The program exits with a value of *1*, to be tested at the shell prompt in $?, a non-zero value meaning that something went wrong.
5   A value for the $*SIG* hash is set. The key is the name of the signal without the *SIG* prefix. The value is the name of the subroutine, called *handler*, that will be called. If <CTRL>+C (both UNIX and Windows), the interrupt key, is pressed while the program is running, the *handler* function is called.
6   *IGNORE* will ignore the hangup signal.
7   The *print* statement is executed and the process sleeps for 10 seconds. If the signal <CTRL>+C arrives, the signal handler routine is called.
8   The *SIGINT* signal is reset to its default state, which is to terminate the process when <CTRL>+C is pressed.

16.5.2　Sending Signals to Processes

The *kill* Function.　If you want to send a signal to a process or list of processes, use the *kill* function. The first element of the list is the signal. The signal is a numeric value or a signal name if quoted. The function returns the number of processes that received the signal successfully. A process group is killed if the signal number is negative. You must own a process to kill it; that is, the effective *uid* and real *uid* must be the same for the process sending the *kill* signal and the process receiving the *kill* signal.

For complex signal handling, see the *POSIX* module in the Perl standard library.

FORMAT

```
kill(LIST);
kill LIST;
```

EXAMPLE 16.69

```
1  $ sleep 100&
2  $ jobs -l
   [1] + 6505 Running    sleep 100&
3  $ perl -e 'kill 9, 6505'
   [1]      Killed       sleep 100
```

EXPLANATION

1   At the UNIX shell prompt, the *sleep* command is executed in the background. The *sleep* command causes the shell to pause for 100 seconds.

2   The *jobs* command lists the processes running in the background. The *sleep* process *pid* is *6505*.

3   Perl is executed at the command line. The *kill* function takes two arguments. The first, signal *9*, guarantees that the process will be terminated. The second argument is the *pid* of the *sleep* process.

The *alarm* Function.   The *alarm* function tells the kernel to send a *SIGALARM* signal to the calling process after some number of seconds. Only one alarm can be in effect at a time. If you call *alarm* and an alarm is already in effect, the previous value is overwritten.

FORMAT

```
alarm (SECONDS);
alarm SECONDS;
```

EXAMPLE 16.70

```
(The Script)
1  alarm(1);
2  print "In a Forever Loop!";
3  for (; ;){ printf "Counting...%d\n", $x++;}

(Output)
2  In a Forever Loop!
3  Counting...0
   Counting...1
   Counting...2
   Counting...3
   Counting...4
      ...
   Counting...294
   Counting...295
4  Alarm Clock
```

1   A *SIGALARM* signal will be sent to this process after 1 second.
2   This statement is printed.
3   The loop starts. We wait for 1 second. The resolution on the actual second may be off. You can use the *syscall* function to call other functions, such as *setitimer* (2) and *getitimer* (2), with better timing resolution.
4   When the alarm goes off, the message *Alarm Clock* is printed.

The *sleep* Function.   The *sleep* function causes the process to pause for a number of seconds or forever if a number of seconds is not specified. It returns the number of seconds that the process slept. You can use the *alarm* function to interrupt the sleep.

FORMAT

```
sleep(SECONDS);
sleep SECONDS;
sleep;
```

EXAMPLE 16.71

```
(The Script)
    use warnings;
1   $|=1          # flush output buffer
2   alarm(5);
    print "Taking a snooze...\n";
3   sleep 100;
4   print "\07 Wake up now.!\n";

(Output)
2   Taking a snooze...   # Program pauses now for 5 seconds
4   (Beep) Wake up now.
```

EXPLANATION

1   The $| variable forces the output buffer to be flushed after it writes and prints.
2   The *alarm* function tells the kernel to send a *SIGALRM* signal to the process in 5 seconds.
3   The process goes to sleep for 100 seconds or until a signal is sent to it.
4   The \07 causes a beep to sound before the statement *Wake up now!*

16.5.3   Attention, Windows Users!

For those Win32 systems, the following functions have not been fully implemented. Primary among these is *alarm()*, which is used in a few Perl modules. Following is a list of unimplemented functions.

Functions for processes and process groups:

- *alarm(), fork(), getpgrp(), getppid(), getpriority(), setpgrp(), setpriority()*

Functions for fetching user and group info:

- *endgrent(), endpwent(), getgrent(), getgrgid(), getgrnam(), getpwent(), getpwnam(), getpwuid(), setgrent(), setpwent()*

System V interprocess communication functions:

- *msgctl(), msgget(), msgrcv(), msgsnd(), semctl(), semget(), semop(), shmctl(), shmget(), shmread(), shmwrite()*

Functions for filehandles, files, or directories:

- *link(), symlink(), chroot()*

Input and output functions:

- *syscall()*

Functions for fetching network info:

- *getnetbyname(), getnetbyaddr(), getnetent(), getprotoent(),getservent(), sethostent(), setnetent(), setprotoent(), setservent(), endhostent(), endnetent(), endprotoent(), endservent(), socketpair()*

See the *perlport* and *perlwin32* documentation pages for more information on the portability of built-in functions in ActivePerl.

16.6 What You Should Know

1. What are system calls?

2. How does Perl make calls to the system?

3. What module is used to traverse a file system?

4. How are directories created and removed?

5. How do you get the date and time with *Time::Piece*?

6. What is meant by the environment?

7. What is a process?

8. What do *fork* and *exec* accomplish?

9. Where can you find modules for Windows processes?

10. How does the system function differ from using command substitution (backquotes) when executing system commands?

11. What is globbing?

12. How does *eval* work with *die*?

13. What are signals?

14. How does Perl deal with signals?

15. How do you rename a file with Perl?

16. How do you remove a file with Perl?

EXERCISE 16
Interfacing with the System

1. From a Perl script:
   a. Create a directory/folder and change to that directory.
   b. Print the current working directory and create a new file in the directory called testing.txt.
   c. Rename the file *junk.txt*.

2. In a Perl script, open up your top-level directory using the opendir function. List all readable files in the directory. Clear the screen.

3. PING means Packet InterNet Groper. It is a program and command that helps testing and debugging network and/or Internet connections. Use the ping command in a Perl script to check network connectivity for your host machine. (Use *ping* for UNIX or *ping -t* for Windows.) It will continuously print output. After 20 seconds, send a signal to the program to stop pinging.

4. Use the *Time::Piece* module to get today's day, week day, month day, and year.

5. Use the *stat* function to get the last time all files in your present working directory were modified.

appendix

A

Perl Built-ins, Pragmas, Modules, and the Debugger

A.1 Perl Functions

The following is a complete list of Perl functions and a short description of what they do. Note: The text in parentheses is a reference to the like-named UNIX system call found in Section 2 of the UNIX manual pages. The like-named UNIX library functions are found in Section 3 of the UNIX manual pages.

Table A.1 Perl Functions

Function	Description
abs	*abs VALUE* Returns the absolute value of its argument ($_ is the default). Ignores signs.
accept	*accept(NEWSOCKET, GENERICSOCKET)* Accepts a socket connection from clients waiting for a connection. *GENERICSOCKET*, a filehandle, has been previously opened by the *socket* function, is bound to an address, and is listening for a connection. *NEWSOCKET* is a filehandle with the same properties as *GENERICSOCKET*. The *accept* function attaches *GENERICSOCKET* to the newly made connection. See accept(2).
alarm	*alarm(SECONDS)* *alarm SECONDS* Sends a *SIGALARM* signal to the process after a number of *SECONDS*. See alarm(3).
atan2	*atan2(X,Y)* Returns the arctangent of X/Y in the range <pi>.

Table A.1 Perl Functions (continued)

Function	Description
bind	bind(SOCKET, NAME) Binds an address, NAME, to an already opened unnamed socket, SOCKET. See bind(2).
binmode	binmode(FILEHANDLE) binmode FILEHANDLE For operating systems that distinguish between text and "binary" mode (not UNIX). Prepares the FILEHANDLE for reading in binary mode.
bless	bless(REFERENCE, CLASS) bless REFERENCE Tells the object referenced by REFERENCE that it is an object in a package (CLASS) in the current package if no CLASS is specified. Returns the reference.
caller	caller(EXPR) caller EXPR caller Returns an array with information about the subroutine call stack, including the package, filename, and line number. With EXPR, a number, the function seeks backward EXPR stack frames before the current one.
chdir	chdir(EXPR) chdir EXPR chdir Changes the present working directory to EXPR. If EXPR is omitted, changes directory to home directory. See chdir(2).
chmod	chmod(MODE, LIST) chmod MODE, LIST Changes permissions of a list of files; first argument is the permission MODE number (octal); the remaining arguments are a list of filenames. Returns the number of files changed. See chmod(2).
chomp	chomp(LIST) chomp(VARIABLE) chomp VARIABLE chomp Chops off the last character of a string, VARIABLE, or the last character of each item in a LIST if that character corresponds to the current value of $/, which is by default set to the newline. Unlike chop (see following), it returns the number of characters deleted.

Table A.1   Perl Functions (continued)

Function	Description
chop	*chop(LIST)* *chop(VARIABLE)* *chop VARIABLE* *chop* Chops off the last character of a string, *VARIABLE*, or the last character of each item in a *LIST* and returns the chopped value. Without an argument, chops the last character off *$_*.
chown	*chown(LIST)* *chown LIST* Changes the owner and group IDs of a list of files. First two elements in the list are the numerical *uid* and *gid*, respectively. The rest of the list are the names of files. Returns the number of files changed. See chown(2).
chr	*chr NUMBER* Returns the ASCII value for *NUMBER*; e.g., *chr(66)* returns *B*.
chroot	*chroot(FILENAME)* *chroot FILENAME* Changes root directory for the current process to *FILENAME*, which is the starting point for pathnames starting with /. Must be superuser to do this. See chroot(2).
close	*close(FILEHANDLE)* *close FILEHANDLE* Closes the file, socket, or pipe associated with *FILEHANDLE*.
closedir	*closedir(DIRHANDLE)* *closedir DIRHANDLE* Closes a directory structure opened by *opendir*. See directory(3).
connect	*connect(SOCKET, NAME)* Connects a process with one that is waiting for an *accept* call. *NAME* is a packed network address. See connect(2).
cos	*cos(EXPR)* *cos EXPR* Returns the cosine of *EXPR* (in radians).
crypt	*crypt(PLAINTEXT, SALT)* The password encryption function, where *PLAINTEXT* is the user's password and *SALT* is a two-character string consisting of characters in the set *[a-zA-Z./]*. See crypt(3).

Table A.1 Perl Functions (continued)

Function	Description
dbmclose	*dbmclose(%ASSOC_ARRAY)* *dbmclose %ASSOC_ARRAY* Breaks the binding between a DBM file and an associative array. Useful only with NDBM, a newer version of DBM, if supported. See *untie*. See dbm(3).
dbmopen	*dbmopen(%ASSOC_ARRAY, DBNAME, MODE)* Binds a DBM or NDBM file to an associative array. Before a database can be accessed, it must be opened by *dbmopen*. The files *file.dir* and *file.pag* must exist. *DBNAME* is the name of the file without the *.dir* and *.pag* extension. If the database does not exist and permission *MODE* is specified, the database is created. See *tie*. See dbminit(3).
defined	*defined(EXPR)* *defined EXPR* Returns a Boolean value *1* if *EXPR* has a real value. Returns a Boolean value *0* if *EXPR* does not have a real value. *EXPR* may be a scalar, array, hash, or subroutine. For a hash, checks only whether the value (not key) is defined.
delete	*delete $ASSOC{KEY}* Deletes a value from an associative array. If successful, returns the deleted value; otherwise, returns an undefined value. If a value in %ENV is deleted, the environment will be modified. The *undef* function can also be used and is faster.
die	*die(LIST)* *die LIST* *die* Prints the *LIST* to *STDERR* and exits with the value of *$!*, the system error message (*errno*). When in an *eval* function, sets the $@ value to the error message, and aborts *eval*. If the value of *LIST* does not end in a newline, the name of the current script, the line number, and a newline are appended to the message.
do	*do BLOCK* *do SUBROUTINE(LIST)* *do EXPR* *do BLOCK* returns the value of the last command in the *BLOCK*. *do SUBROUTINE(LIST)* calls a *SUBROUTINE* that has been defined. *do EXPR* uses *EXPR* as a filename and executes the contents of the file as a Perl script. Used primarily to include subroutines from the Perl subroutine library.

Table A.1   Perl Functions (continued)

Function	*Description*
dump	*dump LABEL* Causes an immediate binary image core dump. The *undump* command, used for undumping a core file, is not part of the Perl 5.6.0 distribution.
each	*each(%ASSOC_ARRAY)* *each %ASSOC_ARRAY* Returns a two-element array, the key and value for the next value of an associative array, in random order.
eof	*eof(FILEHANDLE)* *eof()* *eof* Returns *1* if the next read on *FILEHANDLE* indicates the end of file. If *FILEHANDLE* is omitted, it returns the end of file for the last file read.
eval	*eval(EXPR)* *eval EXPR* Evaluates *EXPR* as a Perl program in the context of the current Perl script. Often used for trapping otherwise fatal errors. Syntax errors or runtime errors or those coming from the *die* function are returned to the $@ variable. The $@ variable is set to NULL if there are no errors. The value returned is the value of the last expression evaluated.
exec	*exec(LIST)* *exec LIST* Executes a system command *LIST* in context of the current program. Never returns. If *LIST* is scalar, checks for *shell* metacharacters and *passes* them to /bin/sh. Otherwise, arguments are passed to the *C* function call *execvp*. Does not flush output buffer.
exists	*exists EXPR* Returns TRUE if a specified key from an associative array exists, even if its corresponding value is undefined.
exit	*exit(INTEGER)* *exit INTEGER* Exits with script with status value of *INTEGER*. If *INTEGER* is omitted, exits with *0*, meaning the program exits with successful status. A nonzero status implies that something went wrong in the program.
exp	*exp(EXPR)* *exp EXPR* The exponential function. Returns *e* to the power of *EXPR*.

Table A.1   Perl Functions (continued)

Function	Description
fcntl	*fcntl(FILEHANDLE, FUNCTION, SCALAR)* Changes properties on an open file. Requires *sys/fcntl.ph*. The *FUNCTION* can duplicate an existing file descriptor, get or set file descriptor flags, get or set file status flags, get or set asynchronous I/O ownership, and get or set record locks. *SCALAR* is an integer for flags. See fcntl(2).
fileno	*fileno(FILEHANDLE)* *fileno FILEHANDLE* Returns the integer file descriptor for *FILEHANDLE*. Descriptors start with *STDIN, STDOUT, STDERR, 0, 1*, and 2, respectively. May not be reliable in Perl scripts if a file is closed and reopened. See ferror(3).
flock	*flock(FILEHANDLE, OPERATION)* Applies or removes advisory locks on files. *OPERATION* specifies an operation on a lock for a file, shared locks, exclusive locks, or nonblocking locks. The *OPERATION* to remove a file is *unlock*. See flock(2).
fork	*fork* Creates a new (child) process. The child is a copy of the parent process. Both child and parent continue execution with the instruction immediately following the *fork*. Returns *0* to the child process and the *pid* of the child to the parent.

format	*format NAME =*
	    picture line
	    value list
	        ...
	    .
	Declares a set of picture lines to describe the layout of corresponding values. The *write* function uses the specified format to send output to a named filehandle represented by *NAME*. If *NAME* is omitted, the default is *STDOUT*.

formline	*formline PICTURE, LIST* An internal function used by *format* to format a list of values according to the picture line. Can also be called directly in a program.
getc	*getc(FILEHANDLE)* *getc FILEHANDLE* *getc* Returns the next character from the input file associated with *FILEHANDLE*. Returns a NULL string at EOF. If *FILEHANDLE* is omitted, reads from *STDIN*.

Table A.1 Perl Functions (continued)

Function	Description
getgrent	*getgrent* *setgrent* *endgrent* Iterates through */etc/group* and returns an entry from */etc/group* as a list, including group name, password, group ID (*gid*), and members. See getgrent(3).
getgrgid	*getgrgid(GID)* Returns a group entry file by group number. See getgrgid(3).
getgrnam	*getgrnam(NAME)* Returns a group file entry by group name. See getgrent(3).
gethostbyaddr	*gethostbyaddr(ADDRESS, AF_INET)* Translates a network address to its corresponding names and alternative addresses. Returns the hostname, aliases, address type, length, and unpacked raw addresses. *AF_INET* is always 2. See gethostbyaddr(3).
gethostbyname	*gethostbyname(HOSTNAME)* Translates a hostname to an entry from the */etc/hosts* file as a list, including the hostname, aliases, addresses. In scalar context, returns only the host address. See gethostbyname(3).
gethostent	*gethostent* *sethostent(STAYOPEN)* *endhostent* Iterates through */etc/hosts* file and returns the entry as a list, including name, aliases, addresss type, length, and alternative addresses. Returns a list from the network host database, */etc/hosts*. See gethostent(3).
getlogin	*getlogin* Returns the current login from */etc/utmp*, if there is such a file. If *getlogin* does not work, try *$loginname = getlogin || (getpwuid($<))[0] || die "Not a user here"* See getlogin(3).
getnetbyaddr	*getnetbyaddr(ADDR, ADDRESSTYPE)* Translates a network address to its corresponding network name or names. Returns a list from the network database, */etc/networks*. In scalar context, returns only the network name. See getnetent(3).

Table A.1   Perl Functions (continued)

Function	Description
getnetbyname	*getnetbyname(NAME)* Translates a network name to its corresponding network address. Returns a list from the network database, */etc/networks*. In scalar context, returns only the network address. See getnetent(3).
getnetent	*getnetent* *setnetent(STAYOPEN)* *endnetent* Iterates through the */etc/networks* file and returns the entry as a list. Returns a list from the network database, */etc/networks*. In scalar context, returns only the network name. See getnetent(3).
getpeername	*getpeername(SOCKET)* Returns the packed *sockaddr* address of other end of the *SOCKET* connection. See getpeername(2).
getpgrp	*getpgrp(PID)* *getpgrp PID* Returns the current process group for the specified *PID* (*PID 0* is the current process). Without *EXPR*, returns the process group of the current process. See getpgrp(2).
getppid	*getppid* Returns the *pid* of the parent process. If *1* is returned, that is the *pid* for *init*. *Init* adopts a process whose parent has died. See getpid(2).
getpriority	*getpriority(WHICH, WHO)* Returns the current priority, *nice* value, for *WHICH*—a process, a process group, or a user. *WHO* is relative to *WHICH* group. A *WHO* value of zero denotes the current process, process group, or user. See getpriority(2).
getprotobyname	*getprotobyname(NAME)* Translates a protocol *NAME* to its corresponding number and returns a list including the protocol name, aliases, and the protocol number. Returns a line from the network protocol database, */etc/protocols*. See getprotoent(3).

Table A.1   Perl Functions (continued)

Function	*Description*
getprotobynumber	*getprotobynumber(NUMBER)* Translates a protocol *NUMBER* to its corresponding name and returns a list including the protocol name, aliases, and the protocol number. Returns a line from the network protocol database, */etc/protocols*. See getprotoent(3).
getprotoent	*getprotoent* *setprotent(STAYOPEN)* *endprotoent* Returns a list from the */etc/protocols* database, including the protocol name, aliases, and the protocol number. If the *STAYOPEN* flag is nonzero, the database will not be closed during subsequent calls. The *endprotoent* function closes the file. In scalar context, returns the protocol name. See getprotoent(3).
getpwent	*getpwent* *setpwent* *endpwent* Iterates through the */etc/passwd* file and returns the entry as a list, username, password, *uid*, *gid*, quotas, comment, *gcos* field, home directory, and startup *shell*. The *endpwent* function closes the file. In scalar context, returns the username. See getpwent(3).
getpwnam	*getpwnam(NAME)* Translates a username to the corresponding entry in */etc/passwd* file. Returns a list, including the username, password, *uid*, *gid*, quotas, comment, *gcos* field, home directory, and startup *shell*. In scalar context, returns the numeric user ID. See getpwent(3).
getpwuid	*getpwuid(UID)* Translates the numeric user ID to the corresponding entry from the */etc/passwd* file. Returns a list, including the username, password, *uid*, *gid*, quotas, comment, *gcos* field, home directory, and startup shell. In scalar context, returns the username. See getpwent(3).
getservbyname	*getservbyname(NAME, PROTOCOL)* From */etc/services* database, translates a port name to its corresponding port number as a scalar and, returns as an array, the service name, aliases, port where service resides and protocol needed from the */etc/services* database. In scalar context, returns only the service port number. See getservent(3).

Table A.1 Perl Functions (continued)

Function	Description
getservbyport	*getservbyport(PORT_NUMBER, PROTOCOL)* From */etc/services* database, translates a port number to its corresponding port name as a scalar and returns as an array the service name, aliases, port where service resides, and protocol needed, from the */etc/services* database. In scalar context, returns only the service port number. See getservent(3).
getservent	*getservent* *setservent(STAYOPEN)* *endservent* Iterates through the */etc/services* database, returning the service name, aliases, port where service resides, and protocol needed. If *STAYOPEN* flag is nonzero, the database will not be closed during subsequent calls and *endservent* closes the file. In scalar context, returns only the service port name. See getservent(3).
getsockname	*getsockname(SOCKET)* Returns the packed sockaddr address of the local end of the *SOCKET* connection. See getsockname(2).
getsockopt	*getsockopt(SOCKET, LEVEL, OPTNAME)* Returns the requested options, *OPTNAME,* associated with *SOCKET* at the specified protocol *LEVEL*. See getsockopt(2).
glob	*glob EXPR* Performs filename expansion on *EXPR* as the *shell* does. Without *EXPR*, $_ is used. Uses the internal <*> operator.
gmtime	*gmtime(EXPR)* *gmtime EXPR* Converts the results of the *time* function to a 9-element array with the Greenwich Mean Time zone, including the second, minute, hour, day of the month, month, year, day of the week, day of the year, and 1 if daylight saving time is in effect. See ctime(3) and *timegm()* in the Perl library module *Time::Local*.
goto	*goto LABEL* *goto EXPR* *goto &NAME* Program branches to the LABEL and resumes execution. Cannot *goto* any construct that requires intialization, such as a subroutine or *foreach* loop. *Goto* never returns a value. The form *goto &NAME* substitutes the currently running subroutine with a call to *NAME* (used by the *AUTOLOAD* subroutine).

Table A.1   Perl Functions (continued)

Function	Description
grep	*grep(EXPR, LIST)* *grep BLOCK LIST* Returns to a new array any element in *LIST* where *EXPR* matches that element. Returns a scalar, the number of matches.
hex	*hex(EXPR)* *hex EXPR* Returns the decimal value of *EXPR* interpreted as a hexadecimal string. Without *EXPR*, uses $_.
import	*import CLASSNAME LIST* *import CLASSNAME* Not a built-in function but a class method defined by modules that will export names to other modules through the *use* function.
index	*index(STR, SUBSTR, POSITION)* *index(STR, SUBSTR)* Returns the position of the first occurrence of *SUBSTR* in *STR*. *POSITION* specifies a starting position for the substring in the string starting with base 0.
int	*int(EXPR)* *int EXPR* Returns the integer portion of *EXPR*. Without *EXPR*, $_ is used.
ioctl	*ioctl(FILEHANDLE, FUNCTION, SCALAR)* Used to control I/O operations, mainly terminal I/O. Requires *sys/ioctl.ph*. *FUNCTION* is an I/O request. *SCALAR* will be read or written depending on the request. See ioctl(2).
join	*join(EXPR, LIST)* Returns a single string by joining the separate strings of *LIST* into a single string where the field separator is specified by *EXPR*, a delimiter.
keys	*keys(%ASSOC_ARRAY)* *keys %ASSOC_ARRAY* Returns a normal array consisting of all the keys in the associative array.
kill	*kill(SIGNAL, PROCESS_LIST)* *kill PROCESS_LIST* Sends a *SIGNAL* to a list of processes. The *SIGNAL* can be either a number or a signal name (signal name must be quoted). (Negative *SIGNAL* number kills process group.) See kill(2).

Table A.1   Perl Functions (continued)

Function	Description
last	*last LABEL* *last* The last command is comparable to *C*'s *break* command. It exits the innermost loop or, if the loop is labeled *last LABEL*, exits that loop.
lc	*lc EXPR* Returns *EXPR* in lowercase. Same as \L \E escape sequence.
lcfirst	*lcfirst EXPR* Returns *EXPR* with the first character in lowercase. Same as \l \E sequence.
length	*length(EXPR)* *length EXPR* Returns the length in characters of scalar *EXPR* or, if *EXPR* is omitted, returns length of $_. Not used to find the size of an array or associative array.
link	*link(OLDFILE, NEWFILE)* Creates a hard link. *NEWFILE* is another name for *OLDFILE*. See link(2).
listen	*listen(SOCKET, QUEUESIZE)* Listens for connections on a *SOCKET* with a *QUEUESIZE* specifying the number of processes waiting for connections. See listen(2).
local	*local(LIST)* Makes variables in *LIST* local for this block, subroutine, or *eval*.
localtime	*localtime(EXPR)* *localtime EXPR* Converts the time returned by the *time* function to a 9-element array for the local time zone. The array consists of seconds minutes hours day of the month number of the month (0 is January) years since 1990 day of the week (0 is Sunday) day of the year (0 is January 1) *isdst* (true if daylight savings is on) See ctime(3).
lock	*lock THING* Places a lock on a variable, subroutine, or object referenced by *THING* until the lock goes out of scope. Used only with threads if they are enabled.

Table A.1   Perl Functions (continued)

Function	Description
log	*log(EXPR)* *log EXPR* Returns the logarithm (base *e*) of *EXPR*. If *EXPR* is omitted, returns *log($_)*.
lstat	*lstat(FILEHANDLE)* *lstat FILEHANDLE* *lstat(EXPR)* Returns a 14-element array consisting of file statistics on a symbolic link, rather than the file the symbolic link points to. The array consists of device file inode number file mode number of hard links to the file user ID of owner group ID of owner raw device size of file file last access time file last modify time file last status change time preferred block size for filesystem I/O actual number of blocks allocated See stat(2).
m	*/PATTERN/* *m/PATTERN/* *m* is the match operator that interprets *PATTERN* as a regular expression and is used when alternative delimeters are needed, such as *m!PATTERN!*.
map	*map(BLOCK LIST)* *map(EXPR, LIST)* Evaluates *BLOCK* or *EXPR* for each element of *LIST* and returns the list value containing the results of the evaluation. The following example translates a list of numbers to characters: *@chars = map chr, @numbers*
mkdir	*mkdir(NAME, MODE)* Creates a directory, *NAME*, with *MODE* permissions (octal). See mkdir(2).
msgctl	*msgctl(MSGID, CMD, FLAGS)* Calls the *msgctl* system call, allowing control operations on a message queue. Has weird return codes. Requires library files *ipc.ph* and *msg.ph*. See System V IPC. See also msgctl(2).

Table A.1   Perl Functions (continued)

Function	Description
msgget	*msgget(KEY, FLAGS)* Calls *msgget* system call. Returns the message queue ID number or, if undefined, an error. See System V IPC. See also msgget(2).
msgrcv	*msgrcv(MSGID, VAR, MSG_SIZE, TYPE, FLAGS)* Calls the *msgrv* system call. Receives a message from the message queue, stores the message in *VAR*. *MSG_SIZE* is the maximum message size, and *TYPE* is the message type. See System V IPC. See also msgrcv(2).
msgsnd	*msgsnd(ID, MSG, FLAGS)* Calls the *msgsnd* system call. Sends the message *MSG* to the message queue. *MSG* must begin with the message type. The *pack* function is used to create the message. See System V IPC. See also msgsnd(2).
my	*my TYPE EXPR : ATTRIBUTES* *my EXPR : ATTRIBUTES* *my TYPE EXPR* *my EXPR* Variables declared with the *my* function are made private; i.e., they exist only within the innermost enclosing block, subroutine, *eval*, or file. Only simple scalars, complete arrays, and hashes can be declared with *my*. *TYPE* and *ATTRIBUTES* optional and experimental at this time.
new	*new CLASSNAME LIST* *new CLASSNAME* Not a built-in function but a constructor method defined by the *CLASSNAME* module for creating *CLASSNAME*-type objects. Convention taken from *C++*.
next	*next LABEL* *next* Starts the next iteration of the innermost or loop labeled with *LABEL*. Like the *C continue* function.
no	*no Module LIST* If a pragma or module has been imported with *use*, the *no* function says you don't want to use it anymore.
not	*not EXPR* Logically negates the truth value of *EXPR*.

Table A.1   Perl Functions (continued)

Function	Description
oct	*oct(EXPR)* *oct EXPR* *oct* Returns the decimal value of *EXPR*, an octal string. If *EXPR* contains a leading *0x*, *EXPR* is interpreted as hex. With no *EXPR*, $_ is converted.
open	*open(FILEHANDLE, EXPR)* *open(FILEHANDLE)* *open FILEHANDLE* Opens a real file, *EXPR*, and attaches it to *FILEHANDLE*. Without *EXPR*, a scalar with the same name as *FILEHANDLE* must have been assigned that filename. <table><tr><td>read</td><td>"FILEHANDLE"</td></tr><tr><td>write</td><td>">FILEHANDLE"</td></tr><tr><td>read/write</td><td>"+>FILEHANDLE"</td></tr><tr><td>append</td><td>">>FILEHANDLE"</td></tr><tr><td>pipe out</td><td>"| UNIX Command"</td></tr><tr><td>pipe in</td><td>"UNIX Command |"</td></tr></table>
opendir	*opendir(DIRHANDLE, EXPR)* Opens a directory structure named *EXPR* and attaches it to *DIRHANDLE* for functions that examine the structure. See directory(3).
ord	*ord(EXPR)* *ord* Returns the unsigned numeric ASCII values of the first character of *EXPR*. If *EXPR* is omitted, $_ is used.
our	*our TYPE EXPR : ATTRIBUTES* *our EXPR : ATTRIBUTES* *our TYPE EXPR* *our EXPR* Declares one or more variables to be valid globals within the enclosing block, file, or *eval*. Like *my* for globals but does not create a new private variable. Useful when the *strict* pragma is turned on and a global variable is wanted.

Table A.1   Perl Functions (continued)

Function	Description
pack	*$packed=pack(TEMPLATE, LIST)* Packs a list of values into a binary structure and returns the structure. *TEMPLATE* is a quoted string containing the number and type of value. *TEMPLATE* is

a	An ASCII string, null padded
A	An ASCII string, space padded
b	A bit string, low-to-high order
B	A bit string, high-to-low order
h	A hexadecimal string, low nybble first
H	A hexadecimal string, high nybble first
c	A signed char value
C	An unsigned char value
s	A signed short value
S	An unsigned short value
i	A signed integer value
I	An unsigned integer value
l	A signed long value
L	An unsigned long value
n	A short in "network" order
N	A long in "network" order
f	A single-precision float in native format
d	A double-precision float in native format
p	A pointer to a string
x	A null byte
X	Back up a byte
@	Null-fill to absolute precision
u	A uuencoded string

Function	Description
package	*package NAMESPACE* A package declaration creates a separate namespace (symbol table) for *NAMESPACE*, the Perl way of creating a class. The *NAMESPACE* belongs to the rest of the innermost enclosing block, subroutine, *eval*, or file. If the package declaration is at the same level, the new one overrides the old one.
pipe	*pipe(READHANDLE, WRITEHANDLE)* Opens a pipe for reading and writing, normally after a *fork*. See pipe(2).
pop	*pop(ARRAY)* *pop ARRAY* Pops and returns the last element of the array. The array will have one less element.

Table A.1   Perl Functions (continued)

Function	*Description*
pos	*pos(SCALAR)* *pos SCALAR* Returns the offset of the character after the last matched search in *SCALAR* left off; i.e., the position where the next search will start. Offsets start at 0. If the *$scalar* is a signed *"hello"* and the search is *$scalar =~ m/l/g*, the *pos* function would return the position of the character after the first *l*, position 3.
print	*print(FILEHANDLE LIST)* *print(LIST)* *print FILEHANDLE LIST* *print LIST* *print* Prints a string or a comma-separated list of strings to *FILEHANDLE* or to the currently selected *FILEHANDLE* or to *STDOUT*, the default. Retuns *1* if successful, *0* if not.
printf	*printf(FILEHANDLE FORMAT, LIST)* *printf(FORMAT, LIST)* Prints a formatted string to *FILEHANDLE* or, if *FILEHANDLE* is omitted, to the currently selected output filehandle. *STDOUT* is the default. Similar to *C's printf*, except * is not supported. See printf(3).
prototype	*prototype FUNCTION* Returns the prototype of a function as a string, where *FUNCTION* is the name of the function. Returns *undef* if there is no prototype.
push	*push(ARRAY, LIST)* Pushes the values in *LIST* onto the end of the *ARRAY*. The array will be increased. Returns the new length of *ARRAY*.
q, qq, qw, qx	*q/STRING/* *qq/STRING/* *qw/LIST/* *qx/COMMAND/* An alternative form of quoting. The *q* construct treats *STRING* as if enclosed in single quotes. The *qq* construct treats *STRING* as if enclosed in double quotes. The *qw* construct treats each element of *LIST* as if enclosed in single quotes, and the *qx* treats *COMMAND* as if in backquotes.
quotemeta	*quotemeta EXPR* Returns the scalar value of *EXPR* with all regular expression metacharacters backslashed.

Table A.1 Perl Functions (continued)

Function	Description
rand	*rand(EXPR)* *rand EXPR* *rand* Returns a random fractional number (scalar) between 0 and *EXPR*, where *EXPR* is a positive number. Without *srand* generates the same sequence of numbers. If *EXPR* is omitted, returns a value between 0 and 1. See rand(3).
read	*read(FILEHANDLE, SCALAR, LENGTH, OFFSET)* *read(FILEHANDLE, SCALAR, LENGTH)* Reads *LENGTH* number of bytes from *FILEHANDLE*, starting at position *OFFSET*, into *SCALAR* and returns the number of bytes read, or *0* if EOF. (Similar to *fread* system call.) See fread(3).
readdir	*readdir(DIRHANDLE)* *readdir DIRHANDLE* Reads the next entry of the directory structure, *DIRHANDLE*, opened by *opendir*. See directory(3).
readline	*readline FILEHANDLE* Reads and returns a line from selected *FILEHANDLE*; e.g., *$line = readline(STDIN)*.
readlink	*readlink(EXPR)* *readlink EXPR* Returns the value of a symbolic link. *EXPR* is the pathname of the symbolic link, and if omitted, *$_* is used. See readlink(2).
readpipe	*readpipe scalar EXPR* *readpipe LIST(proposed)* An internal function that implements the *qw//* quote construct or backquotes for command subsitution; e.g., to print the output of the UNIX *ls* command, type *print reapipe(ls)*.
recv	*recv(SOCKET, SCALAR, LEN, FLAGS)* Receives a message of *LEN* bytes on a socket into *SCALAR* variable. Returns the address of the sender. See recv(2).
redo	*redo LABEL* *redo* Restarts a loop block without reevaluting the condition. If there is a *continue* block, it is not executed. Without *LABEL*, restarts at the innermost enclosing loop.

Table A.1   Perl Functions (continued)

Function	Description
ref	*ref EXPR* Returns a scalar TRUE value, the data type of *EXPR*, if *EXPR* is a reference, else the NULL string. The returned value depends on what is being referenced, a *REF*, *SCALAR*, *ARRAY*, *HASH*, *CODE*, or *GLOB*. If *EXPR* is an object that has been blessed into a package, the return value is the package (class) name.
rename	*rename(OLDNAME, NEWNAME)* Renames a file *OLDNAME* to *NEWNAME*. Does not work across filesystem boundaries. If *NEWNAME* already exists, it is destroyed. See rename(2).
require	*require(EXPR)* *require EXPR* *require* Includes file *EXPR* from the Perl library by searching the *@INC* array for the specified file. Also checks that the library has not already been included. $_ is used if *EXPR* is omitted.
reset	*reset(EXPR)* *reset EXPR* *reset* Clears variables and arrays or, if *EXPR* is omitted, resets ?? searches.
return	*return LIST* Returns a value from a subroutine. Cannot be used outside of a subroutine.
reverse	*reverse(LIST)* Reverses the order of *LIST* and returns an array.
rewinddir	*rewinddir(DIRHANDLE)* *rewinddir DIRHANDLE* Rewinds the position in *DIRHANDLE* to the beginning of the directory structure. See directory(3).
rindex	*rindex(STRING, SUBSTR, OFFSET)* *rindex(STRING, SUBSTR)* Returns the last position of *SUBSTR* in *STRING* starting at *OFFSET*, if *OFFSET* is specified like *index* but returns the last position of the substring rather than the first.
rmdir	*rmdir(FILENAME)* *rmdir FILENAME* Removes a directory, *FILENAME*, if empty.

Table A.1   Perl Functions (continued)

Function	Description
s	*s/SEARCH_PATTERN/REPLACEMENT/[g] [i] [e] [o]* Searches for *SEARCH_PATTERN* and, if found, replaces the pattern with some text. Returns the number of substitutions made. The *g* option is global across a line. The *i* option turns off case sensitivity. The *e* option evaluates the replacement string as an expression; e.g., *s/\d+/$&+5/e*
scalar	*scalar(EXPR)* Forces *EXPR* to be evaluated in a scalar context.
seek	*seek(FILEHANDLE, POSITION, WHENCE)* Positions a file pointer in a file, *FILEHANDLE*, from some position, relative to its postition in the file *WHENCE*. If *WHENCE* is *0*, starts at the beginning of the file; if *WHENCE* is *1*, starts at the current position of the file, and if *WHENCE* is 2, starts at the end of the file. *POSITION* cannot be negative if *WHENCE* is *0*.
seekdir	*seekdir(DIRHANDLE, POSITION)* Sets the *POSITION* for the *readdir* function on the directory structure associated with *DIRHANDLE*. See directory(3).
select	*select(FILEHANDLE)* *select* Returns the currently selected filehandle if *FILEHANDLE* is omitted. With *FILEHANDLE*, sets the current default filehandle for *write* and *print*. See Formatting.
select	*select(RBITS, WBITS, EBITS, TIMEOUT)* Examines the I/O file descriptors to see if descriptors are ready for reading or writing or have exceptional conditions pending. Bitmasks are specified, and *TIMEOUT* is in seconds. See select(2).
semctl	*semctl(ID, SEMNUM, CMD, ARG)* Calls the *semctl* system call, allowing control operations on semaphores. Has weird return codes. Requires library files *ipc.ph* and *sem.ph*. See System V IPC. See also semctl(2).
semget	*semget(KEY, NSEMS, SIZE, FLAGS)* Returns the semaphore ID associated with *KEY*, or undefined if an error. Requires library files *ipc.ph* and *sem.ph*. See System V IPC. See also semget(2).

Table A.1 Perl Functions (continued)

Function	Description
semop	*semop(KEY, OPSTRING)* Calls the *semop* system call to perform operations on a semaphore identified by *KEY*. *OPSTRING* must be a packed array of *semop* structures. Requires library files *ipc.ph* and *sem.ph*. See System V IPC. See also semop(2).
send	*send(SOCKET, MSG, FLAGS,TO)* *send(SOCKET, MSG, FLAGS)* Sends a message on a *SOCKET*. See send(2).
setpgrp	*setpgrp(PID, PGRP)* Sets the current process group for the specified process, process group, or user. See getpgrp(2).
setpriority	*setpriority(WHICH,WHO, PRIORITY)* Sets the current priority, *nice* value, for a process, process group, or user. See getpriority(2).
setsockopt	*setsockopt(SOCKET, LEVEL, OPTNAME, OPTVAL)* Sets the requested socket option on *SOCKET*. See getsockopt(2).
shift	*shift(ARRAY)* shift ARRAY shift Shifts off the first value of the *ARRAY* and returns it, shortening the array. If *ARRAY* is omitted, the @ARGV array is shifted, and if in subroutines, the @_ array is shifted.
shmctl	*shmctl(ID, CMD, ARG)* Calls the *shmctl* system call, allowing control operations on shared memory. Has weird return codes. Requires library file *ipc.ph* and *shm.ph*. See System V IPC. See also shmctl(2).
shmget	*shmget(KEY, SIZE, FLAGS)* Returns the shared memory segment ID associated with the *KEY*, or undefined if an error. The shared memory segment created is of at least *SIZE* bytes. Requires *ipc.ph* and *shm.ph*. See System V IPC. See also shmget(2).

Table A.1 Perl Functions (continued)

Function	Description
shmread	*shmread(ID, VAR, POS, SIZE)* Reads from the shared memory *ID* starting at position *POS* for *SIZE*. *VAR* is a variable used to store what is read. The segment is attached, data is read from, and the segment is detached. Requires *ipc.ph* and *shm.ph*. See System V IPC. See also shmat(2).
shmwrite	*shmwrite(ID, VAR, POS, SIZE)* Writes to the shared memory *ID* starting at position *POS* for *SIZE*. *VAR* is a variable used to store what is written. The segment is attached, data is written to, and the segment is detached. Requires *ipc.ph* and *shm.ph*. See System V IPC. See also shmat(2).
shutdown	*shutdown(SOCKET, HOW)* Shuts down a *SOCKET* connection. If *HOW* is 0, further *receives* will be disallowed. If *HOW* is 1, further *sends* will be disallowed. If *HOW* is 2, then further *sends* and *receives* will be disallowed. See shutdown(2).
sin	*sin(EXPR)* *sin* Returns the sine of *EXPR* (expressed in radians). If *EXPR* is omitted, returns sine of $_.
sleep	*sleep(EXPR)* *sleep EXPR* *sleep* Causes program to sleep for *EXPR* seconds. If *EXPR* is omitted, program sleeps forever. See sleep(3).
socket	*socket(SOCKET, DOMAIN, TYPE, PROTOCOL)* Opens a socket of a specified type and attaches it to filehandle, *SOCKET*. See socket(2).
socketpair	*socketpair(SOCKET, SOCKET2, DOMAIN, TYPE, PROTOCOL)* Creates an unnamed pair of *connect* sockets in the specified domain of the specified type. See socketpair(2).

Table A.1   Perl Functions (continued)

Function	*Description*
sort	*sort(SUBROUTINE LIST)* *sort(LIST)* *sort SUBROUTINE LIST* *sort LIST* Sorts the *LIST* and returns a sorted array. If *SUBROUTINE* is omitted, sorts in string comparison order. If *SUBROUTINE* is specified, gives the name of a subroutine that returns an integer less than, equal to, or greater than 0, depending on how the elements of the array are to be ordered. The two elements compared are passed (by reference) to the subroutine as *$a* and *$b*, rather than @_. *SUBROUTINE* cannot be recursive. See Array Functions.
splice	*splice(ARRAY, OFFSET, LENGTH,LIST)* *splice(ARRAY, OFFSET, LENGTH)* *splice(ARRAY, OFFSET)* Removes elements designated starting with *OFFSET* and ending in *LENGTH* from an array and, if *LIST* is specified, replaces those elements removed with *LIST*. Returns the elements removed from the list. If *LENGTH* is not specified, everything from *OFFSET* to the end of *ARRAY* is removed.
split	*split(/PATTERN/, EXPR, LIMIT)* *split(/PATTERN/, EXPR)* *split(/PATTERN/)* *split* Splits *EXPR* into an array of strings and returns them to an array. The *PATTERN* is the delimiter by which *EXPR* is separated. If *PATTERN* is omitted, whitespace is used as the delimiter. *LIMIT* specifies the number of fields to be split.
sprintf	*$string=sprintf(FORMAT, LIST)* Returns a string rather than sending output to *STDOUT* with the same formatting conventions as the *printf* function. See printf(3).
sqrt	*sqrt(EXPR)* *sqrt EXPR* Returns the square root of *EXPR*. If *EXPR* is omitted, the square root of $_ is returned.
srand	*srand(EXPR)* *srand EXPR* *srand* Sets the random seed for the *rand* function. If *EXPR* is omitted, the seed is the *time* function. See rand(3).

Table A.1   Perl Functions (continued)

Function	Description

stat	*stat(FILEHANDLE)*
	stat FILEHANDLE
	stat(EXPR)
	Returns a 13-element array consisting of file statistics for *FILEHANDLE* or file named as *EXPR*. The array consists of
	    the device
	    the file inode number
	    file mode
	    number of hard links to the file
	    user ID of owner
	    group ID of owner
	    raw device
	    size of file
	    file last access time
	    file last modify time
	    file last status change time
	    preferred block size for filesystem I/O
	    actual number of blocks allocated
	See stat(2).

study	*study(SCALAR)* *study SCALAR* *study* Uses a linked-list mechanism to increase efficiency in searching for pattern matches that are to be repeated many times. Can study only one *SCALAR* at a time. If *SCALAR* is omitted, $_ is used. Most beneficial in loops where many short constant strings are being scanned.
sub	*sub NAME BLOCK* *sub NAME* *sub BLOCK* *sub NAME PROTO BLOCK* *sub NAME PROTO* *sub PROTO BLOCK* The first two declare the existence of named subroutines and return no value. Without a block, *sub NAME* is a forward declaration. The *sub BLOCK* is used to create an anonymous subroutine. The last three are like the first three, except they allow prototypes to describe how the subroutine will be called. A prototype will notify the compiler that a subroutine definition will appear at some later time and can tell the compiler what type and how many arguments the subroutine expects. For example, *sub foo ($$@)* declares that the subroutine *foo* will take three arguments, two scalars and an array. An error will occur if, for example, fewer than three arguments are passed.

Table A.1   Perl Functions (continued)

Function	Description
substr	*substr(EXPR, OFFSET, LENGTH)* *substr(EXPR, OFFSET)* Returns a substring after extracting the substring from *EXPR* starting at position *OFFSET* and, if *LENGTH* is specified, for that many characters from *OFFSET*. If *OFFSET* is negative, starts from the far end of the string.
symlink	*symlink(OLDFILE, NEWFILE)* Creates a symbolic link. *NEWFILE* is symbolically linked to *OLDFILE*. The files can reside on different partitions. See symlink(2).
syscall	*syscall(LIST)* *syscall LIST* Calls the system call specified as the first element in *LIST*, where the system call is preceded with *&SYS_* as in *&SYS_system* call. The remaining items in *LIST* are passed as arguments to the system call. Requires *syscall.ph*.
sysopen	*sysopen(FILEHANDLE, FILENAME, MODE)* *sysopen(FILEHANDLE, FILENAME, MODE, PERMS)* Opens *FILENAME*, using the underlying operating system's version of the *open* call, and assigns it to *FILEHANDLE*. The file modes are system dependent and can be found in the *Fcntl* library module. 0 means read-only, 1 means write-only, and 2 means read/write. If *PERMS* is omitted, the default is 0666. See open(2).
sysread	*sysread(FILEHANDLE, SCALAR, LENGTH, OFFSET)* *sysread(FILEHANDLE, SCALAR, LENGTH)* Reads *LENGTH* bytes into variable *SCALAR* from *FILEHANDLE*. Uses the *read* system call. See read(2).
sysseek	*sysseek(FILEHANDLE, POSITION, WHENCE)* Sets *FILEHANDLE*'s system position, using the syscall *lseek* function, bypassing standard I/O. The values of *WHENCE* are 0 to set the new position to *POSITION*, 1 to set it to the current position plus *POSITION*, and 2 to set it to EOF plus *POSITION* (often negative). See lseek(2).

Table A.1   Perl Functions (continued)

Function	Description
system	*system(LIST)* *system LIST* Executes a shell command from a Perl script and returns. Like the *exec* function, except *forks* first, and the script waits until the command has been executed. Control then returns to script. The return value is the exit status of the program and can be obtained by dividing by 256 or right-shifting the lower 8 bits. See system(3).
syswrite	*syswrite(FILEHANDLE, SCALAR, LENGTH, OFFSET)* *syswrite(FILEHANDLE, SCALAR, LENGTH)* *syswrite(FILEHANDLE, SCALAR)* Returns the number of bytes written to *FILEHANDLE*. Writes *LENGTH* bytes from variable *SCALAR* to *FILEHANDLE*, starting at position *OFFSET*, if *OFFSET* is specified. Uses the *write* system call. See write(2).
tell	*tell(FILEHANDLE)* *tell FILEHANDLE* *tell* Returns the current file position, in bytes (starting at byte 0), for *FILEHANDLE*. Normally the returned value is given to the *seek* function in order to return to some position within the file. See lseek(2).
telldir	*telldir(DIRHANDLE)* *telldir DIRHANDLE* Returns the current position of the *readdir* function for the directory structure, *DIRHANDLE*. See directory(3).

Table A.1   Perl Functions (continued)

Function	Description

tie	*tie(VARIABLE, CLASSNAME, LIST)*
	Binds a *VARIABLE* to a package (*CLASSNAME*) that will use methods to provide the implementation for the variable. *LIST* consists of any additional arguments to be passed to the new method when constructing the object. Most commonly used with associative arrays to bind them to databases. The methods have predefined names to be placed within a package. The predefined methods will be called automatically when the tied variables are fetched, stored, destroyed, etc.
	The package implementing an associative array provides the following methods:
	　TIEHASH $classname, LIST
	　DESTROY $self
	　FETCH $self, $key
	　STORE $self, $key
	　DELETE $self, $key
	　EXISTS $self, $key
	　FIRSTKEY $self
	　NEXTKEY $self, $lastkey
	Methods provided for an array are:
	　TIEARRAY $classname, LIST
	　DESTROY $self
	　FETCH $self, $subscript
	　STORE $self, $subscript, $value
	Methods provided for a scalar are:
	　TIESCALAR $classname, LIST
	　DESTROY $self
	　FETCH $self
	　STORE $self, $value
	
	Example:
	<pre>$object = tie %hash, Myhashclass
	   while($key, $value)=each (%hash){
	   print "$key, $value\n" # invokes the FETCH method
	$object = tie @array, Myarrayclass
	   $array[0]=5 # invokes the STORE method
	$object = tie $scalar, Myscalarclass
	   untie $scalar # invokes the DESTROY method</pre>

tied	*tied VARIABLE* Returns a reference to the object that was previously bound with the *tie* function or undefined if *VARIABLE* is not tied to a package.

Table A.1 Perl Functions (continued)

Function	Description
time	*time* Returns a 4-element array of non-leap-year seconds since January 1, 1970, UTC. Used with *gmtime* and *localtime* functions. See ctime(3).
times	*times* Returns a 4-element array giving the user and system CPU times, in seconds, for the process and its children. See times(3).
tr	*tr/SEARCHPATTERN/REPLACEMENT/[c][d][e]* *y/SEARCHPATTERN/REPLACEMENT/[c][d][e]* Translates characters in *SEARCHPATTERN* to corresponding character in *REPLACEMENT*. Similar to UNIX *tr* command.
truncate	*truncate(FILEHANDLE, LENGTH)* *truncate(EXPR, LENGTH)* Truncate *FILEHANDLE* or *EXPR* to a specified *LENGTH*. See truncate(2).
uc	*uc EXPR* Returns *EXPR* (or *$_* if no *EXPR*) in uppercase letters. Same as \U \E escape sequences.
ucfirst	*ucfirst EXPR* Returns the first character of *EXPR* (or *$_* if no *EXPR*) in uppercase. Same as \u escape sequence.
umask	*umask(EXPR)* *umask EXPR* *umask* Sets the *umask* (file creation mask) for the process and returns the old *umask*. With *EXPR* omitted, returns the current *umask* value. See umask(2).
undef	*undef(EXPR)* *undef EXPR* *undef* Undefines *EXPR*, an *lvalue*. Used on scalars, arrays, hashes, or subroutine names (*&subroutine*) to recover any storage associated with it. Always returns the undefined value. Can be used by itself when returning from a subroutine to determine if an error was made.

Table A.1   Perl Functions (continued)

Function	Description
unlink	*unlink(LIST)* *unlink LIST* *unlink* Removes a *LIST* of files. Returns the number of files deleted. Without an argument, unlinks the value stored in $_. See unlink(2).
unpack	*unpack(TEMPLATE, EXPR)* Unpacks a string representing a structure and expands it to an array value, returning the array value, using *TEMPLATE* to get the order and type of values. Reverse of *pack*. See pack.
unshift	*unshift(LIST)* *unshift* Prepends *LIST* to the beginning of an array. Returns the number of elements in the new array.
untie	*untie VARIABLE* Breaks the binding (unties) between a variable and the package it is tied to. Opposite of *tie*.
use	*use MODULE VERSION LIST* *use MODULE LIST* *use MODULE* *use MODULE()* *use pragma* A compiler directive that imports subroutines and variables from *MODULE* into the current package. *VERSION* is the current version number of Perl. *LIST* consists of specific names of the variables and subroutines the current package will import. Use empty parameters if you don't want to import anything into your namespace. The *-m* and *-M* flags can be used at the command line instead of *use*. Pragmas are a special kind of module that can affect the behavior for a block of statements at compile time. Three common pragmas are *integer, subs*, and *strict*.
utime	*utime(LIST)* *utime LIST* Changes the access and modification times on a list of files. The first two elements of *LIST* are the numerical access and modification times.
values	*values(%ASSOC_ARRAY)* *values ASSOC_ARRAY* Returns an array consisting of all the values in an associative array, *ASSOC_ ARRAY*, in random order.

Table A.1 Perl Functions (continued)

Function	*Description*
vec	*vec(EXPR, OFFSET, BITS)* Treats a string, *EXPR*, as a vector of unsigned integers. Returns the value of the element specified. *OFFSET* is the number of elements to skip over in order to find the one wanted, and *BITS* is the number of bits per element in the vector. *BITS* must be one of a power of 2 from 1 to 32; e.g., 1, 2, 4, 8, 16, or 32.
wait	*wait* Waits for the child process to terminate. Returns the *pid* of the deceased process and *-1* if there are no child processes. The status value is returned in the *$?* variable. See wait(2).
waitpid	*waitpid(PID, FLAGS)* Waits for a child process to terminate and returns true when the process dies or *-1* if there are no child processes or if *FLAGS* specify nonblocking and the process hasn't died. *$?* gets the status of the dead process. Requires *sys/wait.ph*. See wait(2).
wantarray	*wantarray* Returns true if the context of the currently running subroutine wants an array value; i.e., the returned value from the subroutine will be assigned to an array. Returns false if looking for a scalar. Example: *return wantarray ? () : undef*
warn	*warn(LIST)* *warn LIST* Sends a message to *STDERR*, like the *die* function, but doesn't exit the program.
write	*write(FILEHANDLE)* *write FILEHANDLE* *write* Writes a formatted record to *FILEHANDLE* or currently selected *FILEHANDLE* (see *select*); i.e., when called, invokes the format (picture line) for the *FILEHANDLE*, with no arguments. Goes either to *STDOUT* or to the *FILEHANDLE* currently selected by the *select* call. Has nothing to do with the *write*(2) system call. See syswrite.
y	*y/SEARCHPATTERN/REPLACEMENT/[c][d][e]* Translates characters in *SEARCHPATTERN* to corresponding characters in *REPLACEMENT*. Also known as *tr* and similar to UNIX *tr* command or *sed* *y* command.

A.2 Special Variables

Table A.2 Filehandles

Variable	What It Does
$|	If nonzero, forces buffer flush after every write and print on the currently selected filehandle
$%	Current page number of currently selected filehandle
$=	Current page length of currently selected filehandle
$-	Number of lines left on the page for currently selected filehandle
$~	Name of current report format for currently selected filehandle
$^	Name of current top-of-page format for currently selected filehandle

Table A.3 Local to Block

Variable	What It Does
$1.. $9	Contains remembered subpatterns that reference a corresponding set of parentheses (same as \1..\9)
$&	The string matched by the last pattern match (like *sed* editor)
$'	The string preceding what was matched in the last pattern match
$'	The string that follows whatever was matched by the last pattern match
$+	The last pattern matched by the last search pattern

EXAMPLE A.1

```
$str="old and restless";

print "$&\n" if $str =~ /and/;
print "$'\n" if $str =~ /and/;
print "$'\n" if $str =~ /and/;
print "\nold string is: $str\n";
$str=~s/(old) and (restless)/$2 and $1/;
print "new string is: $str\n";
print "\nlast pattern matched: $+\n";

(Output)
and
old
restless
old string is: old and restless
new string is: restless and old
last pattern matched is: restless
```

Table A.4   Global

Variable	What It Does
$_	Default input and pattern-searching space.
$.	Current input line number of last filehandle that was read; must close the filehandle to reset line numbers for next filehandle.
$/	Input record separator, newline by default. (Like RS in *awk*.)
$\	Output record separator for the print function. Does not print a newline unless set: $\="\n"
$,	Output field separator for the print function. Normally delimiter is not printed between comma-separated strings unless set: S,=" ".
$"	Same as $ but applies to printing arrays when in double quotes. Default is space.
$#	Output format for numbers printed with the *print* function. (Like *OMFT* in *awk*.)
$$	The process ID number of the Perl program running this script.
$?	Status returned by last pipe closed, command in backquotes, or system function.
$*	Default is *0*. If set to *1*, does a multiline match within a string; *0* for a match within a single line.
$0	Name of this Perl script.
$[	Index of first element of an array, and first character in a substring. Default is *0*.
$]	The first part of the string is printed out when using *perl -v* for version information.
$;	The subscript separator for multidimensional array emulation. Default is \034. (Like *SUBSEP* in *awk*.)
$!	Yields the current value of *errno* (system error number) if numeric, and the corresponding system error string.
$@	Error message from the last *eval*, *do*, or *require* function.
$<	The real *uid* of this process.
$>	The effective *uid* of this process.
$(	The real *gid* of this process.
$)	The effective *gid* of this process.

Table A.4   Global (continued)

Variable	What It Does
$:	The set of characters after which a string may be broken to fill continuation lines (starting with ^) in a format. Default is \n- to break on whitespace, newline, or colon.
$^A	The accumulator for *formline* and *write* operations.
$^C	TRUE if Perl is run in compile-only mode using command-line option -c.
$^D	Perl's debug flags when -D switch is used.
$^E	Operating-system-dependent error information.
$^F	Maximum file descriptor passed to subprocess, usually 2.
$^H	The current state of syntax checks.
$^I	Current value of inplace-edit extension when -i switch is used. Use *undef* to disable inplace editing.
$^L	Form feed character used in formats.
$^M	Emergency memory pool.
$^O	Name of the operating system.
$^P	Internal Perl debugging flag.
$^S	State of the Perl interpreter.
$^T	Time of day when script started execution. Used by -A, -C, and -M test operators and can be set to any number value returned by *time* to perform file tests relative to the current time.
$^V	The Perl version.
$^W	The current value of the warning switch.
$^X	The full pathname by which this Perl was invoked.
_	An underscore. The special designator for file testing when stating files.
ARGV	The special filehandle array for looping over line arguments.
$ARGV	The variable containing the name of the current file when reading from <ARGV>.
@ARGV	The array containing command-line arguments.
DATA	Special filehandle referring to anything following _ _END_ _.

Table A.4   Global (continued)

Variable	What It Does
@F	The array into which input lines are autosplit when the -a switch is used.
@INC	Array containing pathnames where require and do functions look for files that are to be included in this script.
%INC	Associative array containing entries for files that have been included by calling do or require. The key is the filename and the value is its location.
%ENV	Associative array containing the current environment.
@EXPORT	Default symbols to be exported.
@EXPORT_OK	Symbols to be exported upon request by the user.
%EXPORT_TAGS	Used by Exporter.pm to collectively name sets of symbols.
%SIG	Associative array used to set signal handlers.
STDERR	Special filehandle for standard error.
STDIN	Special filehandle for standard input.
STDOUT	Special filehandle for standard output.

A.3 Perl Pragmas

A pragma is a special "pseudo" module that hints how the compiler should behave. The use declaration allows the importation of compiler directives called pragmas into your Perl program. Pragmas determine how a block of statements will be compiled. They are lexically scoped; the scope is limited to the current enclosing block and can be turned off with the no directive. Pragma names are conventionally lowercase. Table A.5 is a partial list.

Table A.5   Perl Pragmas

Pragma	What It Does
use autouse	Provides a mechanism for runtime demand loading of a module only when a function from that module gets called.
use base	Lets a programmer declare a derived class based on listed parent classes at compile time and eliminates the need for require;
	e.g., use base qw(A B); is equivalent to BEGIN{ require A; require B;; push(@ISA, qw(A B));}

Table A.5 Perl Pragmas (continued)

Pragma	What It Does
use bytes	Prior to Perl 5.6, all strings were treated as a sequence of bytes. Now strings can contain characters wider than a byte that are represented as numbers. The *bytes* pragma allows you to specify that the code is using the older, byte-oriented semantics.
use constant	Declares the named symbol to be a constant with a given scalar or list; For example: *use constant BUFFER_SIZE => 4096;* *use constant OS=> 'Solaris';*
use diagnostics	Forces verbose warning messages beyond the normal diagnostics issued by the Perl compiler and interpreter. Since it affects only the innermost block, the pragma is normally placed at the beginning of the program. Cannot use *no diagnostics*.
use integer	A lexically scoped pragma that tells the compiler to handle all mathematical operations as integer math and truncates the fractional part of floating point numbers when performing such operations.
use locale	A lexically scoped pragma that tells the compiler to enable or disable the use of POSIX locales when dealing with regular expressions, built-in operations, character conversions, etc.
use open	Declares one or more default disciplines for I/O operations; the two disciplines currently supported are *:raw* and *:crlf*.
use overload	Used to redefine the meanings of built-in operations when using objects. See *Math::BigFloat* in the standard Perl library for examples of overloaded operators.
use strict 'vars'	With *'vars'* as an argument, must use lexical (*my*) variables or fully qualified variable names with the package name and the scope operator or imported variables. If not adhered to, will cause a compilation error.
use strict 'ref'	Generates a runtime error if symbolic references are used, such as ypeglobs.
use strict 'subs'	Generates a compile-time error if a bareword is used and it is not a predeclared subroutine or filehandle.
use strict	Generates compile-time errors if symbolic references are used, if non-lexical variables are declared, or if barewords that are not subroutines or filehandles are used.
use vars qw(list)	Used to declare global variables before *our* was introduced.
use warnings	A lexically scoped pragma that permits flexible control over Perl's built-in warnings like the *-w* switch or $^W variable.

Table A.5   Perl Pragmas (continued)

Pragma	What It Does
use lib 'library path'	Loads in the library at compile time, not runtime.
use sigtrap 'signal names'	Initializes a set of signal handlers for the listed signals. Without an argument for a set of default signals. Prints a stack dump of the program and issues an *ABRT* signal.
use subs qw(subroutine list)	Predeclares a list of subroutines allowing the subroutines listed to be called without parentheses and overrides built-in functions.
no integer	To turn off or unimport the pragma, the pragma name is preceded with *no*.

A.4   Perl Modules

Table A.6   General Programming

Module	Description
Benchmark	Checks and compares the speed of running code in CPU time.
Config	Accesses Perl configuration options from the *%Config* hash.
Env	Converts the *%ENV* hash to scalars containing environment variables; e.g., *$ENV{HOME}* becomes *$HOME*.
English	Provides scalars in English or *awk* names for special variables; e.g., *$0* can be represented as *$PROGRAM_NAME*.
Getopt	Provides for processing of command-line options and switches with arguments.
Shell	Used to run shell commands within Perl scripts by treating the commands as subroutines; e.g., *$today=date();*
Symbol	Generates anonymous globs with *gensym()* and qualifies variable names with *qualify()*.

Table A.7   CGI

Module	Description
CGI	CGI (Common Gateway Interface) class.
CGI::Apache	Used with *CGI.pm* and the Perl-Apache API.
CGI::Carp	Handles HTTP error messages and creates error log files.
CGI::Cookie	Interfaces with Netscape cookies.
CGI::Fast	Interfaces with Fast CGI.
CGI::Pretty	Produces pretty formatted HTML code.
CGI::Push	Simple interface to server push.

Table A.8   Error Handling

Module	Description
Carp	Generates *die*-like error messages to report line numbers of the calling routine where the error occurred. The subroutines that can be called from this module are *carp()*, *croak()*, and *confess()*.
Errno	Loads the *libc errno.h* defines.
Sys::Syslog	Provides a Perl interface to the UNIX *syslog(3)* library calls.

Table A.9   File Handling

Module	Description
Cwd	Gets the pathname of the current working directory. Produces an error message if used with the *-w* switch.
DirHandle	Provides an object-oriented interface for directory handles.
Fcntl	Loads the *libc fcntl.h* (file control) defines.
File::Basename	Splits a filename into components or extracts a filename or a directory from full directory path.
File::CheckTree	Runs file tests on a collection of files in a directory tree.
File::Copy	Used to copy files or filehandles.
File::DosGlob	Does DOS-like globbing.
File::Find	Used to traverse a UNIX file tree.
File::Finddepth	Searches depth-first through a file system.

Table A.9   File Handling (continued)

Module	Description
File::Glob	Does UNIX filename globbing.
File::Path	Creates and removes a list of directories.
File::Spec	Performs portable operations on filenames.
FileCache	Allows more files to be opened than permitted by the system.
FileHandle	Provides an object-oriented interface to filehandle access methods.
SelectServer	Saves and restores a selected filehandle.
flush.pl	Writes any data remaining in the filehandle's buffer or prints an expression and then flushes the buffer.
pwd.pl	Sets the *PWD* environment variable to the present working directory after using *chdir*.
stat.pl	Puts the values returned by the *stat* function into scalars—*$st_dev, $st_ino, $st_mode, $st_nlink, $st_uid, $st_rdev, $st_atime, $st_mtime, $st_ctime, $st_blksize, $st_blocks*.

Table A.10   Text Processing

Module	Description
Pod::Text	Converts *pod* documentation to ASCII-formatted text.
Search::Dict	Searches for a string in a dictionary (alphabetically ordered) file and sets the file pointer to the next line.
Term::Complete	Provides a filename-completion-like interface for prompting a user for partial input that can be completed by pressing a Tab key or a complete list of choices by pressing <CTRL>+D.
Text::Abbrev	Creates an abbreviation table, a hash consisting of key/value pairs from a list. The key is the abbreviation and the value is the string that was abbbreviated; e.g., *ma/mail, mo/more*.
Text::ParseWords	Parses a line of text into a list of words like the *shell* does, stripping leading whitespace.
Text::Soundex	Maps words to four character-length codes that roughly correspond to how the word is pronounced or sounds.
Text::Tabs	Expands tabs into spaces and unexpands tabs to spaces.
Text::Warp	Wraps text into a paragraph.

Table A.11   Database Interfaces

Module	Description
AnyDBM_File	A UNIX-based module providing framework for multiple DBMs.
DB_File	Provides access to Berkeley DB manager. See *ftp//ftp.cs.berkeley.edu/ucb/4bsd*.
DBI	Returns a list of DBs and drivers on the system, and functions to interact with the database.
GDBM_File	Provides access to the GNU database manager. See *ftp://prep.ai.mit.edu/pub/gnu*.
NDBM_File	A UNIX-based module providing an interface to NDBM files.
ODBM_File	A UNIX-based module providing an interface to ODBM files.
SDBM_File	A UNIX-based module providing an interface to SDBM files.

Table A.12   Math

Module	Description
bigrat.pl	Enables infinite precision arithmetic on fractions.
Math::BigFloat	Supports arbitary-sized floating point arithmetic.
Math::BigInt	Supports arbitrary-sized integer arithmetic.
Math::Complex	Supports complex numbers to demonstrate overloading.
Math::Trig	Supports trigonometric functions.

Table A.13   Networking

Module	Description
chat2.pl	Allows Perl to manipulate interactive network services such as FTP.
comm.pl	Newer than *chat2.pl*. Allows Perl to manipulate interactive services.
IPC::Open2	Opens a process for reading and writing to allow data to be piped to and from an external program.
IPC::Open3	Opens a process for reading, writing, and error handling so that data can be piped to and from an external program.
Net::Ping	Checks whether a remote machine is up.

Table A.13   Networking (continued)

Module	Description
Socket	Creates sockets and imports socket methods for interprocess communication and loads *socket.h* header file.
Sys::Hostname	Gets the hostname for the system.

Table A.14   Time and Locale

Module	Description
I18N::Collate	Compares 8-bit scalar data according to the current locale.
Time::gmtime	An interface to Perl's built-in *gmtime()* function.
Time::Local	Computes the UNIX time (the number of non-leap-year seconds since January 1, 1970) from local and GMT (UTC) time.
Time::localtime	An interface to Perl's built-in *localtime()* function.

Table A.15   Terminals

Module	Description
Term::Cap	Provides low-level functions to manipulate terminal configurations as a terminal interface to the *termcap* database.

Table A.16   Object-Oriented Module Functions

Module	Description
Autoloader	For large modules, loads in only needed sections of a module.
AutoSplit	Splits module into bite-sized chunks for autoloading.
Devel::SelfStubber	Generates stubs for self-loading modules to ensure that if a method is called, it will get loaded.
DynaLoader	Used to automatically and dynamically load modules.
Exporter	Used by other modules to make methods and variables available through importation.
overload	Used to overload mathmatical operations.
Tie::Hash	Provides methods for tying a hash to a package.
Tie::Scalar	Provides methods for tying a scalar to a package.
Tie::SubstrHash	Provides a hash-table-like interface to an array with constant key and record size.

Table A.17   Language Extension

Module	Description
ExtUtils::Install	For installing and deinstalling platform-dependent Perl extensions.
ExtUtils::Liblist	Determines what libraries to use and how to use them.
ExtUtils::MakeMaker	Creates a *Makefile* for a Perl extension in the extension's library.
ExtUtils::Manifest	Automates the maintenance of *MANIFEST* files, consisting of a list of filenames.
ExtUtils::Miniperl	Writes *C* code for *perlmain.c*, which contains the bootstrap code for making archive libraries needed by modules available from within Perl.
ExtUtils::Mkbootstrap	Is called from the extension's *Makefile* to create a bootstrap file needed to do dynamic loading on some systems.
ExtUtils::Mksysmlists	Writes *linker* option files used by some linkers during the creation of shared libraries for dynamic extensions.
ExtUtils::MM_OS2	Overrides the implementation of methods, causing UNIX behavior.
ExtUtils::MM_Unix	To be used with *MakeMaker* to provide methods for both UNIX and non-UNIX systems.
ExtUtils::MM_VMS	Overrides the implementation of methods, causing UNIX behavior.
Fcntl	Translates the *C fcntl* header file.
POSIX	Provides the Perl interface to IEEE std 1003.1 identifiers.
Safe	Provides private compartments where unsafe Perl code can be evaluated.
Test::Harness	Used by *MakeMaker* to run test scripts for Perl extensions and produce diagnostics.

A.5 Command-Line Switches

Table A.18 Command-Line Switches

Switch	Description
-0	Specify a record separator.
-a	Turns on autosplit mode when used with *-n* or *-p*, performing implicit split on whitespace. Fields are put in @F array.
	``date	perl -ane 'print "$F[0]\n";```
-c	Checks Perl syntax without executing script.
-d	Turns on Perl debugger for script.
-D	Sets Perl debugging flags. (Check your Perl installation to make sure debugging was installed.) To watch how Perl executes a script, use *-D14*.
-e command	Used to execute Perl commands at the command line rather than in a script.
-Fpattern	Specifies a pattern to use when splitting the input line. The pattern is just a regular expression enclosed in slashes or single or double quotes. For example, *-F/:+/* splits the input line on one or more colons. Turned on if *-a* is also in effect.
-h	Prints a summary of Perl's command-line options.
-iextension	Enables in-place editing when using <> to loop through a file. If extension is not specified, modifies the file in place. Otherwise, renames the input file with the extension (used as a backup) and creates an output file with the original filename, which is edited in place. This is the selected filehandle for all *print* statements.
-Idirectory	Used with *-P* to tell the *C* preprocessor where to look for included files, by default */usr/include* and */usr/lib/perl* and the current directory.
-ldigits	Enables automatic line-ending processing. Chops the line terminator if *-n* or *-p* are used. Assigns $\ the value of digits (octal) to add the line terminator back on to *print* statements. Without digits specified, sets $\ to the current value of $/. (See Table A.2, "Filehandles.")
-m[-]module	
-M[-]module	
-M[-]'module'	
-[mM]module=arg[,arg]...	

Table A.18 Command-Line Switches (continued)

Switch	Description
-mmodule	Executes the *use* module before executing the Perl script.
-Mmodule	Executes the *use* module before executing the Perl script. Quotes are used if extra text is added. The dash shown in square brackets means that the *use* directive will be replaced with *no*.
-n	Causes Perl to implicitly loop over a named file, printing only lines specified.
-p	Causes Perl to implicitly loop over a named file, printing all lines in addition to those specified.
-P	Causes script to be run through the C preprocessor before being compiled by Perl.
-s	Enables switch parsing after the script name but before filename arguments, removing any switches found there from the *@ARGV* array. Sets the switch names to a scalar variable of the same name and assigns *1* to the scalar; e.g., *-abc* becomes *$abc* in the script.
-S	Makes Perl use the *PATH* environment variable to search for the script if the *#!/usr/bin/perl* line is not supported.
-T	Forces "taint" checks to be turned on for testing a script, which is ordinarily done only on *setuid* or *setgid* programs. Recommended for testing CGI scripts.
-u	Causes a core dump of script after compilation (UNIX based).
-U	Allows Perl to do unsafe operations; e.g., unlinking directories if superuser.
-v	Prints Perl version information (UNIX based).
-V	Prints a summary of the most important Perl configuration values and the current value of the *@INC* array.
-V:NAME	Prints the value of *NAME*, where *NAME* is a configuration variable.
-w	Prints warnings about possible misuse of reserved words, filehandles, subroutines, etc.
-W	Enables all warnings even if disabled locally using *no warnings*.
-xdirectory	Any text preceding the *#!/usr/bin/perl* line will be ignored. If a directory name is provided as an argument to the -x switch, Perl will change to that directory before execution of the script starts.
-X	Disables all warnings.

A.6 Debugger

A.6.1 Getting Information About the Debugger

Information on how to use the debugger is found by typing at your command line:

```
perldoc perldebug
```

Here is a sample of the output:

NAME
    perldebug - Perl debugging

DESCRIPTION
    First of all, have you tried using the -w switch?

A.6.2 The Perl Debugger

If you invoke Perl with the *-d* switch, your script runs under the Perl source debugger. This works like an interactive Perl environment, prompting for debugger commands that let you examine source code, set breakpoints, get stack backtraces, change the values of variables, and so on. This is so convenient that you often fire up the debugger all by itself just to test out Perl constructs interactively to see what they do. For example:

```
$ perl -d -e 42
```

In Perl, the debugger is not a separate program the way it usually is in the typical compiled environment. Instead, the *-d* flag tells the compiler to insert source information into the parse trees it's about to hand off to the interpreter. That means your code must first compile correctly for the debugger to work on it. Then when the interpreter starts up, it preloads a special Perl library file containing the debugger.

The program will halt **right before** the first runtime executable statement (but see following regarding compile-time statements) and ask you to enter a debugger command. Contrary to popular expectations, whenever the debugger halts and shows you a line of code, it always displays the line it's **about** to execute rather than the one it has just executed.

Any command not recognized by the debugger is directly executed (*eval*'d) as Perl code in the current package. (The debugger uses the DB package for keeping its own state information.)

For any text entered at the debugger prompt, leading and trailing whitespace is first stripped before further processing. If a debugger command coincides with some function in your own program, merely precede the function with something that doesn't look like a debugger command, such as a leading ; or perhaps a +, or by wrapping it with parentheses or braces.

<continues here>

A.6.3   Entering and Exiting the Debugger

To invoke the Perl debugger, use the -d switch. It allows you to examine your program in an interactive-type environment after it has successfully compiled. After each line, the script will stop and ask for a command. The line you will be looking at is the next line that will be executed, not the previous one. The prompt contains the current package, function, file and line number, and the current line. Following is a list of the debug commands.

Once you start the debugger, all the debugging commands are listed by typing h at the debug prompt, or h h if you can't read what is displayed.

To exit the debugger, type q for quit or R for restart.

```
$ perl -d exer.1

Loading DB routines from $RCSfile: perldb.pl,v $$Revision: 4.0.1.2
$$Date: 91/11/05 17:55:58 $
Emacs support available.
Enter h for help.
main'(exer.1:3):        print "Today is ", `date`;
  DB<1> h
T                       Stack trace.
s                       Single step.
n                       Next, steps over subroutine calls.
r                       Return from current subroutine.
c [line]                Continue; optionally inserts a one-time-only
                        breakpoint at the specified line.
<CR>                    Repeat last n or s.
l min+incr              List incr+1 lines starting at min.
l min-max               List lines.
l line                  List line.
l                       List next window.
-                       List previous window.
w line                  List window around line.
l subname               List subroutine.
f filename              Switch to filename.
/pattern/               Search forwards for pattern; final / is optional.
?pattern?               Search backwards for pattern.
L                       List breakpoints and actions.
S                       List subroutine names.
```

t	Toggle trace mode.\
b [line] [condition]	Set breakpoint; line defaults to the current execution line; condition breaks if it evaluates to true, defaults to 1.
b subname [condition]	Set breakpoint at first line of subroutine.
d [line]	Delete breakpoint.
D	Delete all breakpoints.
a [line] command	Set an action to be done before the line is executed. Sequence is: check for breakpoint, print line if necessary, do action, prompt user if breakpoint or step, evaluate line.
A	Delete all actions.
V [pkg [vars]]	List some (default all) variables in package (default current).
X [vars]	Same as "V currentpackage [vars]".
< command	Define command before prompt.
> command	Define command after prompt.
! number	Redo command (default previous command).
! -number	Redo numberth-to-last command.
H -number	Display last number commands (default all).
q or ^D	Quit.
p expr	Same as "print DB'OUT expr" in current package.
= [alias value]	Define a command alias, or list current aliases.
command	Execute as a Perl statement in current package.

```
  DB<1> l
3:      print "Today is ", `date`;
4:      print "The name of this \uperl script\e is $0.\n";
5:      print "Hello. The number we will examine is 125.5.\n";
6:      printf "The \unumber\e  is %d.\n", 125.5;
7:      printf "The \unumber\e  is %d.\n", 125.5;
8:      printf "The following number is taking up 20 spaces and is
        right-justified.\n";
9:      printf "|%-20s|\n", 125;
10:     printf "\t\tThe number in hex is %x\n", 125.5;
11:     printf "\t\tThe number in octal is %o\n", 125.5;
12:     printf "The number in scientific notation is %e\n", 125.5;
  DB<1> q     (quit)
```

A.6.4   Debugger Commands

Getting help:

h	Lists help messages for all debugger commands.
h p	Lists a help message for debugger command *p*.

Listing parts of a script:

l	Lists 10 lines of the program.
l 8	Lists line 8.
l 5–10	Lists lines 5 through 10.
l greetme	Lists statements in subroutine *greetme*.

L	Lists the next line to execute.
w7	Lists a window of lines containing specified line 7. Lists three lines before the specified lines and fills the window with lines after it.
/^abc/	Searches forward for regular expression *abc*, where *abc* is at the beginning of the line.
?abc?	Searches backward for regular expression *abc*.
S	Lists all subroutines in the program by package name, two colons, and the name of the subroutine.
r	Executes the remainder of statements in the current subroutine and then displays the line immediately after the subroutine call.

Stepping line by line:

s	Single step a line at a time through the script.
n	Like s but executes subroutine calls without stepping through them.
Enter	Pressing the Enter key causes the previous s or n command to be repeated.
.	Repeats the last line executed.
-	Repeats all lines preceding the current one.
r	Continues until the currently executing subroutine returns and displays the return value and type after returning.

Getting out of the debugger:

q	Quit the debugger.
<CTRL>+D	Quit the debugger.
R	Restart the debugger and a new session.

Breakpoints:
Breakpoints allow you to set a place where the program will stop so you can examine what's going on. They must be set on lines that start an executable statement.

b 45	Sets breakpoint to line 45. Type *c* to continue and the program will stop execution at line 45.
c	Continue execution.
b greetme	Sets breakpoint to subroutine greetme.
b $x > 10	Triggers a breakpoint only if the condition is true.
w	Creates a window around the breakpoint and marks the line where the breakpoint is found; e.g., *10==>b* (breakpoint is at line 10).
d	Deletes the breakpoint on the line about to execute.
d 12	Deletes the breakpoint at line 12.
D	Deletes all breakpoints.

Printing variable values:

X name	Displays the value of any variables called name. Variable names are NOT preceded by their identifying funny character; e.g., use *x* rather than $x or @x.
V package	Displays all variables within a package.
p $x + 3	Evaluates and prints the expression.

Tracing:

T	Produces a stack backtrace listing of what subroutines were called.
t	Toggles trace mode.

Aliases:

=	Lists all aliases.	
=	*ph print "$hashref->{Science}->{Lou}"*	*ph* is an alias for printing a hash value.

appendix

B

SQL Language Tutorial

B.1 What Is SQL?

When you go to Google and request information, that request is called a **query**, and the search engine will collect any Web pages that match your query. To narrow the search, you might have to refine your request with more descriptive keywords. The same process applies to database lookups. When you make requests to a database, the request follows a certain format, and the database server will try to locate the information and return a result. The way in which you query the database is defined by the query language you are using. The standard language for communicating with relational databases is SQL, the Structured Query Language. SQL is an ANSI (American National Standards Institute) standard computer language, designed to be as close to the English language as possible, making it an easy language to learn. Popular database management systems, such as Oracle, Sybase, and Microsoft SQL Server, all use SQL, and, although some create their own proprietary extensions to the language, the standard basic commands for querying a database, such as *SELECT*, *INSERT*, *DELETE*, *UPDATE*, *CREATE*, and *DROP*, will handle most of the essential tasks you will need to perform database operations.

The SQL language can be traced back to E. F. "Ted" Cobb, an IBM researcher who first published an article in June 1970 that laid the foundations for the theory of relational databases, an English-like language used to communicate with these databases. Cobb's article triggered a major research project at IBM to design a relational database system called System/R and a database language called SEQUEL (Structured English Query Language), which is known today as SQL (often pronounced "see-quell"). In the late 1970s, two other companies were started to develop similar products, which became Oracle and Ingres. By 1985, Oracle claimed to have more than 1,000 installations, and by the early 1990s, SQL had become the standard for database management in medium to large organizations, especially on UNIX and mainframes.

B.1.1   Standarizing SQL

Like the English language, with all its dialects, many flavors of SQL evolved. Today's SQL is based on IBM's original implementation, with a considerable number of additions. Standards are created to help specify what should be supported in a language. In 1986, the ANSI designated the SQL standard. It was then revised in 1989, 1992, and 1999. The most commonly used standard today is SQL92, representing the second revision of the original specification (SQL2). Most commercial databases (MySQL, Oracle, Sybase, Microsoft Access, and Microsoft SQL Server) support the full SQL and claim to be 100 percent compliant with the standard. However, the standard is quite complex, and as with different dialects of the English language, various vendors have added extensions to their version of SQL, making it difficult to guarantee that an application will run on all SQL server databases.

In this appendix, we focus on the basic SQL language and examine such concepts as table creation, insertion, deletion, and selection of data.

B.1.2   Executing SQL Statements

Because the database management system discussed in this book is MySQL, the server being used in the following examples is the MySQL database server, and most of the SQL commands will be executed at the *mysql* command-line client, although you might prefer to use the MySQL Query Browser. Once connected to the database, you simply type the commands in the *mysql* console (command-line window, see Figure B.1) as explained in Chapter 15.

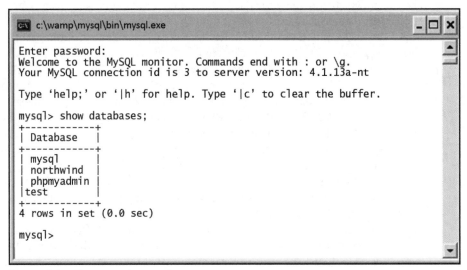

Figure B.1 The *mysql* console.

The MySQL Query Browser.   To run SQL commands in the MySQL Query Browser, type them in the box in the top of the application window and click the Execute button.

Once you click the Execute button (the green button to the right of the query window), the result will be displayed in the center of the application as a Resultset tab (see Figure B.2).

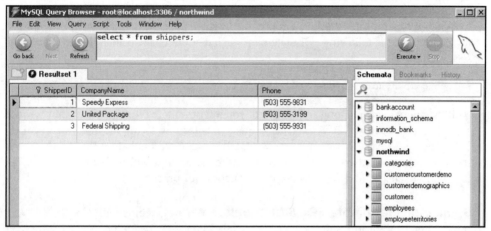

Figure B.2 The MySQL Query Browser.

B.1.3   About SQL Commands/Queries

SQL is a computer language, and like languages in general, SQL has its rules, grammar, and a set of special or reserved words. Different variants of the language have evolved over the years because different relational database vendors offer additional features to manipulate data in the name of competition. This section covers the basic SQL commands and syntax.

Because SQL has so many commands, they are divided into two major categories: the commands to manipulate data in tables and the commands to manipulate the database itself. There are many excellent tutorials on the Web that cover all the SQL commands and how to use them. See *http://www.w3schools.com/sql/default.asp*.

English-like Grammar.   When you create a SQL statement, it makes a request, or "queries" the database, in the form of a statement, similar to the structure of an English imperative sentence, such as "Select your partner," "Show your stuff," or "Describe that bully." The first word in a SQL statement is an English verb, an action word called a command, such as *show, use, select, drop*, and so on. The commands are followed by a list of noun-like words, such as *show databases, use database*, or *create databases*. The statement might contain prepositions, such as *in* or *from*. For example:

```
show tables in database
```

or

```
select phones from customer_table
```

The language also lets you add conditional clauses to refine your query, such as:

```
select companyname from suppliers where supplierid > 20;
```

When listing multiple items in a query, like English, the items are separated by commas; for example, in the following SQL statement, each field in the list being selected is comma-separated:

```
select companyname, phone, address from suppliers;
```

If the queries get very long and involved, you might want to type them into your favorite editor, because once you have executed a query, it is lost. By saving the query in an editor, you can cut and paste it back into the MySQL browser or command line without retyping it. Most important, make sure your query makes sense and will not cause havoc on an important database. MySQL provides a *test* database for practice.

Semicolons Terminate SQL Statements.   When searching with Google for "SQL query," one of the top results is a Web site called *thinkgeek.com*, which sells T-shirts and apparel, electronics, gadgets, and home office and computing items. Its ad for the "SQL query" T-shirt reads:

> Black tshirt with the following SQL query written in white on front "SELECT * FROM users WHERE clue > 0". Unfortunately, zero rows are then returned....uh oh. And hey! there is no freakin semi-colon at the end of this query because not everybody under the sun uses the same database with the same console/shell—and there is more than one way to skin a cat. Umkay? Umkay.

The semicolon is the standard way to terminate each query statement. Some database systems do not require the semicolon, but MySQL does (exceptions are the *USE* and *QUIT* commands), and if you forget it, you will see a secondary prompt, and execution will go on hold until you add the semicolon, as shown in Figure B.3.

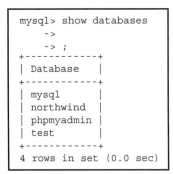
```
mysql> show databases
    ->
    -> ;
+------------+
| Database   |
+------------+
| mysql      |
| northwind  |
| phpmyadmin |
| test       |
+------------+
4 rows in set (0.0 sec)
```

Figure B.3 Missing semicolon and the secondary prompt.

Naming Conventions.   A database and its tables are easier to read when good naming conventions are used.

For example, it makes good sense to make table names plural and field/column names singular. Why? Because a table called *Shippers* normally holds more than one shipper, but the name of the field used to describe each shipper is a single value, such as *Company_Name*, *Phone*, and so on. The first letter in a table or field name is usually capitalized.

Compound names, such as *Company_Name*, are usually separated by the underscore, with the first letter of each word capitalized.

Spaces and dashes are not allowed in any name in the database.

Reserved Words.   All languages have a list of reserved words that have special meaning to the language. The SQL reserved words are listed in Table B.1. Most of these words will be used in this appendix. (See the MySQL documentation for a complete list of all reserved words.)

Table B.1   SQL Reserved Words

ALTER	JOIN
AND	LEFT JOIN
AS	LIKE
CREATE	LIMIT
CROSS JOIN	ON
DELETE	OR
DROP	ORDER BY
FROM	RIGHT JOIN
FULL JOIN	SELECT
GROUP BY	SET
INSERT	UPDATE
INTO	WHERE

Case Senstivity.   Database and table names are case sensitive if you are using UNIX, but not if you are using Windows. A convention is to always use lowercase names for databases and their tables.

SQL commands are not case sensitive. For example, the following SQL statements are equally valid:

```
show databases;
SHOW DATABASES;
```

Although SQL commands are not case sensitive, by convention, SQL keywords are capitalized for clarity, whereas only the first letter of the field, table, and database names is capitalized.

```
SELECT * FROM Persons WHERE FirstName='John'
```

If performing pattern matching with the *LIKE* and *NOT LIKE* commands, then the pattern being searched for is case sensitive when using MySQL.

The Result Set.   A result set is just another table created to hold the results from a SQL query. Most database software systems even allow you to perform operations on the result set with functions, such as *Move-To-First-Record*, *Get-Record-Content*, *Move-To-Next-Record*, and so on. In Figure B.4, the result set is the table created by asking *mysql* to show all the fields in the table called *shippers*.

```
mysql> show fields in shippers;
+-------------------------------------------------------------------------+
| Field       | Type        | Null | Key | Default | Extra          |
+-------------------------------------------------------------------------+
| ShipperID   | int(11)     |      |PRI  | NULL    | auto_increment |
| CompanyName | varchar(40) |      |     |         |                |
| Phone       | varchar(24) | YES  |     | NULL    |                |
+-------------------------------------------------------------------------+
3 rows in set (0.0 sec)
```

Figure B.4   The result set is just a table produced from a query.

B.1.4   SQL and the Database

A database server can support multiple databases. For example, an Oracle or MySQL database server might serve one database for accounting, a second for human resources, a third for an e-commerce application, and so on. To see the available databases, SQL provides the *show* command.

The *show databases* Command.   To see what databases are available on your database server, use the *show databases* command. The list of databases might be different on your machine, but the *mysql* and *test* databases are provided when you install MySQL. The *mysql* database is required because it describes user access privileges, and the *test* database, as the name suggests, is provided as a practice database for testing how things work.

FORMAT

```
SHOW DATABASES;
```

EXAMPLE B.1

```
1   mysql> SHOW databases;
    +------------+
    | Database   |
    +------------+
    | mysql      |
    | northwind  |
    | phpmyadmin |
    | test       |
    +------------+
    4 rows in set (0.03 sec)show databases;
```

The *USE* Command. The *USE* command makes the specified database your default database. From that point on, all SQL commands will be performed on the default database. This is one of the few commands that does not require a semicolon to terminate it.

FORMAT

```
USE database_name;
```

EXAMPLE B.2

```
1   mysql> USE northwind;
    Database changed
```

EXPLANATION

1   The *USE* command changes the database to *northwind*. The command-line client will report that the database has been changed.

B.1.5 SQL Database Tables

A database usually contains one or more tables. Each table is identified by a name, such as *Customers* or *Orders*. The *SHOW TABLES IN* command displays all the tables within a database, as shown in Figure B.5. The *SELECT * FROM* command lists all the fields and rows in a specified table. Tables contain rows, called records, and columns, called fields. The table in Figure B.6 contains three records (one for each shipper) and three columns (*ShipperID*, *CompanyName*, and *Phone*).

```
mysql> show tables in northwind;
+----------------------+
| Tables_in_northwind  |
+----------------------+
| categories           |
| customercustomerdemo |
| customerdemographics |
| customers            |
| employees            |
| employeeterritories  |
| order_details        |
| orders               |
| products             |
| region               |
| shippers             |
| suppliers            |
| territories          |
| usstates             |
+----------------------+
14 rows in set (0.03 sec)
```

Figure B.5   Show all the tables in the *northwind* database.

```
mysql> select * from shippers;
+-------------------------------------------------+
| ShipperID | CompanyName      | Phone            |
+-------------------------------------------------+
|         1 | Speedy Express   | (503) 555-9831   |
|         2 | United Package   | (503) 555-3199   |
|         3 | Federal Shipping | (503) 555-9931   |
+-------------------------------------------------+
3 rows in set (0.00 sec)
```

Figure B.6   Display the contents of a particular table.

The *SHOW* and *DESCRIBE* Commands.   To see what type of data can be assigned to a table, use the *DESCRIBE* command, specific to MySQL, and *SHOW FIELDS IN* command, a standard SQL command. The output displayed is the name of each field and the data types of the values that correspond to each field, as shown in Figure B.7. The data type can be a variable string of characters, a date, a number, and so on. For example, the type *varchar(40)* means a field with up to 40 characters. Also displayed is the primary key that is used to uniquely identify the record.

FORMAT

```
SHOW FIELDS IN table_name;

or

DESCRIBE table_name;
```

```
mysql> show fields in customers;
+------------------------------------------------------------------+
| Field        | Type        | Null | Key | Default | Extra |
+------------------------------------------------------------------+
| CustomerID   | varchar(5)  |      | PRI |         |       |
| CompanyName  | varchar(40) |      | MUL |         |       |
| ContactName  | varchar(30) | YES  |     | NULL    |       |
| ContactTitle | varchar(30) | YES  |     | NULL    |       |
| Address      | varchar(60) | YES  |     | NULL    |       |
| City         | varchar(15) | YES  | MUL | NULL    |       |
| Region       | varchar(15) | YES  | MUL | NULL    |       |
| PostalCode   | varchar(10) | YES  | MUL | NULL    |       |
| Country      | varchar(15) | YES  |     | NULL    |       |
| Phone        | varchar(24) | YES  |     | NULL    |       |
| Fax          | varchar(24) | YES  |     | NULL    |       |
+------------------------------------------------------------------+
11 rows in set (0.05 sec)
```

Figure B.7   The SQL *SHOWS FIELDS IN* command.

The shorter *DESCRIBE* version is shown in Figure B.8.

```
mysql> describe shippers;
+--------------------------------------------------------------------------+
| Field       | Type        | Null | Key | Default | Extra          |
+--------------------------------------------------------------------------+
| ShipperID   | int(11)     |      | PRI | NULL    | auto_increment |
| CompanyName | varchar(40) |      |     |         |                |
| Phone       | varchar(24) | YES  |     | NULL    |                |
+--------------------------------------------------------------------------+
3 rows in set (0.00 sec)
```

Figure B.8   The MySQL *DESCRIBE* command.

B.2   SQL Data Manipulation Language (DML)

SQL is a nonprocedural language providing a syntax for extracting data, including a syntax to update, insert, and delete records.

These query and update commands together form the Data Manipulation Language (DML) part of SQL. We cover the following SQL commands in this section:

- *SELECT*—Extracts data from a database table.
- *UPDATE*—Updates data in a database table.
- *DELETE*—Deletes data from a database table.
- *INSERT INTO*—Inserts new data into a database table.

B.2.1   The *SELECT* Command

One of the most commonly used SQL commands is *SELECT*, mandatory when performing a query. The *SELECT* command is used to retrieve data from a table based on some criteria.

It specifies a comma-separated list of fields to be retrieved, and the *FROM* clause specifies the table(s) to be accessed. The results are stored in a result table known as the result set. The * symbol can be used to represent all of the fields.

FORMAT

```
SELECT column_name(s) FROM table_name
```

Example:
```
SELECT LastName, FirstName, Address FROM Students;
```

EXAMPLE B.3

```
mysql> SELECT CompanyName FROM Shippers;
+------------------+
| CompanyName      |
+------------------+
| Speedy Express   |
| United Package   |
| Federal Shipping |
+------------------+
3 rows in set (0.05 sec)
```

EXPLANATION

The *SELECT* command will retrieve all items in the field *CompanyName FROM* the *Shippers* table. The result-set table is displayed in response to the query.

Select Specified Columns.   To select the columns named *CompanyName* and *Phone* from the *Shippers* table, *SELECT* is followed by a comma-separated list of fields to be selected *FROM* the *Shippers* table. The resulting table is called the result set, as shown in Example B.4.

EXAMPLE B.4

```
mysql> SELECT CompanyName, Phone FROM Shippers;
+------------------+----------------+
| CompanyName      | Phone          |
+------------------+----------------+
| Speedy Express   | (503) 555-9831 |
| United Package   | (503) 555-3199 |
| Federal Shipping | (503) 555-9931 |
+------------------+----------------+
3 rows in set (0.09 sec)
```

Select All Columns.   To select all columns from the *Shippers* table, use an * symbol instead of column names, as shown in Example B.5. The * is a wildcard character used to represent all of the fields (columns).

EXAMPLE B.5

```
mysql> SELECT * FROM Shippers;
+-----------+------------------+------------------+
| ShipperID | CompanyName      | Phone            |
+-----------+------------------+------------------+
|         1 | Speedy Express   | (503) 555-9831   |
|         2 | United Package   | (503) 555-3199   |
|         3 | Federal Shipping | (503) 555-9931   |
+-----------+------------------+------------------+
3 rows in set (0.06 sec)
```

The *SELECT DISTINCT* Statement.   The *DISTINCT* keyword is used to return only distinct (unique) values from the table. If there are multiple values of a specified field, the *DISTINCT* result set will display only one.

In the next example, ALL values from the column named *ShipName* are first selected, and more than 800 records are displayed, but notice that with the *DISTINCT* keyword, fewer than 90 records are retrieved.

FORMAT

```
SELECT DISTINCT column_name(s) FROM table_name
```

EXAMPLE B.6

```
SELECT ShipName from Orders
(Partial Output)
| North/South                   |
| Blauer See Delikatessen       |
| Ricardo Adocicados            |
| Franchi S.p.A.                |
| Great Lakes Food Market       |
| Reggiani Caseifici            |
| Hungry Owl All-Night Grocers  |
| Save-a-lot Markets            |
| LILA-Supermercado             |
| White Clover Markets          |
| Drachenblut Delikatessen      |
| Queen Cozinha                 |
| Tortuga Restaurante           |
| Lehmanns Marktstand           |
| LILA-Supermercado             |
| Ernst Handel                  |
| Pericles Comidas clásicas     |
```

EXAMPLE B.6 (CONTINUED)

```
| Simons bistro                      |
| Richter Supermarkt                 |
| Bon app'                           |
| Rattlesnake Canyon Grocery         |
+------------------------------------+
830 rows in set (0.00 sec)
```

With the *DISTINCT* keyword, fewer than 90 records are retrieved:

```
SELECT DISTINCT ShipName FROM Orders;
| Océano Atlántico Ltda.          |
| Franchi S.p.A.                  |
| Gourmet Lanchonetes             |
| Consolidated Holdings           |
| Rancho grande                   |
| Lazy K Kountry Store            |
| Laughing Bacchus Wine Cellars   |
| Blauer See Delikatessen         |
| North/South                     |
| Cactus Comidas para llevar      |
| Great Lakes Food Market         |
| Maison Dewey                    |
| Trail's Head Gourmet Provisioners |
| Let's Stop N Shop               |
```

Limiting the Number of Lines in the Result Set with *LIMIT*.   If you do not want to display a huge database, you can limit the number of lines to print by using *LIMIT*; for example, the tables in the *northwind* database contain thousands of records. In the previous examples, it would have been better to display a few lines to demonstrate that the query was successful. Because you are getting only a partial list, you might want to know the total number in the table. This can be done by using the *SQL_CALC_FOUND_ROWS* option and the *SQL FOUND_ROWS()* function. SQL will calculate the total number of records, and the *FOUND_ROWS()* function will let you display the results of that calculation.

EXAMPLE B.7

```
mysql> select ShipName from Orders LIMIT 10;
+---------------------------+
| ShipName                  |
+---------------------------+
| Vins et alcools Chevalier |
| Toms Spezialitaten        |
| Hanari Carnes             |
| Victuailles en stock      |
| Suprêmes délices          |
| Hanari Carnes             |
| Chop-suey Chinese         |
| Richter Supermarkt        |
| Wellington Importadora    |
| HILARION-Abastos          |
+---------------------------+
10 rows in set (0.00 sec)
```

EXPLANATION

With one argument, in this case *10*, *LIMIT* specifies the number of rows to return from the beginning of the result set.

EXAMPLE B.8

```
mysql> SELECT SQL_CALC_FOUND_ROWS ShipName from Orders
    -> LIMIT 5;
+---------------------------+
| ShipName                  |
+---------------------------+
| Vins et alcools Chevalier |
| Toms Spezialitaten        |
| Hanari Carnes             |
| Victuailles en stock      |
| Suprêmes délices          |
+---------------------------+
5 rows in set (0.03 sec)

mysql> SELECT FOUND_ROWS();
+--------------+
| FOUND_ROWS() |
+--------------+
|          830 |
+--------------+
1 row in set (0.03 sec)
```

EXPLANATION

SQL will calculate the total number of records, limited to *5*, and the *FOUND_ROWS()* function will let you display the results of that calculation.

The *WHERE* Clause.   What if you want to select fields only when a certain set of conditions is true? For example, you might want to list all the customers who come from Sweden and were paid more than $50,000 last year. The *WHERE* clause is optional and specifies which data values or rows will be selected, based on a condition described after the keyword *WHERE*. To create the conditions, called the selection criteria, SQL provides a set of operators to further qualify what criteria should be specified in the *WHERE* clause. See Table B.2.

FORMAT

```
SELECT column FROM table WHERE column operator value
```

Example:
```
SELECT phone FROM shippers WHERE country like "Sw";
```

Table B.2   SQL Operators

Operator	Description	Example
=	Equal to	where country = 'Sweden'
<>, !=	Not equal to*	where country <> 'Sweden'
>	Greater than	where salary > 50000
<	Less than	where salary < 50000
>=	Greater than or equal	where salary >= 50000
<=	Less than or equal	where salary <= 50000
IS [NOT] NULL	Is NULL (no value) or Not NULL	where birth = NULL
BETWEEN	Between an inclusive range	where last_name BETWEEN 'Dobbins' AND 'Main'
LIKE	Search for a value like a pattern	where last_name LIKE 'D%'
NOT LIKE	Search for a value not like a pattern	where country NOT LIKE 'Sw%'
!, NOT	Logical not for negation	where age ! 10;
||, OR	Logical OR	where order_number > 10 || part_number = 80
&&, AND	Logical AND	where age > 12 && age < 21
XOR	Exclusive OR	where status XOR

* In some versions of SQL, the <> operator can be written as !=.

Using Quotes.   Quotes are always an issue in programming languages. Should you use a set of single quotes or double quotes, and when should you use them?

SQL uses single quotes around text values (most database systems, including MySQL, also accept double quotes). Numeric values should not be enclosed in quotes.

For text values, this example is correct:

```
SELECT * FROM Students WHERE FirstName='Marco'
```

and this example is wrong:

```
SELECT * FROM Students WHERE FirstName=Marco      Marco should be "Marco"
```

For numeric values, this example is correct:

```
SELECT * FROM Students WHERE Year>2004
```

and this example is wrong:

```
SELECT * FROM Students WHERE Year>'2004'     '2004' should be 2004
```

Using the = and <> Operators.   In Figure B.9, the *CompanyName* and *Phone* fields are retrieved from the *Customers* table if the condition following the *WHERE* clause is true; that is, if the string values in the *Country* field are exactly equal to the string *Italy* (they must contain the same number and type of characters). The <> operator can be used to test for "not equal to."

```
mysql> select CompanyName, Phone FROM Customers
    -> WHERE Country='Italy';
+---------------------------------------+
| CompanyName                 | Phone   |
+---------------------------------------+
| Franchi S.p.A.              | 011-4988260 |
| Magazzini Alimentari Riuniti | 035-640230 |
| Reggiani Caseifici          | 0522-556721 |
+---------------------------------------+
3 rows in set (0.00 sec)
```

Figure B.9 The *WHERE* clause with the = operator.

What Is *NULL*?   Null means that there is not a value in a field, or it is unknown, but does not mean a value of zero. If a field is *NULL*, it is empty, and if it is *NOT NULL*, it has data. Fields have *NULL* as a default unless they are specified by *NOT NULL* in the definition of the table.

EXAMPLE B.9

```
mysql> SELECT region, country FROM suppliers
    -> WHERE region IS NULL;
+--------+-------------+
| region | country     |
+--------+-------------+
| NULL   | UK          |
| NULL   | Japan       |
| NULL   | Japan       |
| NULL   | UK          |
| NULL   | Sweden      |
| NULL   | Brazil      |
| NULL   | Germany     |
| NULL   | Germany     |
| NULL   | Germany     |
| NULL   | Italy       |
| NULL   | Norway      |
| NULL   | Sweden      |
| NULL   | France      |
| NULL   | Singapore   |
| NULL   | Denmark     |
| NULL   | Netherlands |
| NULL   | Finland     |
| NULL   | Italy       |
| NULL   | France      |
| NULL   | France      |
+--------+-------------+
20 rows in set (0.00 sec)
```

EXPLANATION

Displays the region and country from the *suppliers* database where the region *IS NULL*; that is, has no value.

EXAMPLE B.10

```
mysql> SELECT region, country FROM suppliers
    -> WHERE region NOT NULL;
+----------+-----------+
| region   | country   |
+----------+-----------+
| LA       | USA       |
| MI       | USA       |
| Asturias | Spain     |
| Victoria | Australia |
```

EXAMPLE B.10 (CONTINUED)

```
| OR       | USA       |
| MA       | USA       |
| NSW      | Australia |
| Québec   | Canada    |
| Québec   | Canada    |
+----------+-----------+
9 rows in set (0.00 sec)
```

EXPLANATION

Displays the *region* and *country* from the *suppliers* database where the region is *NOT NULL*; that is, has a value.

The > and < Operators. The > and < operators are used to select rows where the value of a field is greater or less than some value, such as:

```
SELECT product, price FROM table WHERE price > 50;

SELECT product, price FROM table
WHERE price > 50 && price < 100;
```

You can also use the >= and <= operators to select rows that are greater than or equal to or less than or equal to some value:

```
SELECT product, price FROM table
WHERE price >=50;
```

EXAMPLE B.11

```
mysql> SELECT UnitPrice, Quantity FROM Order_Details
    -> WHERE UnitPrice > 1 && UnitPrice < 3;
+-----------+----------+
| UnitPrice | Quantity |
+-----------+----------+
|    2.0000 |       25 |
|    2.0000 |       60 |
|    2.0000 |       24 |
|    2.0000 |       20 |
|    2.0000 |        8 |
|    2.0000 |       60 |
|    2.0000 |       49 |
|    2.0000 |       50 |
|    2.0000 |       20 |
```

EXAMPLE B.12

```
mysql> SELECT CategoryName from categories WHERE CategoryName < 'D';
+---------------+
| CategoryName  |
+---------------+
| Beverages     |
| Condiments    |
| Confections   |
+---------------+
3 rows in set (0.00 sec)
```

The *AND* and *OR* Operators. *AND* and *OR* operators are used in a *WHERE* clause to further qualify what data you want to select from a table. The *AND* operator tests one or more conditions to see if all the conditions are true; if so, *SELECT* displays the rows. The *OR* operator displays a row if only one of the conditions listed is true. The *AND* operator can be designated by the *&&* symbol, and the *OR* operator can be designated as ||.

EXAMPLE B.13

```
mysql> SELECT ContactName FROM Suppliers
       -> WHERE City = 'Montreal' AND Region = 'Quebec';
+------------------+
| contactname      |
+------------------+
| Jean-Guy Lauzon  |
+------------------+
1 row in set (0.03 sec)
```

EXPLANATION

When using the *&&* (*AND*) operator, both of the conditions being tested in the *WHERE* clause must be true; that is, both the *City* must be *Montreal* **and** the *Region* must be *Quebec*. If both conditions are true, then *SELECT* will print the *ContactName* from the *Suppliers* database.

EXAMPLE B.14

```
mysql> SELECT CompanyName, City FROM Suppliers WHERE
    -> City = 'Montreal' OR City = 'Boston';
+-----------------------------+----------+
| CompanyName                 | City     |
+-----------------------------+----------+
| New England Seafood Cannery | Boston   |
| Ma Maison                   | Montreal |
+-----------------------------+----------+
2 rows in set (0.00 sec)
```

EXPLANATION

When using the || (*OR*) operator, only one of the conditions being tested must be true; that is, if either the *City* is *Montreal* **or** the *City* is *Boston*, then *SELECT* will print the *CompanyName* and *City* from the *Suppliers* database.

The *LIKE* and *NOT LIKE* Conditions. The *LIKE* pattern-matching operator is a powerful operator that can be used as a condition in the *WHERE* clause, allowing you to select only rows that are "like" or match a pattern.

A percent sign (%) can be used as a wildcard to match any possible character that might appear before and/or after the characters specified.

A _ is used to match a single character.

The *LIKE* condition can be used in any valid SQL statement, including *SELECT*, *INSERT*, *UPDATE*, or *DELETE*.

FORMAT

```
SELECT column FROM table WHERE column LIKE pattern
SELECT column FROM table WHERE column NOT LIKE pattern
```

Example:
```
SELECT column FROM customer WHERE last_name LIKE 'Mc%';
```

The next examples will demonstrate how the % and _ are used with *LIKE* and *NOT LIKE* as a wildcard in pattern matching.

Pattern Matching and the % Wildcard. The % wildcard is used to represent one or more of any character when performing pattern matching. For example, if you are looking for all phone numbers in the 408 area code, you could say *408%*, and the % will be replaced by any characters after *408*.

EXAMPLE B.15

```
mysql> SELECT CompanyName, Country FROM Customers
    -> WHERE country like 'Sw%';
+---------------------+-------------+
| CompanyName         | Country     |
+---------------------+-------------+
| Berglunds snabbköp  | Sweden      |
| Chop-suey Chinese   | Switzerland |
| Folk och få HB      | Sweden      |
| Richter Supermarkt  | Switzerland |
+---------------------+-------------+
4 rows in set (0.00 sec)
```

EXPLANATION

The *SELECT* returns all the customers who are from countries that start with *Sw*.

EXAMPLE B.16

```
mysql> SELECT City, Country FROM Suppliers WHERE City LIKE '%o';
+-----------+---------+
| City      | Country |
+-----------+---------+
| Tokyo     | Japan   |
| Oviedo    | Spain   |
| Sao Paulo | Brazil  |
| Salerno   | Italy   |
+-----------+---------+
4 rows in set (0.00 sec)
```

EXPLANATION

The *SELECT* returns all cities and countries where the % matches any city that ends with a letter *o*.

EXAMPLE B.17

```
mysql> SELECT Companyname FROM customers WHERE CompanyName LIKE '%Super%';
+--------------------+
| Companyname        |
+--------------------+
| LILA-Supermercado  |
| Richter Supermarkt |
+--------------------+
2 rows in set (0.00 sec)
```

EXPLANATION

The *SELECT* returns all company names where the % matches any company name that contains the pattern *Super*.

The _ Wildcard.   The next example shows how the underscore (_) wildcard character works. Remember that the _ matches only one character.

EXAMPLE B.18

```
mysql> SELECT extension, firstname FROM employees
    -> WHERE extension LIKE '4_ _';
+-----------+-----------+
| extension | firstname |
+-----------+-----------+
| 428       | Michael   |
| 465       | Robert    |
| 452       | Anne      |
+-----------+-----------+
3 rows in set (0.00 sec)
```

EXPLANATION

This *SELECT* returns all extensions and first names where the extension has three characters and the first character is a 4. The _ symbol is used to match a single character.

The _BETWEEN_ Statement.   The *BETWEEN* keyword allows you select a field based on criteria that represent a range of values. The syntax for the *BETWEEN* clause is as follows.

FORMAT

```
SELECT column  FROM table
WHERE column BETWEEN 'value1' AND 'value2'
```

Example:
```
select age from person where age BETWEEN 10 && 20;
```

EXAMPLE B.19

```
mysql> SELECT ProductName, ProductId
    -> FROM Products WHERE ProductId BETWEEN 30 AND 33;
+-----------------------+-----------+
| ProductName           | ProductId |
+-----------------------+-----------+
| Nord-Ost Matjeshering |        30 |
| Gorgonzola Telino     |        31 |
| Mascarpone Fabioli    |        32 |
| Geitost               |        33 |
+-----------------------+-----------+
4 rows in set (0.06 sec)
```

EXPLANATION

The *SELECT* returns product names and product IDs if the *ProductId* value is in the range between 30 and 33.

Sorting Results with *ORDER BY*.   You can display the output of a query in a particular order by using the *ORDER BY* clause. Rows can be sorted in either ascending (*ASC*, the default) or descending (*DESC*) order where the values being sorted are either strings or numbers.

FORMAT

```
SELECT column FROM table
[WHERE condition]
ORDER BY column [ASC, DESC]
```

Example:
```
SELECT Company, OrderNumber FROM Orders
ORDER BY Company
```

EXAMPLE B.20

```
mysql> SELECT CompanyName, ContactName FROM suppliers
    -> ORDER BY CompanyName LIMIT 10;
+-----------------------------------+----------------------------+
| CompanyName                       | ContactName                |
+-----------------------------------+----------------------------+
| Aux joyeux ecclésiastiques        | Guylène Nodier             |
| Bigfoot Breweries                 | Cheryl Saylor              |
| Cooperativa de Quesos 'Las Cabras' | Antonio del Valle Saavedra |
| Escargots Nouveaux                | Marie Delamare             |
| Exotic Liquids                    | Charlotte Cooper           |
| Forêts d'Trables                  | Chantal Goulet             |
| Formaggi Fortini s.r.l.           | Elio Rossi                 |
| G'day, Mate                       | Wendy Mackenzie            |
| Gai pâturage                      | Eliane Noz                 |
| Grandma Kelly's Homestead         | Regina Murphy              |
+-----------------------------------+----------------------------+
10 rows in set (0.06 sec)
```

EXPLANATION

The *CompanyName* is sorted in ascending order, limited to 10 records.

```
mysql> SELECT CompanyName, ContactName FROM suppliers
    -> ORDER BY CompanyName DESC LIMIT 10;
+------------------------------------------+----------------------------+
| CompanyName                              | ContactName                |
+------------------------------------------+----------------------------+
| Zaanse Snoepfabriek                      | Dirk Luchte                |
| Tokyo Traders                            | Yoshi Nagase               |
| Svensk Sjöföda AB                        | Michael Björn              |
| Specialty Biscuits, Ltd.                 | Peter Wilson               |
| Refrescos Americanas LTDA                | Carlos Diaz                |
| Plutzer Lebensmittelgro-markte AG        | Martin Bein                |
| PB Knackebröd AB                         | Lars Peterson              |
| Pavlova, Ltd.                            | Ian Devling                |
| Pasta Buttini s.r.l.                     | Giovanni Giudici           |
| Norske Meierier                          | Beate Vileid               |
29 rows in set (0.00 sec)
```

The *CompanyName* is sorted in descending order, limited to 10 records.

B.2.2   The *INSERT* Command

The *INSERT INTO* statement is used to insert new rows into a table. After the *VALUES* keyword, a comma-separated list of column names follows.

```
INSERT INTO table_name VALUES (value1, value2,....)
```

You can also specify the columns for which you want to insert data:

```
INSERT INTO table_name (column1, column2,...)
VALUES (value1, value2,....)
```

```
INSERT INTO Shippers (CompanyName, Phone)
VALUES ('Canada Post', '416-555-1221');
+-----------+------------------+----------------+
| ShipperID | CompanyName      | Phone          |
+-----------+------------------+----------------+
|         1 | Speedy Express   | (503) 555-9831 |
|         2 | United Package   | (503) 555-3199 |
|         3 | Federal Shipping | (503) 555-9931 |
|         4 | Canada Post      | 416-555-1221   |
+-----------+------------------+----------------+
```

EXPLANATION

The *INSERT INTO* statement is inserting a new row into the *Shippers* table, first by listing the field name, and then the corresponding values after the *VALUES* keyword. The *ShipperID* value is not included, because when the table was created, *ShipperID* was set as a *PRIMARY KEY* to be autoincremented by the database every time a new shipper record is added. (Letting the database increment the *PRIMARY KEY* ensures that the value is always unique.) To see how the table was originally set up, see the output from the *DESCRIBE* command here:

```
mysql> DESCRIBE shippers;
+-------------+-------------+------+-----+---------+----------------+
| Field       | Type        | Null | Key | Default | Extra          |
+-------------+-------------+------+-----+---------+----------------+
| ShipperID   | int(11)     |      | PRI | NULL    | auto_increment |
| CompanyName | varchar(40) |      |     |         |                |
| Phone       | varchar(24) | YES  |     | NULL    |                |
+-------------+-------------+------+-----+---------+----------------+
```

B.2.3 The *UPDATE* Command

The *UPDATE* statement is used to modify the data in a table. After the *UPDATE* command, you list the name of the table where the data will be changed, followed by the *SET* statement to indicate what field will be changed, and then the new value that will be assigned to the field. The *WHERE* clause further qualifies what data is to be modified, thereby limiting the scope of the update.

In Example B.23, the key is the use of the *WHERE* statement to limit the scope of the update.

FORMAT

```
UPDATE table_name
SET column_name = new_value
WHERE column_name = some_value
```

Example:
```
UPDATE orders SET ShipCountry="Luxembourg" WHERE CustomerId='white';
```

EXAMPLE B.23

```
1   mysql> select * from shippers;
    +-----------+------------------+----------------+
    | ShipperID | CompanyName      | Phone          |
    +-----------+------------------+----------------+
    |         1 | Speedy Express   | (503) 555-9831 |
    |         2 | United Package   | (503) 555-3199 |
    |         3 | Federal Shipping | (503) 555-9931 |
    +-----------+------------------+----------------+
    3 rows in set (0.00 sec)

2   mysql> UPDATE shippers SET PHONE='(777) 444-1234'
    -> WHERE companyname = 'Federal Shipping';
    Query OK, 1 row affected (0.08 sec)
    Rows matched: 1  Changed: 1  Warnings: 0

3   mysql> select * from shippers;
    +-----------+------------------+----------------+
    | ShipperID | CompanyName      | Phone          |
    +-----------+------------------+----------------+
    |         1 | Speedy Express   | (503) 555-9831 |
    |         2 | United Package   | (503) 555-3199 |
    |         3 | Federal Shipping | (777) 444-1234 |
    +-----------+------------------+----------------+
    3 rows in set (0.00 sec)
```

EXPLANATION

1   The *SELECT* command shows all the fields in the *Shippers* table.
2   The *UPDATE* command allows you to change an existing record. The phone number for Federal Shipping is being changed.
3   This *SELECT* command shows that the phone number for Federal Shipping was changed by the previous *UPDATE* command.

B.2.4 The *DELETE* Statement

The *DELETE* statement is used to delete rows in a table and returns the number of rows that were deleted. *DELETE* uses the *FROM* clause to specify the name of the table that contains the data you want to delete, and the *WHERE* clause specifies the criteria to identify what data should be removed.

Be careful! Without a *WHERE* clause, all rows are deleted.[1]

If the *ORDER BY* clause is specified, the rows are deleted in the order that is specified. The *LIMIT* clause places a limit on the number of rows that can be deleted.

---

1. You can set up MySQL so that if you use *DELETE* without a *WHERE* clause, the rows will not be deleted.

FORMAT

```
DELETE FROM table_name
WHERE column_name = some_value
```

The *DELETE* statement is very similar to the *UPDATE* statement. To delete the previous record, you would enter this query:

DELETE FROM Shippers WHERE CompanyName='Canada Post';

B.3   SQL Data Definition Language

The Data Definition Language (DDL) part of SQL permits database objects to be created or destroyed. You can also define indexes (keys), specify links between tables, and impose constraints between database tables. Often, decisions to create and remove databases are handled by a database administrator, and having permission to create and drop tables depends on what access rights are granted.

The most important data definition statements in SQL are:

- *CREATE TABLE*—Creates a new database table.
- *ALTER TABLE*—Alters (changes) a database table.
- *DROP TABLE*—Deletes a database table.
- *CREATE INDEX*—Creates an index (search key).
- *DROP INDEX*—Deletes an index.

B.3.1   Creating the Database

Creating the database is very simple. All you have to do is issue one command, and the only parameter is the database name.

FORMAT

```
CREATE DATABASE database_name
```

In the earlier examples, we used the *northwind* database. Now we will create a database for an art gallery.

EXAMPLE B.24

```
1   mysql> CREATE DATABASE gallerydb;
    Query OK, 1 row affected (0.03 sec)

2   mysql> show databases;
    +------------+
    | Database   |
    +------------+
    | gallerydb  |
    | mysql      |
    | northwind  |
    | phpmyadmin |
    | test       |
    +------------+
    5 rows in set (0.00 sec)
```

EXPLANATION

That's it. The database is now created. Note that just because we created the database, we are still not in that database. The *USE* command in the next example will make the new database the current default database.

EXAMPLE B.25

```
1   mysql> USE gallerydb;
    Database changed
```

EXPLANATION

We are now in the *gallerydb* database, and all the SQL commands will be executed on that database.

B.3.2   SQL Data Types

After creating a database, you will add the tables that make up the database. Before creating a table, you have to decide what kind of data will be stored in it; for example, will you have rows of names, dates, part numbers, Social Security numbers, prices, and so on? The data type specifies what type of data the column can hold. The basic types are string, numeric, and date and time types. For a fully documented list, see *http://dev.mysql.com/doc/refman/5.0/en/data-types.html*.

Table B.3 contains the most common data types in SQL.

Table B.3 Most Common SQL Data Types

Data Type	Description
Numbers	
INTEGER	Holds a 4-byte whole number.
INT UNSIGNED	Holds a 4-byte non-negative whole number.
SMALLINT	Holds a 2-byte whole number.
TINYINT	Holds a 1-byte whole number.
FLOAT(m,d)	A 4-byte fractional number. FLOAT(7,4) for value 999.00009 results in 999.0001. The maximum number of digits is specified in m. The maximum number of digits to the right of the decimal is specified in d.
DOUBLE(m,d)	An 8-byte fractional double-precision number.
DECIMAL(m,d)	A real or fractional 8-byte number. The maximum number of digits is specified in m. The maximum number of digits to the right of the decimal is specified in d.
NUMERIC(m,d)	The DECIMAL and NUMERIC data types are used to store exact numeric data values with exact precision; e.g., monetary data. Hold numbers with fractions.
Strings	
CHAR(SIZE)	Holds a fixed-length string (can contain letters, numbers, and special characters) from 0 to 255 characters long. The fixed size is specified in the parentheses.
VARCHAR(SIZE)	A variable-length string (can contain letters, numbers, and special characters) from 0 to 65,535 in MySQL 5.0.3 and later versions. The maximum size is specified in the parentheses.
TINYTEXT	A string with a maximum length of 255 characters.
TEXT	A variable-length text string with a maximum length of 65,535 characters, used for storing large text files, documents, text areas, etc.
BLOB	Binary large object. A binary string with a maximum length of 65,535 characters, used for storing binary files, images, sounds, etc.
Date and Time	
DATE	(yyyy-mm-dd) year, month, day; e.g., 2006-10-30 (Note: MySQL also allows you to store 0000-00-00 as a "dummy date.")
DATETIME	(yyyy-mm-dd hh:mm:ss) date and time; e.g., 2006-10-30 22:59:59
TIMESTAMP	(yyyy-mm-dd hh:mm:ss) date and time; e.g., 1970-01-01 (date and time of last transaction on a row)
TIME	(hh:mm:ss) time; e.g., 10:30:58
YEAR	(yyyy | yy) year in four or two digits; e.g., 1978 or 78

B.3.3   Creating a Table

Creating a table is a little more complicated than creating the database. The *CREATE TABLE* statement is used to create a new table in the database. First, you must name the new table and then specify all the fields that will be included in the table as well as the data types and any other attributes. A data type can be an integer, a floating point (real) number such as 5.4, a string of characters, a date, a time, and so on. Not all databases will specify data types in the same way. To see what data types and attributes are available for MySQL, see Table B.3 or the MySQL documentation.

Designing your tables correctly is important and a subject that merits further research if you have not worked with databases before. See *http://databases.about.com/od/specificproducts/a/normalization.htm* for an excellent beginner's tutorial on database design. For now, here are some rules to keep in mind when designing the table.

1. Choose the right data type for your fields; for example, use integer types for primary keys, use float and double types for large numbers, use decimal or numeric types for currency, use the correct date format for times and dates, and give yourself ample field width for strings containing variable numbers of characters, such as names and addresses. If you are saving binary data, such as images and sounds, use a data type that supports large amounts of data, such as blob and text types. See Table B.3.

2. Give columns sensible and concise names. Make them unique within the table. Do not have duplicate columns in the same table, as shown here. These should not be three columns all headed with phone.

First_Name	Last_Name	Phone1	Phone2	Phone3
Joe	Blow	415-444-3333	333-111-1233	652-345-1123

3. Store only one value under each column heading in each row; for example, if you have a *Phone* field, you should not have "cell, home, business" all in one table cell, as shown here:

First_Name	Last_Name	Phone
Joe	Blow	415-444-3333, 333-111-1233, 652-345-1123

4. Create separate tables for each group of related items, and give each row a unique column or primary key, as shown here:

User Table:

Customer_Id	First_Name	Last_Name
1	Joe	Blow

Phone Table:

Customer_Id	Cell	Business	Home
1	415-444-3333	333-111-1233	652-345-1123

5. If you still have redundant data, put it in its own table and establish a relation between the tables with foreign keys.

FORMAT

```
CREATE TABLE table_name
(
column_name1 data_type,
column_name2 data_type,
column_name3 data_type   <-- no comma on the last entry
)
```

EXAMPLE B.26

```
1   mysql> CREATE DATABASE pets;
    Query OK, 1 row affected (0.24 sec)
2   mysql> USE pets;
3   mysql> CREATE TABLE dog
    -> ( name varchar(20),
    ->   owner varchar(20),
    ->   breed varchar(20),
    ->   sex char(1),
    ->   birth date,
    ->   death date
    -> );
    Query OK, 0 rows affected (0.16 sec)
4   mysql> describe dog;
    +-------+-------------+------+-----+---------+-------+
    | Field | Type        | Null | Key | Default | Extra |
    +-------+-------------+------+-----+---------+-------+
    | name  | varchar(20) | YES  |     | NULL    |       |
    | owner | varchar(20) | YES  |     | NULL    |       |
    | breed | varchar(20) | YES  |     | NULL    |       |
    | sex   | char(1)     | YES  |     | NULL    |       |
    | birth | date        | YES  |     | NULL    |       |
    | death | date        | YES  |     | NULL    |       |
    +-------+-------------+------+-----+---------+-------+
    6 rows in set (0.00 sec)
```

EXPLANATION

1   A database called *pets* is created.
2   The *pets* database is selected and entered.
3   A table called *dogs* is created with fields and their data types. The *name*, *owner*, and *breed* will consist of a varying number of up to 20 characters. The *sex* is one character, either *f* or *m* for female or male. The *birth* and *death* columns are assigned *date* type.
4   The *DESCRIBE* command is like the *SHOW* command. It displays the layout of the new table.

Now we can insert some data into the new table.

EXAMPLE B.27

```
mysql> INSERT INTO dog(name,owner,breed, sex, birth, death)
    -> VALUES('Fido','Mr. Jones', 'Mutt', 'M', '2004-11-12',
       '2006-04-02');
Query OK, 1 row affected (0.09 sec)
```

B.3.4   Creating a Key

In real life, people can be identified by Social Security numbers, driver's license numbers, and employee numbers; books can be identified by ISBN numbers; and a Web store order can be identified by a purchase order number. These identification numbers must be unique so that no two people have the same Social Security number, no two books have the same ISBN number, and so on. Keys are used to uniquely identify a record in a table. There are two types of keys: **primary** keys and **foreign** keys.

Primary Keys.   Each table typically has a primary key. Primary keys are used to uniquely identify a record in the database. They must be unique, never change, occur only once per table, and are normally numeric types.

You can choose to manually generate this unique number for each record or let the database do it for you. If you let the database generate the primary key, it will generate a unique number, given a starting value (e.g., 1) and then for each new record, increment that number by 1. Even if a record is deleted, that number is never recycled. The database increments its internal counter, guaranteeing that each record will be given a unique "key."

To set a field as a primay key, use the attribute *PRIMARY KEY (field_name)*, and to tell the database to automatically create the unique number, use the *AUTO_INCREMENT* attribute following the field definition. The primary key cannot be null.

The following two examples describe a table called *categories* where the primary key is called *CategoryID*. It will automatically be incremented each time a new category is added to the table.

EXAMPLE B.28

```
mysql> USE northwind;
Database changed
mysql> DESCRIBE categories;
+--------------+-------------+------+-----+---------+----------------+
| Field        | Type        | Null | Key | Default | Extra          |
+--------------+-------------+------+-----+---------+----------------+
| CategoryID   | int(11)     |      | PRI | NULL    | auto_increment |
| CategoryName | varchar(15) |      | MUL |         |                |
| Description  | longtext    | YES  |     | NULL    |                |
| Picture      | longblob    | YES  |     | NULL    |                |
+--------------+-------------+------+-----+---------+----------------+
4 rows in set (0.09 sec)
```

EXPLANATION

The *CategoryID* is the primary key, an integer of up to 11 digits, which will be incremented by 1, initially set to *NULL* (no value). The first time a record is inserted into the database, the value will be 1.

EXAMPLE B.29

```
mysql> SELECT CategoryID, CategoryName FROM categories;
+------------+----------------+
| CategoryID | CategoryName   |
+------------+----------------+
|          1 | Beverages      |
|          2 | Condiments     |
|          3 | Confections    |
|          4 | Dairy Products |
|          5 | Grains/Cereals |
|          6 | Meat/Poultry   |
|          7 | Produce        |
|          8 | Seafood        |
+------------+----------------+
8 rows in set (0.16 sec)
```

EXPLANATION

The primary key is called *CategoryID*. It is used to uniquely identify the different categories in this table from the *northwind* database. When a new category is added to the table, the *CategoryID* will be automatically incremented by 1.

Foreign Keys.   If a primary key is referenced in another table, it is called a foreign key. Foreign keys are used to create relation between tables. In the following example, two tables are described that both reference the *CategoryID* key, although it is primary in one and foreign in the other.

EXAMPLE B.30

```
mysql> DESCRIBE categories;
+--------------+--------------+------+-----+---------+----------------+
| Field        | Type         | Null | Key | Default | Extra          |
+--------------+--------------+------+-----+---------+----------------+
| CategoryID   | int(11)      |      | PRI | NULL    | auto_increment |
| CategoryName | varchar(15)  |      | MUL |         |                |
| Description  | longtext     | YES  |     | NULL    |                |
| Picture      | longblob     | YES  |     | NULL    |                |
+--------------+--------------+------+-----+---------+----------------+
4 rows in set (0.00 sec)

mysql> DESCRIBE products;
+----------------+--------------+------+-----+---------+----------------+
| Field          | Type         | Null | Key | Default | Extra          |
+----------------+--------------+------+-----+---------+----------------+
| ProductID      | int(11)      |      | PRI | NULL    | auto_increment |
| ProductName    | varchar(40)  |      | MUL |         |                |
| SupplierID     | int(11)      | YES  | MUL | NULL    |                |
| CategoryID     | int(11)      | YES  | MUL | NULL    |                |
| QuantityPerUnit| varchar(20)  | YES  |     | NULL    |                |
| UnitPrice      | decimal(19,4)| YES  |     | NULL    |                |
| UnitsInStock   | smallint(6)  | YES  |     | NULL    |                |
| UnitsOnOrder   | smallint(6)  | YES  |     | NULL    |                |
| ReorderLevel   | smallint(6)  | YES  |     | NULL    |                |
| Discontinued   | tinyint(4)   |      |     | 0       |                |
+----------------+--------------+------+-----+---------+----------------+
10 rows in set (0.00 sec)
```

EXPLANATION

1   The *categories* table has a primary key field called *CategoryID*.
2   The *products* table has its own primary key (*ProductID*) in addition to a foreign key called *CategoryID*. If a primary key is referenced in another table, it is called a foreign key.

B.3.5   Relations

A major advantage of the relational database system is the ability to create relations between tables. Simply put, a relation is a connection between a field of one table and a field of another. This relation allows you to look up related records in the database.

The operation of matching rows from one table to another using one or more column values is called a **join**. There are several types of join statements, such as **full joins**, **cross joins**, **left joins**, and so on, but let's start with a simple joining of two tables, called an **inner join**.

Tables can be related to each other with keys. As we discussed earlier, a primary key is a column with a unique value for each row. A matching key in a second table is called a foreign key. With these keys, you can bind data together across tables without repeating all of the data in every table where a certain condition is met.

Consider the previous Example B.30, in which two tables from the *northwind* database are described. One table is called *categories* and the other called *products*. *CategoryID* is a primary key field in the *categories* table, and it is a foreign key in the *products* table. The *CategoryID* key is used to create a relationship between the two tables.

Two Tables with a Common Key.   As discussed previously, both the *categories* table and the *products* table have a *CategoryID* key with the same values, making it possible to create a relation between the two tables.

Let's create a relation in which all the product names are listed if they are in the *Seafood* category. Because every product in the *products* table falls into one of the eight categories in the *categories* table, the two tables can be bound by their common *CategoryID*.

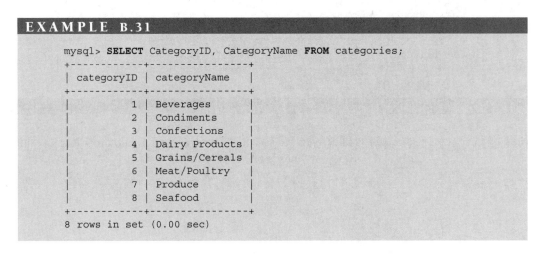

```
EXAMPLE  B.31

mysql> SELECT CategoryID, CategoryName FROM categories;
+------------+----------------+
| categoryID | categoryName   |
+------------+----------------+
|          1 | Beverages      |
|          2 | Condiments     |
|          3 | Confections    |
|          4 | Dairy Products |
|          5 | Grains/Cereals |
|          6 | Meat/Poultry   |
|          7 | Produce        |
|          8 | Seafood        |
+------------+----------------+
8 rows in set (0.00 sec)
```

EXAMPLE B.31 (CONTINUED)

```
mysql> SELECT CategoryID, ProductName FROM products;
(Partial Output)
+------------+----------------------------------+
| CategoryID | ProductName                      |
+------------+----------------------------------+
|          1 | Chai                             |
|          1 | Chang                            |
|          2 | Aniseed Syrup                    |
|          2 | Chef Anton's Cajun Seasoning     |
|          2 | Chef Anton's Gumbo Mix           |
|          2 | Grandma's Boysenberry Spread     |
|          7 | Uncle Bob's Organic Dried Pears  |
|          2 | Northwoods Cranberry Sauce       |
|          6 | Mishi Kobe Niku                  |
|          8 | Ikura                            |
|          4 | Queso Cabrales                   |
|          4 | Queso Manchego La Pastora        |
|          8 | Konbu                            |
|          7 | Tofu                             |
|          2 | Genen Shouyu                     |
```

EXPLANATION

This example displays columns from both the *categories* table and the *products* table. In the *categories* table, the *CategoryID* is the primary field and uniquely identifies all other fields in the table. In the *products* table, the *CategoryID* is a foreign key and is repeated many times for all the products.

Using a Fully Qualified Name and a Dot to Join the Tables. When querying more than one table, a dot is used to fully qualify the columns by their table name to avoid potential ambiguity if two tables have a field with the same name, as shown in Example B.32.

EXAMPLE B.32

```
mysql> SELECT CategoryName, ProductName FROM categories, products
    -> WHERE products.CategoryID = 8 AND categories.CategoryID = 8;
+--------------+----------------------------------+
| CategoryName | ProductName                      |
+--------------+----------------------------------+
| Seafood      | Ikura                            |
| Seafood      | Konbu                            |
| Seafood      | Carnarvon Tigers                 |
| Seafood      | Nord-Ost Matjeshering            |
| Seafood      | Inlagd Sill                      |
| Seafood      | Gravad lax                       |
| Seafood      | Boston Crab Meat                 |
```

EXAMPLE B.32 (CONTINUED)

```
    | Seafood        | Jack's New England Clam Chowder |
    | Seafood        | Rogede sild                     |
    | Seafood        | Spegesild                       |
    | Seafood        | Escargots de Bourgogne          |
    | Seafood        | Röd Kaviar                      |
    +----------------+---------------------------------+
    12 rows in set (0.00 sec)
```

EXPLANATION

In the *SELECT*, two tables (separated by commas) will be joined by the *CategoryID* field. Because the field name is the same in both tables, the table name is prepended to the field name with a dot, as *products.CategoryId* and *categories.CategoryId*. In the *WHERE* clause, the two tables are connected if both tables have a *CategoryID* equal to 8.

Aliases. To make things a little easier by typing less with complicated queries, SQL provides an aliasing mechanism that allows you to use symbolic names for columns and tables. The alias is defined with the *AS* keyword and consists of a single character or an abbreviated string. When the alias is used in the *WHERE* clause to represent a table name, it is appended with a dot and the name of the field being selected from that table.

FORMAT

(Column Alias)
```
SELECT column_name AS column_alias_name
FROM table_name
```

(Table Alias)
```
SELECT column_name
FROM table_name AS table_alias_name
```

EXAMPLE B.33

```
mysql> SELECT CategoryName as Foods FROM categories;
+----------------+
| Foods          |
+----------------+
| Beverages      |
| Condiments     |
| Confections    |
| Dairy Products |
| Grains/Cereals |
| Meat/Poultry   |
| Produce        |
| Seafood        |
+----------------+
8 rows in set (0.00 sec)
```

The column name from table *categories* was named *CategoryName*. An alias called *Foods* is created by using the *AS* keyword after *CategoryName*. Now when the *SELECT* returns a result-set, the output will show *Foods* as the name of the column.

```
mysql> SELECT ProductName FROM products AS p, categories AS c WHERE
    -> p.CategoryID = c.CategoryID AND c.CategoryName="SeaFood";
+----------------------------------+
| ProductName                      |
+----------------------------------+
| Ikura                            |
| Konbu                            |
| Carnarvon Tigers                 |
| Nord-Ost Matjeshering            |
| Inlagd Sill                      |
| Gravad lax                       |
| Boston Crab Meat                 |
| Jack's New England Clam Chowder  |
| Rogede sild                      |
| Spegesild                        |
| Escargots de Bourgogne           |
| Röd Kaviar                       |
+----------------------------------+
12 rows in set (0.00 sec)
```

This example might look a little tricky at first. The table named *products* is given an alias called *p*, and the table name *categories* is given the alias *c*. These aliases are short names, making it easier to type the query when more than one table is involved; for example, instead of typing *products.CategoryID*, we can type *p.CategoryID*, and *categories.CategoryName* can be referenced as *c.CategoryName*.

B.3.6   Altering a Table

When you alter a table, you redefine its structure by adding or dropping new columns, keys, indexes, and tables. You can also use the *ALTER* command to change column names, types, and the table name.

FORMAT

```
ALTER TABLE tablename
ADD column datatype
```

Example:
```
alter table artist add column ArtDate date;
alter table artist drop column "Address";
```

EXAMPLE B.35

```
    use pets;
1   mysql> ALTER TABLE dog ADD pet_id int(11);
    Query OK, 0 rows affected (0.13 sec)
    Records: 0  Duplicates: 0  Warnings: 0
2   mysql> ALTER TABLE dog MODIFY column pet_id int(11)
    -->   auto_increment primary key;
    Query OK, 1 row affected (0.11 sec)
    Records: 1  Duplicates: 0  Warnings: 0
3   mysql> describe dog;
```

Field	Type	Null	Key	Default	Extra
name	varchar(20)	YES		NULL	
owner	varchar(20)	YES		NULL	
breed	varchar(20)	YES		NULL	
sex	char(1)	YES		NULL	
birth	date	YES		NULL	
death	date	YES		NULL	
pet_id	**int(11)**		**PRI**	**NULL**	**auto_increment**

```
    7 rows in set (0.00 sec)
    mysql> select * from dog;
```

name	owner	breed	sex	birth	death	pet_id
Fido	Mr. Jones	Mutt	M	2004-11-12	2006-04-02	1
Lassie	Tommy Rettig	Collie	F	2006-01-10	NULL	2

```
    2 rows in set (0.00 sec)
```

EXPLANATION

1   The *ALTER* command will change the table by adding a new field, called *pet_id*, an integer of 11 digits.

2   Once the *pet_id* field has been created, the *ALTER* command is used again to make this a primary key that will automatically be incremented each time a record is added.

3   The *DESCRIBE* command shows the structure of the table after it was changed. A primary key has been added.

B.3.7 Dropping a Table

To drop a table is relatively simple. Just use the *drop* command and the name of the table:

```
mysql> drop table dog;
Query OK, 20 rows affected (0.11 sec)
```

B.3.8 Dropping a Database

To drop a database, use the *drop database* command:

```
mysql> drop database pets;
Query OK, 1 row affected (0.45 sec)
```

B.4 SQL Functions

The following functions are used to alter or format the output of a SQL query. Functions are provided for strings, numbers, dates, server and information, and so on. They return a result set. Functions are vendor specific, meaning functions supported by MySQL might not be supported by Microsoft SQL Server. See the MySQL documenation for a list of all functions supported.

When using *SELECT* with a function, the function, as it was called, is displayed as the name of the column in the result set as shown in Example B.36.

EXAMPLE B.36

```
1   mysql> SELECT avg(UnitPrice)
    FROM order_details;
    +----------------+
    | avg(UnitPrice) |
    +----------------+
    |     26.21851972 |
    +----------------+
    1 row in set (0.01 sec)

2   mysql> SELECT avg(UnitPrice) as 'Average Price'
    FROM order_details;
    +---------------+
    | Average Price |
    +---------------+
    |    26.21851972 |
    +---------------+
    1 row in set (0.00 sec)
```

EXPLANATION

1   The function is displayed as the name of the column.
2   You can use the *AS* keyword to create an alias or another name for the column where
    the function displays the result set.

B.4.1   Numeric Functions

Suppose you want to get the sum of all the orders or the average cost of a set of items or
to count all the rows in a table based on a certain condition. The aggregate functions will
return a single value based on a set of other values. If used among many other expressions
in the item list of a *SELECT* statement, the *SELECT* must have a *GROUP BY* clause. No
GROUP BY clause is required if the aggregate function is the only value retrieved by the
SELECT statement. The functions and their syntax are listed in Table B.4.

Table B.4   Aggregate Functions

Function	*What It Does*
AVG()	Computes and returns the average value of a column.
COUNT(*expression*)	Counts the rows defined by the expression.
COUNT()	Counts all rows in a table.
MIN()	Returns the minimum value in a column.
MAX()	Returns the maximum value in a column by the expression.
SUM()	Returns the sum of all the values in a column.

EXAMPLE B.37

```
1   mysql> select count(*) from products;
    +----------+
    | count(*) |
    +----------+
    |       81 |
    +----------+
    1 row in set (0.00 sec)

    mysql> SELECT count(*) as 'Number of Rows' FROM products;
    +----------------+
    | Number of Rows |
    +----------------+
    |             81 |
    +----------------+
    1 row in set (0.00 sec)
```

1   The *COUNT()* function counts all rows in a table.

```
1    mysql> SELECT avg(UnitPrice)
     FROM order_details;
     +----------------+
     | avg(UnitPrice) |
     +----------------+
     |     26.21851972 |
     +----------------+
     1 row in set (0.01 sec)

2    mysql> SELECT FORMAT(avg(UnitPrice),2) as 'Average Price'
     FROM  order_details;
     +---------------+
     | Average Price |
     +---------------+
     | 26.22         |
     +---------------+
     1 row in set (0.00 sec)
```

1   The *AVG()* function computes and returns the average value of a column, called *UnitPrice*.

2   The *FORMAT* function returns the result of the *AVG()* function with a precision of two decimal places.

Using *GROUP BY*.   The *GROUP BY* clause can be used with a *SELECT* to collect all the data across multiple records and group the results by one or more columns. This is useful with the aggregate functions, such as *SUM, COUNT, MIN,* or *MAX*. See the following two examples.

EXAMPLE B.39

```
mysql> select CategoryID, SUM(UnitsInStock) as 'Total Units in Stock'
    -> FROM products
    -> GROUP BY CategoryID;
+------------+----------------------+
| CategoryID | Total Units in Stock |
+------------+----------------------+
|       NULL |                    0 |
|          1 |                  559 |
|          2 |                  507 |
|          3 |                  386 |
|          4 |                  393 |
|          5 |                  308 |
|          6 |                  165 |
|          7 |                  100 |
|          8 |                  701 |
+------------+----------------------+
9 rows in set (0.00 sec)
```

EXAMPLE B.40

```
mysql> select C.CategoryName,
    -> SUM(P.unitsInsStock) AS Units
    -> FROM products as P
    -> join categories AS C ON C.CategoryID=
    -> P.CategoryID Group By C.CategoryName;
+----------------+-------+
| CategoryName   | Units |
+----------------+-------+
| Beverages      |   559 |
| Condiments     |   507 |
| Confections    |   386 |
| Dairy Products |   393 |
| Grains/Cereals |   308 |
| Meat/Poultry   |   165 |
| Produce        |   100 |
| Seafood        |   701 |
+----------------+-------+
8 rows in set (0.00 sec)
```

B.4.2   String Functions

SQL provides a number of basic string functions, as listed in Table B.5.

Table B.5   MySQL String Functions

Function	What It Does
CONCAT(string1,string2,...)	Combines column values, or variables, together into one string.
LOWER(string)	Converts a string to all lowercase characters.
SUBSTRING(string, position)	Extracts a portion of a string (see Example B.41).
TRANSLATE	Converts a string from one character set to another.
TRIM(' string ');	Removes leading characters, trailing characters, or both from a character string.
UPPER(string)	Converts a string to all uppercase characters (see Example B.41).

* SQL99 defines a concatenation operator (||) to use with the *CONCATENATE()* function. MySQL uses the *concat()* function shown in Table B.5.

EXAMPLE B.41

```
mysql> select upper(CompanyName) as 'Company' from shippers;
+------------------+
| Company          |
+------------------+
| SPEEDY EXPRESS   |
| UNITED PACKAGE   |
| FEDERAL SHIPPING |
+------------------+
3 rows in set (0.00 sec)

mysql> select lower(CompanyName) as 'Company' FROM shippers;
+------------------+
| Company          |
+------------------+
| speedy express   |
| united package   |
| federal shipping |
+------------------+
3 rows in set (0.00 sec)
```

B.4.3   Date and Time Functions

To get the date and time, MySQL provides the functions shown in Table B.6.

Table B.6   MySQL Date and Time Functions

Function	*Example*

`NOW()`	`select NOW()`
	`--> 2006-03-23 20:52:58`
	(See Example B.42.)

`CURDATE()`	`select CURDATE();`
	`--> '2006-12-15'`
	(See Example B.42.)

`CURTIME()`	`select CURTIME();`
	`--> '23:50:26'`
	(See Example B.42.)

`DAYOFYEAR(date)`	`select DAYOFYEAR('2006-12-15');` `--> 349`
`DAYOFMONTH(date)`	`select DAYOFMONTH('2006-12-15');` `--> 15`
`DAYOFWEEK(date)`	`select DAYOFWEEK('2006-12-15');` `--> 6`
`WEEKDAY(date)`	`select WEEKDAY('2006-12-15');` `--> 4`
`MONTHNAME(date)`	`select MONTHNAME('2006-12-15');` `--> December`
`DAYNAME(date)`	`select DAYNAME('2006-12-15');` `--> Friday`
`YEAR(date)`	`select YEAR('2006-12-15');` `--> 2006`
`QUARTER(date)`	`select QUARTER('2006-12-15');` `--> 4`

EXAMPLE B.42

```
mysql> select NOW();
+---------------------+
| NOW()               |
+---------------------+
| 2006-03-21 00:32:37 |
+---------------------+
1 row in set (0.00 sec)

mysql> select CURDATE();
+------------+
| CURDATE()  |
+------------+
| 2006-03-21 |
+------------+
1 row in set (0.03 sec)

mysql> select CURTIME();
+------------+
| CURTIME()  |
+------------+
| 00:12:46   |
+------------+
1 row in set (0.01 sec)
```

Formatting the Date and Time. When retrieving dates and times from a table, you might find you want to format the output. For example, when selecting the dates of the orders from the orders table in the *northwind* database, the result set is not user friendly. Date values in SQL are always saved in *MM/DD/YY(YY)* format. The *DATE_FORMAT()* and *TIME_FORMAT()* functions (see Example B.43) are provided with a list of parameters (see Table B.7) used to specify how the output should be displayed.

EXAMPLE B.43

```
mysql> select DATE_FORMAT('2006-03-23', '%W %M %d, %Y') as Today;
+------------------------+
| Today                  |
+------------------------+
| Thursday March 23, 2006 |
+------------------------+
1 row in set (0.00 sec)
```

EXAMPLE B.43 (CONTINUED)

```
mysql> select DATE_FORMAT(OrderDate,'%M %e, %Y - %l:%i %p')
            FROM orders LIMIT 5;

+--------------------------------------------------+
| DATE_FORMAT(OrderDate,'%M %e, %Y - %l:%i %p')     |
+--------------------------------------------------+
| July 4, 1996 - 12:00 AM                          |
| July 5, 1996 - 12:00 AM                          |
| July 8, 1996 - 12:00 AM                          |
| July 8, 1996 - 12:00 AM                          |
| July 9, 1996 - 12:00 AM                          |
+--------------------------------------------------+
5 rows in set (0.00 sec)
```

Table B.7 *Date_Format()* and *Time_Format()*

Parameter	What It Means
%a	Weekday abbreviation (Sun, Mon, Tues, etc.)
%b	Month name abbreviation (Jan, Feb, Mar, etc.)
%c	Month (1–12)
%d	Two-digit day of the month (01–31)
%D	Day with a suffix (30th, 31st)
%e	Day of the month (1–31)
%f	Microseconds (000000..999999)
%H	Hour (00..23)
%h	Hour (01..12)
%i	Minutes, numeric (00..59)
%I	Hour (01–12)
%j	Day of year (001–366)
%k	Hour (0..23)
%l	Hour (1–12)
%m	Month with a leading 0 (01, 06, etc.)
%M	Month name (March, April, May, etc.)
%p	AM/PM

(continued)

Table B.7 *Date_Format()* and *Time_Format()* (continued)

Parameter	What It Means
%r	Time, 12-hour (hh:mm:ss followed by AM or PM)
%S	Seconds (00..59)
%s	Seconds (00..59)
%T	Time, 24-hour (hh:mm:ss)
%U	Week (00..53) starting with Sunday
%u	Week (00..53) starting with Monday
%v	Week (01..53) starting with Monday
%V	Week (01..53) starting with Sunday
%W	Weekday (Sunday, Monday, etc.)
%w	Day of the week (0 = Sunday..6 = Saturday)
%Y	Year (1999, 2007)
%y	Two-digit year (99, 07)
%%	A literal % character

The MySQL *EXTRACT* Command. The *EXTRACT* command is an example of a MySQL extension, not described in the SQL standard. It allows you to extract different parts of a date or time, as shown in Table B.8.

Table B.8 Date and Time Parts

Type	Format
SECOND	SECONDS
MINUTE	MINUTES
HOUR	HOURS
DAY	DAYS
MONTH	MONTHS
YEAR	YEARS (see Example B.44)
MINUTE_SECOND	"MINUTES:SECONDS"
HOUR_MINUTE	"HOURS:MINUTES"

(continued)

Table B.8 Date and Time Parts (continued)

Type	Format
DAY_HOUR	"DAYS HOURS"
YEAR_MONTH	"YEARS-MONTHS"
HOUR_SECOND	"HOURS:MINUTES:SECONDS"
DAY_MINUTE	"DAYS HOURS:MINUTES"
DAY_SECOND	"DAYS HOURS:MINUTES:SECONDS"

EXAMPLE B.44

```
mysql> select EXTRACT(YEAR FROM NOW());
+--------------------------+
| EXTRACT(YEAR FROM NOW()) |
+--------------------------+
|                     2006 |
+--------------------------+
1 row in set (0.03 sec)
```

B.5 Appendix Summary

In this appendix, you learned how to use the SQL language to create database schemas and how to insert, update, retrieve, alter, and delete records from a database.

B.6 What You Should Know

1. How do you retrieve all the records from a database table?

2. How do you retrieve a select set of records or a single record from a table based on specific criteria?

3. How do you select and sort records in a database?

4. How do you select a range of rows from a database?

5. How do you create a database?

6. How do you create database tables?

7. How do you assign a primary key to a field?

8. How are records inserted into the database table?

9. How are records updated in a table?

10. How do you delete a record?

EXERCISE B
Do You Speak My Language?

1. Go to the MySQL console and use the *show* command to list all the databases. Use the *mysql* database. Now display all of its tables.

2. Create a new database called *school*. Once you create the database, you need to be able to use it: *use school;*

3. Create a table called *student*. The table will consist of the following fields:

   FirstName
   LastName
   Email
   CellPhone
   Major
   GPA
   StartDate
   StudentId (the primary key)

   The following information is the type of data you will use to define your table. Go online and look for a table similar to this to use as your guide.

Data Type	Description
integer(size)	
int(size)	
smallint(size)	
tinyint(size)	Holds integers only

The maximum number of digits is specified by *size* in parentheses.

----

decimal(size,d)	
numeric(size,d)	Holds numbers with fractions.

The maximum number of digits is specified in *size*. The maximum number of digits to the right of the decimal is specified in *d*.

----

char(size)   Holds a fixed-length string (can contain letters, numbers, and special characters). The fixed size is specified by *size* in parentheses.

varchar(size)   Holds a variable-length string (can contain letters, numbers, and special characters). The maximum size is specified by *size* in parentheses.

----

date(yyyymmdd)   Holds a date.

----

4. Use the SQL *describe* statement to display the information you used to create the *school* database.

5. Insert three rows into the table:

Row 1:   FirstName: John
         LastName: Doe
         Email: johndoe@smileyface.edu
         CellPhone: 408-333-3456
         Major: CIS
         GPA: 2.8
         StartDate: 09/22/2004 (use the correct date format!)
         StudentId: 1

Row 2:   FirstName: Mary
         LastName: Chin
         Email: mchin@qmail.com
         CellPhone: 408-204-1234
         Major: Biology
         GPA: 3.3
         StartDate: 06/22/2003
         StudentId: 2

Row 3:   FirstName: Sadish
         LastName: Pamel
         Email: sadi@univ_ab.edu
         CellPhone: 415-204-1234
         Major: CIS
         GPA: 3.9
         StartDate: 06/22/2003
         StudentId: 2

6. Use the *show* commands to display all the fields.

7. Use *select* statements to display the following (write your query in the blank line):

   a. The data in all of the columns

   b. The first and last names of the students

   c. The student's first and last names and major

   d. The student's cellphone and e-mail addresses

   e. Any distinct majors

   f. Only 2 rows

8. a. Select all students who have a GPA over 3.0.

   b. Select all students who have a GPA between 3.0 and 4.0.

   c. Select students whose cellphones are in the 408 area code.

   d. Display rows for students who started in 2003.

   e. Select student first and last names who are majoring in CIS and have a GPA over 3.5.

   f. Select student first name and e-mail address if the e-mail address ends in *.com*.

9. a. Insert a new entry into the table.

   b. Sort the student table by last names.

   c. Sort the student table by GPA in descending order.

10. Change Mary's phone number to 650-123-4563.

    The next three questions deal with SQL functions:

11. Find the average GPA for all the students.

12. Find the number of rows in the table.

13. Print today's date using a SQL function.

Introduction to Moose (A Postmodern Object System for Perl 5)

Moose offers you an alternative to writing object-oriented Perl the old fashioned way, as described in Chapter 14, "Bless Those Things! (Object-Oriented Perl)." It modernizes Perl's object system by including features that are familiar to *C++* and *Java* programmers and makes Perl OO more consistent, easier to use, and more powerful. (Moose is based on the idea of meta-object programming, or MOP, which means that the object system itself is an object, a framework built on top of the Perl OO system.)

Moose is an extension of the Perl 5 object system which sweetens the process of creating classes by providing a set of exported functions for declaring classes, providing attributes and accessor methods, setting defaults, performing inheritance, type validation, and more. It simplifies the process of writing object-oriented Perl so that you can concentrate on the project rather than the mechanics. But you are not restricted to doing everything the Moose way just because you are using it; it's there to help you and provides powerful extensions for performing a number of OO tasks. To start, check the *Moose::Manual* documentation:

```
perldoc Moose::Manual
```

C.1 Getting Started

To get documentation, at the command line, type:

```
perldoc Moose
```

or go to the Web site, *http://metacpan.org/pod/Moose*.

To start, in your program, type:

```
use Moose;
```

C.2 The Constructor

The parent class will be *Moose::Object* (unless your class already has a parent), although initially we won't worry about *Moose::Object*; just know that it's there. When you load Moose, *strict* and *warnings* are turned on for you. *Moose::Object* provides a default constructor called *new* allowing you to create an object without worrying about shifting off the class name, the "blessing," and so forth.

Moose creates the class, calls the constructor, blesses the object, and returns blessed hashref. (When calling the *new* constructor with an argument, it takes either a hash or a hashref; otherwise, produces an error.) Here is a barebones Moose script:

```
(Module Dog.pm)
package Dog;
use Moose;    # Load Moose

1;
-------------------------------
(user.pl)

use Dog;
my $dogref=Dog->new;
# Call Moose constructor; get back a reference to a hash.

use Data::Dumper;
print Dumper($dogref);
# Displays a blessed object in the Dog class
-------------------------------

(Output)
$VAR1 = bless( {}, 'Dog' );
```

C.3 The Attributes

The next step in your Moose program is to set up the attributes for your object. These attributes, also called properties or slots, are one of the most powerful features of Moose. In fact, you can create a class that consists simply of attributes. What makes the attributes different from those you created before using Moose is that these attributes can serve as accessor methods (getters and setters). For example, if you have a *Dog* class and one of the attributes is *name*, then *name* can be used as both a setter and a getter.

C.3.1 The *has* Function

Moose provides the *has* function to declare an attribute. In the following small snippet, the *dog* has a *name* attribute. The *rw* means that this attribute can be used as a method to both get and set attributes for the object. You can use *name* as a write accessor to set the name this way:

```
$dog->name("Fido");
```

and as a read accessor to get the name this way:

```
$dog->name();
```

or you can simply set the attribute, like so:

```
$dog->{name}="Fido";
```

and create your own method to get the name or use any combination of methods for your setters and getters. In the following example, the class *Dog* has a read/write *name* attribute.

EXAMPLE C.1

```
(The Dog.pm Module)
package Dog;

use Moose;

has 'name' => (is => 'rw');    # Set the attribute

1;
-------------------------------------
And the user of the module:

use Dog;

my $dogref=Dog->new;       # Call default constructor

$dogref->name("Lassie"); # Use 'name' as a setter method

print "The dog's name is ", $dogref->name(),".\n";
            # Use 'name' as a getter method

use Data::Dumper;
print Dumper($dogref);     # Moose blessed the object.

(Ouput)
The dog's name is Fido.
$VAR1 = bless( {
            'name' => 'Fido'
          }, 'Dog' );
```

Attributes can also have defaults, type constraints, delegations, and so forth. (See *Moose::Manual::Attributes*.) The use of attributes as setter or getter methods is optional. Once you have a reference to the object, you can create your own accessor just as you have in non-Moose OO programs. Note that in the previous example, the output from *Data::Dumper* shows that the *dog* object was blessed into the *Dog* class just as it would appear in the non-Moose way.

C.3.2 Before and After Moose Examples

The next two examples demonstrate a program before Moose, using the traditional Perl OO. The second example uses Moose to do the same thing.

Example C.2 shows an object-oriented module before Moose.

EXAMPLE C.2

```
(Class Without Moose)
package House;  # Class
 use strict;
 use warnings;
 sub new{  # Constructor
   my $class = shift;
    # Set properties
   my $house={ Color=>undef,
               Owner=>undef,
               Price=>undef,
             };  # Attributes
   bless($house, $class);  # Blessing
   return $house;  # Return blessed hashref
 }

   sub set_props{  # method/setter
      my $obj = shift;
      my ($color,$owner,$price) = @_;  # Set attributes
      $obj->{Color}=$color;
      $obj->{Owner}=$owner;
      $obj->{Price}=$price;
   }
   sub get_props{   # method/getter
      my $self=shift;
      my $prop = shift;
      return $self->{$prop};
   }
   1;
```

Example C.3 shows the same example, but this time using Moose.

EXAMPLE C.3

```
(House.pm)
1   package House;
2   use Moose;
    # Define attributes for the House class
3   has 'color'=>(
        is => 'rw',
        isa => 'Str',
        predicate => 'has_color',
    );
4   has 'owner'=> (
        is => 'rw',
        isa => 'Str',
    );
5   has 'price'=>(
        is=>'ro',
        isa => 'Int',
6       writer => '_set_price';
    );
7   sub _set_price{
        my $self=shift;
        my $self->{price}=shift;
    );
8 # sub _set_props{  # define your own method
  #     my $self = shift;
  #     my ($color,$owner,$price) = @_;
  #     $self->{color}=$color;
  #     $self->{owner}=$owner;
  #     $self->{price}=$price;
  # }

    1;
```

EXPLANATION

1   The *House* class is defined in a package. All you do to create a class is to declare a package and *use Moose*.

2   Loading Moose automatically turns on strictures (*warnings* and *strict*). A default constructor, called *new*, is also automatically added.

3   This is where you define the attributes for the object. The first attribute is *'color'*. This option accepts either *rw* (read/write) or *ro* (read only). In this example, it creates a read/write accessor of the same name as the attribute, *'color'*, also called a setter/getter method. You don't have to use the attributes as accessor methods. You can create your own methods to set or retrieve the object's values. The *'color'* attribute is also given type => *'Str'* (is a string). The *predicate* method tells you whether or not an an attribute has been set, even *undef* will do, and will return true if it has been set and false if not.

4   The next attribute is the *'owner'*. It can serve as a read/write accessor. The *'owner'* type *isa* => *'Str'* (is a string).

EXPLANATION (CONTINUED)

5   The *'price'* attribute is read only. This means if you try to use it as an accessor method, you **cannot set** the price, but you can get its value. Here is the error you would get if you tried to directly assign a price to the house with the accessor:

```
$h1->price(5000000);
```

Produces the following error (partial output):

```
Cannot assign a value to a read-only accessor at reader House::price
(defined at House.pm line 16) line 3.
   House::price('House2=HASH(0x1010025e0)', 500000) called at
houseMooseuser line 9
```

To handle exceptions with Moose, see: *Moose::Manual::Exceptions* at *cpan.org*.

6   We can explicitly specify the method to be used for reading and writing. In this example, we are making the accessor publically readable, but not writeable. If the user wants to set or change the price, he will have to call the *_set_price* method provided for the attribute.

7   This is the *_set_price* method defined as a *writer* in the *'price'* attribute. This method lets us change or set the price.

8   As stated earlier, Moose doesn't force you to use the attributes as accessors. You can create your own accessor methods just as you have done before you used Moose. Remember, under the hood, Moose is just Perl 5 OO. In this commented segment, we want to pass the attribute information in *set_props* rather than use the accessors created by Moose when defining the attributes. By doing so, we are ignoring the accessors. Since we don't have a *get_props* method, we will use *price*, *owner*, and *color* as accessor methods.

The next example demonstrates how a user would use the House module defined in Example C.3.

EXAMPLE C.4

```
(User of the House module)
   #!/usr/bin/env perl
1  use House;
   use Data::Dumper;
   use v5.16;

2  my $h1 = House->new()  # Call constructor
   my $h2 = House->new();

3  $h1->color("yellow"); # Use 'color' as an accessor
4  print "Has a color \n" if $h1->has_color == 1;
       # use predicate method
5  $h1->owner("B of A");
```

EXAMPLE C.4 (CONTINUED)

```
6    # $h1->price(50000);     # Throws an exception/readonly
7    $h1->_set_price(50000);  # Call 'set_price'
8    $h2->color("yellow");    # set values
     $h2->owner("Mr. Trump");
     $h2->set_price(1000000);

9    say "The price is ", $h1->price;
       # Use 'price' as an accessor method (getter)
     say "The owner is ", $h1->owner;
     say "The color is ", $h1->color, "\n";
10   print Dumper($h1,$h2);

(Output)
Has a color
The price is 50000
The owner is B of A
The color is yellow
$VAR1 = bless( {
                'owner' => 'B of A',
                'color' => 'yellow',
                'price' => 50000
              }, 'House2' );
$VAR2 = bless( {
                'owner' => 'Mr. Trump',
                'color' => 'yellow',
                'price' => 1000000
              }, 'House2' );
```

C.3.3 Moose Types

As seen in the previous Moose example, when you declare an attribute you can use the Moose *isa* option to associate the attribute with a type, such as a *Str* (string), *Int* (integer), *HashRef* (reference to a hash), or a *Bool* (Boolean), and so forth. From the Moose documentation, here is a list of types:

```
Any
   Item
       Bool
       Undef
       Defined
           Value
               Num
                   Int
               Str
                   ClassName
```

```
Ref
     ScalarRef
     ArrayRef
     HashRef
     CodeRef
     RegexpRef
     GlobRef
        FileHandle
     Object
          Role
```

Since Moose has its own type system for attributes, it can also check the parameters; for example, if your property takes a type *ArrayRef,* Moose will throw an exception if you don't obey this constraint. The feature of parameter checking makes it much easier to ensure that you're getting valid data. See *Moose::Manual::Types* for a complete list of types and how to use them.

Let's change the *House* example using a type constraint. This time we may have more than one owner for the house object. The *'owners'* attribute will be of type *ArrayRef*, a reference to an anonymous array where the elements (owners) are strings.

EXAMPLE C.5

```perl
   use v5.16;
1  package House;   # Create the class
2  use Moose;
        # Define attributes for the House class
3  has 'color'=>(
       is => 'rw',
       isa => 'Str',
   );
4  has 'owners'=>(
     is=>'rw',
5    isa => 'ArrayRef[Str]',   # Type is an array reference
6    required => 1,   # Must be provided to constructor
   );
7  has 'price'=>(
     is=>'ro',
     isa => 'Num',
     writer => '_set_price',
   );
8  sub _set_price{
     my $self=shift;
     my $price=shift;
     #$self->price($price);
   }
   1;
```

EXPLANATION

1   Declare the package *House*.

2   Load *Moose*. It will create the class and attributes.

3   The *'color'* attribute is read/write and a *'Str'* (string) type.

4   The *'owners'* attribute is also read/write.

5   The value assigned to the *'owners'* attribute must be an array reference where each of the elements in the array will be of type *'Str'*. If you try to assign something other than an array reference to the *'owners'* attribute, Moose will throw an exception such as:

```
# Attribute (owners) does not pass the type constraint because:
Validation failed for 'ArrayRef[Str]' with value Mr. Trump at /usr/
local/ActivePerl-5.16    /lib/Moose/Meta/Attribute.pm line 1274.
```

6   Normally all attributes are optional. With the *required* attribute set to *1*, Moose says the attribute *'owners'* must be provided when the constructor is called, but does not say what its values should be.

7   You can explicitly specify the method name to be used for reading and writing the value of an attribute by using the *reader* and *writer* attribute options. Since the *'price'* attribute is read only, we can't directly set the price. If you want to use it to set the value of the price, you would call the *_set_price* method defined on line 8 as a *writer* method. The leading underscore indicates that this is a private method even though it can be called from outside the class.

8   The *_set_price* method is defined. Even though the *'price'* attribute was defined as a read-only accessor, we can treat it as a writer accessor by using this method.

Example C.6 shows the user of the *House* module, *house.pl*.

EXAMPLE C.6

```
    #!/usr/bin/env perl
    use Data::Dumper;
    use strict;
    use warnings;
1   my $h1 = House->new('owners'=>[ "Mrs. A", "Mr. B" ]);
2   my $h2 = House->new('owners'=>[]); # Define values later
3   # my $h3 = House->new('owners'=> 'Mr. Trump');
4   $h1->color('red');
    $h1->_set_price(125000);
5   $h2->owners(['Mr. Trump','Mr. Mellon','CityBank']);
    $h2->color('blue');
    $h2->_set_price(5000000);

    say "The price is ", $h1->price;
6   say "The owners are ", join(", ",@{$h1->owners});
    say "The color is ", $h1->color;
    say "The price is ", $h2->price;
```

EXAMPLE C.6 (CONTINUED)

```
7   say "The owners are ", join(", ",@{$h2->owners});
    say "The color is ", $h2->color;
8   #print $h1->dump;
9   print Dumper($h1,$h2);
```

(Output)
```
The owners are Mrs. A, Mr. B
The color is red
The price is 5000000
The owners are Mr. Trump, Mr. Mellon, CityBank
The color is blue
$VAR1 = bless( {
                 'color' => 'red',
                 'owners' => [
                               'Mrs. A',
                               'Mr. B'
                             ],
                 'price' => 125000
               }, 'House' );
$VAR2 = bless( {
                 'color' => 'blue',
                 'owners' => [
                               'Mr. Trump',
                               'Mr. Mellon',
                               'CityBank'
                             ],
                 'price' => 5000000
               }, 'House' );
```

EXPLANATION

1   Call the constructor with an argument, the name of the attribute (*'owners'*), and its value (the required *ArrayRef* and its string values). (Note: the constructor itself requires that you send a hash or hashref as an argument.)

2   Call the constructor with the required *ArrayRef*, this time without values. They will be assigned later. This is fine as long as the constructor gets the *required* type, a reference to an anonymous array.

3   This line threw an exception because Moose tried to validate the argument and it didn't pass the type constraint; meaning, the value for the *'owners'* attribute is not of type *ArrayRef*.

4   The *'color'* attribute is used as a setter to assign a value for the color of the house object.

5   Now we are using the *'owners'* attribute as an accessor method. Note that with *required* turned on, we had to send an *arrayref* to the constructor, but we can assign the values later, as shown here.

6, 7   The *'owners'* attribute is used to access (get) the values for the first and second houses; that is, dereference the reference to the anonymous array returned by the method.

8 Moose provides its own version of *Data::Dumper* with its *dump* method.

9 The *Data::Dumper* module is really helpful in showing that the output for these house objects is the same as for a non-Moose program. You can see that the objects were blessed as hash references into the *House* class and all of the attributes and their values are displayed as expected.

C.3.4 Example Using Moose and Extensions

Changing and extending Moose can be done by adding extensions yourself or by using those that have already been written. Some of the most popular extensions to Moose can be found at *Moose::Manual::MooseX*. The next example shows you how to use two of these extensions: *MooseX::Declare* and *MooseX::ClassAttributes*.

EXAMPLE C.7

```
(The Student Module)
  # Student.pm
  # Written by Daniel Holmes

  #use Moose;
1 use List::MoreUtils;

2 use MooseX::Declare;

3 class Student {
4   use MooseX::ClassAttribute;   # Include Moose extensions
5   class_has student_count => (
        is      => 'rw',
        isa     => "Int",
        default => 0,
    );
6   has 'name' => (
        is       => 'rw',
        isa      => 'Str',
        required => 1,
    );
7   has 'major' => (
        is      => 'rw',
        isa     => 'Str',
        default => "",
    );
8   has 'courses' => (
        is       => 'rw',
9       isa      => 'ArrayRef[Str]',
10      default  => sub {[]},
11      traits   => ['Array'],
```

EXAMPLE C.7 (CONTINUED)

```
12        handles => {
              add_courses => 'push',
              get_courses => 'elements',
          }
      );
13    has 'address' => (
          is      => 'rw',
          isa     => 'Str',
          default => "",
      );
      has 'idnumber' => (
          is       => 'rw',
          isa      => 'Str',
          required => 1,
      );
      has 'startdate' => (
          is      => 'rw',
          isa     => 'Str',
          default => "",
      );
      has 'tuition' => (
          is      => 'rw',
          isa     => 'Int',
          default => -1,
      );
14    sub BUILD {
          my $self = shift;
15        $self->student_count($self->student_count + 1);
      }

16    sub DEMOLISH {
          Student->student_count(Student->student_count - 1);
          print "Demolish\n";
      }

17    sub show_student {
          my $this = shift;

          printf "Name:    %s\n", $this->name;
          printf "ID:      %s\n", $this->idnumber;
          printf "Major:   %s\n", $this->major;
          printf "Courses: @{$this->courses}\n";
          printf "Address: %s\n", $this->address;
          printf "Tuition: %s\n", $this->tuition;
      }
```

EXAMPLE C.7 (CONTINUED)

```
18    sub drop_courses {
          my $self = shift;
          foreach my $course (@_) {
19            my $index = List::MoreUtils::first_index{
                  $_ eq $course} @{$self->courses};
              splice(@{$self->courses}, $index, 1);
          }
      }
  }
  1;
```

EXPLANATION

1   The *List::MoreUtils* module provides functions to deal with lists. In this example, it is used to find an index value in an array.

2   Instead of declaring a package, we will use *MooseX::Declare*. This allows a more declarative style of class generation, familiar to *Java* and *C* users. The *X* in *MooseX* is a conventional symbol meaning "extension." According to the documentation:
The "MooseX::" namespace is the official place to find Moose extensions. These extensions can be found on the CPAN. The easiest way to find them is to search for the extension (*http://search.cpan.org/search?query=MooseX::*), or to examine *Task::Moose*, which aims to keep an up-to-date, easily installable list of Moose extensions.

3   *Student* will be a package, but *MooseX::Declare* lets us use the *class* keyword to create a package with all the extra Moose behavior.

4   *MooseX::ClassAttribute* is used. This module allows you to declare class attributes in exactly the same way as object attributes, using *"class_has()"* instead of *"has()"*; that is, it allows the class to have static data members.

5   The *class_has* function is provided by *MooseX::ClassAttribute*. The *Student* class has a *student_count* property, an integer with a default value of 0.

6   A *Student* object has a *'name'* and *'major'* attribute, both strings. The *'name'* is required, meaning it must be provided when calling the constructor.

7   The *'major'* attribute is not required and defaults to the empty string.

8   The *'courses'* attribute will consist of a list of courses.

9   The courses will be assigned as reference to an array; for example, *[qw(French Math Biology)]*. The course names are strings (*Str*). A student has zero or more courses.

10 A subroutine reference is provided as a default. When called as a method, *courses* will return a reference to an array.

11 The *Array* trait tells Moose that we would like to use a set of *Array* helper functions; meaning, we want to perform common array operations such as *push*, *map*, *shift*, *splice*, *delete*, and so forth, on this property. (See *Moose::Meta::Attribute::Native::Trait::Array* for a complete list of provided methods.)

EXPLANATION (CONTINUED)

12   The *handles* attribute allows you to delegate to standard Perl data structures as if they were objects. Using a hash tells Moose to create your own method names (specified on the left) which invoke the delegated class methods (specified on the right). In this example, the method *'add_courses'* on the left is mapped to the Moose *push* method on the right (push elements onto the array), and *'get_courses'* is mapped to the *elements* method (returns all the elements in an array, not an array reference).

When we call *$student->add_courses*, the courses will be pushed onto this property:

```
$student->add_courses("linear_algebra");
```

'get_courses' works similarly. When we call *'get_courses'* on a an object, it actually delegates a call to the *'elements'* method and returns the list of courses; in other words, *get_courses* tells the *elements* method to get all the courses referenced by the *courses* attribute.

```
$student->get_courses,
```

13   The program continues to define more attributes.

14   The *BUILD* method is called after an object is created. One use of *BUILD* is to check whether an object is valid; another use could be for logging or tracing object creation. In this example, we use it to increment the number of students after each one is created.

15   The class ("static") property *'student_count'* is accessed and altered.

16   When an object is destroyed, Moose calls *DEMOLISH*, a hook for object destruction. You could use Perl's *DESTROY* method as well. *'student_count'* is a *Student* class method and will be called when a student object is demolished.

17   The *show_student* method is defined. This simply prints information about the student.

18   The *drop_courses* method is defined. The *Array* trait does not provide a simple way of performing this action, so we cannot define this method like we defined *push* and *elements*; we have to search for a course in the list and splice it out manually.

19   *List::MoreUtils::first_index* is used to find the index of the first element in the array that matches the course provided. The index found is used in the *splice* function to remove this element from the array.

EXAMPLE C.8

```perl
    (The user of the Student Class)
    #!/usr/bin/env perl
    use strict;
    use warnings;
1   use Student;
    use Data::Dumper;

2   print Student->student_count(), " \n";

3   $student1 = Student->new(
        name     => "Bob",
        idnumber => "123",
        major    => "math",
        courses  => [qw(calculus topology matricies)],
    );
    $student2 = Student->new(
        name     => "Jane",
        idnumber => "321",
        major    => "computer science",
        courses  => [qw(automata algorithms java)],
        tuition  => 5000,  # Override the default
    );

    #$student1->show_student();
    #$student2->show_student();

    #print Dumper($student1);

    print "Schedule change \n";

4      $student1->add_courses("linear_algebra");
       $student1->show_student();
5      $student1->drop_courses("topology");
6      $student1->show_student();

7   print "New courses:   ", join(" ", $student1->get_courses()), " \n";
8   print Student->student_count(), " \n";


9   {
       my $student3 = Student->new(
           name     => "Ethel",
           idnumber => "3210",
           major    => "computer science",
           courses  => [qw(automata algorithms java)],
       );
```

EXAMPLE C.8 (CONTINUED)

```
10   print Student->student_count(), " \n";
   }  # End block

11 print Student->student_count(), " \n";
   # print Dumper($student2);
```

(Output)
```
0
Schedule change
Name:     Bob
ID:       123
Major:    math
Courses: calculus topology matricies
Address:
Tuition: -1
Name:     Bob
ID:       123
Major:    math
Courses: calculus matricies
Address:
Tuition: -1
New courses:    calculus matricies
2
3
Demolish
2
Demolish
Demolish
```

EXPLANATION

1   This script is going to *use* the *Student* class.

2   The number of students is printed. It is zero, the default, which was set when the class was created. We call this method on the class *Student*, and since an object is not needed, it is a class attribute.

3   Two *Student* objects are created, with attributes sent as a has to the new constructor.

4   A course is added to the first student. Because the *'courses'* attribute was given the *Array* trait, we are able to tell Moose that the *'courses'* attribute handles the *'add_courses'* method. *'add_courses'* is a valid method and is associated with the Moose *push* method, the same as the Perl built-in function for adding elements to an array. The next line outputs the student's data, showing that the new course was added. (See *Moose::Meta::Attribute::Native/Trait/Array.pm.*)

5   The student is dropping topology. *'drop_courses'* had to be written manually because the *Array* trait does not include a method for removing an element with *splice* based on the string value.

EXPLANATION (CONTINUED)

6   *'show_student'* is called to show that the course has been removed from the array.
7   The *get_courses* method was defined by the handles option in the *'courses'* attribute. The student's courses are printed. The list contains *linear_algebra* but not *topology*.
8   We have created two new students. The *student_count* accessor is called and returns 2.
9   A new block is created and a lexical variable declared. It will go out of scope when the block ends. It is assigned a new *Student* object, with data. The *DEMOLISH* method will be called and destroy the variable when it goes out of scope; meaning, when the block ends. See *Demolish* in the output.
10 The *student_count* is now *3*.
11 Outside the block, the object, *$student3*, has gone out of scope and is destroyed. Now when we inspect that class attribute again, it is back to 2.

C.3.5   Example Using Inheritance with Moose

We talked about Perl OO and inheritance in Chapter 14, "Bless Those Things! (Object-Oriented Perl)." Also in Chapter 14, we discussed Moose roles (see Section 14.4.4, "Multiple Inheritance and Roles with Moose").

The following Moose examples consist of four files: a parent (*Pet.pm*), two sub classes (*Dog.pm* and *Cat.pm*), and a user (*petuser.pl*). The purpose of these examples is to give you a brief introduction to how Moose simplifies inheritance.

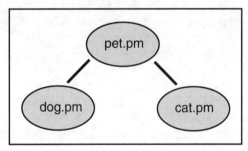

Figure C.1   The parent and subclass hierarchy for the following examples.

EXAMPLE C.9

```
(The Parent Class)
    # Pet.pm
1   package Pet;

2   use Moose;

3   has 'owner' => (
        isa => 'Str',
        is  => 'rw'
    );
```

EXAMPLE C.9 (CONTINUED)

```
4   has 'name' => (
        isa => 'Str',
        is  => 'rw'
    );
5   has 'gender' => (
        isa => 'Str',
        is  => 'rw'
    );

6   sub eat {
        my $self = shift;
7       print $self->name, " says thanks for the ",  @_, "\n";
    }
    1;
```

EXPLANATION

1   The file, *Pet.pm*, defines the *Pet* package. It is a class designed to represent the generic *Pet*. *Dog* and *Cat* are specializations; they are a specific type of *Pet* with specific behavior. This class defines what all *Pets* have in common and what they can do.

2   We use Moose to make this a class.

3   All *Pets* have an owner. The attribute is named *'owner'* and its value will be a *Str* (string) type. It is *rw*, meaning we can both access (read) and change (write) the owner of any Pet. When we create a new *Pet*, we will provide the owner with a value.

4   All pets have a *'name'* attribute with the same options as the *'owner'*.

5   All pets have a *'gender'*. Note now that the program is unable to define *Pets* that have no *'gender'*, such as earthworms or pet rocks. When designing real-world OO systems it is important to realize that the classes you write define how the system can work in the future.

6   All *Pets* can eat. For now, when a *Pet* eats, a message is printed containing the Pet's name. *'name'* was defined as a property of *Pet*, and since this method must be called on an object, then the object (in *$self*) must have a name.

7   The rest of the parameters in @_ are also printed; the *eat* method accepts string data.

EXAMPLE C.10

```
    (The Cat Module)
1   package Cat;
2   use Moose;

3   extends 'Pet';

4   sub speak {
5       my $self = shift;
6       print $self->name, " says Meow\n";
    }
    1;
```

EXPLANATION

1   This file (*Cat.pm*) contains the *Cat* class.

2   We use Moose to handle all the boring and difficult parts of OO as shown in earlier examples.

3   Moose provides the *extends* function to load the parent class, *Pet*. (You don't have to say *use Pet;*.) All *Cats* are now defined as being *Pets* and can do what *Pets* can do. This also means that *Cats* have the same properties as *Pets*; for example, *'name'*, *'owner'*, and *'gender'*.

4   *Cats* can *speak*, but not all *Pets* can *speak*. This is an extension of Pet; meaning, *Cats* can do things that not all other *Pets* can do, such as purr.

5   As with normal Perl OO, the current object (the "context" object) is passed as the first parameter to the object's methods and is shifted from the @_.

6   In *Pet*, we used Moose to declare that *Pets* have names. A *Cat* is a *Pet*; therefore, a *Cat* has a name. The context object will be a *Cat* (a subclass of *Pet*) and therefore have a *'name'*. The name is printed, as well as the assertion that this object says *Meow*.

The next example shows the user of the *Cat.pm* and *Dog.pm* modules.

EXAMPLE   C.11

```
(The Dog Module)

1  package Dog;

2  use Moose;

3  extends 'Pet';

4  sub speak{
      my $self = shift;

5     print $self->name, " says Woof\n";
   }

   1;
```

EXPLANATION

1   This file (*Dog.pm*) contains the *Dog* class. The difference between a class and a module is entirely in how it is used—this module uses Moose, which means it is intended to be used to create objects. That makes it a class.

2   *Use Moose* to make it a class.

EXPLANATION (CONTINUED)

3   Like *Cat*, a *Dog* is a *Pet*. The only difference (in this example) between a *Dog* and a *Cat* is how they *speak*. In a real-world scenario, the differences between these classes will depend on what you are writing code to do. Perhaps your classes will contain the genomes for the particular species; perhaps just the biological classification; perhaps you want to model their behavior differently for a computer game. At any rate, attributes are inherited from the parent class.

4   As with *Cat*, the *Dog* has a *speak* method as well. If you tried to run *speak()* on an object that was not a *Cat* or a *Dog*, but just a basic *Pet*, a runtime error would occur.

5   When *speak* is called on a *Dog* object, it will say *Woof*, whereas *Cat* said *Meow*. We still use the *'name'* property, which we inherited from *Pet*.

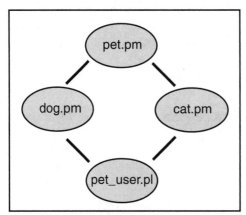

Figure C.2   The parent, subclass, and user hierarchy for the examples..

EXAMPLE C.12

```
# (( Standard Perl script preamble used ))
#!/usr/bin/env perl
# pet_user.pl
1  use Dog;
use Cat;
use warnings;
use strict;

2  my $dog = Dog->new(
owner => "Daniel",
name  => "Fido",
gender   => "M"
);
```

EXAMPLE   C.12 (CONTINUED)

```
3   $cat = Cat->new(
        owner  => "Daniel",
        name   => "Felix",
        gender  => "M"
    );

4   $dog->eat("Table scraps");
5   $dog->speak();

6   $cat->eat("Tuna fish");
7   $cat->speak();

(Output)

4   Fido says thanks for the Table scraps
5   Fido says Woof
6   Felix says thanks for the Tuna fish
7   Felix says Meow
```

EXPLANATION

1   This script will use both the *Dog* and *Cat* classes.
2   A new *Dog* object is created, with the listed attributes, and stored in the variable *$dog*. The dog's name is *Fido*.
3   A new *Cat* object is created. The same attributes are provided, just with different values. The cat's name is *Felix*.
4   The *Dog* object can eat because it is a *Pet*, and *Pets* can eat. The *eat* method prints a message containing the name of the animal. When we call the *eat* method on the *Dog*, the message contains *"Fido"*; and because we gave it the argument *"Table scraps"*, this also appears in the message.
5   When the *Dog* speaks, the version from the *Dog* class runs. The message contains *Fido* and *Woof,* the first being from the object, and the second from the method itself.
6, 7 When we call the same methods on the *Cat* object, the *eat* method behaves similarly because it runs the same code, the *eat* method in the *Pet* class. However, when we call *speak*, it says *Meow*, because it has run the *speak* method from the *Cat* class, and because *$cat* is a *Cat*!

C.4   What About Moo?

You may have heard about Moo (2/3 Moose). This is a lightweight subset of Moose to get you up and running quickly and preferable for programs that only require the minimal features of Moose. For more on this see *https://metacpan.org/pod/Moo.*

C.5 Appendix Summary

There is a lot more to Moose. This appendix has been an introduction to provide you with some Moose examples to help you get started. There is a plethora of information available on the Internet. Some starting points are listed in the following section.

C.6 References

Following are some resources to continue your education on Moose.

1. *Moose::Manual* (a starter)
2. *Moose::Cookbook* (many examples)
3. Moose, "A Postmodern Object System for Perl," *http://moose.iinteractive.com/en.*
4. Perl Maven, "Object Oriented Perl using Moose," *http://perlmaven.com/object-oriented-perl-using-moose.*
5. The Perl Review, "Getting Started with Moose," *http://www.theperlreview.com/articles/moose.html.*
6. The Sysadmin Notebook, "Building Modules and Testing," *http://home.clara.net/drdsl/Perl/Modules.html.*

appendix

D

Perlbrew, CPAN, and *cpanm*

Written by Alastair McGowan-Douglas

Perl comes preinstalled on UNIX systems. Normally, you will find that the preinstalled version is older than the latest Perl release, and in some cases it will be subtly different. This Perl is designed by the system maintainers to work with the rest of the system. When you install packages, such as with the system package manager, the packages you install will have been tested against the version of Perl installed by the system.

Many of those packages are precompiled and tested versions of modules available on CPAN, the Comprehensive Perl Archive Network. This allows you to use those modules and that version of Perl to write your own scripts and applications on your system.

This is fine, until you either want to upgrade Perl or install modules that don't exist in your package manager. It is worthwhile to upgrade Perl so as to be up to date with the latest bug fixes and features. Installing modules from CPAN is a cornerstone of Perl programming; if you can't get things from CPAN, you'll find yourself reinventing wheels, writing nonportable code, and unable to use scripts others have written that rely on CPAN modules.

Upgrading and installing are two separate processes, and they are solved in two different ways, but they are related.

D.1 CPAN and *@INC*

CPAN (traditionally *the* CPAN, but we usually treat it as a proper noun) is the place where all of the community-submitted code resides and where all modules not in core, can be found, fetched, and installed. In Modern Perl, the ability to find and install modules from CPAN is not just encouraged; it is imperative. Without it, you will write code that repeats mistakes others have made before and have already fixed. Your scripts will not be portable because you didn't use a module that wraps up Perl functions in portable ways. You will not be able to use other people's scripts that make heavy use of modules. In general, you will be using Perl as a blunt instrument instead of the Swiss Army Knife it can be, and you will find the community reluctant to help you if you have issues trying to solve a problem that's already been solved.

D.1.1 Finding Modules

When writing code, it is valuable to search first on *http://metacpan.org*[1] to see whether your problem has been solved before. If it has, you can download and use that module. If not, consider solving your problem in a generic way, such that you could upload your module to CPAN for future developers to do what you just tried.

D.1.2 Using Modules

When you *use Module;* Perl looks in various places for *Module.pm*, and loads the first one it finds. If it doesn't find it at all, you will get a compile-time error:

```
use Module;
Can't locate Module.pm in @INC (you may need to install the Module module)
```

(This particular error message was introduced in 5.18; prior to this version, it did not give the hint about installing the module.)

The *use* directive defines a requirement; semantically, it says that the script in question cannot run without the stated module. Hence, Perl refuses to go further without the module. The message states that the file could not be found in *@INC*, which you will recognize as the name of a Perl array. *@INC* is, indeed, an array; the array that contains all the search paths for modules.

You can inspect the contents of *@INC* by either using it as a normal array and printing them, or asking *perl -V* to list them:

```
$ perl -E'say for @INC'²
/etc/perl
/usr/local/lib/perl/5.18.2
/usr/local/share/perl/5.18.2
    ...
    <snip>

$ perl -V
Summary of my perl5 (revision 5 version 18 subversion 2) configuration:
```

---

1. At the time of writing, the traditional CPAN search site (*http://search.cpan.org*) is fluctuating between available and unavailable. That site is being phased out for not being community-run—the code is not available and the community cannot access the server that hosts it. The new site, metacpan, is available on github at *https://github.com/CPAN-API*.
2. *-E* is a new option introduced with 5.10 that is equivalent to *-e'use feature ":5.10"*; *-E* turns on all the features introduced with 5.10. Here, we use it, in order to *use say*.

```
Platform:
  osname=linux, osvers=3.2.0-58-generic, archname=x86_64-linux-
gnu-thread-multi
    ...
      <snip>
    ...
 Compiled at Mar 27 2014 18:30:28
  @INC:
    /etc/perl
    /usr/local/lib/perl/5.18.2
    /usr/local/share/perl/5.18.2
    /usr/lib/perl5
    /usr/share/perl5
    /usr/lib/perl/5.18
    /usr/share/perl/5.18
    /usr/local/lib/site_perl
  .
```

These are all the directories Perl will look in by default.

Listed is the default output for the Perl provided with Linux Mint 17, which comes with 5.18; your output may differ.

These directories are the places Perl looks when your script requests a module. Apart from '.', however, all of these directories are system directories. Only root can write to these. Some of these directories don't even exist! This is just a default set that Perl is built with. The ones that do exist are:

```
/usr/lib/perl5
/usr/share/perl5
/usr/lib/perl/5.18
/usr/share/perl/5.18
.
```

(Of course the current directory exists!) Files in the *lib* directories are architecture-dependent, and therefore are going files that interface between Perl and existing *C* libraries, or else are written in *C* for efficiency purposes. Those in *share* are everything else—pure Perl modules, essentially.

Keep in mind, that all of these files were provided by *apt*, Debian's package manager. None of them were installed manually by the user. What if you want to use a module from CPAN, but *apt* hasn't installed it?

I Already Have It!   In some cases you will already have the module you want. This is most often the case when you are writing the module, so it's not actually on CPAN yet; or it is, but you've updated it and want to use the updated version.

Less often, you will have been provided a module from somewhere other than CPAN. This can happen if you are using code from a third-party vendor. This is very uncommon. Most modules written by third parties go on CPAN anyway, because they interface into proprietary software or services, meaning the company suffers nothing from making the modules themselves free on CPAN.

In all cases, you can tell Perl where to look for modules using the *-I* option to Perl, which prepends the *@INC* array with the requested directory. (Ordinarily you will have a distribution with a script and a *lib* directory containing the script's modules). The *-I* option is shown here:

```
$ perl -I lib example.pl
```

This is the technique *cpan* will use when testing modules prior to installation. With *-I*, the temporary directory with the module in it can be added to *@INC*, and the test scripts run in this context. This ensures the module being tested is the one in the temporary directory, and not an older version installed in system Perl.

For more permanent locations for your modules, you can use the *PERL5LIB* environment variable. Simply set it to a set of colon-separated paths, much like *PATH* itself, and these will be added to *@INC* as well:

```
$ PERL5LIB="$HOME/perl5:$PERL5LIB" perl example.pl
```

D.1.3 Package Manager

For modules you want to get from CPAN, the first thing to check is your package manager, if your system has one. As noted, Debian has *apt*. RedHat and derivatives have *yum,* and FreeBSD has *ports*. If you have access, the easiest way to get a module for the system Perl is to install it via the package manager.

Modules from the package manager have the advantage of having been tested by the vendor; i.e., the people who put the operating system together in the first place. You will often hear the term "vendor Perl" used to refer to the system Perl that your vendor supplies. Additionally, on many systems, the packaged versions are precompiled. This means the procedure for getting a Perl module with *C* dependencies is a simple matter of unpacking it. Later, we will see how otherwise complex this can be.

This method is not without its drawbacks, however, including the following:

- You need root access. If you are working in a corporate environment, you are unlikely to have this access. Sometimes there are procedures in place to request that those who do have access install it for you, but these processes take time and aren't necessarily going to be granted.
- It installs to system Perl. If you are using Perlbrew (discussed later), you will not be able to use a prepackaged version, because Perlbrew creates custom Perl installations independent of vendor Perl.
- The version in the package manager might not be the version containing the features you want. You will have to get the latest version from CPAN if the packaged version is older.
- It might not be there! There are tens of thousands of distributions on CPAN, and it is infeasible for a vendor to package, test, and distribute every one of them. With the recent resurgence of Perl's popularity (the "Modern Perl" movement)

CPAN's popularity has had an equivalent increase in activity. That means that, in many cases, CPAN is gaining new and updated distributions faster than vendors can keep up. Vendors, therefore, have to pick a snapshot of CPAN, compile a popular subset of the modules, and distribute that.

D.1.4 Manually: CPAN

The alternative is to install modules manually. This basically reverses the advantage/drawback listed previously:

- You can have anything.
- You don't need root.
- You can install to a custom Perl.
- You need a *C* compiler, and *C* dependencies.
- It hasn't been thoroughly tested for your particular situation.

Installation of modules from CPAN is done with the *cpan* command that comes with Perl, but it is recommended to fetch and install *cpanm* instead. The *cpan* command is usable but requires setup; while *cpanm* comes with defaults for everything and tries to be as DWIM (Do What I Mean) as possible.

The first thing to realize is that, by default, *cpan* is going to try to install to system Perl directories. This is because *cpan* is a Perl script itself, which means that system Perl will be used to run it! And that requires root access. To avoid that, we will use *local::lib* to create and use a local *lib/* for Perl modules.

local::lib. Using a local lib is considered best practice even if you do have root access. The principal reason for this is a simple tenet: system Perl is not for your use. This applies to many modern languages. The system Perl, with the system modules in the package manager, are all designed to work with the system's Perl-based commands and utilities. If this happens to be the set of requirements for your own purposes, that's great, but as soon as these diverge, you'll end up needing these techniques anyway. It's far better to have a local environment of which you have complete control, making it simple to switch environments at any time, and also protecting you from changes in system Perl.

The following five environment variables are all you will need to create a local Perl setup. With them in effect, *cpan* can work with any directory on the system.

Traditionally, your *$HOME* will be used to contain modules and scripts you want to install without root. This is known as *local* Perl (as opposed to system, or vendor, Perl). Another common location is *site* Perl, which generally refers to that set of modules your organization commonly uses, and hence is installed on all servers by default. For our purposes, we'll be dealing with the most common case, which is to install a local Perl library (a *local lib*) in your home directory.

Listed here are the five environment variables:

```
PATH="/home/altreus/perl5/bin${PATH+:}$PATH"
PERL5LIB="/home/altreus/perl5/lib/perl5${PERL5LIB+:}$PERL5LIB"
PERL_LOCAL_LIB_ROOT="/home/altreus/perl5${PERL_LOCAL_LIB_ROOT+:}$PERL_
LOCAL_LIB_ROOT"
PERL_MB_OPT="--install_base \"/home/altreus/perl5\""
PERL_MM_OPT="INSTALL_BASE=/home/altreus/perl5"
```

The five environment variables listed here all contain the same directory: */home/altreus/perl5*. This is the local Perl directory. You can copy the five environment variables and amend them for your own purposes, or you can use the *local::lib* module.

Unfortunately, you need to install *local::lib* before you can use it to install modules! *local::lib* can usually be installed from package managers, but it is possible to install it to local Perl before you have it in the first place.

https://metacpan.org/pod/local::lib is the *de facto* source for *local::lib*. It contains a section, "The bootstrapping technique," that explains how to install it up front. Essentially it is as follows:

```
$ wget http://cpan.metacpan.org/authors/id/H/HA/HAARG/local-lib-2.000012.
tar.gz
$ tar xzf local-lib-2.000012.tar.gz
$ cd local-lib-2.000012
$ perl Makefile.PL --bootstrap
$ make test && make install
```

The documentation then tells you how to set up your environment for the future:

```
$ echo '[ $SHLVL -eq 1 ] && eval "$(perl -I$HOME/perl5/lib/perl5
-Mlocal::lib)"' >>~/.bashrc
```

The preceding command assumes you are using *bash* as your shell, which is the default shell for most UNIX systems, including Mac OS X. (Users of other shells will need to rewrite the command to adapt to their particular shell syntax.) All the procedure does is automate the exporting of the environment variables mentioned earlier.

Remember to start a new shell if you change your *.bashrc*, so that the new environment variables are loaded; or just source your *.bashrc*. The *source builtin* command works for bash but may be a different command for other shells.

D.2 *cpanm*

The *cpan* command requires a good deal of setup and makes installing modules more awkward than necessary. We can easily install *cpanm* to make everything a lot easier. Recently, some systems have started shipping with *cpanm* by default. If you already have *cpanm* then there's nothing to do! With the *local::lib* environment we just set up, *cpanm* will magically install everything to local Perl.

If you don't have cpanm, go to *http://cpanmin.us* and follow the directions given in the provided script comment section. In keeping with the theme of putting everything in your local *lib*, it is advised to install your own *cpanm,* even if you do already have it.

```
$ curl -L http://cpanmin.us | perl - App::cpanminus
```

However, this can cause problems if your connection breaks while installing. Instead, save the file as *cpanm.pl*, and then run

```
$ perl cpanm.pl App::cpanminus
```

This simply uses a temporary *cpanm* to install a permanent *cpanm*. It will use the *local::lib* we already set up, so you will find *cpanm* in *~/perl5/bin* by default.

Now that we have both *local::lib* and *cpanm* set up, installing a module is a simple matter of running

```
$ cpanm Module::Name
```

You can also use the *--sudo* option if you want to install to site Perl (that's the root-owned area that is not system Perl), but this is not recommended, because it is not guaranteed such a directory is set up. Remember, you can use *local::lib* to specify any directory, so you could easily have a site Perl set up with *local::lib* and then use the *sudo* option so *cpanm* can install to it.

With these tools, you can avoid system Perl entirely; except in one aspect, which is the *perl* runtime itself. For that, we can use Perlbrew.

D.3 Perlbrew

Just as we couldn't assume the system Perl libraries were for our use, neither can we assume the system *perl* runtime is for our use. The fact that it might happen to work for now is something that can change at any time. In corporate environments, it is just too risky to change system-provided software.

Different Perl versions have different requirements when installing modules. That means that modules installed under 5.16 might not be compatible with 5.18 or 5.20. We need to keep these installations separate, so that the install directory is relative to the current Perl version, and we avoid conflicts.

We solve all of this with Perlbrew. This will download and compile any version of Perl currently available in its repository (they're actually on CPAN) and install it into local Perl; which means the whole thing can be done with only user access to the system. (In the next section, we will discuss caveats to this.) We can install as many Perl versions as we like, and simply ask Perlbrew to switch to the one we want to use. That way, *perl* is dependent on our environment, which is what we want; and because the environment changes, *cpanm* knows where to install the modules to avoid conflict.

To install Perlbrew, go to *http://perlbrew.pl/* and follow the instructions:

```
$ \curl -L http://install.perlbrew.pl | bash
```

This installs Perlbrew locally and initializes it. The output says to append the following piece of code to the end of your *~/.bash_profile* and start a new shell. Perlbrew should be up and fully functional from there:

```
source ~/perl5/perlbrew/etc/bashrc
```

Depending on your setup, this might have to go into *~/.bashrc* instead. Perlbrew will also detect other shells and advise on those as relevant. **Note that you should do this *instead of* the line that *local::lib* uses.** Restart your terminal session if you had to switch this out; this *bashrc* detects when you're running with a brewed Perl and sets up a *local::lib* for you.

With that in your shell's RC, you can now compile your own Perl in your home directory, and use that in place of system Perl.

```
$ perlbrew available
  perl-5.21.1
  perl-5.20.0
  perl-5.18.2
    ...
      <snip>
```

You will need the following line to use Perlbrew properly. It simply assists with installing certain versions of Perl, and it's easier if it's just installed always.

```
$ perlbrew install-patchperl
```

Finally, you can install any version of Perl listed. The *perl-* part is optional.

```
$ perlbrew install 5.20.0

      <snip>
```

```
$ perlbrew use 5.20.0
$ perl -V
      <snip>
      ...
 @INC:
    /home/altreus/perl5/perlbrew/perls/perl-5.20.0/lib/site_perl/5.20.0/
x86_64-linux
    /home/altreus/perl5/perlbrew/perls/perl-5.20.0/lib/site_perl/5.20.0
    /home/altreus/perl5/perlbrew/perls/perl-5.20.0/lib/5.20.0/x86_64-linux
    /home/altreus/perl5/perlbrew/perls/perl-5.20.0/lib/5.20.0
```

You can see that your *@INC* contains only a local *lib* for 5.20.0. That means Perl 5.20 will not look in system Perl for modules, because they are unlikely to be compatible. However, the installation process for 5.20 will fetch all the core modules as well, so the directories just listed will not be empty.

Perlbrew can also be used to install *cpanm* locally:

```
$ perlbrew install-cpanm
```

This *cpanm* will always be available, even if you switch out Perl version. That avoids any issue with *cpanm* having been installed into a local *lib* that has suddenly changed.

D.4   Caveats: *C* Dependencies

Perlbrew compiles Perl for you. This means you need a *C* compiler. Although you can theoretically get *gcc* and put it in your home directory (similar to Perl itself), it is normal to use your package manager to install the *C* compiler. This, of course, needs root access. For our purposes, we are creating our local environment for best practice, not because we don't have root; so installing a *C* compiler should not be a problem. You would have to manually install the *gcc* binary into your home directory and amend *$PATH* in order to do it without root.

On Mac OS X, you can install Xcode and the command-line tools for it to get a *C* compiler. On Windows, the *C* compiler is provided with Strawberry Perl.

It is not just Perl itself that requires a *C* compiler. Many modules on CPAN are interfaces into *C* libraries (*XML::LibXML* is an example), and some modules are written in *C* for efficiency (JSON has a version like this). Perl modules that use *C* in some way are known as **XS modules**. XS is the tool used to interface between Perl and *C*, allowing a normal *.pm* to wrap up code written in *C* and expose the interface to Perl. That's why the JSON module has two versions: *JSON::PP* ("Pure Perl") and *JSON::XS*.

Interfaces like JSON can be installed without a *C* compiler because the XS version simply is not installed at all if the *C* compiler is not available at the time. Some modules are XS but don't have a pure Perl equivalent; these ones will require a *C* compiler. But the tricky ones are those that interface into an external library, like *XML::LibXML*.

XML::LibXML is a Perl interface into the *C* library *libxml2*. In order to compile, the development headers for *libxml2* have to be available to the *C* compiler. Exactly how *C* compiles against external libraries is out of the scope of this discussion, but the difficulty arrives in just how to get these third-party dependencies in the first place. The CPAN toolchain (*cpanm*, *Module::Build*, and friends) allows us to list an unlimited chain of dependencies from CPAN itself, but there is no mechanism to list dependencies outside of CPAN. The best we can do is to try to give the user as helpful a message as possible when trying to compile an XS module that interfaces a *C* library like this.

In the case of *XML::LibXML*, we need the *libxml2* development headers. On Debian, this is the *libxml2-dev* package. On OS X, Xcode comes with *libxml2*, but *homebrew* is a common tool for installing various packages on OS X. Dependencies that don't come with Xcode are likely to be available with homebrew.

When it comes to *C* dependencies, then, it is often necessary to install a package. This often requires root access. It is possible to set up the environment so that all the *C* dependencies are discoverable by the *C* compiler in *$HOME*, similar to how Perl itself discovers modules somewhere in *$HOME*. This can be achieved with the *LIBRARY_PATH* environment variable. Normally, when developing, the developer has root access and can avoid this issue.

So, the requirement for root can be avoided in general, but the Perl toolchain (*cpanm*, *perlbrew*) can only help with Perl itself. Any dependencies outside of Perl will have to be dealt with independently of this.

D.5 Windows

On Windows, many modules are included with Strawberry Perl. Strawberry is available with different versions of Perl, each being bundled with the modules built for it. This eradicates the requirement to compile or install most modules.

For those modules not available, Strawberry comes with *cpanm* by default (since 5.14), and ships with a *C* compiler.

Windows being mostly a single-user environment, those external dependencies required for compiling modules that use *C* libraries should be easy to install by locating the Windows installer for that library, installing it, and then trying again. Problems with not having root access don't tend to occur on Windows.

It is possible to have a similar system to the UNIX method, whereby the library is installed to the user's home directory, but it is so rare that this is needed that you are unlikely to find a case where a user has been unable to run their script on Windows due to an external *C* dependency they cannot resolve.

Visit *http://strawberryperl.com* for Strawberry Perl; you can find a full set of release notes at the bottom of the page, listing the distributions shipped with it. Strawberry Perl contains all modules required to run examples in this book.

appendix

E

Dancing with Perl

Written by Alastair McGowan-Douglas

Web work is a very common use of Perl. The Web is a heavily text-based medium, with plain-text HTTP being used to negotiate the transfer of plain-text HTML, XML, or JSON resources.

In the past, CGI (Common Gateway Interface) was used, but today a module called Dancer is a popular alternative. Dancer is a free, open-source micro Web application framework written in Perl that creates Web applications by building a list of HTTP verbs, routes, and methods to handle them. (See *www.perldancer.org/quickstart*.)

Dancer, as well as all the other popular modern Web frameworks (such as Mojolicious and Catalyst), differs from CGI in the principal sense that your entire Dancer application is a single script that you run manually. Compare to CGI, where each CGI script would be run by the Web server, and only when requested.

The following URLs will be used to access the program example we build in this appendix.

- *http://localhost:3000/student.cgi*—CGI style
- *http://localhost:3000/student*—Modern style

The latter URL makes no mention of *how* the student will be served to the client; in particular, there is no mention of CGI (or PHP or ASP or anything like that). This allows us to later rework the underlying code, and clients will not have to change their bookmarks.

A major benefit of the modern style of structuring a Web application is that we don't have to compile and run the script on every single request. We can create a single process that will handle the request and return a response. Having actually launched the application once, means it was compiled once; and if compiled once, we can make much more complex systems that can take as long as needed to actually launch, because we launch them so rarely.

The following example will draw upon the *Student.pm* we created in Appendix C, "Introduction to Moose (A Postmodern Object System for Perl 5)." First, we will show a simple script that contains some example students and allows you to view them; then we will extend the script to create new students.

But first, you will need to install Dancer. For a discussion on setting up your environment for installation of modules (and for a new Perl if you want to upgrade), see Appendix D, "Perlbrew, CPAN, and *cpanm*." Once done, you may simply run

```
cpanm Dancer
```

and Dancer will be installed, ready for use.

E.1 A New Dancer App

Dancer comes with a utility, *dancer*, that creates a Dancer application for you. Simply run *dancer -a Example* and you will get a new directory, *Example*, containing a functional (but featureless) Dancer application. Feel free to replace *Example* with any valid module name—a module by this name will be created for you, and this module will be your whole Web site![1]

At this point, you will be warned that installing YAML is a good idea. In fact, you will need to. Dancer says to run *cpan YAML*; but we want to run *cpanm YAML* to benefit from the environment that we set up in Appendix D.

The new *Example* directory contains everything you will need to run your new application. To test it out is easy.

EXAMPLE E.1

```
(Shell commands)
1   cd Example
2   ./bin/app.pl

(Output)
3   [25877]  core @0.000022> loading Dancer::Handler::Standalone handler
    in [...]/Dancer/Handler.pm l. 45
    [25877]  core @0.000298> loading handler 'Dancer::Handler::Standalone'
    in [...]/Dancer.pm l. 483

4   >> Dancer 1.3126 server 25877 listening on http://0.0.0.0:3000
5   == Entering the development dance floor ...
```

---

1. Avoid choosing *Student* for this example, because then we will have a collision between the *Student.pm* that Dancer creates and the *Student.pm* that we're going to use for the example. Usually this will not be a problem. In the real world, both Student modules would be namespaced differently; e.g., *MyApp::Student* for the object and *MyApp::Web::Route::Student* for the Dancer part. For the purposes of this appendix, it is simpler to avoid this issue instead.

EXPLANATION

1   We switch to the new directory, *Example*, created by Dancer.

2   *app.pl*, located in the *bin* directory, runs our Dancer application. The *dancer* script created this for us, and because it is executable, we don't need to specify *perl* at the command line.

3   These two lines of output inform us that Dancer has loaded the handler that runs the standalone Web server. It is possible also to connect Dancer applications to another Web server, such as Apache or nginx.

4   This line is output from the standalone handler, and gives us the URL that we can use to view our application; in this case, it is *http://0.0.0.0:3000*. When you click on this, you will be greeted by Dancer.

5   This line is Dancer's output when it has finished loading everything. The "development dance floor" is the application running in development mode. This will use the development configuration, which includes the configuration to output extra debugging information. Normally, the development configuration has this set to extra information, while the production configuration has it set to no information (and to log errors). This makes it a lot easier for our application to behave differently in different places without having to be edited.

Congratulations! Your first modern Web app has been created. But it doesn't do anything yet. By following the URL mentioned in Dancer's output (by default, this is *http://0.0.0.0:3000*) you can access the Dancer welcome page (see Figure E.1).

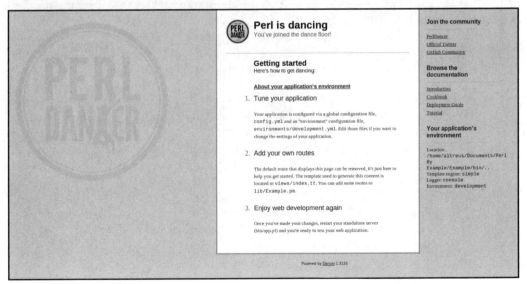

Figure E.1   The Dancer welcome page.

Example E.2 shows the contents of *lib/Example.pm*. This is the file that contains the actual behavior of the application. *app.pl* is just a helper script that launches it. The welcome page, pictured, is simply the contents of *views/index.tt*. Templates and views are explained later in this appendix.

EXAMPLE E.2

```
1   package Example;
2   use Dancer ':syntax';


3   our $VERSION = '0.1';

4   get '/' => sub {
5       template 'index';
    };

6   true;
```

EXPLANATION

1   This is a normal Perl module found in *Example.pm*, and it contains the Example package. Dancer ensures that the *lib* directory is available in *@INC*. *app.pl* uses Dancer and then uses this module. This module then tells Dancer how to behave. It is possible to have *app.pl* directly tell Dancer how to behave, but then we haven't written reusable or testable code. The Example module could be used by a Dancer test suite, and instead of launching the Web server, it could run automated tests that ensure whatever Example does is consistent and correct.

2   This module needs Dancer syntax, but not all the rest of Dancer behavior. The *use* line uses syntax familiar from Exporter (see Chapter 13, "Modularize It, Package It, and Send It to the Library!") to import the *syntax* group. The Dancer docs list exactly what this contains.

3   This is version 0.1 of our Web application—the very first version! This number will normally go up as the application is released, and this information will be used if we put our application as a distribution on CPAN.

4   This is the first part of the real body of the application. Dancer is told that, when a *get* request arrives to / (the root of the Web site), the subroutine should be run. This is a *reference* to an anonymous subroutine.

5   Dancer is told to render the template called *index*.

6   Dancer exports some constants that we can use to make our code more legible. You may prefer to use *1;* like in other modules, because not all modules use Dancer, and so *true* is not always available.

E.1.1   Verbs

The Web uses HTTP to request and send content. That which is requested and served is generally called **resources**; i.e., the *R* in *URL* (Uniform Resource Locater). HTTP uses a URL and a verb to tell the server what we want. We already understand the URL part: *http://localhost:3000/* means "the root resource at localhost on port 3000 via the HTTP protocol." Normally this is an index page listing all the other available resources. In this case, it is a page that confirms to us that we have successfully created a Dancer app.

What that URL doesn't say is that we want to *get* that resource. That is the verb in HTTP. If you use *curl*, you can see exactly that, as shown in Example E.3.

EXAMPLE E.3

```
(Shell commands)
1  curl -v -D- localhost:3000/

(Output (abridged))
   * Connected to localhost (127.0.0.1) port 3000 (#0)
2  > GET / HTTP/1.1
   > User-Agent: curl/7.35.0
3  > Host: localhost:3000
   > Accept: */*
   >
```

EXPLANATION

1   *curl* is used to send a request to the server that we're running. This lets us control what information we see. In this case, we want to see the headers *curl* is sending. With *-v, curl* outputs extra information. With *-D-, curl* dumps the request headers (*-D*) to standard out (*-*).

2   This line in the output shows the first line of the HTTP request that *curl* makes. It is a verb, a URL (just the path) and the HTTP version. The verb is *GET* and the path is */*.

3   This is the other part of the URL. The *Host* header tells the server which host we want. A server like Apache can serve multiple hosts at the same time, and will use this to forward the request to the appropriate application.

The *GET* in the *curl* request just shown corresponds to the *get* in *Example.pm*. The */* in the request corresponds to the *'/'* in *Example.pm*. Dancer, therefore, makes it simple to write Perl that matches closely to the HTTP requests. An HTTP request for *GET /* is handled by *get '/'* in Dancer, and HTTP request for *POST /students* is handled by *post '/students'*.

The common HTTP verbs are *GET, POST, PUT,* and *HEAD*. Others exist, but they are used less often. These are described in Table E.1.

Table E.1 HTTP Verbs

Verb	Meaning
GET	Fetch the resource. This can be run as often as you like (you may get throttled) and the resource will never change. This is a *read-only* operation. The response will be a representation of the resource, or a copy of it (for example, an HTML page).
POST	Create a new sub resource. Every time you send a *POST* request with valid data, a resource will be created underneath the resource you *POST* to. The response will normally contain the URL to the new resource. This is a *write-only* operation.
PUT	Updates a resource with new data. Often, *POST* is used for this because some browsers do not support *PUT*. The difference is that *PUT* edits a resource and *POST* creates one.
HEAD	Fetch just the headers. This is like *GET* except the resource is not actually sent. This is useful for testing whether the resource actually exists.

Dancer allows us to define different handlers for different verbs. That's useful. Instead of having to test whether a *POST* or a *GET* was made, as we did with CGI, or to *POST* to a different place and redirect the user back to the form if there was an error, with this method of structuring the code, we can simply choose which function is run based on what the request is for.

That means that we can create a *GET* / handler that creates a list of students, and a *POST* / handler that adds to the list.

We already have a *GET* / handler, but it doesn't produce a list of students yet. The following is a new *Example.pm* that creates a collection of students and serves it.[2] Remember, *Student* relies on Moose, *MooseX::Declare,* and *MooseX::ClassAttribute*, so you'll have to install these with *cpanm* if you haven't already.

EXAMPLE E.4

```
1   package Example;
2   use Dancer ':syntax';
3   use Student;

    our $VERSION = '0.1';
```

---

2. To use *Student.pm,* you should copy it from wherever you have it (or the Internet if you don't have a copy) and put it next to *Example.pm*. This is uncommon. Normally, *Student.pm* would be part of a larger CPAN release, and you would have, therefore, installed *Student.pm* using *cpanm*, along with a whole suite of other Moose classes that came with the distribution. In that case, your *Student.pm* would already exist in @INC and you would not have to copy the file around at all. The other common setup is that your *Student.pm* and *Example.pm* are in the same distribution, but different directories, using namespacing as suggested in the previous footnote.

EXAMPLE E.4 (CONTINUED)

```
4   my @students = (
        Student->new(
            name     => "Bob",
            idnumber => "123",
            major    => "math",
            courses  => [qw(calculus topology matricies)],
        ),
        Student->new(
            name     => "Jane",
            idnumber => "321",
            major    => "computer science",
            courses  => [qw(automata algorithms java)],
        )
    );

5   get '/' => sub {
6       my $template_data = {
7           students => \@students,
        };
8       template 'index', $template_data;
    };

    true;
```

EXPLANATION

1   We are in the Example module, so we are going to define the *Example* package.
2   As before, *Example.pm* will import the *syntax* group from Dancer to set up route handlers.
3   This time we are also going to use the *Student* module we previously created.
4   A lexically scoped array is created. The alternative (*our*, like *$VERSION*) is a package variable, but we don't want other modules to be able to affect our list of students. Route handlers in this part of the Dancer application (meaning, this file) will be able to interact with this array, but nobody else will. The array is populated with the same two students we used in the example script when we first saw *Student* in Chapter 14, "Bless Those Things! (Object-Oriented Perl)."
5   The *get* handler is defined for the root path. An anonymous *subref* is defined to be run when the root path is requested.
6   An anonymous hashref is created and assigned to the lexical variable *$template_data*.
7   The hash key *students* is associated with the *@students* array. When building data structures in Perl, we have to pass references to non-scalar data, so the *@students* array is passed by reference.
8   Dancer is instructed to render the *'index'* template when the root path is requested. This time, the new variable *$template_data* is also sent to the template. Within the template, the variable *students* will refer to the array reference we put into *$template_data*.

In order to use this new script, we are also going to have to change the template. Dancer is not going to magically know what to do with the template data we provided, after all.

E.1.2   Templating

Templating is a manner of separating the way you **represent** a resource from the way you **produce** the resource. In our example, the list of students we are representing is directly defined inside the module. Every time we quit the application and restart it, the student data will be reset, because the program will be recompiled.

Alternatives to this include storing the data in a file, putting them in a database, or even storing them on somebody else's network! We could easily script our Web site to fetch data from a different Web site—that's how RSS readers work.

You can also represent a resource in different ways. In this case, we are going to assume we want to see the students in HTML form because we're going to assume we are using a browser. However, if we wanted to create an RSS feed of our students, we could use a different template with the same set of students to produce RSS-compliant XML. Or we could represent them as JSON. A Web-based RSS reader would **produce** resources by collecting them from somebody else's Web site; and it would **represent** them by repackaging them into HTML form.

So we really do want to be able to fetch the data in one place and represent it in a different place. This is something we simply couldn't do in the CGI days; in those days, you had to have a different script for different things—and CGI only provided HTML helpers!

Templating is a way of sending data to text files, and thus constructing the text files consistently based on the data we send them. We define a template, which contains the common factors like the header and footer HTML, plus the HTML we use to represent a resource, and into it we put the data items that make one resource different from another. In this example, templating is done with the *Template* module (see *http://template-toolkit.org* for more information), so we install that:

```
cpanm Template
```

Next, we need to change *config.yml* to say *template: "template_toolkit"*. The following is *config.yml* with comments removed for brevity. The reader is encouraged to read the comments in his own copy of the file. (This file is why we installed the YAML module.)

EXAMPLE E.5

```
(config.yml (abridged))

1   appname: "Example"
2   layout: "main"
3   charset: "UTF-8"
4   template: "template_toolkit"
```

1   YAML is a simple data definition language that uses *key: value* syntax. This line defines the name of the application as *"Example"*. Dancer generated this.

2   Dancer supports layouts. This is basically a template that wraps up other templates. In CGI, we would have a *header.html* and a *footer.html*, but that was far too easy to break with mismatched tags. Having a wrapper is much easier. This application is configured to have a layout called *"main"*. This can be found in *views/layouts/main.tt*.

3   HTTP specifies the charset that the resource is using. (Actually, it specifies the encoding, but calls it charset. This is an ancient mistake and it is too late to change it now.) Dancer is configured to encode everything with UTF-8, which is the preferred encoding these days.

4   Dancer is configured to use the *"template_toolkit"* template system. Previously, it was the *"simple"* template system, but *"simple"* does not have loops, and we want to output an array of things.

When the Dancer application launches, the configuration is read from *config.yml*. This sets up Dancer with a default set of configuration, and in this case we are configuring the template system. There are many other configuration options, and you can even set it up so that it uses different values in different environments. This is the mechanism that allows us to put a Web site live without accidentally showing the users messy errors that are only useful to developers debugging the system.

Now that we've told it which template system to use, we turn our attention to the *views* directory. This contains all the templates, and is where Dancer will look if you don't tell it to look elsewhere. **View** is the term we give to the concept of being able to display the same resource in different formats. There may be a *JSON* view, an *HTML* view, an *RSS* view, and so forth. To keep it simple, we'll leave the structure as it is, but it is often beneficial to add subdirectories to *views*, one for each supported format.

The default *index.tt* can be opened to see the HTML that makes up the welcome page that was shown in the browser when the application was first run (Figure E.1). Part of this file uses the <% %> syntax of *Template::Toolkit*, which Dancer's *"simple"* template system also uses, to output information like the Dancer version and the environment data on the right.

Now that we're using *Template::Toolkit* properly (that's what the *tt* stands for in *index.tt*) we can replace *index.tt* with other useful templates. The following example lists the new *index.tt*.

```
1   <div id="page">
2       <div id="content">
          <div id="header">
            <h1>Student List</h1>
          </div>
```

EXAMPLE E.6 (CONTINUED)

```
3              <div id="students">
4                 <% FOREACH student IN students %>
5                    <h2>
6                       <% student.name %>
7                    </h2>
8                    <dl>
9                       <dt>ID</dt>
10                      <dd><% student.idnumber %></dd>
11                      <dt>Major</dt>
                        <dd><% student.major %></dd>
                        <dt>Address</dt>
                        <dd><% student.address %></dd>
                        <dt>Tuition</dt>
                        <dd><% student.tuition %></dd>
                        <dt>Courses</dt>
12                      <% FOREACH course IN student.courses %>
13                         <dd><% course %></dd>
14                      <% END %>
15                   </dl>
16                <% END %>
              </div>
           </div>

    </div>
```

EXPLANATION

1   This file does not start with *<html>* or *<!DOCTYPE>*. Instead, it starts with *<div>*. The
    file will be imported into *views/layouts/main.tt*, and so it only needs to contain the
    HTML specific to the student list page. It is *main.tt* that contains the *DOCTYPE* and
    <html> element. This allows us to create new pages while keeping a consistent theme
    and framing for them.

2   By keeping some of the original HTML, the need to do too much extra styling can be
    avoided. We will keep the *content div* and the *header div* inside it, and this will make
    the new page look similar to the old one.

3   A new *div* is made whose ID is *students*. Later, we can style this with CSS if we want
    to.

4   *Template::Toolkit* defines the *FOREACH* directive, which acts just like a *foreach* loop in
    Perl with a different syntax; for examle, *IN* is used instead of the parentheses in Perl
    syntax. *Template::Toolkit* expects *students* to be an *arrayref*, and iterates over it, assign-
    ing each element in turn to the *student* variable. Dancer configures *Template::Toolkit*
    with the *<% %>* syntax to identify template areas; everything else is output as plain
    text.

5   This is the first line of the *FOREACH* loop body. It defines an *<h2>*. This line will be
    output once for each student in the students array.

6   The name of the student is output. When a variable is put into template tags, the default behavior is to print it. The current student is referenced by the *student* variable, and properties of variables can be accessed using a dot. *Template::Toolkit* is smart enough to understand that *student* is referencing an object, and fetches the *name* property. If *student* were a hashref, it would fetch the value associated with the *name* key. It tries to do the right thing in all situations.

7   The *<h2>* tag is closed. Now the student's name is a level-two heading in the page. Each student will have an *<h2>* with their name in it.

8   A *<dl>* tag is started. This is a description list. Each student will have one of these, thanks to the *FOREACH* loop.

9   A *<dt>* tag contains *ID*. This is the title of the item in the description list (*dt* means "description title"). One of these is used for every property of the *Student* object we want to output.

10   A *<dd>* tag contains the actual value. This is the description itself. Like *name*, the *id-number* property from the *student* variable is accessed and, because there is no other directive inside this *Template::Toolkit* tag, it is output.

11   More *<dt>* and *<dd>* pairs complete the student, using the same information as *show_student* on the class itself.

12   On the Student class, *courses* was defined as an array of data. Another *FOREACH* directive begins a loop over all of the values in the *courses* property of the current Student object, *student* (*student.courses*). Because there is a directive in here (*FOREACH*), *Template::Toolkit* does not output the value of *student.courses* directly. Instead, each course is assigned to the *course* variable, as in a normal *foreach* loop in Perl.

13   One *<dd>* is created for each course in the list, containing the name of the course.

14   The *END* directive completes the most recently opened block directive, in this case *FOREACH*. Indentation is important here because it is easy to lose track of which directive an *END* actually ends.

15   The *</dl>* closes the *<dl>* and concludes all the data output for a single student.

16   The *END* directive closes the other *FOREACH* block directive, the one that loops over students. If there are more students during processing, the whole thing is repeated with the next student. Thus, all students are represented using the same HTML, and only the actual data inside the HTML change.

Because changes were made to *Example.pm*, it is necessary to restart the development Dancer server. Simply kill it with <CTRL>+C (<CTRL>+Z on Windows) and run it again. The script, *app.pl*, does have an option to restart itself when it detects changes to the files, but this can be unreliable, especially on Windows, and so it is often simpler just to restart it manually. Manual restart also means you can change several files several times before you actually restart it.

Once the server process is restarted, reloading the page in the browser will now show a page similar to Figure E.2 utilizing the main principles of Dancer development: server processes (*app.pl*), configuration (*config.yml*), route handling (*get '/'*), and template systems (*index.tt*).

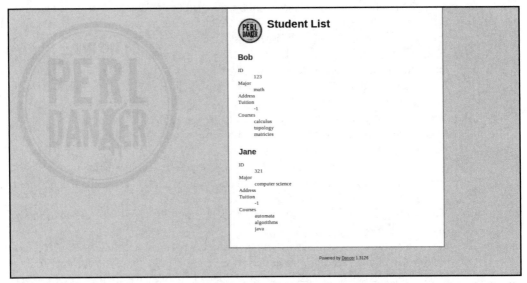

Figure E.2   The (unstyled) student list. The right-hand column was removed when *index.tt* was rewritten, but because *layouts/main.tt* was not changed, the layout did not change.

E.1.3 Parameters

It is not necessarily a given that a *GET* request is complete with just the URL to the resource. Many resources are actually entry points into a set of resources. Our entire application so far is actually an entry point to the whole set of Student resources available to the application. Normally we expect to be able to filter pages like this or to access a single resource.

The modern Web offers two common ways of parameterizing. They differ in how they work, and hence how they should be used. Both of them are part of the URL.

A **query string** is the part of the URL following a question mark. Commonly it is a key/value pair string, where the keys and values are separated by equal signs and the pairs themselves are separated by ampersands:

```
?name=John&courses=java
```

Often, this is referred to as the **GET string**, but this is a misnomer; because it is part of the URL, the HTTP verb used with it is not relevant. A *POST* request can have a query string, and of course it does not have to be an HTTP request in the first place. It is perfectly valid to have a URL like *file:///home/user/html/index.html?user=me*, which doesn't use HTTP at all.[3] Query strings are so called because they are normally used to query the index resource for a more specific set. In the preceding example, it would be expected that we found students with the name "John" and the course "Java".

The other type of parameter is in the path itself. This is usually used to be more specific about exactly which resource we want. If we were dealing with a bigger system, with many schools and universities, we might wish to be more specific about whose students we were after. In this case, the URL might look something like this:

```
http://0.0.0.0:3000/univ/mit/students/
```

This would be built using the techniques we've already seen, plus some techniques we are about to see. The use of *get '/univ'* is almost certainly going to feature here; but once a system gets this big, it is likely that a new module (for example, *University.pm*) will be added to *lib/* in order to keep the system well organized.

Of course, these parameter types can be combined. The following URL might refer to all students at MIT who are named Joe and are doing advanced math:

```
http://0.0.0.0:3000/univ/mit/students/?name=joe&course=advanced_math
```

We can also get a specific student from the whole database using the path form of parameterization, by specifying the student's ID in the path, like so:

```
http://0.0.0.0:3000/students/1
```

This URL has lost the part that specifies "MIT" because a student's ID is unique in the system; therefore, if we know exactly which student we want, it is of no benefit to specify "MIT" any more. This form of parameterization is the most central to the concept of a URL; the URL */students/1* points exactly to a single resource—a specific student. The index resource can show you different things in different situations, but */students/1* will always show you the current state of student 1.

The *students* part of the preceding examples, of course, implies a system larger than our example. Dancer actually makes it simple to augment paths in this way. We can easily add the *students/* part to our example later on. This means it is possible to create parts of systems separately from other parts, and then include them later on as subsections of a bigger site. Later in this appendix, we will see that. For now, let's define a route handler that will get a student based on ID.

The following example is an abridged version of *Example.pm*. The listed code can be added after the existing code, but of course before the *true;* line, which must always come last in the module.

---

3. It may not be meaningful to do this; the point here is to illustrate the difference between the URL and the protocol (HTTP versus file).

EXAMPLE E.7

```
(Example.pm (abridged))
  package Example;
  use Dancer ':syntax';
  use Student;
1 use List::Util qw(first);

2 # [abridged]

3 get '/:id' => sub {
4   my $student = first { $_->idnumber == params->{'id'} } @students;

5   if (! $student) {
6     status 'not_found';
7     send_file '404.html';
    }

8   template 'index', {
9     'students' => [ $student ]
    };
  };
```

EXPLANATION

1   We will use *List::Util's first* function in order to find the first student whose ID matches the parameter. This is only necessary in this situation. If we were to use a database or an external service to find this student, we would simply pass the parameter on. It is customary to have all *use* lines in the same place, at the top.

2   The definitions of *$VERSION* and *@students*, and the route handler for *get '/'* have been omitted for brevity.

3   This new route handler will handle any root request with an ID. The syntax *:id* has two effects. First, it specifies that there must be some part to the path here; and second, it collects whatever it contains into the parameter called *id*. If nothing is provided here, then this route does not match, and the other route handler, *get '/'*, is run as usual.

4   *params* is provided by Dancer and represents a hashref of the parameters available in the request. Because line 3 defined this route to have a parameter called *id*, whenever this route handler is run, Dancer will have collected information into the *id* key in the *params* hashref. *List::Util::first* is used to find the first student whose *idnumber* matches the parameter *id*.

5   If no student was found with this *idnumber*, then this block is entered.

6   Dancer provides the *status* function to change the HTTP status code of the response. *404 Not Found* is a very familiar status code to everyone on the Internet. *status* can either receive *404* or *'not_found'*. If the student was not found, we sensibly set the status code to not found.

EXPLANATION (CONTINUED)

7 Instead of the normal template, the *404.html* file is served. This is found in the *public/* directory of the default Dancer installation. Dancer creates this for us. It is not styled like the other pages, but it suffices to inform the user of the error. *send_file* sends any file from the *public/* directory, and immediately ends the response. Therefore, this line can be considered to return from this sub; line 8 will not be run if line 7 has run.

8 Provided a student was found, the exact same template is used to serve this single student as was used to serve a list of students.

9 The template *index.tt* expects an *array* of students in the *'students'* variable. Arrays are sent to TT as array references. An anonymous array reference is, accordingly, constructed to contain the single student found by the search. The template is rendered with just one student in it—the student defined by *:id*.

Remember to restart the *app.pl* that you ran earlier, in order to compile the new code and gain the new behavior.

Results can be seen simply by adding a number to the URL in the browser. The students defined in the file have *idnumber* values of 123 and 321. Adding these numbers to the URL will, therefore, serve the student with the appropriate *idnumber* (see Figure E.3); any other number will serve the 404 page (see Figure E.4); and no number at all will serve the index of students, as in Figure E.2.

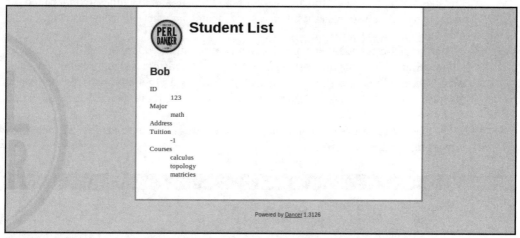

Figure E.3 The response for the URL *http://0.0.0.0:3000/123* is, as expected, Bob, with ID 123.

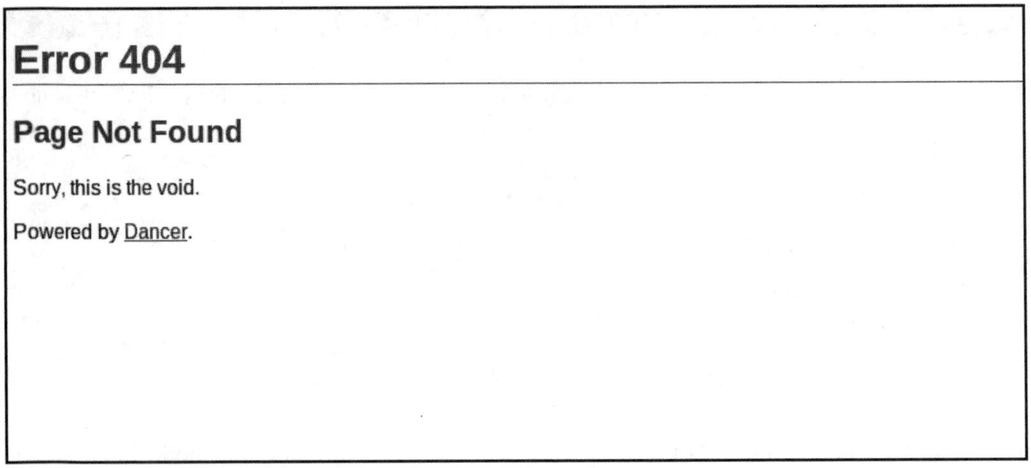

Error 404

Page Not Found

Sorry, this is the void.

Powered by <u>Dancer</u>.

Figure E.4 The response for the URL *http://0.0.0.0:3000/124* is a 404 because that resource was not found.

It is important that we used the same template for this single view as we did for multiple. After all, displaying a single result should be the same, whether it is because we only had one student in the index, or whether we explicitly requested one student. This encourages consistency, which makes it much easier for both humans and machines to understand the pages we return. It also makes it much easier to maintain, when there are many fewer files to understand the purposes of.

Next we address the other type of parameterization: the query string. It is common, but not required, that the query string uses the ampersand/equals sign format of key/value pairs. Dancer will split up this format into the *params* hashref automatically, but it also provides a means to access the query string directly if the route handler does not expect this format.

The following example is a replacement for the existing *get '/'* route handler in *Example.pm*, once again, abridged for brevity.

EXAMPLE E.8

```
(Example.pm (abridged))
   package Example;

   use Dancer ':syntax';
   use Student;
1  use List::Util qw(first);

   # [abridged]

2  get '/' => sub {
3      my @filtered_students;
```

EXAMPLE E.8 (CONTINUED)

```
4       if (! %{params()}) {
5           @filtered_students = @students;
        }
6       else {
7           my $params = params;
8           for my $student (@students) {
9               if ($params->{name}
                    && $student->name =~ /\Q$params->{name}/i) {
10                  push @filtered_students, $student;
11                  next;
                }

12              if ($params->{major}
                    && $student->major =~ /\Q$params->{major}/i) {
                    push @filtered_students, $student;
                    next;
                }

13              if ($params->{course}) {
14                  if (first { $_ eq $params->{course} }
                        @{ $student->courses }) {
15                      push @filtered_students, $student;
16                      next;
                    }
17              }
18          }
        }

19      my $template_data = {
20          students => \@filtered_students,
        };

        template 'index', $template_data;
    };

    # [abridged]
```

EXPLANATION

1   *List::Util::first* will be used as in the last example. It is an efficient way of finding whether something in an array matches. We could also use *List::MoreUtils::any*, but Dancer already has *any*, and we don't want to collide.*

2   The route handler for the root path is defined, *get '/'*.

3   The array *@filtered_students* is defined in preparation for the parameterized version.

---

* An important difference is that *first* can return a false value, if your array contains false values, whereas *any* will always return a true value if the test passes for any element. Since our array contains objects, and objects are refs, and refs are always true, we can use *first*.

4   The hashref returned by *params* is dereferenced and tested. *params* is actually a function exported by Dancer, and the parentheses are required here. Without them, Perl looks for %params, which is not declared, and so causes an error. If the hash that *params* refers to is empty, the block is entered.

5   If the hash referenced by *params* was empty, @*filtered_students* is simply set to all students. Dancer automatically populates *params* with the query string values, just as it does with path segments that use the :*name* syntax used in the previous example.

6   If the hash was *not* empty, this block is entered.

7   The hashref returned by *params* is stored in a temporary variable, $*params*. This variable is lexical to the *else* block, since it will only be useful here. The purpose of this variable is to simplify the rest of the *else* block a bit.

8   Since this request came with query parameters, the array of students is iterated over in order to find those students that match. Each student is successively stored in $*student*, ready for testing.

9   The parameter *name* is tested. If it is a true value, it is used as a regular expression to match against the student's name. The \Q ensures that any special regex characters in the *name* parameter are not treated as such—they are matched literally. The /i part allows the user to enter the student's name in any letter case; the match is case insensitive.

10   Provided that a *name* parameter was specified and that the student's name matches it, the student is pushed onto the @*filtered_students* array, because it passed the *name* test. If no *name* was provided, no student will be added based on the name.

11   The rest of the loop is skipped. This is simpler than using *elsif*. Whenever a student passes one of the tests, the other tests are irrelevant. If all tests were run, we risk adding the same student multiple times to the results array.

12   In the same way, the *major* parameter is tested. If the student's major matches the provided major, the student is added. If *major* is not provided, the student is not added.

13   Courses are handled differently. We only check that *course* was specified in the query. If no course was specified, the student is skipped. If we have gotten this far, and no course is specified, then this student will not be added to the results at all, because this means the other two tests also did not pass.

14   *List::Util::first* is used to find the first course that matches the query parameter *course*. $*student->courses* is known to be an array ref because *Student.pm* declares it so, and provides a default, empty array ref. $*student->courses* is enclosed in the @{} structure that dereferences an arrayref, and the resulting list of courses is tested with *first*. The test uses *eq*, checking that the course matches exactly. If the result of *first* is true, the block is entered. It will only be false if the course was not found.

15   Provided a *course* parameter was specified, and at least one of the student's courses matches *exactly* that course name, then the student is added to the results.

EXPLANATION (CONTINUED)

16 At this time, it is not necessary to skip this student if they pass the *course* test, because *course* is the last test anyway. However, it is good practice, so that a future developer adding more tests to the set does not cause a bug by not noticing that the existing code also needs changing.

17 The last of the three tests ends here. If the student has not been added to the *@filtered_students* array by now, they are not going to be added at all.

18 The loop over *@students* ends here. Once reached, all students have been tested against the parameters, and *@filtered_students* contains everything it is going to contain.

19 The same hashref, *$template_data*, is defined.

20 The only difference between this version of *$template_data* and the previous is that, now, *@filtered_students* is given to the template. If the *params* hashref was empty, that will be the same set as *@students*, but if it was not empty, it may be fewer or even zero students.

We can now use the query string method to query the student index, as in Figure E.5, in which all students whose name contains a *b* or a *B* are returned.

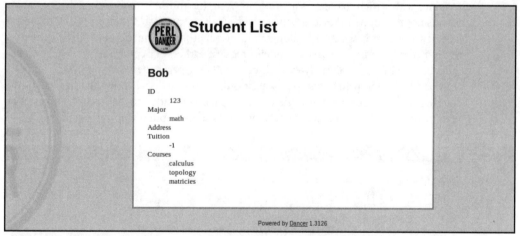

Figure E.5 The response to the URL *http://0.0.0.0:3000/?name=b*.

Astute readers will have realized that if a query is run that returns no results, the page is returned normally, but with no students in it. This differs from the previous example, wherein if the student was not found, a 404 error was returned.

The difference lies in the consideration of **resources**. This same consideration determines whether you want to use the path form of parameterization or the query form. In the first example, the student's ID number was part of the URL's path. That means that the student whose ID is 123 is a **separate resource** from the student whose ID number is 124—a different path represents a different resource. As it happens, the resource where the ID number is 124 does not actually exist, while the resource where the ID was 123 did exist. In the first example, the URL that returned 404 was requesting a different resource from the URL that returned the representation of a student.

In the query string example, the **same** resource was being requested with a different set of query parameters. The student index was being requested in both cases. The index resource always exists, and if your query matches no students, then an empty index is returned. That is to say, the **representation** of the index resource with the query *?name=x* is just representing a resource with no items in it. But the index resource still exists. An empty set is different from a set that does not exist at all.

So a query string does not affect which **resource** is being requested, but a different path does.

E.1.4 POST

It was mentioned that a *POST* request can be made to create a new resource under a given resource. That means that if we want to make a new student, we would probably want to post the data to the index resource. Since the index resource always exists, all we have to do is allow it to handle *POST* requests and define what it should do when it receives one.

We know that a *POST* request should create a new resource, but how would it know the values with which to create this student? Well, the third form of parameterization, one that was not mentioned previously, is in the *body* of the request. When an HTTP request is made, it sends a verb and a URL, along with certain other information like the *Host, Accept,* and *User-Agent* headers we saw in our *curl* request earlier. For certain requests[4] it can also send a *body*, which is essentially everything else. *POST* parameters are sent in the body.

As usual, the following example is abridged. It lists the new route handler to go into *Example.pm*. It can be added anywhere, but it is recommended to organize them based on the route they handle. Since this is *post '/'*, it makes sense to put it after the handler for *get '/'*.

EXAMPLE E.9

```
(Example.pm (abridged))

1  post '/' => sub {
2      my $student = Student->new(
3          name     => params->{name},
4          idnumber => params->{id},
           major    => params->{major},
5          courses  => [ split /,/, params->{courses} ],
       );

6      push @students, $student;
7      redirect '/';
   };
```

---

4. In fact, a *body* can be sent for any request, but it doesn't always make sense to do so, and so sometimes the *body* may be ignored.

EXPLANATION

1   The *POST* handler for '/' is defined. It uses the same principle as the *GET* handler; that is, the verb, then the path, then the code ref that handles it.

2   The variable *$student* is defined as a new *Student* object.

3   The *Student* object is constructed with parameters in a very similar manner to how the initial *Students* were created. This time, each constructor parameter is retrieved from the *POST* body. Once again, Dancer puts parameters into the hashref retrieved by *params*. The *name* property of the new *Student* is the *name* parameter from the *POST* body.

4   The *idnumber* for the new *Student* is the *id* parameter from the *POST* body. It is often tempting to write a loop that does these lines automatically, but that is not recommended. Over time, the names of the *POST* parameters and the names of the properties in the *Student* class may drift apart, meaning the automatic code eventually becomes manual code, or riddled with *ifs*. Being able to have a different set of *POST* parameter names from the set of fields on the class, is often very valuable.

5   The courses will be received in the *POST* body as a set of comma-separated values. An anonymous array ref is created containing the result of splitting this parameter by comma.

6   The new *Student* object is pushed onto the array of *Student* objects.

7   Dancer provides the *redirect* function, which sets the status to *302 Found* and the *Location* header to the provided URL. In this case, it will cause the browser to send a *GET* request to the index page instead, effectively reloading the page with the new data.

Restarting the application now will allow you to send *POST* requests to the index page to create new students. Normally this would be done with a form on the page, but that has not been written yet. Instead, we can issue *curl* requests again:

EXAMPLE E.10

```
Shell code)
1  $ curl -X POST -d 'name=Jill' -d 'id=124' -d 'major=math' -d 'z
   courses=topology,matrices,calculus,perl' 0.0.0.0:3000
```

EXPLANATION

1   *curl* is used to send a *POST* request (*-X POST*) to our running application. Each *-d* provides a *key=value* pair to the *POST* body, and *curl* combines these and sends an appropriately formatted request. The new *Student* is created with *idnumber* of *124*, *name* of *Jill*, *major* of *math*, and with *courses* becoming the array of four values, *topology*, *matrices*, *calculus*, and *perl*.

Having run this *curl* request, refreshing the index page in the browser will produce output similar to Figure E.6.

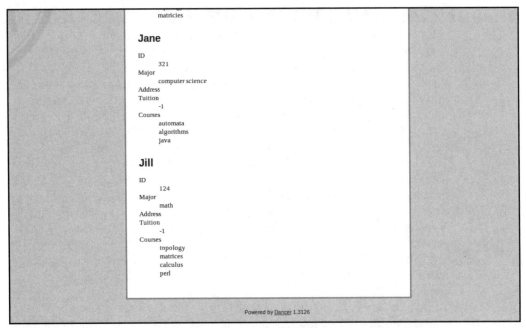

Figure E.6   After running the *POST* request with *curl,* the response to the URL *http://0.0.0.0:3000* now contains three students, rather than two.

Having done this, it may also be noted that the URL that previously returned 404, *http://0.0.0.0:3000/124,* now returns the new student, *Jill.*

Sometimes, in the wild, you will see the query string used to create a resource. This is a bad idea; a page in the browser should be able to be refreshed. The browser will warn if this involves sending *POST* data again, but it is assumed that the query string is safe. The reverse is true; if *POST* is used to query a resource like the student index we just made, the browser will assume it is unsafe and warn the user when refreshing. These behaviors are defined by the HTTP and URI standards, so by contradicting the standards, Web sites cause themselves and their users issues. That is why our student index uses a *GET* request with a query string to fetch students, and a *POST* request with *body* data to create students.

A good way to remember the difference is to ask yourself whether it would make sense for a user to copy the URL from the browser and send it to a friend, in order to share the information. If so, it is probably a *GET* request and should be either the path or the query string of the URL. If not, you are probably creating a resource and you want to *POST* the data.

Remember, it is not only humans with Web browsers that will send requests to your application. Scripts (for example, search indexers) are going to make assumptions based on the standardized meaning of URLs and HTTP verbs.

EXERCISE E
May I Have This Dance?

1. Add a form to *index.tt* that creates a new student. The form should probably have *method="post"* and *action="/"*.

2. What happens when you *POST* invalid data? What should happen? Amend *post '/'* to error sensibly when the *POST* parameters are invalid. Creating a form assists the user in providing the correct field names, but a script or test using *curl* is still likely to get it wrong. Use HTTP status codes to indicate errors. Remember that the 400 range means the user did something wrong, and the 500 range means the server (you) did something wrong.

3. In the user index, create links from each student's name to the full URL for that student (for example, *Bob* should link to *http://0.0.0.0:3000/123*). Note that you can either omit everything before */123* (i.e., just use */123* as the URL, and let the browser behave correctly), or you can use Dancer's *uri_for* function. The former option is defined as standard behavior for browsers to follow (that is, if the browser sees */123*, it will assume the *http://0.0.0.0:3000* part), and the latter option will have to be performed in the route handler, because the templates will not be able to use *uri_for* in the current setup.

4. What happens to the new students when you restart the server process? Why?

5. What happens when you try to run it a second time? This method of writing Web applications is supposed to allow you to run the script as many times as is necessary to handle the amount of traffic to the site. Run the script with *-p 3001* and note the different URL reported to you by Dancer.

6. How will you ensure that, if two copies of the application are running at the same time, they will respond to the same URL with the same information? Tip: you will not be able to have an array *@students* any more, because this array will be unique to each application process, and it cannot be shared. You will have to store the student data externally, and have the script pass on data requests somehow.

7. Amend the application to store *Students* in a new MySQL database created for the purpose. The same three route handlers can be used for this; the only difference is how you fetch and how you store the students. The query parameters in *get '/'* will become bind values in a MySQL query, instead of a loop. Dancer provides a *database* function that you can use to get a handle on your DBI connection, as long as you correctly configure your application.

8. What is the *environments/* directory for? Consider whether your configuration changes are for development, production, or all situations.

9. What goes in *public/*?

10. Spend some time styling up the student index to look a bit more in keeping with the theme of the default template.

11. Investigate Dancer's *prefix* function. This will allow you to prefix all your current route handlers with, for example, */student*. This will mean that your current / handler will be available on */student/*, and */123* will now be */student/123*. This makes sense. You are handling student resources here, so the URLs should say so. Most systems deal with more than just one type of resource, after all.

12. The reader is encouraged to read further on deploying Web apps in this manner. There are many options, but common ones include *plackup* and *Starman*. It is also possible to have Web servers like Apache and nginx run your application as necessary.

Index